Linux User's Resource

Developer's Resource

Prentice Hall PTR
Developer's Resource Series

Java Developer's Resource: A Tutorial and On-line Supplement	Harold
JavaScript Developer's Resource: Client-Side Programming Using HTML, Netscape Plug-ins, and Java Applets	Husain & Levitt
CGI Developer's Resource: Web Programming in Tcl and Perl	Ivler
Powerbuilder 5 Developer's Resource: Client/Server Programming for the Enterprise	Schumacher & Bosworth
JavaBeans Developer's Resource	Sridharan
Linux User's Resource	Mohr
JDBC Developer's Resource	Taylor

Linux User's Resource

Developer's Resource

James Mohr

Prentice Hall PTR
Upper Saddle River, NJ 07458
http://www.prenhall.com/mail_lists/

Library of Congress Cataloging in Publication Data

Mohr, James.
Linux user's resource / James Mohr.
p. cm — (Prentice Hall PTR developer's resource series)
Includes bibliographical references and index.
ISBN 0-13-842378-4 (alk. paper)
1. Linux. 2. Operating systems (Computers) I. Title.
II. Series.
QA76.76.O63M7459 1997
005.4'469--dc21 97-22733
CIP

Editorial/Production Supervision: *Kathleen M. Caren*
Acquisitions Editor: *Mark Taub*
Cover Design Director: *Jerry Votta*
Cover Design: *Design Source*
Manufacturing Manager: *Alexis R. Heydt*
Marketing Manager: *Dan Rush*
Editorial Assistant: *Tara Ruggiero*

Prentice-Hall, Inc.
A Simon & Schuster Company
Upper Saddle River, New Jersey 07458

Prentice Hall books are widely used by corporations and government agencies for training, marketing, and resale.
The publisher offers discounts on this book when ordered in bulk quantities.
For more information, contact: Corporate Sales Department, Phone: 800-382-3419;
FAX: 201-236-7141; E-mail: corpsales@prenhall.com
Or write: Corp. Sales Dept., Prentice Hall PTR, 1 Lake Street, Upper Saddle River, NJ 07458

Printed in the United States of America
10 9 8 7 6 5 4 3 2 1

ISBN 0-13-842378-4

Prentice-Hall International (UK) Limited, *London*
Prentice-Hall of Australia Pty. Limited, *Sydney*
Prentice-Hall Canada Inc., *Toronto*
Prentice-Hall Hispanoamericana, S.A., *Mexico*
Prentice-Hall of India Private Limited, *New Delhi*
Prentice-Hall of Japan, Inc., *Tokyo*
Simon & Schuster Asia Pte. Ltd., *Singapore*
Editora Prentice-Hall do Brasil, Ltda., *Rio de Janeiro*

Dedication

To my family: Anja, Daniel, and David.

Thank you, once again, for your extreme patience and understanding. I love you all.

ACKNOWLEDGMENTS

There were so many people who helped with this book. Many helped with the technical side, while others supported me in the dream I had. I felt it necessary to either just say thanks to everyone at once or to list all their names. Because I am personally grateful to everyone who helped, I feel it necessary to thank everyone personally. The problem with that is that there may be someone I missed. I went over this list and through all my notes. I hope I didn't leave anyone out. If I did, please accept my apologies. The support everyone gave was very much appreciated.

I would first like to thank my parents-in-law, Gerd and Renate Hofmann, for giving me the most wonderful woman in the world.

Thanks again to my editor at Prentice Hall, Mark Taub. His patience in letting me get this project done when it was ready was greatly appreciated.

Very special thanks to Alan Langton. Aside from helping me to keep my English up, he helped to keep my blood pressure down.

Thanks to Lothar Schultheiß for the nice art work he provided for me and for giving me the tips and tricks to create some on my own.

Thanks to Frank Heumann for the great logo and some more great tips.

Thanks to Kalen Delaney of Sound Software Solutions. Aside from being the best SQL Server instructor in the world, she is also a *great* sister.

For giving me the motivation and being an inspiration to my writing in general, I owe a great deal of thanks and gratitude to Bill Leikam, my English teacher at Cupertino High School. Bill, it's all your fault!

Thanks to my reviewers Mark Komarinski, Han Holl, and Alan Cox. You guys did a great job and definitely made the book even better. I owe you all a big one!

Special thanks to Mark Bolzern and the people at WorkGroup Solutions. I really appreciate the support I had from the beginning.

Not enough good things can be said about Ransome Love, Nancy Pomeroy, Lyle Ball, Allan Smart, Nicholas Wells, and Kent Paddock of Caldera, Inc. What a group. Great software and great people!

Thanks again to Jeff Hyman of Cactus International for keeping my Linux system safe with the Linux Lone-Tar backup software.

I would also like to thank Hartmut Lorenz, Achim Knauer, Holger Ranft, and Ralf Schwarz for helping me keep what's left of my sanity.

Thanks to the following people for providing me materials for this book:

Jenny Ahn of Parasoft

Mike Burris, Heather Nelson, Marty Siegel, and Mike Crawford of Stallion Technologies. Now *that's* what you call support!

Frederic Falise of Digital Equipment Corporation

Joel Goldberger of InfoMagic

Astrid Hütte of StarDivision

Randy Just of Just Computers

Nicole Martinez of Craftwork Solutions

Jürgen Neubauer, Michael Stieb, and Franz von Profft of Applix, München. (Now that you have ApplixWare for Linux, you need to get working on the Applix Enterprise help desk.)

Evan Schaffer of Revolutionary Software

Anna Selvia, Lisa Sullivan, and Bob Young of RedHat

Tom Thompson, Ed DeJesus, and John Montgomery of *BYTE* magazine

Jack Velte of Walnut Creek CD-ROM

Also thanks to these people for providing me information and help at different points during this project:

Agus Budy Wuysang, Akasapu V. Appalas, Alan Westhagen, Almond Wong, Anand Rangaraja, Andreas Schiffler, Andrew Piziali, Anthony Greene, Anthony Moscatel, Anton de Wet, Baba Buehler, Benjammin H. Graham, Bill Wright, Brian Talley, Bryan C. Andregg, Chuck Stickelman, Chris Fearnley, Chris Foote, Dan Carter, Dan Merillat, Dan O'Connel,

Dane Wilder, Danny Arseneau, Danny ter Haar, Dave Comer, Dave Hahn, Dave Nuttall, David Bonn, David J. Boatwright, David Wuertele, Don Marti, Donovan Ready, Edmund Humenberger, Emmett Dulaney, Eric Gonzales, Eric L. Green, Erick Gonzales, Frank Konitzer, Frederick Lee Hendrix, Georgios Papadopoulos, Gerard Hynes, Greg Fields, Greg Roelofs, Gregor Gerstmann, Idan Shoham, Jacobus Erasmus, James Youngman, Jan Vicherek, Jan Walter, Jeff Gardner, Jeff Stern, Jeremy Buch, Jim Nicholson, Johann Fiby, Juan A. Pons, Juan Pons, Kamran Karimi, Kerry Schwab, Lydia Kinta, Mark Grennan, Marke Lehrer, Markus Håkansson, Mattias Kregert, Michael Slocombe, Michael Stutz, Mike Black, Mike Knott, Mike York, Nat Makarevitch, Nich Busigin, Nick Atkins, Patrick Giagnocavo, Peter H. Salus, Peter Kreps, Peter-Paul Witta, Reginald Burgess, Richard Goerwitz, Richard Gregory, Robert Fossum, Russ Nelson, Russell Coker, Scott Chistley, Scott Raney, Steve Herber, Steve Mertz, Teddy Tan, Ternton Twining, Terrence Liao, Tim Sailer, Vinchn Pujol, Zanna Knight.

Lastly, thanks to you for using Linux and giving me the reason to write this book.

Although a lot of people provided technical information and reviewed my material, any mistakes that may appear are solely my responsibility. I tried to test everything and check everything I said, but I'm only human. Therefore, there just might be something in here that's wrong. If you find something that you believe is inaccurate, please tell me. Also, please tell me what you might have added, left out, or changed in this book. Most of all, I would like to find out how much you learned from it and whether my efforts were worth it. I can be reached at:

jimmo@jimmo.com

or

100542.2677@compuserve.com

Acknowledgments vii

What this Book is About xix

Chapter 1—Introduction to Operating Systems 1

1.1 What Is an Operating System? 2
1.2 Processes 4
1.3 Files and Directories 11
1.4 Operating System Layers 16
1.5 Moving On 17

Chapter 2—The Linux Basics 21

2.1 What Linux is All About 22
2.1.1 A Guided Tour 22
2.1.2 What Linux Is Made Of 29
2.1.3 What Linux Does 31
2.1.4 What Goes with Linux 34
2.2 Reading All About It: Linux Documentation 35
2.3 What's Next 36

Chapter 3—Shells and Basic Utilities 37

3.1 Talking to Linux: The Shell 38
3.1.1 The Search Path 39
3.1.2 Shell Variables 44
3.1.3 Regular Expressions and Metacharacters 46
3.1.4 Quotes 52
3.1.5 Pipes and Redirection 54
3.1.6 Interpreting the Command 58
3.1.7 Different Kinds of Shells 62
3.1.8 Command Line Editing64
3.1.9 Command Line Completion 65
3.1.10 Functions66
3.1.11 Job Control 68
3.1.12 Aliases 70
3.1.13 A Few More Constructs 71
3.1.14 The C-Shell 72
3.2 Commonly Used Utilities 76
3.2.1 Looking for Files 77
3.2.2 Looking Through Files 82
3.3 Basic Shell Scripting 88
3.3.1 Odds and Ends 97

Chapter 4—Editing Files 105

4.1 Interactively Editing Files with vi 106
4.1.1 Basics 106
4.1.2 Basic Editing and Movement Commands 108
4.1.3 More vi Magic 120
4.1.4 Configuring vi 122
4.2 Interactively Editing Files with `emacs` 123
4.2.1 Starting `emacs` 124
4.2.2 Basic Movement 125
4.2.3 Editing Text 126
4.2.4 Searching and Replacing Text 127
4.2.5 Customizing `emacs` 128
4.3 Noninteractively Editing Files with sed 130
4.4 Programming with awk 134
4.5 Putting Things Together 142
4.6 Perl: The Language of the Web 142

Chapter 5—Basic System Administration 165

5.1 Starting and Stopping the System 166
5.1.1 The Boot Process 166
5.1.2 Run Levels 171
5.1.3 Stopping the System 173
5.2 Users and User Accounts 174
5.3 User Accounts 175
5.3.1 Logging into the System 180
5.3.2 Terminals 184
5.3.3 `cron` 188
5.3.4 User Communication 192
5.4 Printers and Interfaces 195
5.4.1 Advanced Formatting Options 198
5.4.2 The `printcap` File 200
5.4.3 Remote Printing 201
5.4.4 The Next Step 202

Chapter 6—The Operating System and Its Environment 203

6.1 The Kernel: The Heartbeat of Linux 204
6.1.1 Processes 204
6.1.2 The Life Cycle of Processes 212
6.1.3 Process Scheduling 215
6.1.4 Interrupts, Exceptions, and Traps 216
6.1.5 Signals 220
6.1.6 System Calls 220
6.1.7 Paging and Swapping 221
6.1.8 Processes in Action 223
6.2 Rebuilding Your Kernel 226
6.2.1 Installing Your Kernel 231
6.3 Devices and Device Nodes 233
6.3.1 Major and Minor Numbers 233
6.3.2 File Systems and Files 238
6.3.3 Disk Layout 238

Chapter 7—The X-Windows System 247

7.1 Configuring the X-Windows Server 248
7.2 The Basics of X 252

7.3 Displaying Clients 256
7.4 Resources 258
7.5 Colors 261
7.6 Fonts 263
7.7 The Window Manager 268
7.8 The Pager 272
7.9 What Else? 273

Chapter 8—The Computer Itself 275

8.1 Basic Input/Output Services and the System Bus 276
8.2 The Expansion Bus 279
8.2.1 Industry Standard Architecture (ISA) 280
8.2.2 Micro-Channel Architecture (MCA) 285
8.2.3 Extended Industry Standard Architecture (EISA) 288
8.2.4 VESA Local Bus (VLB) 290
8.2.5 Peripheral Component Interconnect (PCI) 291
8.3 The Small Computer Systems Interface (SCSI) 293
8.3.1 Termination 300
8.4 Memory 301
8.4.1 RAM 301
8.4.2 Cache Memory 305
8.4.3 Parity 308
8.5 The Central Processing Unit 309
8.5.1 Intel Processors 310
8.5.2 Alpha Processors 319
8.6 Hard Disks 321
8.7 Floppy Drives 328
8.8 Tape Drives 330
8.9 CD-ROMS 333
8.10 Serial Ports 335
8.11 Parallel Ports 339
8.12 Video Cards and Monitors 341
8.13 Modems 344
8.14 Printers 348

8.15 Mice 351
8.16 Uninterruptable Power Supplies 352

Chapter 9—Talking to Other Machines 355

9.1 TCP/IP 356
9.1.1 Network Services 362
9.1.2 Network Standards 364
9.1.3 IP Addressing 366
9.1.4 Subnet Masks 368
9.1.5 Routing and IP Gateways 370
9.1.6 DNS: Finding Other Machines 376
9.1.7 Configuring the Domain Name System (DNS) 381
9.1.8 Debugging the Name Server 392
9.1.9 Your Own IP Address 397
9.2 NFS 399
9.2.1 The Flow of Things 402
9.2.2 When Things Go Wrong 403
9.2.3 Automount 405
9.3 SAMBA 412
9.4 Serial Network Protocols 419
9.4.1 Serial Line Internet Protocol (SLIP) 419
9.4.2 Point-to-Point Protocol (PPP) 420
9.4.3 Testing the Configuration 421
9.4.4 Automating the Login 424
9.4.5 Starting the Server 425
9.4.6 Setting up a PPP Server 426
9.5 Accessing the Web 427
9.6 Firewalls 430
9.6.1 Securing the Server 432
9.6.2 Securing the Internal Network 434
9.7 Network Technologies 435
9.7.1 Ethernet 435
9.7.2 Token-Ring Network 436
9.7.3 ATM 437
9.7.4 ISDN 437

Chapter 10—Installing and Upgrading 441

10.1 Preparing for the Installation 444
10.1.1 Hardware Requirements 448

10.1.2 Repartitioning 449
10.1.3 Installation Problems 450
10.1.4 Preparing for the Worst 452
10.2 Upgrading an Existing System 453
10.3 Adding Hardware 453
10.3.1 Preparation 454
10.3.2 CPU 457
10.3.3 RAM 458
10.3.4 SCSI Devices 460
10.3.5 Hard Disks 460
10.3.6 Other SCSI Devices 462
10.3.7 Serial Terminals 463
10.3.8 EIDE Drives 464
10.3.9 CD-ROMs 465
10.4 A Treasure Chest of Choices 465
10.4.1 Caldera Open Linux (COL) 466
10.4.2 Craftworks Linux 467
10.4.3 Deutsche Linux Distribution (DLD) 468
10.4.4 Linux PRO 469
10.4.5 RedHat 470
10.4.6 Slackware 471

Chapter 11—System Monitoring 473

11.1 Finding Out About Your System 474
11.1.1 Hardware and the Kernel 475
11.1.2 Terminals 479
11.1.3 Hard Disks and File Systems 480
11.1.4 User Files 481
11.1.5 Network Files 482
11.2 What the System Is Doing Now 485
11.2.1 Users 486
11.2.2 Processes 487
11.2.3 Files and File Systems 490
11.2.4 Checking Other Things 492

Chapter 12—Problem Solving 495

12.1 Solving Problems Yourself 496
12.1.1 Preparation 496
12.1.2 Checking the Sanity of Your System 504

12.1.3 Problem Solving 507
12.1.4 Crash Recovery 511
12.2 Getting Help 513
12.2.1 Calling Support 514
12.2.2 Consultants 525
12.2.3 Other Sources 533

Chapter 13—Linux in Your Business 535

13.1 Supporting Your Users 535
13.1.1 Configuring the System 536
13.1.2 Accessing Information 539
13.2 Security 555
13.2.1 Real Threats 555
13.2.2 Real World Examples 564
13.3 What You Can Do about the Danger 568
13.3.1 Watching Your System 569
13.3.2 The Official Word 578
13.4 User Software 587
13.4.1 Desktops 589
13.4.2 Office Suites 594
13.4.3 Development Software 598
13.4.5 Back-up Software 601
13.4.6 Text and Publishing 601
13.4.7 Databases 602
13.4.8 Wabi 603

Chapter 14—Building an Internet Server 609

14.1 Connecting to the Internet 610
14.1.1 Web Services 610
14.1.2 Web Service Providers 611
14.2 Building the Server 613
14.2.1 Browsing the Web 613
14.2.2 Configuring the Web 614
14.2.3. Anonymous ftp 624
14.3 Building Your Pages 634
14.3.1 HTML: The Language of the Web 634
14.3.2 Connecting Your Pages 652
14.3.3 Tips and Techniques 667

14.3.4 The Next Step 670
14.4 Java 670

Chapter 15—Business on the Internet 673

15.1 Why Do Companies Do Business on the Internet? 674
15.1.1 Corporate Identity and Your Web Site 677
15.1.2 The "World Wide" Web 679
15.2 First Things First 680
15.2.1 Plan 681
15.2.2 Forming Your Team 682
15.2.3 Establish Ownership 684
15.2.4 Wait Until You Are Ready 685
15.3 Developing Your Web Site 686
15.3.1 Accessing the Information 691
15.3.2 Engage the Visitor 694
15.4 Content: Service to Your Customer 696
15.4.1 Information 696
15.4.2 Marketing 699
15.4.3 Customer Service and Technical Support 706
15.4.4 Discussion Lists/Forums 712
15.4.5 The Frequently Asked Questions List 713
15.4.6 Public Relations 714
15.4.7 Sales 715
15.5 Measuring Your Success 720
15.6 Attracting Attention 725
15.7 Things to Consider 726
15.7.1 Legal Issues 726
15.7.2 Intellectual Property 727
15.8 Odds and Ends 727

Appendix A—Glossary 731

Appendix B—Suggested Reading 767

Index 777

WHAT THIS BOOK IS ABOUT

As you picked up this book you may have asked yourself, "Why should I run my business on Linux?" The question is quite understandable considering that Linux started out as one person's college project. It is the work of thousands of volunteers around the world who have contributed the various components. There is no company that has developed it, so there is no "seal of approval" or "100 percent money-back guarantee if you are not completely satisfied."

So why run your business on Linux?

If you are looking to run a system composed of the latest software on the most advanced hardware, Linux is not for you. Commercial UNIX vendors have good working relationships with both software developers and hardware manufacturers and more than likely have tested the most current versions of the software or drivers. In many cases, the product has been on the market for sometime, before the work begins porting it to Linux. Even the sheer number of supported products steers a company toward a commercial operating system.

So why use Linux?

There are dozens of reasons why computer "hackers" like Linux. First of all, it's free. There are none of the same licensing issues as with commercial UNIX products. One copy of Linux can be installed on every machine in your company if you choose to do so. The only costs involved are those in obtaining the first copy. If you have a friend with a copy, nothing prevents you from installing that copy. If not, there are many mail-order houses that sell copies for nominal fees, usually just to cover the media and handling. If you have an Internet connection, copies are available from many sites.

Now that sounds like a contradiction. If the software is free, how are companies selling it? Well, "free" actually has two meanings. If you want, you can download the source to the kernel, along with all of the programs, utilities, and applications. Doing this from work is probably free, but you are likely to annoy your boss. If you do it from home and your Internet provider is a local phone call away, it may also be free. Otherwise, you are looking at a hefty phone bill.

What "free" really means for Linux is that you are free to do with it what you want. That means you are free to copy it as often as you like to as many machines as you like. You are given the complete source code so you are free to change everything about the system that you don't like. This even means that you are free to charge for it. Considering the price of most distributions and what you get for your money, it's close enough to being free that there is no need to argue about it.

Supporting this is the fact that Linux is small. With only 2Mb of RAM and 40Mb of hard disk space, you can install and run Linux successfully. However, if you want and if you can afford the hardware, Linux will run on the fastest Pentium–and even the Pentium Pro–and you can install hundreds of megabytes worth of programs and applications that are available. (My gigabyte partition is almost full of *commercial* Linux software with very little data.)

Also good for the hacker is that the source code is readily available. This does not mean that you must download it from some Internet site. Instead, it is a requirement that all versions that are distributed provide access to the source code. You can twist and tweak the system to your heart's content, changing anything and everything.

But what good does this do a business?

Well, if you think about it for a moment, all of the reasons I just mentioned are valid for using Linux in a business environment as well. Obviously as a business you want the best product for the least amount of money. Obtaining Linux from a commercial distributor might cost you $50, which is certainly reasonable. Some are bundled with other products and, as a result, may up upwards of $200. Based on what you get, this is reasonable, too. If you already have machines in your company, you probably don't have to buy any new hardware to get Linux to run. That will save you money.

Because you have the source code, you can *completely* change the system to fit your needs. You can configure your system to best support your users. UNIX, in general, is customizable. By providing the source code, Linux takes that feature one step further.

What's the point of having free software when you can't use it effectively?

Valid question, but it doesn't apply to Linux. As I said, Linux can run on a wide range of hardware platforms. If you have a 20Mhz 386 (like my son does), Linux runs fine. If you have a 133Mhz Pentium (as I do), Linux runs fine as well. Linux also supports most of the standard bus types like ISA, EISA, PCI, and Localbus. Linux has also been ported to DEC Alpha and SPARC machines, and versions are being developed for Motorola 680x0 and PowerPC (if not already). Major software products such as WordPerfect, Mathematica, CorelDraw, StarWriter and Applixware have been ported as well.

Linux is also a very powerful operating system. It's fast and takes advantage of the multitasking and multi-user capabilities of the hardware, just like commercial UNIX dialects. Because you have complete access to the source code, you can change the behavior of the system to suit your needs *exactly*. In contrast, most commercial versions will allow you to tune certain parameters, but often that is not enough.

Most of the readily available Linux distributions come with all of the tools, applications, and add-ons that you might expect only to find in a larger product offer. These include compilers, The X Window System, TCP/IP, and even a WWW server. Dozens of commercial products are available as well as hundreds of shareware or freeware programs.

Linux is often called a "clone" of UNIX; it just has the "look and feel" of UNIX. However, what is UNIX? The Santa Cruz Operation (SCO) owns the rights to the original AT&T source code. So is the SCO version really UNIX? AT&T produces a version of UNIX, so is the AT&T version really UNIX? In my mind, UNIX is more of a concept than a single entity. There are certain characteristics that an operating system must have to be called UNIX. Linux has the same basic characteristics as all the other dialects, including all of the standard tools. However, Linux has not been official approved by X/Open. However, companies like Caldera are working on it, therefore, we need to call it UNIX-like (or simply Linux).

Users and administrators who know how to work on other dialects of UNIX can easily switch to Linux in a relatively short time. It has all the programs and utilities that UNIX administrators have grown to love. Many have substantially more functionality than their commercial cousins.

Implementing Linux in your business has another advantage as a result of it being free. If you are a developer, Linux can be installed on computers at home, just as easily as those at work. Even if you have a DOS/Windows machine, Linux allows you to install without having to repartition your hard disk. It will allow you to install directly on top of a

DOS (FAT) file system. Because it recognizes the standard PC partition table, Linux can be installed on a separate partition just as easily. You can have your employees working on the same systems at home that they do at work, without incurring extra license fees for the OS.

One advantage that Microsoft has is its sheer numbers. You find Microsoft products everywhere. I know that if I sit down at a Windows machine somewhere, the commands will be the same as what I am used to.

Often, one requirement of MIS managers is to use "shrink-wrapped" software. They want to be able to get a product off-the-shelf, believing that its accessibility is somehow a guarantee that it is good software. Although you won't (yet) find a Microsoft product saying "Cool: It runs on Linux," there is a wide range of software available for Linux. Most distributions come with a very extensive set of application software. However, there are many commercial products available, some of which we will get into later.

You don't need to buy commercial software to do productive work. LIVIA Informatique in Paris, France, has been working on French translations of some of the UNIX books published by O'Reilly & Associates. The latest title available is the French version of *CGI Programming on the World Wide Web* by Shishir Gundavaram. What does LIVIA use to do their work? The `emacs` editor that comes with every Linux system. LIVIA director Nat Makarevitch says, "We edit the documents under `emacs` with the help of a mode named 'AUC TeX.' In fact, `emacs` is here the Swiss (army) knife helping us to tackle all edition-related work."

There is a common misconception that something that's free is not worth much. Everyone knows that you get what you pay for, right? Scott Christley, President of NET-Community, reminds us that free software does not mean the price, but the freedom to change it to fit your needs. Scott goes on to say, "...the cost of the software is generally irrelevant in the big picture. It's the maintenance costs over the lifetime of the software that becomes the biggest slice of the pie." Because you have thousands of people assisting in the maintenance effort, your costs are minimized.

David Bonn of Seattle Software Labs puts its another way: "Consider air. Consider listening to the radio. Consider beers bought by a friend. Linux combines aspects of all three."

If you need the features of commercial products, they are available as well. Products start at the small end with text editors, word processors, spreadsheets, databases, etc., and move on to full-blown office suites. These are not products that are just thrown together or "clones" of the commercial products available for Windows and other operating systems. Instead, these are the same products. Caldera has created their

Internet Office Suite, which contains a complete version of WordPerfect. StarDivision has released a Linux version of their StarOffice suite. There is also the less known Applixware from Applix. Despite the fact that it is not as widespread as some of the other products, Applixware provides a fully integrated office suite, which includes a tool builder and an HTML editor.

What good does all that do when it crashes all the time?

The answer to this question is simple: it doesn't. Linux has been installed on hundreds of thousands of machines and runs virtually trouble-free. Because every administrator has access to the source code, when problems do arise, they can be quickly located and solved, and the remedies are then made available to everyone. Even so, because it is so widely used, it has been tested as much (or more so) than commercial products, making it just as reliable.

In addition to being reliable, an operating system needs to be stable. There is no doubt that Linux is stable. The only times my system is rebooted is when I turn it off at night and when I make changes to the kernel. Minor changes, such as changing your IP address (which, by the way, requires you to restart a Windows machine), are not causes to reboot Linux. Additionally, device drivers can be loaded into the kernel of a running Linux system.

Okay, not having to reboot to load drivers doesn't necessarily mean that a system is stable. However, running an Internet server 24 hours a day, 7 days a week, and then only rebooting to update the kernel is a pretty good indication of the system's robustness. When you add a company with more than 200 offices that run solely on Linux, the evidence is pretty clear.

The fact that some people use Linux does not necessarily mean that it is stable. They may believe that the cost is right to accept a few crashes now and then. Aside from talking to the tens of thousands of people that are using Linux, you can take Linux for a test drive to see just how stable it is.

You might find a reseller that will allow you a trial of NT. SCO is providing a single user version of their OS for free. However, letting you run extended tests (for example, over six months) on a *complete* version is not something that you are likely to find (assuming that you are not planning to lay out several million dollars and the reseller will do anything to get your business).

It's completely different with Linux. For around $50, you can get yourself a complete, unlimited user version of Linux. With the OS, you get a fully functional WWW and FTP server, development tools, text processing, scientific applications, and much more. The nice thing is that it is not a test version–it is the complete version. Once you pay your $50 (probably less), the product is yours to keep–forever!

This gives you a chance to test out the product and see if it fits your needs. If not, you have spent less than what other products would charge just for the shipping. A good approach would be to use Linux as your Internet server. More than 10 percent of Internet servers are already running Linux, which is twice as many as NT. Use Linux in an area where it has already proven itself and then evaluate it for other purposes.

Michael Slocombe, a staff engineer at BBN, describes Linux's stability like this: "In addition, it appears that Unix/Linux operating systems are much more stable than Microsoft operating systems. It seems common when working with PC/Microsoft support people that they recommend a procedure of rebooting the system. If a PC/Microsoft system crashes once a week, that seems to be considered reasonable. If a UNIX system exhibited similar problems, it would be considered broken and the support people would be trying to figure out what was wrong."

Michael Stutz, president of Design Systems Labs (DSL), reminds us that the majority of Linux software is free and free software is written for the "art" of it and not the paycheck.

So whose code are you going to trust more? Someone who writes code because it's their job or someone who writes it because it's their passion? DSL is one company that has taken their confidence in Linux to the extreme. They run every aspect of their business on Linux.

Not every company has the ability to hire a full-time administrator to spend hours digging through source code looking for the cause of problems.

It is difficult to get away from the fact that the support structure for Linux does not have as strong a foundation as Windows NT or SCO. Each of these organizations has dozens of engineers on staff to answer your questions. There are hundreds of companies all over the world that will also provide support.

Originally, I had wanted to say that the support structure was not as extensive. However, within a matter of seconds I realized that the opposite is true. There are tens of thousands of people using Linux on the Internet. It is their devotion to the product that motivates them to provide support. There are few places I have found that are comparable to the enthusiasm in which people provide help, assistance, and support in the various newsgroups and mailing lists. The Linux community is called a "community" for good reason. Thousands of people are willing to help, just because they want to and not because they are getting paid for it.

Although there is no one company that produces Linux where you can call to get tech support, this does not mean you get no support. Not only do you get quick responses from the many different network newsgroups specifically for Linux, many independent companies provide the same kind of support for Linux as you can get for other products. If that's not enough, you have the complete source code that you can look through to find solutions to your problems.

Looking through tens of thousands of lines of source code is not an easy task. Besides, you may need help getting your system designed and configured so you may not have access to the soruce code, yet. Fortunately, there are (as of this writing) 175 consultants world-wide who provide Linux consultant. The Consultant-HOWTO (http://www.cyrius.com/tbm/Consultants-HOWTO) provides you with the necessary contact information to get you on your way.

If you can't spend the time looking for problems in the source code and can't afford a consultant, you can often find the solution yourself. Early in the development of Linux, the Linux Documentation Project was established. Most versions of Linux come with very extensive documentation. This is often more in-depth than you would get for commercial UNIX versions. There are already dozens of excellent books on Linux covering everything from basic user commands to kernel programming. In addition, because Linux is so much like UNIX, books on "generic" UNIX are useful as well.

Aside from just the amount of support and the willingness people have to support the product, there are a couple of other advantages. First, the people who support Linux are people who actually work with Linux. They have had either the same problems themselves or experience with similar problems. Even if no one has the exact answer to your problem, there will be enough discussion of the problem that a solution will be found.

Another key advantage is that the developers themselves read and reply to these messages. And, because they use the products, they are more than interested in finding bugs or anything else that decreases the value of Linux.

In November 1996, I read a message on the Internet from someone who had examined the source code of one program and had determined that there was the *potential* that someone *could* exploit an oversight in the source code to force the system to execute some other code. On the *same* day that this was reported, the developer had posted the patch to the Internet. How often do the developers of commercial products say that the fix *may* be in the next release that is six months away?

However, you don't have to wait for the developer to fix it. Because you have access to the source code, you can fix it yourself. While you spend time and money working around the bugs and shortcoming of other systems in Linux, you are correcting the bugs and making improvements; therefore, you are increasing your own productivity. You can then make these modifications available on the Internet. The developers are always grateful when people make corrections and are willing to provide suggestions to help improve the product even further.

In considering Linux, you have the choice of spending tens of thousands of dollars in initial costs for an OS and continuing support, or you hire a Linux guru who customizes the product exactly to fit your needs. Considering the philosophy of Linux, you can customize it to meet your needs now as well as in the future. This is much more cost-effective than spending hundreds (if not thousands) of dollars on the new version of another OS and hope that it meets your needs.

Solutions to problems and answers to questions are no slower. In most cases, responses come within just a few hours. The key disadvantage of this system is that a few hours may be too slow. If you have a crashed system, you need help now. Being able to call support and get an immediate response is worth the money. There are dozens (hundreds already?) of companies all over the US, and many others throughout the world, that provide Linux services and support. You will find URLs to many of these companies on the accompanying CD.

Jeremy Buch at the University of Colorado feels that not having a single company behind Linux is actually an advantage. It results in a "feeling of 'community' with other users." It is not as "stale" as other systems and because you have the ability to "add your own," it is constantly changing and improving.

Getting support for the software is a major concern for MIS managers. If problems occur, they want two things. First, they want their questions to be answered. All one needs to do is take a look at the various Linux newsgroups and mailing lists to see what kind of support is available. This is often far better than the support you get from commercial vendors, as these are the developers themselves. They have an active, personal concern in the quality of the product and are more than willing to help. Normally you will find that questions are usually answered within hours (depending on your connection to the Internet).

The key problem for MIS managers is the issue of "normally." I have experienced cases in which a question was posted and days passed before someone answered. Maybe the developer was on vacation or was too busy to read his or her mail; there are dozens of reasons. If the problem is urgent, then even waiting a couple of hours is unacceptable.

Second, MIS managers want someone to take responsibility. Or, as Lyle Ball of Caldera put it, "They want someone whose neck they can ring." That's a problem with Linux–there is no single company that takes responsibility. Who is there to "blame" when something goes wrong? In general, the answer is no one. Because of the very nature of Linux, there probably never will be any single entity that takes responsibility for it. Basically, every program, module, and piece of Linux documentation has a disclaimer that "absolves" the developer or writer from any responsibility if the product doesn't work. However, from the standpoint of the MIS manager, there needs to be someone not only to take the responsibility, but also the blame. This certainly will never happen with Linux.

Does this then mean that Linux support is designed to be the ad hoc process it is on the Internet? Certainly not. Although not every Linux distribution comes with free support, many, including the one you find on the accompanying CD, do provide free support. For details on the support that WorkGroup Solutions provides for this CD, check the accompanying README file.

Caldera is another company that provides support. In their case, they will provide up to five free calls during the first 30 days, which is similar to the support that WorkGroup Solutions provides. If necessary, you can also purchase extended support contracts with the service that is provided, which vary in cost. This is no different from what other operating system vendors provide.

Taking this one step further, Caldera is building up a very extensive network of resellers and value-added resellers (VARs) throughout the world that will also provide support. Where major UNIX vendors like SCO are moving away from the low-end workstation toward the server market, companies like Caldera are filling the gap with products like Caldera OpenLinux. In addition, the products that are put on top of the Caldera base are the same that you find on the other systems.

To provide the technology necessary for your business to remain competitive, the operating system must remain current. Until recently, most of the software and hardware vendors have not been taking Linux seriously. Through the efforts of hardware companies like Stallion and software companies like Caldera, this is changing.

Ransome Love, VP of Marketing at Caldera, mentions that one key to success for any operating system is the technology partnerships that it develops. Companies like Microsoft and SCO have developed these partnerships and, as a result, have the latest technologies that the other vendors have to have offer. Caldera has made that step to develop the relationship with companies like Novell and Netscape: they are now including Novell Gateway as well as Netscape Navigator Gold in their products. This, coupled with the other commercial products that they include, ensures that you have the tools necessary to run your business.

Being able to support the product does not mean just putting out distribution and having software to go with it. Support means that you must be an active player in the Linux world. Caldera is doing this by trying to get the X/Open branding for Caldera OpenLinux so that it can finally call itself "UNIX." Other companies, such as WGS, are involved in overseeing the smooth interaction of all the various players. Mark Bolzern, president of WGS, and Ransom Love, VP of Marketing at Caldera, are both on the board of directors of Linux International (*www.linux.org*).

Can it really do what I need?

The answer is a very solid "Yes!" System administrators and users alike want to be able to fit a system to their needs and not have some marketing person tell them where they should go today. If you can't make the software fit your needs, you waste time trying to work around the problem.

Every system administrator realizes that his/her primary responsibility is to provide the technology needed to make other people's work more productive. (Okay, I do know some MIS managers who believe that IS is a goal unto itself.) The best way to make people work more efficiently is to match up their work with the technology–not necessarily buying products that match the way they work, nor changing work habits to match a particular product, but instead, figuring out what works best and matching a product with that work.

This means that the product must be configurable. You will rarely find a product that fits perfectly into your business. There is always some configuration that needs to be done. The more you can make a product fit your needs and the less you have to change your work to fit the product, the better you can work.

UNIX, by its very nature is configurable and extensible. Linux takes this feature to extremes. Not only do you have the full configurability of any UNIX system, Linux also provides you with the source code. This includes both the kernel and the standard applications and programs. If there is some functionality that you need and it is not included in the original program, you can add it yourself.

One aspect of being able to change software is considering what you have to do to make changes take effect. If you have ever run a Windows machine, you know that even something as simple as changing your default gateway, or even your own IP address, requires that you reboot the machine.

Linux, like most dialects of UNIX, require you to reboot only when you add drivers to the system. However, in the case of Linux, there are many drivers you can add (load) as you need, without the need to reboot. Other simpler acts, like changing an IP address, can be done within seconds, without having to reboot.

However, we need to be fair when we talk about configuring your system. As of this writing, Windows NT is much easier to configure than Linux. The point-and-click configuration under Windows NT is much simpler than editing files under Linux. There are a few GUI-based tools provided with most Linux distributions. However, the majority of the configuration needs to be done manually. To configure a Linux system, you therefore need to have more experience and skill than for Windows NT. Just as you need more experience and skill to be a Cordon Bleu chef than to toss a TV dinner into the microwave.

Now, this might sound like a load of propaganda. It's not. I have supported a Windows network of more than 500 PCs and two dozen NT servers. There are things that you simply cannot do with NT that you can with Linux (or other dialects of UNIX, for that matter). Some things require that you re-install the entire system and lose security and other configuration information. Others are simply impossible.

On the other hand, it really is a Microsoft world out there. People have grown accustomed to Microsoft products. In all fairness, I have to admit that they are good products. Like any software, there are bugs and other shortcomings, but the quality of products like Word and Excel are difficult to argue. Forcing your employees to switch to a Linux product just to switch to Linux is not efficient.

Does this mean that you have to run an NT server to support them? Not at all. The Samba package that is available on all newer distributions is a wonderful alternative. It allows you to connect to a Linux machine and use both file and print services.

Because of the design of the configuration file, you can share every user's home directory within 30 seconds. On an NT system, you would need at least that long per user. You can also define default characteristics that are shared among the various resources. There is no need to specifically change them for each resource as with NT. I also created a script that added a list of 20 users to the system within 60 seconds. Because the home directory was automatically shared, I didn't need to explicitly define it as I would in NT.

Admittedly, the security within NT is more extensive than with Linux. File access is defined using an Access Control List (ACL). This enables you to define access to a very fine level, much more than with most dialects of UNIX, in fact. Although the structures exist within the Linux code, no distribution has yet implemented ACLs. In addition, the algorithms used in NT passwords is more complex than those for Linux.

This is a double-edged sword. You are extremely limited in what you can do to your system because of this security. For example, when the system is re-installed (as when you simply want to change its name), all the security information is lost. There is no way to copy it to the new system. All the users must be re-created and the permissions must be set on every single file. There is no tool to say, for example, if the permissions or owner of a file are a certain value, then change them back. Simply put, you had better know exactly how you want your system to be configured before you start.

Then we come back to the ease of configuration. Without a doubt, that which you can configure is much easier to do it with NT. Since what you can configure is limited, making the interface easy to use is not a problem.

Being the ice-breaker in business is not always the best approach.

Don't worry, you're not. There are already thousands of companies that use Linux. In fact, more than 10 percent of all WWW servers run Linux. This is more that several commercial UNIX dialects, such as SCO, HP/UX, AIX, and DEC OSF/1.

The first widespread commercial use of Linux was as an Internet server. However, this has quickly changed to the point where entire businesses are being run on Linux. One German company, Sixt Rent-a-Car, has implemented Linux in more than 200 offices throughout Germany. In addition, there are hundreds of other companies that run Linux alongside other operating systems and a large number of Internet Service Providers that run exclusively on Linux.

So why use Linux in your business?

A better question is why not? If you are strictly a Microsoft house, in that you only use non-Microsoft products when you must, there is probably no need to try to convince you otherwise. However, if you are still trying to decide what the best solution is, have decided to implement a UNIX solution, or haven't decided which direction to take, then maybe I can give you a gentle push.

Running your business on Linux is not an issue of being on the cutting edge. Today, it is more like jumping on the Linux bandwagon as more and more are realizing the business potential of Linux. Chris Fearnley, a Linux and Internet consultant, says that one of Linux's key advantages is the "support for enterprising small businesses." Aside from the monetary savings of the OS itself, there is savings made when fitting the product to the business.

Chris says: "The motivated entrepreneur...can focus on modifying those pre-existing Linux tools to meet her needs (or build an application out of several such tools–this is the power of Unix's 'tool' model of software and after learning how to use it, one will be eternally frustrated by systems that try to do everything in one big application [the silliest recent 'innovation' being the concept of the Web browser as operating system]).

"Free software allows the businessperson the ability to get custom software without the vast expense that that type of software incurs on a commercial OS. Moreover, when the entrepreneur shares the improvements they needed with the rest of the Linux community, they will get helpful feedback about how to improve their contribution."

This statement directly supports the Internet mentality of sharing. The Internet is a value-added community in which you are expected to add to the value by making a contribution to it. Linux takes that philosophy into the world of operating systems.

Another business advantage that Linux has was described by Dan Wilder, a senior engineer for a point-of-sale development company: "Linux brings high reliability and a sticker price where I can have one at home and as many copies at work as I can use, even doing things like dedicating a whole copy to running on an obsolete old 386 box and doing nothing but acting as a print server for a little-used but conveniently placed laser printer."

Many people are getting tired of hearing that they need to buy more expensive and more powerful hardware just for the operating system itself. An operating system, we might add, that does not provide that much more functionality. It just happens to look prettier. You can have the full functionality of a multitasking operating system with just a couple of megabytes of RAM and a 40Mb hard disk.

Benjammin Graham, owner and system administrator of Jammin Internet Services, uses Linux to save money in other ways. Benjammin says, "It can turn a 386 12mhz with 2MB of RAM into a usable server/workstation. Let me see any other OS do that. (I have done it.)" There is no need to throw away "outdated" equipment like this. Linux can be used for a definite competitive advantage.

Another problem that you are likely to run into is your boss. (Assuming that's not you.) It is common for MIS managers and CEOs of big companies to shy away from products that are not also from big companies. After all, if the product was that great, the company would be big, right?

One company that is taking Linux by the hand and leading it though the world of big business is Caldera, Inc. Aside from creating Caldera OpenLinux and a wide range of products like the Caldera Network Desktop and Caldera Internet Office Suite, they are building an international organization of companies that are forming the infrastructure of a Linux business network.

Caldera is becoming the big company with the big name that is supporting Linux. However, that's not all. Red Hat, who provides Red Hat Linux, is also becoming a major player in the Linux world. Both provide not only a Linux distribution, but outstanding commercial-grade business software to go with it.

Linux has it all: stability, software, and support. Plus, you can't argue with the price. In this day of downsizing and cutbacks, Linux is your key to remaining competitive.

What this Book is About

To best describe what this book is about, I need to first tell you what this book is *not* about. First, this is not a book to show you how to use all the different Linux commands and utilities. Because the commands and utilities provided with Linux behave identically to those in other UNIX dialects, generic UNIX books are sufficient. Additionally, there are already several books on the market that provide you with that information.

Also, this is not a book that shows you how to administer and run a Linux system. A lot of that type of information is available in the Linux documentation. Plus, there are good books available that already do this, such as *Running Linux* by Matt Walsh and Lar Kaufman from O'Reilly & Associates and the *Linux Companion* by Mark Komarinski from Prentice Hall.

The intention of this book is not to jump on the Linux bandwagon or to add one more drop to the already present flood of Linux books just to get in on the action. Instead, as the title implies, this book will address those issues that are relevant and important in using Linux in a business. It covers not only the practical aspects such as the actual implementation, but also the strategic issues that every business must address.

If you are looking for a hand-holding, step-by-step introduction to all of Linux's commands, utilities, and functions, then I must disappoint you. This book is not for you. If you're looking for a first aid book that will list out the 1000 most common problems and their solutions, then I must disappoint you again. If you are looking for a how-to book that tells you step-by-step how to configure printers, install a new hard disk, and add users, then this book is also not for you. So why buy this book?

There are already many books on the market that provide information on the commands and the hand-holding. To lure you to buy this book rather than another, I must give you something different. There is already a good introduction to the Linux commands and utilities: the Linux documentation. In addition, SAMS has published *Linux Unleashed*, by Kamran Husain, Timothy Parker, et al. This provides more than a quick reference to all the commands, utilities, and functions. There are also the books that I mentioned earlier. Repeating what is in these books hurts you more than helps you, as you now need to worry about which one you should buy. So why buy this one?

The information provided in this book is based, in part, on my four years of experience in the tech support department of a major UNIX vendor. Common issues arose when dealing with customers that this book addresses. If addressed at all in existing documentation, users and administrators needed to wade through several different manuals, references, and Web sites to get their answers. This book provides a single source that addresses the important issues and their relationship to each other and the Linux system.

While providing phone support, I noticed that many of the same problems kept recurring. Users were trying to accomplish some task and they lacked the basic knowledge to go beyond what was explained in the existing documentation. When they wanted to go beyond the basics or expand on the examples provided, they couldn't. Many people simply ended up calling support for the answers, while others would get themselves into situations that they couldn't easily back out of.

After a couple of years of receiving these kinds of phone calls, it became obvious that many users lacked information about the different aspects of their system–information that is available from many different sources but isn't gathered in one place. Until now.

No book specifically addresses the issues involved in running your business on Linux. The result is that you spend time and money running from book to Web site to consultant just to find out if Linux is right for you, then you do it all over to find out how to implement your choices.

In the following pages, I hope to give you that information, not as a list of facts to store away somewhere, but rather as a collection of interacting processes. Like your body, it is a system that works together to reach a common goal. When one part fails, the whole system can collapse.

This book is not a first-aid handbook. I am not going to list specific issues and specific problems with an explanation of what you need to do to implement that functionality or solve that problem. These books annoy me because they will list 100 things you can do or 100 problems. However, I end up having problem 101 and the book does not go into enough details to expand on what they are saying.

This book is also not a cookbook. I do not provide step-by-step instructions, telling you what to input in what field, what button to press, and what menu option to select. Although cookbooks are good and tell you how to bake a cake, they don't cut it when it comes to administering your computer system. On the other hand, a cookbook that explains how flour, eggs, and milk interact with each other when you put them in the oven enables you not only to bake a cake, but a pie and bread as well. That's what we're going to do here.

This book is intended to be used by the system administrator whose job it is to implement a business strategy using Linux and the MIS manager who is interested in the capabilities of Linux. The system administrator will also have a better understanding of things "behind the scenes," thereby making it easier to identify problems and find solutions. The MIS manager will learn just what Linux can do and how well it can fit into any business strategy.

The information is presented in language that even beginners can understand to give them the tools to understand what is happening and why. I intentionally tried to avoid "buzz-words" and "techno-speak" in an effort to bring my message across to most people. Because of that, some of the more knowledgeable readers will encounter places where I oversimplify or gloss over something. This was unavoidable.

I also tried to make this book easy to read. I did not want to bog you down with long drawn-out explanations, but rather I wanted to show you key concepts. My intention was to provide a book that you could read on the living room couch, not one that required that you have a computer in front of you.

By using real world examples, you will see that the solution to the problem is within your reach. In this way, you will be able to take a completely new situation and solve problems on your own. This is a book that, unlike the Linux documentation, focuses not on the features of the operating system, but rather on real world problems and situations that real world people are experiencing and implementing.

The decision on how to organize the book was difficult. I tried to put things in an order in which subsequent sections and chapters would build on previous material. One major problem that kept cropping up was the chicken-egg/cart-horse business. So often I came to a place where I thought I had to explain one thing first before I started something else, then later I switched things around to limit the amount I had to repeat myself.

Unfortunately that is the nature of the business. Hardware and software work together. You can't have one without the other. You can't explain one without explaining the other. Somewhere along the line you either make assumptions about what people already know and leave things out, or you repeat yourself. I did both. However, I feel that I left out those things that were easily accessed from other sources and only repeated myself when absolutely necessary.

A single book cannot do everything in this regard. Some of you might be disappointed at some of the things I left out. I tried to cover those issues that represented the majority of the calls to support as well as the key issues when implementing Linux in your business. I also attempted to address those issues where people lack knowledge of basic relationships. Because that is one goal of this book, it seemed like a reasonable approach.

I felt that the assumption of certain base knowledge would be more useful than starting with an explanation of bits and bytes. I also tried not to rehash things that you could find in existing material. However, order to make sense in many places, it was necessary to repeat other documentation.

This book will proceed in three phases. We begin with basic concepts of both UNIX in general and the Linux implementation. Subsequent chapters provide information needed on a user level then progress into the more advanced topics that would be needed by a system administrator. The material is presented in a way that relates to the actual use of the product and not just a description of programs and their behavior. Many real situations with customers are used as examples of how the information is useful. This is intended for people who are new to either Linux or UNIX and will provide the base on which later sections will build.

In the second phase, we will discuss the details of the different aspects of a Linux system. What I am going to show you here is not only the inside of a Linux system, but also how things interact with the system as well as with each other. In other words, I am not only going to show you the anatomy of an Linux system, but the physiology as well.

Lastly, we are going to talk about actually implementing Linux in your business. We'll talk about setting up Linux as an Internet server, as well as running your day-to-day operation on Linux.

With this book, you will find a CD containing Linux Pro 4.1. Granted, you will be hard pressed to find a Linux book on the market today that does not have a CD. The one difference is that I included some Web page examples for your enjoyment. Although they are not the best Web sites in the world, they will provide you with a general overview of what is possible and get you started on the road to making the perfect Web site.

Note also that many of the Web page examples are intentionally poor. Again, I was trying to show you what is possible in the least amount of space. You might also want to look through the files themselves with some kind of editor (e.g., vi, `emacs`) just to see how they are put together. On the other hand, if there are some real mistakes in there, I would love to hear from you.

When writing this book, I had a few choices:

- **Being politically correct by saying "he or she" instead of just "he"**
- **Being lazy and just saying "he"**
- **Being grammatically incorrect and saying "they" although I was referring to a single person**

Since I would rather be grammatically incorrect than politically incorrect, I decided to take the third choice. However, I am only human and if I do slip and just say "he", this is not intended as a sexist remark. I am just lazy.

Throughout the book I tell you stories about my experiences in tech support as well as some about supporting end users directly. Often, it may seem like I am trying to make fun of a the customer or user: This is *not* the case. I am trying to use these examples to demonstrate the problems that arise when you do not understand the principles behind what is happening on your system and what you are doing. Once you are done reading this book, you won't have those problems anymore.

I hope you enjoy reading and using this book as much as I enjoyed working on it.

Best regards,

jimmo

Untersiemau, Germany

April 1997

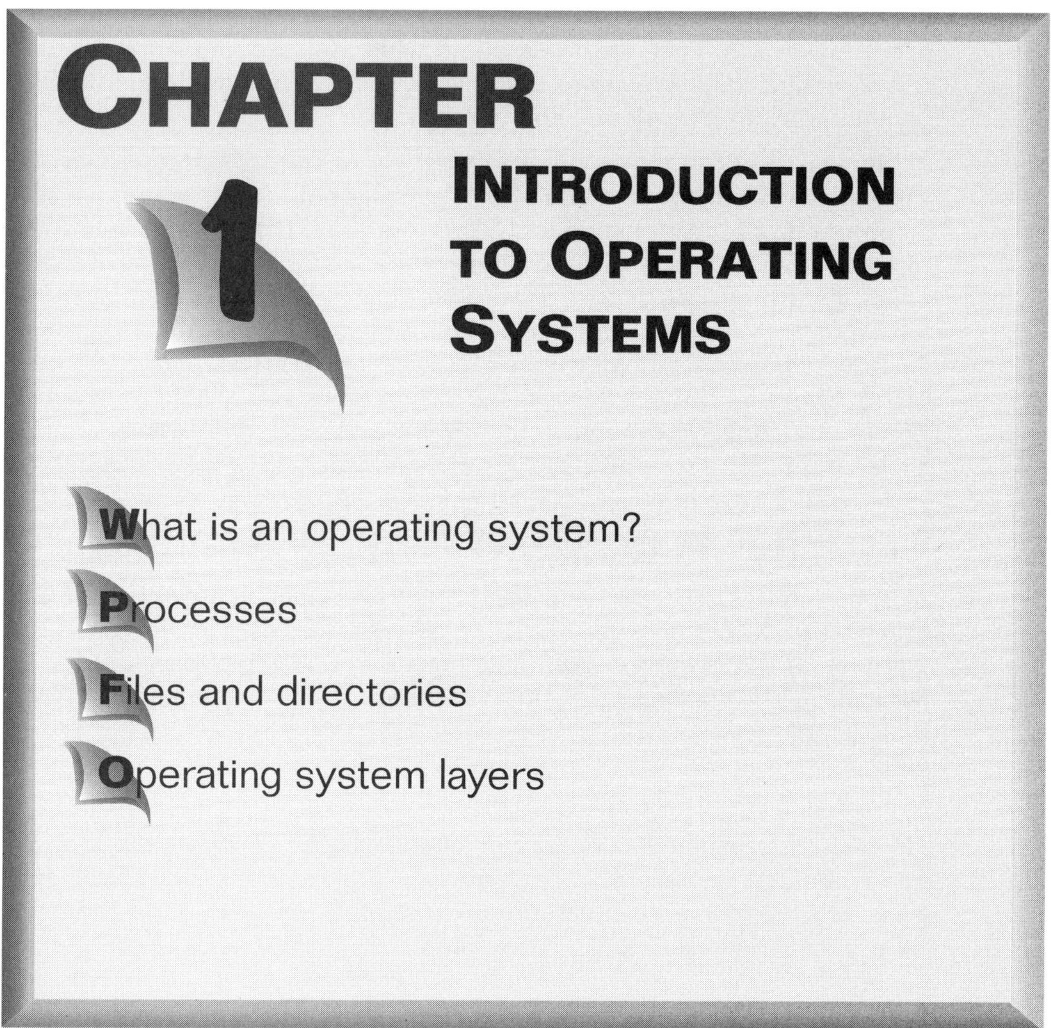

CHAPTER 1 INTRODUCTION TO OPERATING SYSTEMS

- What is an operating system?
- Processes
- Files and directories
- Operating system layers

It is a common occurrence to find users who are not even aware of what operating system they are running. On occasion, you may also find an administrator who knows the name of the operating system, but nothing about the inner workings of it. For many, they have no time as they are often clerical workers or other personnel who were reluctantly appointed to be the system administrator.

Being able to run or work on a Linux system does not mean you must understand the intricate details of how it functions internally. However, there are some operating system concepts that will help you to interact better with the system. They will also serve as the foundation for many of the issues we're going to cover in this book.

In this chapter we are going to go through the basic composition of an operating system. First, we'll talk about what an operating system is and why it is important. We are also going to address how the different components work independently and together.

My goal is not to make you an expert on operating system concepts. Instead, I want to provide you with a starting point from which we can go on to other topics. If you want to go into more detail about operating systems, I would suggest *Modern Operating Systems* by Andrew Tanenbaum, published by Prentice Hall, and *Operating System Concepts* by Silberschatz, Peterson, and Galvin, published by Addison-Wesley. Another comparatively new book on the market (February 1996) is *Inside Linux* by Randolph Bentson, which gives you a quick introduction to operating system concepts from the perspective of Linux.

1.1 What Is an Operating System?

In simple terms, an operating system is a manager. It manages all the available resources on a computer. These resources can be the hard disk, a printer, or the monitor screen. Even memory is a resource that needs to be managed. Within an operating system are the management functions that determine who gets to read data from the hard disk, what file is going to be printed next, what characters appear on the screen, and how much memory a certain program gets.

Once upon a time, there was no such thing as an operating system. The computers of forty years ago ran one program at a time. The computer programmer would load the program he (they were almost universally male at that time) had written and run it. If there was a mistake that caused the program to stop sooner than expected, the programmer had to start over. Because there were many other people waiting for their turn to try their programs, it may have been several days before the first programmer got a chance to run his deck of cards through the machine again. Even if the program did run correctly, the programmer probably never got to work on the machine directly. The program (punched cards) was fed into the computer by an operator who then passed the printed output back to the programmer several hours later.

As technology advanced, many such programs, or jobs, were all loaded onto a single tape. This tape was then loaded and manipulated by another program, which was the ancestor of today's operating systems. This program would monitor the behavior of the running program and if it misbehaved (crashed), the monitor could then immediately load and run another. Such programs were called (logically) monitors.

In the 1960s, technology and operating system theory advanced to the point that many different programs could be held in memory at once.

This was the concept of "multiprogramming." If one program needed to wait for some external event such as the tape to rewind to the right spot, another program could have access to the CPU. This improved performance dramatically and allowed the CPU to be busy almost 100 percent of the time.

By the end of the 1960s, something wonderful happened: UNIX was born. It began as a one-man project designed by Ken Thompson of Bell Labs and has grown to become the most widely used operating system. In the time since UNIX was first developed, it has gone through many different generations and even mutations. Some differ substantially from the original version, like BSD (Berkeley Software Distribution) UNIX or Linux. Others, still contain major portions that are based on the original source code. (A friend of mine described UNIX as the only operating system where you can throw the manual onto the keyboard and get a real command.)

Linux is an operating system like many others, such as DOS, VMS, OS/360, or CP/M. It performs many of the same tasks in very similar manners. It is the manager and administrator of all the system resources and facilities. Without it, nothing works. Despite this, most users can go on indefinitely without knowing even which operating system they are using, let alone the basics of how the operating system works.

For example, if you own a car, you don't really need to know the details of the internal combustion engine to understand that this is what makes the car move forward. You don't need to know the principles of hydraulics to understand what isn't happening when pressing the brake pedal has no effect.

An operating system is like that. You can work productively for years without even knowing what operating system you're running on, let alone how it works. Sometimes things go wrong. In many companies, you are given a number to call when problems arise, you report what happened, and it is dealt with.

If the computer is not back up within a few minutes, you get upset and call back, demanding to know when "that darned thing will be up and running again." When the technician (or whoever has to deal with the problem) tries to explain what is happening and what is being done to correct the problem, the response is usually along the lines of, "Well, I need it back up now."

The problem is that many people hear the explanation, but don't understand it. It is not unexpected for people to not want to acknowledge that they didn't understand the answer. Instead, they try to deflect the other person's attention away from that fact. Had they understood the explanation, they would be in a better position to understand what the technician is doing and that he/she is actually working on the problem.

By having a working knowledge of the principles of an operating system you are in a better position to understand not only the problems that can arise, but also what steps are necessary to find a solution. There is also the attitude that you have a better relationship with things you understand. Like in a car, if you see steam pouring out from under the hood, you know that you need to add water. This also applies to the operating system.

In this section, I am going to discuss what goes into an operating system, what it does, how it does it, and how you, the user, are affected by all this.

Because of advances in both hardware design and performance, computers are able to process increasingly larger amounts of information. The speed at which computer transactions occur is often talked about in terms of *billionths* of a second. Because of this speed, today's computers can give the appearance of doing many things simultaneously by actually switching back and forth between each task extremely fast. This is the concept of multitasking. That is, the computer is working on multiple tasks "at the same time."

Another function of the operating system is to keep track of what each program is doing. That is, the operating system needs to keep track of whose program, or task, is currently writing its file to the printer or which program needs to read a certain spot on the hard disk, etc. This is the concept of multi-users, as multiple users have access to the same resources.

In subsequent sections, I will be referring to UNIX as an abstract entity. The concepts we will be discussing are the same for Linux and any other dialect. When necessary, I will specifically reference where Linux differs.

1.2 Processes

One basic concept of an operating system is the process. If we think of the program as the file stored on the hard disk or floppy and the process as that program in memory, we can better understand the difference between a program and a process. Although these two terms are often interchanged or even misused in "casual" conversation, the difference is very important for issues that we talk about later.

A process is more than just a program. Especially in a multi-user, multitasking operating system such as UNIX, there is much more to consider. Each program has a set of data that it uses to do what it needs. Often, this data is not part of the program. For example, if you are using a text editor, the file you are editing is not part of the program on disk, but is part of the process in memory. If someone else were to be using the same editor, both of you would be using the same program. However, each of you would have a different process in memory. See Figure 1.1 to see how this looks graphically.

Figure 1.1: **From Program to Process**

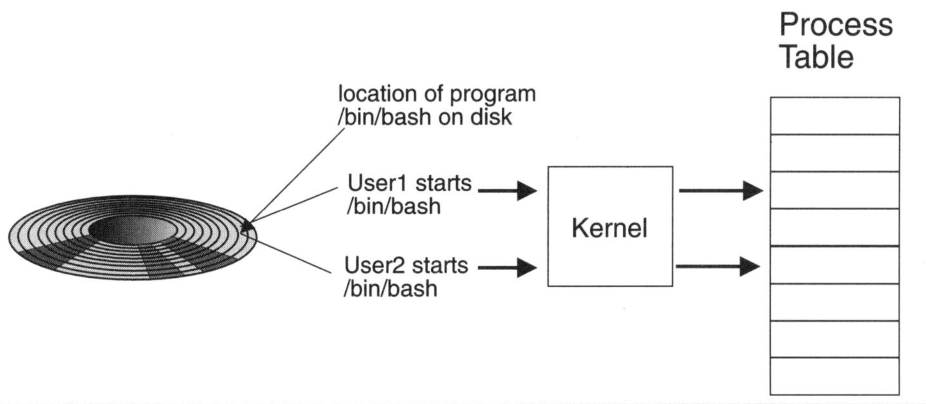

Under UNIX, many different users can be on the system at the same time. In other words, they have processes that are in memory all at the same time. The system needs to keep track of what user is running what process, which terminal the process is running on, and what other resources the process has (such as open files). All of this is part of the process.

When you log onto a UNIX system, you usually get access to a command line interpreter, or shell. This takes your input and runs programs for you. If you are familiar with DOS, you already have used a command line interpreter: the COMMAND.COM program. Under DOS, your shell gives you the C:> prompt (or something similar). Under UNIX, the prompt is usually something like $, #, or %. This shell is a process and it belongs to you. That is, the in-memory (or in-core) copy of the shell program belongs to you.

If you were to start up an editor, your file would be loaded and you could edit your file. The interesting thing is that the shell has not gone away. It is still in memory. Unlike what operating systems like DOS do with some programs, the shell remains in memory. The editor is simply another process that belongs to you. Because it was started by the shell, the editor is considered a "child" process of the shell. The shell is the *parent* process of the editor. (A process has only one parent, but may have many children.)

As you continue to edit, you delete words, insert new lines, sort your text, and write it out occasionally to the disk. During this time, the backup is continuing. Someone else on the system may be adding figures to a spreadsheet, while a fourth person may be inputting orders into a database. No one seems to notice that there are other people on the system. For them, it appears as though the processor is working for them alone.

Another example we see in Figure 1.2. When you login, you normally have a single process, which is your login shell (`bash`). If you start the X Windowing System, your shell starts another process, `xinit`. At this point, both your shell and `xinit` are running, but the shell is waiting for `xinit` to complete. Once X starts, you may want a terminal in which you can enter commands, so you start `xterm`. From the `xterm`, you might then start `ps`, to see what other processes are running. In addition, you might have something like I do, where a clock is automatically started when X starts. At this point, your process tree might look like Figure 1.2.

Figure 1.2: **Relationship of Multiple Processes**

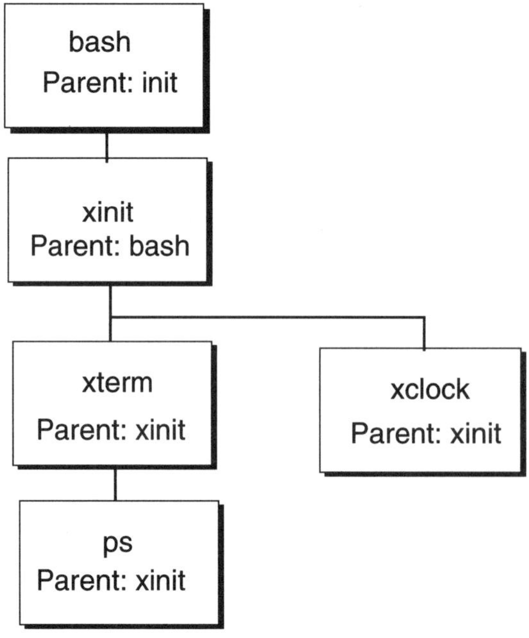

The nice thing about UNIX is that while the administrator is backing up the system, you could be continuing to edit your file. This is because UNIX knows how to take advantage of the hardware to have more than one process in memory at a time. (Note: It is not a good idea to do a backup with people on the system as data may become inconsistent. This was only used as an illustration.)

As I write this sentence, the operating system needs to know whether the characters I press are part of the text or commands I want to pass to the editor. Each key that I press needs to be interpreted. Despite the fact that I can clip along at about thirty words per minute, the Central Processing Unit (CPU) is spending approximately 95 percent of its time doing nothing.

The reason for this is that for a computer, the time between successive keystrokes is an eternity. Let's take my Intel Pentium running at a clock speed of 133Mhz as an example. The clock speed of 133Mhz means that there are 133 million(!) clock cycles per second. Because the Pentium gets close to one instruction per clock cycle, this means that within one second, the CPU can get close to executing 133 million instructions! No wonder it is spending most of its time idle. (Note: This is an oversimplification of what is going on.)

A single computer instruction doesn't really do much. However, being able to do 133 million little things in one second allows the CPU to give the user an impression of being the only one on the system. It is simply switching between the different processes so fast that no one is aware of it.

Each user, that is, each process, gets complete access to the CPU for an incredibly short period of time. On my Linux system, this period of time (referred to as a *time-slice*) is 1/100th of a second. That means that at the end of that 1/100th of a second, it's someone else's turn and the current process is *forced* to give up the CPU. (In reality, it is much more complicated than this. We'll get into more details later.)

Compare this to an operating system like standard Windows (not Windows NT). The program will hang onto the CPU until it decides to give it up. An ill-behaved program can hold onto the CPU forever. This is the cause of a system hanging because nothing, not even the operating system itself, can gain control of the CPU.

Depending on the load of the system (how busy it is), a process may get several time-slices per second. However, after it has run for its time-slice, the operating system checks to see if some other process needs a turn. If so, that process gets to run for a time-slice and then it's someone else's turn: maybe the first process, maybe a new one.

As your process is running, it will be given full use of the CPU for the entire 1/100th of a second unless one of three things happens. Your process may need to wait for some event. For example, the editor I am using to write this in is waiting for me to type in characters. I said that I type about 30 words per minute, so if we assume an average of six letters per word, that's 180 characters per minute, or three characters per second. That means that on average, a character is pressed once every 1/3 of a second. Because a time-slice is 1/100th of a second, more than 30 processes can have a turn on the CPU between each keystroke! Rather than tying everything up, the program waits until the next key is pressed. It puts itself to sleep until it is awoken by some external event, such as the press of a key. Compare this to a "busy loop" where the process keeps checking for a key being pressed.

When I want to write to the disk to save my file, it may appear that it happens instantaneously, but like the "complete-use-of-the-CPU myth," this is only appearance. The system will gather requests to write to or read from the disk and do it in chunks. This is much more efficient than satisfying everyone's request when they ask for it.

Gathering up requests and accessing the disk all at once has another advantage. Often, the data that was just written is needed again, for example, in a database application. If the system wrote everything to the disk immediately, you would have to perform another read to get back that same data. Instead, the system holds that data in a special buffer; in other words, it "caches" that data in the buffer. This is called the *buffer cache.*

Figure 1.3: **The Flow of file Access**

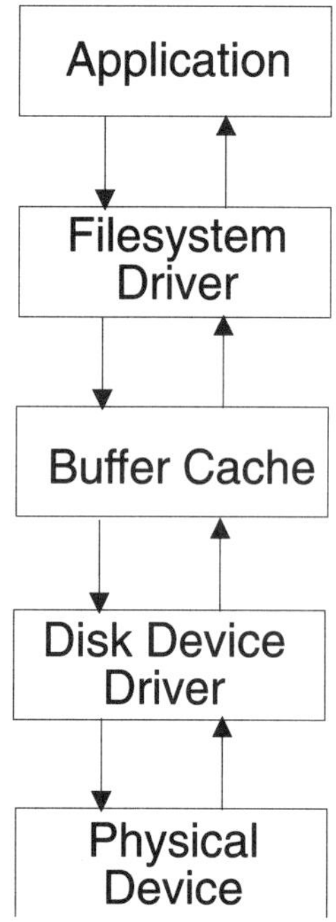

If a file is being written to or read from, the system first checks the buffer cache. If on a read it finds what it's looking for in the buffer cache, it has just saved itself a trip to the disk. Because the buffer cache is in memory, it is substantially faster to read from memory than from the disk. Writes are normally written to the buffer cache, which is then written out in larger chunks. If the data being written already exists in the buffer cache, it is overwritten. The flow of things looks like Figure 1.3.

When your process is running and you make a request to read from the hard disk, you can't do anything until you have completed the write to the disk. If you haven't completed your time-slice yet, it would be a waste not to let someone else have a turn. That's exactly what the system does. If you decide you need access to some resource that the system cannot immediately give to you, you are "put to sleep" to wait. It is said that you are put to sleep waiting on an event, the event being the disk access. This is the second case in which you may not get your full time on the CPU.

The third way that you might not get your full time-slice is also the result of an external event. If a device (such as a keyboard, the clock, hard disk, etc.) needs to communicate with the operating system, it signals this need through the use of an interrupt. When an interrupt is generated, the CPU itself will stop execution of the process and immediately start executing a routine in the operating system to handle interrupts. Once the operating system has satisfied this interrupt, it returns to its regularly scheduled process. (Note: Things are much more complicated than that. The "priority" of both the interrupt and process are factors here. We will go into more detail later.)

As I mentioned earlier, there are certain things that the operating system keeps track of as a process is running. The information the operating system is keeping track of is referred to as the process' context. This might be the terminal you are running on or what files you have open. The context even includes the internal state of the CPU, that is, what the content of each register is.

What happens when a process's time-slice has run out or for some other reason another process gets to run? If things go right (and they usually do), eventually that process gets a turn again. However, to do things right, the process must be allowed to return to the exact place where it left off. Any difference could result in disaster.

You may have heard of the classic banking problem concerning deducting from your account. If the process returned to a place before it made the deduction, you would deduct twice. If the process hadn't yet made the deduction but started up again at a point after which it would have made the deduction, it appears as though the deduction was made. Good for you, but not so good for the bank. Therefore, everything must be put back the way it was.

The processors used by Linux (Intel 80386 and later, as well as the DEC Alpha, and SPARC) have built-in capabilities to manage both multiple users and multiple tasks. We will get into the details of this in later chapters. For now, just be aware of the fact that the CPU assists the operating system in managing users and processes. Figure 1.4 shows how multiple processes might look in memory.

In addition to user processes, such as shells, text editors, and databases, there are system processes running. These are processes that were started by the system. Several of these deal with managing memory and

Figure 1.4: **Multiple Processes in Memory**

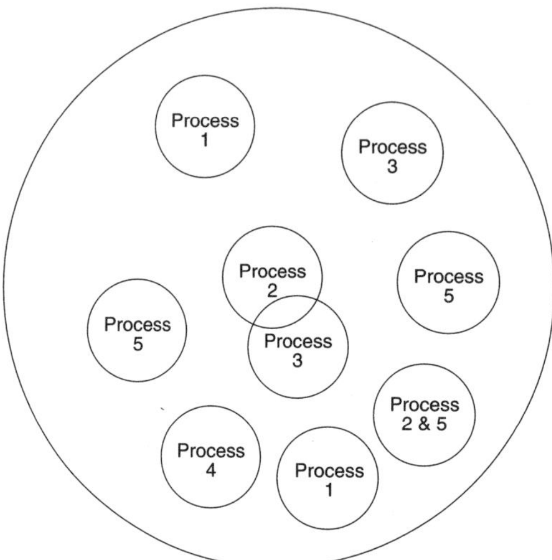

scheduling turns on the CPU. Others deal with delivering mail, printing, and other tasks that we take for granted. In principle, both of these kinds of processes are identical. However, system processes can run at much higher priorities and therefore run more often than user processes.

Many of these system processes are referred to as daemon processes or background processes because they run behind the scenes without user intervention. It is also possible for a user to put one of his or her processes "in the background." This is done by using the ampersand (&) metacharacter at the end of the command line. (I'll talk more about metacharacters in the section on shells.)

What normally happens when you enter a command is that the shell will wait for that command to finish before it accepts a new command. By putting a command in the background, the shell does not wait, but rather is ready immediately for the next command. If you wanted, you could put the next command in the background as well.

I have talked to customers who have complained about their systems grinding to a halt after they put dozens of processes in the background. The misconception is that because they didn't see the process running, it must not be taking up any resources. (Out of sight, out of mind.) The issue here is that even though the process is running in the background and you can't see it, it still behaves like any other process.

1.3 Files and Directories

Another key aspect of any operating system is the concept of a file. A file is nothing more than a related set of bytes on disk or other media. These bytes are labeled with a name, which is then used as a means of referring to that set of bytes. In most cases, it is through the name that the operating system is able to track down the file's exact location on the disk.

There are three kinds of files that most people are familiar with: programs, text files, and data files. However, on a UNIX system, there are other kinds of files. One of the most common is a device file. These are often referred to as *device files* or *device nodes*. Under UNIX, every device is treated as a file. Access is gained to the hardware by the operating system through the device files. These tell the system what specific device driver needs to be used to access the hardware.

Another kind of file is a *pipe*. Like a real pipe, stuff goes in one end and out the other. Some are named pipes. That is, they have a name and are located permanently on the hard disk. Others are temporary and are unnamed pipes. Although these do not exist once the process using them has ended, they do take up physical space on the hard disk. We'll talk more about pipes later.

Unlike operating systems like DOS, there is no pattern for file names that is expected or followed. DOS will not even attempt to execute programs that do not end with .EXE, .COM, or .BAT. UNIX, on the other hand, is just as happy to execute a program called `program` as it is a program called `program.txt`. In fact, you can use any character in a file name except for "/" and NULL.

However, completely random things can happen if the operating system tries to execute a text file as if it were a binary program. To prevent this, UNIX has two mechanisms to ensure that text does not get randomly executed. The first is the file's permission bits. The permission bits determine who can read, write, and execute a particular file. You can see the permissions of a file by doing a long listing of that file. What the permissions are all about, we get into a little later. The second is that the system must recognize a *magic number* within the program indicating that it is a binary executable. To see what kinds of files the system recognizes, take a look in `/etc/magic`. This file contains a list of file types and information that the system uses to determine a file's type.

Even if a file was set to allow you to execute it, the beginning portion of the file must contain the right information to tell the operating system how to start this program. If that information is missing, it will attempt to start it as a shell script (similar to a DOS batch file). If the lines in the file do not belong to a shell script and you try to execute the program, you end up with a screen full of errors.

What you name your file is up to you. You are not limited by the eight-letter name and three-letter extension as you are in DOS. You can still use periods as separators, but that's all they are. They do not have the same "special" meaning that they do under DOS. For example, you could have files called

```
letter.txt
letter.text
letter_txt
letter_to_jim
letter.to.jim
```

Only the first file example is valid under DOS, but all are valid under Linux. Note that even in older versions of UNIX where you were limited to 14 characters in a file name, all of these are still valid. With Linux, I have been able to create file names that are 255 characters long. However, such long file names are not easy to work with. Note that if you are running either Windows NT or Windows 95, you can create file names that are basically the same as with Linux.

One naming convention does have special meaning in Linux: "dot" files. In these files, the first character is a "." (dot). If you have such a file, it will by default be invisible to you. That is, when you do a listing of a directory containing a "dot" file, you won't see it.

However, unlike the DOS concept of "hidden" files, "dot" files can be seen by simply using the `-a` (all) option to `ls`, as in `ls -a`. (`ls` is a command used to list the contents of directories.)

The ability to group your files together into some kind of organizational structure is very helpful. Instead of having to wade through thousands of files on your hard disk to find the one you want, Linux, along with other operating systems, enables you to group the files into a *directory*. Under Linux, a directory is actually nothing more than a file itself with a special format. It contains the names of the files associated with it and some pointers or other information to tell the system where the data for the file actually reside on the hard disk.

Directories do not actually "contain" the files that are associated with them. Physically (that is, how they exist on the disk), directories are just files in a certain format. The directory structure is imposed on them by the program you use, such as `ls`.

The directories have information that points to where the real files are. In comparison, you might consider a phone book. A phone book does not contain the people listed in it, just their names and telephone numbers. A directory has the same information: the names of files and their numbers. In this case, instead of a telephone number, there is an information node number, or *inode* number.

The logical structure in a telephone book is that names are grouped alphabetically. It is very common for two entries (names) that appear next to each other in the phone book to be in different parts of the city. Just like names in the phone book, names that are next to each other in a directory may be in distant parts of the hard disk.

As I mentioned, directories are logical groupings of files. In fact, directories are nothing more than files that have a particular structure imposed on them. It is common to say that the directory "contains" those files or the file is "in" a particular directory. In a sense, this is true. The file that is the directory "contains" the name of the file. However, this is the only connection between the directory and file, but we will continue to use this terminology.

One kinds of files a directory can contain is more directories. These, in turn, can contain still more directories. The result is a hierarchical tree structure of directories, files, more directories, and more files. Directories that contain other directories are referred to as the *parent* directory of the *child* or subdirectory that they contain. (Most references I have seen refer only to parent and subdirectories. Rarely have I seen references to child directories.)

When referring to directories under UNIX, there is often either a leading or trailing slash ("/"), and sometimes both. The top of the directory tree is referred to with a single "/" and is called the "root" directory. Subdirectories are referred to by this slash followed by their name, such as `/bin` or `/dev`. As you proceed down the directory tree, each subsequent directory is separated by a slash. The concatenation of slashes and directory names is referred to as a path. Several levels down, you might end up with a path such as `/home/jimmo/letters/personal/chris.txt`, where `chris.txt` is the actual file and `/home/jimmo/letters/personal` is all of the directories leading to that file. The directory `/home` contains the subdirectory `jimmo`, which contains the subdirectory `letters`, which contains the subdirectory `personal`. This directory contains the file `chris.txt`.

Movement up and down the tree is accomplished by the means of the `cd` (change directory) command, which is part of your shell. Although this is often difficult to grasp at first, you are not actually moving anywhere. One of the things that the operating system keeps track of within the context of each process is the process's *current directory,* also referred to as the *current working directory.* This is merely the name of a directory on the system. Your process has no physical contact with this directory; just that it is keeping its name in memory.

When you change directories, this portion of the process memory is changed to reflect your new "location." You can "move" up and down the tree or make jumps to completely unrelated parts of the directory tree. However, all that really happens is that the current working directory portion of your process gets changed.

Although there can be many files with the same name, each combination of directories and file name must be unique. This is because the operating system refers to every file on the system by this unique combination of directories and file name. In the example above, I have a personal letter called `chris.txt`. I might also have a business letter by the same name. Its path would be `/home/jimmo/letters/business/chris.txt`. Someone else named John might also have a business letter to Chris. John's path might be `/home/john/letters/business/chris.txt`. This might look like Figure 1.5.

Figure 1.5: **Diagram of Directory Tree Structure**

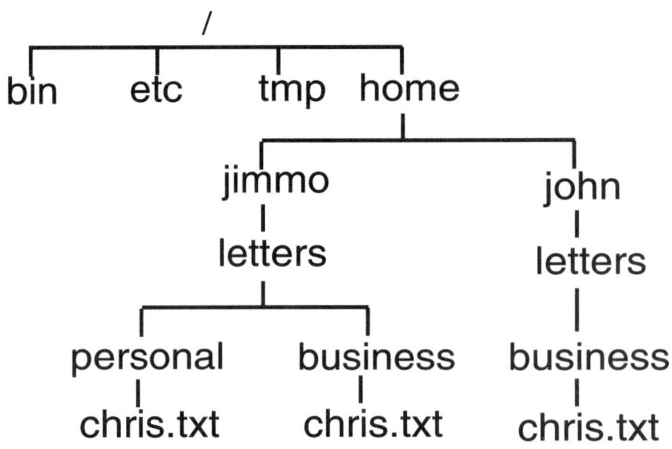

One thing to note is that John's business letter to Chris may be the exact same file as Jim's. I am not talking about one being a copy of the other. Rather, I am talking about a situation where both names point to the same physical locations on the hard disk. Because both files are referencing the same bits on the disk, they must therefore be the same file.

This is accomplished through the concept of a *link*. Like a chain link, a file link connects two pieces together. I mentioned above the "telephone number" for a file was its inode. This number actually points to a special place on the disk called the *inode table*, with the inode number being the offset into this table. Each entry in this table not only contains the file's physical location on this disk, but the owner of the file, the access permissions, and the number of links, as well as many other things. In the case where the two files are referencing the same entry in the inode table, these are referred to as *hard links*. A *soft link* or *symbolic link* is where a file is created that contains the *path* of the other file. We will get into the details of this later.

An inode does *not* contain the name of a file. The name is *only* contained within the directory. Therefore, it is possible to have multiple directory entries that have the same inode. Just as there can be multiple entries in the phone book, all with the same phone number. We'll get into a lot more detail about inodes in the section on filesystems. A directory and where the inodes point to on the hard disk might look like Figure 1.6.

Figure 1.6: **Files and Inodes in a Directory**

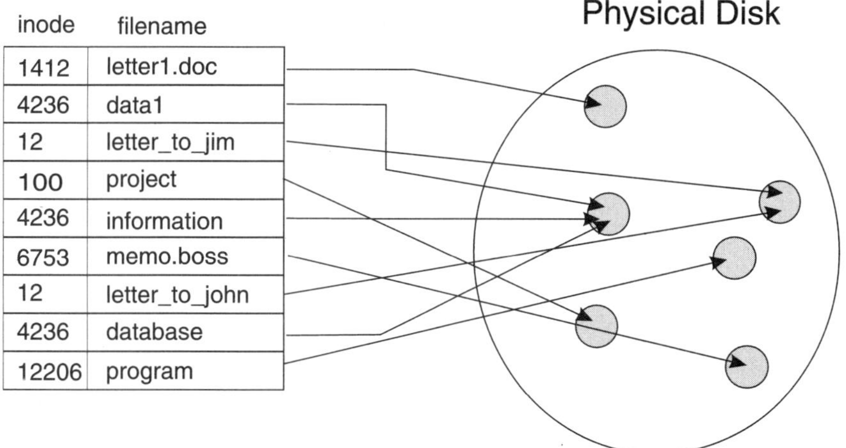

Let's think about the telephone book analogy once again. Although it is not common for an individual to have multiple listings, there might be two people with the same number. For example, if you were sharing a house with three of your friends, there might be only one telephone. However, each of you would have an entry in the phone book. I could get the same phone to ring by dialing the telephone number of four different people. I could also get to the same inode with four different file names.

Under Linux, files and directories are grouped into units called *filesystems.* A filesystem is a portion of your hard disk that is administered as a single unit. Filesystems exist within a section of the hard disk called a *partition*. Each hard disk can be broken down into multiple partitions and the filesystem is created within the partition. Each has specific starting and ending points that are managed by the system. (Note: Some dialects of UNIX allow multiple filesystems within a partition.)

When you create a filesystem under Linux, this is comparable to formatting the partition under DOS. The filesystem structure is laid out and a table is created to tell you where the actual data are located. This table, called the inode table in UNIX, is where almost all the information related to the file is kept.

In an operating system such as Linux, a file is more than just the basic unit of data. Instead, almost everything is either treated as a file or is only accessed through files. For example, to read the contents of a data file, the operating system must access the hard disk. Linux treats the hard disk as if it were a file. It opens it like a file, reads it like a file, and closes it like a file. The same applies to other hardware such as tape drives and printers. Even memory is treated as a file. The files used to access the physical hardware are the device files that I mentioned earlier.

When the operating system wants to access any hardware device, it first opens a file that "points" toward that device (the device node). Based on information it finds in the inode, the operating system determines what kind of device it is and can therefore access it in the proper manner. This includes opening, reading, and closing, just like any other file.

If, for example, you are reading a file from the hard disk, not only do you have the file open that you are reading, but the operating system has opened the file that relates to the filesystem within the partition, the partition on the hard disk, and the hard disk itself (more about these in later chapters). Three additional files are opened every time you log in or start a shell. These are the files that relate to input, output, and error messages.

Normally, when you login, you get to a shell prompt. When you type a command on the keyboard and press enter, a moment later something comes onto your screen. If you made a mistake or the program otherwise encountered an error, there will probably be some message on your screen to that effect. The keyboard where you are typing in your data is the input, referred to as standard input (standard in or *stdin*) and that is where input comes from by default. The program displays a message on your screen, which is the output, referred to as standard output (standard out or *stdout*). Although it appears on that same screen, the error message appears on standard error (*stderr*).

Although stdin and stdout appear to be separate physical devices (keyboard and monitor), there is only one connection to the system. This is one of those device files I talked about a moment ago. When you log in, the file (device) is opened for both reading, so you can get data from the keyboard, and writing, so that output can go to the screen and you can see the error messages.

These three concepts (standard in, standard out, and standard error) may be somewhat difficult to understand at first. At this point, it suffices to understand that these represent input, output, and error messages. We'll get into the details a bit later.

1.4 Operating System Layers

Conceptually, the Linux operating system is similar to an onion. It consists of many layers, one on top of the other. At the very core is the interface with the hardware. The operating system must know how to communicate with the hardware or nothing can get done. This is the most privileged aspect of the operating system.

Because it needs to access the hardware directly, this part of the operating system is the most powerful as well as the most dangerous. What accesses the hardware is a set of functions within the operating system itself (the kernel) called *device drivers*. If it does not behave correctly, a device driver has the potential of wiping out data on your hard disk or "crashing" your system. Because a device driver needs to be sure that it has properly completed its task (such as accurately writing or reading from the hard disk), it cannot quit until it has finished. For this reason, once a driver has started, very little can get it to stop. We'll talk about what can stop it in the section on the kernel.

Above the device driver level is what is commonly thought of when talking about the operating system, the management functions. This is where the decision is made about what gets run and when, what resources are given to what process, and so on.

In our previous discussion on processes, we talked about having several different processes all in memory at the same time. Each gets a turn to run and may or may not get to use up its time-slice. It is at this level that the operating system determines who gets to run next when your time-slice runs out, what should be done when an interrupt comes in, and where it keeps track of the events on which a sleeping process may be waiting. It's even the alarm clock to wake you up when you're sleeping.

The actual processes that the operating system is managing are at levels above the operating system itself. Generally, the first of these levels is for programs that interact directly with the operating system, such as the various shells. These interpret the commands and pass them along to the operating system for execution. It is from the shell that you usually start application programs such as word processors, databases, or compilers. Because these often rely on other programs that interact directly with the operating system, these are often considered a separate level. See Figure 1.7 for what the different levels (or layers) might look like graphically.

Under Linux, there are many sets of programs that serve common functions. This includes things like mail or printing. These groups of related programs are referred to as "System Services." Whereas individual programs such as `vi` or `fdisk` are referred to as utilities. Programs that perform a single function such as `ls` or `date` are referred to as commands.

1.5 Moving On

So you now have an understanding of the basics of how Linux works. We talked about the different functions that the operating system is responsible for, what it manages, and a little about how everything fits

Figure 1.7: **Operating System Layers**

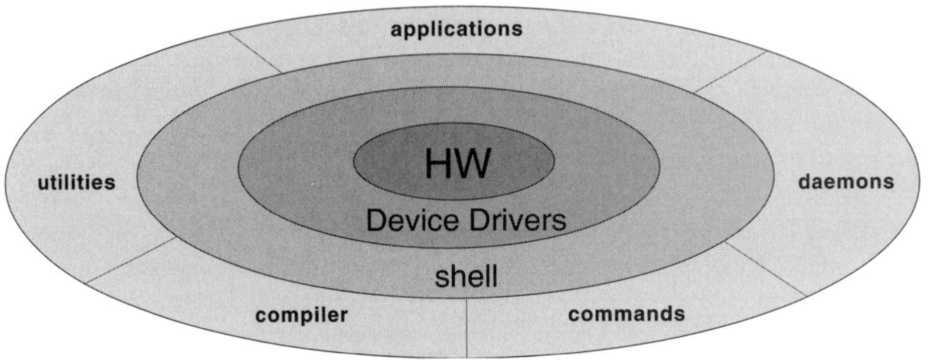

together. As we move on through the book, we'll build on these ideas and concepts to give you a complete understanding of a Linux system.

I need to make one general comment about UNIX before I let you move on. Always remember that UNIX is not DOS. Nor is it any other operating system for that matter. UNIX is UNIX and Linux is Linux. There are probably as many "dialects" of Linux as there are dialects of UNIX. All have their own subtle differences. As you go through this book, keep that in mind.

I came from the DOS world before I started on UNIX. I had many preconceptions about the way an operating system "should" behave and react. The way DOS did things was the "right" way. As I learned UNIX, I began to see a completely different world. The hardest part was not that I had to learn a whole new set of commands, but rather that I was fighting myself because I was so used to DOS.

For example, I believed that the way commands were given arguments or options was better in DOS. Every time I used a UNIX command, I grumbled about how wrong it was to do things like that. As I learned more about UNIX, I came to realize that many of the decisions on how things work or appear is completely arbitrary. There is no right way of doing many things. There is a DOS way and a UNIX way. Neither is right. You might be used to the DOS way or whatever system you use. However, that does not make it right.

When I started working with Linux, I had several years experience with a half-dozen different dialects of UNIX. It was much easier for me to adjust and simply said to myself, "Oh, so this is the way Linux does it."

If you are new to Linux, keep in mind that there are going to be differences. There are even differences among the various distributions. If you keep this in mind, you will have a much more enjoyable time learning about the Linux way.

I have always found that the best way to learn something is by doing it. That applies to learning a new operating system as well. Therefore, I suggest that when you find something interesting in this book, go look at your Linux system and see what it looks like on your system. Play with it. Twist it. Tweak it. See if it behaves the way in which you expect and understand.

With many UNIX systems that are around, the user is unaware that the operating system is a UNIX system. Many companies have point-of-sales systems hooked up to a UNIX host. For example, the users at the cash register may never see what is being run. Therefore, there is really no need to go into details about the system other than for pure curiosity–assuming that users find out that they are running on an UNIX system.

On the other hand, if you do have access to the command line or interact with the system by some other means, knowing how the system is put together is useful information. Knowing how things interact helps expand your knowledge. Knowing what's on your system is helpful in figuring out just what your system can do.

That's what this chapter is about: what's out there. We're going to talk about what makes up Linux. This brings up the question "What is Linux?" There are more than a dozen versions commercially available, in several different countries, all with their own unique characteristics. How can you call any one of them *the* Linux distribution?

The answer is you can't. What I will do instead is to synthesize all the different versions into a single pseudo-version that we can talk about. Although there are differences in the different versions, the majority of the components are the same. There has been a great deal of effort in the past few years to standardize Linux, with a great deal of success. I will therefore address this standard Linux and then mention those areas where specific versions diverge.

2.1 What Linux is All About

Linux is available from many companies and in many versions. Often, a company will produce their own version with specific enhancements or changes. These are then released commercially and called distributions. Although Linux is technically only the kernel, it is commonly considered to be all of the associated programs and utilities. Combined with the kernel, the utilities and often some applications comprise a commercial distribution.

2.1.1 A Guided Tour

Unless you are on familiar ground, you usually need a map to get around any large area. To get from one place to another, the best map is a road map (or street map). If you are staying in one general area and are looking for places of interest, you need a tourist map. Because we are staying within the context of Linux and we're looking for things of interest, what I am going to give you now is a tourist map of Linux directories.

In later chapters, we'll go into detail about many of the directories that we are going to encounter here. For now, I am going to briefly describe where they are and what their function is. As we later get into different sections of the book, it will be a lot easier to move and know how files relate if we already have an understanding of the basic directory structure.

One thing I would like to point out is that (for the most part) the directories of most UNIX systems are laid out according to the functionality of the files and program within the directory. One enhancement that Linux makes is allowing things to be in more than one place. For example, files that the system uses may be in one place and those that normal users need may be in another place. Linux takes advantage of links to allow the necessary files to be in both places. We'll talk more about links as we move on.

One question people often ask is why it is necessary to know what *all* the directories are for. Well, it isn't. It isn't necessary to know them all, just the more important ones. While working in tech support, I have talked numerous times with administrators who were trying to clean up their systems a little. Because they had little experience with UNIX systems, they ended up removing things that they thought were unnecessary, but turned out to be vital for the operation of the system. If they knew more about where things were and what they were for, they wouldn't have made these mistakes.

As we go through these directories, keep in mind that your system may not be like this. I have tried to follow the structure of the Linux Filesystem Standard as well as to find some commonality among the different versions that I installed. On your system, the files and directories may be in a different place, have different names, or may be gone all together.

Note that depending on your distribution and the packages you have installed, these files and directories will look different. In addition, although my system has every conceivable package installed (well, almost), I did not list all the files and directories I have. I included this list with the intention of giving you a representative overview.

With that said, let's have a look.

The top-most directory is the root directory. In verbal conversation, you say "root directory" or "slash," whereas it may be referred to in text as simply "/."

So when you hear someone *talking* about the `/bin` directory, you many hear them say "slash bin." This is also extended to other directories, so `/usr/bin/` would be "slash *user*, slash bin." However, once you get the feeling and begin to talk "Linux-ese," you will start talking about the directories as "bin" or "user bin." Note that `usr` is read as "user."

Under the root, there are several subdirectories with a wide range of functions. Figure 2.1 shows the key subdirectories of /. This representation does not depict every subdirectory of /, just the more significant ones. In subsequent diagrams, I will continue to limit myself to the most significant directories to keep from losing perspective.

One of these files, one could say, is the single *most* important file: `vmlinuz`. This file is the operating system proper. It contains all the functions that make everything go. When referring to the file on the hard disk, one refers to `/vmlinuz`, whereas the in-memory, executing version is referred to as the *kernel*.

The first directory we get to is `/bin`. Its name is derived from the word "*bin*ary." Often, the word "binary" is used to refer to executable pro-

Figure 2.1: **The Root Directory**

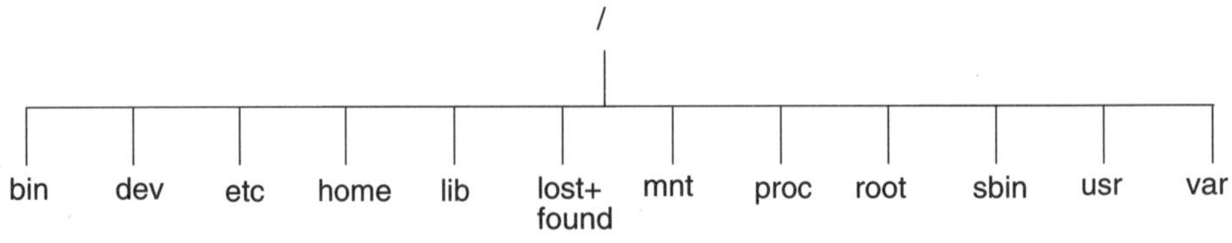

grams or other files that contains non-readable characters. The /bin directory is where many of the system-related binaries are kept, hence the name. Although several of the files in this directory are used for administrative purposes and cannot be run by normal users, everyone has read permission on this directory, so you can at least see what the directory contains.

The /boot directory is used to boot the system. There are several files here that the system uses at different times during the boot process. For example, the files /boot/boot.???? are copies of the original boot sector from your hard disk. Files ending in .b are "chain loaders," secondary loaders that the system uses to boot the various operating systems that you specify.

The /dev directory contains the device nodes. As I mentioned in our previous discussion on operating system basics, device files are the way both the operating system and users gain access to the hardware. Every device has at least one device file associated with it. If it doesn't, you can't gain access to it. We'll get into more detail on individual device files later.

The /etc directory contains files and programs that are used for system configuration. Its name comes from the common abbreviation etc., for *et cetera*, meaning "and so on." This seems to come from the fact that on many systems, /etc contains files that don't seem to fit elsewhere.

Under /etc are several subdirectories of varying importance to both administrators and users Figure 2.2 shows what the subdirectories of /etc would look like graphically.

Next is the /etc/lilo directory, which is used for the Linux loader (lilo). This directory contains a single file, install, which is a link to /sbin/lilo. This file is used (among other things) to install the boot configuration options. We'll get into this more in the section on starting and stopping your system.

The /etc/msgs directory contains the text of various messages that may appear when using ftp. Well get into more detail about ftp when we talk about configuring your system as an Internet server.

The /etc/rc.d directory contains files that the system uses when starting up or shutting down. Which files are read depends on whether

Figure 2.2: **Subdirectories of** `/etc`

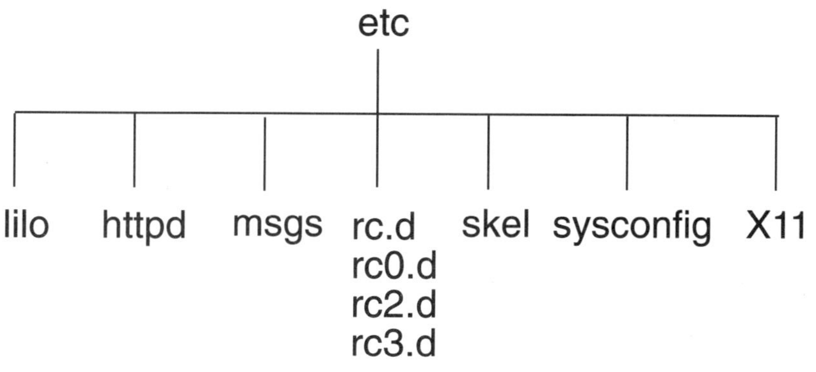

the system is being started or shut down. We'll talk more about these directories and their associated files in the section on starting up and shutting down the system.

The `/etc/skel` directory is used when you create a new user with the `adduser` command. This is the "skeleton" of files that is copied to the user's home directory when it's created (hence the name "`skel`"). If you want to ensure that each user gets other files at startup, place them in here. For example, you may want everyone to have a configuration file for `vi` (`.exrc`) or for mail (`.mailrc`).

The `/etc/sysconfig` directory contains default system configuration information. For example, the `keyboard` file defines which keyboard table is to be used and the `network` file contains network parameters, such as the hostname.

Moving back up to the root directory, we next find `/home`. As its name implies, this is the default location for users' home directories. However, as we'll talk about later, you can have the home directory anywhere.

The `/lost+found` directory is used to store files that are no longer associated with a directory. These are files that have no home and are, therefore, lost. Often, if your system crashes and the filesystem is cleaned when it reboots, the system can save much of the data and the files will end up here. We'll get into more detail about this in the section on filesystems.

If you have installed development tools, the `/lib` directory (for library) will contain the libraries needed for program development.

The `/proc` directory takes a little while to get used to, especially if you come from a non-UNIX world or have used a version of UNIX without this directory. This is a "pseudo-filesystem" that is used to access information in the running system. Rather than having you access kernel memory directly (i.e., through the special device `/dev/kmem`), you can access the files within this directory. There are directories for every running process as well. We will get into more detail about this when we talk about monitoring your system. If you are curious now, check out the `proc`(8) man-page.

The `/root` directory is the home directory for the user root. This is different from many UNIX dialects that have the root's home directory in /.

The `/sbin` directory contains programs that are used (more or less) to administer the system. In other words, the **s**ystem **bin**aries. Many sources say that this is only for system administrators. However, most of these files are executable by normal users. (Whether the support files or device nodes are accessible is another matter.) In general, there are no files here that should be accessible by users.

The `/usr` directory contains many user-related subdirectories. Note the 'e' is missing from "user". In general, one can say that the directories and files under `/usr` are used by and related to users. There are programs and utilities here that users use on a daily basis. Unless changed, `/usr` is where users have their home directory. Figure 2.3 shows what the subdirectories of `/usr` would look like graphically.

Figure 2.3: **Sub-directories of** `/usr`

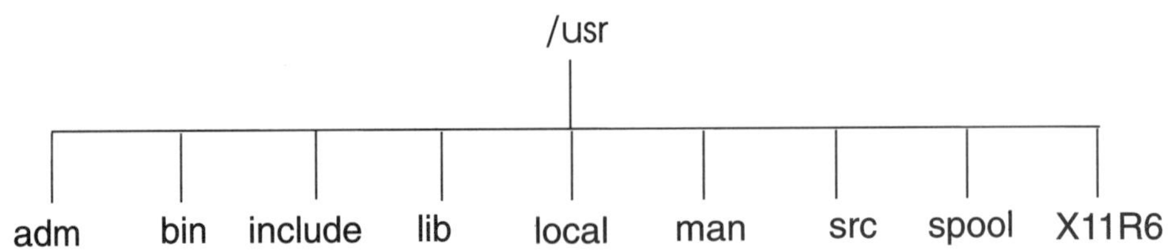

Where `/bin` contains programs that are used by both users and administrators, `/usr/bin` contains files that are almost exclusively used by users. (However, like everything in UNIX, there are exceptions.) Here again, the `bin` directory contains binaries.

The `/usr/adm` directory contains mostly administrative data. The name "adm" comes from "administration," which is no wonder considering this contains a lot of the administrative information that relates to users. This may be a symbolic link to the `/var` directory.

The `/usr/include` directory and its various subdirectories contain all the include files. For normal users and even most system administrators, the information here is more a place to get one's curiosity satisfied. However, for me, that is enough. This directory and its various subdirectories contain information that both the kernel needs when being re-created and programs need when being compiled. (For those of you who know that this is dramatic over-simplification, all I can say is that you already know what this directory is for anyway.)

Many system parameters and values are stored inside the files underneath /usr/src/linux/include. Because of the information provided in many of the files, I will be making reference to them through the book. Rather than spelling out the full path of the directory, I will make a reference to the files relative to the /usr/src/linux/include directory, the same way that it is done in C source code. For example, when I refer to something like <linux/user.h>, I mean the full path /usr/src/linux/include/linux/user.h. When you see something enclosed in angled brackets like this, you can make the expansion yourself.

The /usr/lib directory is difficult to explain. We could say that it contains the user-related library files (based on its name). However, that still does not accurately describe the complete contents. One thing it contains is the library files that are less general than those you find in /lib. This directory contains many of the systemwide configuration files for user-level programs such as perl and emacs.

Figure 2.4 shows what the sub-directories of /usr/lib look like graphically.

Figure 2.4: **Subdirectories of** /usr/lib

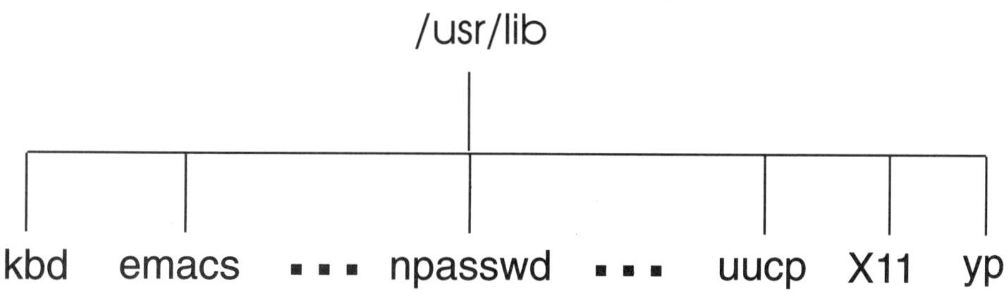

The /usr/lib/kbd directory contains files that are used to configure the system console keyboard. Through these files, you can configure your keyboard to accommodate one of several different languages. You can even configure it for dialects of the same language, such as the German keyboard as used in Switzerland or Germany. You can also change these files to create a totally new keyboard layout, such as the Dvorak.

If you have switched to the more secure npasswd program, the /usr/lib/npasswd directory is used to contain come configuration information.

The /usr/lib/terminfo directory contains both the source files and compiled versions of the terminfo database. Terminfo is the mechanism by which the system can work with so many different types of terminals and know which key is being pressed. For more information, see the terminfo(5) man-page.

When configuring UUCP, all the necessary files are contained in the /usr/lib/uucp directory. Not only are the configuration files here, but this is also home for most of the UUCP programs. UUCP (Unix-to-Unix Copy) is a package that allows you to transfer files and communicate with remote systems using serial lines. We'll talk in more detail about this directory in the section on networking.

There are actually many more directories under `/usr/lib`. (Well, at least on my system.) Most are related to user programs and operations. We'll get to some of them as we move along.

The directory `/usr/X11R6` contains all the X Windows System files. This make upgrading to newer releases of X much easier as the files are not spread out over the entire system. If you have an older version of Linux, you might still have X11R5 or if a newer release comes out you might have X11R7. To simplify things even further, the directory `/usr/X11` is what many things look at instead. This is then linked to the appropriate directory (i.e., `/usr/X11R6`, `/usr/X11R5`).

Underneath this directory are the subdirectories `bin`, `lib`, and `man`, which have the same functionality as those under `/usr`. In most cases, links in other directories point here. For example, you should have a directory `/usr/bin/X11`. This is a symbolic link to the directory `/usr/X11R6/bin`. The directory `/usr/lib/X11` is a symbolic link to `/usr/X11R6/lib`. The reason for this is to maintain the directory structure, but still make upgrading easy. When X11R7 comes out, all that you need to do is make the links point to the X11R7 directories and not copy the individual files.

Next, `/usr/sbin` contains more system binaries, including the daemon programs that run in the background. In other systems (e.g., SCO), these files are probably in `/etc`.

Moving back up to the `/usr` directory, we find the `/usr/local` subdirectory. This may or may not contain anything. In fact, there are no rules governing its contents. It is designed to contain programs, data files, and other information that is specific to your local system, hence the name. There is often a `bin` directory that contains local programs and a `lib` directory that contains data files or libraries used by the programs in `/usr/local/bin`.

Also in the `/usr` directory is `/usr/man`. This is where the man-pages and their respective indices are kept. This directory contains the index files, which you can search through to find a command you are looking for. You can also create and store your own manual pages here. The `/usr/info` and `/usr/doc` directories contain GNU Info documents and other documentation files.

The `/usr/spool` directory is the place where many different kinds of files are stored temporarily. The word "spool" is an acronym for **s**imultaneous **p**eripheral **o**peration **o**ff-**l**ine, the process whereby jobs destined for some peripheral (printer, modem, etc.) are queued to be processed later. This may be a link to `/var/spool`.

Several subdirectories are used as holding areas for the applicable programs. For example, the /usr/spool/cron directory contains the data files used by cron and at. The /usr/spool/lp directory not only contains print jobs as they are waiting to be printed, it also contains the configuration files for the printers.

The /var directory contains files that *vary* as the system is running. This was originally intended to be used when the /usr directory is shared across multiple systems. In such a case, you don't want things like the mail or print spoolers to be shared.

The /var/man/cat? directory is a cache for man-pages when they are formatted. Some are stored in a preformatted form, and those that need to be formatted are cached here in case they are needed again soon.

Many system lock files are kept in /var/lock. These are used to indicate that one program or another is currently using a particular file or maybe even a device. If other programs are written to check in here first, you don't have collisions.

As you might guess, the /var/log directory contains log files. The /var/run contains information that is valid until the system is rebooted. For example, the process ID of the inetd daemon can be found here. It is often important to know this information when changes are made to the system and storing them here makes them quickly accessible.

The /var/yp directory contains the changing files that are used with the Network Information Service (NIS), also know as Yellow Pages, or YP.

As I mentioned before, the /usr/adm directory is a link to /var/adm. There are several key log files stored here. Perhaps, the most important is the messages file that contains all the system service, kernel, and device driver messages. This is where the system logs messages from the syslogd daemon. For more information, see the respective man-page.

Okay, so that's about it. There were many directories that I skipped, as I said I would at the beginning of this section. Think about the comparison that I made to a tourist map. We visited all the museums, 200-year-old churches, and fancy restaurants, but I didn't show you where the office of city planning was. Granted, such offices are necessary for a large city, but you really don't care about them when you're touring the city; just as there are certain directories and files that are not necessary to appreciate and understand the Linux directory structure.

2.1.2 What Linux Is Made Of

There are many aspects of the Linux operating system that are difficult to define. We can refer to individual programs as either utilities or commands, depending on the extent of their functions. However, it is difficult to label collections of files. Often, the labels we try to place on these collections do not accurately describe the relationship of the files. However, I am going to try.

Linux comes with essentially all the basic UNIX commands and utilities that you have grown to know and love (plus some that you don't love so much). Basic commands like `ls` and `cat`, as well as text manipulation programs like `sed` and `awk` are available.

Linux also comes with a wide range of programming tools and environments, including the GNU `gcc` compiler, `make`, `rcs`, and even a debugger. Several languages are available, including Perl, Python, Fortran, Pascal, ADA, and even Modula-3.

Unless you have an extremely low-level distribution, you probably have X11R6 in the form of XFree86 3.x, which contains drivers for a wide range of video cards. There are a dozen text editors (`vi`, `emacs`, `jove`) and shells (`bash`, `zsh`, `ash`, `pdksh`), plus a wide range of text processing tools, like TeX and groff. If you are on a network, there is also a wide range of networking tools and programs.

If you have been working with a Linux or any UNIX dialect for a while, you may have heard of certain aspects of the operating system but not fully understood what they do. In this section, I'm going to talk about functions that the system performs as well as some of the programs and files that are associated with these functions. I'm also going to talk about how many of the system files are grouped together into what are referred to as "packages," and discuss some of the more important packages.

To install, remove, and administer these packages on a Slackware-derived system, use the `/sbin/pkgtool` tool, which is actually a link to the shell script `/usr/lib/setup/cpkgtool`. This tool can be called from the command line directly or by the `/sbin/setup` program. Each package comes on its own set of disks. These packages are

- Base Linux System
- AP, various applications that do not need X
- D Program Development (C, C++, Lisp, Perl, etc.)
- E GNU emacs
- F FAQ lists, HOWTO documentation
- I Info files readable with info, JED, or emacs
- IV InterViews Development + Doc and Idraw apps for X
- N Networking (TCP/IP, UUCP, Mail, News)
- OOP Object-Oriented Programming (GNU Smalltalk 1.1.1)
- Q Extra Linux kernels with custom drivers
- T TeX , text processing system
- TCL Tcl/Tk/TclX, Tcl language and Tk toolkit for X

- X XFree-86 3.1 X Window System
- XAP X applications
- XD XFree-86 3.1 X11 Server Development System
- XV XView 3.2 (OpenLook Window Manager, apps)
- Y games (that do not require X)

Why is it important to know the names of the different packages? Well, for the average user, it really isn't. However, the average user logs on, starts an application and has very little or no understanding of what lies under the application. The mere fact that you are reading this book says to me that you want to know more about the operating system and how things work. Because these packages are the building blocks of the operating system (at least in terms of how it exists on the hard disk), knowing about them is an important part of understanding the whole system.

To be able to do any work on a Linux system, you must first install software. Most people think of installing software as adding a word processing program or database application; but any program on the operating system needs to be installed at one time or another. Even the operating system itself was installed.

Earlier, I referred to the Linux operating system as all the files and programs on the hard disk. For the moment, I want to restrict the definition of "operating system" to just those files that are necessary for "normal" operation. Linux (at least the Slackware) has defined that set of programs and files as the Base Linux System, or Base Package. Although there are many files in the Base Package that could be left out to have a running system, this is the base set that is usually installed.

Many versions of Linux are now using the Red Hat Package format. In fact, the Red Hat format is perhaps the format most commonly found on the Internet. Most sites will have new or updated programs in this format. You can identify this format by the `rpm` extension to the file name.

This has proven itself to be a much more robust mechanism for adding and removing packages, as it is much easier to add and manage single programs than with Slackware. We'll get into more detail about this when I talk about installing. You will also find that RPM packages are grouped into larger sets like those in Slackware, so the concepts are the same.

2.1.3 What Linux Does

On any operating system, a core set of tasks are performed. On mutli-user or server systems such as Linux, these tasks include adding and configuring printers, adding and administering users, and adding new hardware to the system. Each of these tasks could take up an entire chapter in this book. In fact, I do cover all of these, and many others, in a fair bit of detail later on.

I think it's important to briefly cover all of the basic tasks that an administrator needs to perform in one place. There are a couple of reasons for this. First, many administrators of Linux systems are not only novice administrators, they are novice users. They get into the position as they are the only ones in the company or department with computer experience. (They've worked with DOS before.) By introducing the varied aspects of system administration here, I hope to lay the foundation for later chapters.

The average user may not want to get into the details that the later chapters provide. So here I give an overview of the more important components. Hopefully, this will give you a better understanding of what goes into an operating system as well as just how complex the job is that your system administrator does.

The first job of a system administrator is to add users to the system. Access is gained to the system only through user accounts. Although it may be all that a normal user is aware of, these accounts consist of substantially more than just a name and password. Each user must also be assigned one of the shells, a home directory, and a set of privileges to access system resources.

Although the system administrator could create a single user account for all users to use to log in, it ends up creating more problems than it solves. Each user has his/her own password and home directory. If there were a single user, everyone's files would be stored in the same place and everyone would have access to everyone else's data. This may be fine in certain circumstance, but not in most.

Users are normally added to the system through the `adduser` command. Here, when adding a user, you can input that user's default shell, his/her home directory as well as his/her access privileges.

Another very common function is the addition and configuration of system printers. This includes determining what physical connection the printer has to the system, what characteristics the printer has (to choose the appropriate model printer) as well as making the printer available for printing. Generically, all the files and programs that are used to access and manage printers are called the print spool, although not all of them are in the spool directory.

Adding a printer is accomplished like in many UNIX dialects: you do it manually with the primary configuration file, `/etc/printcap` file. The printcap man-page lists all the capabilities that your version of Linux supports. You must also add the appropriate directory and enable printing on the port. We'll get into more detail about it as we move on.

What happens when you want to remove a file and inadvertently end up removing the wrong one (or maybe more than one)? If you are like me with my first computer, you're in big trouble. The files are gone, never to show up again. I learned the hard way about the need to do backups. If you have a good system administrator, he/she has probably already learned the lesson and makes regular backups of your system.

There are several ways of making backups and several different utilities for doing them. Which program to use and how often to make backups completely depends on the circumstances. The system administrator needs to take into account things like how much data need to be backed up, how often the data are changed, how much can be lost, and even how much will fit on the backup media.

There are tasks that an administrator may need to perform at regular intervals, such as backups, cleaning up temporary directories, or calling up remote sites to check for incoming mail. The system administrator could have a checklist of these things and a timer that goes off once a day or every hour to remind him/her of these chores, which he/she then executes manually.

Fortunately, performing regular tasks can be automated. One basic utility in every UNIX version is `cron`. `Cron` (the "o" is short) is a program that sits in the background and waits for specific times. When these times are reached, it starts pre-defined programs to accomplish various, arbitrarily defined tasks. These tasks can be set to run at intervals ranging from once a minute to once a year, depending on the needs of the system administrator.

`Cron` "jobs" (as they are called) are grouped together into files, called *cron tables*, or *crontabs* for short. There are several that are created by default on your system and many users and even system administrators can go quite a long time before they notice them. These monitor certain aspects of system activity, clean up temporary files, and even check to see if you have UUCP jobs that need to be sent.

What about a program that you only want to run one time at a specific time and then never again? Linux provides a mechanism: `at`. Like `cron`, `at` will run a job at a specific time, but once it has completed, the job is never run again.

A third command that relates to `cron` and `at`, the `batch` command, differs from the other two in that `batch` runs the job you submit whenever it has time; that is, when the system load permits.

Linux supports the idea of virtual consoles (VCs), like SCO. With this, the system console (the keyboard and monitor attached to the computer itself) can work like multiple terminals. By default, the system is configured with at least four VCs that you switch between by pressing the ALT key and one of the function keys F1-F6.

Normally, you will only find the first six VCs active. Also, if you are using the X Windowing System, it normally starts up on VC 7.

2.1.4 What Goes with Linux

Throughout this book, we are going to be talking a great deal about what makes up the Linux operating system. In its earliest form, Linux consisted of the base operating system and many of the tools that were provided on a standard UNIX system. For many companies or businesses, that was enough. These companies may have only required a single computer with several serial terminals attached, running a word processor, database, or other application. However, when a single computer is not enough, the base Linux package does not provide you with everything that you need.

Suppose you want to be able to connect all the computers in your company into a computer network. The first thing that you could use is the networking capabilities of UUCP, which is included in Linux's network package. However, this is limited to exchanging files, remotely executing programs, and simple terminal emulation. Also, it is limited to serial lines and the speed at which data can be transferred is limited as well.

So it was in the dark recesses of ancient computer history. Today, products exist that allow simultaneous connection between multiple machines with substantially higher performance. One such product is TCP/IP (Transmission Control Protocol/Internet Protocol). If a company decides it needs an efficient network, it might decide to install TCP/IP, which has become the industry standard for connecting not only UNIX systems, but other systems as well.

There is a problem with TCP/IP that many companies run into. Suppose you want everyone in the company to be able to access a specific set of files. With TCP/IP you could devise a scheme that copies the files from a central machine to the others. However, if the files need to be changed, you need to ensure that the updated files are copied back to your source machine. This is not only prone to errors, but it is also inefficient.

Why not have a single location where the source files themselves can be edited? That way, changes made to a file are immediately available to everyone. The problem is that TCP/IP by itself has nothing built in to allow you to share files. You need a way to make a directory (or set of directories) on a remote machine appear as though it were local to your machine.

Like many operating systems, Linux provides an answer: NFS (Network File System). With NFS, directories or even entire filesystems can appear as if they are local. One central computer can have the files physically on its hard disk and make them available via NFS to the rest of the network.

Two other products are worth mentioning. To incorporate the wonders of a graphical user interface (GUI), you have a solution in the form of X-Windows. And if you just switched to Linux and still have quite a few DOS applications that you can't livc without, Linux provides a solution: dosemu or the DOS Emulator package.

2.2 Reading All About It: Linux Documentation

Software documentation is a very hot subject. It continues to be debated in all sorts of forums from USENET newsgroups to user groups. Unless the product is very intuitive, improperly documented software can be almost worthless to use. Even if intuitive to use, many functions remain hidden unless you have decent documentation. Unfortunately for many, UNIX is not very intuitive. Therefore, good documentation is essential to be able to use Linux to its fullest extent.

Unlike a commercial UNIX implementation, Linux does not provide you with a bound set of manuals that you can refer to. The documentation that is available is found in a large number of documents usually provided with your Linux distribution. Because the documentation was developed by many different people at many different locations, there is no single entity that manages it all.

The Linux Documentation Project (LDP) was organized for this very reason. More and more documents are being produced as Linux develops. There are many HOWTOs available that give step-by-step instructions to perform various tasks. In many cases, these were written by the program developers themselves. You'll find ASCII versions on the CD under the `doc/HOWTO` directory and HTML versions under `doc/HTML`.

Unfortunately, in my experience in tech support, few administrators and even fewer users take the time to read the manuals. This is not good for two important reasons. The first is obviously the wasted time spent calling support or posting messages to the Internet for help on things in the manual. The second is that you miss many of the powerful features of the various programs. When you call support, you usually get a quick and simple answer. Tech support does not have the time to train you how to use a particular program. Two weeks later, when you try to do something else with the same program, you're on the phone again.

The biggest problem is that people see the long list of files containing the necessary information and are immediately intimidated. Although they would rather spend the money to have support explain things rather than spend time "wading" through documentation, it is not as easy with Linux. There is no tech support office. There is an increasing number of consulting firms specializing in Linux, but most companies cannot afford the thousands of dollars needed to get that kind of service.

The nice thing is that you don't have to. You neither have to wade through the manuals nor spend the money to have support hold your hand. Must of the necessary information is available on-line in the form of manual pages (man-pages) and other documentation.

Built into the system is a command to read these man-pages: `man`. By typing `man <command>`, you can find out many details about the command `<command>`. There are several different options to `man` that you can use to find out about by typing `man man`, which will bring up the `man` man-page (or, the man-page for `man`).

You very often will see in Linux documentation, when referring to a particular command, the name followed by a letter or number in parenthesis, such as `ls(1)`. This indicates that the `ls` command can be found in section 1 of the man-pages. This dates back to the time when man-pages came in books (as they often still do). By including the section, you could more quickly find what you were looking for. Here I will be making references to files usually as examples. I will say only what section the files are in when I explicitly point you toward the man-page.

Before installing any Linux system it is best to know if there is anything to watch out for. For commercial software, this is usually the release notes. Often there is a file in the root directory of the CD (if that's what you are installing from) called README or README.1ST which mentions the things to look out for.

2.3 What's Next

After two chapters, we know what an operating system does and what goes into making the Linux product offering. With the understanding of how things interact and what components are available, we can now start thinking about what the system can do for us. We are now ready to begin working with the system to see just what we need to do to get the system to work for us the way we want.

Chapter 3

Shells and Basic Utilities

- Shell fundamentals
- Interacting with the shell
- Differences in the shells
- Basic shell scripting
- Common Linux utilities

Most UNIX users are familiar with "the shell"–it is where you input commands and get output on your screen. Often, the only contact users have with the shell is logging in and immediately starting some application. Some administrators, however, have modified the system to the point where users never even see the shell, or in extreme cases, have eliminated the shell completely for the users.

If you never get to the point where you can actually input commands and see their output, this chapter may be a waste of time. If your only interaction with the operating system is logging in, most of this entire book can only serve to satisfy your curiosity. However, if you are like most users, understanding the basic workings of the shell will do wonders to improve your ability to use the system to its fullest extent.

Up to this point, we have referred to the shell as an abstract entity. In fact, that's the way it is often referred to as there are many different shells that you can use. Each has its own characteristics (or even quirks), but all behave in the same general fashion. Because the basic concepts are the same, I will avoid talking about specific shells until later.

In this chapter, we are going to cover the basic aspects of the shell. We'll talk about how to issue commands and how the system responds. Along with that, we'll cover how commands can be made to interact with each other to provide you with the ability to make your own commands. We'll also talk about the different kinds of shells, what each has to offer, and some details of how particular shells behave.

3.1 Talking to Linux: The Shell

As I mentioned in Chapter 1, the shell is essentially the user's interface to the operating system. The shell is a Command Line Interpreter. Through it, you issue commands that are interpreted by the system to carry out certain actions. Often, the state where the system is sitting at a prompt, waiting for you to type input, is referred to (among other things) as being at the shell prompt or at the command line.

For many years before the invention of graphical user interfaces, such as X-Windows (the X Windowing System, for purists), the only way to input commands to the operating system was through a command line interpreter, or shell. In fact, shells themselves were thought of as wondrous things during the early days of computers because prior to them, users had no direct way to interact with the operating system.

Most shells, be they under DOS, UNIX, VMS, or other operating systems, have the same input characteristics. To get the operating system to do anything, you must give it a command. Some commands, such as the date command under UNIX, do not require anything else to get them to work. If you type in `date` and press Enter, that's what appears on your screen: the date.

Some commands need something else to get them to work: an *argument*. Some commands, like `mkdir` (used to create directories), work with only one argument, as in `mkdir directory_name`. Others, like `cp` (to copy files), require multiple arguments, as in `cp file1 file2`.

In many cases, you can pass flags to commands to change their behavior. These flags are generally referred to as *options*. For example, if you wanted to create a series of subdirectories without creating every one individually, you could run `mkdir` with the `-p` option, like this:

```
mkdir -p one/two/three/four
```

In principle, anything added to the command line after the command itself is an argument to that command. Using the terminology discussed, some arguments are optional and some options are required. The convention is that an option changes the behavior, whereas an argument is acted upon by the command. Generally, options are preceded by a dash (-), whereas arguments are not. I've said it before and I will say it again, nothing is certain when it comes to Linux or UNIX, in general. By realizing that these two terms are often interchanged, you won't get confused when you come across one or the other. I will continue to use *option* to reflect something that changes the command's behavior and *argument* to indicate something that is acted upon.

Each program or utility has its own set of arguments and options, so you will have to look at the man-pages for the individual commands. You can call these up from the command line by typing in

```
man <command_name>
```

where `<command_name>` is the name of the command you want information about. Also, if you are not sure what the command is, many Linux versions have the `whatis` command that will give you a brief description. There is also the `apropos` command, which searches through the man-pages for words you give as arguments. Therefore, if you don't know the name of the command, you can still find it.

Many commands require that an option appear immediately after the command and before any arguments. Others have options and arguments interspersed. Again, look at the man-page for the specifics of a particular command.

Often, you just need a quick reminder as to what the available options are and what their syntax is. Rather than going through the hassle of calling up the man-page, a quick way is to get the command to give you a *usage message*. As its name implies, a usage message reports the usage of a particular command. I normally use `-?` as the option to force the usage message, as I cannot think of a command where `-?` is a valid option. Your system may also support the `--help` (two dashes) option.

3.1.1 The Search Path

It may happen that you know there is a program by a particular name on the system, but when you try to start it from the command line, you are told that the file is not found. Because you just ran it yesterday, you assume it has gotten removed or you don't remember the spelling.

The most common reason for this is that the program you want to start is not in your search path. Your search path is a predefined set of directories in which the system looks for the program you type in from the command line (or is started by some other command). This saves time because the system does not have to look through every directory trying to find the program. Unfortunately, if the program is not in one of the directories specified in your path, the system cannot start the program unless you explicitly tell it where to look. To do this, you must specify either the full path of the command or a path relative to where you are currently located.

Let's look at this issue for a minute. Think back to our discussion of files and directories. I mentioned that every file on the system can be referred to by a unique combination of path and file name. This applies to executable programs as well. By inputting the complete path, you can run any program, whether it is in your path or not.

Let's take a program that is in everyone's path, like `date` (at least it should be). The `date` program resides in the `/bin` directory, so its full path is `/bin/date`. If you wanted to run it, you could type in `/bin/date`, press Enter, and you might get something that looks like this:

```
Sat Jan 28 16:51:36 PST 1995
```

However, because date is in your search path, you need to input only its name, without the path, to get it to run.

You could also start a program by referencing it through a *relative path*, the path in relation to your current working directory. To understand the syntax of relative paths, we need to backtrack a moment. As I mentioned, you can refer to any file or directory by specifying the path to that directory. Because they have special significance, there is a way of referring to either your *current directory* or its *parent directory*. The current directory is referenced by "." and its parent by ".." (often referred to in conversation as "dot" and "dot-dot").

Because directories are separated from files and other directories by a /, a file in the current directory could be referenced as `./file_name` and a file in the parent directory would be referenced as `../file_name`. You can reference the parent of the parent by just tacking on another `../`, and then continue on to the root directory if you want. So the file `../../file_name` is in a directory two levels up from your current directory. This slash (/) is referred to as a forward slash, as compared to a back-slash (\), which is used in DOS to separate path components.

When interpreting your command line, the shell interprets everything up to the last / as a directory name. If we were in the root (upper-most) directory, we could access `date` in one of several ways. The first two, `date` and `/bin/date`, we already know about. Knowing that `./` refers to the current directory means that we could also get to it like this: ./bin/date. This is saying relative to our current directory (./), look in the bin subdirectory for the command date. If we were in the /bin directory, we could start the command like this: ./date. This is useful when the command you want to execute is in your current directory, but the directory is not in your path. (More on this in a moment.)

We can also get the same results from the root directory by starting the command like this: bin/date. If there is a ./ at the beginning, it knows that everything is relative to the current directory. If the command contains only a /, the system knows that everything is relative to the root directory. If no slash is at the beginning, the system searches until it gets to the end of the command or encounters a slash whichever comes *first*. If there is a slash there (as in our example), it translates this to be a subdirectory of the current directory. So executing the command bin/date is translated the same as ./bin/date.

Let's now assume that we are in our home directory, /home/jimmo (for example). We can obviously access the date command simply as date because it's in our path. However, to access it by a relative path, we could say ../../bin/date. The first ../ moves up one level into /home. The second ../ moves up another level to /. From there, we look in the subdirectory bin for the command date. Keep in mind that throughout this whole process, our current directory does not change. We are still in /home/jimmo.

Searching your path is only done for commands. If we were to enter vi file_name (vi is a text editor) and there was no file called file_name in our current directory, vi would start editing a new file. If we had a subdirectory called text where file_name was, we would have to access it either as vi ./text/file_name or vi text/file_name. Of course, we could access it with the absolute path of vi /home/jimmo/text/file_name.

One problem that regularly crops up for users coming from a DOS environment is that the *only* place UNIX looks for commands is in your path. However, even if not specified in your path, the first place DOS looks is in your current directory. This is not so for UNIX. UNIX only looks in your path.

For most users, this is not a problem as the current directory is included in your path by default. Therefore, the shell will still be able to execute something in your current directory. Root does not have the current directory in its path. In fact, this is the way it should be. If you want to include the current directory in root's path, make sure it is the last entry in the path so that all "real" commands are executed before any other command that a user might try to "force" on you.

Assume a malicious user created a "bad" program in his/her directory called `more`. If root were to run `more` in that user's directory, it could have potentially disastrous results. (Note that the current directory normally always appears at the end of the search path. So, even if there was a program called `more` in the current directory, the one in `/bin` would probably get executed first. However, you can see how this could cause problems for root.) To figure out exactly which program is actually being run, you can use the (what else?) `which` command.

It is common to have people working on UNIX systems that have *never* worked on a computer before or have only worked in pure windowing environments, like on a Macintosh. When they get to the command line, they are lost. On more than one occasion, I have talked to customers and I have asked them to type in `cd /`. There is a pause and I hear: click-click-click-click-click-click-click-click-click-click-click-click. "Hmmm," I think to myself, "that's too many characters." So I ask them what they typed, and they respond, "cd-space-slash."

We need to adhere to some conventions throughout this book to make things easier. One is that commands that I talk about will be in your path unless I say otherwise. Therefore, to access them, all you need to do is input the name of the command without the full path.

The second convention is the translation of the phrases "input the command," "enter the command," and "type in the command." These are translated to mean "input/enter/type in the command *and press Enter.*" I don't know how many times I have talked with customers and have said "type in the command" and then asked them for what happens and their response is, "Oh, you want me to press Enter?" Yes! Unless I say otherwise, always press Enter after inputting, entering, or typing in a command.

All this time we have been talking about finding and executing commands, but there is one issue that I haven't mentioned. That is the concept of permissions. To access a file, you need to have permission to do so. If you want to read a file, you need to have read permission. If you want to write to a file, you need to have write permission. If you want to execute a file, you must have execute permission.

Permissions are set on a file using the `chmod` command or when the file is created (the details of which I will save for later). You can read the permissions on a file by using either the `l` command or `ls -l`. At the beginning of each line will be ten characters, which can either be dashes or letters. The first position is the type of the file, whether it is a regular file (-), a directory (d), a block device file (b), and so on. Below are some examples of the various file types.

```
-rw-rw--r-     jimmo support 1988  Sep 15  10:05 letter.txt
crw-rw---   1 root  tty     4,1   Jul  2  10:05 /dev/tty1
brw-rw---   1 root  disk    1,1   Mar  8  07:34 /dev/hda1
drwxr-xr-x  2 root  bin     2048  May 26  14:15 /bin
pr--r—r--   1 root  root    0     Jul  2  09:48 /proc/1/maps
lrwxrwxrwx  1 root  root    5     Mar 28  15:45 /usr/bin/vi->elvis
```

- - regular file
c - character device
b - block device
d - directory
p - named pipe
l - symbolic link

We'll get into the details of these files as we move along. If you are curious about the format of each entry, you can look at the ls man-page. An overview is presented in Figure 3.1.

The next nine positions are broken into three groups. Each group consists of three characters indicating the permissions. They are, in order, read(r), write(w), and execute(x). The first group indicates what permissions the owner of the file has. The second group indicates the permissions for the group of that file. The last group indicates the permissions for everyone else.

If a particular permission is not given, a dash (-) will appear here. For example, `rwx` means all three permissions have been given. In our example above, the symbolic link `/usr/bin/vi` has read, write, and execute permissions for everyone. The device nodes `/dev/tty1` and `/dev/hda1` have permissions `rw-` for the owner and group, meaning only read and write, but not execute permissions have been given. The directory `/bin` has read and execute permissions for everyone (`r-w`), but only the owner can write to it (`rwx`).

For directories, the situation is slightly different than for regular files. If you do not have read permission on a directory, you cannot read the contents of that directory. Also, if you do not have write permission on a directory, you cannot write it. This means that you cannot create a new file in that directory. Execute permissions on a directory mean that you can search it. That is, if the execution bit is not set on a directory but the read bit is, you can see what files are in the directory but cannot execute any of the files or even change into that directory. If you have execution permission but no read permission, you can execute the files, change directories, but not see what is in the files.

Figure 3.1: **Breakdown of File Permissions**

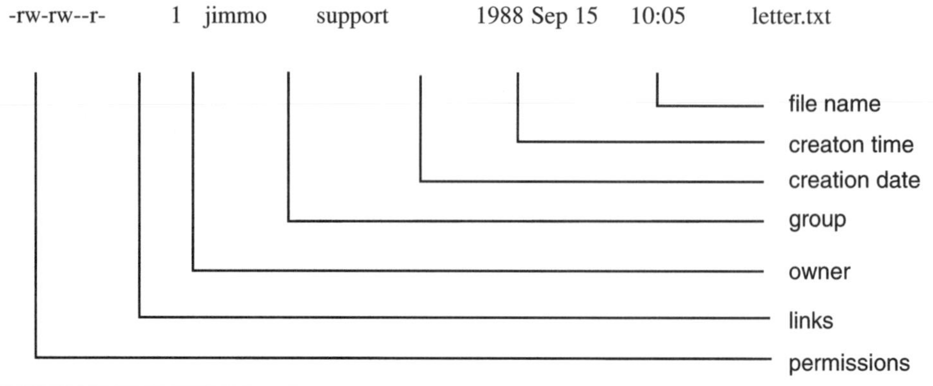

Write permission on a directory also has an interesting side effect. Because you need to have write permission on a directory to create a new file, you also need to have write permission to remove an existing file. Even if you do not have write permission on the a itself, if you can write to the directory, you can erase the file.

At first this sounds odd. However, remember that a directory is nothing more than a file in a special format. If you have write permission to a directory-file, you can remove the references to other files, thereby removing the files themselves.

3.1.2 Shell Variables

Before we talk about specific shells, there are some general shell concepts we need to talk about. The first thing we should talk about is the shell's environment. This is all the information that the shell will use as it runs. This includes such things as your command search path, your *logname* (the name you logged in under), and the terminal type you are using. Collectively, they are referred to as your *environment variables* and individually, as the "so-and-so" environment variable, such as the TERM environment variable, which contains the type of terminal you are using.

When you log in, most of these are set for you in one way or another. (The mechanism that sets all environment variables is shell-dependent, so we will talk about it when we get to the individual shells.) Each environment variable can be viewed by simply typing `echo $VARIABLE`. For example, if I type `echo $LOGNAME`, I get:

```
jimmo
```

Typing `echo $TERM`, I get:

```
ansi
```

One most important environment variable is the `PATH` variable. Remember that the PATH tells the shell where it needs to look when determining what command it should run. One of the things the shell does to make sense of your command is to find out exactly what program you mean. This is done by looking for the program in the places specified by your `PATH` variable.

Although it is more accurate to say that the shell looks in the directories specified by your PATH environment variable, it is commonly said that the shell "searches your path." Because this is easier to type, I am going to use that convention here.

If you were to specify a path in the command name, the shell does not use your `PATH` variable to do any searching. That is, if you issued the command `bin/date`, the shell would interpret that to mean that you wanted to execute the command `date` that was in the `bin` subdirectory of your current directory. If you were in `/` (the root directory), all would be well and it would effectively execute `/bin/date`. If you were somewhere else, the shell might not be able to find a match.

If you do not specify any path (that is, the command does not contain any slashes), the system will search through your path. If it finds the command, great. If not, you get a message saying the command was not found.

Let's take a closer look at how this works by looking at my path variable. From the command line, if I type `echo $PATH`, I get

```
/usr/local/bin:/bin:/usr/bin:/usr/X11/bin:/home/jimmo/
bin:/:. ←WATCH THE DOT!
```

If I type in `date`, the first place in which the shell looks is the `/bin` directory. Because that's where `date` resides, it is executed as `/bin/date`. If I type in `vi`, the shell looks in `/bin`, doesn't find it, then looks in `/usr/bin`, where it does find `vi`. Now I type in `getdev`. (This is a program I wrote to translate major device numbers into the driver name. Don't worry if you don't know what a major number is. You will.) The shell looks in `/usr/local/bin` and doesn't find it. It then looks in `/bin`. Still not there. It then tries `/usr/bin` and `/usr/X11/bin` and still can't find it. When it finally gets to `/home/jimmo/bin`, it finds the `getdev` command and executes it. (Note that because I wrote this program, you probably won't have it on your system.)

What would happen if I had not yet copied the program into my personal `bin` directory? Well, if the `getdev` program is in my current directory, the shell finds a match with the last "." in my path. (Remember that the "." is translated into the current directory, so the program is executed as `./getdev`.) If that final "." was missing or the `getdev` program was somewhere else, the shell could not find it and would tell me so with something like

```
getdev: not found
```

3.1.3 Regular Expressions and Metacharacters

Often, the arguments that you pass to commands are file names. For example, if you wanted to edit a file called `letter`, you could enter the command `vi letter`. In many cases, typing the entire name is not necessary. Built into the shell are special characters that it will use to expand the name. These are called *metacharacters*.

The most common metacharacter is *. The * is used to represent any number of characters, including zero. For example, if we have a file in our current directory called `letter` and we input `vi let*`, the shell would expand this to `vi letter`. Or, if we had a file simply called `let`, this would match as well.

Instead, what if we had several files called `letter.chris`, `letter.daniel`, and `letter.david`? The shell would expand them all out to give me the command

```
vi letter.chris letter.daniel letter.david
```

We could also type in `vi letter.da*`, which would be expanded to

```
vi letter.daniel letter.david
```

If we only wanted to edit the letter to chris, we could type it in as `vi *chris`. However, if there were two files, `letter.chris` and `note.chris`, the command `vi *chris` would have the same results as if we typed in:

```
vi letter.chris note.chris
```

In other words, no matter where the asterisk appears, the shell expands it to match *every* name it finds. If my current directory contained files with matching names, the shell would expand them properly. However, if there were no matching names, file name expansion couldn't take place and the file name would be taken literally.

For example, if there were no file name in our current directory that began with `letter`, the command `vi letter*` could not be expanded and we would end up editing a new file called (literally) `letter*`, including the asterisk. This would not be what we wanted.

What if we had a subdirectory called `letters`? If it contained the three files `letter.chris`, `letter.daniel`, and `letter.david`, we could get to them by typing `vi letters/letter*`. This would expand to be:

```
vi letters/letter.chris letters/letter.daniel letters/
letter.david
```

The same rules for path names with commands also apply to files names. The command vi letters/chris.letter is the same as vi ./letters/letter.chris, which is the same as vi /home/jimmo/letters/letter.chris. This is because the shell is doing the expansion before it is passed to the command. Therefore, even directories are expanded. And the command vi le*/letter.* could be expanded as both letters/letter.chris and lease/letter.joe.

The next wildcard is ?. This is expanded by the shell as one, and only one, character. For example, the command vi letter.chri? is the same as vi letter.chris. However, if we were to type in vi letter.chris? (note that the "?" comes after the "s" in chris), the result would be that we would begin editing a new file called (literally) letter.chris?. Again, not what we wanted. This wildcard could be used if, for example, there were two files named letter.chris1 and letter.chris2. The command vi letter.chris? would be the same as

```
vi letter.chris1 letter.chris2
```

Another commonly used metacharacter is actually a pair of characters: [ ]. The square brackets are used to represent a list of possible characters. For example, if we were not sure whether our file was called letter.chris or letter.Chris, we could type in the command as: vi letter.[Cc]hris. So, no matter if the file was called letter.chris or letter.Chris, we would find it. What happens if both files exists? Just as with the other metacharacters, both are expanded and passed to vi. Note that in this example, vi letter.[Cc]hris appears to be the same as vi letter.?hris, but it is not always so.

The list that appears inside the square brackets does not have to be an upper- and lowercase combination of the same letter. The list can be made up of any letter, number, or even punctuation. (Note that some punctuation marks have special meaning, such as *, ?, and [ ], which we will cover shortly.) For example, if we had five files, letter.chris1-letter.chris5, we could edit all of them with vi letter.chris[12435].

A nice thing about this list is that if it is consecutive, we don't need to list all possibilities. Instead, we can use a dash (-) inside the brackets to indicate that we mean a range. So, the command vi letter.chris[12345] could be shortened to vi letter.chris[1-5]. What if we only wanted the first three and the last one? No problem. We could specify it as vi letter.chris[1-35]. This does not mean that we want files letter.chris1 through letter.chris35! Rather, we want letter.chris1, letter.chris2, letter.chris3, and letter.chris5. All entries in the list are seen as individual characters.

Inside the brackets, we are not limited to just numbers or just letters. we can use both. The command `vi letter.chris[abc123]` has the potential for editing six files: `letter.chrisa`, `letter.chrisb`, `letter.chrisc`, `letter.chris1`, `letter.chris2`, and `letter.chris3`.

If we are so inclined, we can mix and match any of these metacharacters any way we want. We can even use them multiple times in the same command. Let's take as an example the command `vi *.?hris[a-f1-5]`. Should they exist in our current directory, this command would match all of the following:

```
letter.chrisa note.chrisa   letter.chrisb note.chrisb   letter.chrisc
note.chrisc   letter.chrisd note,chrisd   letter.chrise note.chrise
letter.chris1 note.chris1   letter.chris2 note.chris2   letter.chris3
note.chris3   letter.chris4 note.chris4   letter.chris5 note.chris5
letter.Chrisa note.Chrisa   letter.Chrisb note.Chrisb   letter.Chrisc
note.Chrisc   letter.Chrisd note.Chrisd   letter.Chrise note.Chrise
letter.Chris1 note.Chris1   letter.Chris2 note.Chris2   letter.Chris3
note.Chris3   letter.Chris4 note.Chris4   letter.Chris5 note.Chris5
```

Also, any of these names without the leading `letter` or `note` would match. Or, if we issued the command: `vi *.d*`, these would match

```
letter.daniel   note.daniel   letter.david   note.david
```

Remember, I said that the shell expands the metacharacters only with respect to the name specified. This obviously works for file names as I described above; however, it also works for command names as well.

If we were to type `dat*` and there was nothing in our current directory that started with `dat`, we would get a message like

```
dat*: not found
```

However, if we were to type `/bin/dat*`, the shell could successfully expand this to be `/bin/date`, which it would then execute. The same applies to relative paths. If we were in `/` and entered `./bin/dat*` or `bin/dat*`, both would be expanded properly and the right command would be executed. If we entered the command `/bin/dat[abcdef]`, we would get the right response as well because the shell tries all six letters listed and finds a match with `/bin/date`.

An important thing to note is that the shell expands as long as it can before it attempts to interpret a command. I was reminded of this fact by accident when I input `bin/l*`. This yielded the output:

```
-rwxr-xr-x 1 root bin 12292  Apr 29 1995 /bin/ln
-rwxr-xr-x 1 root bin 7268   May  5 1995 /bin/login
-rwxr-xr-x 1 root bin 28676  Apr 29 1995 /bin/ls
```

At first, I expected each one of the files in /bin that began with an "l" (ell) to be executed. Then I remembered that expansion takes place before the command is interpreted. Therefore, the command that I input, /bin/l*, was expanded to be

```
/bin/ln /bin/login /bin/ls
```

Because /bin/ln was the first command in the list, the system expected that I wanted to link the two files together (what /bin/ln is used for). I ended up with error message: /bin/ln: /bin/ls: File exists

This is because the system thought I was trying to link the file /bin/login to /bin/ls, which already existed. Hence the message.

The same thing happens when I input /bin/l? because the /bin/ln is expanded first. If I issue the command /bin/l[abcd], I get the message that there is no such file. If I type in /bin/l[a-n], I get

```
/bin/ln: missing file argument
```

because the /bin/ln command expects two file names as arguments and the only thing that matched is /bin/ln.

I first learned about this aspect of shell expansion after a couple of hours of trying to extract a specific subdirectory from a tape that I had made with the cpio command. Because I made the tape using absolute paths, I attempted to restore the files as /home/jimmo/letters/*. Rather than restoring the entire directory as I expected, it did nothing. It worked its way through the tape until it got to the end and then rewound itself without extracting any files.

At first I assumed I made a typing error, so I started all over. The next time, I checked the command before I sent it on its way. After half an hour or so of whirring, the tape was back at the beginning. Still no files. Then it dawned on me–I hadn't told the cpio to overwrite existing files unconditionally. So I started it all over again.

Now, those of you who know cpio realize that this wasn't the issue either. At least not entirely. When the tape got to the right spot, it started overwriting everything in the directory (as I told it to). However, the files that were missing (the ones that I really wanted to get back) were still not copied from the backup tape.

The next time, I decided to just get a listing of all the files on the tape. Maybe the files I wanted were not on this tape. After a while it reached the right directory and lo and behold, there were the files that I wanted. I could see them on the tape, I just couldn't extract them.

Well, the first idea that popped into my mind was to restore everything. That's sort of like fixing a flat by buying a new car. Then I thought about restoring the entire tape into a temporary directory where I could then get the files I wanted. Even if I had the space, this still seemed like the wrong way of doing things.

Then it hit me. I was going about it the wrong way. The solution was to go ask someone what I was doing wrong. I asked one of the more senior engineers (I had only been there less than a year at the time). When I mentioned that I was using wildcards, it was immediately obvious what I was doing wrong (obvious to him, not to me).

Let's think about it for a minute. It is the *shell* that does the expansion, not the command itself (like when I ran `/bin/l*`). The shell interprets the command as starting with `/bin/l`. Therefore, I get a listing of all the files in `/bin` that start with "`l`". With `cpio` , the situation is similar.

When I first ran it, the shell interpreted the files (`/home/jimmo/data/*`) before passing them to `cpio`. Because I hadn't told `cpio` to overwrite the files, it did nothing. When I told `cpio` to overwrite the files, it only did so for the files that it was told to. That is, only the files that the shell saw when it expanded `/home/jimmo/data/*`. In other words, `cpio` did what it was told. I just told it to do something that I hadn't expected.

The solution is to find a way to pass the wildcards to `cpio`. That is, the shell must ignore the special significance of the asterisk. Fortunately, there is a way to do this. By placing a backslash (\) before the metacharacter, you remove its special significance. This is referred to as "escaping" that character.

So, in my situation with `cpio`, when I referred to the files I wanted as `/home/jimmo/data/\*`, the shell passed the arguments to `cpio` as `/home/jimmo/data/*`. It was then `cpio` that expanded the `*` to mean all the files in that directory. Once I did that, I got the files I wanted.

Another symbol with special meaning is the dollar sign (`$`). This is used as a marker to indicate that something is a variable. I mentioned earlier in this section that you could get access to your login name environment variable by typing:

```
echo $LOGNAME
```

The system stores your login name in the environment variable `LOGNAME` (note no "`$`"). The system needs some way of knowing that when you input this on the command line, you are talking about the variable `LOGNAME` and not the literal string `LOGNAME`. This is done with the "`$`". Several variables are set by the system. You can also set variables yourself and use them later on. I'll get into more detail about shell variables later.

So far, we have been talking about metacharacters used for searching the names of files. However, metacharacters can often be used in the arguments to certain commands. One example is the grep command, which is used to search for strings within files. The name grep comes from Global Regular Expression Print (or Parser). As its name implies, it has something to do with regular expressions. Let's assume we have a text file called documents, and we wish to see if the string "letter" exists in that text. The command might be

```
grep letter documents
```

This will search for and print out every line containing the string "letter." This includes such things as "letterbox," "lettercarrier," and even "love-letter." However, it will not find "Letterman," because we did not tell grep to ignore upper- and lowercase (using the -i option). To do so using regular expressions, the command might look like this

```
grep [Ll]etter documents
```

Now, because we specified to look for either "L" or "l" followed by "etter," we get both "letter" and "Letterman." We can also specify that we want to look for this string only when it appears at the beginning of a line using the caret (^) symbol. For example

```
grep ^[Ll]etter documents
```

This searches for all strings that start with the "beginning-of-line," followed by either "L" or "l," followed by "etter." Or, if we want to search for the same string at the end of the line, we would use the dollar sign to indicate the end of the line. Note that at the beginning of a string, the dollar sign is treated as the beginning of the string, whereas at the end of a string, it indicates the end of the line. Confused? Let's look at an example. Let's define a string like this:

```
VAR=^[Ll]etter
```

If we echo that string, we simply get ^[Ll]etter. Note that this includes the caret at the beginning of the string. When we do a search like this

```
grep $VAR documents
```

it is equivalent to

```
grep ^[Ll]etter documents
```

Now, if write the same command like this

```
grep $VAR$ documents
```

this says to find the string defined by the VAR variable (`^[Ll]etter`), but only if it is at the end of the line. Here we have an example where the dollar sign has *both* meanings. If we then take it one step further:

```
grep ^$VAR$ documents
```

this says to find the string defined by the VAR variable, but only if it takes up the entry line. In other words, the line consists only of the beginning of the line (^), the string defined by VAR, and the end of the line ($).

3.1.4 Quotes

One last issue that causes its share of confusion is quotes. In Linux, there are three kinds of quotes: *double-quotes* ("), *single-quotes* ('), and *back-quotes*(`) (also called back-ticks). On most US keyboards, the single- and double-quotes are on the same key, with the double-quotes accessed by pressing Shift and the single-quote key. Usually this key is on the right-hand side of the keyboard, next to the Enter key. The back-quote is usually in the upper left-hand corner of the keyboard, next to the 1.

To best understand the difference between the behavior of these quotes, I need to talk about them in reverse order. I will first describe the back-quotes, or back-ticks.

When enclosed inside back-ticks, the shell interprets something to mean "the output of the command inside the back-ticks." This is referred to as *command substitution*, as the output of the command inside the back-ticks is substituted for the command itself. This is often used to assign the output of a command to a variable. As an example, let's say we wanted to keep track of how many files are in a directory. From the command line, we could say

```
ls | wc
```

The `wc` command gives me a word count, along with the number of lines and number of characters. The | is a "pipe" symbol that is used to pass the output of one command through another. In this example, the output of the `ls` command is passed or piped through `wc`. Here, the command might come up as:

```
 7      7     61
```

However, once the command is finished and the value has been output, we can only get it back again by rerunning the command. Instead, If we said:

```
count=`ls |wc`
```

the entire line of output would be saved in the variable `count`. If we then say `echo $count`, we get

```
7       7     61
```

showing me that `count` now contain the output of that line. If we wanted, we could even assign a multi-line output to this variable. We could use the `ps` command, like this

```
trash=`ps`
```

then we could type in

```
echo $trash
```

which gives me

```
PID TTY STAT TIME COMMAND 209 06 0:02 -bash 1362 06 0:00 ps
```

This is different from the output that `ps` would give when not assigned to the variable `trash`:

```
PID       TTYSTATTIME COMMAND
209       06    S     0:02 -bash
1362      06    R     0:00 ps
```

The next kind of quote, the single-quote ('), tells the system not to do *any* expansion at all. Let's take the example above, but this time, use single quotes:

```
count='ls |wc'
```

If we were to now type `echo $count`, we would get

```
ls |wc
```

and what we got was exactly what we expected. The shell did no expansion and simply assigned the literal string "`ls | wc`" to the variable `count`. This even applies to the variable operator "`$`." For example, if we simply say

```
echo '$LOGNAME'
```

what comes out on the screen is

```
$LOGNAME
```

No expansion is done at all and even the "$" is left unchanged.

The last set of quotes is the double-quote. This has partially the same effect as single-quotes, but to a limited extent. If we include something inside of double-quotes, everything loses its special meaning except for the variable operator ($), the backslash (\), the back-tick ('), and the double-quote itself. Everything else takes on its absolute meaning. For example, we could say

```
echo "`date`"
```

which gives us

```
Wed Feb 01 16:39:30 PST 1995
```

This is a round-about way of getting the date, but it is good for demonstration purposes. Plus, I often use this in shell scripts when I want to log something. Remember that the back-tick first expands the command (by running it) and then the echo echoes it to the screen.

That pretty much wraps up the characters that have special meaning to the shell. You can get more details from any number of references books on Linux or UNIX in general (if you need it). However, the best way to see what's happening is to try a few combinations and see if they behave as you expect.

Previously, I mentioned that some punctuation marks had special meaning. We already know about the special meaning of `*`, `?`, and `[ ]`. What about the others? Well, in fact, most of the other punctuation marks have special meaning. We'll get into more detail about them when we talk about shell programming.

3.1.5 Pipes and Redirection

Perhaps the most commonly used character is "|", which is referred to as the pipe symbol, or simply pipe. This enables you to pass the output of one command through the input of another. For example, say you would like to do a long directory listing of the `/bin` directory. If you type `ls -l` and then press Enter, the names flash by much too fast for you to read. When the display finally stops, all you see is the last twenty entries or so.

If instead we ran the command `ls -l | more`, the output of the `ls` command will be "piped through `more`". In this way, we can scan through the list a screenful at a time.

In our discussion of standard input and standard output in Chapter 1, I talked about standard input as being just a file that usually points to your terminal. Standard output is also a file that usually points to your terminal in this case. The standard output of the `ls` command is changed to point to the pipe, and the standard input of the more command is changed to point to the pipe as well.

The way this works is that when the shell sees the pipe symbol, it creates a temporary file on the hard disk. Although it does not have a name or directory entry, it takes up physical space on the hard disk. Because both the terminal and the pipe are seen as files from the perspective of the operating system, all we are saying is that the system should use different files instead of standard input and standard output.

Under Linux (as well as other UNIX dialects), there exist the concepts of standard input, standard output, and standard error. When you log in and are working from the command line, standard input is your terminal keyboard and both standard output and standard error are your terminal screen. In other words, the shell expects to be getting its input from the keyboard and showing the output (and any error messages) on the terminal screen.

Actually, the three (standard input, standard output, and standard error) are references to files that the shell automatically opens. Remember that in UNIX, everything is treated as a file. When the shell starts, the three files it opens are usually the ones pointing to your terminal.

When we run a command like `cat`, it gets input from a file that it displays to the screen. Although it may appear that the standard input is coming from that file, the standard input (referred to as stdin) is still the keyboard. This is why when the file is large enough and `more` stops after each page, you can continue by pressing either the Spacebar or Enter key. That's because *standard* input is still the keyboard.

As it is running, `more` is displaying the contents of the file to the screen. That is, it is going to standard output (stdout). If you try to do a `more` on a file that does not exist, the message

```
file_name: No such file or directory
```

shows up on your terminal screen as well. However, although it appears to be in the same place, the error message was written to standard error (stderr). (I'll show how this differs shortly.)

One pair of characters that is used quite often, "<" and ">," also deal with stdin and stdout. The more common of the two, ">," redirects the output of a command into a file. That is, it changes standard output. An example of this would be `ls /bin > myfile`. If we were to run this command, we would have a file (in my current directory) named `myfile` that contained the output of the `ls /bin` command. This is because stdout is the file `myfile` and not the terminal. Once the command completes, stdout returns to being the terminal. What this looks like graphically, we see in Figure 3.2.

Figure 3.2: **File Redirection**

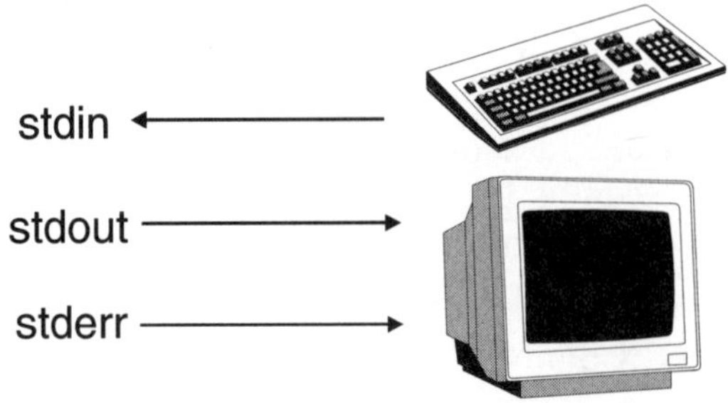

redirection with: *command 2> error.file*

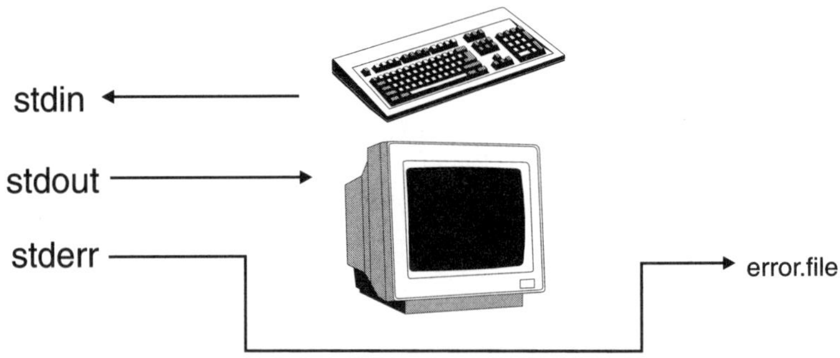

Now, we want to see the contents of the file. We could simply say `more myfile`, but that wouldn't explain about redirection. Instead, we input `more <myfile`. This tells the `more` command to take its standard input from the file `myfile` instead of from the keyboard or some other file. (Remember, even when stdin is the keyboard, it is still seen as a file.)

What about errors? As I mentioned, stderr *appears* to be going to the same place as stdout. A quick way of showing that it doesn't is by using output redirection and forcing an error. If wanted to list two directories and have the output go to a file, we run this command:

```
ls  /bin  /jimmo > /tmp/junk
```

We then get this message:

```
/jimmo not found
```

However, if we look in `/tmp`, there is indeed a file called `junk` that contains the output of the `ls /bin` portion of the command. What happened here was that we redirected stdout into the file `/tmp/junk`. It did this with the listing of `/bin`. However, because there was no directory `/jimmo` (at least not on my system), we got the error `/jimmo not found`. In other words, stdout went into the file, but stderr still went to the screen.

If we want to get the output and any error messages to go to the same place, we can do that. Using the same example with `ls`, the command would be:

```
ls  /bin  /jimmo > /tmp/junk 2>&1
```

The new part of the command is `2>&1`, which says that file descriptor 2 (stderr) should go to the same place as file descriptor 1 (stdout). By changing the command slightly

```
ls  /bin  /jimmo > /tmp/junk  2>/tmp/errors
```

we can tell the shell to send any errors someplace else. You will find quite often in shell scripts throughout the system that the file that error messages are sent to is `/dev/null`. This has the effect of ignoring the messages completely. They are neither displayed on the screen nor sent to a file.

Note that this command does not work as you would think:

```
ls  /bin  /jimmo 2>&1 > /tmp/junk
```

The reason is that we redirect stderr to the same place as stdout *before* we redirect stdout. So, stderr goes to the screen, but stdout goes to the file specified.

Redirection can also be combined with pipes like this:

```
sort < names | head
```

or

```
ps | grep sh > ps.save
```

In the first example, the standard input of the `sort` command is redirected to point to the file `names`. Its output is then passed to the pipe. The standard input of the `head` command (which takes the first ten lines) also comes from the pipe. This would be the same as the command

```
sort names | head
```

which we see in Figure 3.3.

In the second example, the `ps` command (process status) is piped through grep and all of the output is redirected to the file `file.save`.

Figure 3.3: **Data Flow Through a Pipe**

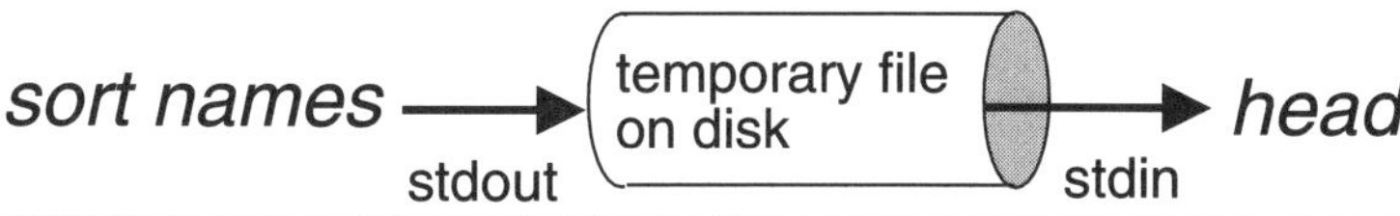

If we want to redirect stderr, we can. The syntax is similar, but it differs slightly from shell to shell. Therefore, I am going to hold off until I talk about the individual shells.

It's possible to input multiple commands on the same command line. This can be accomplished by using a semi-colon (`;`) between commands. I have used this on occasion to create command lines like this:

```
man bash | col -b > man.tmp; vi man.tmp; rm man.tmp
```

This command redirects the output of the man-page for `bash` into the file `man.tmp`. (The pipe through `col -b` is necessary because of the way the man-pages are formatted.) Next, we are brought into the `vi` editor with the file `man.tmp`. After I exit `vi`, the command continues and removes my temporary file `man.tmp`. (After about the third time of doing this, it got pretty monotonous, so I created a shell-script to do this for me. I'll talk more about shell-scripts later.)

3.1.6 Interpreting the Command

One question I had was, "In what order does everything gets done?" We have shell variables to expand, aliases and functions to process, "real" commands, pipes and input/output redirection. There are a lot of things that the shell must consider when figuring out what to do and when.

For the most part, this is not so important. Commands do not get so complex that knowing the evaluation order becomes an issue. However, on a few occasions I have run into situations in which things did not behave as I thought they should. By evaluating the command myself (as the shell would), it became clear what was happening. Let's take a look.

The first thing that gets done is that the shell figures out how many commands there are on the line. (Remember, you can separate multiple commands on a single line with a semicolon.) This process determines how many *tokens* there are on the command line. In this context, a token could be an entire command or it could be a control word such as "if." Here, too, the shell must deal with input/output redirection and pipes.

Once the shell determines how many tokens there are, it checks the syntax of each token. Should there be a syntax error, the shell will not try to start *any* of the commands. If the syntax is correct, it begins interpreting the tokens.

The first thing the shell checks for is functions. Like the functions in programming languages like C, a shell function can be thought of as a small subprogram.

Next, aliases are expanded. Aliases are a way for some shells to allow you to define your own commands. If any token on the command line is actually an alias that you have defined, it is expanded before the shell proceeds. If it happens that an alias contains another alias, they are both expanded before continuing with the next step. We'll go into both aliases and functions shortly.

Once aliases and functions have all been completely expanded, the shell evaluates variables. Finally, it uses any wildcards to expand them to file names. This is done according to the rules we talked about previously.

After the shell has evaluated everything, it is *still* not ready to run the command. It first checks to see if the first token represents a command built into the shell or an external one. If it's not external, the shell needs to go through the search path.

At this point, it sets up the redirection, including the pipes. These obviously must be ready before the command starts because the command may be getting its input from someplace other than the keyboard and may be sending it somewhere other than the screen. Figure 3.4 shows how the evaluation looks graphically.

This is an oversimplification. Things happen in this order, though many more things occur in and around the steps than I have listed here. What I am attempting to describe is the general process that occurs when the shell is trying to interpret your command.

Once the shell has determined what each command is and each command is an executable *binary* program (not a shell script), the shell makes a copy of itself using the `fork()` system call. This copy is a child process of the shell. It then uses the `exec()` system call to overwrite itself with the binary it wants to execute. Keep in mind that even though the child process is executing, the original shell is still in memory, waiting for the child to complete (assuming the command was not started in the background with `&`).

If the program that needs to be executed is a shell-script, the program that is created with `fork()` and `exec()` is another shell. This new shell starts reading the shell-script and interprets it, one line at a time. This is why a syntax error in a shell script is not discovered when the script is started, but rather when the erroneous line is first encountered.

Understanding that a new process is created when you run a shell-script helps to explain a very common misconception under UNIX. When you run a shell-script and that script changes directories, your original shell knows nothing about the change. This confuses a lot of people who are new to UNIX as they come from the DOS world, where changing the directory from within a batch file does change the original shell. This is because DOS does not have the same concept of a process as UNIX does.

Figure 3.4: **Evaluating a Command**

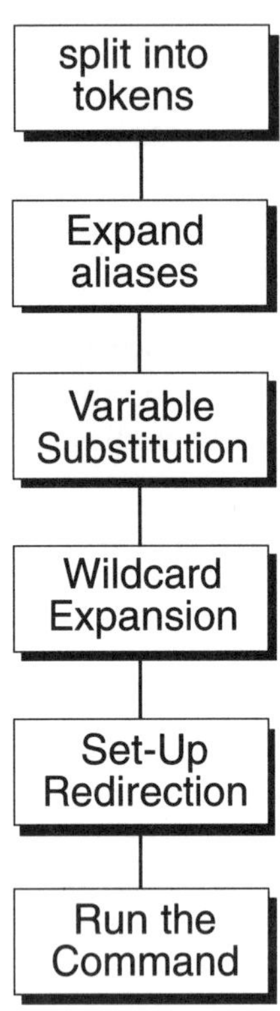

Look at it this way: The sub-shell's environment has been changed because the current directory is different, but this is *not* passed back to the parent. Like "real" parent-child relationships, only the children can inherit characteristics from their parent, not the other way around. Therefore, any changes to the environment, including directory changes, are not noticed by the parent. Again, this is *different* from the behavior of DOS .bat files.

You can get around this by either using aliases or shell functions (assuming that your shell has them). Another way is to use the dot command in front of the shell-script you want to execute. For example:

`. myscript` ←NOTICE THE DOT!

This script will be interpreted directly by the current shell, *without* forking a subshell. If the script makes changes to the environment, it is *this* shell's environment that is changed.

You can use this same behavior if you ever need to reset your environment. Normally, your environment is defined by the start-up files in your home directory. On occasion, things get a little confused (maybe a variable is changed or removed) and you need to reset things. By using the dot command, you can reset your environment. For example, with either sh or ksh, you can write it like this:

```
. $HOME/.profile
```

Or, using a function of bash you can also write

```
. ~/.profile
```

This uses the tilde (~), which I haven't mentioned yet. Under many shells, you can use the tilde as a shortcut to refer to a particular user's home directory.

If you have csh, the command is issued like this:

```
source $HOME/.login
```

One construct that I find very useful is select. With select, you can have a quick menuing system. It takes the form

```
select name in word1 word2 ...
do
      list
done
```

where each word is presented in a list and preceded by a number. Inputting that number sets the value of name to the word following that number. Confused? Let's look at an example. Assume we have a simple script that looks like this:

```
select var in date "ls -l" w exit

do
      $var

done
```

When we run this script, we get

```
1) date
2) ls -l
3) w
4) exit
#?
```

The "#?" is whatever you have defined as the PS3 (third-level prompt) variable. Here, we have just left it at the default, but we could have set it to something else. For example:

```
export PS3="Enter choice: "
```

This would make the prompt more obvious, but you need to keep in mind that PS3 would be valid everywhere (assuming you didn't set it in the script).

In our example, when we input 1, we get the date. First, however, the word "date" is assigned to the variable "var." The single line within the list expands that variable and the line is executed. This gives us the date. If we were to input 2, the variable "var" would be assigned the word "ls -l" and we would get a long listing of the current directory (not where the script resides). If we input 4, when the line was executed, we would exit from the script.

Some shells keep track of your *last* directory in the `OLDPWD` environment variable. Whenever you change directories, the system saves your current directory in `OLDPWD` *before* it changes you to the new location.

You can use this by simply entering `cd $OLDPWD`. Because the variable `$OLDPWD` is expanded before the `cd` command is executed, you end up back in your previous directory. Although this has more characters than just `popd`, it's easier because the system keeps track of my position, current and previous, for me. Also, because it's a variable, I can access it in the same way that I can access other environment variables.

For example, if there were a file in our old directory that we wanted to move to our current one, we could do this by entering:

```
cp $OLDPWD/<file_name> ./
```

However, things are not as difficult as they seem. Typing in `cd $OLDPWD` is still a bit cumbersome. It is a lot less characters to type in `popd`–like in the `csh`. Why isn't there something like that in the `ksh`? There is. In fact, it's much simpler. When I first found out about it, the adjective that first came to mind was "sweet." To change directories to your previous directory, simply type "`cd -`".

3.1.7 Different Kinds of Shells

The great-grandfather of all shells is `/bin/sh`, called simply `sh` or the Bourne Shell, named after its developer, Steven Bourne. When it was first introduced in the mid-1970's, this was almost a godsend as it allowed *interaction* with the operating system. This is the "standard" shell that you will find on every version in UNIX (at least all those I have seen). Although many changes have been made to UNIX, `sh` has remained basically unchanged.

All the capabilities of "the shell" I've talked about so far apply to `sh`. Anything I've talked about that `sh` can do, the others can do as well. So rather than going on about what `sh` can do (which I already did), I am going to talk about the characteristics of some other shells.

Later, I am going to talk about the C-Shell, which kind of throws a monkey wrench into this entire discussion. Although the concepts are much the same between the C-Shell and other shells, the constructs are often quite different. On the other hand, the other shells are extensions of the Bourne Shell, so the syntax and constructs are basically the same.

Be careful here. This is one case in which I have noticed that the various versions of Linux are different. Not every shell is in every version. Therefore, the shells I am going to talk about may not be in your distribution. Have no fear! If there is a feature that you really like, you can either take the source code from one of the other shells and add it, or you can find the different shells all over the Internet, which is much easier.

Linux includes several different shells and we will get into the specific of many of them as we move along. In addition, many different shells are available as either public domain, shareware, or commercial products that you can install on Linux.

As I mentioned earlier, environment variables are set up for you as you are logging in or you can set them up later. Depending on the shell you use, the files used and where they are located is going to be different. Some variables are made available to everyone on the system and are accessed through a common file. Others reside in the user's home directory.

Normally, the files residing in a user's home directory can be modified. However, a system administrator may wish to prevent users from doing so. Often, menus are set up in these files to either make things easier for the user or to prevent the user from getting to the command line. (Often users never need to get that far.) In other cases, environment variables that shouldn't be changed need to be set up for the user.

One convention I will be using here is how I refer to the different shells. Often, I will say "the `bash`" or just "`bash`" to refer to the Bourne-Again Shell as a concept and not the program `/bin/bash`. I will use "`bash`" to refer to the "Bourne Shell" as an abstract entity and not specifically to the program `/bin/sh`.

Why the Bourne-Again Shell? Well, this shell is compatible with the Bourne Shell, but has many of the same features as both the Korn Shell (`ksh`) and C-Shell (`csh`). This is especially important to me as I flail violently when I don't have a Korn Shell.

Most of the issues I am going to address here are detailed in the appropriate man-pages and other documents. Why cover them here? Well, in keeping with one basic premise of this book, I want to show you the relationships involved. In addition, many of the things we are going to look at are not emphasized as much as they should be. Often, users will go for months or years without learning the magic that these shells can do.

Only one oddity really needs to be addressed: the behavior of the different shells when moving through symbolic links. As I mentioned before, symbolic links are simply pointers to files or directories elsewhere on the system. If you change directories into symbolic links, your "location" on the disk is different than what you might think. In some cases, the shell understands the distinction and hides from you the fact that you are somewhere else. This is where the problem lies.

Although the concept of a symbolic link exists in most versions of UNIX, it is a relatively new aspect. As a result, not all applications and programs behave in the same way. Let's take the directory `/usr/spool` as an example. Because it contains a lot of administrative information, it is a useful and commonly accessed directory. It is actually a symbolic link to `/var/spool`. If we are using `ash` as our shell, when we do a `cd /usr/spool` and then `pwd`, the system responds with: `/var/spool`. This is where we are "physically" located, despite the fact that we did a `cd /usr/spool`. If we do a `cd ..` (to move up to our parent directory), we are now located in `/var`. All this seems logical. This is also the behavior of `csh` and `sh` on some systems.

If we use `bash`, things are different. This time, when we do a `cd /usr/spool` and then `pwd`, the system responds with `/usr/spool`. This is where we are "logically". If we now do a `cd ..`, we are located in `/usr`. Which of these is the "correct" behavior? Well, I would say both. There is nothing to define what the "correct" behavior is. Depending on your preference, either is correct. I tend to prefer the behavior of `ksh`. However, the behavior of `ash` is also valid.

3.1.8 Command Line Editing

When I first started working in tech support, I was given a `csh` and once I figured out all it could do, I enjoyed using it. I found the editing to be cumbersome from time to time, but it was better than retyping everything.

One of my co-workers, Kamal (of IguanaCam fame), was an avid proponent of the Korn Shell. Every time he wanted to show me something on my terminal, he would grumble when he forgot that I wasn't using `ksh`. Many times he tried to convert me, but learning a new shell wasn't high on my list of priorities.

I often complained to Kamal how cumbersome `vi` was (at least I thought so). One day I asked him for some pointers on `vi`, because every time I saw him do something in `vi`, it looked like magic. He agreed with one condition–that I at least try the `ksh`. All he wanted to do was to show me one thing and if after that I still wanted to use the csh, that was my own decision. Not that he would stop grumbling, just that it was my own choice.

The one thing that Kamal showed me convinced me of the errors of my ways. Within a week, I had requested the system administrator to change my login shell to ksh.

What was that one thing? There is a way to edit command lines in the ksh as if you were in vi. Once Kamal showed me how to do it, I felt like the csh editing mechanism was like using a sledge-hammer to pound in a nail. It does what you want, but it is more work than you need.

Like the csh, the ksh has a history mechanism. The ksh history mechanism has two major advantages over that of the csh. First, the information is actually saved to a file. This is either defined by the HISTFILE environment variable *before* the shell is invoked, or it defaults to .sh_history in your home directory. At any point you can edit this file and make changes to what the ksh perceives as your command history.

This could be useful if you knew you were going to be issuing the same commands every time you logged in and you didn't want to create aliases or functions. If you copied a saved version of this file (or any other text file) and named it .sh_history, you would immediately have access to this new history. (Rewriting history? I shudder at the ramifications.)

The second advantage is the ability to edit directly any of the lines in your .sh_history file from the command line. If your EDITOR environment variable is set to vi or you use the set -o vi command, you can edit previous commands using many of the standard vi editing commands.

To enter edit mode, press Esc. You can now scroll through the lines of your history file using the vi movement keys (h-j-k-l). Once you have found the line you are looking for, you can use other vi commands to delete, add, change, or whatever you need. If you press "v," you are brought into the full-screen version of vi, which I found out by accident. For more details, check out the vi or ksh man-page or the later section on vi.

One exciting thing that bash can do is extend the command line editing. There are a large number of key combinations to which you can get bash to react. You say that the key combinations are "bound" to certain actions. The command you use is bind. To see what keys are currently bound, use bind -v. This is useful for finding out all the different editing commands to which you can bind keys.

3.1.9 Command Line Completion

Another nice feature of many shells is called *command line completion*, and, as its name implies, you can have the system complete your commands as well as path names for you. In most cases, tell the system that you want it to complete the command line by pressing Tab, provided it is not bound to another key.

For example, if we input `cd /home/jimm` and press Tab, the command is completed:

```
cd /home/jimmo
```

If we type `ema` and press Tab, we get

```
emacs
```

In both cases, press Enter for the system to execute the command. If there is no unique expansion, the shell gives you the list of what it could be. In the first example, if there was also a directory `/home/jimma`, we would get

```
jimma jimmo
```

Although these may not appear to be too useful, command and file completion comes in handy if the file you want to reference has a very long name. Rather than typing the whole name, you just need to input enough to make the name unique.

Note that depending on your shell, this command line expansion works not only for commands, but for arguments as well. Let's say that we have a file in my current directory called `letter.peter`. I input

```
emacs letter[TAB]
```

and the shell automatically expands that to be

```
emacs letter.peter
```

If we have two files, one named `letter.peter` and the other named `letter.klaus`, we can use this as mechanism as well. However, the same command cannot expand to one specific file. Therefore, pressing Tab again gives us a list of matching files.

3.1.10 Functions

Most (all?) shells have the means of creating new "internal" commands. This is done by creating shell *functions*. Shell functions are just like those in a programming language. Sets of commands are grouped together and jointly called by a single name.

The format for functions is:

```
function_name()
{
     first thing to do
     second thing to do
     third thing to do
}
```

Functions can be defined anywhere, including from the command line. All you need to do is simply type in the lines one at a time, similar to the way shown above. The thing to bear in mind is that if you type a function from a command line, once you exit that shell, the function is gone.

Shell functions have the ability to accept arguments, just like commands. A simple example is a script that looks like this:

```
display()
{
echo $1
}

display Hello
```

The output would be

```
Hello
```

Here we need to be careful. The variable `$1` is the positional parameter from the call to the `display` function and not to the script. We can see this when we change the script to look like this:

```
display()
{
echo $1
}

echo $1
display Hello
```

Let's call the script `display.sh` and start it like this:

```
display.sh Hi
```

The output would then look like this:

```
Hi
Hello
```

The first `echo` shows us the parameter from the command line and the second one shows us the parameter from the function.

3.1.11 Job Control

Job control is the ability to move processes between the foreground and background. This is very useful when you need to do several things at once, but only have one terminal. For example, let's say there are several files spread out across the system that we want to edit. Because we don't know where they are, we can't use full paths. Because they don't have anything common in their names, we can't use `find`. So we try `ls -R | more`.

After a minute or two, we find the first file we want to edit. We can then suspend this job by pressing Ctrl+Z. We then see something that looks like this:

```
[1]+   Stopped                    ls -R | more
```

This means that the process has been stopped or suspended. One very important thing to note is that this process is not in the background as if we had put an "&" at the end. When a process is suspended, it stops doing anything, unlike a process in the background, which keeps on working.

Once the `ls` is in the background, we can run `vi`. When we are done with `vi`, we can bring the `ls` command back with the `fg` (foreground) command.

If we wanted to, we could have more than just one job suspended. I have never had the need to have more than two running like this, but I have gotten more than ten during tests. One thing that this showed me was the meaning of the plus sign (+). This is the "current" job, or the one we put into the background last.

The number in brackets is the process's entry in the job table, which is simply a table containing all of your jobs. Therefore, if we already had three jobs, the next time we suspended a job, the entry would look like this:

```
[4]+   Stopped                    ls -R >> output
```

To look at the entire job table, we simply enter the command `jobs`, which might give us

```
[1]       Stopped       ls -R /usr >> output.usr
[2]       Stopped       find / -print > output.find
[3]-      Stopped       ls -R /var >> output.var
[4]+      Stopped       ls -R >> output.root
```

The plus sign indicates the job that we suspended last. So this is the one that gets called if we run `fg` without a job number. In this case, it was Job 4. Note that there is a minus sign (-) right after Job 3. This was the second to last job that we suspended. Now, we bring Job 2 in the foreground with `fg 2` and then immediately suspend it again with Ctrl+Z. The table now looks like this:

```
[1]      Stopped    ls -R /usr >> output
[2]+     Stopped    find / -print > output.find
[3]      Stopped    ls -R /var >> output
[4]-     Stopped    ls -R >> output
```

Note that Job 2 now has the plus sign following it and Job 4 has the minus sign.

In each of these cases, we suspended a job that was running in the foreground. If we had started a job and put it in the background from the command line, the table might have an entry that looked like this:

```
[3]     Running   ls -R /var >> output &
```

This shows us that although we cannot see the process (because it is in the background), it is still running. We could call it to the foreground if we wanted by running `fg 3`. And, if we wanted, we could use the `bg` command to send one of the stopped jobs to the background. So

```
bg %1
```

would send Job 1 to the background just as if we had included `&` from the command line.

One nice thing is that we don't have to use just the job numbers when we are pulling something into the foreground. Because we know that we started a process with the find command, we can get it by using

```
fg %find
```

Actually, we could have used `%f` or anything else that was not ambiguous. In this case, we were looking for a process that *started* with the string we input. We could even look for strings anywhere within the command. To do this, the command might be

```
fg %?print
```

which would have given us the same command. Or, if we had tried

```
fg %?usr
```

we would have gotten Job 1 because it contains the string `usr`.

If we find that there is a job that we want to kill (stop completely), we can use the `kill` command. This works the same way, so `kill %<nr>` kills the job with number `<nr>`, `kill %<string>` kills the job starting with `string`, and so on.

3.1.12 Aliases

What is an alias? It isn't the ability to call yourself Thaddeus Jones when your real name is Jedediah Curry. However, it is the ability to use a different name for a command. In principle, personal aliases can be anything you want. They are special names that you define to accomplish tasks. They aren't shell-scripts, as a shell-script it external to your shell. To start up a shell-script, type in its name. The system then starts a shell as a child process of your current shell to run the script.

Aliases, too, are started by typing them in. However, they are internal to the `csh`. That is, they are internal to your `csh` process. Instead of starting a subshell, the `csh` executes the alias internally. This has the obvious advantage of being quicker, as there is no overhead of starting the new shell or searching the hard disk.

Another major advantage is the ability to create new commands. You can do this with shell-scripts (which we will get into later), but the overhead of creating a new process does not make it worthwhile for simple tasks. Aliases can be created with multiple commands strung together. For example, I created an alias, `t`, that shows me the time. Although the date command does that, all I want to see is the time. So, I created an alias, `t`, like this:

```
alias t='date | cut -c12-16'
```

When I type in `t`, I get the hours and minutes, just exactly the way I want.

Aliases can be defined in either the `.login` or the `.cshrc`. However, as I described above, if you want them for all subshells, they need to go in `.cshrc`. If you are running a Bourne Shell, aliasing may be the first good reason to switch to another shell.

Be careful when creating aliases or functions so that you don't redefine existing commands. Either you end up forgetting the alias, or some other program uses the original program and fails because the alias gets called first. I once had a call from a customer with a system in which he could no longer install software. We tried replacing several programs on his system, but to no avail. Fortunately, he had another copy of the same product, but it, too, died with the same error. It didn't seem likely that it was bad media. At this point, I had been with him for almost an hour, so I decided to hand it off to someone else (often, a fresh perspective is all that is needed).

About an hour later, one of the other engineers came into my cubicle with the same problem. He couldn't come up with anything either, which relieved me, so he decided that he needed to research the issue. Well, he found the exact same message in the source code and it turned out that this message appeared when a command could not run the sort command. Ah, a corrupt sort binary. Nope! Not that easy. What else was there? As it turned out, the customer had created an alias called sort that he used to sort directories in a particular fashion. Because the Linux command couldn't work with this version of sort, it died.

Why use one over the other? Well, if there is something that can be done with a short shell-script, then it can be done with a function. However, there are things that are difficult to do with an alias. One thing is making long, relatively complicated commands. Although you can do this with an alias, it is much simpler and easier to read if you do it with a function. I will go into some more detail about shell functions later in the section on shell scripting. You can also find more details in the bash man-page.

3.1.13 A Few More Constructs

There are a few more loop constructs that we ought to cover as you are likely to come across them in some of the system scripts. The first is for a loop and has the following syntax:

```
for var in word1 word2 ...
do
      list of commands
done
```

We might use this to list a set of pre-defined directories like this:

```
for dir in bin etc usr
do
       ls -R $dir
done
```

This script does a recursive listing three times. The first time through the loop, the variable dir is assigned the value bin, next etc, and finally usr.

You may also see that the do/done pair can be replaced by curly braces ({ }). So, the script above would look like this:

```
for dir in bin etc usr
{
      ls -R $dir
}
```

Next, we have while loops. This construct is used to repeat a loop while a given expression is true. Although you can use it by itself, as in

```
while ( $VARIABLE=value)
```

I almost exclusively use it at the end of a pipe. For example:

```
cat filename | while read line
do
        commands
done
```

This sends the contents of the file `filename` through the pipe, which reads one line at a time. Each line is assigned to variable `line`. I can then process each line, one at a time. This is also the format that many of the system scripts use.

For those of you who have worked with UNIX shells before, you most certainly should have noticed that I have left out some constructs. Rather than turning this into a book on shell programming, I decided to show you the constructs that occur most often in the shell scripts on your system. I will get to others as we move along. The man-pages of each of the shells provide more details.

3.1.14 The C-Shell

One of the first "new" shells to emerge was the `csh` or C-Shell. It is so named because much of the syntax it uses is very similar to the C programming language. This isn't to say that this shell is only for C programmers, or programmers in general. Rather, knowing C makes learning the syntax much easier. However, it isn't essential. (Note: The `csh` syntax is *similar* to C, so don't get your dander up if it's not *exactly* the same.)

The `csh` is normally the shell that users get on many UNIX systems. Every place I ever got a UNIX account, it was automatically assumed that I wanted `csh` as my shell. When I first started out with UNIX, that was true. In fact, this is true for most users. Because they don't know any other shells, the `csh` is a good place to start. You might actually have `tcsh` on your system, but the principles are the same as for `csh`.

As you login with `csh` as your shell, the system first looks in the global file `/etc/cshrc`. Here, the system administrator can define variables or actions that should be taken by every `csh` user. Next, the system reads two files in your home directory: `.login` and `.cshrc`. The `.login` file normally contains the variables you want to set and the actions you want to occur each time you log in.

In both of these files, setting variables have a syntax that is unique to the `csh`. This is one *major* difference between the `csh` and the other two shells. It is also a reason why it is not a good idea to give root csh as its default shell. The syntax for csh is

```
set variable_name=value
```

whereas for the other two, it is simply

```
variable=value
```

Because many of the system commands are Bourne scripts, executing them with csh ends up giving you a lot of syntax errors.

Once the system has processed your .login file, your .cshrc is processed. The .cshrc contains things that you want executed or configured every time you start a csh. At first, I wasn't clear with this concept. If you are logging in with the csh, don't you want to start a csh? Well, yes. However, the reverse is not true. Every time I start a csh, I don't want the system to behave as if I were logging in.

Let's take a look as this for a minute. One of the variables that gets set for you is the SHELL variable. This is the shell you use anytime you do a *shell escape* from a program. A shell escape is starting a shell as a subprocess of a program. An example of a program that allows a shell escape is vi.

When you do a shell escape, the system starts a shell as a new (child) process of whatever program you are running at the time. As we talked about earlier, once this shell exits, you are back to the original program. Because there is no default, the variable *must* be set to a shell. If the variable is set to something else, you end up with an error message like the following from vi:

```
invalid SHELL value: <something_else>
```

where <something_else> is whatever your SHELL variable is defined as.

If you are running csh and your SHELL variable is set to /bin/csh, every time you do a shell escape, the shell you get is csh. If you have a .cshrc file in your home directory, not only is this started when you log in, but anytime you start a new csh. This can be useful if you want to access personal aliases from inside of subshells.

One advantage that the csh offered over the Bourne Shell is its ability to repeat, and even edit, previous commands. Newer shells also have this ability, but the mechanism is slightly different. Commands are stored in a shell "history list," which, by default, contains the last 20 commands. This is normally defined in your .cshrc file, or you can define them from the command line. The command set history=100 would change the size of your history list to 100. However, keep in mind that everything you type at the command line is saved in the history file. Even if you mistype something, the shell tosses it into the history file.

What good is the history file? Well, the first thing is that by simply typing "history" with nothing else you get to see the contents of your history file. That way, if you can't remember the exact syntax of a command you typed five minutes ago, you can check your history file.

This is a nice trick, but it goes far beyond that. Each time you issue a command from the `csh` prompt, the system increments an internal counter that tells the shell how many commands have been input up to that point. By default, the `csh` often has the prompt set to be a number followed by a `%`. That number is the current command, which you can use to repeat those previous commands. This is done with an exclamation mark (`!`), followed by the command number as it appears in the shell history.

For example, if the last part of your shell history looked like this:

```
21 date
22 vi letter.john
23 ps
24 who
```

You could edit `letter.john` again by simply typing in `!22`. This repeats the command `vi letter.john` and adds this command to your history file. After you finish editing the file, this portion of the history file would look like

```
21 date
22 vi letter.john
23 ps
24 who
25 vi letter.john
```

Another neat trick that's built into this history mechanism is the ability to repeat commands without using the numbers. If you know that sometime within your history you edited a file using `vi`, you could edit it again by simply typing `!vi`. This searches backward though the history file until it finds the last time you used `vi`. If there were no other commands since the last time you used `vi`, you could also Enter `!v`.

To redo the last command you entered, you could do so simply by typing in `!!`.

This history mechanism can also be used to edit previously issued commands. Let's say that instead of typing `vi letter.john`, we had typed in `vi letter.jonh`. Maybe we know someone named jonh, but that's not who we meant to address this letter to. So, rather than typing in the whole command, we can edit it. The command we would issue would be `!!:s/nh/hn/`.

At first, this seems a little confusing. The first part, however, should be clear. The "!!" tells the system to repeat the previous command. The colon (:) tells the shell to expect some editing commands. The "s/nh/hn/" says to substitute for pattern nh the hn. (If you are familiar with vi or sed, you understand this. If not, we'll get into this syntax later.)

What would happen if we had edited a letter to john, done some other work and decided we wanted to edit a letter to chris instead. We could simply type !22:s/john/chris/. Granted, this is actually more keystrokes than if we had typed everything over again. However, you hopefully see the potential for this. Check out the csh man-page for many different tricks for editing previous commands.

In the default .cshrc are two aliases that I found quite useful. These are pushd and popd. These aliases are used to maintain a directory "stack". When you run pushd <dir_name>, your current directory is pushed onto (added to) the stack and you change the directory to <dir_name>. When you use popd, it pops (removes) the top of the directory stack and you change directories to it.

Like other kinds of stacks, this directory stack can be several layers deep. For example, let's say that we are currently in our home directory. A "pushd /bin" makes our current directory /bin with our home directory the top of the stack. A "pushd /etc" brings us to /etc. We do it one more time with pushd /usr/bin, and now we are in /usr/bin. The directory /usr/bin is now the top of the stack.

If we run popd (no argument), /usr/bin is popped from the stack and /etc is our new directory. Another popd, and /bin is popped, and we are now in /bin. One more pop brings me back to the home directory. (In all honesty, I have never used this to do anything more than to switch directories, then jump back to where I was. Even that is a neat trick.)

There is another useful trick built into the csh for changing directories. This is the concept of a directory path. Like the execution search path, the directory path is a set of values that are searched for matches. Rather than searching for commands to execute, the directory path is searched for directories to change into.

The way this works is by setting the cdpath variable. This is done like any other variable in csh. For example, if, as system administrator, we wanted to check up on the various spool directories, we could define cdpath like this:

```
set cdpath = /usr/spool
```

Then, we could enter

```
cd lp
```

If the shell can't find a subdirectory named `lp`, it looks in the `cdpath` variable. Because it is defined as `/usr/spool` and there is a `/usr/spool/lp` directory, we jump into `/usr/spool/lp`. From there, if we type

```
cd mail
```

we jump to `/usr/spool/mail`. We can also set this to be several directories, like this:

```
set cdpath = ( /usr/spool /usr/lib /etc )
```

In doing so, each of the three named directories will be searched.

The `csh` can also make guesses about where you might want to change directories. This is accomplished through the `cdspell` variable. This is a Boolean variable (true/false) that is set simply by typing

```
set cdspell
```

When set, the `cdspell` variable tells the `csh` that it should try to guess what is really meant when we misspell a directory name. For example, if we typed

```
cd /sur/bin  (instead of /usr/bin)
```

the `cdspell` mechanism attempts to figure out what the correct spelling is. You are then prompted with the name that it guessed as being correct. By typing in anything other than "n" or "N," you are changing into this directory. There are limitations, however. Once it finds what it thinks is a match, it doesn't search any further.

For example, we have three directories, "a," "b," and "c." If we type "`cd d`," any of the three could be the one we want. The shell will make a guess and choose one, which may or may not be correct.

Note that you may not have the C-Shell on your system. Instead, you might have something called `tcsh`. The primary difference is that `tcsh` does command line completion and command line editing.

3.2 Commonly Used Utilities

There are hundreds of utilities and commands plus thousands of support files in a normal Linux installation. Very few people I have met know what they all do. As a matter of fact, I don't know anyone who knows what they all do. Some are obvious and we use them everyday, such as `date`. Others are not so obvious and I have never met anyone who has used them. Despite their overwhelming number and often cryptic names and even more cryptic options, many commands are very useful and powerful.

I have often encountered users, as well as system administrators, who combine many of these commands into something relatively complicated. The only real problem is that there is often a single command that would do all of this for them.

In this section, we are going to cover some of the more common commands. I am basing my choice on a couple of things. First, I am going to cover those commands that I personally use on a regular basis. These commands are those that I use to do things I need to do, or those that I use to help end users get done what they need to. Next, I will discuss the Linux system itself. There are dozens of scripts scattered all through the system that contain many of these commands. By talking about them here, you will be in a better position to understand existing scripts should you need to expand or troubleshoot them.

Because utilities are usually part of some larger process (such as installing a new hard disk or adding a new user), I am not going to talk about them here. I will get to the more common utilities as we move along.

3.2.1 Looking for Files

There are many ways to do to the things that you want to do. Some use a hammer approach and force the answer out of the system. In many cases, there are other commands that do the exact same thing without all the gyrations. So, what I am going to try to do here is step through some of the logic (and illogic) that I went through when first learning Linux. That way, we can all laugh together at how silly I was and maybe you won't make the same mistakes I did.

Every dialect of UNIX that I have seen has the `ls` command. This gives a directory listing of either the current directory if no argument is given, or a listing of a particular file or directory if arguments are specified. The default behavior under Linux for the `ls` command is to list the names of the files in a single column. Try it and see.

It is a frequent (maybe not common) misconception for new users to think that they have to be in a particular directory to get a listing of it. They will spend a great deal of time moving up and down the directory tree looking for a particular file. Fortunately, they don't have to do it that way. The issue with this misunderstanding is that every command is capable of working with paths, as is the operating system that does the work. Remember our discussion of Linux basics. Paths can be relative to our current directory, such as `./directory`, or absolute, such as `/home/jimmo/directory`.

For example, assume that you have a subdirectory of your current working directory called `letters`. In it are several subdirectories for types of letters, such as business, school, family, friends, and taxes. To get a listing of each of this directories, you could write

```
ls ./letters/business
ls ./letters/school
ls ./letters/family
ls ./letters/friends
ls ./letters/taxes
```

Because the ls command lets you have multiple commands on the same line, you also could have issued the command like this:

```
ls ./letters/business ./letters/school ./letters/family
./letters/friends ./letters/taxes
```

Both will give you a listing of each of the five directories. Even for five directories, typing all of that is a pain. You might think you could save some typing if you simply entered

```
ls ./letters
```

However, this gives you a listing of all the files and directories in ./letters, not the subdirectories. Instead, if you entered

```
ls ./letters/*
```

the shell would expand the wildcard (*) and give you a listing of both the ./letters directory as well as the directories immediately below ./letters, like the second example above. If each of the subdirectories is small, then this might fit onto one screen. If, on the other hand, you have 50 letters in each subdirectory, they are not all going to fit on the screen at once. Remember our discussion on shell basics? You can use the pipe (|) to send the command through something like more so that you could read it a page at a time.

What if the taxes directory contained a subdirectory for each year for the past five years, each of these contained a subdirectory for each month, each of these contained a subdirectory for federal, state, and local taxes, and each of these contained 10 letters?

If we knew that the letter we were looking for was somewhere in the taxes subdirectory, the command ls ./letters/taxes/* would show us the sub-directories of taxes (federal, local, state), and it would show their contents. We could then look through this output for the file we were looking for.

What if the file we were looking for was five levels deeper? We could keep adding wildcards (*) until we reached the right directory, as in:

```
ls ./letters/taxes/*/*/*/*/*
```

This might work, but what happens if the files were six levels deeper. Well, we could add an extra wildcard. What if it were 10 levels deeper and we didn't know it? Well, we could fill the line with wildcards. Even if we had too many, we would still find the file we were looking for.

Fortunately for us, we don't have to type in 10 asterisks to get what we want. We can use the `-R` option to `ls` to do a recursive listing. The `-R` option also avoids the "`argument list too long`" error that we might get with wildcards. So, the solution here is to use the `ls` command like this:

```
ls -R ./letters/taxes | more
```

The problem is that we now have 1,800 files to look through. Piping them through `more` and looking for the right file will be very time consuming. If we knew that it was there, but we missed it on the first pass, we would have to run through the whole thing again.

The alternative is to have `more` search for the right file for you. Because the output is more than one screen, `more` will display the first screen and at the bottom display `--More--`. Here, we could type a slash (`/`) followed by the name of the file and press Enter. Now `more` will search through the output until it finds the name of the file. Now we know that the file exists.

The problem here is the output of the `ls` command. We can find out whether a file exists by this method, but we cannot really tell where it is. If you try this, you will see that `more` jumps to the spot in the output where the file is (if it is there). However, all we see is the file name, not what directory it is in. Actually, this problem exists even if we don't execute a search.

If you use `more` as the command and not the end of a pipe, instead of just seeing `--More--`, you will probably see something like

```
--More--(16%)
```

This means that you have read 16 percent of the file.

However, we don't need to use `more` for that. Because we don't want to look at the entire output–just search for a particular file–we can use one of three commands that Linux provides to do pattern searching: `grep`, `egrep`, and `fgrep`. The names sound a little odd to the Linux beginner, but `grep` stands for **g**lobal **r**egular **e**xpression **p**rint. The other two are newer versions that do similar things. For example, `egrep` searches for patterns that are full regular expressions and `fgrep` searches for fixed strings and is a bit faster.

Let's assume that we are tax consultants and have 50 subdirectories, one for each client. Each subdirectory is further broken down by year and type of tax (state, local, federal, sales, etc.). A couple years ago, a client of ours bought a boat. We have a new client who also wants to buy a boat, and we need some information in that old file.

Because we know the name of the file, we can use grep to find it, like this:

```
ls -R ./letters/taxes | grep boat
```

If the file is called boats, boat.txt, boats.txt, or letter.boat, the grep will find it because grep is only looking for the pattern boat. Because that pattern exists in all four of those file names, all four would be potential matches.

The problem is that the file may not be called boat.txt, but rather Boat.txt. Remember, unlike DOS, UNIX is case-sensitive. Therefore, grep sees boat.txt and Boat.txt as different files. The solution here would be to tell grep to look for both.

Remember our discussion on regular expressions in the section on shell basics? Not only can we use regular expressions for file names, we can use them in the arguments to commands. The term *regular expression* is even part of grep's name. Using regular expressions, the command might look like this:

```
ls -R ./letters/taxes | grep [Bb]oat
```

This would now find both boat.txt and Boat.txt.

Some of you may see a problem with this as well. Not only does Linux see a difference between boat.txt and Boat.txt, but also between Boat.txt and BOAT.TXT. To catch all possibilities, we would have to have a command something like this:

```
ls -R ./letters/taxes | grep [Bb][Oo][Aa][Tt]
```

Although this is perfectly correct syntax and it will find the files it no matter what case the word "boat" is in, it is too much work. The programmers who developed grep realized that people would want to look for things regardless of what case they are in. Therefore, they built in the -i option, which simply says *ignore* the case. Therefore, the command

```
ls -R ./letters/taxes | grep -i boat
```

will not only find boats, boat.txt, boats.txt, and letter.boat, but it will also find Boat.txt and BOAT.TXT as well.

If you've been paying attention, you might have noticed something. Although the grep command will tell you about the existence of a file, it won't tell you where it is. This is just like piping it through more, only we're filtering out something. Therefore, it still won't tell you the path.

Now, this isn't grep's fault. It did what it was supposed to do. We told it to search for a particular pattern and it did. Also, it displayed that pattern for us. The problem is still the fact that the ls command is not displaying the full paths of the files, just their names.

Instead of ls, let's use a different command. Let's use find instead. Just as its name implies, find is used to find things. What it finds is files. If we change the command to look like this:

```
find ./letters/taxes -print | grep -i boat
```

This finds what we are looking for and gives us the paths as well.

Before we go on, let's look at the syntax of the find command. There are a lot of options and it does look foreboding, at first. We find it is easiest to think of it this way:

```
find <starting_where> <search_criteria> <do_something>
```

In this case, the "where" is ./letters/taxes. Therefore, find starts its search in the./letters/taxes directory. Here, we have no search criteria; we simply tell it to do something. That something was to -print out what it finds. Because the files it finds all have a path relative to ./letters/taxes, this is included in the output. Therefore, when we pipe it through grep, we get the path to the file we are looking for.

We also need to be careful because the find command we are using will also find directories named boat. This is because we did not specify any search criteria. If instead we wanted it *just* to look for regular file (which is often a good idea), we could change the command to look like this:

```
find ./letters/taxes -type f -print | grep -i boat
```

Here we see the option -type f as the search criteria. This will find all the files of type f for regular files. This could also be a d for directories, c for character special files, b for block special files, and so on. Check out the find(1) man-page for other types that you can use.

Too complicated? Let's make things easier by avoiding grep. There are many different things that we can use as search criteria for find. Take a quick look at the man-page and you will see that you can search for a specific owner, groups, permissions, and even names. Instead of having grep do the search for us, let's save a step (and time) by having find do the search for us. The command would then look like this:

```
find ./letters/taxes -name boat -print
```

This will find any file named boat and list its respective path. The problem here is that it will only find the files named boat. It *won't* find the files boat.txt, boats.txt, or even Boat.

The nice thing is that find understands about regular expressions, so we could issue the command like this:

```
find ./letters./taxes -name '[Bb]oat' -print
```

(Note that we included the single quote (') to avoid the square brackets ([ ]) from being first interpreted by the shell.)

This command tells find to look for all files named both boat and Boat. However, this won't find boat. We are almost there.

We have two alternatives. One is to expand the find to include all possibilities, as in

```
find ./letters./taxes -name '[Bb][Oo][Aa][Tt]' -print
```

This will find all the files with any combination of those four letters and print them out. However, it won't find boat.txt. Therefore, we need to change it yet again. This time we have

```
find ./letters./taxes -name '[Bb][Oo][Aa][Tt]*' -print
```

Here we have passed the wildcard (*) to find to tell it took find anything that starts with "boat" (upper- or lowercase), followed by anything else. If we add an extra asterisk, as in

```
find ./letters./taxes -name '*[Bb][Oo][Aa][Tt]*' -print
```

we not only get boat.txt, but also newboat.txt, which the first example would have missed.

This works. Is there an easier way? Well, sort of. There is a way that is easier in the sense that there are less characters to type in. This is

```
find ./letters/taxes -print | grep -i boat
```

Isn't this the same command that we issued before? Yes, it is. In this particular case, this combination of find and grep is the easier solution, because all we are looking for is the path to a specific file. However, these examples show you different options of find and different ways to use them.

3.2.2 Looking Through Files

Let's assume for a moment that none of the commands we issued came up with a file. There was not a single match of any kind. This might mean that we removed the file. On the other hand, we might have named it yacht.txt or something similar. What can we do to find it?

We could jump through the same hoops for yacht as we did for boat. However, what if the customer had a canoe or a junk. Are we stuck with every possible word for boat? Yes, unless we know something about the file, even if that something is *in* the file.

The nice thing is that grep doesn't have to be the end of a pipe. One of the arguments can be the name of a file. If you want, you can use several files, because grep will take the first argument as the pattern it should look for. If we were to enter

```
grep [Bb]oat ./letters/taxes/*
```

we would search the contents of all the files in the directory ./letters/taxes looking for the word Boat or boat.

If the file we were looking for happened to be in the directory ./letters/taxes, then all would be well. If things are like the examples above, where we have dozens of directories to look through, this is impractical. So, we turn back to find.

One useful option to find is -exec. When a file is found, you use -exec to execute a command. We can therefore use find to find the files, then use -exec to run grep on them. Because you probably don't have dozens of files on your system related to taxes, let's use an example from files that you most probably have.

Let's find all the files in the /etc directory containing /bin/sh. This would be run as

```
find ./etc -exec grep  /bin/sh {} \;
```

The curly braces ({ }) are substituted for the file found by the search, so the actual grep command would be something like

```
grep /bin/sh ./etc/filename
```

The "\;" is a flag saying that this is the end of the command.

What the find command does is search for all the files that match the specified criteria (in this case there were no criteria, so it found them all) then run grep on the criteria, searching for the pattern [Bb]oat.

Do you know what this tells us? It says that there is a file somewhere under the directory ./letters/taxes that contains either "boat" or "Boat." It *doesn't* tell me what the file name is because of the way the -exec is handled. Each file name is handed off one at a time, replacing the {}. It is as though we had entered individual lines for

```
grep '[Bb]oat' ./letters/taxes/file1
grep '[Bb]oat' ./letters/taxes/file2
grep '[Bb]oat' ./letters/taxes/file3
```

If we had entered

```
grep '[Bb]oat' ./letters/taxes/*
```

grep would have output the name of the file in front of each matching line it found. However, because each line is treated separately when using find, we don't see the file names. We could use the -l option to grep, but that would only give us the file name. That might be okay if there was one or two files. However, if a line in a file mentioned a "boat trip" or a "boat trailer," these might not be what we were looking for. If we used the -l option to grep, we wouldn't see the actual line. It's a catch-22.

To get what we need, we must introduce a new command: xargs. By using it as one end of a pipe, you can repeat the same command on different files without actually having to input the command multiple times.

In this case, we would get what we wanted by typing

```
find ./letters/taxes -print | xargs grep [Bb]oat
```

The first part is the same as we talked about earlier. The find command simply prints all the names it finds (all of them, in this case, because there were no search criteria) and passes them to xargs. Next, xargs processes them one at a time and creates commands using grep. However, unlike the -exec option to find, xargs will output the name of the file before each matching line.

Obviously, this example does not find those instances where the file we were looking for contained words like "yacht" or "canoe" instead of "boat." Unfortunately, the only way to catch all possibilities is to actually specify each one. So, that's what we might do. Rather than listing the different possible synonyms for boat, let's just take the three: boat, yacht, and canoe.

To do this, we need to run the find | xargs command three times. However, rather than typing in the command each time, we are going to take advantage of a useful aspect of the shell. In some instances, the shell knows when you want to continue with a command and gives you a *secondary prompt*. If you are running sh or ksh, then this is probably denoted as ">."

For example, if we typed

```
find ./letters/taxes -print |
```

the shell knows that the pipe (|) cannot be at the end of the line. It then gives us a > or ? prompt where we can continue typing

```
> xargs grep -i boat
```

The shell interprets these two lines as if we had typed them all on the same line. We can use this with a shell construct that lets us do loops. This is the `for/in` construct for `sh` and `ksh`, and the foreach construct in `csh`. It would look like this:

```
for j in boat ship yacht
> do
> find ./letters/taxes -print | xargs grep -i $j
> done
```

In this case, we are using the variable `j`, although we could have called it anything we wanted. When we put together quick little commands, we save ourselves a little typing by using single letters variables.

In the `sh/ksh` example, we need to enclose the body of the loop inside the `do-done` pair. In the `csh` example, we need to include the `end`. In both cases, this little command we have written will loop through three times. Each time, the variable `$j` is replaced with one of the three words that we used. If we had thought up another dozen or so synonyms for boat, then we could have included them all. Remember also that the shell knows that the pipe (|) is not the end of the command, so this would work as well.

```
for j in boat ship yacht
> do
> find ./letters/taxes -print |
> xargs grep -i $j
> done
```

Doing this from the command line has a drawback. If we want to use the same command again, we need to retype everything. However, using another trick, we can save the command. Remember that both the `ksh` and `csh` have history mechanisms to allow you to repeat and edit commands that you recently edited. However, what happens tomorrow when you want to run the command again? Granted, `ksh` has the .sh_history file, but what about `sh` and `csh`?

Why not save commands that we use often in a file that we have all the time? We could use `vi` or some other text editor to create the file. However, we could take advantage of a characteristic of the `cat` command, which is normally used to output the contents of a file to the screen. You can also redirect the `cat` to another file.

If we wanted to combine the contents of a file, we could do something like this:

```
cat file1 file2 file3 >newfile
```

This would combine `file1`, `file2`, and `file3` into `newfile`.

What happens if we leave the names of the source files out? In this instance, our command would look like this:

```
cat >newfile
```

Now, `cat` will take its input from the default input file, `stdin`. We can now type in lines, one at a time. When we are done, we tell `cat` to close the file by sending it an end-of-file character, Ctrl-D. So, to create the new command, we would issue the `cat` command as above and type in our command as the following:

```
for j in boat ship yacht
do
find ./letters/taxes -print |
xargs grep -i $j
done
<CTRL-D>
```

Note that here the secondary prompt, >, does not appear because it is `cat` that is reading our input and not the shell. We now have a file containing the five lines that we typed in that we can use as a shell script.

However, right now, all that we have is a file named `newfile` that contains five lines. We need to tell the system that it is a shell script that can be executed. Remember in our discussion on operating system basics that I said that a file's permissions need to be set to be able to execute the file. To change the permissions, we need a new command: `chmod`. (Read as "change mode" because we are changing the mode of the file.)

The `chmod` command is used to not only change access to a file, but also to tell the system that it should *try* to execute the command. I said "try" because the system would read that file, line-by-line, and would try to execute each line. If we typed in some garbage in a shell script, the system would try to execute each line and would probably report not found for every line.

To make a file execute, we need to give it execute permissions. To give everyone execution permissions, you use the `chmod` command like this:

```
chmod +x newfile
```

Now the file `newfile` has execute permissions, so, in a sense, it is executable. However, remember that I said the system would *read* each line. In order for a shell script to function correctly, it also needs to be readable by the person executing it. In order to read a file, you need to have read permission on that file. More than likely, *you* already have read permissions on the file since you created it. However, since we gave everyone execution permissions, let's give them all read permissions as well, like this:

```
chmod +r newfile
```

You now have a new command called `newfile`. This can be executed just like any the system provides for you. If that file resides in a directory somewhere in your path, all you need to do is type it in. Otherwise, (as we talked about before) you need to enter in the path as well. Keep in mind that the system does not need to be able to *read* binary programs. All it needs to be able to do is execute them. Now you have your first shell script and your first self-written UNIX command.

What happens if, after looking though all of the files, you don't find the one you are looking for. Maybe you were trying to be sophisticated and used "small aquatic vehicle" instead of boat. Now, six months later, you cannot remember what you called it. Looking through every file might take a long time. If only you could shorten the search a little. Because you remember that the letter you wrote was to the boat dealer, if you could remember the name of the dealer, you could find the letter.

The problem is that six months after you wrote it, you can no more remember the dealer's name than you can remember whether you called it a "small aquatic vehicle" or not. If you are like me, seeing the dealer's name will jog your memory. Therefore, if you could just look at the top portion of each letter, you might find what you are looking for. You can take advantage of the fact that the address is always at the top of the letter and use a command that is designed to do look there. This is the head command, and we use it like this:

```
find ./letters/taxes -exec head {} \;
```

This will look at the first 10 (the default for head) lines of each of the files that it finds. If the addressee were not in the first ten lines, but rather in the first 20 lines, we could change the command to be

```
find ./letters/taxes -exec head -20 {} \;
```

The problem with this is that 20 lines is almost an entire screen. If you ran this, it would be comparable to running more on every file and hitting `q` to exit after it showed the first screen. Fortunately, we can add another command to restrict the output even further. This is the tail command, which is just the opposite of head as it shows you the bottom of a file. So, if we knew that the address resided on lines 15-20, we could run a command like this:

```
find ./letters/taxes -exec head -20 {} \; | tail -5
```

This command passes the first 20 lines of each file through the pipe, and then tail displays the last five lines. So you would get lines 15–20 of every file, right? Not quite.

The problem is that the shell sees these as two *tokens*. That is, two separate commands `find ./letters/taxes -exec head -20 {} \;` and `tail -5`. All of the output of the `find` is sent to the pipe and it is the last five lines of this that `tail` shows. Therefore, if the `find | head` had found 100 files, we would not see the contents of the first 99!

The solution is to add two other shell constructs: `while` and `read`. The first command carries out a particular command (or set of commands) while some criteria are true. The `read` can read input either from the command line, or as part of a more complicated construction. So, using `cat` again to create a command as we did above, we could have something like this:

```
find ./letters/taxes -print | while read FILE
do
echo $FILE
head -20 $FILE |  tail -5
done
```

In this example, the `while` and `read` work together. The `while` will continue so long as it can read something into the variable `FILE`; that is, so long as there is output coming from `find`. Here again, we also need to enclose the body of the loop within the `do-done` pair.

The first line of the loop simple `echoes` the name of the file so we can keep track of what file is being looked at. Once we find the correct name, we can use it as the search criteria for a `find | grep` command. This requires looking through each file twice. However, if all you need to see is the address, then this is a lot quicker than doing a `more` on every file.

3.3 Basic Shell Scripting

By now, we have a pretty good idea of how commands can be put together to do a wide variety of tasks. However, to create more complicated scripts, we need more than just a few commands. There are several shell constructs that you need to be familiar with to make complicated scripts. A couple (the `while` and `for-in` constructs) we already covered. However, there are several more that can be very useful in a wide range of circumstances.

There are several things we need to talk about before we jump into things. The first is the idea of arguments. Like binary programs, you can pass arguments to shell scripts and have them use these arguments as they work. For example, let's assume we have a script called `myscript` that takes three arguments. The first is the name of a directory, the second is a file name, and the third is a word to search for. The script will search for all files in the directory with any part of their name being the file name and then search in those files for the word specified. A very simple version of the script might look like this:

```
ls $1 | grep $2 | while read file
do
      grep $3 ${2}/${file}
done
```

The syntax is

```
myscript directory file_name word
```

I discussed the `while-do-done` construct at the beginning of the chapter when I discussed different commands. The one difference here is that we are sending the output of a command through a second pipe before we send it to the while.

This also brings up a new construct: `${2}/${file}`. By enclosing a variable name inside of curly braces, we can combine variables. In this case, we take the name of the directory (`${2}`), and tack on a "`/`" for a directory separator, followed by the name of a file that `grep` found (`${file}`). This builds up the path name to the file.

When we run the program like this

```
myscript /home/jimmo trip boat
```

the three arguments `/home/jimmo`, `trip`, and `boat` are assigned to the *positional parameters* 1, 2, and 3, respectively. "Positional" because the number they are assigned is based on where they appear in the command. Because the positional parameters are shell variables, we need to refer to them with the leading dollar sign ($).

When the shell interprets the command, what is actually run is

```
ls /home/jimmo | grep trip | while read file
do
      grep boat /home/jimmo/${file}
done
```

If we wanted, we could make the script a little more self-documenting by assigning the values of the positional parameters to variables. The new script might look like this:

```
DIR=$1
FILENAME=$2
WORD=$3
ls -1 $DIR | grep $FILENAME | while read file
do
                grep $WORD ${DIR}/${file}
done
```

If we started the script again with the same arguments, first /home/jimmo would get assigned to the variable DIR, trip would get assigned to the variable FILENAME, and boat would get assigned to WORD. When the command was interpreted and run, it would still be evaluated the same way.

Being able to assign positional parameters to variables is useful for a couple of reasons. First is the issue of self-documenting code. In this example, the script is very small and because we know what the script is doing, we probably would not have made the assignments to the variables. However, if we had a larger script, then making the assignment is very valuable in terms of keeping track of things.

The next issue is that you can only reference 10 positional parameters. The first $0 refers to the script itself. What this can be used for, we'll get to in a minute. The others, $1-$9, refer to the arguments that are passed to the script. What happens if you have more than nine arguments? This is where the shift instructions come in. These move the arguments "down" in the positional parameters list.

For example, let's assume we changed the first part of the script like this:

```
DIR=$1
shift
FILENAME=$1
```

On the first line, the value of positional parameter 1 is /home/jimmo and we assign it to the variable DIR. In the next line, the shift moves every positional parameter down. Because $0 remains unchanged, what was in $1 (/home/jimmo) drops out of the bottom. Now, the value of positional parameter 1 is trip, which is assigned to the variable FILENAME, and positional parameter 2 (boat) is assigned to WORD.

If we had 10 arguments, the tenth would initially be unavailable to us. However, once we do the shift, what was the tenth argument is shifted down and becomes the ninth. It is now accessible through the positional parameter 9. If we had more than 10, there are a couple of ways to get access to them. First, we could issue enough shifts until the arguments all moved down far enough. Or, we could use the fact that shift can take as an argument the number of shifts it should do. Therefore, using

```
shift 9
```

makes the tenth argument positional parameter 1.

What about the other nine arguments? Are they gone? If you never assigned them to a variable, then yes, they are gone. However, if you assigned them to a variable *before* you made the shift, you still have access to their values.

Being able to shift positional parameters comes in handy in other instances, which brings up the issue of a new parameter: `$*`. This parameter refers to all the positional parameters (except `$0`). So, we had 10 positional parameters and did a `shift` 2 (ignoring whatever we did with the first two), the parameter `$*` would contain the value of the last eight arguments.

In our sample script above, if we wanted to search for a *phrase* and not just a single word, we could change the script to look like this:

```
DIR=$1
FILENAME=$2
shift 2
WORD=$*
ls -1 $DIR | grep $FILENAME | while read file
do
      grep "$WORD" ${DIR}/${file}
done
```

The first change was that after assigning positional parameters 1 and 2 to variables, we shifted twice, effectively removing the first two arguments. We then assigned the remaining argument to the variable `WORD` (`WORD=$*`). Because this could have been a phrase, we needed to enclose the variable in double-quotes ("`$WORD`"). Now we can search for phrases as well as single words. If we did not include the double quotes, the system would view our entry as individual arguments to `grep`.

Another useful parameter keeps track of the total number of parameters: $#. In the previous script, what would happen if we had only two arguments? The `grep` would fail because there would be nothing for it to search for. Therefore, it would be a good thing to keep track of the number of arguments.

We need to first introduce a new construct: `if-then-fi`. This is similar to the `while-do-done` construct, where the `if-fi` pairs marks the end of the block (`fi` is simply `if` reversed). The difference is that instead of repeating the commands within the block while the specific condition is true, we do it only once, *if* the condition is true. In general, it looks like this:

```
if [ condition ]
then
       do something
fi
```

The conditions are all defined in the `test` man-page. They can be string comparisons, arithmetic comparisons, and even conditions where we test specific files, such as whether the files have write permission. Check out the `test` man-page for more examples.

Because we want to check the number of arguments passed to our script, we will do an arithmetic comparison. We can check if the values are equal, the first is less than the second, the second is less than the first, the first is greater than or equal to the second, and so on. In our case, we want to ensure that there are at *least* three arguments, because having more is valid if we are going to be searching for a phrase. Therefore, we want to compare the number of arguments and check if it is greater than or equal to 3. So, we might have something like this:

```
if [ $# -ge 3 ]
then
      body_of_script
fi
```

If we have only two arguments, the test inside the brackets is false, the `if` fails, and we do not enter the loop. Instead, the program simply exits silently. However, to me, this is not enough. We want to know what's going on, therefore, we use another construct: `else`. When this construct is used with the `if-then-fi`, we are saying that if the test evaluates to true, do one thing; otherwise, do something else. In our example program, we might have something like this:

```
DIR=$1
FILENAME=$2
shift 2
WORD=$*
if [ $# -ge 3 ]
then
ls -1 $DIR | grep $FILENAME | while read file
do
      grep "$WORD" ${DIR}/${file}
done
fi
else
      echo "Insufficient number of arguments"
fi
```

If we only put in two arguments, the `if` fails and the commands between the `else` and the `fi` are executed. To make the script a little more friendly, we usually tell the user what the correct syntax is; therefore, we might change the end of the script to look like this:

```
else
     echo "Insufficient number of arguments"
     echo "Usage: $0 <directory> <file_name> <word>"
fi
```

The important part of this change is the use of the `$0`. As I mentioned a moment ago, this is used to refer to the program itself–not just its name, but rather the way it was called. Had we hard-coded the line to look like this

```
echo "Usage: myscript  <directory> <file_name> <word>"
```

then no matter how we started the script, the output would always be

```
Usage: myscript  <directory> <file_name> <word>
```

However, if we used `$0` instead, we could start the program like this

```
/home/jimmo/bin/myscript /home/jimmo file
```

and the output would be

```
Usage: /home/jimmo/bin/myscript  <directory> <file_name>
<word>
```

On the other hand, if we started it like this

```
./bin/myscript /home/jimmo file
```

the output would be

```
Usage: ./bin/myscript  <directory> <file_name> <word>
```

One thing to keep in mind is that the `else` needs to be within the matching `if-fi` pair. The key here is the word *matching*. We could nest the `if-then-else-fi` several layers if we wanted. We just need to keep track of things. The keys issues are that the ending `fi` matches the *last* `fi` and the else is enclosed within an `if-fi` pair. Here is how multiple sets might look:

```
if [ $condition1 = "TRUE" ]
then
       if [ $condition2 = "TRUE" ]
```

```
        then
                if [ $condition3 = "TRUE" ]
                     echo "Conditions 1, 2 and 3 are true"
                else
                   echo "Only Conditions 1 and 2 are true"
                fi
        else
        echo "Only Condition 1 is true"
        fi
echo "No conditions are true"
else
fi
```

This doesn't take into account the possibility that condition1 is false, but that either condition2 or condition3 is true. However, you should see how to construct nested conditional statements.

What if we had a single variable that could take on several values. Depending on the value that it acquired, the program would behave differently. This could be used as a menu, for example. Many system administrators build such a menu into their user's `.profile` (or `.login`) so that they never need to get to a shell. They simply input the number of the program that they want to run and away they go.

To do something like this, we need to introduce yet another construct: the `case-esac` pair. Like the `if-fi` pair, `esac` is the reverse of `case`. So to implement a menu, we might have something like this:

```
read choice
case $choice in
a) program1;;
b) program2;;
c) program3;;
*) echo "No such Option";;
esac
```

If the value of `choice` that we input is a, b, or c, the appropriate program is started. The things to note are the `in` on the first line, the expected value that is followed by a closing parenthesis, and that there are two semi-colons at the end of each block.

It is the closing parenthesis that indicates the end of the possibilities. If we wanted, we could have included other possibilities for the different options. In addition, because the double semi-colons mark the end of the block, we could have simply added another command before we got to the end of the block. For example, if we wanted our script to recognized either upper- or lowercase, we could change it to look like this:

```
read choice
case $choice in
     a|A) program1
          program2
          program3;;
     b|B) program2
          program3;;
     c|C) program3;;
     *) echo "No such Option";;
esac
```

If necessary, we could also include a range of characters, as in

```
case $choice in
      [a-z] ) echo "Lowercase";;
      [A-Z] ) echo "Uppercase";;
      [0-9] ) echo "Number";;
esac
```

Now, whatever is called as the result of one of these choices does not have to be a UNIX command. Because each line is interpreted as if it were executed from the command line, we could have included anything as though we had executed the command from the command line. Provided they are known to the shell script, this also includes aliases, variables, and even shell functions.

A shell function behaves similarly to functions in other programming languages. It is a portion of the script that is set off from the rest of the program and is accessed through its name. These are the same as the functions we talked about in our discussion of shells. The only apparent difference is that functions created inside of a shell-script will disappear when the shell exits. To prevent this, start the script with a . (dot).

For example, if we had a function inside a script called `myscript`, we would start it like this:

```
. myscript
```

The result is that although the script executes normally, a sub-shell is not started. Therefore, anything you set or define remains, including both functions and variables.

One thing for which I commonly use functions is to clean up for me when things go wrong. In fact, there are quite a few shell-scripts on a standard Linux system that contain "clean-up" functions. Such functions are necessary to return the system to the state it was in before the shell-script was started. What happens when the user presses the interrupt key (usually Delete or Ctrl-C) in the middle of a script? Unless it has been disabled or *trapped*, the script will terminate immediately. This can leave some unwanted things lying around the system. Instead, we can catch or trap the Delete key and run a special clean-up function before we exit.

This is done with the `trap` instruction. The syntax is

```
trap 'command' signals
```

where `command` is the command to run if any of the signals listed in `signals` are received. For example, if we wanted to trap the Delete key (signal 2) and run a clean-up function, the line might look like this:

```
trap 'cleanup' 2
```

After we start the script, any time we press the delete key it will first run the function `cleanup`. You can also set up different traps for different signals, like this:

```
trap 'cleanup1' 1
trap 'cleanup2' 2
```

Note that the KILL signal (signal 9) cannot be ignored and therefore cannot be trapped in this way.

Okay, now you know some of the basic commands and how to put them together into a script. The biggest problem up to this point is figuring out how to create that script. You could continue to use `cat`. However, that will get old fast, especially if you make a lot of typos as I do or want to make changes to your scripts. Therefore, you need a better tool. What you really need is a text editor, which is the subject of the next section.

In a shell-script (or from the command line for that matter), you can input multiple commands on the same line. For example:

```
date; ls | wc
```

would run the date command and then give the word count of the `ls` command. Note that this does not write the output of both commands on the same line; it just allows you to have multiple commands on the same line. First, the date command is executed and then the `ls | wc`. Each time, the system creates an extra process to run that program.

We can prevent the system from creating the extra process by enclosing the command inside of parentheses. For example:

```
(date; ls | wc )
```

This is run by the shell itself and not as subshells.

Up to this point, we have always run our scripts as "shell-scripts." That is, we get our current shell to run the scripts. In other words, our shell becomes the interpreter. Some programs, like sed, awk, and perl, allow us to specify the name of the script that the shell should interpret. However, when you write your script, you can tell the shell yourself what it should use. This is done by including the name of the interpreter as the first line in your script. For example, to use sed, the line would look like this:

```
#!/bin/sed
```

The pound sign and exclamation mark (#!) in front of the command tells the shell to use the following command. This is referred to as "hashpling," as the pound sign in "UNIX-ese" is the hash or hash mark and the exclamation mark is called the "pling" (sometimes "bang").

3.3.1 Odds and Ends

This section includes a few tidbits that I wasn't sure where to put.

You can get the shell to help you debug your script. If you place `set -x` in your script, each command with its corresponding arguments is printed as it is executed. If you want to just show a section of your script, include the `set -x` before that section, then another `set +x` at the end. The `set +x` turns off the output.

If you want, you can capture output into another file, without having it go to the screen. This is done using the fact that output generated as a result of the `set -x` is going to stderr and not stdout. If you redirect stdout somewhere, the output from `set -x` still goes to the screen. On the other hand, if you redirect stderr, stdout still goes to your screen. To redirect sterr to a file start, the script like this:

```
mscript 2>/tmp/output
```

This says to send file descriptor 2 (stderr) to the file /tmp/output.

To create a directory that is several levels deep, you do not have to change directories to the parent and then run mkdir from there. The mkdir command takes as an argument the path name of the directory you want to create. It doesn't matter if it is a subdirectory, relative path, or absolute path. The system will do that for you. Also, if you want to create several levels of directories, you don't have to make each parent directory before you make the subdirectories. Instead, you can use the -p option to mkdir, which will automatically create all the necessary directories.

For example, imagine that we want to create the subdirectory ./letters/personal/john, but the subdirectory letters does not exist yet.

This also means that the subdirectory `personal` doesn't exist, either. If we run `mkdir` like this

```
mkdir -p ./letters/personal/john
```

then the system will create `./letters`, then `./letters/personal`, and then `./letters/personal/john`.

Assume that you want to remove a file that has multiple links; for example, assume that `ls`, `lc`, `lx`, `lf`, etc., are links to the same file. The system keeps track of how many names reference the file through the *link count* (more on this concept later). Such links are called hard links. If you remove one of them, the file still exists as there are other names that reference it. Only when we remove the last link (and with that, the link count goes to zero) will the file be removed.

There is also the issue of symbolic links. A symbolic link (also called a soft link) is nothing more than a path name that points to some other file, or even to some directory. It is not until the link is accessed that the path is translated into the "real" file. This has some interesting effects. For example, if we create a link like this

```
ln -s /home/jimmo/letter.john /home/jimmo/text/letter.john
```

you would see the symbolic link as something like this:

```
drw-r--r--  1 jimmo  support 29  Sep 15 10:06 letter.
john-> /home/jimmo/letter.john
```

Then, the file `/home/jimmo/text/letter.john` is a symbolic link to `/home/jimmo/letter.john`. Note that the link count on `/home/jimmo/letter.john` doesn't change, because the system sees these as two separate files. It is easier to think of the file `/home/jimmo/text/letter.john` as a text file that contains the path to `/home/jimmo/letter.john`. If we remove `/home/jimmo/letter.john`, `/home/jimmo/text/letter.john` will still exist. However, it will point to something that doesn't exist. Even if there are other hard links that point to the same file like `/home/jimmo/letter.john`, that doesn't matter. The symbolic link, `/home/jimmo/text/letter.john`, points to the path `/home/jimmo/letter.john`. Because the path no longer exists, the file can no longer be accessed via the symbolic link. It is also possible for you to create a symbolic link to a file that does exist, as the system does not check until you access the file.

If we were to set the permissions for all users so that they could read, write, and execute a file, the command would look this:

```
chmod 777 filename
```

You can also use symbolic permissions to accomplish the same thing. We use the letters u, g, and o to specify the user(owner), group, and others for this file, respectively. The permissions are then r for read, w for write, and x for execute. So to set the permissions so that the owner can read and write a file, the command would look like this:

```
chmod u=rw filename
```

Note that in contrast to the absolute numbers, setting the permissions symbolically is additive. So, in this case, we would just change the user's permissions to read and write, but the others would remain unchanged. If we changed the command to this

```
chmod u+w filename
```

we would be *adding* write permission for the user of that file. Again, the permissions for the others would be unchanged.

To make the permissions for the group and others to be the same as for the user, we could set it like this

```
chmod go=u filename
```

which simply means "change the mode so that the permissions for the group and others equals the user." We could also have set them all explicitly in one command, like this

```
chmod u=rw,g=rw,o=rw filename
```

which has the effect of setting the permissions for everyone to read and write. However, we don't need to write that much.

Combining the commands, we could have something that looks like this:

```
chmod u=rw, go=u filename
```

This means "set the permissions for the user to read and write, then set the permissions for group and others to be equal to the user."

Note that each of these changes is done in sequence. So be careful what changes are made. For example, let's assume we have a file that is read-only for everyone. We want to give everyone write permission for it, so we try

```
chmod u+w,gu=o filename
```

This is a typo because we meant to say "go=u". The effect is that we added read permissions for the user, but then set the permissions on the group and user to the same as others.

We might want to try adding the write permissions like this:

```
chmod +w filename
```

This works on some systems, but not on the Linux distributions that I have seen. According to the man-page, this will not change those permissions where the bits in the UMASK are set. (More on this later. See the chmod man-page for details.)

To get around this, we use a to specify all users. Therefore, the command would be

```
chmod a+w filename
```

There are a few other things that you can do with permissions. For example, you can set a program to change the UID of the process when the program is executed. For example, some programs need to run as root to access other files. Rather than giving the user the root password, you can set the program so that when it is executed, the process is run as root. This is a Set-UID, or SUID program. If you want to run a program with a particular group ID, you would use the SGID program with the s option to chmod, like this

```
chmod u+s program
```

or

```
chmod g+s program
```

There are a few other special cases, but I will leave it up to you to check out the chmod man-page if you are interested.

When you create a file, the access permissions are determined by their *file creation mask*. This is defined by the UMASK variable and can be set using the umask command. One thing to keep in mind that this is a mask. That is, it masks out permissions rather than assigning them. If you remember, permissions on a file can be set using the `chmod` command and a three-digit value. For example

```
chmod 600 letter.john
```

explicitly sets the permissions on the file `letter.john` to 600 (read and write permission for the user and nothing for everyone else). If we create a new file, the permissions might be 660 (read/write for user and group). This is determined by the `UMASK`. To understand how the `UMASK` works, you need to remember that the permissions are octal values, which are determined by the permissions *bits*. Looking at one set of permissions we have

```
bit:     2   1   0
value:   4   2   1
symbol:  r   w   x
```

which means that if the bit with value 4 is set (bit 2), the file can be read; if the bit with value 2 is set (bit 1), the file can be written to; and if the bit with value 1 is set (bit 0), the file can be executed. If multiple bits are set, their values are added together. For example, if bits 2 and 1 are set (read/write), the value is 4+2=6. Just as in the example above, if all three are set, we have 4+2+1=7. Because there are three sets of permissions (owner, group, others), the permissions are usually used in triplets, just as in the `chmod` example above.

The `UMASK` value *masks* out the bits. The permissions that each position in the `UMASK` masks out are the same as the file permissions themselves. So, the left-most position masks out the owner permission, the middle position the group, and the right most masks out all others. If we have `UMASK=007`, the permissions for owner and group are not touched. However, for others, we have the value 7, which is obtained by setting all bits. Because this is a mask, all bits are unset. (The way I remember this is that the bits are *inverted*. Where it is set in the `UMASK`, it will be unset in the permissions, and vice versa.)

The problem many people have is that the `umask` command does not force permissions, but rather limits them. For example, if we had `UMASK=007`, we could assume that any file created has permissions of 770. However, this depends on the program that is creating the file. If the program is creating a file with permissions 777, the `UMASK` will mask out the last bits and the permissions will, in fact, be 770. However, if the program creates permissions of 666, the last bits are still masked out. However, the new file will have permissions of 660, *not* 770. Some programs, like the C compiler, do generate files with the execution bit (bit 0) set. However, most do not. Therefore, setting the `UMASK=007` does not force creation of executable programs, unless the program creating the file does itself).

Let's look at a more complicated example. Assume we have UMASK=047. If our program creates a file with permissions 777, then our UMASK does nothing to the first digit, but masks out the 4 from the second digit, giving us 3. Then, because the last digit of the UMASK is 7, this masks out everything, so the permissions here are 0. As a result, the permissions for the file are 730. However, if the program creates the file with permissions 666, the resulting permissions are 620. The easy way to figure out the effects of the UMASK are to subtract the UMASK from the default permissions that the program sets. (Note that all negative values become 0.)

As I mentioned, one way the UMASK is set is through the environment variable UMASK. You can change it anytime using the UMASK command. The syntax is simply

```
umask <new_umask>
```

Here the <new_umask> can either be the numeric value (e.g., 007) or symbolic. For example, to set the umask to 047 using the symbolic notation, we have

```
umask u=,g=r,o=rwx
```

This has the effect of removing no permissions from the user, removing read permission from the group, and removing all permissions from others.

The file command can be used to tell you the type of file. With DOS and Windows, it's fairly obvious by looking at the file's extension to determine the file's type. For example, files ending in .exe are executables (programs), files ending in .txt are text files, and files ending in .doc are documents (usually from some word processor). However, a program in UNIX can just as easily have the ending .doc or .exe, or no ending at all.

The file command uses the file /etc/magic to make an assumption about the contents of a file. The file command reads the header (first part of the file) and uses the information in /etc/magic to make its guess. Executables of a specific type (a.out, ELF) all have the same basic format, so file can easily recognize them. However, there are certain similarities between C source code, shell-scripts, and even text files that could confuse file.

For a list of some of the more commonly used commands, take a look at Table 3.1.

FILE MANAGEMENT

Command	Function
`cd`	change directory
`chgrp`	change the group of a file
`chmod`	change the permissions (mode) of a file
`chown`	change the owner of a file
`cp`	copy files
`file`	determine a file's contents
`ls`	list files or directories
`ln`	make a link to a file
`mkdir`	make a directory
`mv`	move (rename) a file
`rm`	remove a file
`rmdir`	remove a directory

FILE MANIPULATION

Command	Function
`awk`	pattern-matching language
`cat`	display a file
`cmp`	compare two files
`csplit`	split a file
`cut`	display columns of a file
`diff`	find differences in two files
`dircmp`	compare two directories
`find`	find files
`head`	show the top portion of a file
`more`	display screenfuls of a file
`perl`	scripting language
`sed`	non-interactive texte editor
`sort`	sort a file
`tail`	display bottom portion of a file
`tr`	translate characters in a file
`uniq`	find unique or repeated lines in a file
`xargs`	process multiple arguments

Even if you're using the X-Windows graphical interface, there are a number of things that you will want to change on your system when you must edit the files directly. One thing you *could* do is use `cat` and redirect it to a file, like this:

```
cat > filename.txt
```

Since there is no argument to cat, it will accept input from stdin. Everything you input up to the end-of-file character (usually CTRL-D) is written to `filename.txt`. This is a quick and simple way of "editing" a file. The downside is that every file has to be created new. Fortunately, the tools that Linux provides makes life much easier.

In this chapter, we're going to cover the basics of the primary tools for manipulating the *contents* of files. Linux provides a handful of programs used to edit files. Depending on the circumstances, each one could be useful.

First are the two text editors: `vi` and `emacs`. Both have their own advantages and disadvantages, which we will cover as we move along.

Next, we'll talk about the stream editor: `sed`. If you have a large amount of text that you need to change, or what you are editing is the output of another program (i.e., a stream), `sed` comes in handy. There are many examples on your system where `sed` is used in system shell-scripts.

Last are two programs that are really programming languages and can do much more than just edit files: `awk` and `perl`. You will find that several scripts on your system use `awk`, but it is rare to find one that has `perl`. The reason I am including `perl` here is that it fits well into the family of text manipulation programs. Although `perl` is a lot more powerful than `awk`, `awk` has been around at least ten years longer than `perl`, and it is available on every UNIX system I am aware of.

4.1 Interactively Editing Files with `vi`

The uses and benefits of any editor like `vi` are almost religious. Often, the reasons people choose one editor over another is purely a matter of personal taste. Each offers its own advantages and functionality. Some versions of UNIX provide other editors, such as `emacs`. However, the nice thing about `vi` is that every dialect of UNIX has it. (Okay, I can think of *one* UNIX dialect that has `emacs` and not `vi`.) You can sit down at any UNIX system and edit a file. For this reason more than any other, I think it is worth learning.

One problem `vi` has is that can be very intimidating. I know I didn't like it at first. I frequently get into discussions with people who have spent less than 10 minutes using it and then have ranted about how terrible it was. Often, I then saw them spending hours trying to find a free or relatively cheap add-on so they didn't have to learn `vi`. The problem with that approach is that if they would have spent as much time learning `vi` as they did trying to find an alternative, they actually could have become quite proficient with `vi`.

4.1.1 Basics

There is more to `vi` than just its availability on different UNIX systems. To me, `vi` is magic. Once you get over the initial intimidation, you will see that there is a logical order to the way the commands are laid out and fit together. Things fit together in a pattern that is easy to remember. So, as we get into it, let me tempt you a little.

Among the "magical" things `vi` can do:

- Automatically correct words that you misspell often
- Accept user-created `vi` commands
- Insert the output of UNIX commands into the file you are editing
- Automatically indent each line
- Shift sets of lines left or right
- Check for pairs of {}, () and [] (great for programmers)
- Automatically wrap around at the end of a line
- Cut and paste between documents

I'm not going to mention every single `vi` command. Instead, I am going to show you a few and how they fit together. At the end of this section, there is a table containing the various commands you can use inside `vi`. You can then apply the relationships to the commands I don't mention.

To see what is happening when you enter commands, first find a file that you can poke around in. Make a copy of the `termcap` file (`/etc/termcap`) in a temporary directory and then edit it (`cd /tmp; cp /etc/termcap . ; vi termcap`). The `termcap` file contains a list of the capabilities of various terminals. It is usually quite large and gives you a lot of things to play with in `vi`.

Before we can jump into the more advanced features of `vi`, I need to cover some of the basics. Not command basics, but rather some behavioral basics. In `vi`, there are two modes: command mode and input mode. While you are in command mode, every keystroke is considered part of a command. This is where you normally start when you first invoke `vi`. The reverse is also true. While in input mode, everything is considered input.

Well, that isn't entirely true and we'll talk about that in a minute. However, just remember that there are these two modes. If you are in command mode, you go into input mode using a command to get you there, such as append or insert (I'll talk about these in a moment). If you want to go from input mode to command mode, press Esc.

When `vi` starts, it goes into full-screen mode (assuming your terminal is set up correctly) and it essentially clears the screen. If we start the command as `vi search`, at the bottom of the screen, you see `"search" [New file]`. Your cursor is at the top left-hand corner of the screen, and there is a column of tildes (~) down the left side to indicate that these lines are nonexistent.

4.1.2 Basic Editing and Movement Commands

Most editing and movement commands are single letters and are almost always the first letter of what they do. For example, to insert text at your current cursor position, press `i`. To append text, press `a`. To move forward to the beginning of the next word, press `w`. To move back to the beginning of the previous word, press `b`.

The capital letter of each command has a similar behavior. Use `I` to insert at the beginning of a line. Use `A` to start the append from the end of the line. To move "real" words, use `W` to move forward and `B` to move back.

Real words are those terminated by whitespaces (space, tab, newline). Assume we wanted to move across the phrase 'static-free bag'. If we start on the 's', pressing 'w', will move me to the '-'. Pressing 'w' again, we move to the 'f and then to the 'b'. If we are on the 's' and press 'W', we jump immediately to the 'b'. That is, to the next "real"weweuswewewe word.

Moving in `vi` is also accomplished in other ways. Depending on your terminal type, you can use the traditional method of arrows keys. If `vi` doesn't like your terminal type, you can use the keys `h-j-k-l`. If we want to move to the left we press 'h'. Makes sense since this in on the left end. This makes sense because `h` is on the left of these four characters. To move right, press `l`. Again, this makes sense as the `l` is on the right end of the row.

Movement up and down is not as intuitive. One of the two remaining characters (`j` and `k`) will move us up and the other will move us down. But which one moves in which direction? Unfortunately, I don't have a very sophisticated way of remembering. If you look at the two letters physically, maybe it helps. If you imagine a line running through the middle of these characters, then you see that `j` hangs down below that line. Therefore, use `j` to move down. On the other hand, `k` sticks up above the middle, so we use `k` to move up. However, in most cases, the arrow keys will work, so you won't need to remember. But it is nice to know them, as you can then leave your fingers on the keyboard.

As I mentioned, some keyboard types will allow you to use the arrow keys. However, you might be surprised by their behavior in input mode. This is especially true if you are used to a word processor where the arrow and other movement keys are the same all the time. The problem lies in the fact that most keyboards actually send more than one character to indicate something like a left-arrow or page-up key. The first of these is normally an escape (`Esc`). When you press one of these characters in input mode, the `Esc` is interpreted as your wish to leave input mode.

If we want to move to the first character on a line, we press '`0`' (zero) or '`^`'. To move to the last character, press `$`. Now, these are not intuitive. However, if you think back to our discussion on regular expressions, you'll remember that ^ (caret) represents the beginning of a line and $ (dollar sign) represents the end of a line. Although, these two characters do not necessarily have an intuitive logic, they do fit in with other commands and programs that you find on a Linux system.

We can also take advantage of the fact that `vi` can count as well as combine movement with this ability to count. By pressing a number before the movement command, `vi` will behave as if we had pressed the movement key that many times. For example, `4w` will move us forward four words or `6j` will move us six lines down.

If we want to move to a particular line we input the number and `G`. So, to move to line 43, we would press `42G`, kind of like 42-Go! If instead of `G` we press `Enter`, we would move ahead that many lines. For example, if we were on line 85, pressing `42` and `Enter` would put us on line 127. (No, you don't have to count lines; `vi` can display them for you, as we'll see in a minute.)

As you might have guessed, we can also use these commands in conjunction with the movement keys (all except `Ctrl-u` and `Ctrl-d`). So, to delete everything from your current location to line 83, we would input `d83G`. (Note that delete begins with `d`.) Or, to change everything from the current cursor position down 12 lines, we would input `c12+` or press `c12 Enter`.

There are a couple other special editing commands. Pressing `dd` will delete the entire line you are on; `5dd` would then delete five complete lines. To open up a line for editing, we press `o` to open the line after the line you are currently on and `O` for the line before. Use `x` to delete the character (including numbers) that the cursor is on.

When we want to move something we just deleted, we put the cursor on the spot where we want it. Then press either `p` to put that text after the current cursor position or `P` to put it before the current position. A nice trick that I always use to swap characters is `xp`. The `x` deletes the character you are on and the `p` immediately inserts it. The result is that you swap characters. So if I had typed the word "into" as "inot," I would place the cursor on the "o" and type `xp`, which would swap the "o" and the "t."

To repeat the edit we just did, be it deleting 18 lines or inputting "I love you," we could do so by pressing "." (dot) from command mode. In fact, any edit command can be repeated with the dot.

CHANGING TEXT

To make a change, press `c` followed by a movement command or number and movement command. For example, to change everything from where you are to the next word, press `cw`. To change everything from where you are to the end of the line, press `C` or `c$`. If you do that, then a dollar sign will appear, indicating how much you intend to change.

If we go back into command mode (press Esc) before we reach the dollar sign, then everything from the current position to the dollar sign is removed. When you think about this, it is actually logical. By pressing C, you tell vi that you want to change everything to the end of the line. When you press Enter, you are basically saying that you are done inputting text; however, the changes should continue to the end of the line, thereby deleting the rest of the line.

To undo the last edit, what would we press? Well, what's the first letter of the word "undo"? Keep in mind that pressing u will only undo the last change. For example, let's assume we enter the following:

```
o        to open a new line and go into input mode
I love
Esc      to go back to command mode
a        to append from current location
you
Esc      to return to command mode
```

The result of what we typed was to open a new line with the text "I love you." We see it as one change, but from the perspective of vi, two changes were made. First we entered "I love," then we entered "you." If we were to press u, only "you" would be removed. However, if u undoes that last change, what command do you think returns the line to its original state? What else: U. As you are making changes, vi keeps track of the original state of a line. When you press U, the line is returned to that original state.

Searching and Replacing

If you are trying to find a particular text, you can get vi to do it for you. You tell vi that you want to enter a search pattern by pressing / (slash). This will bring you down to the bottom line of the screen where you will see your slash. You then can type in what you want to look for. When you press Enter, vi will start searching from your current location down toward the bottom of the file. If you use press ? instead of /, then vi will search from your string toward the top of the file.

If the search is successful, that is, the string is found, you are brought to that point in the text. If you decide that you want to search again, you have three choices. You can press ? or / and input the search string again; press n, which is the first letter of the word "next"; or simply press ? or / with no text following it and vi would continue the search in the applicable direction. If you wanted to find the next string that matches but in the opposite direction, what do you think the command would be? (Hint: the capital form of the "next" command.)

Once you have found what you are looking for, you can edit the text all you want and then continue searching. This is because the search string you entered is kept in a buffer. So, when you press /, ?, n, or N, the system remembers what you were looking for.

You can also include movement commands in these searches. First, you enclose the search pattern with the character used to search (/ or ?), then add the movement command. For example, if you wanted to search forward for the phrase "hard disk" and then move up a line, you would enter `?hard disk?-`. If you wanted to search backward for the phrase "operating system" and then move down three lines, you would enter `/operating system/+3`.

All this time, we have been referring to the text patterns as search strings. As you just saw, you can actually enter phrases. In fact, you can use any regular expression you want when searching for patterns. For example, if you wanted to search for the pattern "Linux," but only when it appears at the beginning of a line, you would enter `/^Linux`. If you wanted to search for it at the end of the line, you would enter `/Linux$`.

You can also do more complicated searches such as `/^new [Bb][Oo][Aa][Tt]`, which will search for the word "new" at the beginning of a line, followed by the word "boat" with each letter in either case.

No good text editor would be complete without the ability to not only search for text but to replace it as well. One way of doing this is to search for a pattern and then edit the text. Obviously, this starts to get annoying after the second or third instance of the pattern you want to replace. Instead, you could combine several of the tools you have learned so far.

For example, let's say that everywhere in the next section you wanted to replace "Unix" with "UNIX." First, do a search on Unix with `/Unix`, tell `vi` that you want to change that word with `cw`, then input `UNIX`. Now, search for the pattern again with /, and simply press **.** (dot). Remember that the dot command repeats your last command. Now do the search and press the dot command again.

Actually, this technique is good if you have a pattern that you want to replace, but not every time it appears. Instead, you want to replace the pattern selectively. You can just press `n` (or whatever) to continue the search without carrying out the replacement.

What if you know that you want to replace every instance of a pattern with something else? Are you destined to search and replace all 50 occurrences? Of course not. Silly you. There is another way.

Here I introduce what is referred to as escape or ex-mode, because the commands you enter are the same as in the `ex` editor. To get to ex-mode, press **:** (colon). As with searches, you are brought down to the bottom of the screen. This time you see the **:** (colon). The syntax is

```
: <scope> <command>
```

An example of this would be:

```
:45,100s/Unix/UNIX/
```

This tells `vi` the scope is lines 45 *through* 100. The command is `s/Unix/UNIX/`, which says you want to substitute (`s`) the first pattern (`Unix`) with the second pattern (`UNIX`). Normally in English, we would say "substitute UNIX for Unix." However, the order here is in keeping with the UNIX pattern of source first, then destination (or, what it was is first, and what it will become is second, like `mv source destination`).

Note that this only replaces the first occurrence on each line. To get all occurrences, we must include `g` for global at the end of each line, like this:

```
:45,100s/Unix/UNIX/g
```

A problem arises if you want to modify only some of the occurrences. In this instance, you could add the modifier `c` for confirm. The command would then look like this:

```
:45,100s/Unix/UNIX/gc
```

This causes `vi` to ask for confirmation before it makes the change.

If you wanted to search and replace on every line in the file, you could specify every line, such as `:1,48.`, assuming there were 48 lines in the file. (By the way, use `Ctrl-g` to find out what line you are on and how many lines there are in the file.) Instead of checking how many lines there are each time, you can simply use the special character `$` to indicate the end of the file. (Yes, `$` also means the end of the line, but in this context, it means the end of the file.) So, the scope of the command would look like `:1,$`.

Once again, the developers of `vi` made life easy for you. They realized that making changes throughout a file is something that is probably done a lot. They included a special character to mean the entire file: `%`. Therefore, the command is written as `% = 1,$`.

Here again, the search patterns can be regular expressions. For example, if we wanted to replace every occurrence of "boat" (in either case) with the word "ship," the command would look like this:

```
%s:/[Bb][Oo][Aa][Tt]/ship/g
```

As with regular expressions in other cases, you can use the asterisk (`*`) to mean any number of the preceding characters or a period (`.`) to mean any single character. So, if you wanted to look for the word "boat" (again, in either case), but only when it was at the beginning of a line and only if it were preceded by at least one dash, the command would look like this:

```
%s:/^--*[Bb][Oo][Aa][Tt]/ship/g
```

The reason you have two dashes is that the search criteria specified at *least* one dash. Because the asterisk can be *any* number, including zero, you must consider the case where it would mean zero. That is, where the word "boat" was at the beginning of a line and there were no spaces. If you didn't care what the character was as long as there was at least one, you could use the fact that in a search context, a dot means any single character. The command would look like this:

```
%s:/^..*[Bb][Oo][Aa][Tt]/ship/g
```

The ex-mode also allows you to do many things with the file itself. Among them are

- `:w` to write the file to disk
- `:q` to quit the file (`:q!` if the file has been changed and you don't want to save the changes)
- `:wq` to write the file and quit
- `:e` to edit a new file (or even the same file)
- `:r` to read in a new file starting at the current location

BUFFERS

Remember when we first starting talking about searching, I mentioned that the expression you were looking for was held in a buffer. Also, whatever was matched by `/[Bb][Oo][Aa][Tt]` can be held in a buffer. We can then use that buffer as part of the replacement expression. For example, if we wanted to replace every occurrence of "UNIX" with "Linux," we could do it like this:

```
:%s/UNIX/Linux/g
```

The scope of this command is defined by the `%`, the shortcut way of referring to the entire text. Or, you could first save "UNIX" into a buffer, then use it in the replacement expression. To enclose something in a buffer, we enclose it within matching pairs of back slashes (\ and \) to define the extent of a buffer. You can even have multiple pairs that define the extent of multiple buffers. These are reference by \#, where # is the number of the buffer.

In this example

```
:%s/\(UNIX\)/Linux \1/g
```

the text, "UNIX," is placed into the first buffer. You then reference this buffer with `\1` to say to `vi` to plug in the contents of the first buffer.

Because the entire search pattern is the same as the pattern buffer, you could also have written it like this

```
:%s/\(UNIX\)/Linux &/g
```

in which the ampersand represents the entire search pattern.

This obviously doesn't save much typing. In fact, in this example, it requires more typing to save "UNIX" into the buffer and then use it. However, if what you wanted to save was longer, you would save time. You also save time if you want to use the buffer twice. For example, assume you have a file with a list of other files, some of them C language source files. All of them end in `.c`. You now want to change just the names of the C files so that the ending is "old" instead of `.c`. To do this, insert `mv` at the beginning of each line as well as produce two copies of the file name: one with `.c` and one with `.old`. You could do it like this:

```
:%s/^\(.*\).c/mv \1.c \1.old\g
```

In English, this line says:

- For every line (`%`).
- substitute (`s`).
- for the pattern starting at the beginning of the line (`^`), consisting of any number of characters (`\(.*\)`) (placing this pattern into buffer #1) followed by `.c`.
- and use the pattern `mv`, followed by the contents of buffer #1 (`\1`), followed by a `.c`, which is again followed by the contents of buffer #1, (`\1`) followed by `.old`.
- and do this for every line (`g`), (i.e., globally)

Now each line is of the form

```
mv file.c file.old
```

We can now change the permissions to make this a shell-script and execute it. We would then move all the files as described above.

Using numbers like this is useful if there is more that one search pattern that you want to process. For example, assume that we have a three-column table for which we want to change the order of the columns. For simplicity's sake, let's also assume that each column is separated by a space so as not to make the search pattern too complicated.

Before we start, we need to introduce a new concept to `vi`, but one that you have seen before: `[ ]`. Like the shell, the square bracket pair (`[ ]`) of `vi` is used to limit sets of characters. Inside of the brackets, the caret (`^`)

takes on a new meaning. Rather than indicating the beginning of a line, here it negates the character we are searching for. So we could type

```
%s/\([^  ]*\)  \([^  ]*\)  \([^  ]*\)/\3 \1 \2/g
  |_____________________________________||_______|
```

Here we have three regular expressions, all referring to the same thing: `\([^ ]*\)`. As we discussed above, the slash pairs(/ and /) delimits each of the buffers, so everything inside is the search pattern. Here, we are searching for `[^ ]*`, which is any number of matches to the set enclosed within the brackets. Because the brackets limit a set, the set is ^, followed by a space. Because the ^ indicates negation, we are placing any number of characters that is not a space into the buffer. In the replacement pattern, we are telling `vi` to print pattern3, a space, pattern1, another space, then pattern2.

In the first two instances, we followed the pattern with a space. As a result, those spaces were not saved into any of the buffers. We did this because we may have wanted to define our column separator differently. Here we just used another space.

I have often had occasion to want to use the pattern buffers more than once. Because they are cleared after each use, you can use them as many times as you want. Using the example above, if we change it to

```
%s/\([^  ]*\)  \([^  ]*\)  \([^  ]*\)/\3  \1  \2  \1/g
  |_____________________________________||______________|
```

we would get pattern3, then pattern2, then pattern2, and at the end, pattern1 again.

Believe it or not, there are still more buffers. In fact, there are dozens that we haven't touched on. The first set is the numbered buffers, which are numbered 1-9. These are used when we delete text and they behave like a stack. That is, the first time we delete something, say a word, it is placed in buffer number 1. We next delete a line that is placed in buffer 1 and the word that was in buffer 1 is placed in buffer 2. Once all the numbered buffers all full, any new deletions push the oldest ones out the bottom of the stack and are no longer available.

To access these buffers, we first tell `vi` that we want to use one of the buffers by pressing the double-quote ("). Next, we specify then the number of the buffer, say 6, then we type either `p` or `P` to put it, as in `"6p`. When you delete text and then do a put without specifying any buffer, it automatically comes from buffer 1.

There are some other buffers, in fact, 26 of them, that you can use by name. These are the named buffers. If you can't figure out what their names are, think about how many of them there are (26). With these buffers, we can intentionally and specifically place something into a particular buffers. First, we say which buffer we want by preceding its name with a double-quote ("); for example, "f. This says that we want to place some text in the named buffer f. Then, we place the data in the buffer, for example, by deleting an entire line with dd or by deleting two words with d2w. We can later put the contents of that buffer with "fp. Until we place something new in that buffer, it will contain what we originally deleted.

If you want to put something into a buffer without having to delete it, you can. You do this by "yanking it." To yank an entire line, you could do one of several things. First, there is yy. Next, Y. Then, you could use y, followed by a movement commands, as in y-4, which would yank the next four lines (including the current one), or y/expression, which would yank everything from your current position up to and including expression.

To place yanked data into a named buffer (rather than the default buffer, buffer number 1), it is the same procedure as when you delete. For example, to yank the next 12 lines into named buffer h, we would do "h12yy. Now those 12 lines are available to us. Keep in mind that we do not have to store full lines. Inputting "x12yw will put the next 12 words into buffer h.

Some of the more observant readers might have noticed that because there are 26 letters and each has both an upper- and lowercase, we could have 52 named buffers. Well, up to now, the uppercase letters did something different. If uppercase letters were used to designate different buffers, then the pattern would be compromised. Have no fear, it is.

Instead of being different buffers than their lowercase brethren, the uppercase letters are the *same* buffer. The difference is that yanking or deleting something into an uppercase buffer appends the contents rather that overwriting them.

You can also have vi keep track of up to 26 different places with the file you are editing. These functions are just like bookmarks in word processors. (Pop quiz: If there 26 of them, what are their names?)

To mark a spot, move to that place in the file, type m for mark (what else?), then a single back quote (`), followed by the letter you want to use for this bookmark. To go back to that spot, press the back quote (`), followed by the appropriate letter. So, to assign a bookmark q to a particular spot, you would enter `q. Keep in mind that reloading the current file or editing a new one makes you lose the bookmarks.

vi MAGIC

I imagine that long before now, you have wondered how to turn on all that magic I said that vi could do. Okay, let's do it.

The first thing I want to talk about is abbreviations. You can tell vi that when you type in a specific set of characters it is supposed to automagically change it to something else. For example, we could have vi always change USA to United States of America. This is done with the abbr command.

To create a new abbreviation, you must get into ex-mode by pressing the colon (:) in command mode. Next, type in abbr, followed by what you want to type in, and what vi should change it to. For example:

```
:abbr USA United States of America.
```

Note that the abbreviation cannot contain any spaces because vi interprets everything after the second word as being part of the expansion.

If we later decide we don't want that abbreviation anymore, we enter

```
:unabbr USA
```

Because it is likely that we will want to use the abbreviation USA, it is not a good idea to use an abbreviation that would normally occur, such as USA. It would be better, instead, to use an abbreviation that doesn't occur normally, like Usa. Keep in mind, that abbreviations only apply to complete words. Therefore, something like the name "Sousa" won't be translated to "SoUSA." In addition, when your abbreviation is followed by a space, Tab, Enter, or Esc, the change is made.

Let's take this one step further. What if we were always spelling "the" as "teh." We could then create an abbreviation

```
:abbr teh the
```

Every time we misspell "the" as "teh," vi would automatically correct it. If we had a whole list of words that we regularly misspelled and created similar abbreviations, then every time we entered one of these misspelled words, it would be replaced with the correctly spelled word. Wouldn't that be automatic spell correction?

If we ever want to "force" the spelling to be a particular way (that is, turn off the abbreviation momentarily), we simply follow the abbreviation with a Ctrl-V. This tells vi to ignore the special meaning of the following character. Because the next character is a white space, which would force the expansion of the abbreviation (which makes the white space special in this case), "turning off" the white space keeps the abbreviation from being expanded.

We can also use vi to re-map certain sequences. For example, I have created a command so that all I need to do to save a file is Ctrl-W (for write). If I want to save the file and quit, I enter Ctrl-X with the "map" command.

The most common maps that I have seen have used control sequences, because most of the other characters are already taken up. Therefore, we need to side-step a moment. First, we need to know how to access control characters from within `vi`. This is done in either command mode or input mode by first pressing `Ctrl-V` and then pressing the control character we want. So to get `Ctrl-W`, I would type `Ctrl-V`, then `Ctrl-W`. This would appear on the screen as `^W`. This looks like two characters, but if you inserted it into a text and moved over it with the cursor, you would realize that `vi` sees it as only one character. Note that although I pressed the lowercase `w`, it will appear as uppercase on the screen.

So, to map Ctrl-W so that every time we press it, we write our current file to disk, the command would be

```
map ^W :w^M
```

This means that when we press `Ctrl-W`, `vi` interprets it as though we actually typed `:w` and pressed `Enter` (the `Ctrl-M`, `^M`). The `Enter` at the end of the command is a good idea because you usually want the command to be executed right away. Otherwise, you would have to press `Enter` yourself.

Also keep in mind that this can be used with the function keys. Because I am accustomed to many Windows and DOS applications in which the `F2` key means to save, I map `F2` to `Ctrl-V`, then `F2`. It looks like this:

```
map ^[[N :w^M     (The ^[[N is what the F2 key displays
on the screen)
```

If we want, we can also use shifted function characters. Therefore, we can map `Shift-F2` to something else. Or, for that matter, we can also use shifted and control function keys.

It has been my experience that, for the most part, if you use `Shift` and `Ctrl` with nonfunction keys, `vi` only sees `Ctrl` and not `Shift`. Also, `Alt` may not work because on the system console, `Alt` plus a function key tells the system to switch to multiscreens.

I try not to use the same key sequences that `vi` already does. First, it confuses me because I often forget that I remapped something. Second, the real `vi` commands are then inaccessible. However, if you are used to a different command set (that is, from a different editor), you can "program" `vi` to behave like that other editor.

Never define a mapping that contains its own name, as this ends up recurringly expanding the abbreviation. The classic example is `:map! n banana`. Every time you typed in the word “banana,” you'd get

```
babababababababababababababababa...
```

and depending on what version you were running, `vi` would catch the fact that this is an infinite translation and stop.

Inserting Command Output

It often happens that we want the output of UNIX commands in the file we are editing. The sledgehammer approach is to run the command and redirect it to a file, then edit that file. If that file containing the command's output already exists, we can use the `:r` from ex-mode to read it in. But, what if it doesn't yet exist. For example, I often want the date in text files as a log of when I input things. This is done with a combination of the `:r` (for read) from ex-mode and a *shell-escape*.

A shell-escape is when we start from one program and jump out of it (escape) to a shell. Our original program is still running, but we are now working in a shell that is a child process of that program.

To do a shell-escape, we need to be in ex-mode. Next, press the exclamation mark (`!`) followed by the command. For example, to see what time it is, type `:!date`. We then get the date at the bottom of the screen with the message to press any key to continue. Note that this didn't change our original text; it just showed us the output of the date command.

To read in a command's output, we need to include the `:r` command, as in `:r!date`. Now, the output of the date is read into the file (it is *inserted* into the file). We could also have the output replace the current line by pressing `!` twice, as in `!!date`. Note that we are brought down to the last line on the screen, where there is a single `!`.

If we want, we can also read in other commands. What is happening is that `vi` is seeing the output of the command as a file. Remember that `:r <file_name>` will read a file into the one we are editing. Why not read from the output of a file? With pipes and redirection, both `stdin` and `stdout` can be files.

We can also take this one step further. Imagine that we are editing a file containing a long list. We know that many lines are duplicated and we also want the list sorted. We could do `:%!sort`, which, if we remember from our earlier discussion, is a special symbol meaning all the lines in the file. These are then sent through the command on the other side of the `!`. Now we can type

```
:%!uniq
```

to remove all the duplicate lines.

Remember that this is a shell-escape. From the shell, we can combine multiple commands using pipes. We can do it here as well. So to save time, we could enter

```
:%!sort | uniq
```

which would sort all the lines and remove all duplicate lines. If we only wanted to sort a set of lines, we could do it like this

```
:45,112!sort
```

which would sort lines 45 through 112. We can take this one step further by either writing lines 45–112 to a new file with `:45,112w file_name` or reading in a whole file to replace lines 45–112 with `:45,112r file_name`.

4.1.3 More `vi` Magic

If we want, we can start editing a file at a point that is part of the way through it, rather than at the beginning. This is done from the command line as follows

```
vi +# filename
```

where # is the line number at which to start. If we omit the number, `vi` will start editing at the end of the file. This is great for hand-written logs and the like.

If we want `vi` to first find a particular phrase and jump there, this is just as easy (as in `vi +/expression`). If we need to, we can also edit multiple files. This is coded as

```
vi file1 file2 file3
```

Once we are editing, we can switch between files with `:n` for the next file and `:p` for the previous one. Keep in mind that the file names do not wrap around. In other words, if we keep pressing `:n` and get to file3, doing it again does not wrap around and bring me to file1. If we know the name of the file, we can jump directly there, with the ex-mode edit command, as in

```
:e file3
```

The ability to edit multiple files has another advantage. Do you remember those numbered and named buffers? They are assigned for a single instance of `vi`, not on a per-file basis. Therefore, you can delete or yank text from one file, switch to the next and then insert it. This is a crude but effective cut and paste mechanism between files.

You can specify line numbers to set your position within a file. If you switch to editing another file (using `:n` or `:r`), or reload an original file (using `:rew!`), the contents of the deletion buffers are preserved so that you can cut and paste between files. The contents of all buffers are lost, however, when you quit `vi`.

ODDS AND ENDS

You will find as you use `vi` that you will often re-use the same `vi` commands over and over again. Here too, `vi` can help. Because the named buffers are simply sequences of characters, you can store commands in them for later use. For example, when editing a file in `vi`, I needed to mark new paragraphs in some way as my word processor normally sees all end-of-line characters as new paragraphs. Therefore, I created a command that entered a "para-marker" for me.

First, I created the command. To do this, I opened up a new line in my current document and typed in the following text:

```
Para
```

Had I typed this from command mode, it would have inserted the text "Para" at the beginning of the line. I next loaded it into a named buffer with "pdd", which deletes the line and loads it into buffer p. To execute it, I entered `@p`. The `@` is what tells `vi` to execute the contents of the buffer.

Keep in mind that many commands, abbreviations, etc., are transitive. For example, when I want to add a new paragraph, I don't write `Para` as the only characters on a line. Instead, I use something less common: `{P}`. I am certain that I will never have `{P}` at the beginning of a line; however, there are contexts where I might have `Para` at the beginning of a line. Instead, I have an abbreviation, `Para`, that I translated to `{P}`.

Now, I can type in `Para` at the beginning of a line in input mode and it will be translated to `{P}`. When I execute the command I have in buffer `p`, it inserts `Para`, which is then translated to `{P}`.

So why don't I just have `{P}` in buffer `p`? Because the curly braces are one set of movement keys that I did not mention yet. The `{` moves you back to the beginning of the paragraph and `}` moves you forward. Because paragraphs are defined by `vi` as being separated by a blank line or delimited by `nroff` macros, I never use them (`nroff` is an old UNIX text processing language). Because `vi` sees the brackets as something special in command mode, I need to use this transitivity.

If you are a C programmer, you can take advantage of a couple of nifty tricks of `vi`. The first is the ability to show you matching pairs of parentheses (`()`), square brackets (`[ ]`), and curly braces (`{}`). In ex-mode (`:`), type set `showmatch`. Afterward, every time you enter the closing parenthesis, bracket, or brace, you are bounced back to its match. This is useful in checking whether or not you have the right number of each.

We can also jump back and forth between these pairs by using `%`. No matter where we are within a curly braces pair (`{}`), pressing `%` once moves us to the first (opening) brace. Press `%` again and we are moved to its match (the closing brace). We can also place the cursor on the closing brace and press `%` to move us to the opening brace.

If you are a programmer, you may like to indent blocks of code to make things more readable. Sometimes, changes within the code may make you want to shift blocks to the left or right to keep the spacing the same. To do this, use << (two less-than signs) to move the text one "shift-width" to the left, and >> (two greater-than signs) to move the text one "shift-width" to the right. A "shift-width" is defined in ex-mode with `set shiftwidth=n`, where `n` is some number. When you shift a line, it moves left or right `n` characters.

To shift multiple lines, input a number before you shift. For example, if you input `23>>`, you shift the next 23 lines one shiftwidth to the right.

There are a lot of settings that can be used with `vi` to make life easier. These are done in ex-mode, using the `set` command. For example, use `:set autoindent` to have `vi` automatically indent. This, along with other `set` commands, can be abbreviated. See the `vi`(C) man-page for more details.

Other useful set commands include

- `wrapmargin=n` automatically "word wraps" when you get to within `n` spaces of the end of the line
- `showmode` tells you whether you are in insert mode
- `number` displays line numbers at the left-hand edge of the screen
- `autowrite` Saves any changes that have been made to the current file when you issue the `:n`, `:rew`, or `:!` command
- `ignorecase` Ignores the case of text while searching
- `list` Prints end-of-line characters such as $ and tab characters such as ^I, which are normally invisible
- `tabstop=n` Sets the number of spaces between each tab stop on the screen to `n`
- `shiftwidth` Sets the number of spaces << and >> shifts each line

4.1.4 Configuring `vi`

When we first started talking about `vi`, I mentioned that there were a lot things we could do to configure it. There are mappings and abbreviations and settings that we can control. The problem is that once we leave `vi`, everything we added is lost.

Fortunately, there is hope. Like many programs, vi has its own configuration file: .exrc (note the dot at the front). Normally, this file does not exist by default, so vi just takes its standard settings. If this file resides in our home directory, it will be valid every time we start vi. The exception is when we have an .exrc file in our current directory. This will then take precedence. Having multiple .exrc files is useful when doing programming as well as when editing text. When writing text, I don't need line numbers or autoindent like I do when programming.

The content and syntax of the lines is exactly the same as in vi; however, we don't have the leading colon. Part of the .exrc file in my text editing directory looks like this:

```
map! ^X :wq

map x :wq
map! ^W :w
map w :w
set showmode
set wm=3
abbr Unix UNIX
abbr btwn between
abbr teh the
abbr refered referred
abbr waht what
abbr Para {P}
abbr inot into
```

THE NEXT STEP

No one can force you to learn vi, just as no one can force you to do backups. However, in my opinion, doing both will make you a better administrator. There will come a time when having done regular backups will save your career. There may also come a time when knowing vi will save you the embarrassment of having to tell your client or boss that you can't accomplish a task because you need to edit a file and the only editor is the system default: vi.

4.2 Interactively Editing Files with emacs

Without a doubt, emacs is a more powerful editor than vi. It can do many more things than vi. As a result, there is more to learn. Because there is more to learn, it takes longer to learn.

Calling emacs a text editor does not do it justice at all. Because of its scale, it is much more appropriate to call it an application. The emacs editor can do much more than simply edit files. One commercial company that implements emacs is LIVIA in Paris, France. They use emacs as their sole tool for editing and preparing layouts of the French translations of many O'Reilly and Associates UNIX books. Director Nat Makarevitch says, "Emacs is here the Swiss (army) knife helping us to tackle all edition-related work."

One major advantage emacs has is its extensibility. It has its own version of the LISP programming language that you can use to write your own macros. In addition, you can also use emacs for reading and sending mail. Because of the macro's language feature, there is a lot that you can do with emacs.

All commands that you want to send to emacs are done by holding down one of the special keys (Ctrl or Alt) and then the command key. For example, to move to the next line, you would hold down Ctrl and press n. By convention, this would be indentified in text as Ctrl-n or just C-n. If we had to press the Alt key, this would appear as Alt-m or A-m. Often the Alt key is referred to as the *Meta* key, so you could see it as Meta-n or M-n.

Perhaps the most important command is C-h, which brings up emacs's on-line help. Here you can get all the information you need about any aspect of emacs. From here, you can even get to an on-line tutorial. This is a good place to start for the beginner. I would recommend that before you do anything with emacs, you take a look at the tutorial.

Aside from running the on-line tutorial, I recommend getting a copy of *Learning GNU Emacs* by Debra Cameron and Bill Rosenblatt from O'Reilly and Associates. This goes into much more detail than I can here and it is easy to follow.

In the next couple of sections, I am going to give you a very brief introduction to emacs. There are several reasons that I covered vi in a lot more detail. First, vi is available on every system. If you learn it, you can edit files anywhere. The next is the size of the programs. What I described in the section on vi covers the vast majority of its functionality. To cover emacs at the same level, I would have to devote an entire chapter just to emacs.

Finally, I am not here to make you Linux gurus, but rather to provide you with the tools you need to implement Linux effectively in your business.

4.2.1 Starting emacs

Like vi, emacs can be started either by itself or with one of many different command line switches, including the name of a file you want to edit.

Because emacs is a full-screen editor, when it comes up, it will fill your screen. If you start it from a window from within X, emacs will catch this and (normally) start Xemacs instead.

Unlike vi, there is neither a command mode nor an input mode. In other words, each key pressed is interpreted for itself and not in regard to whether emacs is expecting a command or text. This is the same basic behavior as word processors, such as MS-Word or WordPerfect. Therefore, you need to tell emacs that what you are sending is a command and not to include it in your file.

When starting emacs, enter one of several different *modes*. The mode you are in is based on the kind of work your are doing and determines the basic behavior of emacs while you are working with it. There are modes for normal text editing, reading mail, C programming, and editing TeX source. LIVIA uses the AUC Tex mode for their work.

The default mode when you give a file name as an argument is the *fundamental* mode. This mode is used for normal text editing because it has the "fundamental" functions in it. I have found that on a lot of machines, if you don't specify a file name, emacs will come up in the *Lisp Interaction* mode.

You can tell what mode you are in by looking at the status line, which looks something like this:

```
--**-Emacs: file.txt      (Fundamental)----All------------------
```

We see the name of the file that we are working on (file.txt), the mode (Fundamental), and some information about where we are in the text. In this case, we have All, which indicates that the entire text is being displayed on the screen. If the file was too large to fit on the screen, we might have something like this:

```
--**-Emacs: file.txt     (Fundamental) --L23--35%---------------
```

This says that we are on line 23 of the file (L23), which is approximately 35 percent of the file. If we were looking at the top or bottom of the file, the status line would show Top and Bottom, respectively.

4.2.2 Basic Movement

As with many word processors, you can use the arrow keys to move around. In some cases, you might have an incorrect or unknown terminal type, so you need to use the keys. I found out the hard way that emacs does not behave the same way as other text editors or word processors at the end of a file. If I press the down arrow, emacs will keep going down. If I have no text after a particular point, `emacs` will just keep adding new lines into my file.

Movement in `emacs` is also accomplished using either the `Ctrl` or `Esc` key and then a letter that indicates the type of movement you want. For example, the word "forward" begins with the letter "f," so use this key to move forward. Use `C-f` to move forward a character and `Esc-f` to move forward a whole word. (An overview of movement commands can be found in Table 4.1.)

Movement up and down screenfuls at a time is accomplished using `v`. To move down a screen, use `C-v`; to move up, use `M-v`. Note that there is an overlap when you do this. For example, if the last line on the screen is line 56 and you move down a screen, line 56 will now be at the top of the screen.

Table 4.1: `emacs` **Movement Commands**

Character	Action
`C-b`	move backward one character
`C-f`	move forward one character
`Esc-b`	move backward one word
`Esc-f`	move forward one word
`C-p`	move to previous line
`C-n`	move to next line
`C-a`	move to beginning of line ("a" is first letter of alphabet)
`C-e`	move to end of line
`C-v`	move forward one screen (lines numbers increase)
`Esc-v`	move backward one screen (lines numbers decrease)
`Esc->`	move to end of buffer (file)
`Esc-<`	move to start of buffer (file)

4.2.3 Editing Text

By editing text, I don't mean simply typing and deleting characters. I also mean selecting blocks of text to copy, delete, or move around your file. You can see some of the basic commands in Table 4.2.

Like a word processor, the region of text that you want to delete or move must first be marked. This is done by using either `C-@` or `C-space`, after which you move the cursor to the place where you want to end the block. This area (or region) is now marked and you can either copy the region into a buffer or delete it into the buffer. This buffer is referred as the "kill-ring." To delete a region into the kill-ring, use `C-w`; to copy it into the kill-ring, use `Esc-w`.

If you want, you could also delete text without first marking a region. For example, `C-d` will delete a word and `C-k` will delete a line. In both cases, the deleted text will end up in the kill-ring.

Once you have something in the kill-ring, you can move to another part of the text and insert it. Note that `emacs` calls this process yanking, whereas in `vi`, yanking is putting text into the buffer. Yank a text with `C-y`.

Table 4.2: `emacs` **Text Editing Commands**

Character	Action
`C-d`	delete character under cursor
`Del`	delete previous character
`Esc-Del`	delete previous word
`Esc-d`	delete word the cursor is on
`C-k`	delete line
`C-w`	delete marked region
`Esc-w`	copy marked region
`C-y`	yank (insert) text from kill-ring
`C-@` or `C-space`	set start of region

4.2.4 Searching and Replacing Text

As one might hope, `emacs` gives you ways to both search for text and replace the text it finds. The most powerful feature of the search mechanism is to do an *incremental* search. You start the search with `C-s` and just below the status line, you should see something like this:

```
I-search:
```

As you type characters, they will appear here, one at a time. As you type, `emacs` will start searching, matching all the characters. For example, if you were searching the `termcap` file and wanted to find a specific occurrence of the word "ansi," you would press `C-s` and start typing. When you press the `a`, the line would look like this

```
I-search: a
```

and emacs would find the first "a" in the file. When you type the "n," you then have

```
I-search: an
```

and emacs would find the first occurrence of "an." When you finally type in the whole word, and it is still not in the right place, you could continue to press C-s and emacs would search for the next occurrence. At any time, you could continue to type characters and this would be the new search pattern.

If you want to use regular expressions, you can. By pressing M-C-s, you will see the following at the bottom of the screen:

```
Regexp I-search:
```

Here you can use standard Linux regular expressions.

If you are not just searching for text, but want to replace it as well, emacs lets you do that. Enter M-%, and emacs will prompt you for the search string and then the string that you want to replace it with. Once you find a string, you have a few choices. See Table 4.3.

Normally, you will have some text in a file that you want to replace and you know what it is, so you don't need to search. For example, to change every occurrence of UNIX to Linux, press M-x. Here again, you will be prompted for both the search and replace strings.

Table 4.3: emacs **Search and Replace Commands**

Character	Action
C-s	search forward incrementally
C-r	search backward incrementally
Esc or period	end search
space or Y	replace string (query replace)
C-g	cancel search and return to start
Del	delete incorrect character in the search string
Esc-w	copy marked region
Esc-%	enter query-replace

4.2.5 Customizing emacs

Like vi, emacs has its own configuration file, .emacs, which normally resides in your home directory. This is a text file that contains the emacs

LISP code that is used to define functions, key bindings, and other aspects of emacs.

Using key binding, every key can be configured. Be default, many of the keys are mapped to internal functions of emacs. For example, C-n maps to the internal function, *next-line*. Another example is calling help with C-h.

Each function is enclosed within a pair of parentheses with the following syntax:

```
(function_name arguments)
```

The most common functions are those that define behavior when specific keys are pressed. These are referred to as key *bindings*. There are three functions involved with key bindings: define-key, global-set-key, and local-set-key.

Before we jump into that, we need to talk about the concept of a *keymap*. A keymap is a table or array of key bindings. The global-map contains the basic emacs key bindings. These are valid no matter what mode you are in. Local keymaps are normally used with specific modes and each mode generally has its own keymap. When you press a key, first the local map is checked, and if it's not there, the global map is checked.

Some commands are actually bound to multiple keystrokes. Here, you type one key to get emacs ready and then the second key starts the command. For example, the keystrokes to insert a file would be C-x i: First press C-x and then press i.

Such commands are kept in the *Ctrl-x-map*. In addition, there is an *Esc-map* for those commands that are reach by pressing the Esc key.

So, to define the next-line function in the global-map, the function would look like this:

```
(define-key global-map "\C--n" 'next-line)
```

Here, the function name is define-key and the remainder of the line is made up of arguments. After the map name (global-map) is the key we want to define, in this case, Ctrl-n. Next we have a single-quote to indicate that what follows is the emacs command that should be executed.

Because we are defining the global-map, the previous function could also be defined as

```
(global-set-key "\C-n" 'next-line)
```

Note that in this case, we did not specify the map because by using the `global-set-key`, we use the global-map by default.

As you might guess, `local-set-key` defines the key bindings for the local-map.

4.3 Noninteractively Editing Files with `sed`

Suppose you have a file in which you need to make some changes. You could load up `vi` and make the changes that way, but what if what you wanted to change was the output of some command before you sent it to a file? You could first send it to a file and then edit that file, or you could use `sed`, which is a stream editor that is specifically designed to edit data streams.

If you read the previous section or are already familiar with either the search and replace mechanisms in `vi` or the editor `ed`, you already have a jump on learning `sed`. Unlike `vi`, `sed` is noninteractive, but can handle more complicated editing instructions. Because it is noninteractive, commands can be saved in text files and used over and over. This makes debugging the more complicated `sed` constructs much easier. For the most part, `sed` is line-oriented, which allows it to process files of almost any size. However, this has the disadvantage that `sed` cannot do editing that is dependent on relative addressing.

Unlike the section on `vi`, I am not going to go into as many details about `sed`. However, `sed` is a useful tool and I use it often. The reason I am not going to cover it in too much detail is three-fold. First, much of what is true about pattern searches, addressing, etc., in `vi` is also true in `sed`. Therefore, I don't feel the need to repeat. Second, it is not that important that you become a `sed` expert to be a good system administrator. In a few cases, scripts on a Linux system will use `sed`. However, they are not that difficult to understand, provided you have a basic understanding of `sed` syntax. Third, `sed` is like any programming language–you can get by with simple things. However, to get really good, you need to practice and we just don't have the space to go beyond the basics.

In this section, I am going to talk about the basics of `sed` syntax, as well as some of the more common `sed` commands and constructs. If you want to learn more, I recommend getting *sed & awk* by Dale Dougherty from O'Reilly and Associates. This will also help you in the section on `awk`, which is coming up next.

The way sed works is that it reads input one line at a time, and then carries out whatever editing changes you specify. When it has finished making the changes, it writes them to stdout. Like commands such as grep and sort, sed acts like a filter. However, with sed you can create very complicated programs. Because I normally use sed as one end of a pipe, most of the sed commands that I use have the following structure:

```
first_cmd | sed <options> <edit_description>
```

This is useful when the edit descriptions you are using are fairly simple. However, if you want to perform multiple edits on each line, then this way is not really suitable. Instead, you can put all of your changes into one file and start up sed like this

```
first_cmd | sed -f editscript
```

or

```
sed -f editscript <inputfile
```

As I mentioned before, the addressing and search/replace mechanisms within sed are basically the same as within vi. It has the structure

```
[address1[,address2]] edit_description [arguments]
```

As with vi, addresses do not necessarily need to be line numbers, but can be regular expressions that sed needs to search for. If you omit the address, sed will make the changes globally, as applicable. The edit_description tells sed what changes to make. Several arguments can be used, and we'll get to them as we move along.

As sed reads the file, it copies each line into its *pattern space*. This pattern space is a special buffer that sed uses to hold a line of text as it processes it. As soon as it has finished reading the line, sed begins to apply the changes to the pattern space based on the edit description.

Keep in mind that even though sed will read a line into the pattern space, it will only make changes to addresses that match the addresses specified and does not print any warnings when this happens. In general, sed either silently ignores errors or terminates abruptly with an error message as a result of a syntax error, not because there we no matches. If there are no lines that contain the pattern, no lines match, and the edit commands are not carried out.

Because you can have multiple changes on any given line, sed will carry them each out in turn. When there are no more changes to be made, sed sends the result to its output. The next line is read in and the whole process starts over. As it reads in each line, sed will increment an internal line counter, which keeps track of the *total* number of lines read, not lines per file. This is an important distinction if you have multiple files that are being read. For example, if you had two 50-line files, from sed's perspective, line 60 would be the tenth line in the second file.

Each sed command can have 0, 1, or 2 addresses. A command with no addresses specified is applied to every line in the input. A command with one address is applied to all lines that match that address. For example:

```
/mike/s/fred/john/
```

substitutes the first instance of "john" for "fred" only on those lines containing "mike". A command with two addresses is applied to the first line that matches the first address, then to all subsequent lines until a match for the second address is processed. An attempt is made to match the first address on subsequent lines, and the process is repeated. Two addresses are separated by a comma.

For example

```
50,100s/fred/john/
```

substitutes the first instance of "john" for "fred" from line 50 to line 100, inclusive. (Note that there should be no space between the second address and the s command.) If an address is followed by an exclamation mark (!), the command is applied only to lines that do not match the address. For example

```
50,100!s/fred/john/
```

substitutes the first instance of "john" for "fred" everywhere except lines 50 to 100, inclusive.

Also, sed can be told to do input and output based on what it finds. The action it should perform is identified by an argument at the end of the sed command. For example, if we wanted to print out lines 5-10 of a specific file, the sed command would be

```
cat file | sed -n '5,10p'
```

The -n is necessary so that every line isn't output in *addition* to the lines that match.

Remember the script we created in the first section of this chapter, where we wanted just lines 5–10 of every file. Now that we know how to use sed, we can change the script to be a lot more efficient. It would now look like this:

```
find ./letters/taxes -print | while read FILE
do
echo $FILE
cat $FILE |  sed -n '5-10p'
done
```

Rather than sending the file through head and then the output through tail, we send the whole file through sed. It can keep track of which line is line 1, and then print the necessary lines.

In addition, sed allows you to write lines that match. For example, if we wanted all the comments in a shell-script to be output to a file, we could use sed like this:

```
cat filename |  sed -n '/^#/w filename'
```

Note that there must be exactly one space between the w and the name of the file. If we wanted to read in a file, we could do that as well. Instead of a w to write, we could use an r to read. The contents of the file would be appended after the lines specified in the address. Also keep in mind that writing to or reading from a file are independent of what happens next. For example, if we write every line in a file containing the name "John," but in a subsequent sed command change "John" to "Chris," the file would contain references to "John," as no changes are made. This is logical because sed works on each line and the lines are already in the file before the changes are made.

Keep in mind that every time a line is read in, the contents of the pattern space are overwritten. To save certain data across multiple commands, sed provides what is called the "hold space." Changes are not made to the hold space directly, rather the contents of either one can be copied into the other for processes. The contents can even be exchanged, if needed. Table 4.4 contains a list of the more common sed commands, including the commands used to manipulate the hold and pattern spaces.

Table 4.4: `sed` **Commands**

`a`	append text to the pattern space
`b`	branch to a label
`c`	append text
`d`	delete text
`D`	delete all the characters from the start of the pattern space up to and including the first new line
`g`	overwrite the pattern space with the holding area
`G`	appends the holding area to the pattern space, separated with a new line
`h`	overwrite holding area with pattern space
`H`	appends the pattern space to the holding area, separated by a newlinewith a new line
`i`	insert text
`l`	list the contents of the pattern space
`n`	add a new line to the pattern space
`N`	append the next input line to the pattern space, separated lines with a new line
`p`	print the pattern space
`P`	print from the start of the pattern space up to and including the first new line
`r`	read in a file
`s`	substitute patterns
`t`	branch only if a substitution has been made to the current pattern space
`w`	writes to a file
`x`	interchange the contents of the pattern space and the holding area (the maximum number of addresses is two)

4.4 Programming with `awk`

Another language that Linux provides and is standard on many (most?) UNIX systems is `awk`. The abbreviation `awk` is an acronym composed of the first letter of the last names of its developers: Alfred Aho, Peter Weinberger, and Brian Kernighan. Like `sed`, `awk` is an interpreted pattern-matching language. In addition, `awk`, like `sed`, can also read `stdin`. It can also be passed the name of a file containing its arguments.

The most useful aspect of awk (at least useful for me and the many Linux scripts that use it) is its idea of a field. Like sed, awk will read whole lines, but unlike sed, awk can immediately break into segments (fields) based on some criteria. Each field is separated by a *field separator.* By default, this separator is a space. By using the -F option on the command line or the FS variable within an awk program, you can specify a new field separator. For example, if you specified a colon (:) as a field separator, you could read in the lines from the /etc/password file and immediately break it into fields.

A programming language it its own right, awk has become a staple of UNIX systems. The basic purposes of the language are manipulating and processing text files. However, awk is also a useful tool when combined with output from other commands, and allows you to format that output in ways that might be easier to process further. One major advantage of awk is that it can accomplish in a few lines what would normally require dozens of lines in sh or csh shell-script, or may even require writing something in a lower-level language, like C.

The basic layout of an awk command is

```
pattern { action }
```

where the action to be performed is included within the curly braces ({}). Like sed, awk reads one input a line at a time, but awk sees each line as a record broken up into fields. Fields are separated by an input Field Separator (FS), which by default is a Tab or space. The FS can be changed to something else, for example, a semi-colon (;), with FS=;. This is useful when you want to process text that contains blanks; for example, data of the following form:

```
Blinn, David;42 Clarke Street;Sunnyvale;California;95123;33
Dickson, Tillman;8250 Darryl Lane;San Jose;Calfifornia;95032;34
Giberson, Suzanne;102 Truck Stop Road;Ben Lomond;California;26
Holder, Wyliam; 1932 Nuldev Street;Mount Hermon;California;95431;42
Nathanson, Robert;12 Peabody Lane;Beaverton;Oregon;97532;33
Richards, John;1232 Bromide Drive;Boston;Massachusettes;02134;36
Shaffer, Shannon;98 Whatever Way;Watsonville;California;95332;24
```

Here we have name, address, city, state, zip code, and age. Without using ; as a field separator, Blinn and David;42 would be two fields. Here, we would want to treat each name, address city, etc., a single unit, rather than as multiple fields.

The basic format of an awk program or awk script, as it is sometimes called, is a pattern followed by a particular action. Like sed, each line of the input is checked by awk to see if it matches that particular pattern. Both sed and awk do well when comparing string values, However, whereas checking numeric values is difficult with sed, this functionality is an integral part of awk.

If we wanted, we could use the data previously listed and output only the names and cities of those people under 30. First, we need an awk script, called awk.scr, that looks like this:

```
FS=;    $6 < 30  { print $1, $3 }
```

Next, assume that we have a data file containing the seven lines of data above, called awk.data. We could process the data file in one of two ways. First

```
awk -f awk.scr awk.data
```

The -f option tells awk that it should read its instructions from the file that follows. In this case, awk.scr. At the end, we have the file from which awk needs to read its data.

Alternatively, we could start it like this:

```
cat awk.data | awk -f awk.scr
```

We can even make string comparisons. as in

```
$4 == "California"  { print $1, $3 }
```

Although it may make little sense, we could make string comparisons on what would normally be numeric values, as in

```
$6 == "33"  { print $1, $3 }
```

This prints out fields 1 and 3 from only those lines in which the sixth field equals the string 33.

Not to be outdone by sed, awk will also allow you to use regular expressions in your search criteria. A very simple example is one where we want to print every line containing the characters "on." (Note: The characters must be adjacent and in the appropriate case.) This line would look like this:

```
/on/ {print $0}
```

However, the regular expressions that awk uses can be as complicated as those used in sed. One example would be

```
/[^s]on[^;]/ {print $0}
```

This says to print every line containing the pattern on, but only if it is *not* preceded by an ^s nor followed by a semi-colon (^;). The trailing semi-colon eliminates the two town names ending in "on" (Boston and

Beaverton) and the leading s eliminates all the names ending in "son." When we run awk with this line, our output is

```
Giberson, Suzanne;102 Truck Stop Road;Ben Lomond;Cali-
fornia;96221;26
```

But doesn't the name "Giberson" end in "son"? Shouldn't it be ignored along with the others? Well, yes. However, that's not the case. The reason this line was printed out was because of the "on" in Ben Lomond, the city in which Giberson resides.

We can also use addresses as part of the search criteria. For example, assume that we need to print out only those lines in which the first field name (i.e., the person's last name) is in the first half of the alphabet. Because this list is sorted, we could look for all the lines between those starting with "A" and those starting with "M." Therefore, we could use a line like this:

```
/^A/,/^M/ {print $0}
```

When we run it, we get

What happened? There are certainly several names in the first half of the alphabet. Why didn't this print anything? Well, it printed exactly what we told it to print. Like the addresses in both vi and sed, awk searches for a line that matches the criteria we specified. So, what we really said was "Find the first line that starts with an 'A' and then print all the lines up to and including the last one starting with an 'M'." Because there was no line starting with an "A," the start address didn't exist. Instead, the code to get what we really want would look like this:

```
/^[A-M]/ {print $0}
```

This says to print all the lines whose first character is in the *range* A–M. Because this checks every line and isn't looking for starting and ending addresses, we could have even used an unsorted file and would have gotten all the lines we wanted. The output then looks like this:

```
Blinn, David;42 Clarke Street;Sunnyvale;California;95123;33
Dickson, Tillman;8250 Darryl Lane;San Jose;Calfifornia;95032;34
Giberson, Suzanne;102 Truck Stop Road;Ben Lomond;California;96221;26
Holder, Wyliam; 1932 Nuldev Street;Mount Hermon;California;95431;42
```

If we wanted to use a starting and ending address, we would have to specify the starting letter of the name that actually existed in our file. For example:

```
/^B/,/^H/ {print $0}
```

Because printing is a very useful aspect of awk, it's nice to know that there are actually two ways of printing with awk. The first we just mentioned. However, if you use printf instead of print, you can specify the format of the output in greater detail. If you are familiar with the C programming language, you already have a head start, as the format of printf is essentially the same as in C. However, there are a couple of differences that you will see immediately if you are a C programmer.

For example, if we wanted to print both the name and age with this line

```
$6 >30 {printf"%20s %5d\n",$1,$6}
```

the output would look like this:

```
          Blinn, David     33
       Dickson, Tillman    34
         Holder, Wyliam    42
      Nathanson, Robert    33
         Richards, John    36
```

The space used to print each name is 20 characters long, followed by five spaces for the age.

Because awk reads each line as a single record and blocks of text in each record as fields, it needs to keep track of how many records there are and how many fields. These are denoted by the NR variable.

Another way of using awk is at the end of a pipe. For example, you may have multiple-line output from one command or another but only want one or two fields from that line. To be more specific, you may only want the permissions and file names from an ls -l output. You would then pipe it through awk, like this

```
ls -l | awk '{ print $1" "$9 }'
```

and the output might look something like this:

```
-rw-r--r-- mike.letter
-rw-r--r-- pat.note
-rw-r--r-- steve.note
-rw-r--r-- zoli.letter
```

This brings up the concept of variables. Like other languages, awk enables you to define variables. A couple are already predefined and come in handy. For example, what if we didn't know off the tops of our heads that there were nine fields in the ls -l output? Because we know that we wanted the first and the last field, we can use the variable that specifies the number of fields. The line would then look like this:

```
ls -l | awk '{ print $1" "$NF }'
```

In this example, the space enclosed in quotes is necessary; otherwise, awk would print $1 and $NR right next to each other.

Another variable that awk uses to keep track of the number of records read so far is NR. This can be useful, for example, if you only want to see a particular part of the text. Remember our example at the beginning of this section where we wanted to see lines 5–10 of a file (to look for an address in the header)? In the last section, I showed you how to do it with sed, and now I'll show you with awk.

We can use the fact that the NR variable keeps track of the number of records, and because each line is a record, the NR variable also keeps track of the number of lines. So, we'll tell awk that we want to print out each line between 5 and 10, like this:

```
cat datafile | awk '{NR >=5 && NR <= 10 }'
```

This brings up four new issues. The first is the NR variable itself. The second is the use of the double ampersand (&&). As in C, this means a logical AND. Both the right and the left sides of the expression must be true for the entire expression to be true. In this example, if we read a line and the value of NR is greater than or equal to 5 (i.e., we have read in at least five lines) *and* the number of lines read is not more than 10, the expression meets the logical AND criteria. The third issue is that there is no print statement. The default action of awk, when it doesn't have any additional instructions, is to print out each line that matches the pattern. (You can find a list of other built in variable in Table 4.5)

Table 4.5: awk **Comparison Operators**

Operator	Meaning
<	less than
<=	less than or equal to
==	equal to
!=	not equal to
>=	greater than or equal to
>	greater than

The last issue is the use of the variable NR. Note that here, there is no dollar sign ($) in front of the variable because we are looking for the value of NR, not what it points to. We do not need to prefix it with $ unless it is a field variable. Confused? Let's look at another example.

Let's say we wanted to print out only the lines where there were more than nine fields. We could do it like this:

```
cat datafile | awk '{ NF > 9 }'
```

Compare this

```
cat datafile | awk '{ print $NF }'
```

which prints out the last field in every line. (You can find a list of other built in variable in Table 4.6)

Table 4.6: **Default Values of `awk` Built-in Variables**

Variable	Meaning	Default
ARGC	number of command-line arguments	-
ARGV	Aay of command-line arguments	-
FILENAME	name of current input file	-
FNR	record number in current file	-
FS	input field separator	space or tab
NF	number of fields in the current record	-
NR	number of records read	-
OFMT	numeric output format	%.6g
OFS	output field separator	space
ORS	output record separator	new line
RS	input record separator	new line

Up to now, we've been talking about one line `awk` commands. These have all performed a single action on each line. However, `awk` has the ability to do multiple tasks on each line as well as a task before it begins reading and after it has finished reading.

We use the `BEGIN` and `END` pair as markers. These are treated like any other pattern. Therefore, anything appearing after the `BEGIN` pattern is done before the first line is read. Anything after the `END` pattern is done after the last line is read. Let's look at this script:

```
BEGIN { FS=";"}
{printf"%s\n", $1}
{printf"%s\n", $2}
{printf"%s, %s\n",$3,$4}
{printf"%s\n", $5}
END {print "Total Names:" NR}
```

Following the `BEGIN` pattern is a definition of the field separator. This is therefore done before the first line is read. Each line is processed four times, where we print a different set of fields each time. When we finish, our output looks like this:

```
Blinn, David
42 Clarke Street
Sunnyvale, California
95123

Dickson, Tillman
8250 Darryl Lane
San Jose, California
95032

Giberson, Suzanne
102 Truck Stop Road
Ben Lomond, California
96221

Holder, Wyliam
1932 Nuldev Street
Mount Hermon, California
95431

Nathanson, Robert
12 Peabody Lane
Beaverton, Oregon
97532

Richards, John
1232 Bromide Drive
Boston, Massachusetts
02134

Shaffer, Shannon
98 Whatever Way
Watsonville, California
95332

Total Names:7
```

Aside from having a pre-defined set of variables to use, `awk` allows us to define variables ourselves. If in the last `awk` script we had wanted to print out, let's say, the average age, we could add a line in the middle of the script that looked like this:

```
{total = total + $6 }
```

Because $6 denotes the age of each person, every time we run through the loop, it is added to the variable `total`. Unlike other languages, such as C, we don't have to initialize the variables; awk will do that for us. Strings are initialized to the null string and numeric variables are initialized to 0.

After the END, we can include another line to print out our sum, like this:

```
{print "Average age: " total/NR}
```

Is that all there is to it? No. In fact, we haven't even touched the surface. awk is a very complex programming language and there are dozens more issues that we could have addressed. Built into the language are mathematical functions, if and while loops, the ability to create your own functions, strings and array manipulation, and much more.

Unfortunately, this is not a book on UNIX programming languages. Some readers may be disappointed that I do not have the space to cover awk in more detail. I am also disappointed. However, I have given you a basic introduction to the constructs of the language to enable you to better understand the more than 100 scripts on your system that use awk in some way.

4.5 Putting Things Together

Because my intent here is not to make you shell or awk programming experts, there are obviously things that we didn't have a chance to cover. However, I hope I have given you the basics to create your own tools and configure at least your shell environment the way you need or want it.

Like any tool or system, the way to get better is to practice. Therefore, my advice is that you play with the shell and programs on the system to get a better feeling for how they behave. By creating your own scripts, you will become more familiar with both `vi` and shell-script syntax, which will help you to create your own tools and understand the behavior of the system scripts. As you learn more, you can add awk and `sed` components to your system to make some very powerful commands and utilities.

4.6 `Perl`: The Language of the Web

If you plan to do anything serious on the Web, I suggest that you learn `perl`. In fact, if you plan to do anything serious on your machine, then learning perl is also a good idea. Although not available on a lot of commercial versions, perl is almost universally available with Linux.

Now, I am not saying that you shouldn't learn sed, awk, and shell programming. Rather, I am saying that you should learn all four. Both sed and awk have been around for quite a while, so they are deeply ingrained in the thinking of most system administrators. Although you could easily find a shell-script on the system that didn't have elements of sed or awk in it, you would be very hard pressed to find a script that had no shell programming in it. On the other hand, most of the scripts that process information from other programs use either sed or awk. Therefore, it is likely that you will eventually come across one or the other.

perl is another matter all together. None of the standard scripts have perl in them. This does not say anything about the relative value of perl, but rather the relative availability of it. Because it can be expected that awk and sed are available, it makes sense that they are commonly used. perl may not be on your machine and including it in a system shell-script might cause trouble.

In this section, I am going to talk about the basics of perl. We'll go through the mechanics of creating perl scripts and the syntax of the perl language. There are many good books on perl, so I would direct you to them to get into the nitty-gritty. Here we are just going to cover the basics. Later on, we'll address some of the issues involved with making perl scripts to use on your Web site.

One aspect of perl that I like is that it contains the best of everything. It has aspects of C, shell, awk, sed and many other things. perl is also free. The source code is readily available and the versions that I have came with configuration scripts that determined the type of system I had and set up the make-files accordingly. Aside from Linux, I was able to compile the exact same source on my DEC OSF/1 workstation. Needless to say, the scripts that I write at home run just as well at work.

I am going to make assumptions as to what level of programming background you have. If you read and understood the sections on sed, awk, and the shell, then you should be ready for what comes next. In this section, I am going to jump right in. I am not going to amaze you with demonstrations of how perl can do I/O, as that's what we are using it for in the first place. Instead, I am going to assume that you want to do I/O and jump right into how to do it.

Let's create a shell-script called hello.pl. The pl extension has no real meaning, although I have seen many places where it is always used as an extension. It is more or less conventional to do this, just as text files traditionally have the extension .txt, shell scripts end in .sh, etc.

We'll start off with the traditional

```
print "Hello, World!\n";
```

This shell-script consists of a single perl statement, whose purpose is to output the text inside the double-quotes. Each statement in perl is followed by a semi-colon. Here, we are using the perl print function to output the literal string "Hello, World!\n" (including the trailing new line). Although we don't see it, there is the implied file handle to stdout. The equivalent command with the explicit reference would be

```
print STDOUT "Hello, World!\n";
```

Along with STDOUT, perl has the default file handlers STDIN and STDERR. Here is a quick script that demonstrates all three as well as introduces a couple of familiar programming constructs:

```
while (<STDIN>)
{
      if ( $_ eq  "\n" )
      {
                print STDERR "Error: \n";
      } else {
                print STDOUT "Input: $_ \n";
      }
}
```

Functioning the same as in C and most shells, the while line at the top says that as long as there is something coming from STDIN, do the loop. Here we have the special format (<STDIN>), which tells perl where to get input. If we wanted, we could use a file handle other than STDIN. However, we'll get to that in a little bit.

One thing that you need to watch out for is that you must include blocks of statements (such as after while or if statements) inside the curly braces ({}). This is different from the way you do it in C, where a single line can follow while or if. For example, this statement is not valid in perl:

```
while ( $a < $b )
      $a++;
```

You would need to write it something like this:

```
while ( $a < $b ) {
      $a++;
}
```

Inside the while loop, we get to an if statement. We compare the value of the special variable $_ to see if it is empty. The variable $_ serves several functions. In this case, it represents the line we are reading from STDIN. In other cases, it represents the pattern space, as in sed. If the latter is true, then just the Enter key was pressed. If the line we just read in is equal to the newline character (just a blank line), we use the print function, which has the syntax

```
print [filehandler] "text_to_print";
```

In the first case, filehandler is stderr and in the second case stdout is the filehandler. In each case, we could have left out the filehandler and the output would go to stout.

Each time we print a line, we need to include a newline (\n) ourselves.

We can format the print line in different ways. In the second print line, where the input is not a blank line, we can print "Input:" before we print the line just input. Although this is a very simple way of outputting lines, it gets the job done. More complex formatting is possible with the perl printf function. Like its counterpart in C or awk, you can come up with some very elaborate outputs. We'll get into more details later.

One more useful function for processing lines of input is split. The split function is used to, as its name implies, to split a line based on a field separator that you define. Say, for example, a space. The line is then stored in an array as individual elements. So, in our example, if we wanted to input multiple words and have them parsed correctly, we could change the script to look like this:

```
while (<STDIN>)
{
@field = split(' ',$_);
if ( $_ eq  "\n" )
{
        print STDERR "Error: \n";
} else {
        print STDOUT "$_ \n";
        print $field[0];
        print $field[1];
        print $field[2];
}
}
```

The split function has the syntax

```
split(pattern,line);
```

where pattern is our field separator and line is the input line. So our line

```
@field = split(' ',$_);
```

says to split the line we just read in (stored in $_) and use a space ( ) as the field separator. Each field is then placed into an element of the array field. The @ is needed in front of the variable field to indicate that it's an array. In perl, there are several types of variables. The first kind we have already met before. The special variable $_ is an example of a scalar variable. Each scalar variable is preceded by a dollar sign ($) and can contain a single value, whether a character string or a number. How does perl tell the difference? It depends on the context. perl will behave correctly by looking at what you tell it to do with the variable. Other examples of scalars are

```
$name = "jimmo";
$initial = 'j';
$answertolifetheuniverseandeverything = 42;
```

Another kind of variable is an array, as we mentioned before. If we precede a variable with %, we have an array. But don't we have an array with @? Yes, so what's the difference? The difference is that arrays, starting with the @, are referenced by numbers, while those starting with the % are referenced by a string. We'll get to how that works as we move along.

In our example, we are using the split function to fill up the array @field. This array will be referenced by number. We see the way it is referenced in the three print statements toward the end of the script.

If our input line had a different field separator (for example, %), the line might look like this:

```
@field = split('%',$_);
```

In this example, we are outputting the first three words that are input. But what if there are more words? Obviously we just add more print statements. What if there are fewer words? Now we run into problems. In fact, we run into problems when adding more print statements. The question is, where do we stop? Do we set a limit on the number of words that can be input? Well, we can avoid all of these problems by letting the system count for us. Changing the script a little, we get

```
while (<STDIN>)
{
      @field = split(' ',$_);
      if ( $_ eq  "\n" )
      {
               print STDERR "Error: \n";
      } else {
               foreach $word (@field){
               print $word,"\n";
               }
      }
}
```

In this example, we introduce the `foreach` construct. This has the same behavior as a `for` loop. In fact, in `perl`, for and `foreach` are interchangeable, provided you have the right syntax. In this case, the syntax is

```
foreach $variable (@array)
```

where `$variable` is our loop variable and `@array` is the name of the array. When the script is run, `@array` is expanded to its components. So, if we had input four fruits, our line might have looked like this:

```
foreach $word ('apple','bananna','cherry','orange');
```

Because I don't know how many elements there are in the array field, `foreach` comes in handy. In this example, every word separated by a space will be printed on a line by itself, like this:

```
perl script.pl
one two three
one
two
three
^D
```

Our next enhancement is to change the field separator. This time we'll use an ampersand (&) instead. The `split` line now looks like this:

```
@field = split('&',$_);
```

When we run the script again with the same input, what we get is a bit different:

```
# perl script.pl

one two three
one two three
```

The reason why we get the output on one line is because the space is no longer a field separator. If we run it again, this time using `&`, we get something different:

```
# perl script.pl
one&two&three
one
two
three
```

This time, the three words were recognized as separate fields.

Although it doesn't seem too likely that you would be inputting data like this from the keyboard, it is conceivable that you might want to read a file that has data stored like this. To make things easy, I have provided a file that represents a simple database of books. Each line is a record and represents a single book, with the fields separated by `%`.

To be able to read from a file, we must create a file handle. To do this, we add a line and change the `while` statement so it looks like this:

```
open ( INFILE,"< bookdata.txt");
while (<INFILE>)
```

The syntax of the open function is

```
open(file_handle,openwhat_&_how);
```

The way we open a file depends on the way we want to read it. Here, we use standard shell redirection symbols to indicate how we want to read the specified file. In our example, we indicate redirection *from* the file `bookdata.txt`. This says we want to read *from* the file. If we wanted to open the file for writing, the line would look like this:

```
open ( INFILE,"> bookdata.txt");
```

If we wanted to append to the file, we could change the redirections so the line would look like this:

```
open ( INFILE,">> bookdata.txt");
```

Remember I said that we use standard redirection symbols. This also includes the pipe symbol. As the need presents itself, your `perl` script can open a pipe for either reading or writing. Assuming that we want to open a pipe for writing that sends the output through `sort`, the line might look like this:

```
open ( INFILE,"| sort ");
```

Remember that this would work the same as from the command line. Therefore, the output is not being written to a file; it is just being piped through sort. However, we could redirect the output of sort, if we wanted. For example:

```
open ( INFILE,"| sort > output_file");
```

This opens the file `output_file` for writing, but the output is first piped through sort. In our example, we are opening the file `bookdata.txt` for reading. The `while` loop continues through and outputs each line read. However, instead of being on a single line, the individual fields (separated by `&`) are output on a separate line.

We can now take this one step further. Let's now assume that a couple of the fields are actually composed of subfields. These subfields are separated by a plus sign (+). We now want to break up every field containing + into its individual subfields.

As you have probably guessed, we use the `split` command again. This time, we use a different variable and instead of reading out of the input line (`$_`), we read out of the string `$field`. Therefore, the line would look like this:

```
@subfield = split('\+',$field);
```

Aside from changing the search pattern, I added the back slash (\) because + is used in the search pattern to represent one or more occurrences of the preceding character. If we don't escape it, we generate an error. The whole script now looks like this:

```
open(INFILE,"<bookdata.txt");
while (<INFILE>)
{
      @data = split('&',$_);
      if ( $_ eq  "\n" )
      {
                print STDERR "Error: \n";
      } else {
      foreach $field (@data){
               @subfield = split('\+',$field);
               foreach $word (@subfield){
                        print $word,"\n";
                        }
      }
      }
}
```

If we wanted, we could have written the script to split the incoming lines at both `&` and `+`. This would have given us a `split` line that looked like this:

```
@data = split('[&\+]',$_);
```

The reason for writing the script like we did was that it was easier to separate subfields and still maintain their relationships. Note that the search pattern used here could have been any regular expression. For example, we could have split the strings every place there was the pattern

`Di` followed by `e`, `g`, or `r`, but not if it was followed by `i`. The regular expression would be

```
Di[reg][^i]
```

so the split function would be:

```
@data = split('Di[reg][^i]',$_);
```

At this point, we can read in lines from an ASCII file, separate the lines based on what we have defined as fields, and then output each line. However, the lines don't look very interesting. All we are seeing is the content of each field and do not know what each field represents. Let's change the script once again. This time we will make the output show us the field names as well as their content.

Let's change the script so that we have control over where the fields end up. We still use the `split` statement to extract individual fields from the input string. This is not necessary because we can do it all in one step, but I am doing it this way to demonstrate the different constructs and to reiterate that in `perl`, there is always more than one way do to something. So, we end up with the following script:

```
open(INFILE,"< bookdata.txt");
while (<INFILE>)
{
@data = split('&',$_);
if ( $_ eq  "\n" )
{
        print STDERR "Error: \n";
} else {
      $fields = 0;
      foreach $field (@data){
               $fieldarray[$fields] = $field;
               print $fieldarray[$fields++]," ";
               }
      }
}
```

Each time we read a line, we first split it into the array `@data`, which is then copied into the `fields` array. Note that there is no new line in the print statement, so each field will be printed with just a space and the newline read at the end of each input line will then be output. Each time through the loop, we reset our counter (the variable `$fields`) to 0.

Although the array is re-filled every time through the loop and we lose the previous values, we could assign the values to specific variables.

Let's now make the output a little more attractive by outputting the field headings first. To make things simpler, let's label the fields as follows

```
title, author, publisher, char0, char1, char2, char3,
char4, char5
```

where `char0-char5` are simply characteristics of a book. We need a handful of `if` statements to make the assignment, which look like this:

```
foreach $field (@data){
if  ( $fields = = 0 ){
       print "Title: ",$field;
}
if  ( $fields = = 1 ){
       print "Author: ",$field;
}
*
*
*
if  ( $fields = = 8 ){
       print "Char 5: ",$field;
}
```

Here, too, we would be losing the value of each variable every time through the loop as they get overwritten. Let's just assume we only want to save this information from the first line (our reasoning will become clear in a minute). First we need a counter to keep track of what line we are on and an `if` statement to enter the block where we make the assignment. Rather than a `print` statement, we change the line to an assignment, so it might look like this:

```
$title = $field;
```

When we read subsequent lines, we can output headers for each of the fields. We do this by having another set of `if` statements that output the header and then the value, which is based on its position.

Actually, there is a way of doing things a little more efficiently. When we read the first line, we can assign the values to variables on a single line. Instead of the line

```
foreach $field (@data) {
```

we add the if statement to check if this is the first line. Then we add the line

```
($field0,$field1,$field2,$field3,$field4,$field5,$field6,
$field7,$field8)=split('&',$_);
```

Rather than assigning values to elements in an array, we are assigning them to specific variables. (Note that if there are more fields generated by the split command than we specified variables for, the remaining fields are ignored.) The other advantage of this is that we saved ourselves a lot of space. We could also call these `$field1`, `$field2`, etc., thereby making the field names a little more generic. We could also modify the `split` line so that instead of several separate variables, we have them in a single array called `field` and we could use the number as the offset into the array. Therefore, the first field would be referenced like this:

```
$field[0]
```

The split command for this would look like this

```
@field=split('&',$_);
```

which looks like something we already had. It is. This is just another example of the fact that there are always several different ways of doing things in `perl`.

At this point, we still need the series of `if` statements inside of the `foreach` loop to print out the line. However, that seems like a lot of wasted space. Instead, I will introduce the concept of an associated list. An associated list is just like any other list, except that you reference the elements by a label rather than a number.

Another difference is that associated arrays, also referred to as associated lists, are always an even length. This is because elements come in pairs: label and value. For example, we have:

```
%list= ('name','James Mohr', 'logname','jimmo',
'department,'IS');
```

Note that instead of `$` or `@` to indicate that this is an array, we use `%`. This specifies that this is an associative array, so we can refer to the value by label; however, when we finally reference the value, we use `$`. To print out the name, the line would look like this:

```
print "Name:",$list{name};
```

Also, the brackets we use are different. Here we use curly braces (`{}`) instead of square brackets (`[]`).

The introduction of the associate array allows us to define field labels within the data itself and access the values using these labels. As I mentioned, the first line of the data file containing the field labels. We can use these labels to reference the values. Let's look at the program itself:

```
open(INFILE,"< bookdata.txt");
$lines=0;
while (<INFILE>)
{
      chop;
      @data = split('&',$_);
      if ( $lines == 0 )
      {
           @headlist=split('&',$_);
           foreach $field (0..@headlist-1){
                    %headers = ( $headlist[$field],'' );
                 }
      $lines++;
      } else {
              foreach $field (0..@data-1){
              $headers{$headlist[$field]}=@data[$field];
              print $headlist[$field],": ", $headers
{$headlist[$field]},"\n";
              }
      }
}
```

At the beginning of the script, we added the chop function, which "chops" off the last character of a list or variable and returns that character. If you don't mention the list or variable, chop affects the $_ variable. This function is useful to chop off the newline character that gets read in. The next change is that we removed the block that checked for blank lines and generated an error.

The first time we read a line, we entered the appropriate block. Here, we just read in the line containing the field labels and we put each entry into the array headlist via the split function. The foreach loop also added some new elements:

```
foreach $field (0..@headlist-1){
        %headers = ( $headlist[$field],'' );
}
```

The first addition is the element (0.. @headlist-1). Two numbers separated by two dots indicate a range. We can use @headlist as a variable to indicate how many elements are in the array headlist. This returns a human number, not a computer number (one that starts at 0). Because I chose to access all my variables starting with 0, I needed to subtract 1 from the value of @headlist. There are nine elements per line in the file bookdata.txt; therefore, their range is 0..9-1.

However, we don't need to know that! In fact, we don't even know how many elements there are to make use of this functionality. The system knows how many elements it read in, so we don't have to. We just use `@headlist-1` (or whatever).

The next line fills in the elements of our associative array:

```
%headers = ( $headlist[$field],'' );
```

However, we are only filling in the labels and not the values themselves. Therefore, the second element of the pair is empty (`''`). One by one, we write the label into the first element of each pair.

After the first line is read, we load the values. Here again, we have a foreach loop that goes from 0 to the last element of the array. Like the first loop, we don't need to know how many elements were read, as we let the system keep track of this for us. The second element in each pair of the associative list is loaded with this line:

```
$headers{$headlist[$field]}=@data[$field];
```

Let's take a look at this line starting at the left end. From the array `@data` (which is the line we just read in), we are accessing the element at the offset that is specified by the variable `$field`. Because this is just the counter used for our foreach loop, we go through each element of the array data one by one. The value retrieved is then assigned to the left-hand side.

On the left, we have an array offset being referred to by an array offset. Inside we have

```
$headlist[$field]
```

The array `headlist` is what we filled up in the first block. In other words, the list of field headings. When we reference the offset with the `$field` variable, we get the field heading. This will be used as the string for the associative array. The element specified by

```
$headers{$headlist[$field}
```

corresponds to the field value. For example, if the expression

```
$headlist[$field}
```

evaluated to `title`, the second time through the loop, the expression `$headers{$headlist[$field}` would evaluate to "2010: Odyssey Two."

At this point, we are ready to make our next jump. We are going to add the functionality to search for specific values in the data. Let's assume that we know what the fields are and wish to search for a particular value. For example, we want all books that have `scifi` as field char0. Assuming that the script was called book.pl, we would specify the field label and value like this:

```
perl book.pl char0=scifi
```

Or we could add #!/usr/bin/perl to the top of the script to force the system to use perl as the interpreter. We would run the script like this:

```
book.pl char0=scifi
```

The completed script looks like this:

```
($searchfield,$searchvalue) = split('=',$ARGV[0]);
open(INFILE,"< bookdata.txt");
$lines=0;
while (<INFILE>)
{
chop;
@data = split('&',$_);
if ( $_ eq  "\n" )
{
print STDERR "Error: \n";
} else {
if ( $lines == 0 )
{
        @headlist=split('&',$_);
        foreach $field (0..@headlist-1){
        %headers = ( $headlist[$field],'' );
}
$lines++;
} else { foreach $field (0..@data-1){
        $headers{$headlist[$field]}=@data[$field];
        if ( ($searchfield eq $headlist[$field] ) &&
                  ($searchvalue eq $headers{$headlist
[$field]} )) {
        $found=1;
        }
        }
}
}
if ( $found == 1 )
{
foreach $field (0..@data-1){
      print $headlist[$field],": ", $headers{$headlist
[$field]},"\n";
}
}
$found=0;
}
```

We added a line at the top of the script that splits the first argument on the command line:

```
($searchfield,$searchvalue) = split('=',$ARGV[0]);
```

Note that we are accessing `ARGV[0]`. This is not the command being called, as one would expect in a C or shell program. Our command line has the string `char0=scifi` as its `$ARGV[0]`. After the split, we have `$searchfield=char0` and `$searchvalue=scifi`.

Some other new code looks like this:

```
        if ( ($searchfield eq $headlist[$field] ) &&
                  ($searchvalue eq $headers{$headlist
[$field]} )) {
        $found=1;
```

Instead of outputting each line in the second `foreach` loop, we are changing it so that here we are checking to see if the field we input, `$searchfield`, is the one we just read in `$headlist[$field]` and if the value we are looking for, (`$searchvalue`), equals the one we just read in.

Here we add another new concept: logical operators. These are just like in C, where `&&` means a logical AND and `||` is a logical OR. If we want a logical comparison of two variables and each has a specific value, we use the logical AND, like

```
if ( $a == 1 && $b = 2)
```

which says if `$a` equals 1 AND `$b` equals 2, execute the following block. If we wrote it like this

```
if ( $a == 1 || $b = 2)
```

it would read as follows: if `$a` equals 1 OR `$b` equals 2, execute the block. In our example, we are saying that if the search field (`$searchfield`) equals the corresponding value in the heading list (`$headlist[$field]`) AND the search value we input (`$searchvalue`) equals the value from the file (`$headers{$headlist[$field]}`), we then execute the following block. Our block is simply a flag to say we found a match.

Later, after we read in all the values for each record, we check the flag. If the flag was set, the `foreach` loop is executed:

```
if ( $found == 1 )
{
foreach $field (0..@data-1){
```

```
        print $headlist[$field],": ", $headers{$headlist
[$field]},"\n";
  }
```

Here we output the headings and then their corresponding values. But what if we aren't sure of the exact text we are looking for. For example, what if we want all books by the author Eddings, but do not know that his first name is David? It's now time to introduce the `perl` function `index`. As its name implies, it delivers an index. The index it delivers is an offset of one string in another. The syntax is

```
index(STRING,SUBSTRING,POSITION)
```

where `STRING` is the name of the string that we are looking in, `SUBSTRING` is the substring that we are looking for, and `POSITION` is where to start looking. That is, what position to start from. If `POSITION` is omitted, the function starts at the beginning of `STRING`. For example

```
index('pie','applepie');
```

will return 5, as the substring pie starts at position 5 of the string `applepie`. To take advantage of this, we only need to change one line. We change this

```
if ( ($searchfield eq $headlist[$field] ) &&
      ($searchvalue eq $headers{$headlist[$field]} )) {
```

to this

```
if ( (index($headlist[$field],$searchfield)) != -1 &&
       index($headers{$headlist[$field]},$searchvalue)
!= -1 ) {
```

Here we are looking for an offset of `-1`. This indicates the condition where the substring is *not* within the string. (The offset comes before the start of the string.) So, if we were to run the script like this

```
script.pl author=Eddings
```

we would look through the field `author` for any entry containing the string `Eddings`. Because there are records with an author named Eddings, if we looked for `Edding`, we would still find it because Edding is a substring of "David Eddings."

As you might have noticed, we have a limitation in this mechanism. We must ensure that we spell things with the right case. Because Eddings is uppercase both on the command line and in the file, there is no problem. Normally names are capitalized, so it would make sense to input them as such. But what about the title of a book? Often, words like "the" and "and" are not capitalized. However, what if the person who input the data, input them as capitals? If you looked for them in lowercase, but they were in the file as uppercase, you'd never find them.

To consider this possibility, we need to compare both the input and the fields in the file in the same case. We do this by using the `tr` (translate) function. It has the syntax

```
tr/SEARCHLIST/REPLACEMENTLIST/[options]
```

where `SEARCHLIST` is the list of characters to look for and `REPLACEMENTLIST` is the characters to use to replace those in `SEARCHLIST`. To see what options are available, check the `perl` man-page. We change part of the script to look like this:

```
foreach $field (0..@data-1){
     $headers{$headlist[$field]}=@data[$field];

($search1 = $searchfield) =~ tr/A-Z/a-z/;
($search2 = $headlist[$field] ) =~ tr/A-Z/a-z/;
($search3 = $searchvalue)=~tr/A-Z/a-z/;
($search4 = $headers{$headlist[$field]})=~tr/A-Z/a-z/;

if ( (index($search2,$search1) != -1) &&
(index($search4,$search3) != -1) ) {
       $found=1;
       }
}
```

In the middle of this section are four lines where we do the translations. This demonstrates a special aspect of the `tr` function. We can do a translation as we are assigning one variable to another. This is useful because the original strings are left unchanged. We must change the statement with the `index` function and make comparisons to reflect the changes in the variables.

So at this point, we have created an interface in which we can access a "database" and search for specific values.

When writing conditional statements, you must be sure of the condition you are testing. Truth, like many other things, is in the eye of the beholder. In this case, it is the `perl` interpreter that is beholding your concept of true. It may not always be what you expect. In general, you can say that a value is true unless it is the null string ("), the number zero (0), or the literary string zero ("0").

One important feature of `perl` is the comparison operators. Unlike C, there are different operators for numeric comparison and for string comparison. They're all easy to remember and you have certainly seen both sets before, but keep in mind that they are different. Table 4.7 contains a list of the `perl` comparison operators and Table 4.8 contains a list of `perl` operations.

Table 4.7: `perl` **Comparison Operators**

Numeric	String	Comparison
==	eq	equal to
!=	ne	not equal to
>	gt	greater than
<	lt	less than
>=	ge	greater than or equal to
<=	le	less than or equal to
<=>	cmp	equal to and sign is returned (0 - strings equal, 1 - first string less, -1 - first string greater)

Another important aspect that you need to keep in mind is that there is really no such thing as a numeric variable. Well, sort of. `perl` is capable of distinguishing between the two without you interfering. If a variable is used in a context where it can only be a string, then that's they way `perl` will interpret it–as a string.

Let's take two variables: `$a=2` and `$b=10`. As you might expect, the expression `$a < $b` evaluates to true because we are using the numeric comparison operator <. However, if the expression were `$a lt $b`, it would evaluate to false. This is because the string "10" comes before "2" lexigraphically (it comes first alphabetically).

Besides simply translating sets of letters, `perl` can also do substitution. To show you this, I am going to show you another neat trick of `perl`. Having been designed as a text and file processing language, it is very common to read in a number of lines of data and processing them all in turn. We can tell `perl` that it should assume we want to read in lines although we don't explicitly say so. Let's take a script that we call `fix.pl`. This script looks like this:

```
s/James/JAMES/g;
s/Eddings/EDDINGS/g;
```

This syntax is the same as you would find in `sed`; however, `perl` has a much larger set of regular expressions. Trying to run this as a script by itself will generate an error; instead, we run it like this:

```
perl -p fix.pl bookdata.pl
```

Table 4.8: `perl` **Operations**

Example Assignment	Function	Result
`$x = $y`	Assignment	Assign the value of $b to $a
`$x +=$y`	Addition	Add the value of $b to $a
`$x -=$y`	Subtraction	Subtract the value of $b from $a
`$x .=$y`	Append	Append string $y onto $x
String Operations		
`index($x,$y)`	Index	Delivers offset of string $y in string $x
`substr($x,$y,$len)`	Substring	Delivers substring on $x, starting at $y of length $len
`$x.$y`	Concatenation	$x and $y considered a single string, but each remains unchanged
`$x x $y`	Repetition	String $x is repeated $y times
Pattern Matching		
`$var =~ /pattern/`	Match	True if $var contains "pattern"
`$var =~ s/par/repl/`	Substitution	Substitutes "repl" for "pat"
`$var =~ tr/a=z/A-Z/`	Translation	Translate lowercase to uppercase
Math Operations		
`$x + $y`		Sum of $x and $y
`$x - $y`		Difference of $x and $y
`$x * $y`		Product of $x and $y
`$x/$y`		Sum of $x and $y
`$x % $y`		Sum of $x and $y
`$x ** $y`		Sum of $x and $y
`$x++, ++$x`		Sum of $x and $y
`$x--, --$x`		Sum of $x and $y
Logic Operation		
`$x && $y`	logical AND	True if both $x and $y are true
`$x || $y`	logical OR	True if either $x or $y is true
`!$ $x`	logical NOT	True if $x is *not* true

The `-p` option tells `perl` to put a wrapper around your script. Therefore, our script would behave as though we had written it like this:

```
while (<>) {
s/James/JAMES/g;
s/Eddings/EDDINGS/g;
} continue {
      print;
}
```

This would read each line from a file specified on the command line, carry out the substitution, and then print out each line, changed or not. We could also take advantage of the ability to specify the interpreter with `#!`. The script would then look like

```
#!/usr/bin/perl -p
s/James/JAMES/g;
s/Eddings/EDDINGS/g;
```

Another command line option is `-i`. This stands for "in-place," and with it you can edit files "in-place." In the example above, the changed lines would be output to the screen and we would have to redirect them to a file ourselves. The `-i` option takes an argument, which indicates the extension you want for the old version of the file. So, to use the option, we would change the first line, like this:

```
#!/usr/bin/perl -pi.old
```

With `perl`, you can also make your own subroutines. These subroutines can be written to return values, so that you have functions as well. Subroutines are first defined with the sub keyword and are called using `&`. For example:

```
#!/usr/bin/perl
sub usage {
print "Invalid arguments: @ARGV\n";
print "Usage: $0 [-t] filename\n";
}
if ( @ARGV < 1 || @ARGV > 2 ) {
      &usage;
}
```

This says that if the number of arguments from the command line `@ARGV` is less than 1 or greater than 2, we call the subroutine `usage`, which prints out a usage message.

To create a function, we first create a subroutine. When we call the subroutine, we call it as part of an expression. The value returned by the subroutine/function is the value of the *last* expression evaluated.

Let's create a function that prompts you for a yes/no response:

```
#!/usr/bin/perl
if (&getyn("Do you *really* want to remove all the
files in this directory? ")
      eq "y\n" )
{
      print  "Don't be silly!\n"
```

```
}

sub getyn{
print @_;
$response = (<STDIN>);
}
```

This is a very simple example. In the subroutine `getyn`, we output everything that is passed to the subroutine. This serves as a prompt. We then assign the line we get from `stdin` to the variable `$response`. Because this is the last expression inside the subroutine to be evaluated, this is the value that is returned to the calling statement.

If we enter "y" (which would include the new line from the Enter key), the calling `if` statement passes the actual prompt as an argument to the subroutine. The `getyn` subroutine could then be used in other circumstances. As mentioned, the value returned includes the new line; therefore, we must check for "y\n." This is *not* "y" or "n," but rather "y#" followed by a newline.

Alternatively, we could check the response inside the subroutine. In other words, we could have added the line

```
$response =~ /^y/i;
```

We addressed the =~ characters earlier in connection with the `tr` function. Here as well, the variable on the left-hand side is replaced by the "evaluation" of the right. In this case, we use a pattern-matching construct: `/^y/i`. This has the same behavior as `sed`, where we are looking for a `y` at the beginning of the line. The trailing `i` simply says to ignore the case. If the first character begins with a `y` or `Y`, the left-hand side (`$response`) is assigned the value 1; if not, it becomes a null string.

We now change the calling statement and simply leave off the comparison to "y\n". Because the return value of the subroutine is the value of the last expression evaluated, the value returned now is either "1" or "." Therefore, we don't have to do any kind of comparison, as the if statement will react according to the return value.

I wish I could go on. I haven't even hit on a quarter of what `perl` can do. Unfortunately, like the sections on `sed` and `awk`, more details are beyond the scope of this book. Instead, I want to refer you to a few other sources. First, there are two books from O'Reilly and Associates. The first is *Learning* `perl` by Randal Schwartz. This is a tutorial. The other is *Programming* `perl` by Larry Wall and Randal Schwartz. If you are familiar with other UNIX scripting languages, I feel you would be better served by getting the second book.

The next suggestion I have is that you get the `perl` CD-ROM from Walnut Creek CD-ROM (*www.cdrom.com*). This is loaded with hundreds of megabytes of `perl` code and the April 1996 version, which I used, contains the source code for `perl4` (4.036) and `perl5` (5.000m). In many cases, I like this approach better because I can see how to do the things I need to do. Books are useful to get the basics and reminders of syntax, options, etc. However, seeing someone else's code shows me how to do it.

Another good CD-ROM is the Mother of `PERL` CD from InfoMagic (*www.infomagic.com*). It, too, is loaded with hundreds of megabytes of `perl` scripts and information.

There are a lot of places to find sample scripts while you are waiting for the CD to arrive. One place is the Computers and Internet: Programming Languages: `Perl` hierarchy at Yahoo. (`www.yahoo.com`). You can use this as a springboard to many sites that not only have information on `perl` but data on using `perl` on the Web (e.g., in CGI scripts).

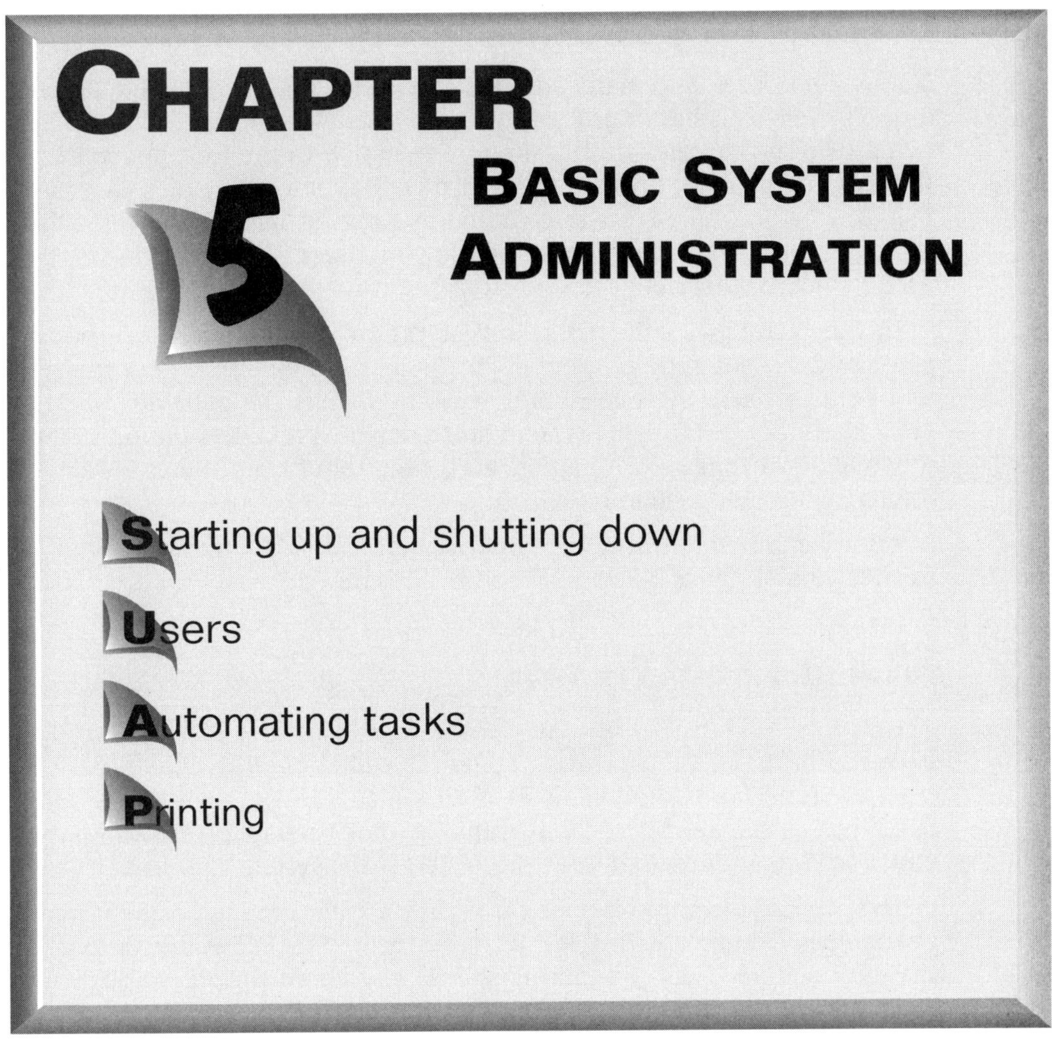

It's difficult to put together a simple answer when I'm asked about the job of a system administrator. Every aspect of the system can fall within the realm of a system administrator. Entire books have been written about just the software side, and for most system administrators, hardware, networks, and even programming fall into their laps.

In this chapter, we are just going to go through the basics. We won't necessarily be talking about individual steps or processes the administrator goes through, but rather about functional *areas*. With this, I hope to be able to give you enough background to use the programs and utilities that the system provides for you.

5.1 Starting and Stopping the System

Almost every user, and many administrators, never see what is happening as the system as is booting. Those who do often are not sure what is happening. From the time you flip the power switch to the time you get that first `login:` prompt, dozens of things must happen, many of which happen long before the system knows that its running Linux. Knowing what is happening as the system boots and in what order it is happening is very useful when your system does not start the way it should.

In this chapter, I will first talk about starting your system. Although you can get it going by flipping on the power switch and letting the system boot by itself, there are many ways to change the behavior of your system as it boots. How the system boots depends on the situation. As we move along through the chapter, we'll talk about the different ways to influence how the system boots.

After we talk about how to start your system, we'll look at a few ways to alter your system's behavior when it shuts down.

5.1.1 The Boot Process

The process of turning on your computer and having it jump through hoops to bring up the operating system is called *booting*, which derives from the term *bootstrapping*. This is an allusion to the idea that a computer pulls itself up by its bootstraps, in that smaller pieces of simple code start larger, more complex pieces to get the system running.

The process a computer goes through is similar among different computer types, whether it is a PC, Macintosh, or SPARC Workstation. In the next section, I will be talking specifically about the PC, though the concepts are still valid for other machines.

The first thing that happens is the Power-On Self-Test (POST). Here the hardware checks itself to see that things are all right. It compares the hardware settings in the CMOS (Complementary Metal Oxide Semiconductor) to what is physically on the system. Some errors, like the floppy types not matching, are annoying, but your system still can boot. Others, like the lack of a video card, can keep the system from continuing. Often, there is nothing to indicate what the problem is, except for a few little "beeps."

Once the POST is completed, the hardware jumps to a specific, predefined location in RAM. The instructions located here are relatively simple and basically tell the hardware to go look for a boot device. Depending on how your CMOS is configured, the hardware first checks your floppy and then your hard disk.

When a boot device is found (let's assume that it's a hard disk), the hardware is told to go to the 0th (first) sector (cylinder 0, head 0, sector

0), then load and execute the instructions there. This is the master boot record, or MBR for you DOS-heads (sometimes also called the master boot block.) This code is small enough to fit into one block but is intelligent enough to read the partition table (located just past the master boot block) and find the active partition. Once it finds the active partition, it begins to read and execute the instructions contained within the first block.

It is at this point that viruses can affect/infect Linux systems. The master boot block is the same format for essentially all PC-based operating systems. All the master boot block does is find and execute code at the beginning of the active partition, or it could contain code that tells it to go to the very last sector of the hard disk and execute the code there. If that last sector contains code that tells the system to find and execute code at the beginning of the active partition, you would never know anything was wrong.

Let's assume that the instructions at the very end of the disk are larger than a single 512-byte sector. If the instructions took up a couple of kilobytes, you could get some fairly complicated code. Because it is at the end of the disk, you would probably never know it was there. What if that code checked the date in the CMOS and, if the day of the week was Friday and the day of the month was 13, it would erase the first few kilobytes of your hard disk? If that were the case, then your system would be infected with the Friday the 13th virus, and you could no longer boot your hard disk.

Viruses that behave in this way are called "boot viruses," as they affect the master boot block and can only damage your system if this is the disk from which you are booting. These kinds of viruses can affect all PC-based systems. Some computers will allow you to configure the CMOS (more on that later) so that you cannot write to the master boot block. Although this is a good safeguard against older viruses, the newer ones can change the CMOS to allow writing to the master boot block. So, just because you have enabled this feature does not mean your system is safe. However, I must point out that boot viruses can only affect Linux systems if you boot from an infected disk. This usually will be a floppy, more than likely a DOS floppy. Therefore, you need to be especially careful when booting from floppies.

Now back to our story...

As I mentioned, the code in the master boot block finds the active partition and begins executing the code there. On an MS-DOS system, these are the `IO.SYS` and `MSDOS.SYS` files. On an Linux system, this is often the `lilo` or Linux loader "program." Although `IO.SYS` and `MSDOS.SYS` are "real" files that you can look at and even remove if you want to, the lilo program is not. The `lilo` program is part of the partition, but not part of the file system; therefore, it is not a "real" file.

Often, `lilo` is installed in the master boot block of the hard disk itself. Therefore, it will be the first code to run when your system is booted. In this case, `lilo` can be used to start other operating systems. On one machine, I have `lilo` start either Windows 95 or one of two different versions of Linux.

In other cases, `lilo` is installed in the boot sector of a given partition. In this case, it is referred to as a "secondary" boot loader and is used just to load the Linux installed on that partition. This is useful if you have another operating system such as OS/2 or Windows NT and you use the boot software from that OS to load any others. However, neither of these was designed with Linux in mind. There, I usually have `lilo` loaded in the boot sector and have it do all the work.

You can configure `lilo` with a wide range of options. Not only can you boot with different operating systems, but with Linux you can boot different versions of the kernel as well as use different root file systems. This is useful if you are a developer because you can have multiple versions of the kernel on a single system. You can then boot them and test your product in different environments.

In addition, I always have three copies of my kernel on the system and have configured `lilo` to be able to boot any one of them. The first copy is the current kernel I am using. When I rebuild a new kernel and install it, it gets copied to `/vmlinuz.old`, which is the second kernel I can access. I then have a copy called `/vmlinuz.orig`, which is the original kernel from when I installed that particular release. This, at least, contains the drivers necessary to boot and access my hard disk and CD-ROM. If I can get that far, I can reinstall what I need to.

During the course of this writing this book, I often had more than one distribution of Linux installed on my system. It was very useful to see whether the application software provided with one release was compatible with the kernel from a different distribution. Using various options to `lilo`, I could boot one kernel but use the root file system from a different version. This was also useful on at least one occasion when I had one version that didn't have the correct drivers in the kernel on the hard disk and I couldn't even boot it.

Once your system boots, you will see the kernel being loaded and started. As it is loaded and begins to execute, you will see screens of information flash past. For the uninitiated, this is overwhelming, but after you take a closer look at it, most of the information is very straightforward.

Once you're booted, you can see this information in the file `/usr/adm/messages`. Depending on your system, this file might be in `/var/adm` or even `/var/logs`. In the messages file, as well as during the boot process, you'll see several types of information that the system logging daemon (syslogd) is writing. The syslogd daemon usually continues logging as the system is running, although you can turn it off if you want.

The general format for the entries is:

```
time hostname program: message
```

where time is the system time when the message is generated, hostname is the host that generated the message, program is the program that generated the message, and message is the text of the message. For example, a message from the kernel might look like this:

```
May 13 11:34:23 localhost kernel: ide0: do_ide_reset:
success
```

As the system is booting, all you see are the messages themselves and not the other information. Most of what you see as the system boots are messages from kernel, with a few other things, so you would see this message just as

```
ide0: do_ide_reset: success
```

Much of the information that the syslogd daemon writes comes from device drivers that perform any initialization routines. If you have hardware problems on your system, this is *very* useful information. One example I encountered was with two pieces of hardware that were both software-configurable. However, in both cases, the software wanted to configure them as the same IRQ. I could then change the source code and recompile so that one assigned a different IRQ.

You will also notice the kernel checking the existing hardware for specific capability, such as whether an FPU is present, whether the CPU has the hlt (halt) instruction, and so on.

What is logged and where it is logged is based on the /etc/syslog.conf file. Each entry is broken down into facility.priority, where facility is the part of the system such as the kernel or printer spooler and security and priority indicate the severity of the message. The facility.priority ranges from none, when no messages are logged, to emerg, which represents very significant events like kernel panics. Messages are generally logged to one file or another, though emergency messages should be displayed to everyone (usually done by default). In general, the log files are under /usr/adm or /var/adm. See the syslog.conf man-page for details.

One last thing that the kernel does is start the init process, which reads the /etc/inittab file. It looks for any entry that should be run when the system is initializing (the entry has a sysinit in the third field) and then executes the corresponding command. (I'll get into details about different run-levels and these entries shortly.)

The first thing init runs out of the inittab is the script /etc/rc.d/rc.sysinit , which is similar to the bcheckrc script on other systems. As with everything else under /etc/rc.d, this is a shell-script, so you can take a look at it if you want.

Among the myriad of things done here are checking and mounting file systems, removing old lock and PID files, and enabling the swap space.

Note that if the file system check notes some serious problems, the rc.sysinit will stop and bring you to a shell prompt, where you can attempt to clean up by hand. Once you exit this shell, the next command to be executed (aside from an echo) is a reboot. This is done to ensure the validity of the file systems.

Next, init looks through inittab for the line with initdefault in the third field. The initdefault entry tells the system what run-level to enter initially, normally run-level 3.Other systems have the default run-level 1 to bring you into single-user or maintenance mode. Here you can perform certain actions without worrying users or too many other things going on your system. (Note: You can keep users out simply by creating the file /etc/nologin. See the nologin man-page for details.)

What kind of actions can you perform here? One action with the most impact is adding new or updating software. Often, new software will effect old software in such a way that it is better not to have other users on the system. In such cases, the installation procedures for that software should keep you from installing unless you are in maintenance mode.

This is also a good place to configure hardware that you added or otherwise change the kernel. Although these actions rarely impact users, you will have to do a kernel rebuild. This takes up a lot of system resources and degrades overall performance. Plus, you need to reboot after doing a kernel rebuild and it takes longer to reboot from run-level 3 than from run-level 1.

If the changes you made do not require you to rebuild the kernel (say, adding new software), you can go directly from single-user to multi-user mode by running init 3. The argument to init is simply the run level you want to go into, which, for most purposes, is run-level 3. However, to shut down the system, you could bring the system to run-level 0 or 6. (See the init man-page for more details.)

Init looks for any entry that has a 3 in the second field. This 3 corresponds to the run-level where we currently are. Run-level 3 is the same as multi-user mode.

Within the inittab, there is a line for every run level that starts the script /etc/rc.d/rc, passing the run level as an argument. The /etc/rc.d/rc script, after a little housekeeping, then starts the scripts for that run level. For each run level, there is a directory underneath `/etc/rc.d`, such as `rc3.d`, which contains the scripts that will be run for that run level.

In these directories, you may find two sets of scripts. The scripts beginning with K are the kill scripts, which are used to shutdown/stop a particular subsystem. The S scripts are the start scripts. Note that the kill and start scripts are links to the files in `/etc/rc.d/init.d`. If there are K and S scripts with the same number, these are both linked to the same file.

This is done because the scripts are started with an argument of either `start` or `stop`. The script itself then changes its behavior based on whether you told it to start or stop. Naming them something (slightly) different allows us to start only the K scripts if we want to shut things down and only the S script when we start things.

When the system changes to a particular run level, the first scripts that are started are the K scripts. This stops any of the processes that should not be running in that level. Next, the S scripts are run to start the processes that should be running.

Let's look at an example. Run-level 1 is *almost* the same as run-level 2. The only difference is that in run-level 2, NFS is not running. If you were to change from run-level 3 to run-level 2, NFS would go down. In run-level 1 (maintenance mode), almost everything is stopped.

5.1.2 Run Levels

Most users are only familiar with two run states or run levels. The one that is most commonly experienced is what is referred to a multiuser mode. This is where logins are enabled on terminals when the network is running and the system is behaving "normally." The other run level is system maintenance or single-user mode, when only a single user is on the system (root), probably doing some kind of maintenance tasks.

On every system that I have encountered, Linux will automatically boot into run-level 3. This is the normal operating mode. To get to a lower run level (for example, to do system maintenance), the system administrator must switch levels manually.

It is generally said that the "system" is in a particular run-level. However, it is more accurate to say that the `init` process is in a particular run level, because `init` determines what other processes are started at each run-level.

In addition to the run levels most of us are familiar with, there are several others that the system can run in. Despite this fact, few of them are hardly ever used. For more details on what these run levels are, take a look at the `init` man-page.

The system administrator can change to a particular run level by using that run level as the argument to `init`. For example, running `init 2` would change the system to run-level 2. To determine what processes to start in each run level, `init` reads the `/etc/inittab` file. This is defined by the second field in the `/etc/inittab` file. Init reads this file and executes each program defined for that run level in order. When the system boots, it decides what run level to go into based on the `initdefault` entry in `/etc/inittab`.

The fields in the `inittab` file are

- id — unique identity for that entry
- rstate — run level in which the entry will be processed
- action — tells init how to treat the process specifically
- process — what process will be started

One thing I need to point out is that the entries in `inittab` are not run *exactly* according to the order in which they appear. If you are entering a run level other than S for the first time since boot-up, `init` will first execute those entries with a boot or `bootwait` in the *third* column. These are those processes that should be started before users are allowed access to the system, such as checking then mounting the status of the file systems.

In run-level 3, the `/etc/getty` process is started on the terminals specified. The getty process gives you your `login:` prompt. When you have entered your logname for the first time, `getty` starts the `login` process, which asks you for your password. If your password is incorrect, you are prompted to input your logname again. If your password is correct, then the system starts your "login shell." Note that what gets started may not be a shell at all, but some other program. The term "login shell" is the generic term for whatever program is started when you login. This is defined by the *last* field of the corresponding entry in `/etc/passwd`.

Keep in mind that you can move in either direction, that is, from a lower to higher run level or from a higher to lower run level without having to first reboot. `init` will read the `inittab` and start or stop the necessary processes. If a particular process is not defined at a particular run level, then `init` will kill it. For example, assume you are in run-level 3 and switch to run-level 1. Many of the processes defined do not have a 1 in the second field. Therefore, when you switch to run-level 1, those processes and all their children will be stopped.

If we look at the scripts in `rc1.d`, we see there all the scripts are kill scripts, with the exception of one start script. It is this start script that actually kills all the processes. It does `exec init -t1 S`, which brings the system into maintenance mode in one (`-t1`) minute.

To shutdown the system immediately, you could run

```
init 0
```

which will bring the system immediately into run-level 0. As with run-level 1, there is only one start script for run-level 0. It is this script that kills all the processes, unmounts all the file systems, turns off swap, and brings the system down.

After it has started the necessary process from `inittab`, `init` just waits. When one of its "descendants" dies (a child process of a child process of a child process, etc., of `init` started by a process that `init` started), `init` rereads the `inittab` to see what should be done. If, for example, there is a `respawn` entry in the third field, `init` will start the specified process again. This is why when you log out, you immediately get a new `login:` prompt.

Because `init` just waits for processes to die, you cannot simply add an entry to `inittab` and expect the process to start up. You have tell `init` to reread the `inittab`. However, you can *force* `init` to reread the `inittab` by running `init` (or `telinit`) `Q`. This is the only time you should use the `init` program yourself.

In addition to the run levels we discussed here, several more are possible. Unfortunately, this is one of those cases in which I have to put off further discussion because these other run levels are rarely, if ever, used. If you're curious, take a look at the `init`(8) man-page.

5.1.3 Stopping the System

For those of you who hadn't noticed, Linux isn't like DOS. Despite the superficial similarity at the command prompt, they have little in common. One very important difference is the way you stop the system.

In DOS, you are completely omnipotent. You know everything that's going on. You have complete control over everything. If you decide that you've had enough and flip the power switch, you are the only one doing so will effect. However, with dozens of people working on an Linux system and dozens more using its resources, simply turning off the machine is not something you want to do. Despite the fact that you will annoy quite a few people, it can cause damage to your system, depending on exactly what was happening when you killed the power. (Okay, you could also create problems with a DOS system, but with only one person, the chances are less likely.)

On a multiuser system like Linux, many different things are going on. You many not see any disk activity, but the system may still have things its buffers are waiting for the chance to write to the hard disk. If you turn off the power before this data is written, what is on the hard disk may be inconsistent.

Normally, pressing `Ctrl-Alt-Del` *will* reboot your system. You can prevent this by creating the file `/etc/shutdown.allow`, which contains a list (one entry per line) of users. If this file exists, the system will first check whether one of the users listed in `shutdown.allow` is logged in on the system console. If none are, you see the message

```
shutdown: no authorized users logged in.
```

To make sure that things are stopped safely, you need to shut down your system "properly." What is considered proper can be a couple of things, depending on the circumstances. Linux provides several tools to stop the system and allows you to decide what is proper for your particular circumstance. Flipping the power switch is *not* shutting down properly.

The first two tools are actually two links to the same file: `/sbin/halt` and `/sbin/reboot`. If either of these is called and the system is not in run-level 0 or 6, then `/sbin/shutdown` is called instead.

Running `shutdown` is really the safest way of bringing your system down, although you *could* get away with running `init 0`. This would bring the system down, but would not give the users any warning. Shutdown can be configured to give the users enough time to stop what they are working on and save all of their data.

Using the `shutdown` command, you have the ability not only to warn your users that the system is going down but also to give them the chance to finish up what they were doing. For example, if you were going to halt the system in 30 minutes to do maintenance, the command might look like this:

```
shutdown -h +30 "System going down for maintenance.
Back up after lunch."
```

This message will appear on everyone's screen immediately, then at increasing intervals, until the system finally goes down.

If you have rebuilt your kernel or made other changes that require you to reboot your system, you can use shutdown as well, by using the `-r` option.

5.2 Users and User Accounts

Unlike most other dialects of UNIX, it is not uncommon to find a Linux system that does not have users on it. As the number of Linux applications grows, businesses begin adding Linux machines to server users. To run a Linux system effectively, the administrator must know how to configure the system to work with users.

Although there are "system" users that have the same characteristics as human users, these are not what we normally think of when we talk about users. For us, a user is a person who interacts with the system, from logging in and getting to a shell prompt to accessing files on a remote system by using various networking programs.

Users are what computers are made for. One key advantage that UNIX has over operating systems like DOS and all flavors of Windows is that it was designed to run with multiple users, all accessing the same system and resources. It is important that the system be able not only to distinguish between different users but also make decisions about what each user can and cannot do.

In this chapter, we are going to talk about what makes a user. We'll look at what the operating system sees as a user; in other words, what files, values and data goes into the system's interpretation of a user. We'll also talk about what a user can and cannot do, plus the mechanisms that are in place to prevent a user from doing something he or she shouldn't. This is the whole idea behind system security.

5.3 User Accounts

Users gain access to the system only after the system administrator has created *user accounts* for them. These accounts are more than just a user name and password; they also define the environment the user works under, including the level of access he or she has.

Users are added to Linux systems in one of two ways. You could create the necessary entries in the appropriate file, create the directories, and copy the start-up files manually. Or, you could use the `adduser` command, which does that for you.

Adding a user to a Linux system is often referred to as "creating a user" or "creating a user account." The terms "user" and "user account" are often interchanged in different contexts. For the most part, the term "user" is used for the person actually working on the system and "user account" is used to refer to the files and programs that create the user's environment when he or she logs in. However, these two phrases can be interchanged and people will know what you are referring to.

When an account is created, a shell is assigned along with the default configuration files that go with that shell. Users are also assigned a home directory, which is their default directory when they login, usually in the form `/home/<username>`. Note that the parent of the user's home directories may be different.

When user accounts are created, each user is assigned a User Name (login name or logname), which is associated with a User ID (UID). Each is assigned to at least one group, with one group designated as their *login group*. Each group has an associated Group ID (GID). The UID is numbers used to identify the user. The GID is a number used to identify the login group of that user. Both are used to keep track of that user and determine what files he or she can access.

In general, programs and commands that interact with us humans report information about the user by logname or group name. However, most identification from the operating systems point of view is done through the UID and GID. The UID is associated with the user's logname. The GID is associated with the user's login group. In general, the group a user is a part of is only used for determining access to files.

If you look on your system, you will see that everyone can read both of these files. Years ago, my first reaction was that this was a security problem, but when I was told what this was all about, I realized that this was necessary. I was also concerned that the password be accessible, even in encrypted format. Because I know what my password is, I can compare my password to the encrypted version and figure out the encryption mechanism, right? Nope! It's not that easy.

At the beginning of each encrypted password is a seed. Using this seed, the system creates the encrypted version. When you login, the system takes the seed from the encrypted password and encrypts the password that you input. If this matches the encrypted password, you are allowed in.

Nowhere on the system is the unencrypted password stored, nor are any of the utilities or commands generate it.

Next, let's talk about the need to be able to access this information. Remember that the operating system knows only about numbers. When we talked about operating system basics, I mentioned that the information about the owner and group of a file was stored as a number in the inode. However, when you do a long listing of a file (`ls -l`), you don't see the number, but rather, a name. For example, if we do a long listing of `/bin/mkdir`, we get:

```
-rwxr-xr-x  1 root   root   7593 Feb 25  1996 /bin/mkdir
```

The entries are:

```
permissions links owner group size date filename
```

Here we see that the owner and group of the file is root. Because the owner and group are stored as numerical values in the inode table, the system *must* be translating this information before it displays it on the screen. Where does it get the translation? From the `/etc/passwd` and `/`

etc/group files. You can see what the "untranslated" values are by entering `ls -ln /bin/mkdir`, which gives us

```
-rwxr-xr-x   1 0     0        7593 Feb 25  1996 /bin/mkdir
```

If we look in /etc/passwd, we see that the 0 is the UID for root, and if we look in /etc/group, we see that 0 is also the GID for the group root, which are the numbers we got above. If the /etc/passwd and /etc/group files were not readable by everyone, then no translation could be made like this without some major changes to most of the system commands and utilities.

On a number of occasions, I have talked to customers who claimed to have experienced corruption when transferring files from one system to another. Sometimes it's with cpio, sometimes it's tar. In every case, files have arrived on the destination machine and have had either "incorrect" owners or groups and sometimes both. Sometimes, the "corruption" is so bad that there are no names for the owner and group, just numbers.

Numbers, you say? Isn't that how the system stores the owner and group information for the files? Exactly. What does it use to make the translation from these numbers to the names that we normally see? As I mentioned, it uses /etc/passwd and /etc/group. When you transfer files from one system to another, the only owner information that is transferred are the numbers. When the file arrives on the destination machine, weird things can happen. Let's look at an example.

At work, my user name was jimmo and I had UID 12709. All my files were stored with 12709 in the owner field of the inode. Let's say that I create a user on my machine at home, also named jimmo. Because there are far fewer users on my system at home than at work, jimmo ended up with UID 500. When I transferred files from work to home, the owner of all "my" files was 12709. That is, where there normally is a name when I do a long listing, there was the number 12709, not jimmo.

The reason for this is that the owner of the file is stored as a number in the inode. When I copied the files from my system at work, certain information from the inode was copied along with the file, including the owner. *Not* the user's name, but the numerical value in the inode. When the files were listed on the new system, there was no user with UID 12709, and therefore no translation could be made from the number to the name. The only thing that could be done was to display the number.

This makes sense because what if there were no user jimmo on the other system? What value should be displayed in this field? At least this way there is some value and you have a small clue as to what is going on.

To keep things straight, I had to do one of two things. Either I create a shell-script that changed the owner on all my files when I transferred them or I figure out some way to give jimmo UID 12709 on my system at home. So I decided to give jimmo UID 12709.

Here, too, there are two ways I can go about it. I could create 12208 users on my system so the 12709th would be jimmo. (Why 12208? By default, the system starts with a UID 500 for normal users.) This bothered me though, because I would have to remove the user jimmo with UID 500 then create it again. I felt that this would be a waste of time.

The other alternative was to change the system files. Now, there is nothing that Linux provides that would do that. I could change many aspects of the user jimmo; however, the UID was not one of them. After careful consideration, I realized that there was a tool that Linux provided to make the changes: vi. Because this information is kept in simple text files, you can use a text editor to change them. After reading the remainder of this chapter, you should have the necessary information to make the change yourself.

One thing I would like to point out is that vi is not actually the tool you should use. Although you could use it, something could happen while you are editing the file and your password file could get trashed. Linux provides you with a tool (that's actually available on many systems) specifically designed to edit the password file: vipw (for "vi password").

What vipw does is create a copy of the password file, which is what you actually edit. When you are finished editing, vipw replaces the /etc/passwd with that copy. Should the system go down while you are editing the file, the potential for problems is minimized. Note that despite its name, the editor that is called is defined by your EDITOR environment variable.

On many systems, the adduser program is used to add users (what else?). Note that when you create a user, you are assigned a value for the UID, usually one number higher than the previously assigned UID. Because adduser is a shell-script, you can change the algorithm used, if you really want to.

When the first customer called with the same situation, I could immediately tell him why it was happening, how to correct it, and assure him that it worked.

You can also change a user's group if you want. Remember, however, that all this does is change the GID for that user in /etc/passwd. Nothing else! Therefore, all files that were created before you make the change will still have the old group.

You can change your UID while you are working by using the su command. What does su stand for? Well, that's a good question. I have seen several different translations in books and from people on the Internet. I say that it means "switch UID," as that's what it does. However, other possibilities include "switch users" and "super-user." This command sets your UID to a new one. The syntax is

```
su <user_name>
```

where <user_name> is the logname of the user whose UID you want to use. After running the command, you have a UID of that user.

The shortcoming with this is that all that is changed is the UID and GID; you still have the environment of the original user. If you want the system to "pretend" as though you had actually logged in, include a dash (-). The command would then be

```
su - <user_name>
```

What is actually happening is that you are running a new shell as that user. (Check the ps output to see that this is a new process.) Therefore, to switch back, you don't need to use su again, but just exit that shell.

We need to remember that a shell is the primary means by which users gain access to the system. Once they do gain access, their ability to move around the system (in terms of reading files or executing programs) depends on a two things: permissions and privileges.

In general, there is no need to switch groups. A user can be listed in more than one group in /etc/group and the system will grant access to files and directories accordingly.

Permissions are something that most people are familiar with if they have ever worked on an Linux (or similar) system before. Based on what has been granted, different users have different access to files, programs, and directories. You can find out what permissions a particular file has by doing a long listing of it. The permissions are represented by the first 10 characters on the line. This is something that we covered in a fair bit of detail in the section on shell basics, so there is no need to repeat it here.

Removing users is fairly straightforward. Unfortunately, I haven't found a utility that will remove them as simply as you can create them. Therefore, you will need to do it manually. The simplest way is to use vipw to remove the user's entry from /etc/passwd and to remove its home directory and mailbox.

However, this is not necessarily the best approach. I have worked in companies where once a user was created, it was never removed. This provides a certain level of accountability.

Remember that the owner is simply a number in the inode table. Converting this number to a name is done through the entry in /etc/passwd. If that entry is gone, there can be no conversion. If a new user were to get the UID of an old, removed user, it may suddenly have access to a file that it shouldn't (i.e., a file owned by the old user that it now owns).

Even if no new users get that UID, what do you do if you find an "unowned" file on your system, that is, one with just a number as the owner and without associated entry in `/etc/passwd`? What you do is up to your company, but I think it is safer to "retire" that user.

You could remove its home directory and mailbox. However, change its password to something like `NOLOGIN`. This password is shorter than an encrypted password, so it is *impossible* that any input password will encrypt to this. Then change its login shell to something like `/bin/true`. This closes one more door. By making it `/bin/true`, no error message will be generated to give a potential hacker a clue that there is "something" about this account. Alternatively, you could replace the login shell with a message to say that the account has been disabled and the owner should report to have it re-activated. This helps to dissuade would-be hackers.

Another useful tool for thwarting hackers is password shadowing. With this, the encrypted password is not kept in `/etc/passwd`, but rather `/etc/shadow`. This is useful when someone decides to steal your password file. Why is this a problem? I will get into details about it later, but let's say now that the password file could be used to crack passwords and gain access to the system.

Because you must have the `/etc/passwd` file word-readable to make translations from UID to user name, you cannot protect it simply by changing the permission. However, the `/etc/shadow` password, where the real password is stored, is not readable by regular users and therefore is less of a security risk. (I say "less" because if an intruder gets in as root, all bets are off).

Unfortunately, the shadow package is *not* standard with a lot of distributions, including the one on the accompanying CD-ROM. You can find the current version at `sunsite.unc.edu/pub/Linux/system/Admin/shadow*`. However, you will find a `HOWTO` on the CD-ROM that goes into more detail about password shadowing and the shadow package.

5.3.1 Logging into the System

Users gain access to the system through "accounts." This is the first level of security. Although it is possible to configure applications that start directly on specific terminals, almost everyone has logged into an Linux system at least once. More that likely, if you are one of those people who never login, you never see a shell prompt and are probably not reading this book.

Figure 5.1: **The Login Process**

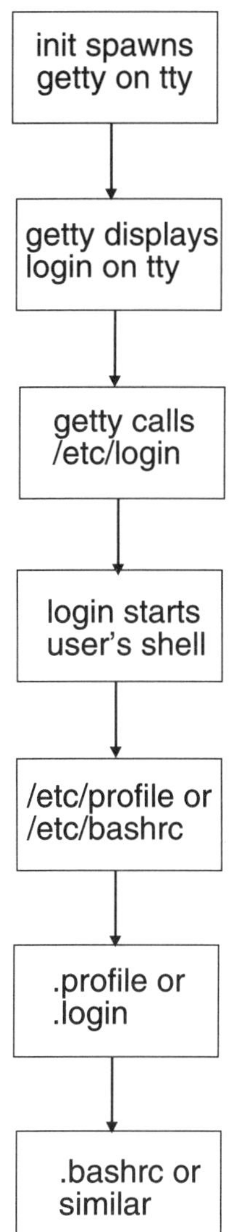
init spawns getty on tty
getty displays login on tty
getty calls /etc/login
login starts user's shell
/etc/profile or /etc/bashrc
.profile or .login
.bashrc or similar

Most Linux systems have a standard login. Figure 5.1 shows what the login process looks like. You see the name of the system, followed by a brief message (the contents of `/etc/issue`) and the login prompt, which usually consists of the system name and the word `login`. This is a text file, so you can edit it as you please. Because it is read dynamically, the changes will appear the next time some tries to log in. After the contents of `/etc/issue`, you see the login prompts, such as

```
jmohr!login:
```

When you log in, you are first asked your user name and your password. Having been identified and your password verified, you are allowed access to the system. This often means that the system starts a shell for you. However, many programs can be used in place of a shell.

One entry in the password file is your home directory, the directory that you have as your current directory when you log in. This is also the place to which the shell returns you if you enter `cd` with no arguments.

After determining your login shell and placing you in your home directory, the system will set up some systemwide defaults. If you have a Bourne or Bourne Again-shell, these are done through the `/etc/profile` file. If `bash` is your login shell, the system runs through the commands stored in the `.profile` in your home directory then the `.bashrc` file, provided they exist. If you have `sh`, then there is no equivalent for the `.bashrc` file. If you have a Z-shell, the system defaults are established in the `/etc/zprofile` file. The system then executes the commands in the `.zshrc` and `.zlogin` files in your home directory, provided they exist. See the appropriate man-page and the section on shell basics for more details.

During the login process, you are shown several pieces of information about the local system. Before the login prompt, you usually see the contents of the `/etc/issue` file, as I mentioned earlier. After your login is successful, you will normally see a message about the last login and the message of the day. The message of the day is the contents of the file `/etc/motd`.

In some cases, all of this information is bothersome. For example, many businesses have either menus that their users log into or applications that start from their users' `.profile` or `.login`. In some cases, the information is of little value.

In some cases, even knowing that this is an UNIX system could be a problem. There are many hackers in the world who would just love the chance to try to crack your security. By not even telling them what kind of system you have, you reduce the amount by which they are tempted. At least, that's one more piece of information that they need to figure out. Therefore, we need a way to disable these messages.

The two obvious ways are by using `/etc/issue` and `/etc/motd`. By default, both of these files contain information about your system. By either changing the contents or removing the files all together, you can eliminate that source of information.

The way is the `login:` prompt itself. Again, by default, this prompt contains the name of your system. This may not concern most system administrators; however, in cases where security is an issue, I might like to disable it. The prompt comes from the `/etc/gettydefs` file. The `gettydefs` file contains information the getty program uses when it starts the login program on a terminal. The more common lines in the `gettydefs` file contain an entry that looks like this:

```
@S login:
```

Take a look at the `login:` prompt and you will see that it also contains the literal string `login:` immediately following the name of the system. The name of the system comes from `@S`. By changing either of the parts (or both), you can change the appearance of your login prompt, even removing the name of the system, if you want.

The `getty`(1m) man-page contains a list of the different information that you can include with the `login:` prompt. If you are providing PPP services, I recommend that you do not use anything that changes in your login prompt, such as the date/time or the port name. This makes creating chat scripts difficult. (For more information on this, see the section on PPP.)

At this point, we are left with the last login messages. Unfortunately, these are not contained in files that are as easily removed as `/etc/motd` and `/etc/issue`. However, by *creating* a file, the file `.hushlogin` in your home directory, we can remove them. It has no contents; rather, the existence of this file is the key. You can create it simply by changing to a user's home directory (*yours*, if you are that user) and running

```
touch .hushlogin
```

Often administrators want to keep users' knowledge of the system as limited as possible. This is particularly important for systems with a high level of security in which users start applications and never see the shell prompt. One give-away to what kind of system you are on is the following line when you login:

```
Last login: ...
```

System administrators often call support asking for a way to turn this feature off. Fortunately, there is a way. This, too, is disabled by creating the `.hushlogin` file. Once this functionality is enabled, you can simplify things by having this file created every time a new user is created. This is done by simply adding the `.hushlogin` file to the `/etc/skel` directory. As with every other file in this directory, it will be copied to the user's home directory whenever a new user is created.

One thing to consider before you turn this feature off is that seeing when the last login was done may indicate a security problem. If you see that the last login was done at a time when you were not there, it may indicate that someone is trying to break into your account.

You can see who is currently logged in by running either the `who` or `w` command. These commands are kept in the file `utmp` in your system log directory (`/usr/adm`, `/var/log`, etc). Once the system reboots, this information is gone.

You can also see the history of recent logins by using the last command. This information is kept in `wtmp` in the system log directory. This command is kept between reboots and, depending on how active your system gets, I have seen this file grow to more than a megabyte. Therefore, it might not be a bad idea to truncate this file at regular intervals. (Note that some Linux distributions do this automatically.)

One way to limit security risks is to keep the root account from logging in from somewhere other than the system console. This is done by setting the appropriate terminals in `/etc/securetty`. If root tries to log into a terminal that is not listed here, it will be denied access. It is a good idea to list only terminals that are on the system console (`tty1`, `tty2`, etc.).

If you really need root access, you can use `telnet` from a regular account and then `su` to root. This then provides a record of who used `su`.

5.3.2 Terminals

Unless your Linux machine is an Internet server or gateway machine, there probably will be users on it. Users need to access the system somehow, either across a network using a remote terminal program like `telnet`, `rlogin.`, or accessing file systems using NFS, or they might log in directly to the system. This (probably) is done from a terminal and the system must be told how to behave with the specific terminal that you are using.

TERMINAL SETTINGS

Whenever you work with an application, what you see is governed by a couple of mechanisms. If you have a serial terminal, the flow of data is controlled by the serial line characteristics, including the baud rate, the number of data bits, parity, and so on. One aspect that is often forgotten or even unknown to many users is the terminal characteristics, which are used to control the physical appearance on the screen.

As I mentioned previously, the serial line characteristics are initially determined by the `gettydefs` file. The characteristics are often changed within the user's startup scripts (`.profile`, `.login`, etc.). In addition, you can change them yourself by using the `stty` command. Rather than jumping to changing them, let's take a look at what our current settings are, which we also do with the `stty` command. With no arguments, `stty` might give us something like this:

```
speed 38400 baud; line = 0;
-brkint ixoff -imaxbel
-iexten -echoctl
```

This is pretty straightforward. Settings that are Boolean values (on or off) are listed by themselves if they are on (`ixoff`) or have a minus sign in front if they are turned off (`-brkint`). Settings that can take on different values (like the baud rate) appear in two formats: one in which the value simply follows the setting name (`speed 38400 baud`) and one in which an equal sign is between them (`line=0`).

In general, if a setting has discrete values, like the baud rate, there is no equal sign. There is only a discrete number of baud rates you could have (i.e., there is no 2678 baud). If the `stty` setting is for something that could take on "any" value (like the interrupt key), then there is an equal sign. Normally, the interrupt key it's something like `Ctrl-C` or the `Delete` key. However, it could be the `f` key or the Down-Arrow or whatever.

This example shows the more "significant" terminal (`stty`) settings. The top line shows the input and output speed of this terminal, which is 38400. On the second line, we see that sending a break sends an interrupt signal (`-brkint`).

Setting these values is very straightforward. For Boolean settings (on or off), the syntax is simply

```
stty <setting>
```

to turn it on or

```
stty -<setting> (note the minus sign in front)
```

to turn it off.

For example, if I wished to turn on input stripping (in which the character is stripped to 7 bits), the command would look like this:

```
stty istrip
```

Settings that require a value have the following syntax:

```
stty <setting> <value>
```

So, to set the speed (baud rate) to 19200, the syntax would look like this:

```
stty speed 19200
```

To set the interrupt character to `Ctrl-`, we would enter

```
stty intr ^C
```

Note that ^c is not two separate characters. Instead, when you type it, hold down the Ctrl key and press "c." Here, the letter appears as capital although you pressed the lowercase letter.

If the default output does not show some characteristics, you can use the -a option to show all the characteristics. You might end up with output like this:

```
speed 38400 baud; rows 25; columns 80; line = 0;
intr = ^C; quit = ^\; erase = ^?; kill = ^U; eof = ^D; eol = <undef>;
eol2 = <undef>; start = ^Q; stop = ^S; susp = ^Z; rprnt = ^R; werase = ^W;
lnext = ^V; flush = ^O; min = 1; time = 0;
-parenb -parodd cs8 hupcl -cstopb cread -clocal -crtscts
-ignbrk -brkint -ignpar -parmrk -inpck -istrip -inlcr -igncr icrnl ixon ixoff
-iuclc -ixany -imaxbel
opost -olcuc -ocrnl onlcr -onocr -onlret -ofill -ofdel nl0 cr0 tab0 bs0 vt0  ff0
isig icanon -iexten echo echoe echok -echonl -noflsh -xcase -tostop -echoprt
-echoctl echoke
```

For details on what each of these entries mean, please see the stty(1L) man-page.

To save, change, and then restore the original values of your stty settings, use the -g option. This option outputs the stty settings as a strings of hexadecimal values. For example, I might get something like this:

```
stty -g
500:5:d050d:3b:7f:1c:8:15:4:0:0:0:0:0:1a:11:13:0:0:0:0:0:0:0:0:0
```

We can run the stty command to get these values and make the changes, then run stty again and use these values as the argument. We don't have to type in everything manually; we simply take advantage of the fact that variables are expanded by the shell before being passed to the command. You could use this to add an additional password to your system:

```
echo "Enter your password: \c"
oldstty=`stty -g`
stty -echo intr '^-'
read password
stty $oldstty
```

Assign the output of the stty command to the variable old, then change the stty settings so that the characters you input are not echoed to the screen and the interrupt key is disabled (this is done with stty -echo intr '^-'). Then read a line from the keyboard and reset the stty settings to their old value.

If you are interacting with the system solely through command line input, you have few occasions to encounter the terminal capabilities. As the name implies, terminal capabilities determine what the terminal is capable of. For example, can the terminal move the cursor to a specific spot on the screen?

The terminal capabilities are defined by one of two databases. Older applications generally use `termcap`, while newer ones use `terminfo`. For the specifics on each, please see the appropriate man-page. Here I am going to talk about the concept of terminal capabilities and what it means to you as a user.

Within each of these databases is a mapping of the character or character sequence the terminal expects for certain behavior. For example, on some terminals, pressing the backspace key sends a `Ctrl-` character. On others, `Crtl-` is sent. When your `TERM` environment variable is set to the correct one for your terminal, pressing the backspace key sends a signal to the system which, in turn, tells the application that the backspace characteristic was called. The application is told not just that you pressed the key with the left arrow (←) on it. Instead, the application is told that that key was the backspace. It is then up to the application to determine what is to be done.

The key benefit of a system like this is that you do not have to recompile or rewrite your application to work on different terminals. Instead, you link in the appropriate library to access either `termcap` or `terminfo` and wait for the capability that OS will send to you. When the application receives that capability (*not* the key), it reacts accordingly.

There are three types of capabilities. The first capabilities are Boolean, which determine whether that terminal has a particular feature. For example, does the terminal have an extra "status" line? The next type is numeric values. Examples of this capability are the number of columns and lines the terminal can display. In some cases, this may not remain constant, as terminals such as the Wyse 60 can change between 80- and 132-column mode. Last are the string capabilities that provide a character sequence to be used to perform a particular operation. Examples of this would be clearing the line from the current cursor position to the end of the line and deleting the contents of an entire line (with or without removing the line completely).

Despite that there are hundreds of possible capabilities, any given terminal will have only a small subset of capabilities. In addition, many of the capabilities do not apply to terminals, but rather to printers.

Both the termcap and terminfo databases have their own advantages and disadvantages. The termcap database is defined by the file /etc/termcap, an ASCII file that is easily modified. In contrast to this is the terminfo database, which starts out as an ASCII file but must be compiled before it can be used.

termcap entries can be converted to terminfo with the captoinfo and then compiled using tic, the terminfo compiler. The tic utility will usually place the compiled version in a directory under /usr/lib/terminfo based on the name of the entry. For example, the ANSI terminal ends up in /usr/lib/terminfo/a and Wyse terminals end up in /usr/lib/terminfo/w.

5.3.3 cron

cron is a commonly confusing and misconfigured aspect of the operating system. Technically, cron is just the clock daemon (/usr/sbin/crond) that executes commands at specific times. However, a handful of configuration files and programs go into making up the cron package. cron is a system process that never ends.

The controlling files for cron are the cron-tables or crontabs. The crontabs are located in /var/spool/cron/crontab. The names of the files are the names of the users that submit the cron jobs.

Unlike other UNIX dialects, cron does not sleep until the next cron job is ready. When cron completes one job, it will keep checking once a minute for more jobs to run. Also, you should not edit the files directly. You can edit them with a text editor like vi, though there is the potential for messing things up. Therefore, you should use the tool that Linux provides: crontab.

The crontab utility has several functions. It is the means by which files containing the cron jobs are submitted to the system. Second, it can list the contains of your crontab. If you are root, it can also submit and list jobs for *any* user. The problem is that jobs cannot be submitted individually. Using crontab, you must submit all of the jobs at the same time.

At first, that might sound a little annoying. However, let's take a look at the process of "adding" a job. To add a cron job, you must first list out the contents of the existing crontab with the -l option. If you are root and wish to add something to another user's crontab, use the -u option followed by the user's logname. Then redirect this crontab to a file, which you can then edit. (Note that on some systems crontab has -e [for "edit"], which will do all the work for you. See the man-page for more details.)

For example, let's say that you are the root user and want to add something to UUCP's crontab. First, get the output like this:

```
crontab -l -u uucp >/tmp/crontab.uucp
```

To add an entry, simply include a new line. Save the file, get out of your editor, and run the crontab utility again. This time, omit the -l to list the file but include the name of the file. The crontab utility can also accept input from stdin, so you could leave off the file name and crontab would allow you to input the cronjobs on the command line. Keep in mind that any previous crontab is removed no matter what method you use.

The file /tmp/crontab.uucp now contains the contents of UUCP's crontab. It might look something like this:

```
39,9 * * * * /usr/lib/uucp/uudemon.hour > /dev/null
10 * * * * /usr/lib/uucp/uudemon.poll > /dev/null
45 23 * * * ulimit 5000; /usr/lib/uucp/uudemon.clean >
/dev/null
48 10,14 * * 1-5 /usr/lib/uucp/uudemon.admin > /dev/null
```

Despite its appearance, each crontab entry consists of only six fields. The first five represent the time the job should be executed and the sixth is the actual command. The first five fields are separated by either a space or a tab and represent the following units, respectively:

- minutes (0-59)
- hour (0-23)
- day of the month (1-31)
- month of the year (1-12)
- day of the week (0-6, 0=Sunday)

To specify all possible values, use an asterisk (*). You can specify a single value simply by including that one value. For example, the second line in the previous example has a value of 10 in the first field, meaning 10 minutes after the hour. Because all of the other four time fields are asterisks, this means that the command is run every hour of every day at 10 minutes past the hour.

Ranges of values are composed of the first value, a dash, and the ending value. For example, the fourth line has a range (1-5) in the day of the week column, meaning that the command is only executed on days 1-5, Monday through Friday.

To specify different values that are not within a range, separate the individual values by a column. In the fourth example, the hour field has the two values 10 and 14. This means that the command is run at 10 a.m. and 2 p.m.

Note that times are additive. Let's look at an example:

```
10 * 1,16 * 1-5 /usr/local/bin/command
```

The command is run 10 minutes after every hour on the first and sixteenth, as well as Monday through Friday. If either the first *or* the sixteenth were on a weekend, the command would still run because the day of the month field would apply. However, this does not mean that if the first is a Monday, the command is run twice.

The `crontab` entry can be defined to run at different intervals than just *every* hour or *every* day. The granularity can be specified to every two minutes or every three hours without having to put each individual entry in the `crontab`.

Lets say we wanted to run the previous command not at 10 minutes after the hour, but every ten minues. We could make an entry that looked like this.:

```
0,10,20,30,40,50 * 1,16 * 1-5 /usr/local/bin/command
```

This runs every 10 minutes: at the top of the hour, 10 minutes after, 20 minutes after, and so on. To make life easier, we could simply create the entry like this:

```
*/10 * 1,16 * 1-5 /usr/local/bin/command
```

This syntax may be new to some administrators. (It was to me.) The slash (/) says that within the specific interval (in this case, every minute), run the command every so many minutes; in this case, every 10 minutes.

We can also use this even when we specify a range. For example, if the job was only supposed to run between 20 minutes after the hour and 40 minutes after the hour, the entry might look like this:

```
20-40 * 1,16 * 1-5 /usr/local/bin/command
```

What if you wanted it to run at these times, but only every three minutes? The line might look like this:

```
20-40/3 * 1,16 * 1-5 /usr/local/bin/command
```

To make things even more complicated, you could say that you wanted the command to run every two minutes between the hour and 20 minutes after, every three minutes between 20 and 40 minutes after, then every 5 minutes between 40 minutes after and the hour.

```
0-20/2,21-40/3,41-59/5 * 1,16 * 1-5 /usr/local/bin/command
```

One really nice thing that a lot of Linux dialects do is allow you to specify abbreviations for the days of the week and the months. It's a lot easier to remember that `fri` is for Friday instead of 5.

With the exception of certain errors in the time fields, errors are not reported until cron runs the command. All error messages *and* output is mailed to the users. At least that's what the crontab man-page says and what is basically true. However, as you see in the previous examples, you are redirecting stdout to /dev/null. If you wanted to, you could also redirect stderr there and you would never see whether there were any errors.

Output is mailed to the user because there is no real terminal on which the cronjobs are being executed. Therefore, there is no screen to display the errors. Also, there is no keyboard to accept input. Does that mean you cannot give input to a cron job? No. Think back to the discussion on shell scripts. We can redefine stdin, stdout and stderr. This way they can all point to files and behave as we expect.

One thing I would like to point out is that I do not advocate doing redirection in the command field of the crontab. I like doing as little there as possible. Instead, I put the absolute path to a shell-script. I can then test the crontab entry with something simple. Once that works, I can make changes to the shell-script without having to resubmit the cronjob.

Keep in mind that cron is not exact. It synchronizes itself to the top of each minute. On a busy system in which you loose clock ticks, jobs may not be executed until a couple minutes after the scheduled time. In addition, there many be other processes with higher priorities that delay cron jobs.

Access is permitted to the cron facility through two files, both in /etc. If you have a file cron.allow, you can specify which users are allowed to use cron. The cron.deny says who are specifically not allowed to use cron. If neither file exists, only the system users have access. However, if you want everyone to have access, create an entry cron.deny file. In other words, no one is denied access.

The next command in the cron "suite" is at. Its function is to execute a command at a specific time. The difference is that once the at job has run, it disappears from the system. As for cron, two files, at.allow and at.deny, have the same effect on the at program.

The batch command is also used to run command once. However, commands submitted with batch are run when the system gets around to it, which means when the system is less busy, for example, in the middle of the night. It's possible that such jobs are spread out over the entire day, depending on the load of the system.

One thing to note is the behavior of at and batch. Both accept the names of the commands from the command line and not as arguments to the command itself. You must first run the command to be brought to a new line, where you input the commands you want execute. After each command, press Enter. When you are done, press Ctrl-D.

Because these two commands accept commands from stdin, you can input the command without having to do so on a new line each time. One possibility is to redirect input from a file. For example

```
at now +1 hour < command_list
```

where command_list is a file containing a list of commands. You could also have at (or batch) as the end of a pipe

```
cat command_list | at now + 1 hour
```

or

```
cat command_list | batch
```

Another interesting thing about both at and batch is that they create a kind of shell-script to execute your command. When you run at or batch, a file is created in /usr/spool/cron/atjobs. This file contains the system variables that you would normally have defined, plus some other information that is contained in /usr/lib/cron.proto. This essentially creates an environment as though you had logged in.

5.3.4 User Communication

If you are running a multiuser system like Linux, you should expect to find other users on your system. (I guess that's why it is a multi-user system) Although there are many built-in mechanisms to keep users separated, there may be some cases in which you don't want to be separate. Sometimes you will want to communicate with other users.

Linux provides several tools to do this, depending on exactly what you want to accomplish. If you simply want to send a quick message to someone, for example, to remind him or her of a meeting, you might use the write program, which sends (writes) a message to his or her terminal.

In contrast to some other systems (say, the winpop mechanism under Windows), each line is sent when you press Enter. If you are on the receiving end of the message, the system lets you know who sent you the message.

If the person you are trying to contact is logged in more than once, you need to specify the terminal to which you want to send the message. So, if I wanted to talk to the user jimmo on terminal tty6, the command would look like this:

```
write jimmo tty6
```

If you omit the terminal, write is kind enough to let you select which terminal to which you want to send the message.

It might happen that someone tries the above command and receives the following message:

```
write: jimmo has messages disabled.
```

This message means that `jimmo` has used the `mesg` command to turn off such messages. The syntax for this command is

```
mesg n
```

to turn it off and

```
mesg y
```

to turn it on. Unless the system administrator has decided otherwise, the command is on by default. I have worked on some systems in which the administrator changed the default to off.

If you want to have an interactive session, you could send `write` messages back and forth. On the other hand, you could use the `talk` program that was designed to do just that. When `talk` first connects to the other user, that other user sees on his or her screen

```
Message from TalkDaemon@source_machine...
talk: connection requested by callers_name@his_machine
talk: respond with: talk callers_name@his_machine
```

As the message indicates, to respond, you would enter

```
talk callers_namer@his_machine
```

You might have noticed that you can use `talk` to communicate with users on other machines. If you omitted the machine name, `talk` would try to contact the user on the local machine (`localhost`). The preceding message would simply say

```
talk: connection requested by callers_name@localhost
```

instead of

```
instead of talk: connection requested by
callers_name@his_machine
```

You can also disable `talk` by using the `mesg` command.

It is common practice to use a couple of terms from radio communication when using `talk`. Because you cannot always tell when someone is finished writing, it is common to end the line with `-o` (or use a separate line) to indicate that your turn is "over." When you are finished with the conversation and wish to end it, use `oo` (over and out).

Both of these mechanisms have some major problems if the user is not logged in: they don't work! Instead, there's mail or, more accurately, electronic mail (or e-mail).

On most UNIX systems (including Linux), e-mail is accessed through the `mail` command. Depending on your system, the `mail` program may be linked to something else. On my system, the default was to link to `/usr/bin/mail`.

There are several different programs for sending and viewing mail. You could use one mail program (or mailer) to send the message and another to read it. Often the program that you use to read your mail is called a mail reader or, simply, reader. Before we go on to the more advanced mail programs, I want to talk about the most common mail program and the one that is most likely to be on your system. (From here on, I will be referring to e-mail simply as mail.)

Mail comes in units called *messages*. Whether you use UUCP or the Internet, mail is sent back and forth in messages. However, once the message has reached its destination, it is usually tacked onto the end of an existing mail file. There is usually one mail file per user, but that single file contains all of a user's messages (that is, all those that haven't yet been deleted).

To read your mail, you can use three primary programs: `elm`, `pine`, and the default reader, `mail`. Actually, you can use all three programs to send mail as well as read it. Each program has its own advantages and disadvantages. Although the `mail` interface looks menu-driven, it simply scrolls the information across the screen. Both `elm` and `pine` have much more complex menuing systems. Because of this, `mail` is easier to learn, but you can do much more with the other two programs.

All three programs understand the concept of a "folder" in which you can store messages. This allows you to develop a hierarchy of files that is no different from the normal file system. How the folders are created and managed depends on the program you are using. Therefore, I would suggest that once you decide to use a specific program, stick with it because the files may not be compatible.

In keeping with the basic premise of this book, I must treat these programs as applications. Therefore, I won't go into any more detail about them. Instead, I suggest that you install all three and see which one suits your needs best. If you have the space, you may consider providing all three for your users. The man-pages provide a great deal of information and each program has its own on-line help.

5.4 Printers and Interfaces

Under Linux, printing is managed and administered by several commands and files located in various parts of the system. The primary administrative directory is /usr/spool/. Each printer that you have configured has its own subdirectory, /usr/spool/<name>, where <name> is the name of the printer. In this subdirectory, you will find status information about the printer, as well as information about the jobs currently being printed.

The actual printing is done by the `lpd` daemon. On system start-up, `lpd` is started through one of the `rc` scripts (normally somewhere under /etc/rc.d). As it starts, `lpd` looks through the printer configuration file, /etc/printcap, and prints any files still queued (normally after a system crash).

In each spool directory is a lock file that contains the process id (PID) of the `lpd` process. The PID helps keeps multiple printer daemons from running and potentially sending multiple jobs to the same printer at the same time. The second line in the lock file contains the control file for the current print job.

Management of the print system, or print spool, is accomplished through the `lpc` utility. This is much more than a "command" because it performs a wide range of functions. One function is enabling printing on a printer. By default, there is probably one printer defined on your system (often `lp`). The entry is a very simple print definition that basically sends the all characters in the file to the predefined port. (For the default printer on a parallel port, this is probably /dev/lp1.)

When a job is submitted to a local printer, two files are created in the appropriate directory in /usr/spool. (For the default printer, this would be /usr/spool/lp1). The first file, starting with `cf`, is the control file for this print job. Paired with the `cf` file is the data file, which starts with `df` and is the data to be printed. If you are printing a pre-existing file, the `df` file will be a copy of that file. If you pipe a command to the `lpr` command, the `df` file will contain the output of the command. Using the `-s` option, you can force the system to create a symbolic link to file to be printed.

The `cf` file contains one piece of information on each of several lines. The first character on each line is an abbreviation that indicates the information contained. The information contained within the `cf` file includes the name of the host from which the print job was submitted (`H`), the user/person who submitted the job (`P`), the job name (`J`), the classification of the print job (`C`), the literal string used on the banner page to identify the user (`L`), the file containing the data (this is the `df` file) (`f`), which file to remove or "unlink" when the job is completed (*U*), and the name of the file to include on the banner page (N). If you check the lpd man-page, you will find about a dozen more pieces of information that you could include in the cf file. However, this list represents the most common ones.

In the same directory, you will find a status file for that printer. This file is called simply "status" and normally contains a single line such as

```
printing disabled
```

If you were to re-enable the printer, the line would then change to

```
lp is ready and printing
```

Looking at this line, you might have noticed something that might seem a little confusing. (Well, at least it confused me the first time.) That is, we've been talking about the directory lp1 all along, but this says the printer is lp. Does this mean that we are talking about two separate printers? No, it doesn't. The convention is to give the directory the same name as the printer, but there is no rule that says you have to. You can define both the printer name and the directory any way you want.

This is probably a good time to talk about the printer configuration file, /etc/printcap. This file contains not only the printer definitions but the printer "capabilities" as well. In general, you can say the printcap file is a shortened version of the termcap file (/etc/termcap), which defines the capabilities of terminals.

In the printcap file, you can define a wide range of capabilities or characteristics, such as the length and width of each line, the remote machine name (if you are remote printing), and, as we discussed, the name of the spool directory. I will get into shortly what each of the entries means.

As we talked about a moment ago, the lpc command is used to manage the print spooler. Not only can you use it to start and stop printing, but you can use it to check the status of all the printer queues and even change the order in which jobs are printed.

There are two ways of getting this information and to manage printer queues. The first is to call lpc by itself. You are then given the lpc> prompt, where you can type in the command you want, such as start, disable, or any other administrative command. Following the command name, you must either enter "all," so the command will be for all printers, or the name of the printer.

The lpc program will also accept these same commands as arguments. For example, to disable our printer, the command would be

```
lpc disable lp1
```

For a list of options, see the lpc man-page. A list of printer queue commands can be found in Table 5.1.

One aspect of the Linux print system that might be new to you is that you enable or the printing functionality within the kernel. Even though printer functionality is configured, you may not be able to print if you have hardware conflicts. When your run make configure one of the options is to enable printing.

Once you have added the printer support to the kernel, the first thing you should do is test the connectivity by using the ls command and sending the output to the printer device. This will probably be /dev/lp0, /dev/lp1, or /dev/lp2, which corresponds to the DOS device LPT1, LPT2, and LPT3, respectively. For example, to test the first parallel port you could use

```
ls > /dev/lp0
```

What results is

```
INSTALL@      dead.letter      linux@          lodlin15.txt
lodlin15.zip                    mbox
sendmail.cf                                 tests/
```

However, if you were to issue the command without the redirection, it would probably look like this:

```
INSTALL@
        dead.letter
                   linux@
                         lodlin15.txt
                                    lodlin15.zip
mbox
    sendmail.cf
              tests/
```

The reason for this is that the ls command puts a single new-line character at the end of the line. Normally, the shell sees that new-line character and is told to add a carriage return onto the line. However, the printer has been told. Therefore, when it reaches the end of the line with the sendmail.cf, just a new line is sent. Therefore, the printer drops down to the next (new) line and starts printing again. This behavior is called “stairstepping” because the output looks like stair steps. When a carriage return is added, the shell returns back to the left of the screen as it adds the new line.

Table 5.1: Print Queue Commands

Command	Function
`/usr/sbin/lpc`	Printer control program
`/usr/sbin/lpd`	Print spooler daemon
`/usr/bin/lpr`	Print program
`/usr/bin/lpq`	Print queue administration program
`/usr/bin/lprm`	Remove jobs from print queue
`/usr/sbin/pr`	Convert text files for printing

5.4.1 Advanced Formatting Options

Being able to output to paper is an important issue for any business. Just having something on paper is not all of the issue. Compare a letter that you type on a typewriter to what you print with a word processor. With a word processor, you can get different sizes or types of fonts and sometimes you can even create drawings directly in the word processor.

Many of you who have dealt with UNIX before might have the misconception that UNIX is only capable of printing simple text files. Some of you might have seen UNIX systems with a word processor that did fancy things with the output. Fortunately for us, these fancy tricks are not limited to the word processing packages. Using `vi` and a couple of commonly available tools, you can output in a wide range of styles.

Readily available from a number of sites, the TeX or LaTeX (pronounced Tech and Lahtech) text formatting package can be used to create professional-looking output. Many academic and research institutions running UNIX use (La)TeX as their primary text processing system. Not only is it free but the source code is also available, allowing you to extend it to suit your needs. (In many cases, the only way to get it onto your system is to get the source code and compile it.)

Like the `*roff` family, TeX is input directly by the writer. These source files are then run through a processor that formats the output based on codes that were input. This process generates a device independent file, usually with the extension `.dvi`. The `.dvi` files are analogous to `.o` files in C because they need to be manipulated further to be useful. Unfortunately, this does not work for every kind of printer.

If your printer does not understand the `.dvi` file, the `dvips` program will convert the `.dvi` file to PostScript. If your printer doesn't support PostScript, you can use ghostview to output to a format your printer can understand.

Included on your system (provided you installed the TeX package) is the `dvips` program, which converts the `.dvi` files to PostScript. These PostScript files can be printed out on any compatible printer.

At first this may sound a little confusing and annoying. You have to use so many tools just to get a simple printout. First, if all you really need is a simple printout, you probably won't need to go through all of these steps. This demonstrates that no matter what standard you choose to use, there are Linux tools available to help you get your job done.

Many different programs are available to allow you to print out, view, and manipulate PostScript files. `Ghostscript` is a program used to view PostScript files. These need not be files that you generated on your local machine, but any PostScript files you have. `Ghostscript` can also be used to print PostScript files to print the file to non-PostScript-compatible printers.

`Ghostscript` supports the resolutions that most printers can handle. However, if you are printing to a dot-matrix printer, you need to be especially careful about getting the right resolution because it is not normally the standard 300 dpi.

I have to pause here to remind you about working with PostScript files and printers. Sometimes the printer is PostScript-compatible, but you have to tell it to process the file as PostScript and not as raw text. This applies to older models of certain laser jet printers. Once, I wanted to print out a 50-page document and forgot to set the flag to say that it was a PostScript file. The result was that instead of 50 pages, I ended up with more than 500 pages of PostScript source.

Under Linux, printers are not the only way you can get words on paper. As of this writing, there are at least three packages with which you can fax documents from your Linux system. First, however, you must have a fax modem with which you can connect.

Here I need to side-step for a minute. The older type of fax, Class 1 faxes, did not have as much processing power distributed in the hardware. Instead, the software took over this job. It works fine on single-user systems like Windows, but under "pre-emptive" multitasking systems like Linux, you can run into timing problems. (Pre-emptive multitasking is where the operating system decides which process will run and therefore can pause the fax program at a crucial moment.)

In addition to Class 1, faxes fall into different groups. To work correctly, the fax software needs to convert the document you are sending into a group-III-compatible image. This can be done with Ghostscript.

The GNU `netfax` program accepts several different file formats (as of this writing, PostScript, `dvi`, and ASCII). Originally available from *prep.ai.mit.edu*, it is no longer supported by the GNU. More extensive than `netfax` is HylaFlex (renamed from FlexFax available to avoid trademark conflicts). This is available (as of this writing) with ftp from `sgi.com` under `/sgi/fax/`. With this package, not only can you send faxes, but you can configure it to receive them as well. In addition, Caldera OpenLinux includes the Seyon fax package.

Man-pages are something that you may need print. If you have files in ASCII format (the cat pages), this is not an issue. However, with pages that have been formatted with `*roff` formatting, you have a couple of choices. The man program has the ability to process files with `*roff` formatting. By redirecting the output on `man` to a file (often piping it through `col`), you can get clean ASCII text that you can then print.

5.4.2 The printcap File

As with the `termcap` file, each entry in the `printcap` file is separated by a colon. Boolean characteristics, such as suppressing the header (`sh`), exist by themselves. Characteristics that can take on a value, such as the name of the output device, are followed by an equal sign (=) and the value (`lp=/dev/lp1`). For a complete list of characteristics, see the printcap man-page.

Each entry in the `/etc/printcap` file consists of single logical line. There is one entry for each printer on your system. To make the entry easier to read, you can break each logical line into several physical lines. As an example, let's look at the entry for the default, generic printer:

```
lp:lp=/dev/lp1:sd=/usr/spool/lp1:sh
```

The first part of the line is the name of the printer, in this case, `lp`. Each field is separated from the others with a colon, so in this example, there are three fields (plus the printer name).

If we were to break this example into multiple physical lines, it might look like this:

```
lp:\
    :lp=/dev/lp1:\
    :sd=/usr/spool/lp1:\
    :sh
```

At the end of each physical line, there is a back-slash to tell lpd that the logical line continues. You'll also see that each field now has a colon before it and after it.

Although it is not necessary, you may find a file minfree in each of the spool directories. This is a simple text file that contains the number of disk blocks that should be left to keep the print spooler from filling up the disk. As a safety mechanism on system with a lot of print jobs, the spool directory can be put on a separate file system. Should it fill up, the rest of the system won't suffer.

Often, data is sent directly to the printer devices, either because it is supposed to be raw ASCII text or because the program that created the data did its own formatting. This is referred to as raw data as the system doesn't do anything with it.

Sometimes the data is sent by the `lpd` daemon through another program that processes the data in preparation of sending it to the printer. Such programs are called filters. The `stdin` of the input filters receive what the lpd puts out. The `stdout` of the filter then goes to printer. Such filters are often called input filters and are specified in the `printcap` file `with if=`.

Because of this behavior, a print filter can be anything that understands the concept of `stdin` and `stdout`. In most cases on Linux, the input filters that I have seen are simply shell-scripts. However, they can also be `perl` scripts.

With the exception of an input filter or a log file (which is specified using `lf=`), I have rarely used any other option for local printing. However, using the `printcap` file, you can configure your printer to print on a remote system, which is the subject of the next section.

5.4.3 Remote Printing

Setting up your system to print from another machine requires just a couple of alterations in your printcap file. Use the `rm=` field to specify the remote machine and the `rp=` field to specify the remote printer on that machine. Sending the print job to the printer is the last thing happens, so any other options, including input filters, are also honored.

On the destination side, you must be allowed to access the other machine. If you are already a trusted host and have an entry in `/etc/hosts.equiv`, then there is no problem. If not, you will be denied access. (This is a good time to start thinking about a log file.)

If the sole reason the remote machine needs to trust your machine is to do remote printing, I would recommend *not* including it in the `hosts.equiv` file. This opens up more holes. Instead, put your host name in the file `/etc/hosts.lpd`. The only thing this file does is decide who can access the printers remotely. Putting remote machine names here is much safer.

5.4.4 The Next Step

Is that it? Unfortunately not. I haven't even hit on half of what you need to know about printers, let alone administering your system. Unfortunately, this is unavoidable because system administration is the subject of books, not just a single chapter. I hope to have given you the tools you need to start administering your system. The suggested reading list in Appendix B gives you some places to look for more detailed information, plus you will find all the HOWTOs on your CD-ROM.

Chapter 6

The Operating System and Its Environment

- Inside the kernel
- Processes
- Files and file systems

In this chapter, I am going to go into some detail about what makes an Linux operating system. I am not talking about the product Linux or either of the bundled distributions such as Slackware, Caldera Open Linux or LinuxPro. Here, I am talking strictly about the software that manages and controls your computer.

Because an operating system is of little use without hardware and other software, we are going to discuss how the operating system interacts with other parts of the various Linux distributions. I will also talk about what goes into to making the kernel, what components it is made of, and what you can do to influence the creation of a new kernel.

Much of this information is far beyond what many system administrators are required to have for their jobs. So why go over it? Because what is required and what the administrator should know are two different things. Many calls I received while in tech support and many questions posted to newsgroups could have been avoided had the administrator understood the meaning of a message on the system console or the effects of making changes. By going over the details of how the kernel behaves, I hope to put you in a better position to understand what is happening.

6.1 The Kernel: The Heartbeat of Linux

If any single aspect of a Linux distribution could be called "Linux," then it would be the kernel. So what is the kernel? Well, on the hard disk, it is *represented* by the file `/vmlinuz`. Just as a program like `/bin/date` is a collection of bytes that isn't very useful until it is loaded in memory and running, the same applies to `/vmlinuz`.

However, once the `/vmlinuz` program is loaded into memory and starts its work, it becomes "the kernel" and has many responsibilities. Perhaps the two most important responsibilities are process management and file management. However, the kernel is responsible for many other things. One aspect is I/O management, which is essentially the accessing of all the peripheral devices.

In the following sections, we are going to look at what's under the hood of your Linux system. Rather than turning this into a book on operating system theory, I am going to have to gloss over some things. I will go into detail about those issues that can and *will* effect your ability to run and administer a Linux system, however.

These sections will be based on the Intel 386 (i386) architecture. Linux also runs on 486, Pentium, and Pentium Pro processors, and these concepts are common to all of them. Linux has been ported to other processor types, however; it was originally designed for the i386. In addition, these versions are all newer, and because this book can't be a "do-all" and "be-all" for everyone, I felt it necessary to limit the bulk of my discussion to the i386 because it is the most widespread version.

6.1.1 Processes

From the user's perspective, perhaps the most obvious aspect of a kernel is process management. This is the part of the kernel that ensures that each process gets its turn to run on the CPU. This is also the part that makes sure that the individual processes don't "trounce" on other processes by writing to areas of memory that belong to someone else. To do this, the kernel keeps track of many different structures that are maintained both on a per-user basis as well as systemwide.

As we talked about in the section on operating system basics, a process is the running instance of a program (a program simply being the bytes on the disks). One of the most powerful aspects of Linux is its ability not only to keep many processes in memory at once but also to switch to them fast enough to make it appear as though they were all running at the same time. (Note: In much of the Linux code, the references are to *tasks*, not to *processes*. Because process seems to be more common in UNIX literature and I am used to that term, I will be using process. However, there is no difference between a task and a process, so you can interchange them to your heart's content.)

As a process is running, it works within its *context*. It is also common to say that the CPU is operating within the context of a specific process. The context of a process is all of the characteristics, settings, values, etc., that that particular program uses as it runs, as well as those that it *needs* to run. Even the internal state of the CPU and the contents of all its registers are part of the context of the process. When a process has finished having its turn on the CPU and another process gets to run, the act of changing from one process to another is called a *context switch*. This is represented graphically by Figure 6.1.

Figure 6.1: **Context Switch**

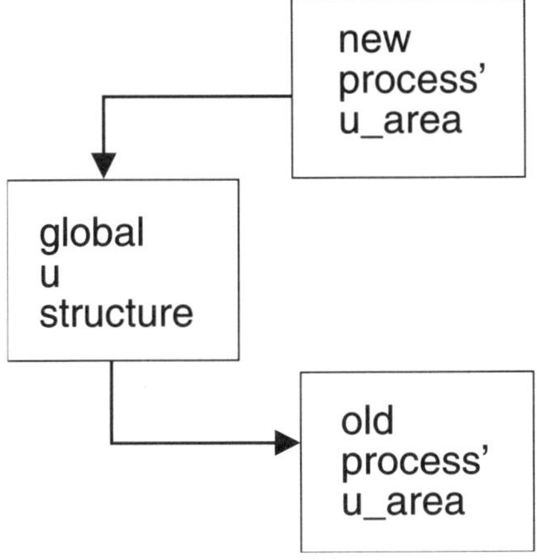

We can say that a process's context is defined by two structures: its *task structure* (also called its `ublock` in some operating system text) and its *process table entry*. These contain the necessary information to manage the each process, such as the user ID (UID) of the process, the group ID (GID), the system call error return value, and dozens of other things. To see where it is all kept (that is, the structure of the task structure), see the `task_struct` in `<linux/sched.h>`.

There is a special part of the kernel's private memory that holds the task structure of the currently running process. When a context switch occurs, the task structure is switched out. All other parts of the process remain where they are. The task structure of the next process is copied into the exact same place in memory as the task structure for the old process. This way the kernel does not have to make any adjustments and knows exactly where to look for the task structure. It will always be able to access the task structure of the currently running process by accessing the same area in memory. This is the `current` process, which is a pointer of type `task_struct`.

One piece of information that the process table entry (PTE) contains is the process's *Local Descriptor Table* (LDT). A descriptor is a data structure the process uses to gain access to different parts of the system (that is, different parts of memory or different *segments*). Despite a common misunderstanding, Linux does use a segmented memory architecture. In older CPUs, segments were a way to get around memory access limitations. By referring to memory addresses as offsets within a given segment, more memory could be addressed than if memory were looked at as a single block. The key difference with Linux is that each of these segments are 4GB and not the 64K they were originally.

The descriptors are held in *descriptor tables*. The LDT keeps track of a process's segments, also called a region. That is, these descriptors are *local* to the process. The *Global Descriptor Table* (GDT) keeps track of the kernel's segments. Because there are many processes running, there will be many LDTs. These are part of the process's context. However, there is only one GDT, as there is only one kernel.

Within the task structure is a pointer to another key aspect of a process's context: its *Task State Segment* (TSS). The TSS contains all the registers in the CPU. The contents of all the registers define the state in which the CPU is currently running. In other words, the registers say what a given process is doing at any given moment, Keeping track of these registers is vital to the concept of multitasking.

By saving the registers in the TSS, you can reload them when this process gets its turn again and continue where you left off because all of the registers are reloaded to their previous value. Once reloaded, the process simply starts over where it left off as though nothing had happened.

This brings up two new issues: system calls and stacks. A system call is a programming term for a very low-level function, functions that are "internal" to the operating system and that are used to access the internals of the operating system, such as in the device drivers that ultimately access the hardware. Compare this to library calls, which are made up of system calls.

A stack is a means of keeping track where a process has been. Like a stack of plates, objects are *pushed* onto the stack and *popped* off the stack. Therefore, objects that are pushed onto the stack *last* are the *first* to pop off. When calling routines, certain values are pushed onto the stack for safe-keeping, including the variables to be passed to the function and the location to which the system should return after completing the function. When returning from that routine, these values are retrieved by being popped off the stack.

Part of the task structure is a pointer to that process's entry in the process table. The process table, as its name implies, is a table containing information about all the processes on the system, whether that process is currently running or not. Each entry in the process table is defined in `<linux/sched.h>`. The principle that a process may be in memory but not actually running is important and I will get into more detail about the life of a process shortly.

The size of this table is a set value and is determined by the kernel parameter `NR_TASKS`. Though you could change this value, you needed to build a new kernel and reboot for the change to take effect.

If there is a runaway process that keeps creating more and processes or if you simply have a very busy system, it is possible that the process table will fill up. If it were to fill up, root would be unable to even stop them because it needs to start a new process to do so (even if root were logged in already.) The nice thing is that there is a set number of processes reserved for root. This is defined by `MIN_TASKS_LEFT_FOR_ROOT` in `<linux/tasks.h>`. On my system, this defaults to 4.

Just how is a process created? First, one process uses the `fork()` system call. Like a fork in the road, the `fork()` system call starts off as a single entity and then splits into two. When one process uses the `fork()` system call, an *exact* copy of itself is created in memory and the task structures are essentially identical. However memory is not copied, but rather the new pages tables are made to point to the same place as the old ones. When something in those pages changes, a copy is made (copy on write).

The value in each CPU register is the same, so both copies of this process are at the exact same place in their code. Each of the variables also has the exact same value. There are two exceptions: the process ID number and the return value of the `fork()` system call. (You can see the details of the `fork()` system call in `kernel/fork.c`.) How the `fork()-exec()` look graphically you can see in Figure 6.2.

Like users and their UID, each process is referred to by its process ID number, or PID, which is a unique number. Although your system could have approximately 32K processes at a time, even of the busiest systems it rarely gets that high.

You may, however, find a very large PID on your system (running `ps`, for example): This does not mean that there are actually that many processes. Instead, it demonstrates the fact that the system does not immedi-

Figure 6.2: **Creating a New Process**

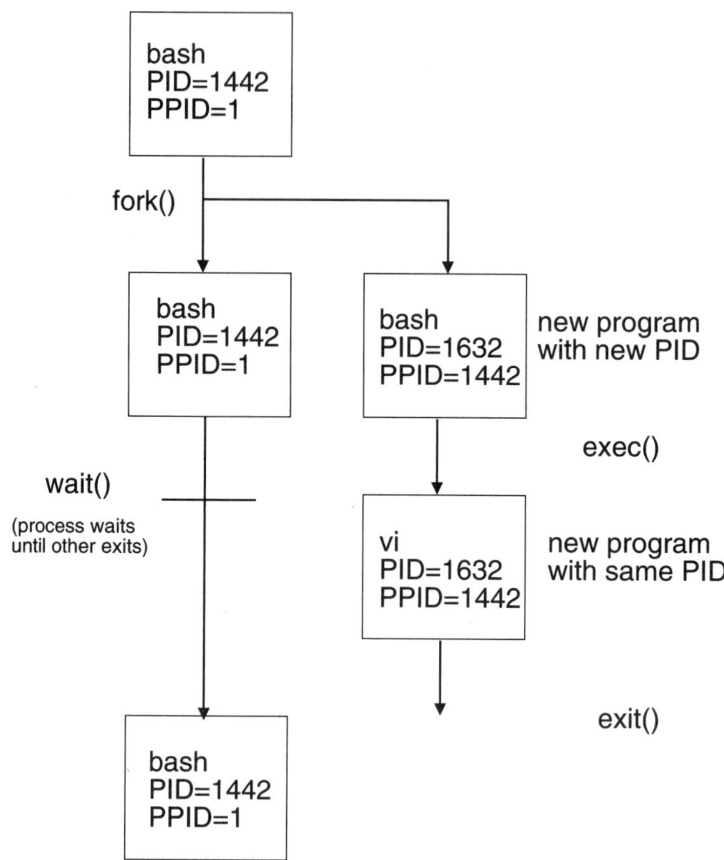

ately re-use the PID. This is is prevent a "race condition", for example where one process sends a signal (message) to a another process, but before the message arrives, the other process has stopped. The result is that the wrong process could get the message which might be telling it to terminate.

When a `fork()` system call is made, the value returned by the `fork()` to the calling process is the PID of the newly created process. Because the new copy didn't actually make the `fork()` call, the return value in the copy is 0. This is how a process *spawns* or *forks* a *child* process. The process that called the `fork()` is the parent process of this new process, which is the child process. Note that I intentionally said *the* parent process and a child process. A process can fork many child processes but has only one parent.

Almost always, a program will keep track of that return value and will then change its behavior based on that value. It is very common for the child to issue an `exec()` system call. Although it takes the `fork()` system call to create the space that will be utilized by the new process, it is the `exec()` system call that causes this space to be overwritten with the new program.

At the beginning of every executable program is an area simply called the "header." This header describes the contents of the file; that is, how the file is to be interpreted. The header contains the locations of the text and data segments. As we talked about before, a segment is a portion of the program. The portion of the program that contains the executable instructions is called the text segment. The portion containing *pre-initialized* data is the data segment. Pre-initialized data are variables, structures, arrays, etc. that have their value already set even before the program is run. The process is given descriptors for each of the segments.

In contrast to other operating systems running on Intel-based CPUs, Linux has only one segment each for the text, data, and stack. I haven't mentioned the stack segment until now because the stack segment is created when the process is created. Because the stack is used to keep track of where the process has been and what it has done, there is no need create it until the process starts.

Another segment that I haven't talked about until now is not always used. This is the shared data segment. Shared data is an area of memory that is accessible by more than one process. Do you remember from our discussion on operating system basics when I said that part of the job of the operating system was to keep processes from accessing areas of memory that they weren't supposed to? So, what if they *want* to? What if they are *allowed* to? That is where the shared data region comes in.

If one process tells the other where the shared memory segment is (by giving a pointer to it), then any process can access it. The way to keep unwanted processes away is simply not to tell them. In this way, each process that is allowed can use the data and the segment only goes away when that last process disappears. Figure 6.3 shows how several processes would look in memory.

In Figure 6.3, we see three processes. In all three instances, each process has its own data and stack segments. However, process A and process B share a text segment. That is, process A and process B have called the same executable off the hard disk. Therefore, they are sharing the same instructions. Note that in reality, this is much more complicated because the two process may be not be executing the exact same instructions at any given moment.

Each process has at least a text, data, and stack segment. In addition, each process is created in the same way. An existing process will (normally) use the `fork()-exec()` system call pair to create another process. However, this brings up an interesting question, similar to "Who or what created God?": If *every* process has to be created by another, who or what created the first process?

Figure 6.3: **Process Segments**

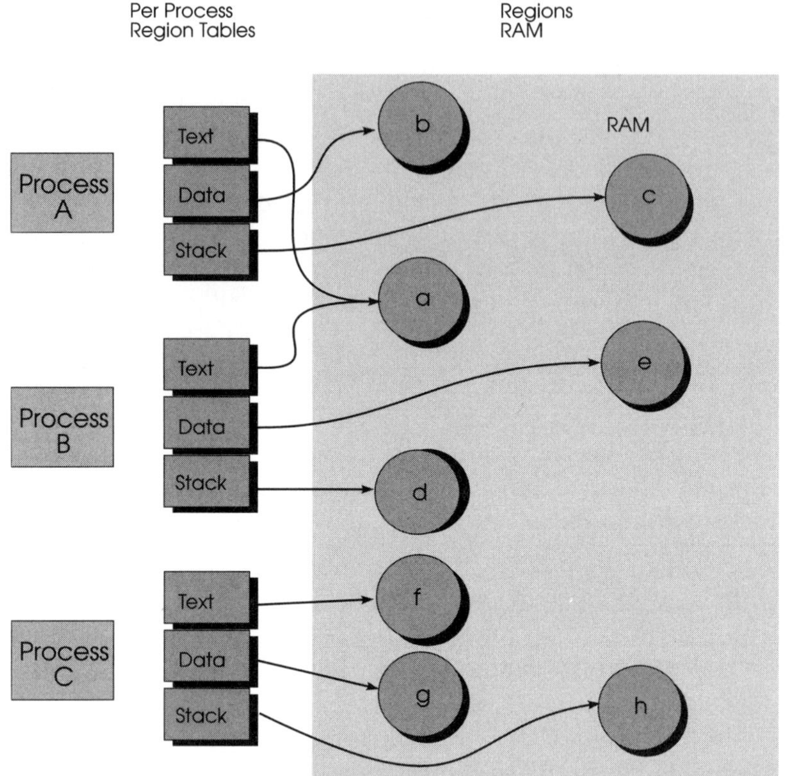

When the computer is turned on, it goes through some wild gyrations that we will talk about later. At the end of the boot process, the system loads and executes the `/vmlinuz` binary, the kernel itself. One of the last things the kernel does is "force" the creation of a single process, which then becomes the great-grandparent of all the other processes.

The first created process is `init`, with a PID of 1. All other processes can trace their ancestry back to `init`. It is `init`'s job to read the entries in the file `/etc./inittab` and execute different programs. One thing it does is start the `getty` program on all the login terminals, which eventually provides every user with its shell.

Another system process is `bdflush`, the buffer flushing daemon. Its job is to clean out any "dirty" buffers inside the system's buffer cache. A dirty buffer contains data that has been written to by a program but hasn't yet been written to the disk. It is the job of `bdflush` to write this out to the hard disk (probably) at regular intervals. These intervals are 30 seconds for data buffers and 5 seconds for metadata buffers. (Metadata is the data used to administer the file system, such as the superblock.)

You may find on your system that two daemons are running, `bdflush` and update. Both are used to write back blocks, but with slightly different functions. The update daemon writes back modified blocks (including superblocks and inode tables) after a specific period of time to ensure that blocks are not kept in memory too long without being written to the disk. On the other hand, bdflush writes back a specific number of dirty blocks buffers. This keeps the ratio of dirty blocks to total blocks in the buffer at a "safe" level.

All processes, including those I described above, operate in one of two modes: user or system mode (see Figure 6.4 Process Modes). In the section on the CPU in the hardware chapter, I will talk about the privilege levels. An Intel 80386 and later has four privilege levels, 0-3. Linux uses only the two most extreme: 0 and 3. Processes running in user mode run at privilege level 3 within the CPU. Processes running in system mode run at privilege level 0 (more on this in a moment).

Figure 6.4: **Process Modes**

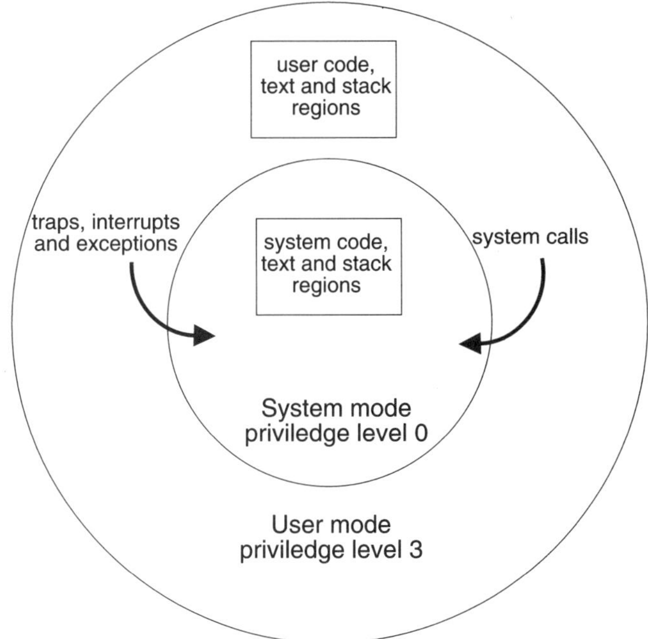

In user mode, a process executes instructions from within its own text segment, references its own data segment, and uses its own stack. Processes switch from user mode to kernel mode by making system calls. Once in system mode, the instructions within the kernel's text segment are executed, the kernel's data segment is used, and a system stack is used within the process' task structure.

Although the process goes through a lot of changes when it makes a system call, keep in mind that this is *not* a context switch. It is still the same process but it is just operating at a higher privilege.

6.1.2 The Life Cycle of Processes

From the time a process is created with a `fork()` until it has completed its job and disappears from the process table, it goes through many different states. The state a process is in changes many times during its "life." These changes can occur, for example, when the process makes a system call, it is someone else's turn to run, an interrupt occurs, or the process asks for a resource that is currently not available.

A commonly used model shows processes operating in one of six separate states, which you can find in `sched.h`:

1. executing in user mode
2. executing in kernel mode
3. ready to run
4. sleeping
5. newly created, not ready to run, and not sleeping
6. issued exit system call (zombie)

The states listed here describe what is happening conceptually and do not indicate what "official" state a process is in. The official states are listed in Table 6.1.

Table 6.1: **Process States in `sched.h`**

`TASK_RUNNING`	task (process) currently running
`TASK_INTERRUPTABLE`	process running
`TASK_UNINTERRUPTABLE`	process terminated but not waited for
`TASK_ZOMBIE`	process stopped by a debugger
`TASK_STOPPED`	process being created
`TASK_SWAPPING`	process is on the processor

In my list of states, there was no mention of a processes actually being on the processor (`TASK_RUNNING`). Processes that are running in kernel mode or in user mode are both in the `TASK_RUNNING` state. Although there is no 1:1 match-up, I hope you'll see what each state means as we go through the following description. You can see how this all looks graphically in Figure 6.5.

A newly created process enters the system in state 5. If the process is simply a copy of the original process (a `fork` but no `exec`), it then begins to run in the state that the original process was in (1 or 2). (Why none of the other states? It has to be running to fork a new process.) If an

Figure 6.5: **Process States**

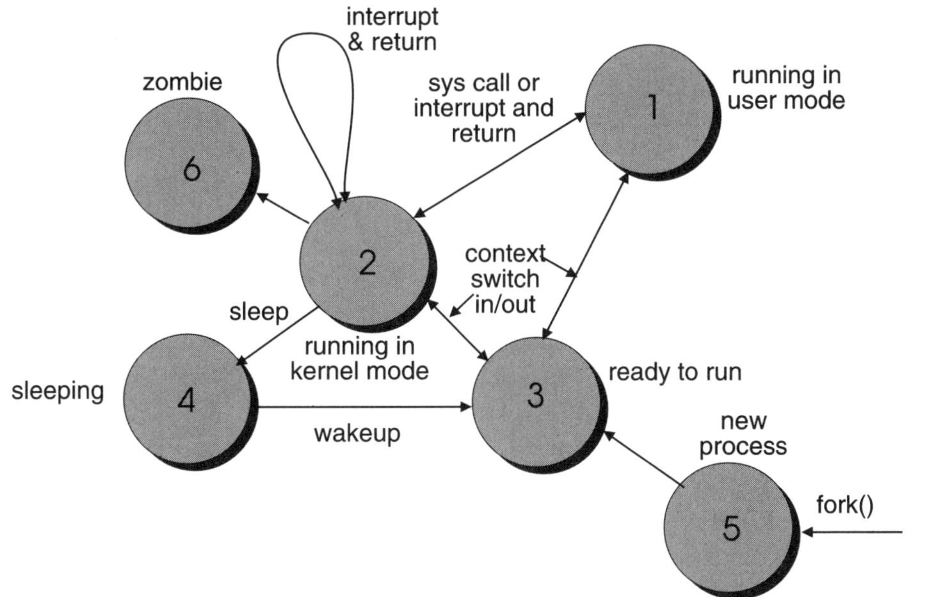

exec() is made, then this process will end up in kernel mode (2). It is possible that the fork()-exec() was done in system mode and the process *never* goes into state 1. However, this highly unlikely.

When a process is running, an interrupt may be generated (more often than not, this is the system clock) and the currently running process is pre-empted (3). This is the same state as state 3 because it is still ready to run and in main memory. The only difference is that the process was just kicked off the processor.

When the process makes a system call while in user mode (1), it moves into state 2 where it begins to run in kernel mode. Assume at this point that the system call made was to read a file on the hard disk. Because the read is not carried out immediately, the process goes to sleep, waiting on the *event* that the system has read the disk and the data is ready. It is now in state 4. When the data is ready, the process is woken up. This does not mean it runs immediately, but rather it is once again ready to run in main memory (3).

If a process that was asleep is awakened (perhaps when the data is ready), it moves from state 4 (sleeping) to state 3 (ready to run). This can be in either user mode (1) or kernel mode (2).

A process can end its life by either explicitly calling the exit() system call or having it called for them. The exit() system call releases all the data structures that the process was using. One exception is the slot in the process table, which is the responsibility of the init process. The reason for hanging around is that the slot in the process table is used for the exit code of the exiting process. This can be used by the parent process to determine whether the process did what it was supposed to do or whether it ran into problems. The process shows that it has terminated by putting itself into state 8, and it becomes a "zombie." Once here, it can never run again because nothing exists other than the entry in the process table.

This is why you cannot "kill" a zombie process. There is nothing there to kill. To kill a process, you need to send it a signal (more on signals later). Because there is nothing there to receive or process that signal, trying to kill it makes little sense. The only thing to do is to let the system clean it up.

If the exiting process has any children, they are "inherited" by `init`. One value stored in the process structure is the PID of that process's parent process. This value is (logically) referred to as the *parent process ID* or PPID. When a process is inherited by `init`, the value of its PPID is changed to 1 (the PID of `init`).

A process's state change can cause a context switch in several different cases. One case is when the processes voluntarily goes to sleep, which can happen when the process needs a resource that is not immediately available. A very common example is your login shell. You type in a command, the command is executed, and you are back to a shell prompt. Between the time the command is finished and you input your next command, a very long time could pass–at least two or three seconds.

Rather than constantly checking the keyboard for input, the shell puts itself to sleep while waiting on an event. That event is an interrupt from the keyboard to say "Hey! I have input for you." When a process puts itself to sleep, it sleeps on a particular *wait channel* (WCHAN). When the event that is associated with that wait channel occurs, every process waiting on that wait channel is woken up.

There is probably only one process waiting on input from your keyboard at any given time. However, many processes could be waiting for data from the hard disk. If so, there might be dozens of processes all waiting on the same wait channel. All are woken up when the hard disk is ready. It may be that the hard disk has read only the data for a subset of the processes waiting. Therefore, if the program is correctly written, the processes check to see whether their data is ready for them. If not, they put themselves to sleep on the same wait channel.

When a process puts itself to sleep, it is *voluntarily* giving up the CPU. It may be that this process had just started its turn when it noticed that it didn't have some resource it needed. Rather than forcing the other process to wait until the first one gets its "fair share" of the CPU, that process is nice and lets some other process have a turn on the CPU.

Because the process is being so nice to let others have a turn, the kernel will be nice to the process. One thing the kernel allows is that a process that puts itself to sleep can set the priority at which it will run when it wakes. Normally, the kernel process scheduling algorithm calculates the priorities of all the processes. In exchange for voluntarily giving up the CPU, however, the process is allowed to choose its own priority.

6.1.3 Process Scheduling

Like many dialects of UNIX, the process scheduler is a function inside the kernel, not a separate process. Actually, it's better to say that process scheduling is done by two functions working together, both of which are a part of `sched.c`. The first function is `schedule()`, which does the actual scheduling. The other is `do_timer()`, which is called at different times and whose function is to update the times of each process. Essentially, this is used to keep track of how long each process has been running it, how long it has had the processors, how long it has been in user mode, how long it has been in kernel mode, etc.

In the section on operating system basics, I mentioned that each process gets a time slice that's 1/100th of a second long. At the end of each time slice, the `do_timer()` function is called and priorities are recalculated. Each time a system call returns to user mode, `do_timer()` is also called to update the times.

Scheduling processes is not as easy as finding the process that has been waiting the longest. Some operating systems do this kind of scheduling, which is referred to as "round-robin." The processes could be thought of as sitting in a circle. The scheduling algorithm could then be though of as a pointer that moves around the circle, getting to each process in turn. The Linux scheduler does a modified version of round-robin scheduling, however, processes with a higher priority get to run more often and longer.

Linux also allows you to be nice to your fellow processes. If you feel that your work is not as important as someone else's, you might want to consider being nice to them. This is done with the nice command, the syntax of which is

```
nice <nice_value> <command>
```

For example, if you wanted to run the date command with a lower priority, you could run it like this:

```
nice  -10 date
```

This decreases the start priority of the date command by 10. Note that only root can increase a process's priority, that is, use a negative nice value. The nice value only affects running processes, but child processes inherit the nice value of their parent. By default, processes that users start have a nice value of 20.

The numeric value calculated for the priority is the opposite of what we normally think of as priority. A better way of thinking about it is like the pull-down number tickets you get at the ice cream store. The lower the number, the sooner you'll be served. So it is for processes as well.

The number of times the clock interrupts per second, and therefore the numbers of times the priority is recalculated, is defined by the HZ system variable. This is defined by default to be 100HZ, or 100 times a second. However, we are assuming that the priorities are only calculated once a second instead of 100 times.

6.1.4 Interrupts, Exceptions, and Traps

Normally, processes are asleep, waiting on some event. When that event happens, these processes are called into action. Remember, it is the responsibility of the `sched` process to free memory when a process runs short of it. So, it is not until memory is needed that `sched` starts up. How does `sched` know?

In Chapter 1, I talked about virtual memory and mentioned page faults. When a process makes reference to a place in its virtual memory space that does not yet exist in physical memory, a page fault occurs.

Faults belong to a group of system events called *exceptions*. An exception is simply something that occurs outside of what is normally expected. Faults (exceptions) can occur either before or during the execution of an instruction.

For example, if an instruction that is not yet in memory needs to be read, the exception (page fault) occurs *before* the instruction starts being executed. On the other hand, if the instruction is supposed to read data from a virtual memory location that isn't in physical memory, the exception occurs *during* the execution of the instruction. In cases like these, once the missing memory location is loaded into physical memory, the CPU can start the instruction.

Traps are exceptions that occur *after* an instruction has been executed. For example, attempting to divide by zero will generate an exception. However, in this case it doesn't make sense to restart the instruction because every time we to try to run that instruction, it still comes up with a Divide-by-Zero exception. That is, all memory references are read before we start to execute the command.

It is also possible for processes to generate exceptions intentionally. These programmed exceptions are called software interrupts.

When any one of these exceptions occurs, the system must react to the exception. To react, the system will usually switch to another process to deal with the exception, which means a context switch. In our discussion of process scheduling, I mentioned that at every clock tick the priority of every process is recalculated. To make those calculations, something other than those processes have to run.

In Linux, the system timer (or clock) is programmed to generate a hardware interrupt 100 times a second (as defined by the HZ system parameter). The interrupt is accomplished by sending a signal to a special chip on the motherboard called an interrupt controller. (I will go into more detail about these in the chapter on hardware.) The interrupt controller then sends an interrupt to the CPU. When the CPU receives this signal, it knows that the clock tick has occurred and it jumps to a special part of the kernel that handles the clock interrupt. Scheduling priorities are also recalculated within this same section of code.

Because the system might be doing something more important when the clock generates an interrupt, you can turn them off. In other words, there is a way to *mask out* interrupts. Interrupts that can be masked out are called *maskable interrupts*. An example of something more important than the clock would be accepting input from the keyboard. This is why clock ticks are lost on systems with a lot of users inputting a lot of data. As a result, the system clock appears to slow down over time.

Sometimes events occur on the system that you want to know about *no matter what*. Imagine what would happen if memory was bad. If the system was in the middle of writing to the hard disk when it encountered the bad memory, the results could be disastrous. If the system recognizes the bad memory, the hardware generates an interrupt to alert the CPU. If the CPU is told to ignore all hardware interrupts, it would ignore this one. Instead, the hardware has the ability to generate an interrupt that cannot be ignored or masked out, called a *nonmaskable interrupt*. Nonmaskable interrupts are generically referred to as NMIs.

When an interrupt or an exception occurs, it must be dealt with to ensure the integrity of the system. How the system reacts depends on whether it was an exception or interrupt. In addition, what happens when the hard disk generates an interrupt is going to be different than when the clock generates one.

Within the kernel is the *Interrupt Descriptor Table* (IDT), which is a list of descriptors (pointers) that point to the functions that handle the particular interrupt or exception. These functions are called the *interrupt* or *exception handlers*. When an interrupt or exception occurs, it has a particular value, called an identifier or vector. Table 6.2 contains a list of the defined interrupt vectors.

Table 6.2: **Interrupt Vectors**

Identifier	Description
0	Divide error
1	Debug exception
2	Nonmaskable interrupt
3	Breakpoint
4	Overflow
5	Bounds check
6	Invalid opcode
7	Coprocessor not available
8	Double fault
9	(reserved)
10	Invalid TSS
11	Segment not present
12	Stack exception
13	General protection fault
14	Page fault
15	(reserved)
16	Coprocessor error
17	alignment error (80486)
18-31	(reserved)
32-255	External (HW) interrupts

These numbers are actually indices into the IDT. When an interrupt, exception, or trap occurs, the system knows which number corresponds to that event. It then uses that number as an index into the IDT, which in turn points to the appropriate area of memory for handling the event.

It is possible for devices to share interrupts; that is, multiple devices on the system are configured to the same interrupt. In fact, certain kinds of computers are designed to allow devices to share interrupts (I'll talk about them in the hardware section). If the interrupt number is an offset into a table of pointers to interrupt routines, how does the kernel know which one to call?

As it turns out, there are two IDTs: one for shared interrupts and one for nonshared interrupts. During a kernel rebuild (more on that later), the kernel determines whether the interrupt is shared. If it is, it places the pointer to that interrupt routine into the shared IDT. When an interrupt is generated, the interrupt routine for each of these devices is called. It is up to the interrupt routine to check whether the associated device really generated an interrupt. The order in which they are called is the order in which they are linked.

When an exception happens in user mode, the process passes through a trap gate. At this point, the CPU no longer uses the process's user stack, but rather the system stack within that process's task structure (each task structure has a portion set aside for the system stack). At this point, that process is operating in system (kernel) mode; that is, at the highest privilege level, 0.

The kernel treats interrupts very similarly to the way it treats exceptions: all the general purpose registers are pushed onto the system stack and a common interrupt handler is called. The current interrupt priority is saved and the new priority is loaded. This prevents interrupts at lower priority levels from interrupting the kernel as it is handling this interrupt. Then the real interrupt handler is called.

Because an exception is not fatal, the process will return from whence it came. It is possible that a context switch occurs immediately on return from kernel mode. This might be the result of an exception with a lower priority. Because it could not interrupt the process in kernel mode, it had to wait until it returned to user mode. Because the exception has a higher priority than the process when it is in user mode, a context switch occurs immediately after the process returns to user mode.

If another exception occurs while the process is in kernel mode, this is not a normal occurrence. Exceptions are the result of software events. Even a page fault can be considered a software event. Because the entire kernel is in memory all the time, a page fault should not happen. When a page fault does happen when in kernel mode, the kernel panics. Special routines have been built into the kernel to deal with the panic to help the system shut down as gracefully as possible. Should something else happen to cause another exception while the system is trying to panic, a double panic occurs.

This may sound confusing because I just said that a context switch could occur as the result of another exception. What this means is that the exception occurred in user mode, so there must be a jump to kernel mode. This does not mean that the process continues in kernel mode until it is finished. It may (depending on what it is doing) be context-switched out. If another process has run before the first one gets its turn on the CPU again, that process may generate the exception.

Unlike exceptions, another interrupt could possibly occur while the kernel is handling the first one (and therefore is in kernel mode). If the second interrupt has a higher priority than the first, a context switch will occur and the new interrupt will be handled. If the second interrupt has the same or lower priority, then the kernel will "put it on hold." These are not ignored, but rather saved (queued) to be dealt with later.

6.1.5 Signals

Signals are a way of sending simple messages to processes. Most of these messages are already defined and can be found in `<linux/signal.h>`. However, signals can only be processed when the process is in user mode. If a signal has been sent to a process that is in kernel mode, it is dealt with immediately on returning to user mode.

Many signals (such as signal 9, SIGKILL), have the ability to immediately terminate a process. However, most of these signals can be either ignored or dealt with by the process itself. If not, the kernel will take the default action specified for that signal. You can send signals to processes yourself by means of the `kill` command, as well as by the `Delete` key and `Ctrl+/`. However, you can only send signals to processes that you own. If you are root, however, you can send signals to any process.

It's possible that the process to which you want to send the signal is sleeping. If that process is sleeping at an *interruptible* priority, then the process will awaken to handle the signal.

The kernel keeps track of pending signals in the `p_sig` entry in each process's process structure. This is a 32-bit value in which each bit represents a single signal. Because it is only one bit per signal, there can only be one signal pending of each type. If there are different kinds of signals pending, the kernel has no way of determining which came in when. It will therefore process the signals starting at the lowest numbered signal and moving up.

6.1.6 System Calls

If you are a programmer, you probably know what a system call is and have used it many times in your programs. If you are not a programmer, you may not know what it is, but you still use it thousands of times a day. All "low-level" operations on the system are handled by system calls, including such actions as reading from the disk or printing a message on the screen. System calls are the user's bridge between user space and kernel space. This also means that it is the bridge between a user application and the system hardware.

Collections of system calls are often combined into more complex tasks and put into *libraries*. When using one of the functions defined in a library, you call a *library function* or make a *library call*. Even when the library routine is intended to access the hardware, it will make a system call long before the hardware is touched.

Each system call has its own unique identifying number. The kernel uses this number as an index into a table of system call entry points, which point to where the system calls reside in memory along with the number of arguments that should be passed to them.

When a process makes a system call, the behavior is similar to that with interrupts and exceptions. Like exception handling, the general purpose registers and the number of the system call are pushed onto the stack. Next, the system call handler is invoked, which calls the routine within the kernel that will do the actual work.

Although there are hundreds of library calls, each of these will call one or more systems calls. In total, there are about 150 system calls, all of which have to pass through this one call gate to ensure that user code moves up to the higher privilege level at a specific location within the kernel (a specific address). Therefore, uniform controls can be applied to ensure that a process is not doing something it shouldn't.

As with interrupts and exceptions, the system checks to see whether a context switch should occur on return to user mode. If so, a context switch takes place. This is possible in situations where one process made a system call and an interrupt occurred while the process was in kernel mode. The kernel then issued a `wake_up()` to all processes waiting for date from the hard disk.

When the interrupt completes, the kernel may go back to the first process that made the system call. But, then again, there may be another process with a higher priority.

6.1.7 Paging and Swapping

In Chapter 1, I talked about how the operating system uses capabilities of the CPU to make it appear as though you have more memory than you really do. This is the concept of virtual memory. Later, I'll go into detail about how this is accomplished, that is, how the operating system and CPU work together to keep up this illusion. However, to make this section on the kernel complete, I should talk about this a little from a software perspective.

One basic concept in the Linux implementation of virtual memory is the concept of a *page*. A page is a 4Kb area of memory and is the basic unit of memory with which both the kernel and the CPU deal. Although both can access individual bytes (or even bits), the amount of memory that is managed is usually in pages.

If you are reading a book, you do not need to have all the pages spread out on a table for you to work effectively–just the page you are currently using. I remember many times in college when I had the entire table top covered with open books, including my notebook. As I was studying, I would read a little from one book, take notes on what I read, and, if I needed more details on that subject, I would either go to a different page or a completely different book.

Virtual memory in Linux is very much like that. Just as I only need to have open the pages I was working with currently, a process needs to have only those pages in memory with which it is working. Like me, if the process needs a page that is not currently available (not in physical memory), it needs to go get it (usually from the hard disk).

If another student came along and wanted to use that table, there might be enough space for him or her to spread out his or her books as well. If not, I would have to close some of my books (maybe putting bookmarks at the pages I was using). If another student came along or the table was fairly small, I might have to put some of the books away. Linux does that as well. Consider the text books to represent the unchanging text portion of the program and the notebook to represent the changing data which might make things a little clearer.

It is the responsibility of both the kernel and the CPU to ensure that I don't end up reading someone else's textbook or writing in someone else's notebook. That is, both the kernel and the CPU ensure that one process does not have access to the memory locations of another process (a discussion of cell replication would look silly in my calculus notebook). The CPU also helps the kernel by recognizing when the process tries to access a page that is not yet in memory. It is the kernel's job to figure out which process it was, what page is was, and to load the appropriate page.

It is also the kernel's responsibility to ensure that no one process hogs all available memory, just like the librarian telling me to make some space on the table. If there is only one process running (not very likely), there may be enough memory to keep the *entire* process loaded as it runs. More likely is the case in which dozens of processes are in memory and each gets a small part of the total memory. (Note: Depending on how much memory you have, it is still *possible* that the entire program is in memory.)

Processes generally adhere to the *principle of spatial locality*. This means that over a short period of time, processes will access the same portions of their code over and over again. The kernel could establish a *working set* of pages for each process, the pages that have been accessed with the last *n* memory references. If *n* is small, the processes may not have enough pages in memory to do their job. Instead of letting the processes work, the kernel is busy spending all of its time reading in the needed pages. By the time the system has finished reading in the needed pages, it is some other process's turn. Now, some other process needs more pages, so the kernel needs to read them in. This is called *thrashing*. Large values of *n* may lead to cases in which there is not enough memory for all the processes to run.

The solution is to use a portion of hard disk as a kind of temporary storage for data pages that are not currently needed. This area of the hard disk is called the *swap space* or *swap device* and is a separate area used solely for the purpose of holding data pages from programs.

The size and location of the swap device is normally set when the system is first installed. Afterward, more swap space can be added if needed. (Swap space is added with the `mkswap` command and the system is told to use it with the with the `swapon` command.)

Eventually, the process that was swapped out will get a turn on the CPU and will need to be swapped back in. Before it can be swapped back in, the system needs to ensure that there is enough memory for at least the task structure and a set of structures called *page tables*. Page tables are an integral part of the virtual memory scheme and point to the actual pages in memory. I talk more about this when I talk about the CPU in the hardware section.

Often you don't want to swap in certain pages. For example, it doesn't make sense to swap in pages for a process that is sleeping on some event. Because that event hasn't occurred yet, swapping them in means that it will just need to go right back to sleep. Therefore, only processes in the `TASK_RUNNING` state are eligible to have pagesswapped back in. That is, only the processes that are runnable get pages swapped back in.

Keep in mind that accessing the hard disk is hundreds of times slower than accessing memory. Although swapping does allow you to have more programs in memory than the physical RAM will allow, using it does slow down the system. If possible, it is a good idea to keep from swapping by adding more RAM.

The Linux memory manager limits the size of each swap area to 127.5 MB. You can create a larger swap space, but only the first 127.5 MB will be used. However, a system can have up to 16 swap spaces for a total of 2GB in swap space.

6.1.8 Processes in Action

If you are like me, knowing how things work in theory is not enough. You want to see how things work on your system. Linux provides several tools for you to watch what is happening. The first tool is perhaps the only one that the majority of users have ever seen. This is the `ps` command, which gives you the process status of particular processes.

Although users can look at processes using the `ps` command, they cannot look at the insides of the processes themselves. This is because the `ps` command simply reads the process table, which contains only the control and data structures necessary to administer and manager the process and not the process itself. Despite this, using `ps` can not only show you a lot about what your system is doing but can give you insights into how the system works. Because much of what I will talk about is documented in the `ps` man-page, I suggest in advance that you look there for more details.

If you start ps from the command with no options, the default behavior is to show the processes running for the user who ran the ps. With a logon on two terminals, it looks something like this:

```
PID    TTY    STAT    TIME    COMMAND
72     v04    S       0:00    -bash
73     v05    S       0:01    -bash
830    v05    S       0:05    vi letter.han
833    v04    R       0:00    ps
```

This shows the process ID (PID), the terminal that the process is running on (TTY), the status of the process (STAT; what state it is in), the total amount of time the process has had on the CPU (TIME), and the command that was run (COMMAND).

Although this is useful in many circumstances, it doesn't say much about these processes, Let's see what the long output looks like. This is run as `ps -l`.

```
F UID    PID  PPID PRI NI SIZE RSS  WCHAN  STAT TTY  TIME COMMAND
0 12709  72   1    4   0  372  520  11d0c0 S    v04  0:00 -bash
0 12709  73   1    1   0  384  544  11d0c0 S    v05  0:01 -bash
0 12709  853  72   25  0  57   188  0      R    v04  0:00 ps 1
0 12709  830  73   1   0  189  336  18a04f S    v05  0:00 vi letter.han
```

This output looks a little better. At least there are more entries, so maybe it is more interesting. The columns PID, TTY, STAT, TIME, and COMMAND are the same as in the previous output.

Here we see that the bash process (line 1) is sleeping. Although I can't tell from the output, I know that the event, which is waiting, is the completion of the ps command. The PID and PPID columns, the Process ID and Parent Process ID, respectively, are one indication. Notice that the PPID of the ps process (line 3) is the *same* as the PID of the bash process. This is because I started the ps command from the bash command line and the bash had to do a fork()-exec() to start up the ps. This makes ps a child process of the bash. Because I didn't start the ps in the background, I *know* the bash is waiting on the completion of the ps. (More on this in a moment.)

The ps process is on the processor (state R-RUNNABLE). As a matter of fact, I have *never* run a ps command where ps was not RUNNABLE. Why? Well, the only way for ps to read the process table is to be running and the only way for a process to be running is to be runnable.

Because I am running these processes as the user jimmo, the UID column, which shows the User ID of the owner of that processes, is 12709. This is the same UID as in the /etc./passwd file and is the only way for the system to keep track of who is who. The owner is almost always the user who started the process. However, you can change the owner of a process using the setuid() or the seteuid() system call.

The PRI column is the process's priority and along with the nice value (the NI column), the scheduler calculates the scheduling priority of this process. The RSS column is the "resident set size," or how many kilobytes of the program is in memory.

The WCHAN column is the wait channel for the process, the event on which the process is waiting. Because ps is currently running, it is not waiting on an any event. Therefore, there is a 0 in this column. The WCHAN that the bash is waiting on is 11d0c0. Although I have nothing here to prove it, I *know* that this event is the completion of the ps.

Though I can't prove this, I can make some inferences. First, let's look at the ps output again. This time, let's start ps in the background, which gives us the following output:

```
F  S UID PID  PPID C  PRI NI  ADDR     SZ  WCHAN    TTY  TIME       CMD
20 S 0   608  607  3  75  24  fb11b9e8 132 f01ebf4c ttyp 000:00:02 ksh
20 O 0   1221 608  20 37  28  fb11cb60 184 -        ttyp 000:00:00 ps
```

Next, let's make use of the ability of ps to display the status of processes running on a specific terminal. You can then run the ps command from another terminal and look at what's happening on ttyp0. Running the command

```
ps -lt ttyp0
```

you get something like this:

```
F  S UID PID PPID C PRI  NI ADDR     SZ  WCHAN    TTY   TIME     CMD
20 S 0   608 1295 3 75   24 fb11b9e8 132 f01ebf4c ttyp0 00:00:02 ksh
```

In the first example, ksh did a fork-exec, but because we put it in the background, it returned to the prompt and didn't wait for the ps to complete. Instead, it was waiting for more input from the keyboard. In the second example, ksh did nothing. I ran the ps from another terminal and it showed me only the ksh. Looking back at that screen, I see that it is sitting there, waiting for input from the keyboard. Notice that in both cases the WCHAN is the same. Both are waiting for the same event: input from the keyboard. However, in the previous example, we did not put the command in the background, so the WCHAN was the completion of ps.

Now, wouldn't you say that having just the address of the wait channel is annoying? So do the kernel developers. If you run the program psupdate, the next time you run ps, you won't see the address, but rather, you'll see the name of the kernel function. If necessary, you could then search the kernel code for that function to find out exactly what is going on. A command you could use is

```
find /usr/src/linux -name '*.c' | xargs -t grep <function_name>
```

where <function_name> is the name of the function for which you are looking. By using `xargs -t`, we not only get the name of the file, but the associated lines as well. Alternatively, you could run

```
find /usr/src/linux -name '*.c' | grep -l <function_name>
```

However, this will only show you the file name.

6.2 Rebuilding Your Kernel

Rebuilding your kernel is the process by which you compile all the components of your source code to create a kernel from which you can then install and boot. A rebuild is important (actually, *necessary*) when you want to add or remove drivers or change parameters. Often, changes or updates to the kernel are made that you want to include to keep yourself up to date. (Note that adding new drivers does not always require you to rebuild your kernel and reboot. This is where kernel modules come in, which we talk about later.)

Usually, the updates and or patch come too fast for commercial distributions to keep up with them and include them on their CD-ROM. Normally, new CD-ROMs are created only for minor releases and not revisions. So, if you want to keep up to date, you will have to implement them you yourself. This is also nice because you don't need to get a new CD-ROM every time.

One very important thing to keep in mind is that many applications require specific kernel versions to run correctly (specifically `ps`). Therefore, if you are planning to install a new version of a program or applications, make sure that it is compatible with your kernel.

The kernel source code (normally) is kept in `/usr/src/linux`. Usually, on a fresh installation, the Linux directory is a symbolic link to a directory whose name is based on the kernel release number (for example, `linux-2.0.14`). A README file lists this version number and instructions on how to update the kernel. The version numbers take the following form:

```
major_release.minor_release.patch_level
```

To find out what release you are on, you can run

```
uname -a
```

```
Linux jmohr 2.0.14#1 Sun May 7 15:19:16 CDT 1995 i486
```

Here we have 2.0.14.

When problems (that is, bugs) are discovered in either the kernel or programs, patches are released. Depending on the extent of the patch, the patch level will change. It is a convention that the even numbered releases 1.2.? are "stable" releases. When patches are added to stable releases, they are only bug fixes and contain no new features. When a new feature is to be added, this gets an odd numbered version 1.3.?. These are called development releases. This probably also contains bug fixes as well. Often both the stable even number version and the development odd number version are being worked on (for example, 1.2 and 1.3).

When bug fixes are made, they are added to both versions, but only the 1.3 would get new features. When it becomes stable enough, the version might be changed to 1.4 and the entire process begins again.

Patches are available from all the Linux ftp sites, for example, *sunsite.unc.edu*, as well as many other places. The best idea is to check the newsgroups or one of the Web search engines like Yahoo (*www.yahoo.com*).

Normally, patches are compressed tar archives. The files within the patch are actually the output of the `diff` command. The old version of the source is compared to the new version and the differences are written to the patch file. The `patch` command (which is used to apply the patches) then compares the source code on your system and makes the appropriate changes. Because the `patch` command compares lines in a particular location and makes changes, it is *vital* that patches be put in the correct order. Otherwise changes might be made where they don't belong and nothing works anymore.

Before applying a patch, I would suggest making a backup copy of your entire source directory. First, change to the source directory (`/usr/src`) and run

```
cp -R linux linux.010997
```

Use `-R` for recursive so that all the subdirectories are included. At the end, include the data, so that you know when the copy was made.

To decompress and extract the new source directory at the same time, the command would be

```
tar xzf v.1.4.0.tar.gz
```

Let's assume that you have a patch file called `patch.42`. The command would be

```
gunzip -c patch.42 | patch -p0
```

where the `-c` option to `gunzip` tells it to write the output to `stdout` and the `-p0` option says not to strip of the path names. Often there are multiple patches between the release you installed and the current release, so you need to get all the patch files.

Some more clever administrators might think about putting all the patch files into a single directory and running a single command using wild cards, such as

```
gunzip -c patch.* | patch -p0
```

The problem with this is the way the shell expands the wild cards. The shell doesn't understand the concept of numbers as we do. All it knows is ASCII, so `patch.*` would expand to something like this:

```
patch1
patch10
patch11
patch2
```

If you were to do this, you'd put the patches in the wrong order!

Even if you are going to apply only one patch, you need to be careful what version you have and what patch you are applying. You may find the script `patch-kernel` in the `/usr/src/linux/tools` directory, which will allow you to put on multiple patches and will figure out what order in which they should be applied.

Also keep in mind that the development kernel (those with odd numbered minor releases) are in development (that is, experimental). Just because a driver is included in the development kernel does not mean it will work with all devices. Speaking from experience, I know the problems this will cause. Several versions of Linux that I installed were still in a 1.2 kernel. However, the driver for my host adapted (AHA-2940 was not included). On the CD-ROM was a copy of a 1.3 kernel that contained the driver. I created a floppy using the driver and all was well, I thought.

I was able to install the entire system and get everything configured, and things looked good. Then my SCSI tape drive arrived and I added it to the system. Well, the host adapter driver recognized the tape drive correctly, but immediately after printing the message with the tape drive model, the system stopped. The message on the screen said a SCSI command had timed out.

The kernel that was booting was the one from the installation floppy and, therefore, the 1.3 kernel. However, the source on the hard disk was for the 1.2 kernel. I added the patch, rebuilt the kernel, and rebooted. It was smooth sailing from then on. (Note that the 2.0 kernel already included the changes. This was an attempt to see what worked and not just to get the system working.)

In the kernel source directory /usr/src/linux is a standard make file. Running make config will ask you a series of questions about what drivers to include in your kernel. These are yes/no questions that are pretty straightforward, provided you know about your system.

If you are new to Linux, you should consider running make menuconfig instead. This is a menu interface to the configuration routines that even has extensive on-line help. If you are running X, you should look at running "make xconfig," which will bring you a full GUI front-end. The commercial vendors can learn something from this baby!

The defaults that the systems provide are fine for normal operations, but you need to know how your system is configured. (Now are you beginning to understand why we got to this so far into the book?) In a lot of cases, the responses you make will add functionality, while others simply change parameters.

I can't go step-by-step through the rebuild process without explaining how make files work, but there are a few key points that I need to address. First, there are major changes between 1.2 and 2.0. A large number of drivers have been added and the overall flow is different. In several cases, you were prompted to configure one specific aspect but now are able to be more specific in what you define.

In /usr/src/linux, there is a new subdirectory: documentation. This contains, as you might expect, documentation for the kernel source. Before you reconfigure your kernel, I would suggest taking a look at this subdirectory. It has some very good information on what options to select depending on the hardware you have.

When you rebuild, what is actually run is a script in the arch/<type> subdirectory, where <type> is the type of architecture you have. If you run it on an Intel machine, then the script that is run is /usr/src/linux/arch/i386/config.in. This is the script that prompts your for all of the configuration options. After each question, you will see a cryptic name. This is the variable that will be defined (or undefined, depending on your answer).

Based on your input, variables are set to particular values. These appear as #define statements and are written to a temporary file as the configuration script is being run. If something stops the configuration process (such as you pressing the interrupt key or you inputting an unacceptable value), this temporary file can be ignored. Once the configuration is complete, the temporary file is used as the new version of <linux/autoconf.h>. If you look in the autoconf.h file, you'll see all of those cryptic variables names that you encountered when you ran the configure script.

If we have a Boolean variable (one that is either defined or undefined), then you'll have the applicable definition in the autoconf.h file. For example, on my machine, I answered yes to configuring normal floppy support, so the line in `autoconf.h` looks like this:

```
#define CONFIG_BLK_DEV_FD 1
```

Here we have defined the constant `CONFIG_BLK_DEV_FD` to 1. Certain parts of the kernel source code or the make file will test for this value and include certain modules or otherwise change its behavior based on how the constant is defined.

Let's look at an example. Because all I have is a SCSI hard disk, there was no need to include support for IDE hard disks, so it must be undefined. The entry looks like this:

```
#undef  CONFIG_ST506
```

If you want to add support for a particular device without having to go through the configuration script each time, all you need to do is edit the `autoconf.h` file.

Next, gather the dependencies for the sources and include them in the various make files used during the kernel rebuild. This is done with `make dep`.

If you have done a kernel rebuild before, there may be a lot of files left lying around, so it's a good idea to run `make clean`. Finally, run make with no options to start the kernel rebuilt.

One advantage that Linux has over other OSs is that it is completely component-based and is not distributed as a complete, nondivisible unit. This allows you to update/upgrade those components that have changed and leave the rest intact. This has been made very simple through the Red Hat Package Manager (RPM). (See the chapter on installing for more details.)

Unfortunately, this process is not always "plug-n-play": Often, differences between the kernel and programs (or between different programs) can cause problems. For example, when the kernel was updated to 2.0, I simply tossed the source code onto a system that had the 1.2 kernel, rebuilt the kernel, and rebooted. All looked well. However, on shutting down the system, I encountered a stream of errors that occur only with the 2.0 kernel. However, installing the distribution with the 2.0 kernel in its entirely did not cause this problem.

A fairly new concept is the idea of a loadable module. These are parts of the kernel that are not linked directly to the kernel but are pulled in when you need them. For example, you only use your tape drive when you do backups, so what's the point of having it in your kernel all the time? If you load it only when you need it, you save memory for other tasks.

To be able to use kernel modules like these, your kernel must support it. When you run `make config`, you are asked this question, among others. Modules can be loaded into the kernel by hand, using the `insmod` command, or automatically, using the `kerneld` daemon. See the kernel HOWTO or the kernel mini-HOWTO for more specifics.

6.2.1 Installing Your Kernel

Once you have rebuilt your kernel, you must install it to be able to boot it. Because it is the simplest to use and available on all current distributions, I am only going to talk about the Linux Loaded (LILO) as a method to install your kernel.

LILO is actually a general-purpose boot manager that can boot almost every OS that you installed on your system. LILO normally is run from the hard disk, but you can configure it to run from a floppy as well. LILO can act as a primary boot loader (that is, it is started from the master boot block) or a secondary loader (started by the primary loader).

There are some problems when you run OS/2 or NT because they have their own boot managers. Therefore you will probably have to use their manager as the primary boot loader and have LILO on the Linux partition to boot Linux.

LILO's configuration is in `/etc/lilo.conf`, which is a text file that can be edited with any text editor (`vi`, `emacs`, etc.). On many systems, there is a configuration program `liloconfig`, which will prompt you for some basic configuration parameters that are then written to `/etc/lilo.conf`.

To get a better idea of what this is all about, let's look at the `lilo.conf` file from one of my systems with a Linux and DOS file system. (Most of this was the default.)

```
# LILO configuration file
#
# Start LILO global section
boot = /dev/hda2
delay = 50
vga = normal     # force sane state
ramdisk = 0      # paranoia setting
# End LILO global section
# Linux bootable partition config begins
image = /vmlinuz
root = /dev/hda2
label = Linux
read-only # Non-UMSDOS filesystems should be mounted
read-only for checking
```

```
# Linux bootable partition config ends
# DOS bootable partition config begins
other = /dev/hda1
label = dos
table = /dev/hda
# DOS bootable partition config ends
```

The first part of the file are the basic configuration parameters. The `boot` line defines the device that LILO should install itself onto, in this case, device `/dev/hda2`, which is the second partition of the first drive. If we were to install LILO as the master boot record, this line would read `boot = /dev/had`. Note that this is what it is on an IDE drive; on an SCSI drive, the device would be `/dev/sda2`.

The delay line specifies the number of *tenths* of seconds LILO should wait before booting the first image. Here we have 50, so this means 5 seconds. The `VGA` line specifies the text mode the system should use when booting. Normal means to select 80x25 text mode. The `ramdisk` line specifies the size of the RAM disk to create; in this case, it won't be created because the size is 0.

Next is the section that defines a particular OS to boot. The image line specifies the image to load. In the first case, this is the file `vmlinuz` in the root file system. Next we define the root file system; here it is the device `/dev/hda2`, which is the second partition on the first disk (which coincidentally is where LILO is loaded).

The label is the name you use to specify which OS you want to boot. Also, when the LILO prompt comes, press `TAB` to display this label, in this case, Linux. The next line says the root file system should be mounted read-only. This seems to contradict logic and experience because the root file system ought to be writable. Actually, this is only used for checking when the system first boots; later, other routines will remount the file system as read-write.

In the next section is the description for the DOS partition, which is on the first partition, `/dev/hda1`. The table line specifies the device, here `/dev/hda` (the first hard disk). If this line is omitted, LILO does not pass partition information. Many more options include the geometry. For more options, see the boot HOW-TO.

When the `lilo.conf` file is set up as you want, you need to run `/sbin/lilo` to install it. If you are using Windows NT, which likes to take control and prescribe everything, you will need to configure LILO as a "secondary" boot loader. You can also do this if you don't want LILO to be your boot manager. In the previous example, this is what we have done; if this was the primary, it would be `/dev/had`.

If LILO is installed as your master boot record, you can "remove" it by overwriting the MBR. From DOS, you can remove it with `fdisk /mbr`.

The original boot block is stored in the /boot directory as either boot.3?? for IDE drives or boot.8?? for SCSI devices, where ?? is the device where the master boot block was. You can then use the dd command to copy it back to the hard disk. The syntax of dd follows:

```
dd if=input_file of=output_file  bs=block_size\
count=block_count
```

For example:

```
dd if=/boot/boot.0300 of=/dev/hda bs=446 count=1
```

Although the size of the file in /boot is 512 bytes, only the first 446 contain information. You need to be very careful here. If you make a mistake, for example, count=10, you can overwrite important information on the first partition.

6.3 Devices and Device Nodes

In UNIX, nothing works without devices. I mean *nothing*. Getting input from a keyboard or displaying it on your screen both require devices. Accessing data from the hard disk or printing a report also require devices. In an operating system like DOS, all of the input and output functions are almost entirely hidden from you. Drivers for these devices must exist for you to be able to use them, though they are hidden behind the cloak of the operating system.

Although they access the same physical hardware, device drivers under UNIX are more complex than their DOS cousins. Although adding new drivers is easier under DOS, Linux provides more flexibility in modifying those you already have. Linux provides a mechanism to simplify adding these input and output functions. There is a set of tools and utilities to modify and configure your system.

6.3.1 Major and Minor Numbers

To UNIX, everything is a file. To write to the hard disk, you write to a file. To read from the keyboard is to read from a file. To store backups on a tape device is to write to a file. Even to read from memory is to read from a file. If the file from which you are trying to read or to which you are trying to write is a "normal" file, the process is fairly easy to understand: the file is opened and you read or write data. If, however, the device you want to access is a special device file (also referred to as a device node), a fair bit of work needs to be done before the read or write operation can begin.

One key aspect of understanding device files lies in the fact that different devices behave and react differently. There are no keys on a hard disk and no sectors on a keyboard, though you can read from both. The system, therefore, needs a mechanism whereby it can distinguish between the various types of devices and behave accordingly.

To access a device accordingly, the operating system must be told what to do. Obviously, the manner in which the kernel accesses a hard disk will be different from the way it accesses a terminal. Both can be read from and written to, but that's about where the similarities end. To access each of these totally different kinds of devices, the kernel needs to know that they are, in fact, different.

Inside the kernel are functions for each of the devices the kernel is going to access. All the routines for a specific device are jointly referred to as the device driver. Each device on the system has its own device driver. Within each device driver are the functions that are used to access the device. For devices such as a hard disk or terminal, the system needs to be able to (among other things) open the device, write to the device, read from the device, and close the device. Therefore, the respective drivers will contain the routines needed to open, write to, read from, and close (among other things) those devices.

The kernel needs to be told how to access the device. Not only does the kernel need to be told what kind of device is being accessed but also any special information, such as the partition number if it's a hard disk or density if it's a floppy, for example. This is accomplished by the major and minor number of that device.

The major number is actually the offset into the kernel's device driver table, which tells the kernel what kind of device it is (whether it is a hard disk or a serial terminal). The minor number tells the kernel special characteristics of the device to be accessed. For example, the second hard disk has a different minor number than the first. The COM1 port has a different minor number than the COM2 port.

It is through this table that the routines are accessed that, in turn, access the physical hardware. Once the kernel has determined what kind of device to which it is talking, it determines the specific device, the specific location, or other characteristics of the device by means of the minor number.

The major number for the `hd` (IDE) driver is hard-coded at 3. The minor numbers have the format

```
(<unit>*64)+<part>
```

where `<unit>` is the IDE drive number on the *first* controller, either 0 or 1, which is then multiplied by 64. That means that all `hd` devices on the first IDE drive have a minor number less than 64. <part> is the partition number, which can be anything from 1 to 20. Which minor numbers you will be able to access will depend on how many partitions you have and what kind they are (extended, logical, etc.). The minor number of the device node that represents the whole disk is 0. This has the node name `hda`, whereas the other device nodes have a name equal to their minor number (i.e., `/dev/hda6` has a minor number 6).

If you were to have a second IDE on the first controller, the unit number would be 1. Therefore, all of the minor numbers would be 64 or greater. The minor number of the device node representing the whole disk is 1. This has the node name `hba`, whereas the other device nodes have a name equal to their minor number plus 64 (i.e., `/dev/hdb6` has a minor number 70).

If you have more than one IDE controller, the principle is the same. The only difference is that the *major* number is 22.

For SCSI devices, the scheme is a little different. When you have an SCSI host adapter, you can have up to seven hard disks. Therefore, we need a different way to refer to the partitions. In general, the format of the device nodes is

```
sd<drive><partition>
```

where `sd` refers to the SCSI disk driver, `<drive>` is a letter for the physical drive, and `<partition>` is the partition number. Like the hd devices, when a device refers to the entire disk, for example the device `sda` refers to the first disk.

The major number for all SCSI drives is 8. The minor number is based on the drive number, which is multiplied by 16 instead of 64, like the IDE drives. The partition number is then added to this number to give the minor.

The partition numbers are not as simple to figure out. Partition 0 is for the whole disk (i.e., `sda`). The four DOS primary partitions are numbered 1–4. Then the extended partitions are numbered 5–8. We then add 16 for each drive. For example:

```
brw-rw----   1 root  disk   8,  22 Sep 12  1994 /dev/sdb6
```

Because `b` is after the `sd`, we know that this is on the second drive. Subtracting 16 from the minor, we get 6, which matches the partition number. Because it is between 4 and 8, we know that this is on an extended partition. This is the second partition on the first extended partition.

The floppy devices have an even more peculiar way of assigning minor numbers. The major number is fairly easy–it's 2. Because the names are a little easier to figure out, let's start with them. As you might guess, the device names all begin with `fd`. The general format is

```
fd<drive><density><capacity>
```

where `<drive>` is the drive number (0 for A:, 1 for B:), `<density>` is the density (d-double, h-high), and `<capacity>` is the capacity of the drive (360Kb, 1440Kb). You can also tell the size of the drive by the density letter–a lowercase letter indicates that it is a i5.25" drive and an uppercase letter indicates that it is a 3.5" driver. For example, a low-density 5.25" drive with a capacity of 360Kb would look like

```
fd0d360
```

If your second drive was a high-density 3.5" drive with a capacity of 1440Kb, the device would look like

```
fd1H1440
```

What the minor numbers represents is a fairly complicated process. In the `fd`(4) man-page there is an explanatory table, but it is not obvious from the table why specific minor numbers go with each device. The problem is that there is no logical progression as with the hard disks. For example, there was never a 3.5" with a capacity of 1200Kb nor has there been a 5.25" with a capacity of 1.44Mb. So you will never find a device with H1200 or h1440. So to figure out the device names, the best thing is to look at the man-page.

The terminal devices come in a few forms. The first is the system console, which are the devices `tty0-tty?`. You can have up to 64 virtual terminals on you system console, although most systems that I have seen are limited five or six. All console terminals have a major number of 4. As we discussed earlier, you can reach the low numbered ones with `ALT-Fn`, where `n` is the number of the function key. So `ALT-F4` gets you to the fourth virtual console. Both the minor number and the `tty` number are based on the function key, so `/dev/tty4` has a minor number 4 and you get to it with `ALT-F4`. (Check the `console(4)` man-page to see how to use and get to the other virtual terminals.)

Serial devices can also have terminals hooked up to them. These terminals normally use the devices `/dev/ttySn`, where `n` is the number of the serial port (0, 1, 2, etc.). These also have a minor number of 4, but the minor numbers all start at 64. (That's why you can only have 63 virtual consoles.) The minor numbers are this base of 64, plus the serial port number (0–4). Therefore, the minor number of the third serial port would be 64+3=67.

Related to these devices are the modem control devices, which are used to access modems. These have the same minor numbers but have a major number of 5. The names are also based on the device number. Therefore, the modem device attached to the third serial port has a minor number of 64+3=67 and its name is `cua3`.

Another device with a major number of 5 is `/dev/tty`, which has a minor number of 0. This is a special device and is referred to as the "controlling terminal." This is the terminal device for the currently running process. Therefore, no matter where you are, no matter what you are running, sending something to `/dev/tty` will always appear on your screen.

The pseudoterminals (those that you use with network connections or X) actually come in pairs. The "slave" is the device at which you type and has a name like `ttyp?`, where `?` is the `tty` number. The device that the process sees is the "master" and has a name like `ptyn`, where `n` is the device number. These also have a major number 4. However, the master devices all have minor numbers based on 128. Therefore, `pty0` has a minor number of 128 and `pty9` has a minor number of 137 (128+9). The slave device has minor numbers based on 192, so the slave device `ttyp0` has a minor number of 192. Note that the `tty` numbers do not increase numerically after 9 but use the letter `a–f`.

Other oddities with the device numbering and naming scheme are the memory devices. These have a major number of 1. For example, the device to access physical memory is `/dev/mem` with a minor number of 1. The kernel memory device is `/dev/kmem`, and it has a minor number of 2. The device used to access IO ports is `/dev/port` and it has a minor number of 4.

What about minor number 3? This is for device `/dev/null`, which is nothing. If you direct output to this device, it goes into nothing, or just disappears. Often the error output of a command is directed here, as the errors generated are uninteresting. If you redirect from `/dev/null`, you get nothing as well. Often I do something like this:

```
cat /dev/null > file_name
```

If `file_name` doesn't exist yet, it is created with a length of zero. If it does exist, the file is truncated to 0 bytes.

The device `/dev/zero` has a major number of 5 and its minor number is 5. This behaves similarly to `/dev/null` in that redirecting output to this device is the same as making it disappear. However, if you direct input *from* this device, you get an unending stream of zeroes. Not the number 0, which has an ASCII value of 48–this is an ASCII 0.

Are those all the devices? Unfortunately not. However, I hope that this has given you a start on how device names and minor numbers are configured. The file `<linux/major.h>` contains a list of the currently used (at least well known) major numbers. Some nonstandard package might add a major number of its own. Up to this point, they have been fairly good about not stomping on the existing major numbers.

As far as the minor numbers go, check out the various man-pages. If there is a man-page for a specific device, the minor number will probably be under the name of the driver. This is in `major.h` or often the first letter of the device name. For example, the parallel (printer) devices are `lp?`, so check out man `lp`.

The best overview of all the major and minor numbers is in the `/usr/src/linux/Documentation` directory. The `devices.txt` is considered the "authoritative" source for this information.

6.3.2 File Systems and Files

Any time you access a Linux system, whether locally, across a network, or through any other means, both files and file systems are involved. Every program that you run starts out as a file. Most of the time you are also reading or writing a file. Because files (whether programs or data files) reside on file systems, every time you access the system, you also access a file system.

Knowing what and how a file is represented on the disk and how the system interprets the contents of the file is useful for you to understand what the system is doing. With this understanding, you can evaluate both the system and application behavior to determine whether it is proper.

6.3.3 Disk Layout

Originally, you could only get four partitions on a hard disk. Though this was not a major issue at first, as people got larger hard disks, there was a greater need to break things down in a certain structure. In addition, certain OSs needed a separate space on which to swap. If you had one partition for your root file system, one for swap, one for user information, and one for common data, you would have just run out.

To solve the problem and still maintain backward compability, DOS-based machines were able to create an extended partition that contained logical partitions within it. Other systems, like SCO, allow you to have multiple file systems within a single partition to overcome the limitation.

To be able to access data on your hard disk, there has to be some predefined structure. Without structure, the unorganized data end up looking like my desk, where there are several piles of papers that I have to look though to find what I am looking for. Instead, the layout of a hard disk follows a very consistent pattern–so consistent that it is even possible for different operating systems to share the hard disk.

Basic to this structure is the concept of a *partition*. A partition defines a portion of the hard disk to be used by one operating system or another.

The partition can be any size, even the entire hard disk. Near the very beginning of the disk is the *partition table*. The partition table is only 512 bytes but can still define where each partition begins and how large it is. In addition, the partition table indicates which of the partitions is *active*. This decides which partition the system should go to when looking for an operating system to boot. The partition table is outside of any partition.

Once the system has determined which partition is active, the CPU knows to go to the very first block of data within that partition and begin executing the instructions there. However, if LILO is setup to run out of your master boot block, it doesn't care about the active partition. It does what you tell it.

Often, special control structures that impose an additional structure are created at the beginning of the partition. This structure makes the partition a *file system*.

There are two control structures at the beginning of the file system: the *superblock* and the *inode table*. The superblock contains information about the type of file system, its size, how many data blocks there are, the number of free inodes, free space available, and where the inode table is. On the ext2 filesystem, copies of the superblock are stored at regular intervals for efficiency and in case the original gets trashed.

Many users are not aware that different file systems reside on different parts of the hard disk and, in many cases, on different physical disks. From the user's perspective, the entire directory structure is one unit from the top (/) down to the deepest subdirectory. To carry out this deception, the system administrator needs to *mount* file systems by mounting the device node associated with the file system (e.g., `/dev/home`) onto a mountpoint (e.g., `/home`). This can be done either manually, with the `mount` command line, or by having the system do it for you when it boots. This is done with entries in `/etc/fstab`.

Conceptually, the mountpoint serves as a detour sign for the system. If there is no file system mounted on the mountpoint, the system can just drive through and access what's there. If a file system is mounted, when the system gets to the mountpoint, it sees the detour sign and immediately diverts in another direction. Just as roads, trees, and houses still exist on the other side of the detour sign, any file or directory that exists underneath the mountpoint is still there. You just can't get to it.

Let's look at an example. You have the `/dev/home` file system that you are mounting on `/home`. Let's say that when you first installed the system and before you first mounted the `/dev/home` file system, you created some users with their home directories in `/home`. For example, `/home/jimmo`. When you do finally mount the `/dev/home` file system onto the `/home` directory, you no longer see `/home/jimmo`. It is still there, but once the system reaches the `/home directory`, it is redirected somewhere else.

The way Linux accesses its file systems is different from the way a lot of people are accustomed to it. Let's consider what happens when you open a file. All the program needs to know is the name of the file, which it tells the operating system, which then has to convert it to a physical location on this disk. This usually means converting it to an inode first.

Because the conversion between a file name and the physical location on the disk will be different for different file system types, Linux has implemented a concept called the Virtual File system layer. When a program makes a system call that accesses the file system (such as `open`), the kernel actually calls a function within the VFS layer. It is then the VFS's responsibility to call the file-system-specific code to access the data. Figure 6.6 shows what this looks like graphically.

Figure 6.6: File System Layers

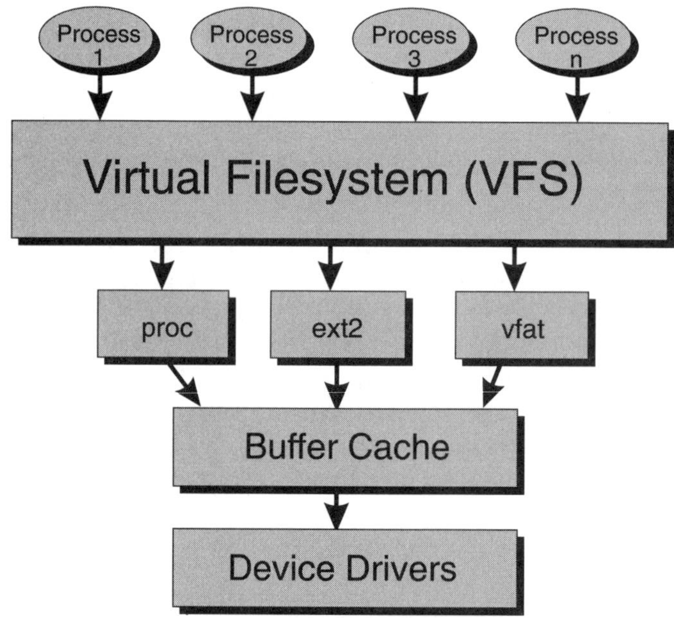

Because it has to interact with every file system type, the VFS has a set of functions that every file system implements. It has to know about all the normal operations that occur on a file such as opening, reading, closing, etc., as well as know about file system structures, such as inodes.

The newest Linux file system is the Second Extended File System (`ext2fs`). This is an enhanced version of the Extended File System (`extfs`). The `ext2fs` was designed to fix some problems in the `extfs`, as well as add some features. Linux also supports the Minix File System and the XIA FS, though these two are less often used.

One benefit of the `ext2fs` over the `extfs` is the size of the file systems that can be managed. Currently (after some enhancements in the

VFS layer), the ext2fs can access file systems as large as 4TB. In contrast to other UNIXs, the ext2fs uses a variable length directory and can have files names that are as long as 255 characters.

When creating the file system, the ext2fs enables you to choose what size block you want. Using larger blocks will speed up the data transfer because the head disk does not need to look (seek) as much. However, if you have a lot of small files, a larger block size means you waste more space.

Also to speed up access, the ext2fs uses a technique called a "fast symbolic link." On many UNIX systems, the files to which symbolic links point are stored as files themselves. This means that each time a file is read as a symbolic link, the disk is accessed to get the inode of the link, the path is read out of the file, and its inode needs to be read, and then the actual file can be accessed.

With a fast symbolic link, the path to the file is stored in the inode. This not only speeds up access but also saves the space that the file is no longer taking on the hard disk. The only drawback is that when the path to the real file has more than 60 characters, it cannot fit in the inode and must sit in a file. Therefore, if you are using symbolic links and want to increase performance, make sure the path has fewer than 60 characters.

Another of the ext2fs's advantages is its reliability. The ext2fs is made of what are called "block groups." Each block group has a block group descriptor, which provides an information copy of the superblock, as well as a block bitmap, inode bitmap, a piece of the inode table, and data blocks.

There is also an entry that contains the number of directories within the group block. When creating a new directory, the system will try to put the directory into the block group with the fewest directories. This makes accessing any one directory quicker.

Because the block group contains copies of the primary control structures, it can be repaired by these copies should the superblock at the start of the disk get corrupted. In addition, because the inode table, as such, is spread out across the disk, you have to search less. Plus, the distance between the inode table and the data block is reduced, thereby increasing performance ever further.

There's still more! The ext2fs will preallocate up to eight adjacent blocks when it allocates a block for a file. This gives the file a little room to grow. By preallocating the blocks, you have a file that is located in the same area of the disk. This speeds up all sequential accesses.

The directories entries in the ext2fs are in a singly linked list, as compared to an array with fixed entry lengths on some systems. Within the directory entry, you will find the name of the file as well as the inode number. Note that this is the only place where the name of the file appears. In addition, there's a field that has the total length of the record in bytes (which is always a multiple of 4) that is then used to calculate the start of the next block. Therefore, there are no pointers as in other linked lists.

When a file is deleted, the inode is set to 0 and the previous entry "takes over" the slot. This saves time because no shifts are required. There may be a slight loss in space, but if a new entry that will fill up the old slot is created, it will fill up the old slot. Because of this scheme, you can implement long file names without wasting space. In some systems, specific-length fields are set aside. If the file name doesn't fill up the slot, the space is just wasted.

Among other things that the inode keeps track of are file types and permissions, number of links, owner and group, size of the file, and when it was last modified. In the inode, you will find 15 pointers to the actual data on the hard disk.

Note that these are *pointers* to the data and not the data itself. Each one of the 15 pointers to the data is a block address on the hard disk. For the following discussion, please refer to Figure 6.7.

Figure 6.7: **Inodes Pointing to Disk Blocks**

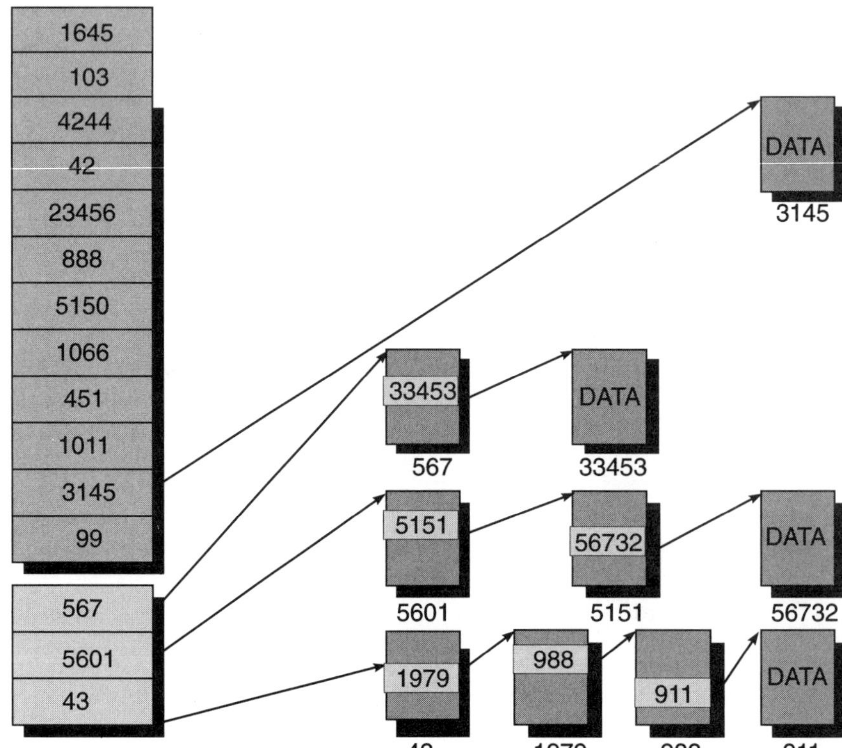

Each of these blocks is 1,024 bytes. Therefore, the maximum file size on a Linux system is 15Kb. Wait a minute! That doesn't sound right, does it? It isn't. If (and that's a big if) all of these pointers pointed to data blocks, then you could only have a file up to 15Kb. However, dozens of files in the `/bin` directory alone are larger than 15Kb. How's that?

The answer is that only 12 of these blocks actually point to data, so there is really only 12Kb that you can access directly. These are referred to as *direct data blocks*. The thirteenth pointer points to a block on the hard disk that actually contains the real pointers to the data. These are the *indirect data blocks* and contain 4-byte values, so there are 128 of them in each block. In Figure 6.7, the thirteenth entry is a pointer to block 567. Block 567 contains 128 pointers to indirect data blocks. One of these pointers points to block 33453, which contains the actual data. Block 33453 is an indirect data block.

Because the data blocks that the 128 pointers pointed to in block 567 each contain 512 bytes of data, there is an additional 65K of data. So, with 12K for the direct data blocks and 65K for the indirect data blocks, we now have a maximum file size of 77K.

Hmmm. Still not good. There are files on your system larger than 77K. So that brings us to triplet 12. This points not to data blocks, not to a block of pointers to data blocks, but to blocks that point to blocks that point to data blocks. These are the *double-indirect data blocks*.

In Figure 6.7, the fourteenth pointer contains a pointer to block 5601. Block 5601 contains pointers to other blocks, one of which is block 5151. However, block 5151 does not contain data, but more pointers. One of these pointers points to block 56732, and it is block 56732 that finally contains the data.

We have a block of 128 entries that each point to a block that each contains 128 pointers to 512 byte data blocks. This gives us 8Mb, just for the double-indirect data blocks. At this point, the additional size gained by the single-indirect and direct data blocks is negligible. Therefore, let's just say we can access more than 8Mb. Now, that's much better. You would be hard-pressed to find a system with files larger than 8Mb (unless we are talking about large database applications). However, we're not through yet. We have one pointer left.

So, not to bore too many of you, let's do the math quickly. The last pointer points to a block containing 128 pointers to other blocks, each of which points to 128 other blocks. At this point, we already have 16,384 blocks. Each of these 16,384 blocks contain 128 pointers to the actual data blocks. Here we have 2,097,152 pointers to data blocks, which gives us a grand total of 1,073,741,824, or 1Gb, of data (plus the insignificant 8MB we get from the double-indirect data blocks). As you might have guessed, these are the triple-indirect data blocks.In Figure 6.7 pointer 13 contains a pointer to block 43. Block 42 contains 256 pointers, one of which points to block 1979. Block 1979 also contains 256 pointers, one of which points to block 988. Block 988 also contains 256 pointers, though *these* pointers point to the actual data. For example, block 911.

If we increase the block size to 4k (4,096 bytes), we end up with more pointers in each of the indirect blocks so they can point to more blocks. In the end, we have files the size of 4Tb. However, because the size field in the inode is a 32-bit value, we max out at 4Gb.

Linux's support for file systems is perhaps the most extensive of any operating system. In addition to the "standard linux" file system, there is also support for FAT, VFAT, ISO9660 (CD-ROM), NFS, plus file systems mounted from Windows machines using Samba (via the SMB protocol). Is that all? Nope! There are also drivers to support several compressed formats such as stacker and double-space. The driver for the Windows NT file system (NTFS) can even circumvent that annoying security.

File System Tools

When you are working with file systems, you need to be aware of several tools. The first tool is not specifically for file systems, but without it you cannot create one. This tool is `fdisk`, which is used to create partitions. The file systems are then created on the partition.

Next is `mke2fs`, which is used to make the file system. If you install a system from scratch, the installation process will run this for you with some fairly legitimate defaults. However, if you are adding a new hard disk to your system, the device nodes may be there, but the file systems are not. Therefore, you will need to create them.

Note that the `mke2fs` program will only make ext2fs file systems. Other programs can make these file systems, but I will continue to restrict our discussion to the ext2fs.

Think back to the discussion on the file system structure. By default, the system creates the inode table with a ratio of one inode for every 4,096 bytes. If you have several large files, the file system will be full before you run out of inodes. However, if you are running a news or mail server, the average size of the files is less than 4,096 bytes. Therefore, you will probably run out of inodes before the file system fills up.

Therefore, if you have a news or mail server, it is a good idea to use `mke2fs` manually to create the file system *before* you add any files. Remember that the inode table is at the beginning of the file system and takes up as much room as it needs for a given number of inodes. If you want to have more inodes, you must have a larger inode table. The only place for the inode table to grow is into your data. Therefore, you would end up overwriting data. Besides, running `mke2fs` "zeroes" out your inode table so the pointers to the data are lost anyway.

The `tune2fs` is also just for the ext2fs and is used to modify the file system parameters. You can adjust the behavior on errors, the maximum interval between forced cleanings. Using the `-l` option will show you the current configuration parameters.

Last is one program that you *don't* want to learn very well: `e2fsck`. This is the file system checker. This program is designed to check *and* fix your file system. The only time you get to know it very well is when there is something wrong with your file system that you need to correct.

If for some reason your system goes down improperly, the file system will not be marked as "clean." In some cases, not being clean (also called being dirty) simply means that the system didn't set the clean bit. When you reboot, `e2fsck` checks the file system, all is well and you can continue to work.

If your luck is not with you, however, there are times when not clean is not good. You might have opened files when the system went down and the data weren't written to the disk, so when the system came back up you had empty files. You may have situations in which the directory entry is trashed and the files exist in the file system (it has an inode and occupies data `blocks`) though there is no entry in any directory.

When you run `e2fsck`, it goes through several phases to check the sanity of each file system and to clean up as necessary. In the first phase or pass, `e2fsck` checks all the files in the file system. Rather, it is more accurate to say that it checks all the inodes. The human concept of a file includes the file name, though when `e2fsck` checks things during the first pass, it only checks the inode, which includes making sure that the mode (permissions of the file) is valid, all the data blocks point to valid block numbers, etc.

Part of this check is to see that now two inodes point to the same data blocks. Remember that you can have two file names point to the same inode, as is the case with both hard and symbolic links. However, they represent the same set of blocks on the hard disk. Having two inodes accessing the same data blocks is not a good thing. Also during this pass, the inode and block bitmaps are checked.

If `e2fsck` noticed any problems, it runs though again (pass 1b–1d) to make sure things are straightened out.

Next, in pass 2, directories are checked. The directories are checked as "unconnected" objects, that is, unrelated to inodes. First, the dot (`.`) entry is checked to see that it exists and points to the current directory and that the dot-dot (`..`) exists. Note that checking the dot-dot entry to ensure that it points to the parent directory is not done until pass 3. This is to keep the directories unconnected.

At this point, `e2fsck` has looked at all of the directories and all of the inodes at least once. Part of what `e2fsck` does to speed things up is to keep all of this information in memory. Therefore, it doesn't have to go back to the disk again. Instead, the remainder of the checks are all performed in memory.

In pass 3, `e2fsck` first checks the directories as connected objects. Here, the paths of each directory are traced back to the root. To do this, `e2fsck` needs to check each of the dot-dot (`..`) entries to make sure it is valid. Any directories that cannot be traced back are linked into the `lost+found` directory.

In pass 4, `e2fsck` checks the reference count of all inodes. Part of this is to make sure that there are as many files pointing to a particular inode as the inode thinks there are. If a file exists but does not point to a valid inode, it is also linked into `/lost+found`.

In the last pass, `e2fsck` checks the validity of the system information, such as the block and inode bitmaps against which we computed what is actually on the hard disk. Because what is in memory was just verified, this would overwrite what is on the hard disk.

I've seen the X-Windows system described as a "distributed, graphical method of working," and that probably fits the best. It's distributed because you could run the display on your monitor in Virginia even though the program is actually running on a computer in California or Calcutta, and it's graphical because you see a lot of nice pictures on your screen.

Despite the extent to which it has spread in the UNIX world, the X-Windows system is not a UNIX product. The X-Windows system, affectionately called X, was developed by the Massachusetts Institute of Technology and runs on a wide range of computers, even MS-Windows-based versions.

The first version was developed at MIT in 1984. Several versions have been developed since, with the most current version, X version 11 (X11), first released in 1987. X11 has been adopted as the industry standard windowing system, with the support of a consortium of major computer industry companies such as DEC, HP, SUN, and IBM.

Although you could probably find a system that is still running release 5, the newest release (as of this writing) is release 6. You will see references to the release as X11Rn, where n is the release number. So, the current release would be X11R6.

7.1 Configuring the X-Windows Server

On all current distributions (as far as I can tell), you will be getting a copy of the Xfree86 X-Windows system. Although this is almost completely compatible with commercial versions, this one is free like other products under the GNU public license.

Although you can get away with 4Mb of physical RAM and an additional 12Mb of swap space, you won't be happy. With this minimal configuration, you will probably get X started and a couple of windows open and then you will want to start swapping. Experience has taught me that without at least 16Mb of physical RAM, the system is too slow to be enjoyable to work in. Considering how low RAM prices have dropped, there really isn't any excuse any more not to purchase more RAM.

When you install your copy of Linux, you will (should) be asked a series of questions about your video system to configure your X server. Even if you don't know what video chipset you use or the video card manufacturer, you can get away with using the standard SVGA card. However, the performance and appearance will dramatically improve if you are able to specify exactly what you have.

Even if there isn't an exact match, you can try something close and still get decent performance. If it is an exact match, I would recommend using a low resolution, like 640x480, to test the configuration. Once you are sure that everything works correctly, you can move to higher resolutions.

Once X-Windows is running, you can use the configuration program `xf86config`, which will again ask you a series of questions about your configuration. Here you really ought to know about the hardware, including your monitor. What hardware X-Windows supports is listed in the latest Xfree86 HOWTO, which you should find on your CD-ROM.

When you install your X server, note that you are not running just a single program. Instead, quite a few different programs are running. Which one runs depends on the options you specified during the configuration. Because most only run on a single video card or chipset, you definitely need to know about your hardware.

Keep in mind that just because you can run the Linux command line does not mean that Linux supports your video card. The command line is run in text mode, which uses well-known standard video modes to access the video card. However, once the X server is running, you are accessing the video card directly and need to know all the details.

Also available are several commercial X servers such as Accelerated-X and Metro-X, which provide better performance than the default X servers Xfree86 provides.

The primary configuration file for your X server is (normally) `/etc/XF86Config` or `/etc/X11/XF86Config`. This is a text file, which is generated new every time you run `xf86config`. This is broken down into three sections. The Screen section is the primary section and often comes last. It defines what you see on the screen based on the other two sections. The Device section describes your video card (which is often referred to as a video device). The Monitor section describes, as you might expect, your monitor.

Each section has a header line that defines what section it is and an `EndSection` line to close it up. The general form is

```
Section "SectionName"
section info
EndSection
```

Because the X server decides what to show on the screen based on the Screen section, that is probably a good place for me to start. Within the Screen section, the server can give you several subsections for each of the "Display" types. The subsections are the logical configurations of your monitor and determine such things as the number of colors that can be displayed, the resolution, and whether there is a "logical" screen.

The Screen section on one of my machines looks like this:

```
Section "Screen"
  Driver      "accel"
  Device      "SPEA Mercury 64"
  Monitor     "Sony17sf"
  Subsection "Display"
    Depth       8
    Modes       "800x600" "1024x768"
    ViewPort    0 0
    Virtual     800 600
  EndSubsection
  Subsection "Display"
```

```
    Depth       16
    Modes       "800x600" "1024x768"
    ViewPort    0 0
    Virtual     1024 768
  EndSubsection
  Subsection "Display"
    Depth       32
    Modes       "800x600"
    ViewPort    0 0
    Virtual     800 600
  EndSubsection
EndSection
```

The Driver line indicates which X server will be used. In this case, I am using the "accel" driver for "accelerated" servers, which basically means that they have faster performance than other cards. The other kinds of drivers are vga2 (for vga cards in 2-color mode), vga16 (16-color vga), and svga (super-VGA, 256 color, 640x480).

The Device line indicates the name of the video card. Because that's the card I have, this line is set to "SPEA Mercury 64." The monitor indicates the monitor type. Note that in my case there was a specific entry for the SPEA Mercury card. However, there was no specific entry for my monitor, though one was close. The system uses this information to choose the best driver for you. However, you can still choose another driver.

As I mentioned previously, the Display subsection determines what is displayed on your screen. In this case, we have three different Display subsections, which are distinguished by the Depth line, which defines the color depth, or number of colors, that can be displayed. This indicates the number of bytes that are used to describe the colors. Therefore, in the first entry, we have 8 bits, or a total of 256 possible colors.

The Modes line defines the possible resolutions that your monitor can support. Normally, the lower the depth, the more modes the server can handle. In my case, the system did not configure this. Each of the modes has an entry for 640x480. Because I never wanted my server coming up in that mode, I was able to remove the modes. (Note that this is one option in the `xf86config` program.)

When it starts up, the X server will take the first entry it finds. In my case, this is 800x600 and 256 colors. However, you can use options to `startx`, which then passes the first entry on to `xinit`. If I wanted to increase the color depth to 24 bits, I could start the server like this:

```
startx -- -bpp 24
```

The Device section describes the characteristics of your video card. On my machine, it looks like this:

```
Section "Device"
  Identifier  "SPEA Mercury 64"
  VendorName  "Unknown"
  BoardName   "Unknown"
  VideoRam    2048
EndSection
```

The Identifier entry is used in other sections to match displays with Devices. Although the VendorName in this case is SPEA and the BoardName is Mercury 64, it does not matter that these two fields are empty.

Last, we get to the Monitor section. An excerpt from the monitor section on my system follows (with a *lot* of things removed to save spaces). Note that you could have multiple Monitor sections if you were going to connect different monitors.

```
Section "Monitor"
Identifier  "Sony17sf"
  VendorName  "Sony"
  ModelName   "17sfII"

HorizSync   31.5 - 57.0

VertRefresh 50-70

# 640x400 @ 70 Hz, 31.5 kHz hsync
Modeline "640x400"   25.175  640   664  760  800   400 409  411  450
# 640x480 @ 60 Hz, 31.5 kHz hsync
Modeline "640x480"     25.175 640  664  760  800   480  491  493  525
# 800x600 @ 56 Hz, 35.15 kHz hsync
ModeLine "800x600"     36      800  824  896 1024   600  601  603  625
# 1024x768 @ 87 Hz interlaced, 35.5 kHz hsync
Modeline "1024x768"    44.9   1024 1048 1208 1264   768  776  784  817
```

Like the Devices section, the Identifier is used to match monitors and displays. Here the physical characteristics of the monitor are described, including the vertical refresh rate (how many times per second the screen can be redrawn) and the horizontal synchronization (which is based on the resolution and vertical refresh rate).

The most important part of the Monitor section are the modeline entries. If you have a common video card and monitor, you don't have to worry about this because the `xf86config` utility will create them for you. If you do need to create them, you should check the latest Xfree86 HOWTO.

7.2 The Basics of X

An X session is usually composed of several windows, each running a separate program or client. Like programs on any other system, programs running under X vary in functionality. Some interact completely with the user, like the `xTerm` terminal emulator. Others simply display output on the screen, like the `xload` system monitor.

The background window is referred to as the root window. Application windows, or clients, are displayed on top of the root window. Like UNIX processes, these windows are grouped together, or related, in a family hierarchy. As `init` is the great-grandmother of all processes, the root window is the great-grandmother of all windows. Clients displayed on the root window are children of the root window, and the root window is their parent. This hierarchy actually extends to different parts of a window. For example, menus are often considered children of the parent window as they inherit characteristics, but also can be configured and react independently of the parent window.

X consists of two sides: a server side and a client side. The basic functionality is similar to the way all client-server models work in that the X server has certain resources that it provides to the client. It is a common misconception that the server and clients are on the same machine. Because X is integrated with the TCP/IP stacks, requests can come from any client and can be requested of any server. In addition, because X is not a program but more a protocol, machines can communicate with completely different architectures. For example, a Digital OSF/1 server can provide services to both a Linux and an AIX client, as well as either of the others providing services to the OSF/1 machine. Just like other network applications, a single machine can be both client and server.

The server acts as the interface between the client programs and the physical hardware. When you input data through either the keyboard or pointer, the server accepts that input and is responsible for passing it along to the client. This information is passed to the client an event. Pressing a key or moving the pointer causes an event, to which the client may react. Often that reaction is in the form of changing the display on the screen. For example, a client receives the event that a particular menu was clicked on. It responds by requesting the server to display the pull-down menu. The server then passes the information on to the hardware, which shows the pull-down menu as a screen. It gives it to the server, which then passes it to the hardware. As a result of this separation of functionality, one client could display information on more than one server.

To start anything, an X server needs to be running somewhere. Despite that fact that you can access servers anywhere on the network, a common configuration is one in which the server is running on the same machine as the client.

Some systems have a graphic login that automatically starts when the system boots (for example, the Common Desktop Environment). Another common way for the system to start is through the `startx` shell-script, which reads the two files `.xinitrc` and `.xserverrc` file in your home directory and treats them in the same way as your shell would treat the `.cshrc` and `.kshrc` files. Here is where your initial clients are started, such as terminal emulator and the window manager. If you don't have a `.xinitrc` file in your home directory, then `startx` will read the system default file `/etc/X11/xinit/xinitrc`. In reality, the X server is started by the `xinit` program. However, `startx` starts `xinit` for you.

Contrary to popular belief, neither the X server nor the clients are responsible for the appearance of the windows on the screen as we understand them. Instead, this falls to a window "manager." Most Linux distributions provide two window managers: The F(?)[1] Virtual Window Manager (`fvwm`) and the Tab Windows Manager (`twm`). In most cases (that I have seen), the default window manager is `fvwm`.

What you can do to each part of a window is important in understanding the basic concepts of X. These parts are shown in Figure 7.1. A *click* is used to active a button. This is done by quickly pressing down and releasing one of the mouse buttons. Because there is only one mouse button on many systems, the mouse button used to click is usually button number one. On a right-handed mouse, this is the left button. A double-click is when the button is clicked twice in rapid succession.

To drag an object, select that object by placing the pointer somewhere on that object, then pressing down and holding the first mouse button. In many cases, such as in XTerm, you must click on the title bar. You then see the outline of that window, which you can move to a new location. You can also select the window by clicking Move in the Window Menu. To drop the object onto another, drag that object over another object and release the mouse button. This only works in appropriate circumstances, for example, dropping a document onto the printer icon to print it.

It can also be said that you, the user, manage the windows. You determine the size and location of the window, as well as determine which is the active window. You can change the size of the window in several dif-

1. What the F stands for has been lost through the ages.

Figure 7.1: **Description of the Various Parts of a Window**

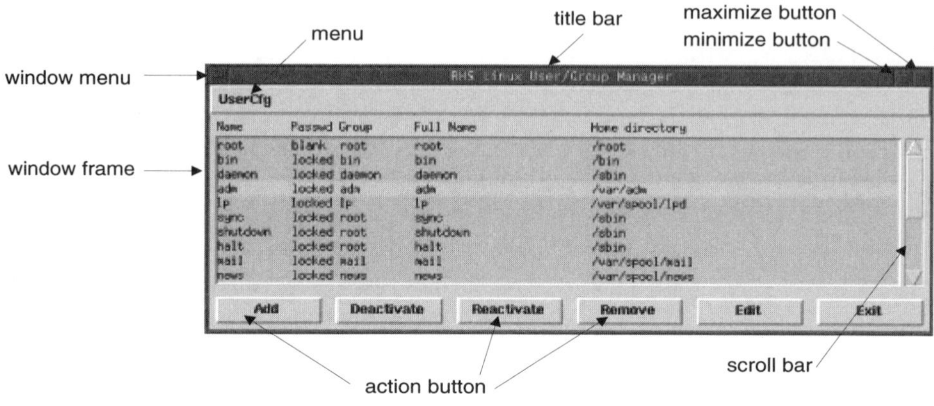

ferent ways. By moving the pointer, you can *grab* any corner of the window by pressing and holding down the left mouse button. You can then move that corner in any direction, thus changing both the horizontal and vertical proportions of the window. You can also grab an edge and change the horizontal or vertical edge, depending on which edge you grab. In addition, you can choose the Size option from the window menu and then move the pointer to the edge or corner with which you want to resize. This time, though, do not hold down the left mouse button.

There are also two buttons in the upper right hand corner of the window. The inner button is the maximize button. When you click it, the window will fill the screen (it maximizes). When you click it again, it returns to its previous size–not the default, but the size it was before you clicked the maximize button. The other button is the iconify button. This turns the window into a miniature version of its former self. This is a "representation" of that window. These little images are referred to as icons. Double-clicking the icon returns it to the size it was before you clicked it to iconify it.

When you choose which window is active, you *set the focus*. There are two types of focus policies used: explicit and pointer. In explicit focus, you must click somewhere within the window to set the focus. In pointer focus, the focus is set when the pointer enters a window.

If the default is explicit focus, I suggest you leave it as such until you are very familiar with moving around windows or have a compelling reason to change it. The problem with pointer focus is that you could be typing away in one window and accidentally push the mouse so the pointer is in another window allowing, all of a sudden, the new window to accept input. On slower machines, the opposite effect might happen. You may move the pointer intentionally to a new window and start typing.

However, because the focus takes a moment to "catch up" with you, the input is sent to the previous window.

To change this, edit your `.fvwmrc` file and look for the entry that says AutoRaise. This item defines how long (in milliseconds) the system will wait until it automatically raises the window over which you have moved the cursor. This is pointer focus. Comment out this entry by placing a pound-sign (#) in fron of the line. Just below it, is the entry ClickToFocus. This is the explicit mode. This means that you have to explicitely click on a window to change the focus.

In the `.fvmwrc` file, these focus modes are referred to as *auto-raise* mode and *focus-follows mouse* mode. Most of the other documentation refers to explicit and auto focus; use what you like.

Common to every windowing system (at least every one I have ever seen) is the concept of a menu. Like a menu in a restaurant, a menu in X presents a list of choices. Windows in X come in two types: pull-down and pop-up. Pull-down menus are almost universally associated with a particular location on the window. When you click on that location, a menu appears to drop down from that location. In a sense, you are pulling down that menu. By default, each window has Window Menu, which is a small square with a horizontal bar running through it, located in the upper left corner. Some people describe it as looking like a filing cabinet drawer with a handle. When you click on the Window Menu, you are give options that are related to the window itself. These include moving, resizing, or changing the window's position in the windows "stack" (raising or lowering it).

Pop-up menus are usually not associated with any particular location on the window. These menus "pop-up" from the current cursor position. An example of a pop-up menu is the Root Menu that pops up anytime you click on an exposed area of the root window.

Earlier I mentioned that the window manager determines the "look and feel" of an application. This is not entirely true. Although what is presented is a function of the window manager, the underlying routines used to represent a button or a scrollbar can be different. Many of the Linux-provided clients use a set of routines called the X Toolkit (Xt), which is actually two libraries (the X Toolkit Intrinsics and the Athena Widget set [Xaw]) used to create the interface components (buttons, menus, etc.), referred to as "widgets."

Keep in mind that X does not provide a graphical-user interface (GUI). X is simply the windowing mechanism, but some other component provides the GUI. To produce such a GUI, the Open Software Foundation (OSF) developed the Motif Toolkit, which is based on the X Toolkit Intrinsics and a set of widgets developed by DEC and HP. This was originally designed to emulate the look and feel of the IBM/ Microsoft Presentation Manager used in OS/2.

On Linux, you will find both Motif and standard X applications. Motif applications are those that use the Motif Toolkit and all have a common look and feel. One standard X application is the xclipboard. If you run it along with some other application such as `xv` (a graphics viewer), you will notice some distinct differences, the most dramatic of which is the overall appearance. Motif-based applications appear three-dimensional, whereas standard X applications look "flat" (two-demensional).

7.3 Displaying Clients

When the clients connect to the server, one key piece of information it needs is the display name. The display is of the form

```
hostname:displaynumber.screennumber
```

The `hostname` identifies the name of the machine to which the display is physically connected. The most common form of `hostname` is simply the node name, as more than likely the server is in the same network. However, it is possible to use a fully qualified domain or even an IP address for the `hostname`.

Unless you have some special hardware, you probably have only one physical display per server. However, each display is given a number starting at 0. If you only have one, then you will always access `hostname:0`. The screen number is only used in cases where a single keyboard and mouse are associated with multiple monitors. Like displays, screens are counted starting at 0. Because multiple screens are far less common than multiple displays, you can omit the screen number when specifying the display. Generally, the default display is stored in the DISPLAY variable, which is then used by default. However, many X clients have a `-display` option, with which you can specify the display.

The next important issue is the concept of *geometry*. One advantage of a system like X is the ability not only to move windows around the screen but also to change their size and shape as well. Rather than using the window manager to change the shape of the window, you can specify the shape and size when the application is started by specifying the client's geometry.

The geometry is represented by four characteristics: width, height, the distance from left or right, and the distance from the top or bottom. These are referenced by width, height, xoff, and yoff, respectively. Depending on the application, the height and width are measured in either pixels or characters, whereas the xoff and yoff values are measured only in pixels. Both xoff and yoff are measured in relationship to the screen. The general syntax of the geometry specification is

```
application -geometry widthxheight+xoff+yoff
```

Here the + (plus sign) before xoff and yoff indicate a distance from the left and top edges of the screen, respectively. By changing + to -, you change the offset to be from the right and bottom instead of left and top. For example, if you wanted to start the analog clock 30 pixels to the right of the upper left corner, the command would look like this:

```
oclock -geometry 90x90+30+0 &
```

(It's a good idea to run all clients in the background, otherwise you don't get your prompt back until the client terminates.) Now, if we wanted to start the clock 30 pixels to the left of the upper right corner, the command would look like this:

```
oclock -geometry 90x90-30+0 &
```

Now, if we wanted to start the clock 30 pixels to the left of the lower right corner, the command would look like this:

```
oclock -geometry 90x90-30-0 &
```

The four corners are thus mapped like this:

```
+0+0      -0+0
+0-0      -0-0
```

You can also specify negative offsets that would then start the client outside of the respective edge of the screen. For example, if we change the above command to look like this

```
oclock -geometry 90x90--30+0 &
```

It will start the client so that right edge of the clock is 30 pixels outside of the right edge of the screen. (Be careful not to have spaces in there.) This does not mean that the entire clock is outside of the right edge of the screen. This is a misconception that many people have (including me, at first). On many systems, there is something magical about the upper left corner of the client. Offsets from the edge of the screen are in relationship to this magical corner. This is not so with X.

A `+xoff` value is the distance of the *left* edge of the client from the left edge of the screen. A `-xoff` value is the distance of the *right* edge of the client from the right edge of the screen. This also means that a `+yoff` value is the distance of the *top* of the client to the top of the screen, and `-yoff` is the distance from the *bottom* of the client to the bottom of the screen.

Note that the geometry is specified in pairs. So, if you specify the height, you must also specify the width. Also, if you specify the x-offset, you must also specify the y-offset. However, you don't have to specify the offsets if you only want to specify the size. Therefore, you could start the clock like this:

```
oclock -geometry 90x90 &
```

This gives me a 90x90 clock at the default location. If you only want the offset to take the default size, it might look like this:

```
oclock -geometry +100+42 &
```

The thing that bothers me about this clock is that it is pretty boring. The colors are drab and it really doesn't have any life to it. The nice thing is that we can change the colors. With the analog clock, we can change several different things. If we wanted the background color to be cornflower blue, we would enter the command

```
oclock -bg cornflowerblue &
```

This creates an analog clock with the default size at the default location with a background of cornflower blue. However, it still looks boring. I want a foreground of red. So, let's run the command like this:

```
oclock -bg cornflowerblue -fg red &
```

Now it's beginning to have a little life to it. However, having both hands red is still not good enough. I want the hour hand red but the minute hand white, and I want the jewel at the top of the clock yellow. The command would then look like this:

```
oclock -bg cornflowerblue -hour red -minute white -jewel yellow &
```

That's not all. We can use a couple more options. However, these are listed in the `oclock(X)` man-page, so you can take a look there if you want. Other clients have different options because some of them don't make sense with an analog clock. For example, the digital clock (`dclock`) has an option to specify the font (`-fn`). Because there are no characters on the analog clock, an option to change the font wouldn't make sense.

7.4 Resources

If we wanted, we also could have included the geometry along with the colors, which would give us a command that is almost too long for the screen. Even now it is a long command that takes a long time to type in, and you can easily make mistakes. One solution would be to write everything in a shell-script and start that script instead of typing everything on the command line.

The nice thing is we don't have to do this. X provides a mechanism to change the appearance and sometimes the behavior of a client to fit our personal preferences. This is the concept of a resource. Up to now, we have specified the resource from the command line, such as foreground color and geometry. However, there are resource files that we can edit to change the default characteristics of a given client.

Resource files for most applications are found in `/usr/lib/X11/app-defaults`. The general form of the resource specification is

```
appname*subname*subsubname...: value
```

The application is the name of the program you are starting, usually with the first letter capitalized. Note the word "usually." I don't know how many times I've tried to change a resource and not have it work, only to find out that this one application's name is written in lowercase. In the case of the files in `/usr/lib/X11/app-defaults`, no `appname` is necessary because there is one file for each client and X knows what client is meant when it reads these files. If set, X will search the path specified by the `XFILESEARCHPATH` variable for the resource information.

Unless you want to change the system defaults, I suggest that you leave these files alone. Instead, you can create a user- or machine-specific resource file. Normally, this is `$HOME/.Xdefaults--hostname`, where `hostname` is the name of the host to which these resource specifications apply. If the `.Xdefaults` file is to apply to the local host, you can omit the hostname. If you want to specify an alternative file, you can use the `XENVIRONMENT` variable.

These resources are organized into classes, which enables you to set groups of individual resources all at once. Individual resources are referred to as an instance. By convention, the class name begins with an uppercase letter and the instance begins with a lowercase letter. We can generally say that a resource (both class and instance) is named for the aspect of appearance that it controls. For example, the class called Foreground sets the foreground color. An instance of the Foreground class would be specified with a lowercase "F": foreground. Keep in mind that different parts of the clients are affected by the class Foreground, such as the text color, cursor color, and pointer color.

Basically all applications have resources. In each case, the class name has an initial capital. Examples of this are

`background`	window background color
`borderWidth`	width in pixels of the window border
`borderColor`	window border color
`foreground`	window foreground color

The distinction between classes and instances is very useful if you want to set several resources at once. For example, if you define the foreground color for all aspects of the XTerm, the resource definition would look like this:

```
XTerm*Foreground: blue
```

This would be equivalent to

```
XTerm*foreground: blue
XTerm*cursorColor: blue
XTerm*pointerColor: blue
```

This means that the foreground color of text, cursor, and pointer are all blue. If we then defined the `pointerColor` instance to be something else, only it changes. For example, if we made the following definition

```
XTerm*pointerColor: red
```

the color is now red, although all the others remain blue.

Although the asterisk is perhaps the most commonly used delimiters, it's not the only one. The asterisk delimiter is used to indicate a *loose binding*, in which there can be several layers in the object hierarchy. It's easy to think of the asterisk as having the same function as on the command line, that is, as a wild card. Here, the asterisk represents 0 or more intermediate layers between the root object and the resource we are defining.

If there are no intermediate layers between the objects, this referred to as a *tight binding*. If you wanted this, you *could* specify the binding with the asterisk because it means 0 or more intermediate levels. However, the symbol used to explicitly specify a tight binding is a dot (`.`). Because I know that the level just before the `pointerColor` in the hierarchy is "ansi," I can make the specification like this:

```
XTerm*.ansi.pointerColor: red
```

However, because the loose binding specifier (`*`) can be used any place though the tight binding specifier (`.`) can be used only when appropriate, it is easier always to use the loose binding specifier.

Both the resource specifications and binding can bring up some conflicts. In the example above, we said to use blue for *every* foreground color related to the client "XTerm." We also said to use red for the foreground color of pointer. Now this seems like a conflict, which it is. However, in this case, the instance of the `pointerColor` took precedence over the class of Foreground.

Consider these lines from an .Xdefaults file:

```
XTerm*Foreground: blue
XTerm*pointerColor: red
XTerm*ansi.pointerColor: green
```

We first defined the Foreground class to be blue. Next, we defined the instance of the `pointerColor` to be red. Both of these are done with loose bindings. We then defined the instance of the `pointerColor` for an ANSI terminal to be green. Because tight bindings have precedence over loose bindings, the pointer is green.

Taking this one step further, we change the class specification so it contains a tight binding. However, we leave the instance specification a loose binding. So, we end up with these two lines:

```
XTerm*ansi.Foreground: blue
XTerm*pointerColor: red
```

In this case, there is a tightly bound class specification that is followed by a loosely bound instance specification. When we start the XTerm, the pointer is blue, not red. In general, we can say that the more specific a specification is, the greater the precedence.

There are a limited number of options that we can use from the command line, although there are many more resources that we might want to change. To accommodate a large number of resource without increasing the number of options, we use the `-xrm` option. For example, if we wanted to change the `tty` modes of `XTerm` (what the characters are for erase, delete, quit, etc.), we could do this using the `-xrm` option and specifying an instance of the `TtyModes` class. For example, to change the interrupt key from the default of `Del` to `Ctrl+C`, the command would look like this:

```
XTerm -xrm 'XTerm*ttyModes: intr ^C ' &
```

Keep in mind that this resource specification is only valid for this one XTerm that we are starting here. If we wanted it to be valid for all XTerms, we would either change the default in `/usr/lib/X11/app-defaults` or define the resource in the `.Xdefaults` file.

7.5 Colors

Although you may be satisfied with the default colors that X gives you, I am sure that eventually you will want to make some changes. In previous sections, I talked about how you can change the color of X clients either from the command line or by changing the appropriate resource. The only problem with that is you might not like the colors that Linux offers.

You might ask, "Why doesn't the system just give me a list with every possible color?" Well, you would need to have that list in a file somewhere. If you did, you would have a list that was more than 20Mb because of the way Linux stores colors.

Each color is represented by one byte for each of the three colors: red, green, and blue (referred to as the RGB scheme). Each byte can have one of 256 values that represent the intensity of each color. In other words, the value represents how much of each color is included in a shade. If all three colors have the value 255, the shade is pure white. If each color has the value 0, the shade is black.

The `/usr/lib/X11/rgb.txt` file contains names of colors and, often, variations in that name. This is usually the case when the name of the color actually consists of two words, for example, antique white. In such a case, you would also find the color antiquewhite. Each entry contains the RGB values and the name of the color. For example, the antique white entry would look like this:

```
250 235 215 antiquewhite
```

This means that the intensity of red in this color is 250/255 of full intensity, the intensity of green is 235/255, and the intensity of blue is 215/255. What this really means is how much energy is sent to each phosphor. For details on what phosphors are and what part they play in displaying an image, see the section on monitors in the chapter on hardware.

If you specify the color as a resource (either from the command line or a resource file), you specify the color as a hexadecimal value. The key thing to note is that you must specify the value for each color, even if it is 0. Because the hexadecimal values range from 0000 to FFFF, you have many more possible combinations of colors. When you specify colors in this way, the hex string you use must be preceded by a pound-sign (#).

If you don't want to specify all four hexidecimal digits, you do not have to. However, all three colors need to be represented with the same number of digits because the system would not be able to tell what value goes with which settings. If we look at an example, this will be clearer.

Let's assume you want to set the intensity of red to F, the intensity of green to 4, and the intensity of blue to 2. You might then have a resource specification that looked like this:

```
*background: #F42
```

If we wanted the intensity of green to be 45 instead of 4, the resource specification might look like this:

```
*background: #F452
```

So what is it? Do we have red at F4, green at 5, and blue at 2? Or do we have red at F, green at 4, and blue at 52? The *only* way to keep things straight is if there are the same number of digits for each color.

Remember that not all video systems are created equal. You may not get the same color on your system as someone else does, even if you use the exact same hex values.

7.6 Fonts

Although not applicable to every client, fonts play a major role in many applications. Defined as a set of characters for displaying text and symbols, fonts share a common appearance in terms of size, boldness, and other physical characteristics. Fonts themselves can be grouped together into font families. Additionally, font families are grouped by resolutions (dots-per-inch, or DPI) into directories. Font families are so named because they were initially stored together in the same directory in the file system. Each directory contains a database that the server uses to translate font names into data that the server uses to display the characters on the screen. How the name of a font is translated, we see in Figure 7.2.

If the X client has a font menu like MS-Windows or Macintosh, life would be easy when it came to fonts. Instead, you need to choose the font as you start the application. If you were tired of the boring font used by default on XTerms, you could choose something a little more fancy, perhaps one that looked like cursive. For example, we could start `xterm` like this:

```
xterm -fn -bitstream-charter-bold-i-normal--12-120-75-
75-p-74-iso8859-1
```

At first, this appears rather intimidating. There are several hundred fonts on an Linux system and learning them all is a pain. More than that, it is a waste of time. Two utilities make like easier for you: `xlsfont` and `xfontsel`. The `xlsfont` utility simply lists all the available fonts with their complete name, as in the previous example. The `xfontsel` is a real X client that enables you to pick and choose a font based on different criteria. What those criteria are is helpful in understanding more about fonts.

The *foundry* is the font's developer. Here we have bitstream, which, as one might guess, is from the company Bitstream, the same people who develop so many fonts for MS-Windows. The font family (here, charter)

Figure 7.2: **Characteristics of the Font Name**

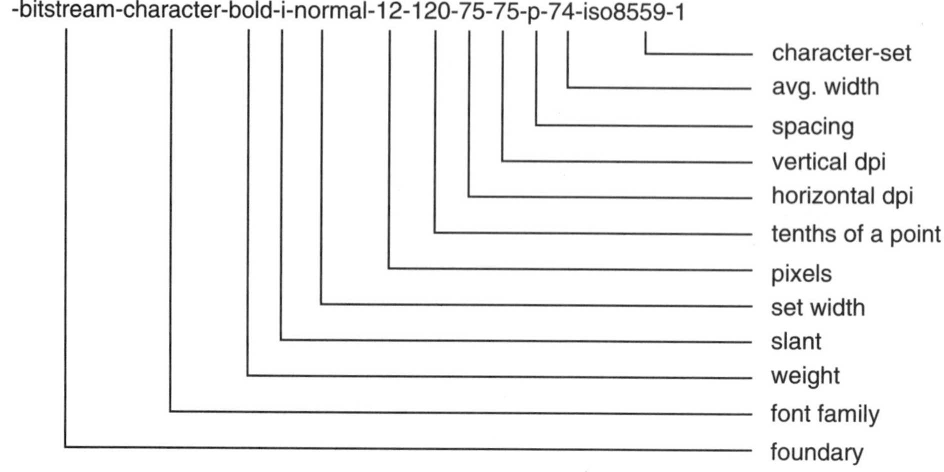

is a convenient way of organizing the fonts by certain appearance characteristics.

The weight of a font can be thought of as its thickness. Common weights are medium and bold. The slant, as you might guess, is the change in orientation of the character from the vertical. A roman slant is upright, italic is tilted, but the characters are given a slightly different shape to make them more aesthetically pleasing, and oblique is just tilted with no changes to the characters' shape. In the example in Figure 7.2 we have an italic slant.

The set width is a general description of the average width. Common set widths are normal, condensed, and double-width. The size of the font on the screen is determined by several aspects of the font name. These characteristics are the pixels, points, and both vertical and horizontal DPI. Because the appearance on your screen depends on your monitor as well as what fonts you choose, it's safe to gauge the font size by the points. A point is an old printer's measurement that represents 1/72 of an inch. In the example in Figure 7.2 we have 120 tenths of a pitch, therefore the size of each character is 1/6 of an inch.

Another important characteristic is the font spacing, which determines whether the font is *proportional* or *monospaced*. A proportional font is one in which the width of each character is different. Although this looks good on paper or on a word processor, it is not really suited for applications like terminal emulators. The monospaced font, in which every character takes up the same space, is better for such applications.

The character set is basically another way of saying what letters are represented. In this example and most others in Linux, this field will be iso8859-1, which represents the ISO Latin 1 character set, which is a superset of the standard ASCII character set. In addition to American English characters, iso8859-1 contains the special characters used in most European languages.

So now that we know what goes into font name, we can easily come up with the right font. Well, maybe. Fortunately, we don't have to. We can use a wild card for the parts of the font that we either don't think are important or don't want to guess at. Any one of the specifications can be wild carded and the system will do its best to find a match. By "do its best," I mean that there can and will be cases in which multiple fonts match the specification. A rather simple example would be

```
XTerm -fn '-bitstream-charter*'
```

On most systems there are 60 matches. So, which one does the system choose? Easy enough: the first one it finds. Unless you are more specific or know that the first one the system will find is the font you want, you might not get the font you want. Fonts are sorted in alphabetical order, and because bold comes before medium, we get the bold version of this font instead of the medium.

Pop quiz: Why did we enclose the font name in this example inside single quotes though we didn't in the first example? Remember that the shell expands everything into tokens before it passes things off to the command. If we didn't use the single quotes, the shell would try to expand the font name and we would get a message indicating that the system cannot find that font.

Life is even simpler than that. We don't need remember any long, drawn-out font names or try 20 different combinations to find the font we want. We can take advantage of the fact that the system understands font aliases, whichs are stored in the font directories in the file `fonts.alias`. These files are ASCII files with the alias in the first column and the font name in the second column.

There are two things to keep mind. First, although you can edit these files and make changes, the system will not recognize the new alias unless you reset the font path with the `xset` command, which is simply done as

```
xset fp
```

Next, unless you are absolutely positive about what fonts each user is using and how they are being referenced, it is not a good idea to remove aliases. If you remove an alias that some client is expecting, the results are unpredictable.

If you always want to use a particular font with a particular application, you don't need to always specify the `-fn` option when starting the client. Because the font is just another resource, you can instead make the change to your resource definition file. An example in our `.Xdefaults` file might look like this:

```
XTerm*font: ibm10x20
```

If you looked though the directory files, you wouldn't find a font simply named `ibm10x20`; this is actually an alias. However, you could specify the full name of the font. Also, just like specifying the font from the command line, we can use wild cards to specify the "we-don't-cares."

The directories in which the fonts are found by the server are referred to by the font path. This is the `XFONTS` variable, which defaults to `/usr/lib/X11/fonts` but can be changed using the `xset` command. Because the server displays the information on the screen, the font path is on the server, not on the client machine. Therefore it is important to ensure that the server is able to display a particular font before changing it for any given client. There are five subdirectories under `/usr/lib/X11/fonts` varying in size and appearance.

The font database is contained in the `fonts.dir` file in each directory. You use this database when you select a font. The system knows what file to read to be able to show the proper characters on the screen. The `fonts.dir` files are ASCII files with the name of the font file in the first column and the font name in the second column. When the system is installed, the `mkfontdir` reads the font files found in the font path and creates the `fonts.dir` files. You can use `mkfontdir` yourself, but the details of fonts creation and management goes beyond the scope of this book.

Rather than requiring every machine on the network to have a full compliment of fonts, the system has something called a *font server*. Like a file server that provides files across the network, a font server provides fonts across the network. Just like files, if the font you want is not available by the server but is available locally, there is no problem. You can access it as well.

The font server program, `xfs`, is not started by default but can be started in one of several different ways. Although starting it manually might be good for testing purposes, it is more efficient to have the font server start up every time the system goes into multiuser mode. As with many of the different aspects of the system, this is accomplished through a script in the `/etc/rc.d` directory. However, there is no script there by default. Obviously, you could write the script yourself, but you ought to let the system do it for you.

Starting the font server from the command line is not recommended for everyday use. To be able to use the fonts provided by the font server, you need to tell your X session about it. The best place to do this is inside your `$HOME/.xinitrc` file. Although the system administrator (you?) can change the `/etc/xinitrc` file, everyone using the default gets to use it, so you need to remember those people who already have their own `.startxrc` file. Before any clients are started, use the `xset` command to specify where the font server is. The general syntax is

```
xset fp=tcp/server:port
```

where the server is the name of the machine on which the font server is running, and port is the TCP broadcast port, which is 7000 by default. For example, to access the font server on the machine siemau, the command would be

```
xset fp=tcp/siemau:7000
```

Or, if you want to use local fonts as well, the line might look like this:

```
xset fp=tcp/boston:7000,/usr/X11/fonts/100dpi
```

The font server's configuration file is `/usr/lib/X11/fs/config`. Here you can limit what fonts will be made available through the font server by changing the catalogue entry and specifying the full paths to the directories with the appropriate fonts. For example, if you only wanted to have access to the 100 dpi fonts, the line might look like this:

```
catalogue = /usr/lib/X11/fonts/100dpi
```

To make the changes take effect, either stop and restart the font server or use the `/etc/fontserv` command to re-read the configuration file and flush the cached entries:

```
fontserv re-read
fontserv flush
```

Like name servers in TCP/IP, which get name information from other name servers, you can have font server get fonts from other font servers. This is also done with the catalogue entry. For example, if I wanted to make the local 100 dpi fonts available, as well as the from the remote host scoburg, the entry might look like this

```
catalogue = /usr/lib/X11/fonts/100dpi,tcp/scoburg:7000
```

assuming that scoburg has its font server configured to use port 7000. Changing the port is also accomplished by changing the `/usr/lib/X11/fs/config` file. On a line by itself, add a line specifying the appropriate port. For example, if you wanted to change it to 7042, the entry would look like this:

```
port=7042
```

Once the change is made, the font server needs to be stopped and restarted. If any other machines were using this server, they need to be told that it is now set for port 7042.

You can use the `-cf` option when starting the font server to specify an alternate configuration file. Reconfigure any X servers that use the font server. Note: Use care when you reference other font servers. Font server connections place a heavy demand on network resources and bandwidth. Also, be careful not to let the number of references to other font servers become so large that your system font server becomes unmanageable.

7.7 The Window Manager

Because the window manager is an important aspect of X, I need to cover it in more detail. As I mentioned earlier, in most versions of Linux, you will find a couple of window managers. The `fvwm` seems to be the most common, although I do see `twm` quite often.

The following sections describe the basic default behavior of windows, icons, the icon box, input focus, and window stacking. The appearance and behavior of the window manager can be altered by changing the configuration of specific resources.

One way to control your windows is though *accelerator keys* (also called hotkeys). By default, several accelerator keys perform various functions. It's quite possible that on your system these bindings have been commenting out of your `.fvwmrc` file. I'll get to how to change entries in a moment.

These functions (probably) can be reached through the window menu as well. It all depends on what is configured in your `.fvwmrc` file. Any windows managed by fvwm will have these keys, which are explicitly defined and can be changed by modifying the appropriate resource (which I'll get to in a moment). These keys are

`Alt+F1`	Run popup "Utilities"
`Alt+F2`	Run popup "Window Ops"
`Alt+F3`	Run FvwmWinList Module
`Alt+F4`	Iconify the window
`Alt+F5`	Move the window
`Alt+F6`	Resize the window
`Alt+F7`	Circulate window up
`Alt+F8`	Circulate window down
`Alt+F9`	Iconify the window

The window manager is also responsible for managing icons. As I mentioned earlier, icons are small graphic representations of clients. Iconifying (turning into an icon) a client is a good way to reduce the space taken by clients that are currently not being used. Although the pager enables you to move clients from one virtual screen to another, icons are a good way of being able to instantly access a particular client. This is done with an "icon box." The icon box that you will find on your system is called FvwmIconBox and, in most cases, you will have to configure the system to start it. (I'll discuss this shortly.)

A nice thing about the icon box is that it represents all running clients, not just those that have been iconified. This makes finding the client you want easy, because by double-clicking its icon in the icon box, it immediately is made the active window and is brought to the front.

If you have a lot of icons, using the icon box is a good way to manage them. The author of the FvwmIconBox describes it as a "clutter-reduction program." The icon box is simply another client that manages the icon images. The icon box can be moved and resized, even iconified. If there are more icons in the icon box that can be shown in the box, scroll bars will appear.

One strong point of both window managers is the ability to configure them to our tastes. Up to now we have basically been talking about the appearance of `fvwm`. What is really fun is to modify its behavior. One way to accomplish this is through the resource description file, which contains descriptions of resources that are easily defined in the resource files. The descriptions of resources include such things as the behavior when buttons are pressed and the individual entries in each menu.

The default resource description file is `/etc/X11/fvwm/system.fvwmrc` or `/etc/X11/fvwm/system.twmrc`. Here again, unless you want to institute systemwide changes, I recommend that you copy the appropriate file into the user's home directory. This copy then has the name `$HOME/.fvwmrc` or `$HOME/.twmrc`. Here is where your default menus and default bindings are defined. When you click the root window, the root menu pops up, as defined in the `.fvwmrc` or `.twmrc` file, which is very easy to modify to your personal tastes and preferences.

Three types of resources can be described here: buttons, keys, and menus. It is said that window manager functions are *bound* to button or key-press events. The relationship between the button or key press is called a *binding*.

Because the resource description file is an ASCII text file, it is easy to edit to make the changes you want. The format of each type of resource is slightly different, but in each case, the fields are separated by white spaces. Any text from an unquoted pound sign (#) to the end of the line is considered a comment. Therefore, if any description must be contained the #, it must be quoted. Single characters can be "quoted" by escaping them (using the back-slash). Any line containing a ! (exclamation mark) as the first character is also treated as a comment.

When an event occurs (button or key is pressed or menu item is selected), a particular window manager function is called. In general, we can say that the functions have the following syntax:

```
function function_arguments
```

You can call dozens of functions that relate to everything from resizing the particular window or icon to shuffling the order, moving, and all the other functions we talked about. All of these are detailed in the `fvwm` man-page, so I don't feel the need to cover them all. However, I will discuss some of the more common functions as I describe the syntax of the resource descriptions.

The first thing we'll talk about is the idea of a popup menu. This is not like the menus in most programs where you see a list of options at the top of the screen and when you click the list, a menu suddenly appears. These are called pull-down menus because you pull them down from the menu list. Popup menus seem to popup out of nowhere. With other window managers, popups are referred to as menus.

You will probably see on your system that when you click an open area of your desktop with the left mouse button, a menu called "Program Menu" will pop up. This menu is defined in your .fvwmrc file. Each popup menu is defined with the following syntax:

```
Popup "Popup Name"
     functions to call
EndPopup
```

In the case of our "Program Menu," the popup's name is actually "Applications," so look for the line

```
Popup "Applications"
```

When you find it, you will see all the same entries that would appear when you click the desktop. When you click one entry in the list, that particular program or module will start. (A module is a program used by the window manager and cannot be started in any other way.)

You'll see that some of the entries have an arrow on the right side. When you click the arrow, it brings up another popup that is defined somewhere else in the `.fvwmrc` file. These popups could then have entries that go to other popups. Although I have tested this to five levels deep, I have never really had a need to go beyond three levels of popup menus.

To start a particular program or module from within the menu, use the Exec function. The syntax for the `Exec` definition is

```
Exec name  exec <arguments>
```

An example would be

```
Exec "Looking Glass" exec lg &
```

The name in each line is the symbol that will appear in the menu pane for that entry, here, "`Looking Glass`." Labels containing spaces or tabs must be enclosed within double quotes, as in our example. To start another popup, the syntax would be

```
Popup    "Menu Entry" Popup_Name
```

Here the "Menu Entry" is just what appears in the menu. The `Popup_Name` is what it actually will be called.

The `title` function within a popup is what appears at the top of the menu when it's started. For example, our applications popup was called "Applications" and that is how the system referred to it. However, when we started it, the words "Program Menu" appeared at the top. This is the title of the menu and has no other function.

If the function called is the `no-operation function` (`Nop`), the function is invalid and/or is the equivalent of adding a separator in other window manager. If you use just two double quotes (`"  "`) as the name, you will see a line between entries. However, you could include a line of something like an equal sign (=) to give your menu a different effect.

The accelerator key's syntax is

```
Key <keyname> <context> <modifiers> <function>
```

Here `<keyname>` is the name of a key like `F1` for the `F1` function key or `Tab` for the `Tab` key. The `<context>` is when this keypress should be valid. Unlike mouse actions, a keypress should be valid in all cases, so you can use an A. The `<modifiers>` is used for an addition key that should be pressed as well, such as "C" for the `Ctrl` key, "A" for the `Alt` key, "M" for the `Meta` key, and "S" for the `Shift` key. As I mentioned earlier, your accelerator keys may have been commented out, so look for the section starting "Keyboard Accelerators."

One example looks like this:

```
Key F1   A M Popup "Utilities"
```

Note that in contrast to keypresses, key bindings to window manager functions are just for the key *presses*. Key releases have no meaning in this context. Also, the modifiers are exclusive, which means that no other modifier key can be pressed. Because I specified just `Meta+F1` and not `SHIFT+Meta+F1`, pressing `SHIFT+Meta+F1` would have no effect (unless I had defined it to something already). If you want, you could use something like "SM" to indicate pressing both the `Shift` and `Meta` keys.

Each button binding has the following syntax:

```
Mouse button context modifier function
```

The button field defines what button to which this function should apply (1, 2, 3). The context is when the particular function should be in effect. Valid contexts are

`A`	A -Any context except for the title bar
`R`	Root window
`W`	Application window
`T`	Window title bar
`S`	Window side, top, or bottom
`F`	Window frame (corners)
`I`	Icon window

You can define certain characteristics of the windows. You can define certain characteristics, such as the foreground and background color, geometry, etc., when the client is started or by defining that particular resource, using the `Style` command within `.fvwmrc`. In many cases, resources define the same characteristics. See the `fvwm` man-page for details.

The syntax of the Style command is

```
Style <windowname> <options>
```

The `<windowname>` can be something other than the window's name, for example, a class or resource string. The `<options>` are a common separated list of values. Some options require arguments like `Icon`, which requires the name of the icon that you want to use when the window is iconified.

7.8 The Pager

One problems I, as well as many other users, face is that we often do not have the luxury of large monitors. Having more than a handful of clients running, we usually end up with them either overlapping or sometimes completely hidden. Often to avoid clutter, we will iconify the less frequently used clients to make room for others. However, this cures the symptom but not the illness. The obvious solution is to get a bigger monitor, but even that doesn't solve everything because you can't have a monitor that's infinitely large. Or can you?

This is where the pager comes in. It established a virtual monitor that can be dozens of times the size of your "real" monitor. With the push of a button or click of a mouse, you move around this virtual workspace with an amount of freedom comparable to having a larger monitor. Just like virtual memory has drawbacks over "real" memory, virtual screens have a drawback over a larger monitor. However, even if you do have a 21" monitor, the pager can provide you with even more work space.

Functionally, the pager behaves like a *viewport* or *viewfinder* into the larger virtual screen. You can move around and place your windows anywhere within the workspace. Movement can be in increments equal to the size of your "real" screen or you can move around in smaller steps, allowing finer control over what your viewfinder is currently viewing.

When you look at the pager, you will see smaller images of the currently active clients. When you click another workspace, the clients that you saw will suddenly disappear. However, you will still see their images in the pager. You can have the clients follow you around by making them "sticky," which is done from the Window Menu under the entry (Un)Stick, which is a toggle. That means that if your window is currently unstuck, selecting this will make it stick, and vice versa. Another way of doing this is by setting the Style within the `.fvwmrc` to Sticky.

When it starts, you will see the pager "viewer" on the left side (by default). It is divided into four workspaces (again, by default). These are numbered 0–3.

Each workspace is the size of your screen. To select a particular workspace, click the workspace within the pager, which will move you completely into a workspace. That is, if you click one of the workspaces, you are brought to that workspace and the viewfinder is completely within that workspace. Even if the viewfinder is over portions of multiple work areas (entirely possible), clicking a workspace takes you there and will move the viewfinder.

If you hold down button 3, you can drag the viewport to any arbitrary point within the pager.

7.9 What Else?

In this chapter, I *briefly* covered some of the basics of X-Windows regarding one specific window manager (`fvwm`). Although most Linux distributions come with another such manager (`twm`), the concepts are the same. To find out the specifics, I suggest that you read the applicable documentation.

Not all distributions will have the programs and tools that I talked about. Some will have them but in a slightly different form. One good example is the Craftworks distribution, which comes with a desktop that is very similar to Windows 95, including the task bar at the bottom of the screen and the general appearance of the windows.

You can buy several additional packages. One is the Common Desktop Environment (CDE) from X Inside, Inc., which replaces your normal desktop and has a lot of features that the standard desktop does not have. Another is the Caldera Network Desktop, which takes a slightly different approach. I will go into more details about these packages later.

In closing, I'd like to say that the principles of X may appear overwhelming at first. Once you understand that the different aspects of X-Windows can be considered as different layers building on each other, it'll be easier to understand their interactions. My suggestion now is to play around with your X system, make some changes, and see how the changes effect the behavior and appearance of your windows and the entire work area. Don't worry too much. The worst that can happen is that you'll need to reinstall.

Chapter 8

The Computer Itself

- Hardware basics
- How hardware interacts with the system
- Configuring peripherals

Hardware is my life. I love working with it. I love installing it. I love reading about it. I am by no means an expert in such a way that I can tell you about every chip on the motherboard. In fact, I enjoy being a "jack-of-all-trades." Of all the trades, I enjoy hardware the most.

It's difficult to say why. There is, of course, that without the hardware, nothing works. Software, without hardware, is just words on a page. However, it's something more than just that. I like the idea that it all started out as rocks and sand and now it can send men to the moon and look inside atoms.

I think that this is what it's all about. Between the hardware and the operating system (I also love operating systems), you've pretty much got the whole ball of wax.

During the several years I spent on the phone in tech support, it was common for people to call in with no idea of what kind of computer they had. I remember one conversation with a customer in which he answered "I don't know" to every questioned I asked about his hardware. Finally, he got so frustrated and said, "Look! I'm not a computer person. I just want you to tell me what's wrong with my system."

Imagine calling your mechanic to say there is something wrong with your car. He asks you whether is car has four or eight cylinders, whether it has fuel injection, whether it is automatic or manual, and whether it uses unleaded or leaded gas. You finally get frustrated and say, "Look. I'm not a engine person. I just want you to tell me what's wrong with my car."

The solution is to drive your car to the mechanic to have it checked. However, you can't always do that with your computer system. Dozens of people rely on it to do their work. Without it, the business stops. To better track down and diagnose hardware problems, you need to know what to look for.

This section should serve as a background for many issues I've covered in elsewhere. This chapter is designed to familiarize you with the concepts rather than make you an expert on any aspect of the hardware. If you want to read more about PC hardware, an excellent book is the *Winn Rosch Hardware Bible* from Brady Books (it's more than 1000 pages and, as of this writing, it's in third edition).

In the following sections, I will be talking primarily about PC hardware. Many of the concepts are the same as on Alpha machines or Macs, but when I talk about specific interactions with the hardware, they probably only apply to the PC, for two reasons. Despite the fact that Linux runs on several platforms, it was first developed on the PC and only recently successfully ported to the other architectures. The second reason is that my expertise is in PCs. I have several of them myself and have worked with them for years, so I have the experience to know what I am talking about.

In addition, the first commercial port to the Alpha is fairly recent. Therefore, there are not as many people using them. However, keep in mind that although the DEC Alpha is a different processor, the rest of the hardware is usually the same.

8.1 Basic Input/Output Services and the System Bus

A key concept for this discussion is the bus. So, just what is a bus? In computer terms, it has a similar meaning as your local county public transit–it is used to move something from one place to another. The county transit bus moves people; a computer bus moves information.

The information is transmitted along the bus as electric signals. If you have ever opened up a computer, you probably saw that there is one central printed circuit board with the CPU, the expansion cards, and several chips sticking out of it. The electronic connections between these parts is referred to as a bus.

The signals that move along a computer bus comes in two basic forms: control and data. Control signals do just that: they control things. Data signals are just that: data. I will get to how this happens and what each part does as we move along.

In today's PC computer market, there are several buses, many of which have the same functions but approach things quite differently. In this section, I am going to talk about the different bus types, what goes on between the different devices on the bus, and what the main components are that communicate along the bus.

Despite differences in bus types, certain aspects of the hardware are common with among all PCs. The Basic Input Output System (BIOS), interrupts, Direct Memory Access channels, and base addresses are just a few. Although once the kernel is loaded, Linux almost never needs the system BIOS, understanding its function and purpose is useful in understanding the process that the computer goes through from the time you hit the power switch to when Linux has full control of the hardware.

The BIOS is the mechanism DOS uses to access the hardware. DOS (or a DOS application) makes BIOS calls that then transfer the data to and from the devices. Except for the first few moments of the boot process and the last moment of a shutdown, Linux may never use it again.

The standard BIOS for PCs is the IBM BIOS, but that's simply because "PC" is an IBM standard. However, "standard" does not mean "most common," as there are several other BIOS vendors, such as Phoenix and AMI.

DOS or a DOS application makes device *independent* calls to the BIOS to transfer data. The BIOS then translates this into device *dependent* instructions. For example, DOS (or the application) requests that the hard disk read a certain block of data. The application does not care what kind of hard disk hardware there is, nor should it. It is BIOS's job to make that translation to something the specific hard disk can understand.

In Linux, on the other hand, a special program called a device driver handles the functions of the BIOS. As we talked about in the section on the kernel, device drivers are sets of routines that directly access the hardware, just as the BIOS does.

The fact that Linux by-passes the BIOS and goes directly to the hardware is one reason why some hardware will work under DOS but not under Linux. In some instances, the BIOS has been specially designed for the machine on which it runs. Because of this, it can speak the same dialect of "machine language" that the rest of the hardware speaks. However, because UNIX does not speak the same dialect, things get lost in the translation.

The Intel 80x86 family of processors has an I/O space that is distinct from memory space. What this means is that memory (or RAM) is treated differently than I/O. Other machine architectures, such as the Motorola 68000 family, see accessing memory and I/O as the same thing. Although the addresses for I/O devices appears as "normal" memory addresses and the CPU is performing a read or write as it would to RAM, the result is completely different.

When accessing memory, either for a read or write, the CPU utilizes the same address and data lines as it does when accessing RAM. The difference lies in the M/IO# line on the CPU. For those not familiar with digital electronics, this can also be described as the Memory/Not IO line. That is, if the line is high, the CPU addresses memory. If it is low, it addresses an I/O device.

Although the Linux operating system is much different from DOS, it still must access the hardware in the same fashion. There are assembly language instructions that allow an operating system (or any program for that matter) to access the hardware correctly. By passing these commands, the base address of the I/O device, the CPU knows to keep the M/IO# line low and therefore access the device and not memory.

You can often see the base address of each device on the system when you boot. The hardware screen shows you the devices it recognizes along with certain values such as the base address, the interrupt vector, and the DMA channel. You can also see this same information by looking in the `/var/logs/messages` and several files in the `/proc` file system.

If your motherboard only uses 10 address lines, devices on the motherboard that have I/O address (such as the DMA controller and PIC) will appear at their normal address, as well as at "image" addresses. This is because the higher 6 bits are ignored, so any 16-bit address in which the lower 10 bits match will show up as an "image" address. Because 6 bits are ignored, there are 63 possible "image" addresses (64 minus the one for the "real" address).

These image addresses may cause conflicts with hardware that have I/O addresses higher than 0x3FF (1023), which is the highest possible with only 10 address lines. Therefore, if your motherboard only has 10 bits of I/O addresses, you shouldn't put devices at addresses higher than 0x3FF.

When you install, it is vital that no two devices have overlapping (or identical) base addresses. Though you can share interrupts and DMA channels on some machines, you can never share base addresses. If you attempt to read a device that has an overlapping base address, you may get information from both devices.

If you are installing a board whose default base address is the same as the one already on the system, you must change one address before they both will work. Additionally, you are almost always asked for the base address of a card when you install it. Therefore, you will need to keep track of address. See the section on troubleshooting for tips on maintaining a notebook with this kind of information.

Table 8.1 contains a list of the more common devices and the base address ranges that they use.

Table 8.1: **Common Hex Addresses**

HexRange	Device
000-0ff	Motherboard devices (DMA Controller, PIC, timer chip, etc.)
1f0-1f8	Fixed disk controller (WD10xx)
2f8-2ff	Serial port 2
378-37f	Parallel port 1
3bc-3bf	Monochrome display and parallel port 2
3c0-3cf	EGA or VGA adapter
3d0-3df	CGA, EGA, or VGA adapter
3f0-3f7	Floppy disk controller
3f8-3ff	Serial port 1

8.2 The Expansion Bus

It is generally understood that the speed and capabilities of the CPU is directly related to the performance of the system as a whole. In fact, the CPU is a major selling point of PCs, especially among less-experienced users. One aspect of the machine that is less understood and therefore less likely to be an issue is the expansion bus.

The expansion bus, simply put, is the set of connections and slots that enable users to add to, or expand, their system. Although it's not really an "expansion" of the system, you often find video cards and hard disk controllers attached to the "expansion" bus.

Anyone who has opened his or her machine has seen parts of the expansion bus. The slots used to connect cards to the system are part of this bus. Note that people will often refer to this bus as "the bus." Though it will be understood what is meant, there are other buses on the system. Just keep this in mind as you go through this chapter.

Most people are aware of the differences in CPUs, whether the CPU is 16-bit or 32-bit, what the speed of the processor is, whether there is a math co-processor, and so on. The concepts of BIOS and interrupts are also commonly understood.

One part of the machine's hardware that is somewhat less known and often causes confusion is the bus architecture. This is the basic way in which the hardware components (usually on the motherboard) all fit together. Linux will run on several different kinds of buses. The most common are those in PCs, which I will talk about first. (Note: Here I am referring to the *main* system bus, although Linux can access devices on other buses.)

The three major types of bus architectures used are the Industry Standard Architecture (ISA), the Extended Industry Standard Architecture (EISA), and the Micro-Channel Architecture (MCA). Both ISA and EISA machines are manufactured by a wide range of companies, but only a few (primarily IBM) manufacture MCA machines. As of this writing, no commercial distributions are available for MCA, but a development project is underway.

In addition to these three architectures, a few other bus types can be used in conjunction with or to supplement the three, including the Small Computer System Interface (SCSI), Peripheral Component Interconnect (PCI), and the Video Electronics Standards Association Local Bus (VLB or VL-Bus).

Both PCI and VLB exist as separate buses on the computer motherboard. Expansion cards exist for both these types of buses. You will usually find either PCI or VLB in addition to either ISA or EISA. Sometimes, however, you can also find *both* PCI and VLB in addition to the primary bus. In addition, it is possible to have machines that only have PCI because it is a true system bus and not an expansion bus like VLB. Because of the advantages of the PCI-Bus, some manufacturers are beginning to manufacture machines with only the PCI-Bus. However, as of this writing, only a few machines provide PCI-only expansion buses.

SCSI, on the other hand, complements the existing bus architecture by adding an additional hardware controller to the system. There are SCSI controllers (more commonly referred to as host adapters) that fit in ISA, EISA, MCA, PCI, or VLB slots.

8.2.1 Industry Standard Architecture (ISA)

As I mentioned before, most people are generally aware of the relationship between CPU performance and system performance. However, every system is only as strong as its weakest component. Therefore, the expansion bus also sets limits on the system performance.

There were several drawbacks with the original expansion bus in the original IBM PC. First, it was limited to only 8 data lines, which meant that only 8 bits could be transferred at a time. Second, the expansion bus was, in a way, directly connected to the CPU. Therefore, it operated at the same speed as the CPU, which meant that to improve performance with the CPU, the expansion bus had to be altered as well. The result would have been that existing expansion cards would be obsolete.

In the early days of PC computing, IBM was not known to want to cut its own throat. It has already developed quite a following with the IBM PC among users and developers. If it decided to change the design of the expansion bus, developers would have to re-invent the wheel and users would have to buy all new equipment. There was the risk that users and developers would switch to another platform instead of sticking with IBM.

Rather than risk that, IBM decided that backward compatibility was a paramount issue. One key change was severing the direct connection between the expansion bus and CPU. As a result, expansion boards could operate at a different speed than the CPU, enabling users to keep existing hardware and enabling manufacturers to keep producing their expansion cards. As a result, the IBM standard became the industry standard, and the bus architecture became known as the Industry Standard Architecture, or ISA.

In addition to this change, IBM added more address and data lines. They doubled the data lines to 16 and increased the address lines to 24. This meant that the system could address up to 16 megabytes of memory, the maximum that the 80286 CPU (Intel's newest central processor at the time) could handle.

When the 80386 came out, the connection between the CPU and bus clocks were severed completely because no expansion board could operate at the 16MHz or more that the 80386 could. The bus speed does not need to be an exact fraction of the CPU speed, but an attempt has been made to keep it there because by keeping the bus and CPU synchronized, it is easier to transfer data. The CPU will only accept data when it coincides with its own clock. If an attempt is made to speed the bus a little, the data must wait until the right moment in the CPUs clock cycle to pass the data. Therefore, nothing has been gained by making it faster.

One method used to speed up the transfer of data is Direct Memory Access, or DMA. Although DMA existed in the IBM XT, the ISA-Bus provided some extra lines. DMA enables the system to move data from place to place without the intervention of the CPU. In that way, data can be transferred from, let's say, the hard disk to memory while the CPU is working on something else. Keep in mind that to make the transfer, the DMA controller must have complete control of both the data and the address lines, so the CPU itself cannot access memory at this time. What DMA access looks like graphically we see in Figure 8.1.

Let's step back here a minute. It is somewhat incorrect to say that a DMA transfer occurs without intervention from the CPU, as it is the CPU

Figure 8.1: **Direct Memory Access**

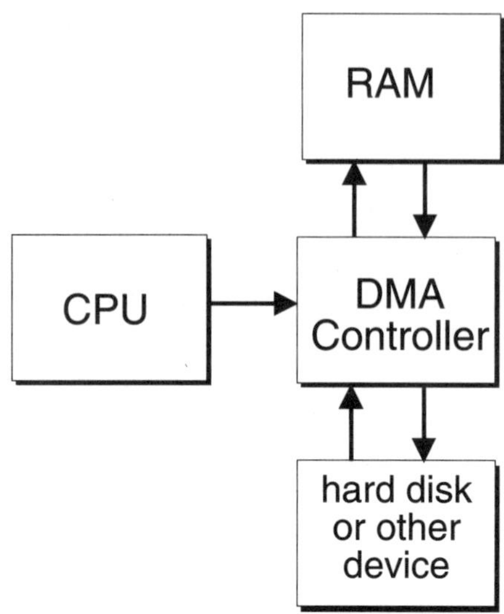

that must initiate the transfer. Once the transfer is started, however, the CPU is free to continue with other activities. DMA controllers on ISA-Bus machines use "pass-through" or "fly-by" transfers. That is, the data is not latched or held internally but rather is simply passed through the controller. If it were latched, two cycles would be needed: one to latch into the DMA controller and another to pass it to the device or memory (depending on which way it was headed).

Devices tell the DMA controller that they wish to make DMA transfers through one of three "DMA Request" lines, numbered 1–3. Each of these lines is given a priority based on its number, 1 being the highest. The ISA-Bus includes two sets of DMA controllers: four 8-bit channels and four 16-bit channels. The channels are labeled 0–7, 0 having the highest priority.

Each device on the system capable of doing DMA transfers is given its own DMA channel. The channel is set on the expansion board usually by means of jumpers. The pins to which these jumpers are connected are usually labeled DRQ, for DMA Request.

The two DMA controllers (both Intel 8237), each with four DMA channels, are cascaded together. The master DMA controller is the one connected directly to the CPU. One of its DMA channels is used to connect to the slave controller. Because of this, there are actually only seven channels available.

Everyone who has had a baby knows what an interrupt-driven operating system like Linux goes through on a regular basis. Just like a baby when it needs its diaper changed, when a device on the expansion bus needs servicing, it tells the system by generating an interrupt (the baby cries). For example, when the hard disk has transferred the requested data to or from memory, it signals the CPU by means of an interrupt. When keys are pressed on the keyboard, the keyboard interface also generates an interrupt.

On receiving such an interrupt, the system executes a set of functions commonly referred to as an Interrupt Service Routine, or ISR. Because the reaction to a key being pressed on the keyboard is different from the reaction when data is transferred from the hard disk, there needs to be different ISRs for each device. Although the behavior of ISRs is different under DOS than UNIX, their functionality is basically the same. For details on how this works under Linux, see the chapter on the kernel.

On the CPU, there is a single interrupt request line. This does not mean that every device on the system is connected to the CPU via this single line, however. Just as a DMA controller handles DMA requests, an interrupt controller handles interrupt requests. This is the Intel 8259 Programmable Interrupt Controller, or PIC.

On the original IBM PC, there were five "Interrupt Request" lines, numbered 2–7. Here again, the higher the number, the lower the priority. (Interrupts 0 and 1 are used internally and are not available for expansion cards.)

The ISA-Bus also added an additional PIC, which is "cascaded" off the first PIC. With this addition, there were now 16 interrupt values on the system. However, not all of these were available to devices. Interrupts 0 and 1 were still used internally, but so were interrupts 8 and 13. Interrupt 2 was something special. It, too, was reserved for system use, but instead of being a device of some kind, an interrupt on line 2 actually meant that an interrupt was coming from the second PIC, similar to the way cascading works on the DMA controller.

A question I brought up when I first started learning about interrupts was "What happens when the system is servicing an interrupt and another one comes in?" Two mechanism can help in this situation.

Remember that the 8259 is a "programmable" interrupt controller. There is a machine instruction called Clear Interrupt Enable, or CLI. If a program is executing what is called a *critical section* of code (a section that should not be stopped in the middle), the programmer can call the CLI instruction and disable acknowledgment of all incoming interrupts. As soon as the critical section is finished and closed, the program should execute a Set Interrupt Enable, or STI, instruction somewhat shortly afterward.

I say "should" because the programmer doesn't have to do this. A CLI instruction could be in the middle of a program somewhere and if the STI is never called, no more interrupts will be serviced. Nothing, aside from common sense, prevents the programmer from doing this. Should the program take too long before it calls the STI, interrupts could get lost. This is common on busy systems when characters from the keyboard "disappear."

The second mechanism is that the interrupts are priority based. The lower the interrupt request level, or IRQ, the higher the priority. This has an interesting side effect because the second PIC (or slave) is bridged off the first PIC (or master) at IRQ2. The interrupts on the first PIC are numbered 0–7, and on the second PIC the interrupts are numbered 8–15. However, the slave PIC is attached to the master at interrupt 2. Therefore, the actual priority is 0, 1, 8–15, 3–7.

Table 8.2 contains a list of the standard interrupts.

Table 8.2: **Default Interrupts**

IRQ	Device
0	System timer
1	Keyboard
2	Second level interrupt
3	COM 2
4	COM 1
5	Printer 2
6	Floppy
7	Printer 1
8	Clock
9	Not assigned
10	Not assigned
11	Not assigned
12	Not assigned
13	Math coprocessor
14	Hard Disk
15	Hard Disk

There's one thing you should consider when dealing with interrupts. On XT machines, IRQ 2 was a valid interrupt. Now on AT machines, IRQ 2 is bridged to the second PIC. So, to ensure that devices configured to IRQ 2 work properly, the IRQ 2 pin on the all the expansion slots are connected to the IRQ 9 input of the second PIC. In addition, all the devices attached to the second PIC are associated with an IRQ value where they are attached to the PIC, and they generate an IRQ 2 on the first PIC.

The PICs on an ISA machine are *edge-triggered*, which means that they react only when the interrupt signal is making the transition from low to high, that is, when it is on a transition *edge*. This becomes an issue when you attempt to share interrupts, that is, where two devices use the same interrupt.

Assume you have both a serial port and floppy controller at interrupt 6. If the serial port generates an interrupt, the system will "service" it. If the floppy controller generates an interrupt before the system has finished servicing the interrupt for the serial port, the interrupt from the floppy is lost. There is another way to react to interrupts called "level triggered," which I will get to shortly.

As I mentioned earlier, a primary consideration in the design of the AT Bus (as the changed PC-Bus came to be called) was that it maintain compatibility with it predecessors. It maintains compatibility with the PC expansion cards but takes advantage of 16-bit technology. To do this, connectors were not changed, only added. Therefore, you could slide cards designed for the 8-bit PC-Bus right into a 16-bit slot on the ISA-Bus, and no one would know the difference.

8.2.2 Micro-Channel Architecture (MCA)

The introduction of IBM's Micro-Channel Architecture (MCA) was a redesign of the entire bus architecture. Although IBM developed the original AT architecture, which later became ISA, many companies produced machines that followed this standard. The introduction of MCA meant that IBM could produce machines to which it alone had the patent rights.

One of the most obvious differences is the smaller slots required for MCA cards. ISA cards are 4.75 x 13.5 inches, compared with the 3.5 x 11.5-inch MCA cards. As a result, the same number of cards can fit into a smaller area. The drawback was that ISA cards could not fit into MCA slots, and MCA cards could not fit into ISA slots. Although this might seem as though IBM had decided to cut its own throat, the changes they made in creating MCA made it very appealing.

Part of the decrease in size was a result of surface mount components, or surface mount technology (SMT). Previously, cards used "through-hole" mounting, in which holes were drilled through the system board (hence the name). Chips were mounted in these holes or into holders that were mounted in the holes. Surface mount does not use this and as a result, looks "flattened" by comparison. This saves not only space but also time and money, as SMT cards are easier to produce. In addition, the spacing between the pins on the card (0.050") corresponds to the spacing on the chips, which makes designing the boards much easier.

Micro-Channel also increases speed because there is a ground on every fourth pin, which reduces interference, and as a result, the MCA-Bus can operate at ten times the speed of non-MCA machines and still comply with FCC regulations in terms of radio frequency interference.

Another major improvement was the expansion of the data bus to 32 bits. This meant that machines were no longer limited to 16 megabytes of memory, but could now access 4 gigabytes.

One key change in the MCA architecture was the concept of *hardware-mediated bus arbitration*. With ISA machines, devices could share the bus, and the OS was required to arbitrate who got a turn. With MCA, that arbitration is done at the hardware level, freeing the OS to work on other things. This also enables multiple processors to use the bus. To implement this, the bus has several new lines. Four lines determine the *arbitration bus priority level*, which represents the 16 different priority levels that a device could have. Who gets the bus depends on the priority.

From the user's perspective, the installation of MCA cards is much easier than that of ISA cards due to the introduction of the Programmable Option Select, or POS. With POS, the entire hardware configuration is stored in the CMOS. When new cards are added, you are required to run the machine's *reference disk*. In addition, each card comes with an *options disk* that contains configuration information for the card. With the combination of reference disk and options disk, conflicts are all but eliminated.

Part of the MCA spec is that each card has its own unique identifying number encoded into the firmware. When the system boots, the settings in the CMOS are compared to the cards that are found on the bus. If one has been added or removed, the system requires you to boot using the reference disk to ensure that things are set up correctly.

As I mentioned, on each options disk is the necessary configuration information. This information is contained within the Adapter Description File (ADF). The ADF contains all the necessary information for your system to recognize the expansion card. Because it is only a few kilobytes big, many ADF files can be stored on a floppy. This is useful in situations like those we had in tech support. There were several MCA machines in the department with dozens of expansion cards, each with its own ADF file. Rather than having copies of each disk, the analysts who supported MCA machines (myself included) each had a single disk with all the ADF files. (Eventually that, too, became burdensome, so we copied the ADF files into a central directory where we could copy them as needed.) Any time we needed to add a new card to our machines for testing, we didn't need to worry about the ADF files because they were all in one place.

Because each device has its own identification number and this number is stored in the ADF, the reference diskette can find the appropriate number with no problem. All ADF files have names such as `@BFDF.ADF`, so it isn't obvious what kind of card the ADF file is for just by looking at the name. However, because the ADF files are simply text files, you can easily figure out which file is which by looking at the contents.

Unlike ISA machines, the MCA architecture enables *interrupt sharing*. Because many expansion boards are limited to a small range of interrupts, it is often difficult, if not impossible, to configure every combination on your system. Interrupt sharing is possible on MCA machines because they use something called *level-triggered interrupts*, or *level-sensitive interrupts*.

With *edge-triggered interrupts*, or edge-sensitive interrupts, (the standard on ISA buses), an interrupt is generated and then is dropped. This sets a flag in the PIC, which figures out which device generated the interrupt and services it. If interrupts were shared with edge-triggered interrupts, any interrupt that arrived between the time the first interrupt is generated and serviced would be lost because the PIC has no means of knowing that a second interrupt occurred. All the PIC sees is that an interrupt occurred. Figure 8.2 shows how each of these elements relate to each other in time.

Figure 8.2: **Interrupt Signal**

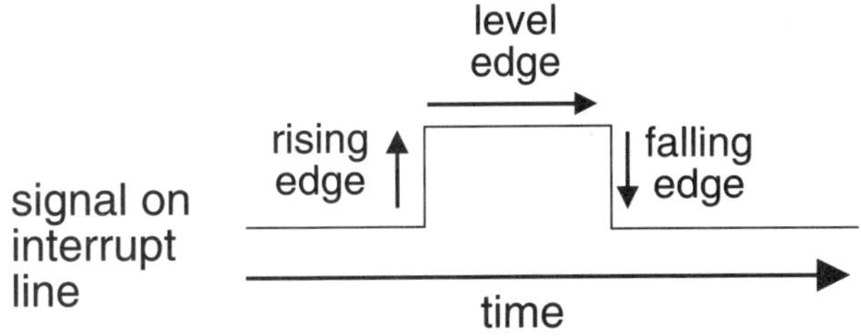

With level-triggered interrupts, when an interrupt is generated, it is held high until the PIC forces it low after the interrupt has been serviced. If another device were on the same interrupt, the PIC would try to pull down the interrupt line; however, the second device would keep it high. The PIC would then see that it was high and would be able to service the second device.

Despite the many obvious advantages of the MCA, there are a few drawbacks. One primary drawback is the interchangeability of expansion cards between architectures. MCA cards can only fit in MCA machines. However, it is possible to use an ISA card in an EISA machine, and EISA machines is what I will talk about next.

8.2.3 Extended Industry Standard Architecture (EISA)

To break the hold that IBM had on the 32-bit bus market with the Micro-Channel Architecture, a consortium of computer companies, lead by Compaq, issued their own standard in September 1988. This new standard was an extension of the ISA-Bus architecture and was (logically) called the Extended Industry Standard Architecture (EISA). EISA offered many of the same features as MCA but with a different approach.

Although EISA provides some major improvements, it has maintained backward compatibility with ISA boards. Therefore, existing ISA boards can be used in EISA machines. In some cases, such boards can even take advantage of the features that EISA offers.

To maintain this compatibility, EISA boards are the same size as their ISA counterparts and provide connections to the bus in the same locations. The original designed called for an extension of the bus slot, similar to the way the AT slots were an extension on the XT slots. However, this was deemed impractical because some hardware vendors had additional contacts that extended beyond the ends of the slots. There was also the issue that in most cases, the slots would extend the entire length of the motherboard, which meant that the motherboard would need to be either longer or wider to handle the longer slots.

Instead, the current spec calls for the additional connections to be intertwined with the old ones and extend lower. In what used to be gaps between the connectors are now leads to the new connectors. Therefore, EISA slots are deeper than those for ISA machines. Looking at EISA cards, you can easily tell them from ISA cards by the two rows of connectors.

Figure 8.3 shows what the ISA and EISA connections look like. Note that the adapters are not to scale.

Another major improvement of EISA over ISA is the issue of *bus arbitration*. Bus arbitration is the process by which devices "discuss" whose turn it is on the bus and then let one of them go. In XT and AT class machines, the CPU completely managed control of the bus. EISA includes additional control hardware to take this job away from the CPU, which does two important things. First, the CPU is now "free" to carry on more important work, and second, the CPU gets to use the bus only when its turn comes around.

Hmmm. Does that sound right? Because the CPU is the single most important piece of hardware on the system, shouldn't it get the bus whenever it needs it? Well, yes and no. The key issue of contention is the use of the word "single." EISA was designed with multiprocessing in mind; that is, computers with more than one CPU. If there is more than one CPU, which one is more important?

Figure 8.3: **Comparison of ISA and EISA Connections**

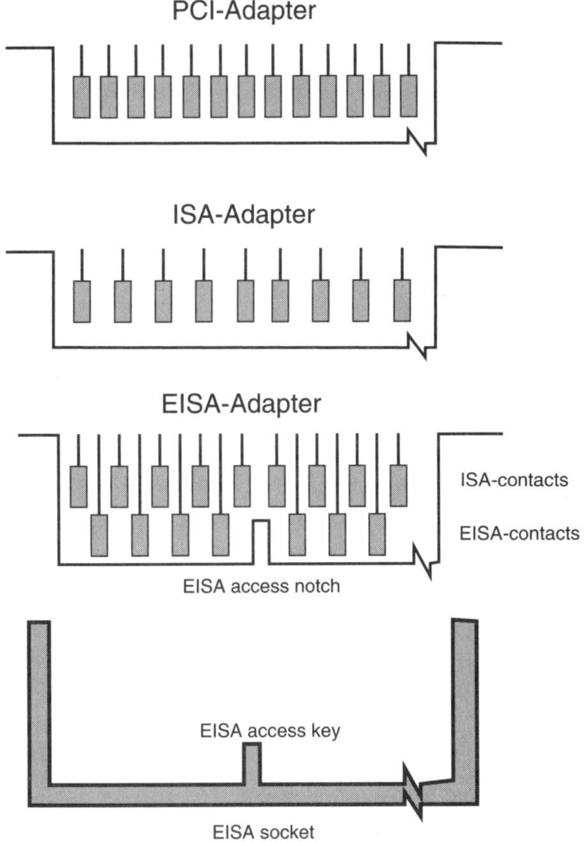

The term used here is *bus arbitration*. Each of the six devices that EISA allows to take control of the bus has its own priority level. A device signals its desire for the bus by sending a signal to the Centralized Arbitration Control (CAC) unit. If conflicts arise (e.g., multiple requests), the CAC unit resolves them according to the priority of the requesting devices. Certain activity such as DMA and memory refresh have the highest priority, with the CPU following close behind. Such devices are called "bus mastering devices" or "bus masters" because they become the master of the bus.

The EISA DMA controller was designed for devices that cannot take advantage of the bus mastering capabilities of EISA. The DMA controller supports ISA, with ISA timing and 24-bit addressing as the default mode. However, it can be configured by EISA devices to take full advantage of the 32-bit capabilities.

Another advantage that EISA has is the concept of dual buses. Because cache memory is considered a basic part of the EISA specification, the CPU can often continue working for some time even if it does not have access to the bus.

A major drawback of EISA (as compared with MCA) is that to maintain the compatibility to ISA, EISA speed improvements cannot extend into memory. This is because the ISA-Bus cannot handle the speed requirements of the high-speed CPUs. Therefore, EISA requires separate memory buses. This results in every manufacturer having its own memory expansion cards.

In the discussion on ISA, I talked about the problems with sharing level-triggered interrupts. MCA, on the other hand, uses edge-triggered interrupts, which enables interrupt sharing. EISA uses a combination of the two. Obviously, EISA needs to support edge-triggered interrupts to maintain compatibility with ISA cards. However, it enables EISA boards to configure that particular interrupt as either edge- or level-triggered.

As with MCA, EISA enables each board to be identified at boot up. Each manufacturer is assigned a prefix code to make the identification of the board easier. EISA also provides a configuration utility similar to the MCA reference disk to enable configuration of the cards. In addition, EISA supports automatic configuration, which enables the system to recognize the hardware at boot-up and configure itself accordingly. This can present problems for a Linux system because drivers in the kernel rely on the configuration to remain constant. Because each slot on an EISA machine is given a particular range of base addresses, it is necessary to modify your kernel before making such changes. This is often referred to as the EISA-config, EISA Configuration Utility, or ECU.

8.2.4 VESA Local Bus (VLB)

As I've said before and will say again, the system is only as good as its weakest link. With computer systems, that weakest link has been the IO subsystem for many years. CPUs got faster, but the system was still limited by slow communication with the outside world. The 32-bit buses of MCA and EISA made significant advances and increased throughput by a factor of five or more, but this was not enough.

The Video Electronics Standards Association, or VESA (a consortium of more than 120 companies), came up with an immediate solution to this problem. Although originally intended as a means of speeding up video transfer, the VESA local bus, or VLB, can achieve data transfer speeds that make it a worthy partner to fast 80386 and 80486 CPUs and even the Intel Pentium.

Like EISA, the VLB is a hybrid. That is, it is not a complete change from ISA, as is MCA. Whereas EISA interleaves the new connections with the old, the VLB extends the existing slots, something EISA decided not to do. Because of the load put on the system by the VLB, usually only three slots on the mother board have the VLB extension. The other remain as just ISA, EISA, or MCA.

The reason for the three-card limit is one of performance. There is the slight cost increase for adding the extra connectors and traces, however, the lure of the increased performance would outweigh the cost. Alas, things are not that easy. The CPU directly accesses the control, addresses, and data pins of the VLB cards (that's why it's called local). However, unless you want to reduce the speed of the CPU (which isn't likely), the CPU just can't handle more than three external loads. In practice, this means that although there are three slots, the CPU can't have more than one or two at speeds greater than 33MHz.

However, on the other hand, it is relatively inexpensive to change an existing ISA or EISA design into a VLB. There are a few new chips, a couple of new traces on the motherboard, and two or three new connectors. There isn't even a change to the BIOS.

VLB is not intended to be a replacement for ISA, although MCA and EISA sell themselves as such (or a replacement for each other, depending on whose literature you read). Current technology doesn't seem to allow it. As I mentioned, you can only have one or two VLB devices before you have to consider reducing your CPU speed. Therefore, you must have some other kind of bus slots as well.

Figure 8.4 shows that standard ISA/ESIA slots are the same length and VLB slots hang down "below" them. Because the VLB slots are an extension of the existing slots, it is not necessary to leave those slots empty if you have only one or two VLB cards. In fact, all the slots with the VLB extension can be filled with other cards (ISA, EISA, or MCA).

Watch out for machines that are advertised as "local bus." It is true that they might be, but there is a catch. Sometimes these machines have an SVGA chip or hard disk controller built onto the motherboard that are connected directly to the CPU and are therefore "local," though they do not adhere to the VLB spec.

8.2.5 Peripheral Component Interconnect (PCI)

More and more machines you find on the market today are including PCI local buses. One advantage that PCI offers over VLB is the higher performance, automatic configuration of peripheral cards, and superior compatibility. A major drawback with the other bus types (ISA, EISA, MCA) is the I/O bottleneck. Local buses overcome this by accessing memory using the same signal lines as the CPU. As a result, they can operate at the full speed of the CPU as well as utilize the 32-bit data path. Therefore, I/O performance is limited by the card and not the bus.

Figure 8.4: **Comparison of ISA/EISA Bus Slots to VLB**

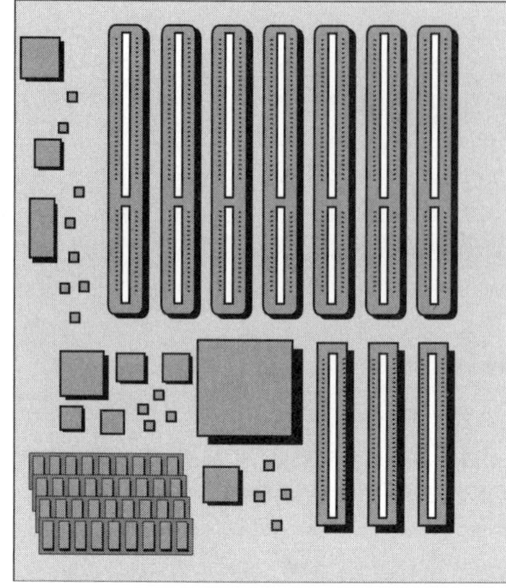

Although PCI is referred to as a local bus, it actually lies somewhere "above" the system bus. As a result, it is often referred to as a "mezzanine bus""" and has electronic "bridges" between the system bus and the expansion bus. As a result, the PCI-Bus can support up to five PCI devices, whereas the VLB can only support two or three. In addition, the PCI-Bus can reach transfer speeds four times that of EISA or MCA.

Even though PCI is called a mezzanine bus, it could replace ISA-, EISA-, or MCA-Buses, although in most cases, PCI is offered as a supplement to the existing bus type. If you look at a motherboard with PCI slots, you will see that they are completely separate from the other slots, whereas VLB slots are extensions of the existing slots. (You see this graphically in Figure 8.5)

Another advantage of PCI over the VLB is the VLB cannot keep up with the speed of the faster CPUs, especially if multiple VLB devices are on the system. Because PCI works with the CPU, it is much more suited to multitasking operating systems like UNIX, whereas the CPU cannot work independently if a VLB device is running.

Like EISA and MCA, PCI boards have configuration information built into the card. As the computer is booting, the system can configure each card individually based on system resources. This configuration is done "around" existing ISA, EISA, and MCA cards on your system.

To overcome PCI's shortcoming in transferring data, Intel (the designer and chief proponent of PCI) has come up with PCI-specific chip sets that enable data to be stored on the PCI controller, freeing the CPU to do other work. Although this may delay the *start* of the transfer, once the data flow starts, the transfer should continue uninterrupted.

Figure 8.5: **Comparison of ISA/EISA Bus Slots to PCI Slots**

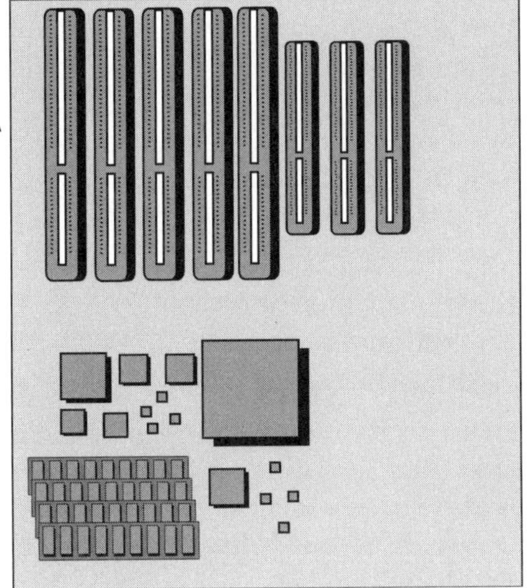

Another of PCI's shortcomings is that though you can swap ISA and EISA cards for VLB cards without any major problems, this is not so for PCI cards. Significant changes must be made to both the kernel and device drivers to account for the differences.

Also, although the number of PCI boards is growing rapidly, it is still a very small fraction of the number of ISA boards available. However, it is becoming more common to find PCI-Bus slots in a PC. PCI is on its way to becoming a *de facto* standard, if not *de jure*.

On the other hand, the PCI-Bus is not processor-dependent; you can install PCI in Pentium machines as well as Alpha machines. You can therefore run the same SCSI host adapter (or whatever). Because it is 64-bits wide, neither the Pentium nor Alphas are slowed down (too much) by the bus.

8.3 The Small Computer Systems Interface (SCSI)

The SCSI-Bus is an extension of your existing bus. A controller card, called a host adapter, is placed into one of your expansion slots. A ribbon cable that contains both data and control signals then connects the host adapter to your peripheral devices.

There are several advantages to having SCSI in your system. If you have a limited number of bus slots, adding a single SCSI host adapter enables you to add up to seven more devices by taking up only one slot with older SCSI systems and up to 15 devices with Wide-SCSI. SCSI has higher throughput than either IDE or ESDI. SCSI also supports many more different types of devices.

There are serveral different types of SCSI devices. The original SCSI specification is commonly referred to as SCSI-1. The newer specification, SCSI-2, offers increased speed and performance, as well as new commands. Fast SCSI increases throughput to more than 10MB per second. Fast-Wide SCSI provides a wider data path and throughput of up to 40MB per second and up to 15 devices. There there are Ultra-SCSI and Ultra-Wide-SCSI.

The last type, SCSI-3, is still being developed as of this writing and will provide the same functionality as Fast-Wide SCSI as well as support longer cables and more devices.

Each SCSI device has its own controller and can send, receive, and execute SCSI commands. As long as it communicates with the host adapter using proper SCSI commands, internal data manipulation is not an issue. In fact, most SCSI hard disks have an IDE controller with a SCSI interface built onto them.

Because there is a standard set of SCSI commands, new and different kinds of devices can be added to the SCSI family with little trouble. However, IDE and ESDI are limited to disk-type devices. Because the SCSI commands need to be “translated” by the device, there is a slight overhead, which is compensated for by the fact that SCSI devices are intrinsically faster than non-SCSI devices. SCSI devices also have higher data integrity than non-SCSI devices. The SCSI cable consists of 50 pins, half of which are ground. Because every pin has its own ground, it is less prone to interference and therefore it has higher data integrity.

On each SCSI host adapter are two connectors. One connector is at the top of the card (opposite the bus connectors) and is used for internal devices. A flat ribbon cable is used to connect each device to the host adapter. On internal SCSI devices, only one connector is on the device itself. Should you have external SCSI devices, there is a second connector on the end of the card (where it attaches to the chassis). Here SCSI devices are “daisy chained” together.

The SCSI-Bus must be closed to work correctly. By this I mean that each end of the bus must be terminated. There is usually a set of resistors (or slots for resistors) on each device. The devices at either end of the SCSI-Bus must have such resistors. This process is referred to as terminating the bus and the resistors are called terminating resistors.

It's fine to say that the SCSI-Bus needs to be terminated. However, that doesn't help your understanding of the issue. As with other kinds of devices, SCSI devices react to the commands sent along the cable to them. Unless otherwise impeded, the signals reach the end of the cable and bounce back. In such cases, there are two outcomes, both of which are undesirable: either the bounced signal interferes with the valid one, or the devices react to a second (unique in its mind) command. By placing a terminator at the end of the bus, the signals are "absorbed" and, therefore, don't bounce back.

Figure 8.6 and Figure 8.7 show examples of how the SCSI-Bus should be terminated. Note that Figure 8.6 says that it is an example of "all external devices." Keep in mind that the principle is still the same for internal devices. If all the devices are internal, then the host adapter would be still be terminated, as would the last device in the chain.

Figure 8.6: **Example of SCSI Bus with All External Devices**

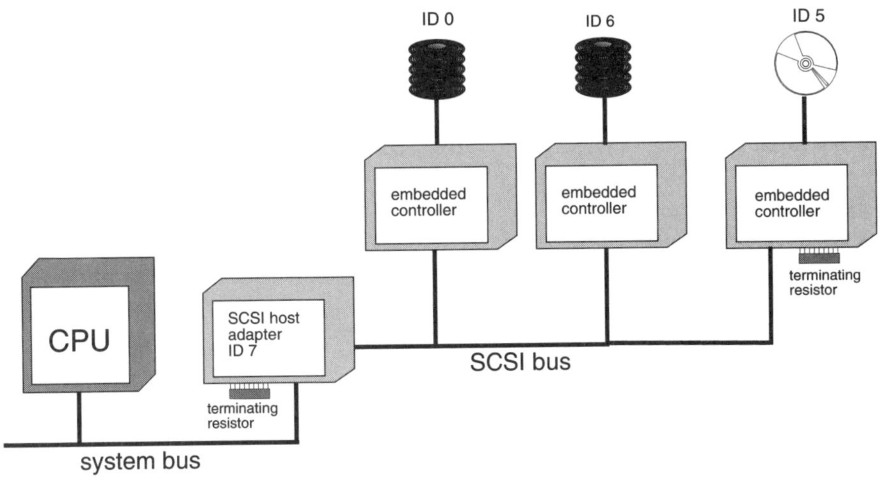

If you don't have any external devices (or only have external devices), the host adapter is at one end of the bus. Therefore, it too must be terminated. Many host adapters today have the ability to be terminated in software, so there is no need for terminating resistors (also known as resistor packs).

Each SCSI device is "identified" by a unique pair of addresses, which are the controller addresses that are also referred to as the SCSI ID. This pair of addresses is usually set by jumpers or dip switches on the device itself. Keep in mind that the ID is something that is set on the device itself and is not related to location on the bus. Note that in Figure 8.6, the SCSI ID of the devices are ordered ID 0, 6, and 5. Also the SCSI ID is often set using a combination of jumpers with no 1:1 relationship. (That is a pair of pins labled ID 0 through ID 7) Therefore, you should always read the hardware documentation to determine how to set the ID.

This sounds pretty obvious, but some people don't make sure. They make assumptions about what they see on the device regarding how the ID is set and do not fully understand what it means. For example, I have

Figure 8.7: **Example of SCSI Bus with Both External and Internal Devices**

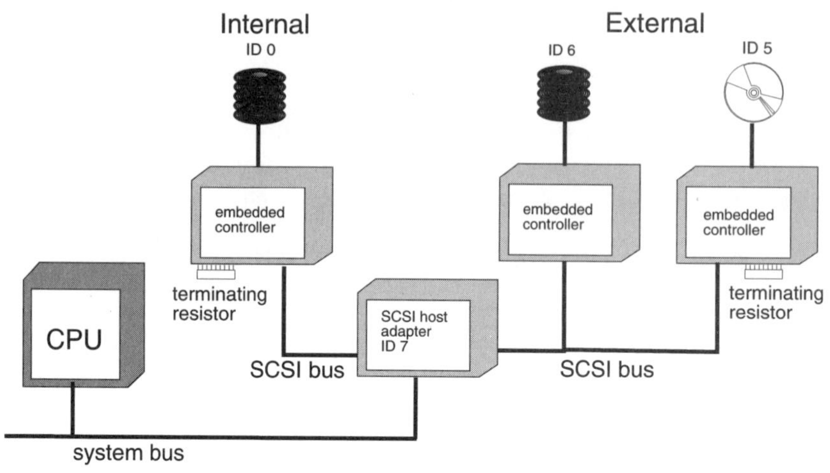

an Archive 5150 SCSI tape drive. On the back are three jumpers, labeled 0, 1, and 2. I have had customers call in with similar hardware with their SCSI tape drive set at 2. After configuring the tape drive and rebooting, they still couldn't access the tape drive. Nothing else was set at ID 2, so there were no conflicts. The system could access other devices on the SCSI-Bus, so the host adapter was probably okay. Different SCSI devices can be plugged into the same spot on the SCSI cable, so it wasn't the cable. The SCSI-Bus was terminated correctly, so that wasn't the problem.

Figure 8.8: **Examples of Binary for SCSI IDs**

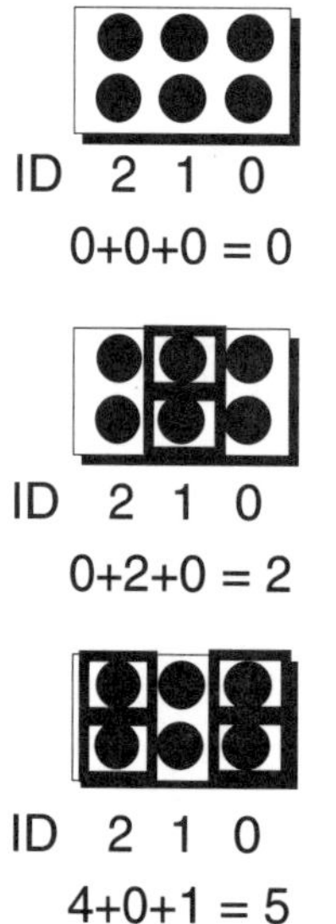

Rather than simply giving up and saying that it was a hardware problem, I suggested that the customer change the SCSI ID to 3 or 4 to see if that worked. Well, the customer couldn't, because the jumpers on the back only allowed him to change the SCSI ID to 0, 1, or 2. It then dawned on me what the problem was: the jumpers in the back are in binary! To set the ID to 2, the jumper needs to be on jumper 1, *not* jumper 2. Once the customer switched it to jumper 1 and rebooted, all was well. (Note: I helped this customer *before* I bought the Archive tape drive. When I got my drive home and wanted to check the SCSI ID, I saw only three jumpers. I then did something that would appall most users: I read the manual! Sure enough, it explained that the jumpers for the SCSI ID were binary.)

An additional problem to this whole SCSI ID business is that manufacturers are not consistent among each other. Some might label the jumpers (or switches) 0, 1, and 2. Others label them 1, 2, and 4. Still others label them ID0, ID1, and ID2. I have even seen some with a dial on them with 8 settings, which makes configuration a lot easier. The key is that no matter how they are labeled, the three pins or switches are binary and their values are added to give you the SCSI ID.

Let's look at Figure 8.8, which represents the jumper settings on a SCSI device. In the first example, none of the jumpers is set, so the SCSI ID is 0. In the second example, the jumper labeled 1 is set. This is 2^1 or 2, so the ID here is 2. In the last example, the jumpers labeled 2 and 0 are set, which is $2^2 + 2^0 = 4 + 1$, or 5.

On an AT-Bus, the number of devices added is limited only by the number of slots (granted, the AT-Bus is limited in how far away the slot can be from the CPU and therefore is limited in the number of slots). On a SCSI-Bus, however, there can be only seven devices in addition to the host adapter. Whereas devices on the AT-Bus are distinguished by their base addresses, devices on the SCSI-Bus are distinguished by their ID number.

ID numbers range from 0–7 and, unlike base addresses, the higher the ID, the higher the priority. Therefore, the ID of the host adapter should always be a 7. Because it manages all the other devices, it should have the highest priority. On the newer Wide SCSI-Buses, there can be up to 15 devices, plus the host adapter, with SCSI IDs ranging from 0 to 15.

Now back to our story...

The device address is known as the logical unit number (LUN). On devices with embedded controllers, such has hard disks, the LUN is always 0. All the SCSI devices directly supported by Linux have embedded controllers. Therefore, you are not likely to see devices set at LUNs other than 0.

In theory, a single-channel SCSI host adapter can support 56 devices. Devices called bridge adapters connect devices without embedded controllers to the SCSI-Bus. Devices attached to the bridge adapter have LUNs between 0 and 7. If there are seven bridge adapters, each with eight LUNs (relating to eight devices), 56 total devices are therefore possible.

The original SCSI-1 spec only defined the connection to hard disks. The SCSI-2 spec has extended this connection to such devices as CD-ROMS, tape drives, scanners, and printers. Provided these devices all adhere to the SCSI-2 standard, they can be mixed and matched even with older SCSI-1 hard disks.

One common problem with external SCSI devices is that the power supply is external as well. If you are booting your system with the power to that external device turned off, once the kernel gets past the initialization routines for that device (the hardware screen), it can no longer recognize that device. The only solution is to reboot. To prevent this problem, it is a good idea to keep all your SCSI devices internally. (This doesn't help for scanners and printer, but because Linux doesn't yet have drivers for them, it's a moot point.)

Although the number of host adapter manufacturers has steadily decreased in the past few years, Adaptec, the premier name in host adapters, has bought up both Trantor and Future Domain. Adaptec's biggest competitor for years, Buslogic, was no longer able to compete and was taken over by Mylex (a motherboard manufacturer, among other things). Despite the decrease in number of manufacturers, the number of models is still overwhelming.

Most host adapter manufacturers provide more than just a single model–many provide models for the entire spectrum of buses and SCSI types. ISA, EISA, PCI, Fast SCSI, Wide SCSI, and Ultra-Wide SCSI are part of the alphabet soup of SCSI devices. You can connect Wide SCSI disks onto a Fast SCSI adapter, although it will still only get 8 bits instead of the Wide SCSI's 16 bits, so it therefore only gets 10Mbytes per second compared to 20Mbytes per second of Wide SCSI.

Ultra SCSI disks can also be connected with the same limitations (it is an 8-bit bus). It can also handle Ultra-Wide SCSI and get 40Mbps. This is not too big of an issue, as most of the devices available today can only handle 10Mbps.

When looking at the performance of a SCSI device, you need to be careful of the manufacturer's test results–they can be deceiving. If a test reads 200MB from the disk in 10 seconds, you get an average of 20MB per second. What if those 100MB are all from the same track? The disk hardware reads the track and keeps it in its own cache. When the host adapter requests a new block from that track, the hard disk doesn't need to find the block on the disk–it delivers it from the cache. This decreases the access time and increases the *apparent* transfer rate of the drive dramatically. The manufacturer can say, in all honesty, that the host adapter has a transfer rate of 20Mbps, though the drive can only do half of this at most. Again, the chain is only as strong as its weakest link.

This does not mean that Wide SCSI or Ultra SCSI are only useful for the companies' marketing departments. SCSI has the advantage of being able to talk to multiple devices. For example, it can request data from one drive and, rather than waiting for the data, free the SCSI-Bus (disconnect). When the drive (or other device) is ready, it requests the bus again (reconnect) and the data is transferred. While the drive searches for the data, the host adapter can request data from another device. While this device is looking for the data, the first device can transfer the data to the host adapter. Being able to read or write devices like this means that a host adapter could get a *sustained* transfer rate of more that what *individual* devices can handle. (Note that both the host adapter and device must support disconnect/reconnect.)

Wide SCSI gets its performance gain by the fact it is wide (16 bits versus 8 bits). Ultra SCSI, on the other hand, gets the increase through a shorter cycle time. This is an important aspect because this makes for a steeper edge on the signal (the time from a low to high signal is much shorter, and vice versa). This means that the SCSI-Bus has higher requirements regarding the cabling.

Internal devices usually are connected by flat cable ribbons and present few new problems with Fast SCSI. The maximum length of the cable is half of what it could be with older SCSI devices and you must follow the specs exactly. Round cables for external devices have to be created specifically for Ultra SCSI and are therefore more expensive. Although the actual data transfer rate between the host adapter and the device is only as high as the device can handle, the steepness of the edges is the same. This means that if you connect Fast SCSI devices to Ultra SCSI host adapters, you still need the special Ultra SCSI cables.

Another consideration is that Ultra SCSI requires *active* termination. On the host adapter side, this isn't a problem because the host adapters are designed to give active termination. However, many older devices support only passive termination and therefore can't work on Ultra SCSI host adapters. This really comes into play when larger amounts of data are being transferred.

PCI devices can generally behave as either masters or slaves. For slave devices, the CPU is responsible for all the activity. This is a disadvantage for slave devices because the CPU is often busy transferring data and issuing commands instead of doing other work. This is really an issue in multitasking operating systems (like Linux) that have "better" things to do. Master devices, on the other hand, have an advantage here. The CPU only needs to tell them where to transfer the data, and they do the work themselves.

Regardless of whether a device acts as a master or slave, it will take up an interrupt line. Single function devices, such as host adapters, are given the interrupt INT-A. This means that the actual IRQ (between 5 and 15) will be determined by the system BIOS.

8.3.1 Termination

With Ultra SCSI, termination plays an more important role. A steeper edge means that the reflection has a stronger effect than with Fast SCSI. Moreover, a faster cycle means that the bus is more sensitive to interference. In principle, SCSI termination, even with Ultra SCSI, is simple: both ends of the bus (that is, the *physical* ends of the bus) must be terminated.

If you have fewer devices than connectors on your SCSI cable, I advise you to connect devices at both ends of the cable, terminating both of them. Loose ends can definitely lead to problems with reflection. By having devices at the physical ends of the cable, there is no question which device is at the end of the bus. Keep in mind that the order of the devices on the bus is independent of this.

You run into problems when the device has no possibility of being terminated or functions only with passive termination. Although no termination is rarely found, many (especially older) devices support only passive termination. Such devices include a lot of CD-ROMS and tape drives. Read the hardware documentation to find out what type of termination your drive supports or contact the manufacturer before you purchase the drive.

You need to be careful with some hard disks. There is often a jumper labeled TERM, which does not enable/disable the termination, but rather enables/disables the power for the active termination.

If you do have a device with active termination, this device belongs at one end of the SCSI cable. The other end is usually the host adapter. PCI host adapters are almost exclusively produced with active termination.

If both external and internal devices are present, the host adapter must not be terminated because it is now in the middle of the bus and no longer at the end. The termination is now on the device at the end of the other cable. Note that older, 50-pin Centronics connectors are almost exclusively passive terminators. Therefore, if you replace your existing host adapter with an Ultra-SCSI adaptor, you really should change the termination to active.

Wide SCSI presents its own termination and cabling problems. On most Wide-SCSI host adapters, you'll find an 8-bit and 16-bit connector, both of which you can use. However, keep in mind that *both* must be terminated.

8.4 Memory

Memory is the part of the computer where your program and data are while they are being used by the CPU. Contrast this to a hard disk or floppy, where the program is sitting on the disk and is not being used. (Of course with operating systems like Linux, parts of both the program and the data can be stored on the disk, even as the program is running.) There are two types of memory that are most common talked about: RAM and cache.

8.4.1 RAM

A computer stores the data it works with in three ways, often referred to as memory. Long-term memory, which remains in the system even when there is no power, is called nonvolatile memory and exists in such places as hard disks or floppies, which are often referred to as secondary storage. Short-term memory, or volatile memory, is stored in memory chips called RAM (random-access memory). RAM is often referred to as primary storage. The third class of memory is often ignored, or at least not often though of. This type of memory exists in hardware on the system but does not disappear when power is turned off. This is called ROM, or read-only memory.

I need to clarify one thing before we go on. Read-only memory is, as it says, read-only. For the most part, you cannot write to it. However, like random-access memory, the locations within it can be accessed in a "random" order, that is, at the discretion of the programmer. Also, read-only memory isn't always read-only, but that's a different story that goes beyond the scope of this book.

The best way to refer to memory to keep things clear (at least the best way in my opinion) is to refer to the memory we traditional call RAM as "main" memory. This is where our programs and the operating system actually reside.

There are two broad classes of memory: Dynamic RAM, or DRAM (pronounced dee-ram), and Static RAM, or SRAM (pronounced es-ram). DRAM is composed of tiny capacitors that can hold their charge only a short while before they require a "boost." SRAM is static because it does not require an extra power supply to keep its charge. As a result of the way it works internally, SRAM is faster and more expensive than DRAM. Because of the cost, the RAM that composes main memory is typically DRAM.

DRAM chips hold memory in ranges of 64KB to 16MB and more. In older systems, individual DRAM chips were laid out in parallel rows called banks. The chips themselves were called DIPPs, for Dual In-Line Pin Package. These look like the average, run-of-the-mill computer chip, with two rows of parallel pins, one row on each side of the chip. If memory ever went bad in one of these banks, it was usually necessary to replace (or test) dozens of individual chips. Because the maximum for most of these chips was 256 kilobits (32KB), it took 32 of them for each megabyte!

On newer systems, the DIPP chips have been replaced by Single In-Line Memory Modules, or SIMMs. Technological advances have decreased the size considerably. Whereas a few years ago, you needed an area the size of standard piece of binder paper to hold just a few megabytes, today's SIMMs can squeeze twice as much into an area the size of a stick of gum.

SIMMs come in powers of 2 megabytes (1, 2, 4, 8, etc.,) and are generally arranged in banks of four or eight. Because of the way the memory is accessed, you sometimes cannot mix sizes. That is, if you have four 2Mb SIMMs, you cannot simply add an 8Mb SIMM to get 16Mb. Bear this in mind when you order your system or order more memory. You should first check the documentation that came with the motherboard or the manufacturer.

Many hardware salespeople are not aware of this distinction. Therefore, if you order a system with 8MB that's "expandable" to 128Mb, you may be in for a big surprise. True, there are eight slots that can contain 16Mb each. However, if the vendor fills all eight slots with 1Mb SIMMs to give you your 8MB, you may have to throw *everything* out if you ever want to increase your RAM.

However, this is not always the case. My motherboard has some strange configurations. The memory slots on my motherboard consist of two banks of four slots each (which is typical of many machines). Originally, I had one bank completely full with four 4Mb SIMMs. When I installed Open Server, this was barely enough. When I decided to start X-Windows and Wabi, this was much too little. I could have increased this by 1Mb by filling the first bank with four 256K SIMMs and moving the four 4Mb SIMMs to the second bank. However, if I wanted to move up to 20Mb, I could use 1Mb instead of 256K. So, here is one example where everything does not have to match. In the end, I added four 4MB SIMMs to bring my total up to 32MB. The moral of the story: Read the manual!

Another issue that you should consider with SIMMs is that the motherboard design may require you to put in memory in multiples of either two or four because this is the way the motherboard accesses that memory. Potentially, a 32-bit machine could read a byte from four SIMMs at once, essentially reading the full 32 bits in one read. Keep in mind that the 32 bits are probably not being read simultaneously. However, being able to read them in succession is faster that reading one bank and then waiting for it to reset.

Even so, this requires special circuitry for each of the slots, called address decode logic. The address decode logic receives a memory address from the CPU and determines which SIMM it's in and where it is on the SIMM. In other words, it decodes the address to determine which SIMM is needed for a particular physical address.

This extra circuitry makes the machine more expensive because this is not just an issue with the memory but with the motherboard design as well. Accessing memory in this fashion is called "page mode" because the memory is broken into sets of bytes, or pages. Because the address decode logic is designed to access memory in only one way, the memory that is installed must fit the way it is read. For example, my motherboard requires each bank to be either completely filled or completely empty. Now, this requires a little bit of explanation.

As I mentioned earlier, DRAM consists of little capacitors for each bit of information. If the capacitor is charged, then the bit is 1; if there is no charge, the bit is 0. Capacitors have a tendency to drain over time, and for capacitors this small, that time is *very* short. Therefore, they must be regularly (or dynamically) recharged.

When a memory location is read, there must be some way of determining whether there is a charge in the capacitor. The only way to do that is to discharge the capacitor. If the capacitor can be discharged, that means that there was a charge to begin with and the system knows the bit was 1. Once discharged, internal circuitry recharges the capacitor.

Now, assume that the system wanted to read two consecutive bytes from a single SIMM. Because there is no practical way for the address decode logic to tell that the second read is not just a re-read of the first byte, the system must wait until the first byte has recharged itself. Only then can the second byte be read.

By taking advantage of the fact that programs run sequential and rarely read the same byte more than once at any given time, the memory subsystem can interleave its reads. That is, while the first bank is recharging, it can be reading from the second, and while the second is recharging, it can be reading from the third, and so on. Because subsequent reads must wait until the previous read has completed, this method is obviously not as fast as simultaneous reads. This is referred to as "interleaved" or "banked" memory.

Because all of these issues are motherboard-dependent, it best to check the hardware documentation when you change or add memory. Additionally, you may need to adjust settings, or jumpers, on the motherboard to tell it how much RAM you have and in what configuration.

Another issue that addresses speed is the physical layout of the SIMM. SIMMs are often described as being arranged in a "by-9" or "by-36" configuration, which refers to the number of bits that are immediately acces-

Figure 8.9: **Comparison of 30-pin and 72-pin SIMMs**

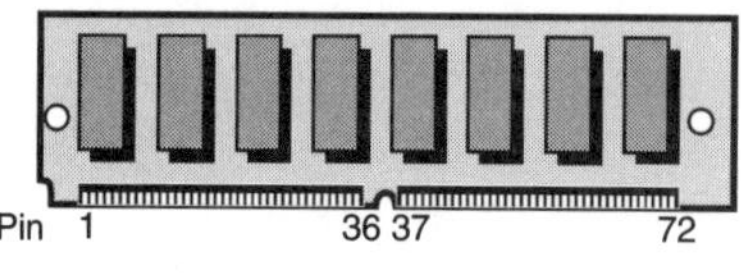

sible. So, in a "by-9" configuration, 9 bits are immediately accessible, with 1 bit used for parity. In a "by-36" configuration, 36 bits are available with 4 bits for parity (one for each 8 bits). The "by-9" configuration comes on SIMMs with 30 pins, where the "by-36" configuration comes on SIMMs with 72 pins. The 72-pin SIMMs can read 32 bits simultaneously, so they are even faster than 30-pin SIMMs at the same speed. Figure 8.9 shows give you a comparison of the older SIMMs and PS/2 SIMMs.

There are also different physical sizes for the SIMM. The 30-pin SIMMs are slightly smaller than 72-pin SIMMs. The larger, 72-pin variety are called PS/2 SIMMs because they are used in IBM's PS/2 machines. As well as being slightly larger, the PS/2 SIMM has a notch in the center so it is impossible to mix up the two. In both cases, there is a notch on one end that fits into a key in the slot on the motherboard, which makes putting the SIMM in backward almost impossible.

SIMMs come in several different speeds. The most common today are between 60 and 80 nanoseconds. Although there is usually no harm in mixing speeds, there is little to be gained. However, I want to emphasize the word *usually*. Mixing speeds has been known to cause panics. Therefore, if you mix speeds, it is best keep all the SIMMS within a single bank at a single speed. If your machine does not have multiple banks, then it is best not to mix speeds. Even if you do, remember that the system is only as fast as its slowest component.

Recently, the computer industry has begun to shift away from the old SIMMs toward extended data out RAM or EDORAM. Although as of this writing, EDORAM is still more expensive than SIMM, it is expected that by early 1997, the demand for EDORAM will be such that the price difference will disappear.

The principle behind EDORAM is an extension of the fast-page-mode (FPM) RAM. With FPM RAM, you rely on the fact that memory is generally read sequentially. Because you don't really need to wait for each memory location to recharge itself, you can read the next location without waiting. Because you have to wait until the signal is stabilized, though, there is still some wait, though it is much less of a wait than waiting for the memory to recharge. At CPU speeds greater than 33Mhz, the CPU requests memory faster than memory can deliver it, and the CPU needs to wait.

EDORAM works by "latching" the memory, which means adding secondary memory cells. These detect the data being out from memory and store the signals so the CPU can retrieve it. This works at bus speeds of 66Mhz. This process can be made even faster by including "burst" EDO-RAM, which extends the locality principle even further. Because the system is going to read sequentially, why doesn't it anticipate the processor and read more than just that single location? In some cases, the system will read 128 bits at once.

Part of the reason why EDORAM hasn't simply taken over the market is the similar to the reason why PS/2 didn't take over standard SIMMs: the hardware needed to support them is different. You cannot just install EDORAM in your machine and expect it to work–you need a special chip set on your motherboard. One such chip set is the Intel Triton chip set.

8.4.2 Cache Memory

Based on the principle of spatial locality, a program is more likely to spend its time executing code around the same set of instructions. This is demonstrated by the tests that have shown that most programs spend 80 percent of their time executing 20 percent of their code. Cache memory takes advantage of that.

Cache memory, or sometimes just cache, is a small set of very high-speed memory. Typically, it uses SRAM, which can be up to ten times more expensive than DRAM, which usually makes it prohibitive for anything other than cache.

When the IBM PC first came out, DRAM was fast enough to keep up with even the fastest processor. However, as CPU technology increased, so did its speed. Soon, the CPU began to outrun its memory. The advances in CPU technology could not be used unless the system was filled with the more expensive, faster SRAM.

The solution to this was a compromise. Using the locality principle, manufacturers of fast 386 and 486 machines began to include a set of cache memory consisting of SRAM but still populated main memory with the slower, less expensive DRAM.

To better understand the advantages of this scheme, let's cover the principle of locality in a little more detail. For a computer program, we deal with two types of locality: temporal (time) and spatial (space).

Because programs tend to run in loops (repeating the same instructions), the same set of instructions must be read over and over. The longer a set of instructions is in memory without being used, the less likely it is to be used again. This is the principle of temporal locality. What cache memory does is enable us to keep those regularly used instructions "closer" to the CPU, making access to them much faster. This is shown graphically in Figure 8.10.

Figure 8.10: **Level 1 and Level 2 Caches**

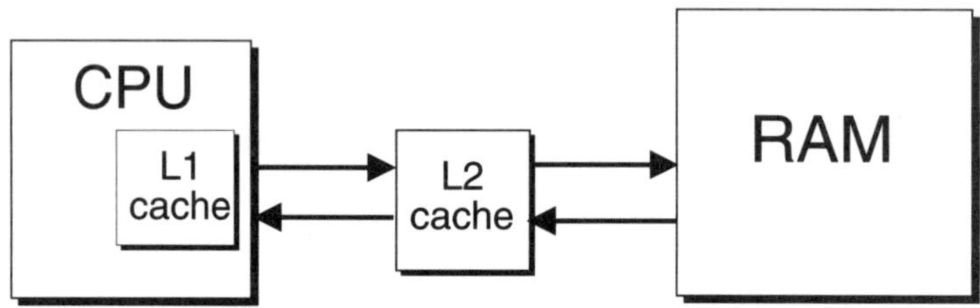

Spatial locality is the relationship between consecutively executed instructions. I just said that a program spends more of its time executing the same set of instructions. Therefore, in all likelihood, the next instruction the program will execute lies in the next memory location. By filling cache with more than just one instruction at a time, the principle of spatial locality can be used.

Is there really such a major advantage to cache memory? Cache performance is evaluated in terms of *cache* hits. A hit occurs when the CPU requests a memory location that is already in cache (that is, it does not have to go to main memory to get it). Because most programs run in loops (including the OS), the principle of locality results in a hit ratio of 85 to 95 percent. Not bad!

On most 486 machines, two levels of cache are used: level 1 cache and level 2 cache. Level 1 cache is internal to the CPU. Although nothing (other than cost) prevents it from being any larger, Intel has limited the level 1 cache in the 486 to 8k.

The level 2 cache is the kind that you buy separately from your machine. It is often part of the ad you see in the paper and is usually what people are talking about when they say how much cache is in their systems. Level 2 cache is external to the CPU and can be increased at any time, whereas level 1 cache is an integral part of the CPU and the only way to get more is to buy a different CPU. Typical sizes of level 2 cache range from 64K to 256K, usually in increments of 64K.

There is one major problem with dealing with cache memory: the issue of consistency. What happens when main memory is updated and cache is not? What happens when cache is updated and main memory is not? This is where the cache's *write policy* comes in.

The write policy determines if and when the contents of the cache are written back to memory. The write-through cache simply writes the data through the cache directly into memory. This slows writes, but the data is consistent. Buffered write-through is a slight modification of this, in which data are collected and everything is written at once. Write-back improves cache performance by writing to main memory only when necessary. Write-dirty is when it writes to main memory only when it has been modified.

Cache (or main memory, for that matter) is referred to as "dirty" when it is written to. Unfortunately, the system has no way of telling whether anything has changed, just that it is being written to. Therefore it is possible, but not likely, that a block of cache is written back to memory even if it is not actually dirty.

Another aspect of cache is its organization. Without going into detail (that would take most of a chapter itself), I can generalize by saying there are four different types of cache organization.

The first kind is fully associative, which means that every entry in the cache has a slot in the "cache directory" to indicate where it came from in memory. Usually these are not individual bytes, but chunks of four bytes or more. Because each slot in the cache has a separate directory slot, any location in RAM can be placed anywhere in the cache. This is the simplest scheme but also the slowest because each cache directory entry must be searched until a match (if any) is found. Therefore, this kind of cache is often limited to just 4Kb.

The second type of cache organization is *direct-mapped* or *one-way set associative cache*, which requires that only a single directory entry be searched. This speeds up access time considerably. The location in the cache is related on the location in memory and is usually based on blocks of memory equal to the size of the cache. For example, if the cache could hold 4K 32-bit (4-byte) entries, then the block with which each entry is associated is also 4K x 32 bits. The first 32 bits in each block are read into the first slot of the cache, the second 32 bits in each block are read into the second slot, and so on. The size of each entry, or line, usually ranges from 4 to 16 bytes.

There is a mechanism called a tag, which tells us which block this came from. Also, because of the very nature of this method, the cache cannot hold data from multiple blocks for the same offset. If, for example, slot 1 was already filled with the data from block 1 and a program wanted to read the data at the same location from block 2, the data in the cache would be overwritten. Therefore, the shortcoming in this scheme is that when data is read at intervals that are the size of these blocks, the cache is constantly overwritten. Keep in mind that this does not occur too often due to the principle of spatial locality.

The third type of cache organization is an extension of the one-way set associative cache, called the *two-way set associative*. Here, there are two entries per slot. Again, data can end up in only a particular slot, but there are two places to go within that slot. Granted, the system is slowed a little because it has to look at the tags for both slots, but this scheme allows data at the same offset from multiple blocks to be in the cache at the same time. This is also extended to four-way set associative cache. In fact, the cache internal to 486 and Pentium has a four-way set associate cache.

Although this is interesting (at least to me), you may be asking yourself, "Why is this memory stuff important to me as a system administrator?" First, knowing about the differences in RAM (main memory) can aide you in making decisions about your upgrade. Also, as I mentioned earlier, it may be necessary to set switches on the motherboard if you change memory configuration.

Knowledge about cache memory is important for the same reason because you may be the one who will adjust it. On many machines, the write policy can be adjusted through the CMOS. For example, on my machine, I have a choice of write-back, write-through, and write-dirty. Depending on the applications you are running, you may want to change the write policy to improve performance.

8.4.3 Parity

In most memory today, an extra bit is added for each byte. This is a parity bit. Parity is a simple way of *detecting* errors within a memory chip (among other things). If an odd number of bits is set, the parity bit will be set to make the total number of bits set an even number (most memory uses even parity). For example, if three bits are set, the parity bit will also be set to make the total bits set four.

When data is written, the number of set bits is calculated and the parity bit is set accordingly. When the data is read, the parity bit is also read. If the total number of bits set is even, all is well. However, if an odd number of data bits is set and the parity bit is not set, or if an even number of data bits is set and the parity bit is set, a parity error has occurred.

When a parity error occurs in memory, the state of the system is uncertain. To prevent any further problems, the parity checking logic generates a Nonmaskable Interrupt (NMI), and the CPU immediately jumps to special codes called NMI service routines.

When Linux is interrupted with an NMI as the result of a parity error, it too realizes things are not good, and the system panics. The panic causes the system to stop everything and shut down. Certain machines support ECC (Error Correcting Code) RAM, which corrects parity problems before it kills your system.

8.5 The Central Processing Unit

Sometimes people just don't understand. At first, I thought that they "didn't have a clue," but that's was really the problem. They had a clue, but a single clue doesn't solve a crime, nor does it help you run a Linux system. You can easily copy a program from a DOS disk onto an Linux system, particularly if Linux is running on your DOS partition. In all likelihood, the permissions are already set to be executable. So you type in the name of the program and press Enter. Nothing happens, or you get an error about incorrect format. Hmmm. The software manual says that it runs on a 386 or higher (which you have), a VGA monitor (which you have), and at least 2Mb of hard disk space (which you have). Why doesn't it work?

This is a true story. A customer called in saying that the system I was supporting at the time (not Linux) was broken. This customer had a program that worked fine on his DOS PC at home. It, too, was a 386, so there shouldn't be a problem, right? Unfortunately, wrong. Granted, in both cases, the CPU is reading machine instructions and executing them, but in fact, they are the same machine instructions. They have to be. The same also applies to a Linux system.

The problem is comparable to German and English. Although both use (basically) the same alphabet, words (sets of characters) written in German are not understandable by someone reading them as English, and vice versa. Sets of machine instructions that are designed to be interpreted under DOS will not be understood under Linux. (Actually, the problem is a little more complicated, but you get the basic idea.)

Just as your brain has to be told (taught) the difference between German and English, a computer needs to be told the difference between DOS and UNIX programs.

In this section, I will talk about the CPU, the brains of the outfit. It is perfectly reasonable for users and administrators alike to have no understanding of what the CPU does internally. However, a basic knowledge of some of the key issues is important so you can completely understand some of the issues I'll get into elsewhere.

It's like trying to tune-up your car. You don't really need to know how oxygen mixes with gasoline to be able to adjust the carburetor. However, knowing that it happens makes adjusting the carburetor that much easier.

I won't go into detail about the CPU's instruction cycle, that is, how it receives and executes instructions. Though I'm interested in things like that and would love to talk about them, it isn't really necessary to understand what we need to talk about here. Instead, I am going to talk mostly about how the CPU enables the operating system to create a scheme whereby many programs can be in memory simultaneously. These are the concepts of paging and multitasking.

Until recently, only the commercial distributions of Linux were available for Intel processors. RedHat released a version for the Digital Electronics Corporation (DEC) Alpha processor, and others have since followed.

In the next section, I will go into a little depth about the Intel process and how Linux interacts with it. Afterwards, I will talk briefly about the DEC Alpha to give you an idea of what it is about. Because of the number of Intel distributions and Intel-based machines, I won't go into the same depth for the Alpha. The concepts a basically the same, though the names of registers, etc., are different.

8.5.1 Intel Processors

Although it is an interesting subject, the ancient history of microprocessors is not really important to the issues at hand. It might be nice to learn how the young PC grew from a small, budding 4-bit system to the gigantic, strapping 64-bit Pentium. However, there are many books that have covered this subject and unfortunately, I don't have the space. Besides, the Intel chips on which Linux runs are only the 80386 (or 100-percent compatible clones) and higher processors.

So, instead of setting the way-back machine to Charles Babbage and his Analytic Engine, we leap ahead to 1985 and the introduction of the Intel 80386. Even compared to its immediate predecessor, the 80286, the 80386 (386 for short) was a powerhouse. Not only could it handle twice the amount of data at once (now 32 bits), but its speed rapidly increased far beyond that of the 286.

New advances were added to increase the 386's power. Internal registers were added and their size was increased. Built into the 386 was the concept of virtual memory, which was a way to make it appear as though there was much more memory on system than there actually was. This substantially increased the system efficiency. Another major advance was the inclusion of a 16-byte, pre-fetch cache. With this, the CPU could load instructions before it actually processed them, thereby speeding things up even more. Then the most obvious speed increase came when the speed of the processor was increased from 8Mhz to 16Mhz.

Although the 386 had major advantages over its predecessors, at first its cost seemed relatively prohibitive. To allow users access to the multitasking capability and still make the chip fit within their customers' budgets, Intel made an interesting compromise: By making a new chip in which the interface to the bus was 16-bits instead of 32-bits, Intel made their chip a fair bit cheaper.

Internally, this new chip, designated the 80386SX, is identical to the standard 386. All the registers are there and it is fully 32 bits wide. However, data and instructions are accessed 16 bits at a time, therefore requiring two bus accesses to fill the registers. Despite this shortcoming, the 80386SX is still faster than the 286.

Perhaps the most significant advance of the 386 for Linux as well as other PC-based UNIX systems was its paging abilities. I talked a little about paging in the section on operating system basics, so you already have a general idea of what paging is about. I will also go into more detail about paging in the section on the kernel. However, I will talk about it a little here so you can fully understand the power that the 386 has given us and see how the CPU helps the OS.

There are UNIX-like products that run on a 80286, such as SCO XENIX. In fact, there was even a version of SCO XENIX that ran on the 8086. Because Linux was first released for the 386, I won't go into anymore detail about the 286 or the differences between the 286 and 386. Instead, I will just describe the CPU Linux used as sort of an abstract entity. In addition, because most of what I will be talking about is valid for the 486 and Pentium as well as the 386, I will simply call it "the CPU" instead of 386, 486, or Pentium.

(Note: Linux will also run on non-Intel CPUs, such as those from AMD or Cyrix. However, the issues I am going to talk about are all common to Intel-based or Intel-derived CPUs.)

I need to take a side-step here for a minute. On PC-Buses, multiple things are happening at once. The CPU is busily processing while much of the hardware is being access via DMA. Although these multiple tasks are occurring simultaneously on the system, this is not what is referred to as multitasking.

When I talk about multitasking, I am referring to multiple processes being in memory at the same time. Because of the time the computer takes to switch between these processes, or tasks, is much shorter than the human brain can recognize, it appears as though the processes are running simultaneously. In reality, each process gets to use the CPU and other system resources for a brief time and then it's another process's turn.

As it runs, the process could use any part of the system memory it needs. The problem with this is that a portion of RAM that one process wants may already contain code from another process. Rather than allowing each process to access any part of memory it wants, protections keep one program from overwriting another one. This protection is built in as part of the CPU and is called, quite logically, "protected mode." Without it, Linux could not function.

Note, however, that just because the CPU is in protected mode does not necessarily mean that the protections are being utilized. It simply means that the operating system can take advantage of the built-in abilities if it wants.

Although this capability is built into the CPU, it is not the default mode. Instead, the CPU starts in what I like to call "DOS-compatibility mode." However, the correct term is "real mode." Real mode is a real danger to an operating system like UNIX. In this mode, a there are no protections (which makes sense because protections exist only in protected mode). A process running in real mode has complete control over the entire system and can do anything it wants. Therefore, trying to run a multiuser system on a real-mode system would be a nightmare. All the protections would have to be built into the process because the operating system wouldn't be able to prevent a process from doing what it wanted.

A third mode, called "virtual mode," is also built in. In virtual mode, the CPU behaves to a limited degree as though it is in real mode. However, when a process attempts to directly access registers or hardware, the instruction is caught, or trapped, and the operating system is allowed to take over.

Let's get back to protected mode because this is what makes multitasking possible. When in protected mode, the CPU can use virtual memory. As I mentioned, this is a way to trick the system into thinking that there is more memory than there really is. There are two ways of doing this. The first is called swapping, in which the entire process is loaded into memory. It is allowed to run its course for a certain amount of time. When its turn is over, another process is allowed to run. What happens when there is not enough room for both process to be in memory at the same time? The only solution is that the first process is copied out to a special part of the hard disk called the swap space, or swap device. Then, the next process is loaded into memory and allowed its turn. The second is called paging and we will get to it in a minute.

Because it takes such a large portion of the system resources to swap processes in and out of memory, virtual memory can be very inefficient, especially when you have a lot of processes running. So let's take this a step further. What happens if there are too many process and the system spends all of its time swapping? Not good.

To avoid this problem, a mechanism was devised whereby only those parts of the process that are needed are in memory. As it goes about its business, a program may only need to access a small portion of its code. As I mentioned earlier, empirical tests show that a program spends 80 percent of its time executing 20 percent of its code. So why bother bringing in those parts that aren't being used? Why not wait and see whether they are used?

To make things more efficient, only those parts of the program that are needed (or expected to be needed) are brought into memory. Rather than accessing memory in random units, the memory is divided into 4K chunks, called pages. Although there is nothing magic about 4K per se, this value is easily manipulated. In the CPU, data is referenced in 32-bit

(4-byte) chunks, and 1K (1,024) of each chunk is a page (4,096). Later you will see how this helps things work out.

As I mentioned, only that part of the process currently being used needs to be in memory. When the process wants to read something that is not currently in RAM, it needs to go out to the hard disk to pull in the other parts of the process; that is, it goes out and reads in new pages. This process is called paging. When the process attempts to read from a part of the process that is not in physical memory, a "page fault" occurs.

One thing you must bear in mind is that a process can jump around a lot. Functions are called, sending the process off somewhere completely different. It is possible–likely, for that matter–that the page containing the memory location to which the process needs to jump is not currently in memory. Because it is trying to read a part of the process not in physical memory, this, too, is called a page fault. As memory fills up, pages that haven't been used in some time are replaced by new ones. (I'll talk much more about this whole business later.)

Assume that a process has just made a call to a function somewhere else in the code and the page it needed is brought into memory. Now there are two pages of the process from completely different parts of the code. Should the process take another jump or return from the function, it needs to know whether it is going into memory. The operating system could keep track of this, but it doesn't need to–the CPU will keep track for it.

Stop here for a minute! This is not entirely true. The OS must first set up the structures that the CPU uses. However, the CPU uses these structures to determine whether a section of a program is in memory. Although not part of the CPU, but rather RAM, the CPU administers the RAM utilization through page tables. As their names imply, page tables are simply tables of pages. In other words, they are memory locations in which other memory locations are stored.

Confused? I was at first, so let's look at this concept another way. Each running process has a certain part of its code currently in memory. The system uses these page tables to keep track of what is currently memory and where it is located. To limit the amount the CPU has to work, each of these page tables is only 4K, or one page, in size. Because each page contains a set of 32-bit addresses, a page table can contain only 1,024 entries.

Although this would imply that a process can only have 4K x 1,024, or 4Mb, loaded at a time, there is more to it. Page tables are grouped into page directories. Like the page table, the entries in a page directory point to memory locations. However, rather than pointing to a part of the process, page directories point to page tables. Again, to reduce the CPU's work, a page directory is only one page. Because each entry in the page directory points to a page, this means that a process can only have 1,024 page tables.

Is this enough? Let's see. A page is 4K or 4,096 bytes, which is 212. Each page table can refer to 1,024 pages, which is 2^{10}. Each page directory can refer to 1,024 page tables, which is also 2^{10}. Multiplying this out, we have

(page size) x (pages in page table) x (page tables in page directory)

or

$(2^{12}) \times (2^{10}) \times (2^{10}) = 2^{32}$

Because the CPU is only capable of accessing 2^{32} bytes, this scheme allows access to every possible memory address that the system can generate.

Are you still with me?

Inside of the CPU is a register called the Control Register 0, or CR0 for short. In this register is a single bit that turns on this paging mechanism. If this paging mechanism is turned on, any memory reference that the CPU receives is interpreted as a combination of page directories, page tables, and offsets, rather than an absolute, linear address.

Built into the CPU is a special unit that is responsible for making the translation from the virtual address of the process to physical pages in memory. This special unit is called (what else?) the paging unit. To understand more about the work the paging unit saves the operating system or other parts of the CPU, let's see how the address is translated.

When paging is turned on, the paging unit receives a 32-bit value that represents a virtual memory location within a process. The paging unit takes theses values and translates them, as shown in Figure 8.11. At the top of the figure, we see that the virtual address is handed to the paging unit, which converts it to a linear address. This is *not* the physical address in memory. As you see, the 32-bit linear address is broken down into three components. The first 10 bits (22–31) are offset into the page directory. The location in memory of the page directory is determined by the Page Directory Base Register (PDBR).

The page directory entry contains 4 bits that point to a specific page table. The entry in the page table, as you see, is determined by bits 12–21. Here again, we have 10 bits, which means each entry is 32 bits. These 32-bit entries point to a specific page in *physical* memory. Which byte is referenced in physical memory is determined by the offset portion of the linear address, which are bits 0–11. These 12 bits represent the 4,096 (4K) bytes in each physical page.

Keep in mind a couple of things. First, page tables and page directories are not part of the CPU. They can't be. If a page directory were full, it would contain 1,024 references to 4K chunks of memory. For the page tables alone, you would need 4Mb! Because this would create a CPU hundreds of times larger than it is now, page tables and directories are stored in RAM.

Figure 8.11: **Translation of Virtual-to-Physical Address**

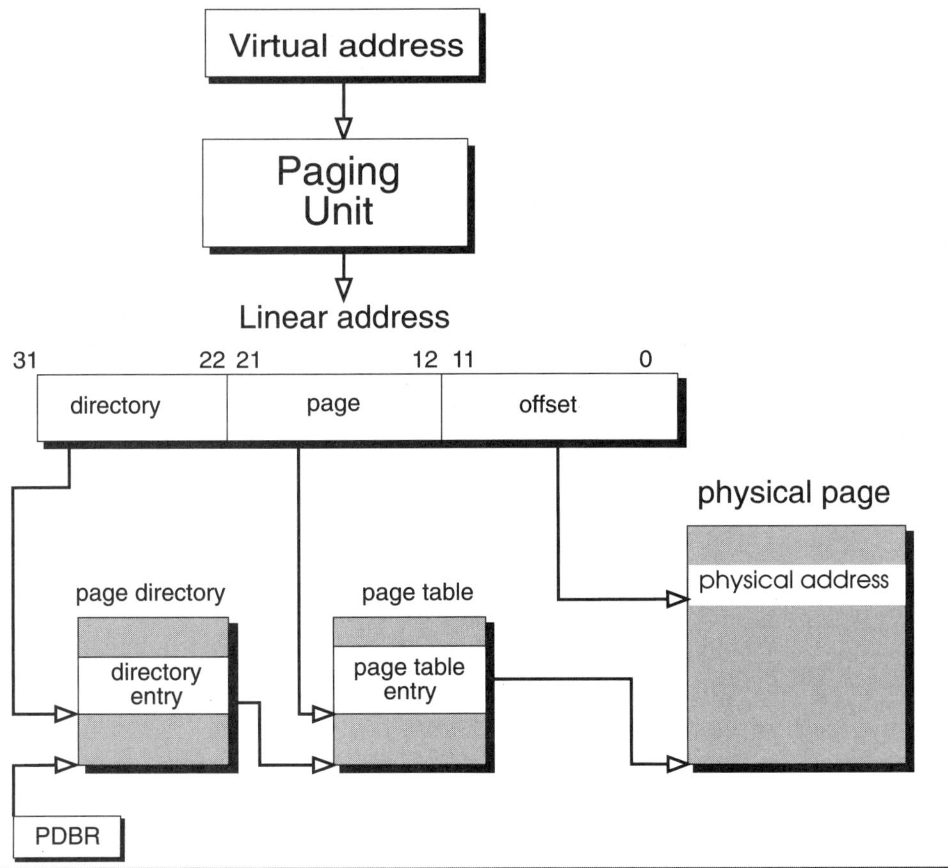

Next, page tables and page directories are abstract concepts that the CPU knows how to utilize. They occupy physical RAM, and operating systems such as Linux know how to switch this capability on within the CPU. All the CPU does is the "translation" work. When it starts, Linux turns this capability on and sets up all the structures. These structures are then handed off to the CPU, where the paging unit does the work.

As I said, a process with all of its page directory entries full would require 4Mb just for the page tables. This implies that the entire process is somewhere in memory. Because each of the page table entries points to physical pages in RAM, you would need 16Gb of RAM. Not that I would mind having that much RAM, though it is a bit costly and even if you had 16Mb SIMMs, you would need 1000 of them.

Like pages of the process, it's possible that a linear address passed to the paging unit translates to a page table or even a page directory that was not in memory. Because the system is trying to access a page (which contains a page table and not part of the process) that is not in memory, a page fault occurs and the system must go get that page.

Because page tables and the page directory are not really part of the process but are important only to the operating system, a page fault causes these structures to be *created* rather than read in from the hard disk or elsewhere. In fact, as the process starts up, all is without form and is void: no pages, no page tables, and no page directory.

The system accesses a memory location as it starts the process. The system translates the address, as I described above, and tries to read the page directory. It's not there. A page fault occurs and the page directory must be created. Now that the directory is there, the system finds the entry that points to the page table. Because no page tables exist, the slot is empty and another page fault occurs. So, the system needs to create a page table. The entry in the page table for the physical page is found to be empty, and so yet another page fault occurs. Finally, the system can read in the page that was referenced in the first place.

This whole process sounds a bit cumbersome, but bear in mind that this amount of page faulting only occurs as the process is starting. Once the table is created for a given process, it won't page fault again on that table. Based on the principle of locality, the page tables will hold enough entries for a while, unless, of course, the process bounces around a lot.

The potential for bouncing around brings up an interesting aspect of page tables. Because page tables translate to physical RAM in the same way all the time, virtual addresses in the same area of the process end up in the same page tables. Therefore, page tables fill up because the process is more likely to execute code in the same part of a process rather than elsewhere (this is spatial locality).

There is quite a lot there, yes? Well, don't get up yet because we're not finished. There are a few more issues that I haven't addressed.

First, I have often referred to page tables and *the* page directory. Each process has a single page directory (it doesn't need any more). Although the CPU supports multiple page directories, there is only one directory for the *entire* system. When a process needs to be switched out, the entries in the page directory for the old process are overwritten by those for the new process. The location of the page directory in memory is maintained in the Control Register 3 (CR3) in the CPU.

There is something here that bothered me in the beginning and may still bother you. As I have described, each time a memory reference is made, the CPU has to look at the page directory, then a page table, then calculate the physical address. This means that for *every* memory reference, the CPU has to make two more references just to find out where the next instruction or data is coming from. I though that was pretty stupid.

Well, so did the designers of the CPU. They have included a functional unit called the Translation Lookaside Buffer, or TLB. The TLB contains 32 entries and, as the internal and external caches point to sets of instructions, points to pages. If a page that is being searched is in the TLB, a TLB hit occurs (just like a cache hit). As a result of the principle of spatial locality, there is a 98-percent hit rate using the TLB.

When you think about it, this makes a lot of sense. The CPU does not just execute one instruction for a program then switch to something else–it executes hundreds or even thousands of instructions before it is another program's turn. If each page contains 1,024 instructions and the CPU executes 1000 before it's another program's turn, all 1000 will most likely be in the same page. Therefore, they are all TLB hits.

Now, let's take a closer look at the page table entries themselves. Each is a 32-bit value that points to a 4K location in RAM. Because it points to an area of memory larger than a byte, it does not need all 32 bits to do it. Therefore, some bits are left over. Because the page table entry points to an area that has 2^{20} bytes (4,096 bytes = 1 page), it doesn't need 12 bits. These are the low-order 12 bits and the CPU uses them for other purposes related to that page. A few of them are unused and the operating system can, and does, use them for its own purposes. Intel also reserves a couple, and they should not be used.

One bit, the 0th bit, is the present bit. If this bit is set, the CPU knows that the page being referenced is in memory. If it is not set, the page is not in memory and if the CPU tries to access it, a page fault occurs. Also, if this bit is not set, none of the other bits has any meaning. (How can you talk about something that's not there?)

Another important bit is the accessed bit. Should a page be accessed for either read or write, the CPU sets this bit. Because the page table entry is never filled in until the page is being accessed, this seems a bit redundant. If that was all there was to it, you'd be right. However, there's more.

At regular intervals, the operating system clears the access bit. If a particular page is never used again, the system is free to reuse that physical page if memory gets short. When that happens, all the OS needs to do is clear the present bit so the page is considered "invalid."

Another bit used to determine how a page is accessed is the dirty bit. If a page has been written to, it is considered dirty. Before the system can make a dirty page available, it must make sure that whatever was in that page is written to disk, otherwise the data is inconsistent.

Finally, we get to the point of what all this protected mode stuff is all about. The protection in protected mode essentially boils down to two bits in the page table entry. One bit, the user/supervisor bit, determines who has access to a particular page. If the CPU is running at user level, then it only has access to user-level pages. If the CPU is at supervisor level, it has access to all pages.

I need to say here that this is the maximum access a process can have. Other protections may prevent a user-level or even supervisor-level process from getting even this far. However, these are implemented at a higher level.

The other bit in this pair is the read/write bit. As the name implies, this bit determines whether a page can be written to. This single bit is really just an on-off switch. If the page is there, you have the right to read it if you can (that is, either you are a supervisor-level process or the page is a user page). However, if the write ability is turned off, you can't write to it, even as a supervisor.

If you have a 386 CPU, all is well. If you have a 486 and decide to use one of those bits that I told you were reserved by Intel, you are now running into trouble. Two of these bits were not defined in the 386 but are now defined in the 486: page write-through (PWT) and page cache disable (PCD).

PWT determines the write policy (see the section on RAM) for external cache regarding this page. If PWT is set, then this page has a write-through policy. If it is clear, a write-back policy is allowed.

PCD decides whether this page can be cached. If clear, this page cannot be cached. If set, then caching is allowed. Note that I said "allowed." Setting this bit does not mean that the page will be cached–other factors that go beyond what I am trying to get across here are involved.

Well, I've talked about how the CPU helps the OS keep track of pages in memory. I also talked about how the CR3 register helps keep track of which page directory needs to be read. I also talked about how pages can be protected by using a few bits in the page table entry. However, one more thing is missing to complete the picture: keeping track of which process is currently running, which is done with the Task Register (TR).

The TR is not where most of the work is done–the CPU simply uses it as a pointer to where the important information is kept. This pointer is the Task State Descriptor (TSD). Like the other descriptors that I've talked about, the TSD points to a particular segment. This segment is the Task State Segment (TSS). The TSD contains, among other things, the privilege level at which this task is operating. Using this information along with that in the page table entry, you get the protection that protected mode allows.

The TSS contains essentially a snapshot of the CPU. When a process's turn on the CPU is over, the state of the entire CPU needs to be saved so that the program can continue where it left off. This information is stored in the TSS. This functionality is built into the CPU. When the OS tells the CPU a task switch is occurring (that is, a new process is getting its turn), the CPU knows to save this data *automatically*.

If we put all of these components together, we get an operating system that works together with the hardware to provide a multitasking, multiuser system. Unfortunately, what I talked about here are just the basics.

I could spend a whole book just talking about the relationship between the operating system and the CPU and still not be done.

One thing I didn't talk about was the difference between the 80386, 80486, and Pentium. With each new processor comes new instructions. The 80486 added an instruction pipeline to improve the performance to the point where the CPU could average almost one instruction per cycle. The Pentium has dual instructions paths (pipelines) to increase the speed even more. It also contains *branch prediction logic*, which is used to "guess" where the next instruction should come from.

The Pentium (as well as the newer PentiumPro) has a few new features that make for significantly more performance. This first feature is multiple instruction paths or pipelines, which allow the CPU to work on multiple instructions at the same time. In some cases, the CPU will have to wait to finish one before working on the other, though this is not always necessary.

The second improvement is called dynamic execution. Normally, instructions are executed one after other. If the execution order is changed, the whole program is changed. Well, not exactly. In some instances, upcoming instructions are not based on previous instructions, so the processor can "jump ahead" and start executing the executions before others are finished.

The next advance is branch prediction. Based on previous activity, the CPU can expect certain behavior to continue. For example, the odds are that once the CPU is in a loop, the loop will be repeated. With more than one pipeline executing instruction, multiple possibilities can be attempted. This is not always right, but is right more than 75 percent of the time!

The PentiumPro (P6) introduced the concept of data flow analysis. Here, instructions are executed as they are ready, not necessarily in the order in which they appear in the program. Often, the result is available before it normally would be. The PentiumPro (P6) also introduced speculative execution, in which the CPU takes a guess at or anticipates what is coming.

The P6 is also new in that it is actually two separate chips. However, the function of the second chip is the level 2 cache. Both an external bus and a "private" bus connect the CPU to the level 2 cache, and both of these are 64 bits.

8.5.2 Alpha Processors

The Alpha procressor from the Digital Equipment Corporation (DEC) is the first non-Intel-based processor on which Linux was commerically available and is substantially different from its Intel cousins. The most significant difference is that the Alpha is a Reduced Instruction Set Computer (RISC), as compared to the Intel, which is a Complex Instruction Set Computer (CISC). Without turning this book into a textbook on microprocessor design, I can simply say that the difference is that RISC has fewer instructions (the instruction set is reduced) and therefore takes more instructions to do a specific job. A CISC processor has more instructions and takes fewer instructions to do the same job.

Imagine someone told you to stand up and open the door. The CISC instruction might simply say, "Go open the door." Using what's built into your CPU (your brain), you know to translate this to "stand up and open the door." On the other hand, the RISC instructions might be "Stand up. Turn left and take two paces forward. Turn right, and take three paces forward. Raise right hand, etc." There might then be a CISC instruction that says, "Go open the window." However, the RISC instructions might be "Stand up. Turn left, and take two paces forward. Turn left, and take three paces forward, etc."

Not only does the CISC give fewer instructions, it also requires less logic circuitry. As a result, an Alpha processor can run at higher speeds than an Intel. This does *not* make the Alpha intrinsically faster! Take our example. I simply tell you to open the window, and you do it. However, giving you each instruction individually takes more time. One significant difference is that the PentiumPro just recently broke the 200Mhz barrier, whereas the Alphas are more than twice that.

Even if the increase in clock speed is not considered, the design of the Alpha enables it to do more work per cycle. Several issues were addressed to help eliminate any aspect of the processor that would hinder multiple instruction issues. For example, there are no branch delay or skip instructions. As a result of its design, the Alpha (as of this writing) can get up to 10 new instructions per cycle.

In addition, the Alpha was designed to run with multiple processors, though that's not to say that it can't run as a single processor. The Alpha was designed with several instructions that simplify adding multiple processors. Unlike other processors, this functionality was designed from the beginning and didn't have to be built onto an existing system.

One advantage of Alpha is that it doesn't have a lot of baggage to carry around. The Intel 80x86 family is based on the 8086 and is completely backward-compatible. If you have an 8086 program, it will run on an PentiumPro. The Alpha was developed with a full 64-bit architecture, although it has a few 32-bit operations for backward compatibility.

Part of the 64-bit architecture is the Alpha's 64-bit virtual address space. All values (registers, addresses, integers, etc.) are operated on as full 64-bit quantities. Unlike with the Intel processors, there are no segmented addresses. In some cases, the operating system may restrict the number of bits that is used to translate the virtual address; however, at least 43 bits are used.

Like the Intel, Alpha's memory protection is done on a per-page basis. The design of the paging mechanism in Intel specifies a 4KB page, but the Alpha can have 8KB, 16KB, 32KB, or even 64KB pages. In addition, the Alpha also uses many-to-one page mapping, as does the Intel, so that multiple processors can have a virtual memory address that references the same page in physical memory.

8.6 Hard Disks

You've got to have a hard disk. You could actually run Linux from a floppy (even a high-density 5.25" floppy), but life is so much easier when you run from the hard disk. Not only do you have space to save your files, you have access to all the wonderful tools that Linux provides.

A hard disk is composed of several (probably) aluminum-coated disks with either an "oxide" media (the stuff on the disks) or "thin film" media. Because "thin film" is thinner than oxide, the denser (that is, larger) hard disks are more likely to have thin film. Each disk is called a platter, and the more platters you have, the more data you can store.

Platters are usually the same size as floppies. Older platters were 5.25" round, and the newer ones are 3.5" round. (If someone knows the reason for this, I would love to hear it.) In the center of each platter is a hole though which the spindle sticks. In other words, the platters rotate around the spindle. The functionality is the same as with a phonograph record. (Remember those?)

The media that coats the platters is very thin–about 30 millionths of an inch. The media has magnetic properties that can change its alignment when it is exposed to a magnetic field. That magnetic field comes in the form of the hard disk's read/write heads. It is the change in alignment of this magnetic media that enables data to be stored on the hard disk.

As I said earlier, a read/write head does just that: it reads and writes. There is usually one head per surface of the platters (top and bottom). That means that there are usually twice as many heads as platters. However, this is not always the case. Sometimes the top- and bottom-most surfaces do not have heads.

The head moves across the platters that are spinning several thousand times a minute (at least 60 times a second!). The gap between the head and platter is smaller that a human hair, smaller than a particle of smoke. For this reason, hard disks are manufactured and repaired in rooms where the number of particles in the air is fewer than 100 particles per cubic meter.

Because of this very small gap and the high speeds in which the platters are rotating, if the head comes into contact with the surface of a platter, the result is (aptly named) a head crash. More than likely this will cause some physical damage to your hard disk. (Imagine burying your face into an asphalt street going even only 20 MPH!)

The heads move in and out across the platters by the older stepping motor or the new, more efficient voice-coil motor. Stepping motors rotate and monitor their movement based on notches or indentations. Voice-coil motors operate on the same principle as a stereo speaker. A magnet inside the speaker causes the speaker cone to move in time to the music (or with the voice). Because there are no notches to determine movement, one surface of the platters is marked with special signals. Because the head above this surface has no write capabilities, this surface cannot be used for any other purpose.

The voice-coil motor enables finer control and is not subject to the problems of heat expanding the disk because the marks are expanded as well. Another fringe benefit is that because the voice-coil operates on electricity, once power is removed, the disk moves back to its starting position because it no longer is resisting a "retaining" spring. This is called "automatic head parking."

Physically, data is stored on the disk in concentric rings. The head does not spiral in like a phonograph record but rather moves in and out across the rings, which are called tracks. Because the heads move in unison across the surface of their respective platters, data are usually stored not in consecutive tracks but rather in the tracks that are positioned directly above or below them. The set of all tracks that are the same distance from the spindle are called a *cylinder*. Therefore, hard disks read from successive tracks on the same cylinder and not the same surface.

Think of it this way. As the disk is spinning under the head, it is busy reading data. If it needs to read more data than what fits on a single track, it has to get it from a different track. Assume data were read from consecutive tracks. When the disk finished reading from one track, it would have to move in (or out) to the next track before it could continue. Because tracks are rings and the end is the beginning, the delay in moving out (or in) one track causes the beginning of the next track to spin past the position of the head before the disk can start reading it. Therefore, the disk must wait until the beginning comes around again. Granted, you could stager the start of each track, but this makes seeking a particular spot much more difficult.

Let's now look at when data are read from consecutive tracks (that is, one complete cylinder is read before it goes on). Once the disk has read the entire contents of a track and has reached the end, the beginning of the track just below it is just now spinning under the head. Therefore, by switching the head it is reading from, the disk can begin to read (or write) as though nothing was different. No movement must take place and the reads occur much faster.

Each track is broken down into smaller chunks called sectors. The number of sectors into which each track is divided is called sectors per track, or sectors/track. Although any value is possible, common values for sectors/track are 17, 24, 32, and 64. (These are shown graphically in Figure 8.12.)

Each sector contains 512 bytes of data. However, each sector can contain up to 571 bytes of information. Each sector contains information that indicates the start and end of the sector, which is only ever changed by a low-level format. In addition, space is reserved for a checksum contained in the data portion of the sector. If the calculated checksum does not match the checksum in this field, the disk will report an error.

Figure 8.12: **Logical Components of a Hard Disk**

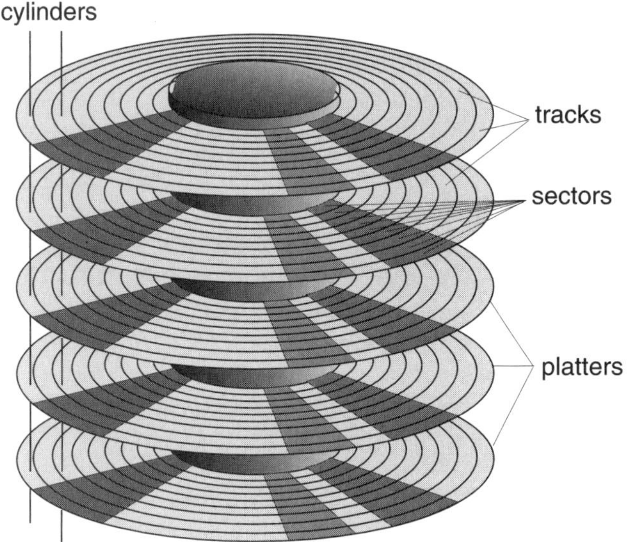

This difference between the total number of bytes per sector and the actual amount of data has been cause for a fair amount of grief. For example, in trying to sell you a hard disk, the salesperson might praise the tremendous amount of space that the hard disk has. You might be amazed at the low cost of a 1G drive.

There are two things to watch out for. Computers count in twos, humans count in tens. Despite what the salesperson wants you to believe (or believes himself), a hard disk with 1 billion bytes is *not* a 1 gigabyte drive–it is only 10^9 bytes. One gigabyte means 2^{30} bytes. A hard disk with 10^9 (1 billion) is only about 950 megabytes. This is five percent smaller!

The next thing is that seller will often state is the *unformatted* storage capacity of a drive. This is the number that you would get if you multiplied all the sectors on the disk by 571 (see the preceding discussion). Therefore, the unformatted size is irrelevant to almost all users. Typical formatted MFM drives give the user 85 percent of the unformatted size, and RLL drives give the user about 89 percent. (MFM and RLL are formatting standards, the specifics of which are beyond the scope of this book.)

This brings up an interesting question. If the manufacturer is telling us the unformatted size and the formatted size is *about* 85 percent for MFM and 89 percent for SCSI/IDE (using RLL), how can I figure out how much usable space there really is? Elementary, my dear Watson: It's a matter of multiplication.

Let's start at the beginning. Normally when you get a hard disk, it comes with reference material that indicates how many cylinders, heads, and sectors per track there are (among other things). The set of all tracks at the same distance from the spindle is a cylinder. The number of cylinders is therefore simply the number of tracks because a track is on one surface and a cylinder is all tracks at the same distance. Because you can only use those surfaces that have a head associated with them, you can calculate the number of total tracks by multiplying the number of cylinders by the number of heads. In other words, take the number of tracks on a surface and multiply it by the number of surfaces. This gives you the total number of tracks.

From our discussion of tracks, you know that each track is divided into a specific number of sectors. To find the total number of sectors, simply multiply the number of total tracks that we calculated above by the sectors per track. Once you have the total number of sectors, multiply this by 512 (the number of bytes of *data* in a sector). This give us the total number of bytes on the hard disk. To figure out how may megabytes this is, simply divide this number by 1,048,576 (1024 x 1024 = 1MB).

For those of you who need to see it as an equation (I always hated word problems myself)

$$\frac{\text{cylinders} \times \text{heads} \times \text{sectors per track} \times 512}{\text{1Mb}} = \text{total megabytes}$$

All PC-based operating systems need to break down the hard disk into units called partitions. A partition can be any size, from just a couple of megabytes to the entire disk. Each partition is defined in a *partition table* that appears at the very beginning of the disk. This partition table contains information about the kind of partition it is, where it starts, and where it ends. This table is the same whether you have a DOS-based PC, UNIX, or both.

Because the table is the same for DOS and UNIX, there can be only four partitions total because there are four entries in the table. DOS gets around this by creating *logical* partitions within one physical partition. This is a characteristic of DOS, *not* the partition table. Both DOS and UNIX must first partition the drive before installing the operating system and provide the mechanism during the installation process in the form of the `fdisk` program. Although their appearances are very different, the DOS and Linux `fdisk` commands perform the same function.

When you run the Linux `fdisk` utility, the values you see and input are all in tracks. To figure out how big each `fdisk` partition is, simply multiply that value by 512 and by the number of sectors per track. (Remember that each sector holds 512 bytes of data.)

To physically connect itself to the rest of the computer, the hard disk has five choices: ST506/412, ESDI, SCSI, IDE, and the newest Enhanced IDE (EIDE). However, the interface the operating system sees for ST506/412 and IDE are identical, and there is no special option for an IDE drive. At the hardware level, though, there are some differences that I need to cover for completeness.

To be quite honest, only ESDI and ST506/412 are really disk interfaces. SCSI and IDE are referred to as "system-level interfaces" and they incorporate ESDI into the circuitry physically located on the drive.

The ST506/412 was developed by Seagate Technologies (hence the ST) for its ST506 hard disk, which had a whopping 5Mb formatted capacity. (This was in 1980 when 360K was a *big* floppy.) Seagate later used the same interface in their ST412, which doubled the drive capacity (which is still less hard disk space than I have RAM. Oh well). Other drive manufacturers decided to incorporate this technology, and over the years, it has become a standard. One of its major drawbacks is that is 15-year-old technology, which can no longer compete with the demands of today's hard disk users.

In 1983, the Maxtor Corporation established the Enhanced Small Device Interface (ESDI) standard. The enhancements ESDI provided offered higher reliability because Maxtor had built the encoder/decoder directly into the drive and therefore reduced the noise, high transfer rates, and the ability to get drive parameters directly from this disk. This meant that users no longer had to run the computer setup routines to tell the CMOS what kind of hard disk it had.

One drawback that I have found with ESDI drives is the physical connection between the controller and the drive itself. Two cables were needed: a 34-pin control cable and a 24-pin data cable. Although the cables are different sizes and can't (easily) be confused, the separation of control and data is something of which I was never a big fan. The connectors on the drive itself were usually split into two unequal halves. In the connector on the cable, a small piece of plastic called a key prevented the connector from being inserted improperly. Even if the key was missing, you could still tell which end was which because the pins on the hard disk were labeled and the first line on the cable had a colored stripe down its side. (This may not always be the case, but I have never seen a cable that wasn't colored like this.)

Another drawback that I have found is that the physical location on the cable determines which drive is which. The primary drive is located at the end of the cable, and the secondary drive is in the middle. The other issue is the number of cables: ESDI drives require three separate cables. Each drive has its own data cable and the drives share a common control cable.

Although originally introduced as the interface for hard cards (hard disks directly attached to expansion cards), the IDE (integrated drive electronics) interface has grown in popularity to the point where it is perhaps the most commonly used hard-disk interface today (rapidly being replaced by SCSI). As its name implies, the controller electronics are *integrated* onto the hard disk itself. The connection to the motherboard is made through a relatively small adapter, commonly referred to as a "paddle board." From here, a single cable attaches two hard disks in a daisy chain, which is similar to the way floppy drives are connected, and often, IDE controllers have connectors and control electronics for floppy drives as well.

IDE drives often play tricks on systems by presenting a different face to the outside world than is actually on the disk. For example, because IDE drives are already preformatted when they reach you, they can have more physical sectors in the outer tracks, thereby increasing the overall amount of space on the disk that can be used for storage. When a request is made to read a particular block of data on the drive, the IDE electronics translate this to the actual physical location.

Because IDE drives come preformatted, you should never low-level format an IDE drive unless you are specifically permitted to do so by the manufacturer. You could potentially wipe out the entire drive to the point at which it must be returned to the factory for "repair." Certain drive manufacturers, such as Maxtor, provide low-level format routines that accurately and *safely* low-level format your drive. Most vendors that I am aware of today simply "zero" out the data blocks when doing a low-level format. However, *don't* take my word for it! Check the vendor.

The next great advance in hard disk technology was SCSI. SCSI is not a disk interface, but rather a semi-independent bus. More than just hard disks can be attached to a SCSI-Bus. Because of its complex nature and the fact that it can support such a wide range of devices, I talked in more detail about SCSI earlier in this chapter. However, a few specific SCSI issues relate to hard disks in general and the interaction between SCSI and other types of drives.

The thing to note is that the BIOS inside the PC knows nothing about SCSI. Whether this is an oversight or intentional, I don't know. The SCSI spec is more than 10 years old, so there has been plenty of time to include it. Because the BIOS is fairly standard from machine to machine, including SCSI support might create problems for backward compatibility.

On the other hand, the BIOS is for DOS. DOS makes BIOS calls. To be able to access all the possible SCSI devices through the BIOS, it must be several times larger. Therefore, every PC-based operating system needs to have extra drivers to be able to access SCSI devices.

Because the BIOS does not understand about SCSI, you have to trick the PC's BIOS a little to boot from a SCSI device. By telling the PC's BIOS that no drives are installed as either C: or D:, you force it to quit before it looks for any of the other types. Once it quits, the BIOS on the SCSI host adapter has a chance to run.

The SCSI host adapter obviously knows how to boot from a SCSI hard disk and does so wonderfully. This is assuming that you enabled the BIOS on the host adapter. If not, you're hosed.

There is also the flip side of the coin. The official doctrine says that if you have a non-SCSI boot driver, you *have* to disable the SCSI BIOS because this can cause problems. However, I know people who have IDE boot drives and still leave the SCSI BIOS enabled. Linux normally reacts as though the SCSI BIOS were not enabled, so, what do to? I suggest that you see what works. I can only add that if you have multiple host adapters, only one should have the BIOS enabled.

Another thing is that once the kernel boots from a SCSI device, you loose access to other kinds of drives. Just because it doesn't boot from the IDE (or whatever), does this mean you cannot access it at all? Unfortunately, yes. This is simply the way the kernel is designed. Once the kernel has determined that it has booted off a SCSI hard disk, it can no longer access a non-SCSI hard disk.

The newest member of the hard disk family is Enhanced IDE, or EIDE. The most important aspect of this new hard disk interface is its ability to access more than 504 megabytes. This limitation is because the IDE interface can access only 1,024 cylinders, 16 heads, and 63 sectors per track. If you multiply this out using the formula I gave you earlier, you get 504Mb.

EIDE also has other advantages such as higher transfer rates, ability to connect more than just two hard disks, and attach more than just hard disks. One drawback the EIDE had at the beginning was part of its very nature. To overcome the hard disk size limit that DOS had, EIDE drives employ a method called *logical block addressing* (LBA).

The idea behind LBA is that is that the system's BIOS would "rearrange" the drive geometry so that drives larger than 528Mb could still boot. Because Linux does not use the BIOS to access the hard disk, the fact that the BIOS could handle the EIDE drive meant nothing. New drivers needed to be added to account for this.

8.7 Floppy Drives

A customer once called in to tech support about a system that would not boot. For some unknown reason, the system crashed and would no longer boot from the hard disk. It got to a particular point in the boot process and hung. Even an old copy of the kernel hung in the same way.

Fortunately, the customer had an emergency boot floppy that enabled him to boot and gain access to the hard disk. The customer stuck the floppy in the drive and pressed the reset button. After a few seconds, there were the normal messages the system presented at boot up. For the moment, things looked fine. Suddenly the messages stopped and I could hear over the phone how the floppy drive was straining. It finally came up with the dreaded "floppy read error." Rather than giving up, I decided to try it again. Same thing.

At that point I started to get concerned. The hard disk booted, but the kernel hung. The floppy booted, but somewhere in the middle of loading the kernel, there was a bad spot on the floppy. This was not a good thing.

The floppy disk was brand new and the customer had tested it out immediately after he had made it. The most logical thing that caused this problem was putting the floppy too close to a magnetic field. Nope! That wasn't it, either. The customer had been told to keep this floppy in a safe place, and that's what the customer did.

What was that safe place? The customer had tacked it to the bulletin board next to the monitor, not through the hub or at one of the corners, but right through the floppy itself. The customer was had been careful not to stick the pin through the media access hole because he was told never to touch the floppy media itself.

In this section, I'm going to talk about floppy disks, lovingly referred to as floppies. They come in different sizes and shapes, but all floppies serve the same basic functions. Interaction with floppies can be a cause of great heartache for the unprepared, so, I'm going to talk about what they are like physically, how they are accessed, and what kinds of problems you can have with them.

Although they hold substantially less data than hard disks, floppies appear and behave very much like hard disks. Like hard disks, floppies are broken down into sectors, tracks, and even cylinders. Like hard disks, the number of tracks tells us how many tracks are on a given surface. Therefore, a floppy described as 40 tracks (such as a 360Kb floppy) actually contains 80 tracks, or 40 cylinders.

Other common characteristics are the header and trailer of each sector, which results in 571 bytes per sector, 512 of those being data. Floppy disks almost universally use MFM data encoding.

Linux floppy drivers support a wide range of floppies: from the ancient 48 tracks per inch/8 sectors per track, 5.25" floppies to the newest 135 tracks per inch/36 sector per track, 3.5" floppies that can hold almost 3Mb of data. More commonly however, the floppy devices found on systems today are somewhere in between these two types.

Because they are as old as PCs themselves, floppies have changed little except for their size and the amount of data that can be stored on them. As a result, very few problems are encountered with floppies. One most common problem is that customers are unsure which floppy device goes to which type of drive. Sometimes customers do know the difference and try to save money by forcing the floppy to format in a density higher than it was designed for.

The truth of the matter is, you *can't* format floppies higher than you're supposed to, that is, higher than the manufacturer specifies. To some extent, you might get away with punching holes in single-sided floppies to make them double-sided. However, forcing a floppy to a format at a higher density (if it works) isn't worth risking your data.

To understand why this is so, I need to talk about the concept of coercivity, that is, how much energy (how strong the magnetic field) must be used to make a proper recording on a disk. Older floppies had a lower coercivity and therefore required a weaker magnetic field to hold the signal; that is, less energy was required to "coerce" them into a particular pattern.

This seems somewhat contradictory, but look at it another way. As densities increased, the magnetic particles got closer together and started to interfere with each other. The result was to make the particles weaker magnetically. The weaker the particles are magnetically, the stronger a force was needed to "coerce" them into the proper patterns to hold data. Therefore, high-density disks have a higher coercivity.

As the capacity of drives increased, the tracks became narrower. The low density 5.25" floppies had 48 tracks per inch and could hold 360K of data. The high density 5.25" floppies have twice as many tracks per inch and can hold 1.2Mb (the added increase is also due to the fact they have 15 sectors per track instead of nine). Because there are more tracks in a given space, they are thinner. Problems arise if you use a disk formatted at 360K in a 1.2Mb drive. Because the 1.2 Mb drive writes the thinner tracks, not all of the track of the 360K floppy is overwritten. This may not be a problem in the 1.2Mb drive, but if you ever try to read that floppy in a 360K drive, the data will run together. That is, the larger head will read data from more than one track.

Formatting a 360K floppy as a 1.2Mb usually fails miserably because of the different number of tracks, so you usually can't get yourself into trouble. However, with 3.5" floppies, the story is a little different. For both the 720Kb and 1.44Mb floppies, there are 80 tracks per side. The difference is that the 1.44Mb floppies are designed to handle 18 sectors per track instead of just nine. As a result, formatting appears to go well. It is only later that you discover that the data is not written correctly.

The reason for this is that the magnetic media for the lower-density 720Kb floppies is less sensitive. By formatting it as 1.44Mb, you subject it to a stronger magnetic field than you should. After a while, this "overdose" causes the individual magnetic fields to begin to interfere with one another. Because high-density, 1.44Mb floppies cost much less than $1.00 apiece, it's not worth risking data by trying to force low-density to high-density to save money.

While I'm on the subject of money, note that buying unformatted floppies to save money is becoming less and less the smart thing to do. If you figure that formatting floppies takes at least two minutes apiece and the cost difference between a package of ten formatted floppies and ten unformatted is $2, then it would only make sense (or cents) to have someone format these if they were making only $6.00 an hour. Rarely does a company have someone whose sole job is to format floppies. That job usually falls on those people who use them and most of them get more than $6.00 an hour. Therefore, you may as well buy the formatted floppies.

(I actually did some consulting work for a company whose president insisted that they buy *unformatted* floppies. Because the only people who used the floppies were his programmers and system administrators, they earned more than $6.00 an hour. In one case, I calculated that turning a package of 10 unformatted floppies into formatted floppies worked out to costing twice as much for the unformatted as for the formatted ones. That didn't phase him a bit because the system administrators were on salary and were paid no matter what. By saving the few dollars by buying unformatted ones, his profit margin looked better, at least on paper.)

8.8 Tape Drives

For the longest time, tape drives were a block to me. Although I understood the basic concept (writing to a tape similar to a music cassette), it took me quite a bit of time before I felt comfortable with them.

Because this device has the potential for either saving your data or opening up career opportunities for you to flip burgers, knowing how to install and use them is an important part of your job as a system administrator. Because the tape device node is usually read/write, regular users can also back up their own data with it.

The first tape drives supported under Linux were quarter-inch cartridge tapes, or QIC tapes. QIC is not just an abbreviation for the size of the media; it is also a standard.

In principle, a QIC tape is like a music cassette. Both consist of a long, two-layer tape. The "backing" is usually made of cellulose acetate (photographic film) or polyester (1970s leisure suits), polyester being more common today. The "coating" is the actual media that holds the magnetic signals.

The difference is in the way the tapes are moved from the supply reel to the take-up reel. In cassette tapes, movement is accomplished by a capstan and the tape is pinched between two rollers. QIC tapes spread the driving pressure out over a larger area by means of a drive belt. Additionally, more care is taken to ensure that the coating touches only the read/write heads. Another major difference is the size. QIC tapes are much larger than cassette tapes (and a little bit smaller than a VHS video tapes).

Initially, the QIC tape was 300 feet long and held approximately 30Mb of data. This was a DC300 tape. The tape that next appeared was a DC600, which was 600 feet long and could hold about 60Mb. As with other technologies, tape drives got better and longer and were able to hold more data. The technology advanced to the point where the same tapes could be used in new drives and could store as much as twice as much as they could before.

There are currently several different QIC standards for writing to tape drives, depending on the tape and tape drive being used. Older, 60Mb drives used a QIC-24 format when writing to 60Mb tapes. Newer drives use the QIC-525 format to write to several different kinds of tapes. As a result, different tapes yield different capacity depending on the drive on which they are written.

For example, I have an Archive 5150 tape drive that is "officially" designed to work with 150MB tapes (DC6150). However, I can get 120Mb from a DC600. Why? The DC600 is 600 feet long and the DC6150 is only 20 feet longer. A tape drive designed to use DC600 tapes only writes in 9 tracks, however, and a tape that uses DC6150s (like mine) writes in 15 tracks. In fact, you can use many different combinations of tapes and drives.

One thing I would like to point out from a technical standpoint is that there is no difference between 150Mb and 250Mb QIC drives. When the QIC standard was enhanced to include 1000-foot tapes, 150Mb drives automatically became 250Mb drives. (I wish I had known this before I bought so many DC6150 tapes. Oh, well–live and learn.)

A similar thing happened with 320Mb and 525Mb tapes. The QIC-320 standard was based on 600-foot tapes. However, the QIC committee decided to go with the QIC-525 standard based on 1000-foot tape. That's why a 600-foot tape writing with the QIC-525 standard writes 320Mb.

Notice that this entire time, I never referred to QIC--02 tapes. That's because QIC-02 is not a tape standard, but a controller standard.

An interesting side note is just how the data is actually written to the tape. QIC tape drives use a system called "serpentine recording." Like a serpent, it winds its way back and forth along the length of the tape. It starts at one end and writes until it reaches the other end. The tape drive then reverses direction and begins to write toward the other end.

Other common tape drives are QIC-40 and QIC-80 tape drives, which provide 40Mb and 80Mb, respectively. These provide an inexpensive backup solution. These tape drives are connected to standard floppy controllers and, in most cases, the standard floppy cables can be used. The size of the tapes used for this kind of drive is about the same as a pack of cigarettes.

Aside from using the same type of controller, QIC-40/80 tape drives are similar to with floppy drives in other ways as well. Both use *modified frequency modulation* (MFM) when writing to the device. Sectors are assigned in similar fashion and each tape has the equivalent of a file allocation table to keep track of where each file is on the media.

QIC-40/80 tapes must be formatted before they are used, just like floppies. Because the size of data storage is substantially greater than for a floppy, formatting takes substantially longer. Depending on the speed of the tape drive, formatting can take up to an hour. Preformatted tapes are also available and, like their floppy counterparts, the prices are only slightly higher than unformatted tapes.

Because these tape drives run off the floppy controller, it is often a choice between a second floppy drive and a tape drive. The deciding factor is the floppy controller. Normally, floppy controllers can only handle two drives, so this is usually the limit.

However, this limit can be circumvented if the tape drive supports soft select (sometimes called "phantom select"), whereby the software chooses the device number for the tape drive when it is using it. The ability to soft select depends on the drive. Though more floppy tape drives support this capability, many of the older drives do not. I will get into more detail about this in the second part of the book when I talk about installing and using tape drives.

On larger systems, neither QIC nor mini-tapes can really handle the volume of data being stored. While some QIC tapes can store up to 1.3Gb, they cannot compare to digital audio tape (DAT) devices. Such devices use Digital Data Storage (DDS) media. Rather than storing signals similar (or analogous) to those coming across the bus, DDS stores the data as a series of numbers or digits on the tape, hence, the name "digital." The result is much higher reliability.

Physically, DATs are the smallest tapes that Linux supports. The actual media is 4mm, so DATs are sometimes referred to as 4mm tapes.

Hewlett-Packard DATs can be divided into multiple logical tapes. This is useful when making backups if you want to store different file systems to different "tapes" and you don't want to use any extra physical tapes.

Device nodes are created to represent these different logical tapes. DAT drives can quickly scan for the location of subsequent partitions (as they are called), making searches much faster than with backups to single tapes.

One thing to watch out for is that data written to DATs are not as standardized as data written to QIC tapes. Therefore, it is possible that data written on one DAT drive cannot be read on another.

There are two reasons for this problem. This first is the blocking factor, which is the minimum space each file will take up. A 1Kb file with a blocking factor of 20 will have 19Kb of wasted space. Such a situation is faster in that the tape drive is streaming more, though there is a lot of wasted space. DAT drives use either a variable or fixed block size. Each drive has a default blocking factor that is determined by the drive itself.

Another problem is data compression, which, if it is done, is performed at the hardware level. Because there is no standard for data compression, it is very unlikely that two drives from different manufactures that both do data compression will be able to read each other's tapes.

Keep in mind that that's not all. There are many more standards that I didn't list here. One place to start is the QIC consortium's home page at *www.qic.org*, which lists dozens of tape standards and associated documents.

8.9 CD-ROMS

Linux distribution media is becoming more and more prevalent on CD-ROMs. One CD-ROM takes a lot less space than 50 floppies or even one QIC tape, so the media is easier to handle. In fact, I would be hard-pressed to find a version that is still being distributed on floppies. Added to this, CD-ROMs are significantly faster than either floppies or tape media.

Another important aspect of CD-ROMs when it comes to installing media is their size. Therefore, it is possible to get numerous products on the CD-ROM. You can get a single CD-ROM that contains a runnable copy of Linux and the source code with room to spare.

CD-ROMs, in fact CD-ROM's technology in general, have always fascinated me. I am amazed that you could get so much information into such a small place and still have such quick access to your data.

The basic principle behind data storage on a CD-ROM is really nothing more than Morse code. A series of light and dark (dots and dashes) compose the encoded information on the disk. Commercial CD-ROMs, whether music or data, almost universally have data on one side of the disk. Although there is nothing technologically preventing a CD-ROM from having a flip side, current convention limits data to just a single side. This is enough when you consider that you can get more than 600Mb of data on a single CD-ROM. As the technology improves, the amount is steadily increasing. In addition, certain manufacturers are working on dual-sided CD-ROMs.

On the surface of the disk are a series of dents, or holes, called "lands." The areas between the lands are called "pits." A laser is projected onto the surface of the disk and the light is either reflected by the pits or scattered by the lands. If reflected, the light reaches a light-sensing receptor, which then sends an electrical signal that is received by the control mechanism of the CD-ROM drive. Just as the pattern of alternating dots and dashes forms the message when using Morse code, it is the pattern of reflected light and no light that indicates the data stored on the disk.

When I first thought of CD-ROMs, I conceptualized them as being like WORM (Write-Once, Read-Many) drives, which they are, somewhat. I visualized them as being a read-only version of a hard disk. However, after looking more closely at the way data is stored, I saw that CD-ROMs have less in common with hard disks.

As you remember from our discussion of hard disks, each surface is composed of concentric rings called tracks, and each track is divided into sectors. The disk spins at a constant speed as the heads move in and out across the drive's surface. Therefore, the tracks on the outer edges move faster than those on the inside.

For example, take a track that is a half-inch away from the center of the disk. The diameter of the circle representing the track is one inch, so the radius of that circle is approximately 3.1415 inches. Spinning 60 times a second, the track goes at a speed of about 190 inches per second. Now, take a track at one inch from the center, or twice as far. The diameter of the circle representing that track is 6.2830 inches. It, too, is going around at 60 revolutions per second. However, because it has to travel twice as far in each revolution, it has to go twice as fast.

A CD-ROM isn't like that. CD-ROMS rotate in a manner called "constant linear velocity." The motor keeps the CD-ROM moving at the same speed, regardless of where the CD-ROM reader is reading from. Therefore, as the light detector moves inward, the disks slows down so that each revolution takes the same amount of time per track.

Let's look at hard disks again. They are divided into concentric tracks that are divided into sectors. Because the number of sectors per track remains constant, the sectors must get smaller toward the center of the disk (because the circumference of the circle representing the track is getting smaller as you move in).

Again, a CD-ROM isn't like that. Actually, there is no reason why it should work that way. Most CD-ROMs are laid out in a single spiral, just like a phonograph record. There are no concentric circles, so there is no circumference to get smaller. As a result, the sectors in a CD-ROM can remain the same size no matter what. The added advantage of sectors remaining the same size means there can be more on the disk and therefore more data for the user.

Currently, CD-ROMS have a capacity of *at least* 650Mb, although I am aware of some that are already more than 700Mb. Several companies are currently working on technology to get even more out of them. The simplest technology involves making the CD-ROM writable on *both* sides, which simply doubles the capability. Others involve storing the data in different layers on the CD-ROM and using light that is polarized differently to read the different layers.

The single-speed CD-ROM drives are the oldest and have a transfer rate of about 150Kb a second. Recently (as of this writing), eight-speed CD-ROM drives are available. I often see both four-speed and six-speed drives sold in machines, but the single- and double-speed drives are slowly dying out.

Most CD-ROMS are formatted with the ISO-9660 format, which allows them to be read by a wide range of machines, including DOS/Windows, Macintosh, as well as Linux and other UNIX dialects. The shortcoming, though, is just that: short, as in short file names. The ISO-9660 format only recognizes the DOS 8.3 file names, so the long file names that we have grown to love in UNIX are not possible. As a result, the Rock Ridge Extensions to the ISO-9660 format allow many of the typical UNIX file stuff, like longer file names, file ownership, and even symbolic links, etc.

Another standard is the PhotoCD, which was developed by Kodak to store photographic information. Not every CD-ROM drive can access these CD-ROMs, which require special software. (As a side note, one system administrator working on the PhotoCD project at Kodak had Linux installed to do network monitoring!)

CD-ROMs first became popular as SCSI devices. However, because most people could not afford a SCSI host adapter, companies began producing CD-ROM drives that ran on IDE controllers, and therefore looked just like a hard disk, or would run on their own controllers. Some even enabled you to run the CD-ROM off a sound card or through your parallel port. For details on how to get these to work correctly, see the CD-ROM HOWTO.

8.10 Serial Ports

Most machines sold today come attached with two serial ports. These can be built into the motherboard, as part of a serial/parallel card, or as part of an "all-in-one" card that has serial ports, parallel ports, games ports, and even hard disk and floppy controllers.

A serial board is an expansion card that translates bus signals in which at least eight bits arrive simultaneously into signals that send single bits at a time. These bits are encapsulated into groups of one byte. The encapsulation contains other signals that represent the start and end of the byte, as well as a parity bit. Additionally, the number of bits used to represent data can be either 7 or 8.

Parity is the mechanism by which single-bit errors can be detected during transmission. The number of bits set to one is counted and based on whether even or odd parity is used, and the parity bit is set. For example, if even parity is used and there are three bits set, then the parity bit is also set to make the total number of bits set an even number. However, if odd parity is used, the number of bits set is already odd, therefore the parity bit is left unset. When you use some other means to detect errors, you can turn parity off, and you are said to be using no parity. This is the default for modems in Linux.

Serial communication parameters must be agreed upon by both ends. These parameters are often referred to in triples, such as 8-1-N (read as eight-one-none). In this instance, there are eight data bits, 1 stop bit, and no parity is used. This is the default for Linux systems.

One key element of a serial board is the Universal Asynchronous Receiver-Transmitter, or UART. The transmitter portion takes a byte of parallel data written by the serial driver to the card and transmits it one bit at a time (serially). The receiver does just the opposite: It takes the serial bits and converts them into parallel data that is sent down the bus and is read by the serial driver.

Originally, Linux only provided drivers for standard serial ports; intelligent boards are often installed to allow many more logins (or other connections) to the system. The most significant difference is that intelligent serial boards (often referred to as smart serial boards) have a built-in CPU, which allows it to take all responsibility for processing the signals away from the system CPU.

In the newer versions, you can find drivers for commercial multiport boards, such as the Stallion Easy IO, which allows you to quickly extend the number of serial ports on your system as the drivers are built in. Stallion is very supportive of the Linux world and even advertises the fact that their boards run on Linux.

In addition, intelligent serial boards can better buffer incoming signals that keep them from getting lost. With nonintelligent boards, the system may be so busy that it does not get around in time to read characters off the board. Although the 16550 UART, common on most serial boards today, contains 16-byte buffers, this is often not enough. Under heavy load, the serial driver does not react fast enough and the characters are overwritten.

Serial board performance is also increased by intelligent boards. Because signals are buffered and sent in large chunks, there is less overhead on a per-character basis. With nonintelligent boards, single characters are often transmitted, so the per-character overhead is much larger. In fact, most nonintelligent boards generate and interrupt the associated overhead with *each* character.

It is possible to obtain supported serial boards that have multiple ports. Although such boards have multiple UARTs, they do not have the performance of intelligent boards, though they do provide a low-cost alternative. For a discussion on the device nodes used for such boards, see the section on the device directory.

Originally designed to connect mainframe computers to modems, the RS-232 standard is used exclusively for serial ports on PCs. Two kinds of devices are considered with RS-232: Data Terminal Equipment (DTE) and Data Communication Equipment (DCE). DTE is the serial port side and DCE is the modem side.

Two types of connections are used: DB25 (with 25 pins) and DB9 (with 9 pins). Although they both serve the same basic function, the numbering of the pins is slightly different. Table 8.3 lists the main pins of the DB25 connector, their functions, and a mnemonic that is commonly used to refer to them. Table 8.4 lists the pins for the DB9 connector. The physical layout of the pins is shown in Figure 8.13.

Table 8.3: **Common Pins on the DB25 Connector**

Pin	Function	Mnemonic
2	Transmit	TXD or TX
3	Receive	RXD or RX4
4	Request to send	RTS
5	Clear to send	CTS
6	Data set ready	DSR
7	Signal ground	GND
8	Carrier detect	CD
20	Data terminal ready	DTR
22	Ring indicator	RI

Table 8.4: Pins on DB9 Connector

Pin	Function	Mnemonic
1	Carrier detect	CD
2	Receive	RXD or RX
3	Transmit	TXD or TX
4	Data terminal ready	DTR
5	Signal ground	GND
6	Data set ready	DSR
7	Request to send	RTS
8	Clear to send	CTS
9	Ring indicator	RI

Figure 8.13: **The Physical Layout of Pins on Serial Cables**

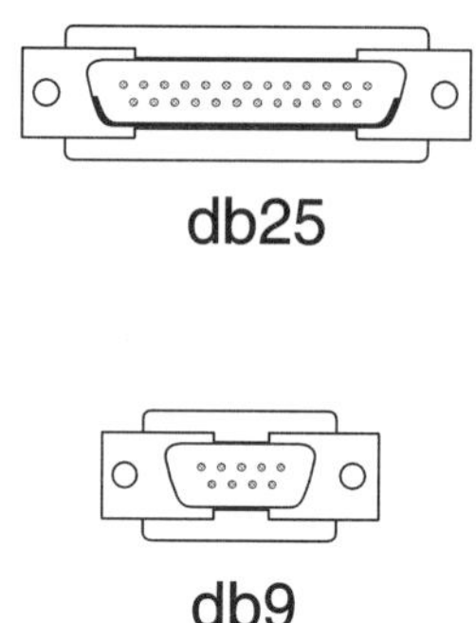

Note that on a DB25 connector, pin 1 is *chassis ground*, which is different from signal ground. Chassis ground ensures that both serial connectors are operating at the same electric potential and keeps you from getting a shock.

To communicate properly, the DTE device must say that it is ready to work by sending a signal on the DTR line. The DCE device must do the same on the DSR line.

One side indicates that it has data by sending a signal on the RTS line (it is requesting to send data). If ready, the other side says that it is ready by sending a signal on the CTS line (the sender is clear to send the data). What happens when the receiving side can't keep up (that is, if the sending side is sending too fast)? If the receiving side needs to stop (perhaps a buffer is full), it stops the CTS signal (meaning the sender is no longer clear to send the data). This causes the sending side to stop. This process is referred to as *hardware handshaking*, *hardware flow control*, or *RTS/CTS flow control*.

Problems arise when connecting other types of devices. Some devices, such as printers, are themselves DTE devices. If you tried to connect a standard RS-232 cable, TX is connected to TX, RX is connect to RX, DSR is connected to DSR, and DTR is connected to DTR. The result is that nothing happens. The solution is a cross-over cable, which internally swaps the appropriate signals and makes sure they go to the right place.

If you have a terminal, things are easier. First, though the data is going in both directions, the data coming from the terminal will never exceed the speed of the serial port (I'd like to see you type 240 characters per second). Data heading toward the terminal is displayed on the screen, which will display it as quickly as it comes. Therefore, you only need three signals: send, transmit, and ground.

If the terminal displays the data too fast for you to read, you can stop it by sending an XOFF character back to the system. This is usually Ctrl+S and unless it is turned off, it will stop incoming data. To turn the flow of data back on again, send the system an XON (`Ctrl+Q`) character. This type of flow control is called *software flow control* or *XON/XOFF* flow control. In some cases, depending on how the terminal is configured, sending any character restarts the flow.

8.11 Parallel Ports

Parallel ports are a common way printers are attached to an Linux system. Although many different problems arise with printers attached to parallel ports, not many issues arise with parallel ports themselves.

First, let's take a look at how parallel ports work.

One key difference between parallel and serial ports is the way data is sent. From our discussion of serial ports, you know that data goes across a serial line one bit at a time across a single data line. Parallel ports send data across a byte (eight bits) at a time across eight data lines.

Another key difference is the cable. Looking at the computer end, you can easily confuse the cable with a serial connector. Both have 25 pins in the same layout. On the printer end, though, things are different. There is a special kind of 36-pin connector called a *Centronics* connector, named after the printer manufacturer Centronics. A cable that has a 25-pin *D-shell* connector on one end and a 36-pin on the other is called a Centronics or parallel cable (see Figure 8.14). Unlike serial cables, there are not different kinds of cables (like straight-through or crossed). Because of this, all you usually need to do is to plug in the cable at both ends and go.

Although some devices allow communication in both directions along a parallel port, Linux does not support this communication. In fact, the only thing that Linux directly supports on parallel ports are printers.

Figure 8.14: **Comparison of Centronic and DB25 Connectors**

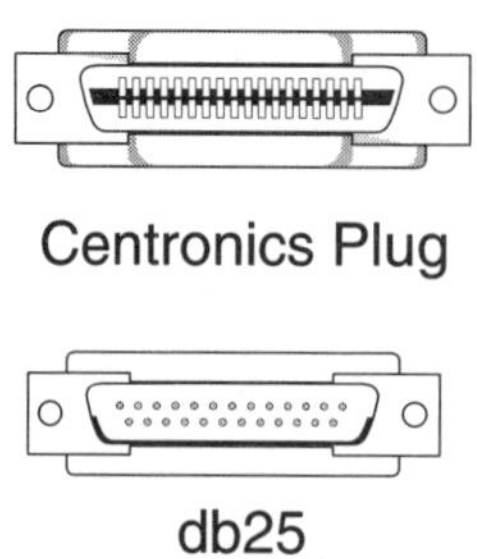

Because there is no guarantee that all the data bits arrive at the port at the same time, there must be some way of signaling the printer that the data is ready. This is done with the *strobe* line. Once a character (or any byte of data) is ready, the system sends a signal along the strobe line. Using the strobe line also prevents characters from being read more than once.

Often, the printer cannot keep up with the data flow from the parallel port. Just like RTS-CTS flow control on serial ports, parallel ports also need a way to be told to stop. This is done with the *busy* line. Actually, the busy line is set after each character in case the printer cannot process the character fast enough. Once the character is processed, the printer can turn off the busy signal.

However, this is not enough to get the parallel port to send the next character. The printer must first tell the parallel port it has received the character by sending a signal along the *acknowledge* line. Note that this acknowledge occurs after *every* character.

The printer also uses other control lines. One is the select, which indicates that the printer has been selected or is on-line. There is also a special line that indicates when the paper source is empty. This is the *paper empty* line. If the problem is unknown, the printer can send a signal along the *fault* line that says that "something" is wrong.

One thing that comes up regularly is the confusion about which physical parallel port is related to which `lp` device. For your parallel ports to work correctly, you must configure them according to Table 8.5.

Table 8.5: **Default Parallel Port Devices**

Device name	Address	IRQ
/dev/lp0	0x378	7
/dev/lp1	0x3BC	7
/dev/lp2	0x278	5

8.12 Video Cards and Monitors

Without a video card and monitor, you don't see anything. In fact, every PC that I have ever seen won't even boot unless there is a video card in it. Granted, your computer could boot and even work without being attached to a monitor (and I have seen those), but it's no fun unless you get to see what's going on.

When PCs first hit the market, there was only one kind of video system. High resolution and millions of colors were something you read about in science-fiction novels. Times changed and so did graphics adapters. The first dramatic change was with the introduction of color with IBM's color graphics adapter (CGA), which required a completely new (and incompatible) video subsystem. In an attempt to integrate color and monochrome systems, IBM came out with the enhanced graphics adapter (EGA).

But I'm not going to talk about those. Why? First, no one buys them anymore. I doubt that anyone still makes them. If you could find one, there would be no problem at all to install them and get them to work. The second reason why I am not going to talk about them is because they are not that common. Because "no one" uses them any more, the time I spend telling you why I won't tell you about them is already too much.

What are we going to talk about instead? Well, the first thing is Video Graphics Array (VGA). VGA is the standard by which virtually all video card manufacturers base their products. Though enhancements to VGA (Super VGA or SVGA) exists, it is all based on VGA.

When talking about VGA, I first need to talk about some basics of video technology. The first issue is just how things work. Digital signals are sent by the operating system to the video card, which sends them through a digital-to-analog converter (DAC). Usually a single chip contains three DACs, one for each color (red, green, and blue, or RGB). The DAC has a look-up table that determines the voltage to be output on each line for the respective color.

The voltage that the DAC has found for a given color is sent to the three electron guns at the back of the monitor's cathode ray tube (CRT), again, one for each color. The intensity of the electron stream is a result of this voltage.

The video adapter also sends a signal to the *magnetic deflection yoke*, which aims the electron beams to the right place on the screen. This signal determines how far apart the dots are, as well as how often the screen is redrawn. The dots are referred to as pixels, the distance apart they are is the *pitch*, and how often the screen is redrawn is the *refresh rate*.

To keep the beams precisely aligned, they first pass through a *shadow mask*, a metal plate containing hundreds of thousands of little holes. The dot pitch is how closely the holes are aligned. The closer the holes, the higher the pitch. A higher pitch means a sharper image.

The electrons from the electron guns strike the phosphors inside the monitor screen and make them glow. Three different phosphors are used, one for each color. The stronger the beams, the more intense the color. Colors other than RGB are created by varying the amount displayed each of these three colors, that is, changing the intensity of each color. For example, purple would be created by exciting red and blue but no green phosphors. After the beams stops hitting the phosphor, it still continues to glow for a short time. To keep the image on the screen, the phosphor must be recharged by the electron beam again.

The electron beams are moved across the screen by changing the deflection yoke. When the beams reach the other side, they are turned off and returned to the starting side, just below the line where they left off. When the guns reach the last line, they move back up to the top. This is called *raster scanning* and it is done approximately 60 times a second.

When the beam has completed a line, it needs to return to the other end to begin the new line. This is called *horizontal retrace*. Similarly, when the beam has reached the bottom, it needs to move back to the top again. This is the *vertical retrace*. In both cases, the beam's intensity is reduced to the point that nothing is drawn on the screen. (This is called *blanking*.)

Some monitor manufacturers try to save money by using less expensive components. The trade off is that the beams cannot scan every line during each pass. Instead, they scan every other line during the first pass then scan the lines they missed during the second pass. This is called interlacing because the scan lines are *interlaced*. Although this provides higher resolutions in less expensive monitors, the images will "flicker" because the phosphors begin to fade before they can be recharged. (This flickering gives me, and other people, a headache.)

For most users, the most important aspect is the *resolution*. Resolution determines the total number of pixels that can be shown on the screen. In graphics mode, standard VGA has a resolution of 640 pixels horizontally and 480 pixels vertically. By convention, you say that your resolution is 640-by-480.

A pixel is actually a set of three phosphors rather than just a single phosphor. So, in essence, a pixel is a single spot of color on the screen. What color is shown at any given location is an *interaction* between the operating system and the video card. Years ago, the operating system (or program) had to tell the video card where each dot on the screen was. It had an internal array (or table) of pixels, each containing the appropriate color values. Today, some video cards can be told to *draw*. They don't need to know that there is a row of red dots between points A and B.

Instead, they are simply told to draw a red line from point A to point B. This results in faster graphics because the video card has taken over much of the work.

In other cases, the system still needs to keep track of which colors are where. If we had a truly monochrome video system, any given pixel would either be on or off. Therefore, a single bit can be used to store that information. If we go up to 16 colors, we need 4 bits, or half a byte of information ($2^4 = 16$). If we go to a whole byte, then we can have 256 colors at once (2^8). Many video cards use three bytes to store the color data, one for each of the primary colors (RGB). In this way, they can get more than 16 million colors!

Now, 16 million colors seems like a lot, and it is. However, it's actually too much. Humans cannot distinguish that many colors, so much of the ability is wasted. Add to that that most monitors are limited to just a few hundred thousand colors. So, no matter what your friends tell you about how wonderful their video card is that does 16 million colors, you need not be impressed. The odds are the monitor can't handle them and you certainly can't see them.

However, don't think that the makings of video cards are trying to rip us off. In fact, it's easier to design cards that are multiples of whole bytes. If we had a 18-bit display (which is needed to get the 250K of colors that monitors could handle), we either use 6 bits of three different bytes or two whole bytes and 2 bits of the third. Either way, things are wasted and you spend time processing the bits. If you know that you have to read three whole bytes, one for each color, then there is not as much processing.

How many pixels and how many colors a video card can show are interdependent of each other. When you bought it, your video card came with a certain amount of memory. The amount of memory it has limits the total number of pixels and colors you can have. If you take the standard resolution of a VGA card of 640x480 pixels, that's 307,200 pixels. If we want to show 16 colors, that's 307,200 x 4 bits or 1,228,800 bits. Dividing this by eight gives you 153,600 bytes needed to display 640x480 in 16 colors. Because memory is usually produced in powers of two, the next smallest size is 256 Kilobytes. Therefore, a video card with 256K of memory is needed.

Maybe this is enough. For me, I don't get enough on the screen with 640x480, and only 16 colors looks terrible (at least to me). However, if you never run any graphics applications on your machines, such as X-Windows, then there is no need for anything better. Operating in *text mode*, your video card does fine.

As I said, I am not happy with this–I want more. If I want to go up to the next highest resolution (800x600) with 16 colors, I need 240,000 bytes. I still have less than the 256K I need for 640x480 and 16 colors. If, instead, I want 256 colors (which requires 8 bits per pixel), I need at least 480,000. I now need 512K on the video card.

Now I buy a great big monitor and want something closer to "true color." Let's not get greedy, but say I wanted a resolution of 1,024x768 (the next highest up) and "only" 65,635 colors. I now need 1,572,864 bytes of memory. Because my video card has only 1Mb of memory, I'm out of luck!

But wait a minute! Doesn't the VGA standard only support resolutions up to 640x480? True. However, the Video Electronics Standards Association (VESA) has defined resolutions more than 640x480 as Super VGA. In addition to the resolutions I mentioned previously (800x600 and 1,024x768), SVGA also includes 1,280x1,024 and 1,600x1,200.

Okay. The mere fact that you have a video card that handle SVGA resolutions does not mean you are going to get a decent picture (or at least not the picture you want). Any system is only as good as its worst component, and this also applies to your video system. It is therefore important to understand a characteristic of your monitor: pitch. I mentioned this briefly before, but it is important to talk about it further.

When shopping for a monitor, you will often see that among the characteristics used to sell it is the pitch. The values you would see could be something like .39 or .28, which is the spacing between the holes in the shadow mask, measured in millimeters. Therefore, a pitch of .28 is just more than one-quarter of a millimeter. The lower the pitch, the closer together the holes and the sharper the image. Even if you aren't using any graphics-oriented programs, it's worth the few extra dollars to get a lower pitch and the resulting sharper image.

8.13 Modems

Up to this point, I've talked about things that almost every computer user has and almost always come with the system. We are now moving into a new area, where we get one computer to talk to another. In my opinion, this is where computers begin to show their true power.

Perhaps the earliest means of getting computers to talk to one another (at least over long distances) was the modem. Modem stands for Modulator/Demodulator, which is its basis of operation. It takes the digital signals that come across the bus from the CPU and converts them into a signal that can be understood by the telephone wires. This process is called *modulation*. On the other end, the signals are converted back from telephone signals into computer signals by a process called *demodulation*. Graphically this looks like Figure 8.15.

The underlying concept of the transmission of data across the telephone line is that of a *carrier*. A carrier is a signal that runs along the

Figure 8.15: **Transfer of Data Across Modems**

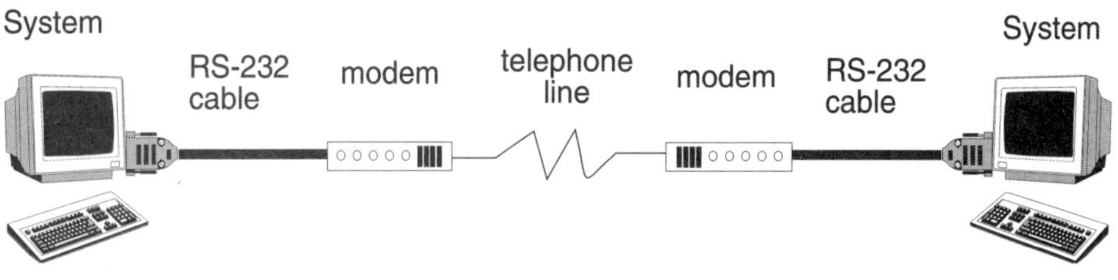

phone line that is at a constant strength (amplitude), frequency, and phase. Because all of these are known values, changes in them can be detected. It is the changes that are used to encode the data.

When data are sent at relatively low speeds, the exact timing of that data being sent is not important. Markers, the start and stop bits, used within the transmitted data indicate the beginning and the end of each piece of data. (Note: You could have two stop bits.) If each modem is set to the same values, it knows when one piece of data stops and the next one begins. This is called asynchronous transfer.

How big is that piece of data? Usually just a single character. All the modems that I have ever seen have either 7 or 8 bits for data. That means that there are 7 or 8 bits between the start-stop bit pairs. This, too, is something that both modems need to agree on.

Parity works like this. Let's assume that a specific byte has 3 bits that are set. If you are using even parity, then the parity bit would be set to make the total number set four, which is an even number. If you are using odd parity, the number of the bit is already an odd number (three), and the parity bit would not be set.

When the settings at which your modem must be are determined, the order is usually the number of data bits, followed by the number of stop bits, then the parity. By default, Linux uses eight data bits, one stop bit, and no parity. It is common to refer to this as "eight, one, and none," or "8-1-N." Other settings might be 7-2-E for seven data bits, two stop bits, and even parity.

Another important characteristic is the speed at which the modem transmits the data. Although the exact timing is not critical, signals must be received within a certain time or problems happen. (For example, you could be waiting for months if the connection suddenly dropped.)

Now, let's go back to the modulated carrier wave. The term for the number of changes in the carrier wave per second is baud, named after the French telegraph expert, J. M. E. Baudot. One way of encoding data, based on the changes to the carrier wave, is called *frequency shift keying*, or FSK. The number of changes that can take place per second is the number of bits of information that can be sent per second (one change ⇔ one bit).

Let's consider a modem connection that operates at 2400 baud, eight data bits, one stop bit, and no parity. This gives us a total of 10 bits used for each character sent. (Did you forget the start bit?) Because baud is a measurement of the number of bits sent per second, 2400 baud means that 240 characters can be sent per second.

Other encoding methods result in getting more bits per baud. For example, the Bell 212A standard operates at 300 baud. However, because it gets four bits of data per baud, it gets 1,200 bits per second for those 300 baud. This rate is accomplished by changing more than just the frequency. If you changed both frequency and amplitude, you have four distinct values that you could use.

Have you ever had someone tell you that you have a 9600 baud modem? Don't believe them! There is no such thing. In fact, the fastest baud rate is only 2400. So what are people taking about when they say their modem goes 9,600 or 14,400? They are talking about the *bits-per-second* (bps). If you get one bit-per-baud, then these terms are synonymous. However, all 9600 modems get more than that. They operate at 2400 baud but use a modulation technique that yields 4 bits per baud. Thus, a 2400 baud modem gives 9,600 bits per second.

As with all the other kinds of hardware I've talked about, modems must have standards to be useful. Granted, you could have a modem that can only communicate with another from the same manufacturer, but even that is a kind of standard.

Modem standards are like opinions: everyone has one. There are the AT&T standards, the Bell standards, the International Telecommunications Union (ITU) standards (which was formally the Comite Consultatif International Telegraphique et Telephoneique, or CCITT), and the Microcom Networking Protocol (MNP) standards.

As of this writing, the two most common standards are the CCITT and MNP. The MNP standards actually work in conjunction with modems that adhere to the other standards and for the most part define technologies rather than speeds or other characteristics.

The CCITT/ITU standards define (among other things) modulation methods that allow speeds up to 9,600bps for the V.32 standard and 14,00bps for the V.32 bis standard. The new V.34 standard supports 2,800bps. One newer standard, V.42, is accepted worldwide and provides error-correction enhancements to V.32 and V.32 bis. The V.42 standard also incorporates the MNP 4 standard, enabling one modem that supports V.42 to communicate with another that supports MNP 4. (For much more detail on the different modem standards, see *The Winn L. Rosch Hardware Bible*, Third Edition, and the *Modem Reference*, Second Edition, by Michael Banks. Both are published by Brady Books.)

One standard we need to go into is the *Hayes command set.* This set was developed by and named for the modem manufacturer Hayes and is used by almost every modem manufacturer. It consists of dozens of commands that are used to modify the functionality as well as read the characteristics of your modem. Most of the commands in this set begin with AT (which is short for "attention"), so this is often referred to as the AT command set. Note that the AT and almost every other letter is capitalized.

Several AT commands can be combined in a single string, and this is often used to initialize the modem before first use. These commands can set the default speed, whether the modem should automatically answer when someone calls in, and even how many rings it should wait for. I'll talk about these in more detail later when I talk about configuring modems.

Modems come in two forms: internal and external. Because a modem is a serial device (it communicates serially as opposed to parallel), it will always take up a serial port. With an external modem, you must physically make the connection to the serial port, so you are more conscious of the fact that the modem is taking up a port. Internal modems also take up a serial port, but it is less obvious. Because you don't actually see the modem, some users don't realize that they no longer have a COM1 (or COM2).

External modems are usually connected to the computer via a 25-pin RS-232 connector. Some serial ports have only a 9-pin serial port, so you need an adapter to convert the 25-pin to 9-pin, because every modem I have every seen has a 25-pin connector.

So, what happens when I want to dial into another site or send an e-mail message to my sister in Washington? Well, the communications software (maybe `cu` or `uucp`) sends a signal (an increase in voltage) along pin 20 (data terminal ready, or DTR) to tell the modem that it is ready to transmit data. On the modem, the equivalent pin is pin 6, data set ready, or DSR.

The modem is told to go "off hook" via the transmit data line (TX, line 2). Shortly thereafter, the system sends the AT-commands to start the modem dialing either with pulses (ATDP) or with tones (ATDT). The modem acknowledges the commands via line 3 (receive data, or RX).

The modem dials just like a phone and tries to connect to some device on the other end, probably a modem. If *auto answer* is enabled, the modem being called should answer, or *pick up*, the modem. When the connection is made, the calling modem sends a high-pitched signal to tell the receiving modem that a modem is calling. The receiving modem sends a higher-pitched acknowledgment. (You can hear this if your modem has a speaker.)

The carrier signal is then established between the two modems, which is kept at a steady, predetermined frequency. This is the signal that is then modulated actually to transmit the data. When the modem has begun to receive this carrier signal, it sends another signal back to the system via line 8 (carried detect, or CD). This signal is held active for the duration of the call.

The two modems must first decide how they will transmit data. This negotiation is called a handshake. The information exchanged includes many of the things that are defined in the different standards I talked about earlier.

When the system is ready to send data, it first raises line 4 (request to send, or RTS). If it is ready, the modem says okay by raising line 5 (clear to send, or CTS). Data then are sent out on line 2 and received on line 3. If the modem cannot keep up, it can drop the CTS line to tell the system to stop for a moment.

8.14 Printers

Although more and more companies are trying to transform into a "paperless office," you will undoubtedly see a printer somewhere. Even if the office is paperless internally, it will have to use paper of some kind to communicate with the rest of the world.

Printers come in many different shapes, sizes, formats, means of connection to the system, ways of printing characters, speeds, and so on. The two most common ways to connect printers are by serial port or parallel port. Linux also supports Hewlett-Packard Laser Jet printers equipped with JetDirect cards. These cards allow the printer to be attached directly to a network, thereby increasing its speed. I'll talk more about these later. In addition, although they are not supported by Linux as of this writing, SCSI printers have appeared on the market.

In previous sections, we talked about serial and parallel connections, so I don't need to go into detail about them. I do talk about these connections in more detail in the second part of the book, however, when I talk about installing and configuring printers.

There are two kinds of printers that, although were once very common, are now making way for more advanced successors: the daisy-wheel and chain printers. The distinction these printers had is that they had preformed characters.

In the case of a daisy-wheel printer, printing was accomplished by means of a wheel, where the characters were at the end of thin "leaves," which made the daisy shape. The wheel rotated very fast and as the appropriate letter came into position, it was struck with a hammer that forced the leaf with the character on it against the ink ribbon, which then struck the paper. This mechanism uses the same principle as a normal typewriter. In fact, there are typewriters that use the same daisy-wheel principle.

Chain printers also have preformed letters. Instead of a wheel, however, the letters are on a long strip called a chain. Instead of rotating, the chain moves back and forth to bring the appropriate letter into position.

Although these printers are fairly quick, they are limited in what they can print. You could get pretty tricky in which characters you use, and come up with some rather cute pictures. However, these mechanisms aren't able to do anything very detailed.

The next step in printers was the impact dot-matrix printer. These, too, had hammers, but rather than striking preformed letters, the hammers themselves struck the ink ribbon. Instead of a single hammer, there was a column of usually 9 or 24 hammers, or pins. Such printers are called 9-pin or 24-pin printers.

As the printer prints, the heads move across the page and print out columns of dots. Depending on what character is to be printed, some of the pins do not strike the ink ribbon. For example, when a dash is printed, only the middle pin(s) strike the ribbon. When printing a more complex character like an ampersand (&), the pins strike at different times as the print head moves across the page.

As with monitors, the more dots you have, the sharper the image. Therefore, a 24-pin printer can produce a sharper image than one with only 9 pins. In most cases, the type of printer used is obvious the moment you see something printed with a 9-pin printer. Some 24-pin printers require a closer look before you can tell.

Next, printers began to get rid of the ink ribbon and replace the pins with little sprayers connected to a supply of ink. Instead of striking something, these sprayers squirt a little dot of ink onto the paper. The result, similar to that of an impact dot-matrix printer, is what an ink jet printer does.

Ink jet printers have two advantages over impact dot-matrix printers. First is the issue of noise. Because no pins are striking the ink ribbon, the ink jet printer is much quieter. Second, by extending the technology a little, the manufacturer increased the number of jets in each row. Also, instead of just squirting out black ink, you could squirt out colored ink, which is how many color printers work.

The drawback is the nature of the print process itself. Little sprayers squirting ink all over the place is messy. Without regular maintenance, ink jets can clog up.

Using a principle very similar to video systems, laser printers can obtain very high resolution. A laser inside the printer (hence the name) scans across a rotating drum that has been given a static-electric charge. When the laser hits a spot on the drum, that area looses its charge. Toner then spreads across the drum and sticks to those areas that retain the charge. Next, the drum rolls the paper across, smashing the toner onto the paper. Finally, the toner is fused into the paper by means of a heating element.

Although laser printers may appear to print a solid image, they still work with dots. The dots are substantially smaller than those of a 24-pin dot matrix, but they are still dots. As with video systems, the more dots, the sharper the image. Because a laser is used to change the characteristics of the drum, the areas effected are very small. Therefore, with laser printers, you can get resolutions of even 300dpi on even the least expensive printers. Newer printers are approaching 1,200dpi, which is comparable to photographs.

Some laser printers, like HP's LaserJet, use a technology called resolution enhancement. Although there are still a limited number of dots-per-inch, the size of each dot can be altered, thereby changing the *apparent* resolution.

Keep in mind that printers have the same problem with resolution as do video systems. The more dots desired, the more memory is needed to process them. An 8 1/2" x 11" page with a resolution of 300dpi takes almost a megabyte of memory to print.

With printers such as daisy-wheel and chain printers, you really don't have this issue. Even a buffer as small as 8K is more than sufficient to hold a whole page of text, including *control characters* that can change the way the other characters appear. While such control characters may cause the text to be printed bold or underlined, they are relatively simple in nature. For example, underlining normally consists of printing the character, backing up one space, then printing an underline.

Multiple-character sets or fonts is something that this kind of printer just can't handle. Different character sets (e.g., German) or changing the character's form (e.g., italic) can easily be accomplished when the letter is created "on-the-fly" with dot-matrix printers. All that is needed is to change the way the dots are positioned, which is usually accomplished by using escape sequences. First, an *escape character* (ASCII 27) is sent to the printer to tell it that the next character (or characters) is a command to change its behavior.

Different printers react differently to different escape sequences. Although there is a wide range of sets of escape sequences, the two most common sets are those for IBM Proprinters and Epson printers. Most dot-matrix printers can be configured to behave like one of these. Some, like my Panasonic KX-P1123, can be configured to behave like either one.

The shortcoming with this is that you are limited to a small range of character types and sizes. Some printers, like mine, can get around this limitation because they can print in graphics modes as well. By viewing the page as a one complete image composed of thousands of dots, they can get any font, any size, with any attribute (assuming the software can handle this). This is how printers like mine can print charts, tables, and, to some extent, pictures.

Viewing the page as a complete image works when you have graphics or diagrams, but it's a waste of memory when you're dealing with straight text. Therefore, most laser printers operate in *character-mapped mode,* in which the characters are stored in memory and are the dots are generated as the page goes through the printer.

Printers are controlled by other means than just escape sequences of treating the page as a single image. One most widely used means of control is Adobe System's Postscript page description language, which is as much a language as the programming languages C or Pascal, with syntax and vocabulary. To use it, both the software and the printer have to support it. However, the advantage is that many applications allow you to print Postscript to a file. That file can then be transferred to a remote site with a Postscript printer. The file is then sent to a printer (as raw data) and the output is the same as though it were printed directly from the application. The nice thing is that the remote site does not even have to have the same application as long as its printer is Postscript-capable.

8.15 Mice

The basic principle is that by moving the mouse, the cursor (pointer) on the screen moves in the same manner. Actions can be carried out by clicking one of up to three buttons on the mouse.

As the mouse is moved across a surface, a ball underneath rolls along with it. This ball turns small wheels (usually three of them) inside the mouse. The amount each wheel turns is measured and this movement is translated into the movement of the cursor.

Because the ball underneath must roll for the mouse to work, it has to remain on a flat surface. The surface must also have a certain amount of friction for the ball to roll. Although you can get a certain amount of movement by shaking the mouse, picking it up and expecting the cursor to move is a waste of time.

Originally, mice were connected by a thin cable to the computer. As technology has progressed, the cable was done away with and replaced with a light-emitting diode (LED) on the mouse and a photodetector near the computer. This has the advantage of preventing the cable from tangling or getting buried under a pile of papers and thereby limiting the mouse's movement. The disadvantage is that the LED must remain within the line-of-sight of the photodetector to function. Some manufacturers have overcome this disadvantage by using an alternate form of light that does not depend on line-of-sight: radio.

Another major problem with all of these kinds of mice is desk space. My desk is not neat. Space is at a premium. Even the small space needed for a mouse pad is a luxury that I rarely have. Fortunately, companies such as Logitech have heard my cries and come to the rescue. The solution is, as an old UNIX guru called it, a dead mouse.

This is a mouse that lies with its feet (or, at least, the ball) sticking up. Rather than moving the mouse to move the ball to move the wheels to move the cursor, you simply move the ball. The ball is somewhat larger than the one inside of a mouse, which makes it a lot easier to move. Such a mouse is called a trackball and is very common with laptop computers. Provided the signals sent to the operating system are the same, a trackball behaves similarly to a mouse.

The mouse's interface to the operating system can take one of three forms. The mouse is referred to, based on this interface, as a *serial mouse*, *bus mouse*, or *keyboard mouse*.

As its name implies, a serial mouse is attached to your computer through a serial port. Bus mice have their own interface card that plugs into the bus. Keyboard mice, despite their name, usually do not plug into the keyboard. Though I have seen some built into the keyboard, these were actually serial mice. Instead, a keyboard mouse is plugged into its own connector, usually next to the keyboard connector, which is then attached directly to the motherboard. These mice are usually found on IBM PS/2 and some Compaq computers, though more computer manufacturers are providing a connector for a keyboard mouse.

When people talk about the movement of the mouse, you often hear the term *resolution*. For a mouse, resolution is referred to in terms of clicks per inch, or CPI. A click is simply the signal sent to the system to tell it that the mouse has moved. The higher the CPI, the higher resolution. Both mice and trackballs have resolution, because both rely on the movement of a ball to translate the movement of the cursor.

Keep in mind that despite how it appears at first, a mouse with a higher resolution is not necessarily more precise. In fact, almost the opposite is true. Higher resolution means that the mouse moves *further* for each given movement on the ball. The result is that the movement is *faster*, not more precise. Because precision is really determined by your own hand movement, experience has shown me that you get better precision with a mouse that has a lower resolution.

8.16 Uninterruptable Power Supplies

The first thing I want to address here is the concept of uninterruptable power. If you take that term literally, a power supply that goes out at all has been interrupted. In that case, many UPS are not correctly named because there is a brief moment (ca. 30 milliseconds) between the time the computer notices the power has gone out and the battery kicks in. This time is too short for the computer to notice, but it is there. (Normally, power must be out for at least 300 milliseconds before the computer will notice.) As a result, most UPS should be referred to as stand-by power supply (SPS) because they switch to the battery when the primary supply shuts off. Because Underwriter's Laboratories uses UPS to describe both, that's what I will do here.

The basic UPS provides limited power conditioning (keeping the voltage within a specific range) but no protection against surges and spikes. This is useful if the power goes out but doesn't protect you if the voltage suddenly jumps (such as the result of a lightning strike). A *double-conversion* model provides the power when the main power fails and also provides protection against surges by first passing the power through the batteries. Although this does provide protection, it is less efficient because power is constantly drawn from the battery.

Although no UPS vendor directly supports Linux, there are several sources for programs that can take advantage of existing UPSs. The best place to start is the UPS HOWTO.

CHAPTER 9

TALKING TO OTHER MACHINES

- TCP/IP fundamentals
- Configuring DNS and NFS
- Troubleshooting your network
- SAMBA
- Getting connected

Long ago (at least in terms of the history of electronic data processing), having two computers at the same time was something you read about in science fiction novels. As systems became more common, the time did come when a company or university would have two computers. The need then arose that data be exchanged between the two machines. This was the beginning of SNEAKER-Net (Slow, Non-Electrical Activity, Keeping Everyone Running), which was developed in the 1950s. With SNEAKER-Net, the technician would copy data onto a tape or other media and, using his sneakers, would run the tape over to the other machine to load it. In many organizations, SNEAKER-Net is still employed today because this is often the only type of network they think they can afford.

In 1976, researchers at AT&T Bell Laboratories came to the rescue. They developed a serial line protocol to exchange data between UNIX machines, which came to be known as UUCP, for Unix-to-Unix Copy. Over the years, there were several changes, upgrades, revisions, etc. In 1983, AT&T released a new version that came to be known as Honeydanber UUCP because it had been developed by Peter Honeyman, David A. Nowitz, and Brian E. Redman.

Although UUCP was a good thing, it was limited by the speed of the serial line connecting the two computers. Because the system could only be as fast as its slowest component, there had to be a way to speed up that slowest component. Serial line speeds increased, but that still was not enough. In the 1970s, Xerox came out with Ethernet, which made high-speed communication between computers possible. It was now possible for users to access remote computers and expect response times to compare to being logged in locally, rather than experiencing delays, which was common with the serial line communication of the day. (I'll get into more detail on Ethernet later; see Section 9.7.1, Ethernet.)

Today, both are still widespread. Although prices have dropped to the point at which Ethernet networks are common place (I even have one in my house), UUCP is still used regularly when distance prevents other types of connection or when the connection will be quick or short-term and the administrator doesn't want the added hassle of first installing the Ethernet cards.

Unfortunately, going into detail about UUCP is beyond the scope of this book, so I leave it to you to take a look at the UUCP HOWTO if you are interested in getting UUCP configured.

9.1 TCP/IP

Before I talk about the details of networking, I should first talk about the process of network communication. Let's take a network program such as `telnet`. The `telnet` program allows you to login to a remote system. You end up with a shell just as though you had logged in locally. Although you input commands on your local keyboard and the output appears on your local screen, all other activity happens on the remote machine.

For simplicity's sake, I can say that there is a `telnet` program running on each computer. When you input something on local keyboard, the local copy of `telnet` accepts input. It passes the information through the network to the `telnet` on the remote machine. The command is executed and the output is handed to the remote `telnet`. That information is passed back through the network to the local `telnet`, which then displays the information on your screen.

Although it may appear as though there is a constant flow of information between your local machine and the remote one, this is not what is happening. At any given time, there may be dozens if not hundreds of programs using the network. Because only one can use the network at a time, there needs to be some mechanism to allow each program to have its turn.

Think back on our discussion on the kernel (see Section 6.1, The Kernel: The Heatbeat of Linux). When you need something from the hard disk, the system does not read everything at once. If it did, one process could dominate the computer if it needed to read in a large file. Instead, disk requests are sent in smaller chunks and the program only thinks that it's getting everything it wants. Something similar is done with network connections.

Computers are like humans beings in that they need to speak the same language to communicate. Regardless of how they are connected, be it serially or by Ethernet, the computers must know how to talk to each other. The communication is carried out in a predefined manner, called a *protocol*. Like the protocol diplomats and politicians go through, computer protocol determines how each side behaves and how it should react to its counterpart's behavior. Roughly speaking, even the interaction between the computer and the hardware, such as the hard disk, can be considered a protocol.

The most common protocol used by UNIX variants, including Linux, is TCP/IP. However, it is more accurate to call TCP/IP a protocol suite, or protocol family because TCP/IP actually consists of several different protocols. Even the name consists of two different protocols, as TCP/IP stands for Transmission Control Protocol/Internet Protocol.

TCP/IP is often referred to as protocol suite because it contains many different protocols and therefore many different ways for computers to talk to each other. However, TCP/IP is not the only protocol suite. There are dozens, if not hundreds of different protocol suites, though only a small portion of them have gained wide acceptance. Linux only uses a few itself, although the TCP/IP family is delivered by default and is most commonly used.

Although the name refers to two specific protocols, TCP/IP usually refers to an entire suite of protocols and programs. The result of many years of planning and discussion, the TCP/IP suite includes a set of standards that specify how computers ought to communicate. By following these standards, computers "speak" the same language and can therefore communicate. In addition to the actual means of communication that the TCP/IP suite defines, it also defines conventions for connecting different networks and routing traffic through routers, bridges, and other types of connections.

The TCP/IP suite is result of a Defense Advanced Research Projects Agency (DARPA) research project on network connectivity. Its availability has made it the most commonly installed network software. Many versions provide source code that reside in the public domain, allowing users to adapt it to many new systems. Most vendors of network hardware (e.g., bridges, routers) support the TCP/IP suite.

Whereas the data transferred to and from the hard disk is talked about in terms of blocks, the unit of information for transfer across a network connection is in terms of a packet. Depending on the program you use, this packet can be different sizes. In any event, it is small enough to send across the network fast enough for no one process to dominate the network. In addition, the packets go across the network so fast that you don't notice that your data are broken into packets. This is similar to the way the CPU manages processes. Each process gets a very small turn on the processor. Because it switches so fast between processes, it only seems as though you have the processor to yourself.

If you take a step back and look at the process of network communication more abstractly, you see each portion supported by and supporting another. You can say that each portion sits on top of another or, in other words, the protocols are *stacked* on top of each other. Therefore, TCP/IP is often referred to as a *protocol stack*. To see how these layers look graphically, take a look at Figure 9.1.

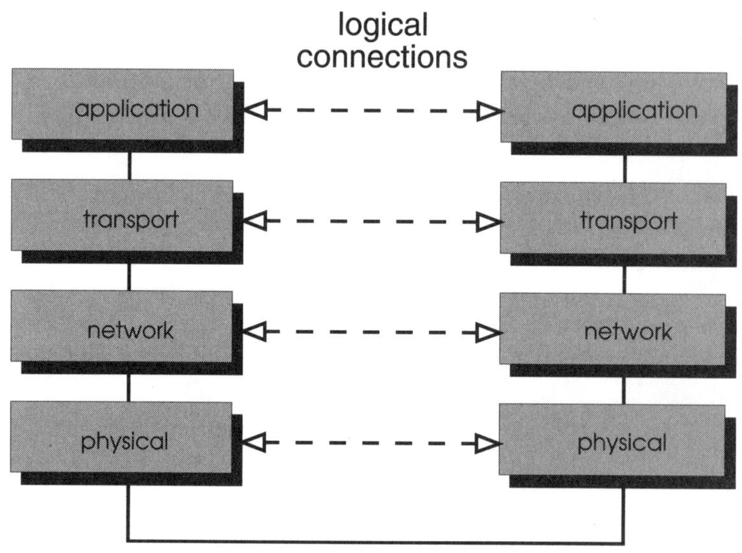

Figure 9.1: Network Layers

Each portion of the stack is referred to as a *layer*. At the bottom of the stack is the physical layer, which is responsible for the physical connection between the two computers. Sitting on top of the physical layer is the network layer, which is responsible for the network portion of the stack. That is, it ensures that packets either stay on the network or get to the right network and at the same time ensures that packets get to the right network address.

On top of the network layer is the transport layer, which ensures that the packets have been transmitted correctly. That is, that there are no errors and all packets have been received. Finally, at the top of all of this is the layer that the user sees. Because the programs that we use are often called applications, this upper layer is called the application layer.

Conceptually, each layer talks to its counterpart on the other system. That is, `telnet` on the local machine is passing data to `telnet` on the remote machine. TCP on the remote machine sends an acknowledgment to TCP on the local machine when it receives a packet. IP on the local machine gets information from IP on the remote machine that tells it that this packet is destined for the local machine. Then there are the network interface cards that communicate with each other using their specific language. This communication between corresponding layers is all conceptual. The actual communication takes place between the different layers on each machine, *not* the corresponding layers on both machines.

When the application layer has data to send, it prepends an *application header* onto the data it needs to send. This header contains information necessary for the application to get the data to the right part of the application on the receiving side. The application then calls up TCP to send the information along. TCP wraps that data into a TCP packet, which contains a *TCP header* followed by the application data (including header). TCP then hands the packet (also called a TCP *segment*) to IP. As with the layers before it, IP wraps up the packet and prepends an *IP header* to create an IP *datagram*. Finally, IP hands it off to the hardware driver. If it is Ethernet, this includes both an Ethernet header and Ethernet trailer, which creates an *Ethernet frame*. See Figure 9.2 for how the encapsulation looks graphically.

As you see, the application talks to the TCP layer. TCP sticks the data from the application into a kind of envelope (the process is called *encapsulation*) and passes it to the IP layer. Just as the operating system has a mechanism to keep track of which area of memory belongs to which processes, the network has a means of keeping track of which data belong to what process. This is TCP's job. It is also TCP's responsibility to ensure that the packets are delivered with the correct contents and then put in the right order.

Error detection is the job of the TCP *envelope*, which contains a checksum of the data contained within the packet. This checksum information sits in the packet header and is checked on all packets. If the checksum doesn't match the contents of the packet or the packet doesn't arrive at all, it is TCP's job to ensure that packet is resent. On the sending end, TCP waits for an acknowledgment that each packet has been

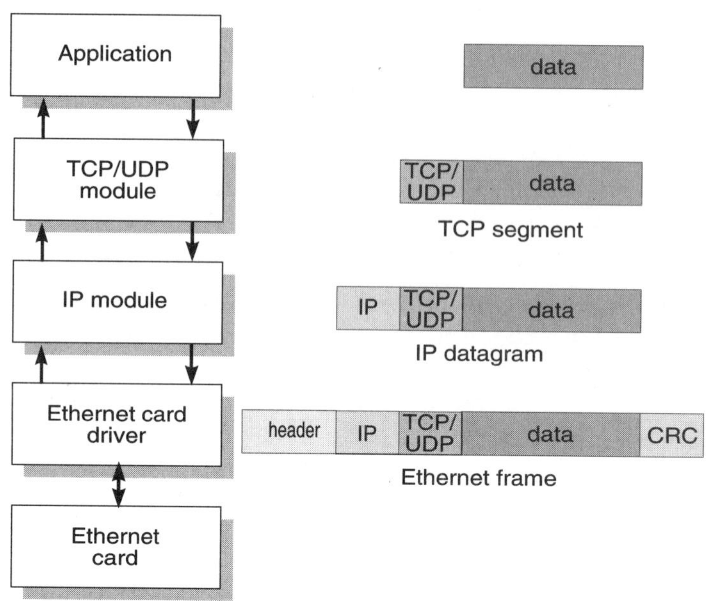

Figure 9.2: Encapsulation

received. If it hasn't received one within a specific period, it will resend that packet. Because it uses this checksum and resends packets, TCP is considered a *reliable connection*.

Another protocol that is often used is the User Datagram Protocol (UDP). Like TCP, UDP sits on top of IP. However, UDP provides a *connectionless* transport between applications. Services, such as the Network File Service (NFS), that utilize UDP must provide their own mechanism to ensure delivery and correct sequencing of packets. Because it can be either broadcast or multicast, UDP also offers one-to-many services. Because UDP does no checking, it is considered unreliable.

Closest to the hardware level, IP is a protocol that provides the delivery mechanism for the protocols. The IP layer serves the same function as your house address, telling the upper layers how to get to where they need to go. In fact, the information IP uses to get the pieces of information to their destinations are called IP addresses. However, IP does not guarantee that the packets arrive in the right order or that they arrive at all. Just as a letter to your house is required to be registered to ensure that it is delivered with the content intact, IP depends on the upper layers to ensure the integrity and sequencing of the packets. Therefore, IP is considered unreliable.

Because the hardware–that is, the network cards–do the actual, physical transfer of the packets, it is important that they are somehow addressed. Each card has its own, unique identifier called the Media Access Control, or MAC, address. The MAC address is a 48-bit number that is usually represented by six pairs of hexadecimal numbers separated by (usually) dashes or colons. Each network card manufacturer is assigned a specific range of addresses that usually are specified by the first three pairs of numbers.

When sending a packet, the IP layer has to figure out how to do so. If the destination is on a different physical network, IP needs to send it to the appropriate gateway. If the destination machine is on the local network, however, the IP layer uses the Address Resolution Protocol (ARP) to determine the MAC address of the Ethernet card with that IP address.

To figure this out, ARP will broadcast an ARP packet across the entire network, asking which MAC address belongs to a particular IP address. Though every machines receives this broadcast, only the one that matches will respond. The IP layer then stores this in its internal ARP table. You can look at the ARP table at any time by running the following command:

```
arp -a
```

This command would give you a response similar to

```
siemau 194.113.47.147 at 0:0:2:c:8c:d2
```

which has the general format

```
<machine name> (IP address) at <MAC address>
```

Because the ARP table is cached, IP does not have to send out an ARP request every time it needs to make a connection. Instead, it can quickly look in the ARP table to make the IP-MAC translation. Then, the packet is sent to the appropriate machine.

Status and error information is exchanged between machines through the Internet Control Message Protocol (ICMP). Other protocols can use this information to recover from transmission problems and system administrators can use it to detect problems in the network. One most commonly used diagnostic tool, PING (Packet Internet Groper), makes use of ICMP.

At the bottom of the pile is the hardware or link layer. As I mentioned earlier, this can be represented by many different kinds of physical connections: Ethernet, Token-Ring Network, fiber optics, ISDN, and RS-232, to name a few.

This four-layer model (hardware, IP, TCP, and application) is common when referring to computer networks. This is the most commonly used model and the one that I will use throughout the book. Another model, the OSI model, consists of seven layers, but I won't be using it here. To learn more about your TCP/IP configuration, see Table 9.3 on page 398.

9.1.1 Network Services

In the preceding discussion, I used the `telnet` command as an example of one of the programs that uses TCP/IP. However, many others provide additional services, such as transferring of files, electronic mail, network printing, and access to remote file systems. Other products, such as database applications, may have one central machine that contains all the data and gains access from the other machines via TCP/IP. Often this access is invisible to the user, who just sees the "front end" of the database.

This configuration, in which one machine contains the data or resource that another machine uses, is very common in computer networking. The machine *with* the resource it provides to other machines is referred to as the server because it serves the resource to the other machines. The machine that uses the resource is called the *client*. This model, in which one machine is the server and the other is the client, is referred to as a *client-server model*.

Another common network model is the *peer-to-peer model*. In this model, no one central machine has all the resources. Instead, all machines are on equal status. Often, these two models blend together. In Linux networks, it is possible to have multiple servers, each providing many of the same resources. Multiple machines all can also have resources that others need, so everyone acts as both a client and a server, which is similar to peer-to-peer, which is common in Microsoft Windows networks.

On Linux systems, dozens of resources are available, many of which are well-known, such as `telnet`. Others, such as `ntp`, are more obscure. As when you call into a large office building with a central switchboard, your server needs to know which numbers are associated with which programs to make the proper connection, in the same regard that you need to know which office you want to reach before you call. In some cases, you can call and say you want a particular extension; in other cases, you say you want a particular office. In a office building, there is a list of available "services" called a phone book. On a Linux system, the phone book is the file `/etc/services`.

The `/etc/services` file contains a list of the services a particular machine may have to offer. The concept of a service is slightly different than the concept of a resource. A machine may provide many resources in the form of login shells that it provides to remote users, however, all of them access the machine through the one service: `telnet`.

In addition to the service the machine provides, `/etc/services` also lists the port. To understand the idea of a port, think about it as being the telephone number. When I call in to a machine (say using `telnet`), I am connected to the `telnet` program on the other side through a particular port, as though I were calling a large office building with a single switchboard. When I reach that switchboard, I tell the operator which office or person I want to talk to. In the ancient history of telephones, that operator had to make the connection between the incoming line and the office manually.

A port can also be thought of as the socket into which the operator plugs the phone lines. As in that office building, a set of these sockets, or ports, may be directly connected to a specific person (i.e., service). These are *well-known* ports. Offices may have their own operators (or maybe just a receptionist) who passes the incoming phone call to the right person or may even pick someone else to take the call (such as when you call a government agency with a generic question and there is no one person responsible for that area).

On an Linux system using TCP/IP, the principle is the same. There are dozens of services to which you can connect, but there is only one way into the system: through your network interface card. For you to be able to connect to the right service, there must be something like an operator to make the connection for you. This operator is the program `/etc/inetd`, the "Internet Daemon" often referred to as a "super server" because its responsibility is to wait for requests to access the other servers on your system and pass you along.

As in our office building, you may know what number you want, that is, which port. When you make the connection to `inetd`, your process tells it to which port you want to connect and `inetd` makes the connection. On the other hand, you may have a program that does not have a well-known port, so a new port must be created.

The `inetd` daemon "listens" for the connections. You can say that it listens on multiple ports in the sense that it manages all the ports. However, `inetd` makes the connection between the incoming connection and the local port and, therefore, to the local server. This mechanism saves memory because you don't need to start up the servers you aren't going to use. This is similar to having a central switchboard and not requiring every office to have their own switchboard. You can see how this concept looks graphically in Figure 9.3.

Normally, `inetd` starts during system start-up from a script under `/etc/rc.d`. When the script starts, `inetd` reads its configuration file (`/etc/inetd.conf`) to obtain the necessary information to start the various servers. It then builds the logical connection between the server and its respective port, kind of like laying the cable from the central switchboard to the various offices. Technically it creates a *socket*, which is *bound* to the port for that server.

When `inetd` gets a connection request (the phone rings) for a connection-based port, it "accepts" the incoming call, creating a new socket. That is, there is a logical connection between the incoming request and the server. Now `inetd` can continue to listen on the original port for additional incoming calls.

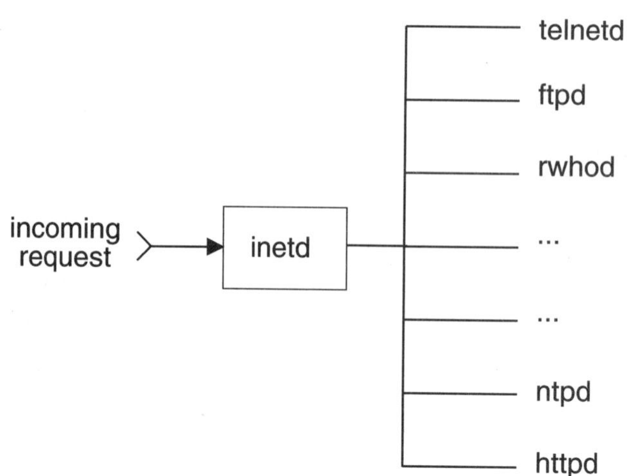

Figure 9.3: The `inetd` Daemon

If the port is connectionless (UDP), the behavior depends on entries in the `/etc/inetd.conf` file. If `inetd` is told to wait (there is a `wait` in the fourth column), the server that was called must process the incoming message before `inetd` can go on. If `inetd` was told not to wait (there is a `nowait` in the fourth column), `inetd` will continue to process incoming requests on that port. If you look in `/etc/inetd.conf`, you see that almost exclusively TCP ports are nowait and UDP ports are wait.

9.1.2 Network Standards

Here I need to side step a little. I must first talk about what goes into making a standard. Without standards, communication among computers of different types is very difficult. Just as you have bus standards, like ISA and PCI, so hardware can communicate with the CPU, you need some kind of standard for the network.

In the Internet community, standards are both suggested and established through Request for Comments or RFCs. To some extent, this is the law. If one product claims to comply with a particular RFC, you know that any other applications that do so should be able to communicate with it. However, RFCs include other things such as lists of previous RFCs and basic introductions to things like TCP.

Becoming a standard is a three-step process. Usually, the first few paragraphs of an RFC will tell you to what stage it applies, assuming, of course, that the RFC is part of a standards proposal. First, the standard is proposed. Organizations then decide to implement the proposed standard. The proposed standard must go through three separate implementations before it becomes a standard. Finally, it becomes a standard. (This is an oversimplification of the process because there will also be a lot of discussion via emailabout the proposed standard, via email, newsgroups, etc.)

If you need information about a specific network standard, the first place to look is the most current RFC index, which is also published as an RFC. Not only does this index list all the RFCs, but it will also tell you if one RFC has been replaced and if so, by which one.

Originally, I had planned to include a list of the more commonly used and significant RFCs. I eventually realized that this was an unending task. When I started this book, there were just more than 1,800 RFCs. The last time I checked before wrapping up this book, there were more than 1,900. Instead, I will simply tell you where to get them.

The first place is from the "central repository." These are obtainable using ftp from `ftp.ds.internic.net`. There is an `rfc` directory that contains the RFCs in ASCII as well as many in PostScript format. If you know what RFC you want, you can obtain it by sending an e-mail message to *mailserv@ds.internic.net*. List each RFC you want in the format

```
document-by-name rfcXXXX
```

where XXXX is the number of the RFC. You can obtain the index by including the following entry:

```
document-by-name rfc-index
```

In addition, the RFCs are available from archives all over the Internet. Rather than tying up the Internet bandwidth with a lot of copies of files you may not need, however, check out *www.cdrom.com* or mail *info@cdrom.com*. This is Walnut Creek CD-ROM, who sell a CD-ROM packed with thousands of documents related to the Internet, including RFCs. Another site with pretty much the same kind of offering is InfoMagic. You can reach them at *www.infomagic.com* or *info@infomagic.com*.

For Linux systems running TCP/IP, one most important standard deals with Ethernet. The encapsulation (packaging) of IP datagrams is defined for Ethernet in RFC 894. Developed in 1982 by Digital Equipment Corporation (DEC), Intel, and Xerox, Ethernet is a standard rather than a physical entity. Several years later, the 802 Committee of the Institute of Electrical and Electronic Engineers (IEEE or I-triple E) published standards of its own that differed in many ways from the original Ethernet standard. Collectively, these are referred to as the 802 IEEE standards. The 802.3 standard covers networks similar to Ethernet. The IEEE 802 encapsulation was defined in RFC 1042. Both of these use an access method called Carrier Sense, Multiple Sense with Collision Detection, or CSMA/CD.

Both of these framing types (RFC 894 and RFC 1042) use a 48-bit addressing scheme. These are generally referred to as the MAC or hardware addresses. The 6 bytes of both the destination and source machines are included in the header of both framing types. However, the remainder of the frame is different. As I talked about earlier (see Section 9.1,

TCP/IP), this layer is responsible for sending and receiving the IP datagrams. It is also responsible for sending and receiving other kinds of packets as well. These are packets from the Address Resolution Protocol (ARP) and the Reverse Address Resolution Protocol (RARP). I'll talk about both later on.

9.1.3 IP Addressing

In today's world of interconnected computers, you may have a connection to hundred of thousands of other machines. Granted, no single cable connects all of these computers, though there is a logical connection in that you can use the `telnet` program from your PC in California and connect to a machine in Germany. The problem is, how do the packets get from one end to another? Added to that, how do you keep your local network in California from getting overloaded with packets that are being sent between machines in Germany and, at the same time, make sure that those `telnet` packets get through? The answer is provided by the Internet Protocol (IP).

Just as a street address is not always sufficient to get your letter delivered, so is the IP not always sufficient to get the packet delivered. If I sent you a letter, it could go to a single, central post office whose job it is to distribute mail throughout the entire U.S. Because of the incredibly large number of pieces of mail, this is impractical. Instead, there are thousands of offices all over the country whose job it is to route the mail for us.

If you lived in a small town, the local post office could catch a letter destined for a local address before it goes further. Mail with addresses outside could be sent to other post offices to be processed.

A similar situation applies to IP addresses. In local, self-contained networks, the IP address alone is sufficient. However, when multiple networks are combined, machines spend more time trying to figure out whether the packet belongs to them than actually processing information. The solution is a network mask. Just as a zip code tells a postal worker whether to process a particular piece of mail locally or not, the network mask (or netmask) tells machines whether or not they can simply ignore a packet or need to process it further. I'll get to how this works in a moment.

Every machine on the network needs to have its own, unique IP address, just as every house has a unique mail address. If that network is connected to the rest of the world, that address must not only be unique within the local network but unique within the rest of the world as well. As of this writing, IP addresses are 32-bit values that are usually represented by four sets of numbers, ranging from 0–255 separated by dots (.). This is referred to as dotted-decimal notation. In *dotted-decimal notation*, an address might look like this:

147.132.42.18

Because each of these numbers ranges between 0–255, each can be represented by 8 bits and are therefore referred to as an *octet*. This IP address is often thought of as being composed of a network portion (at the beginning) and a node (or machine) portion at the end. This would be comparable to writing a street address as

95061.Main_Street.42

where 95061 is the zip code, Main Street is the street, and 42 is the address on that street. You write the street address in this fashion because the IP address moves from the general to the specific.

Currently, three classes of networks are in common use each of which is broken down by both the range used in the first octet and the number of octets used to identify the network. Class A networks are the largest and use the first octet as the network address. Networks in the class will have the first octet in the range 1–126. Class B networks use the first two octets, the first being in the range 128–192. The smallest networks, class C, use the first three octets in the network address, the first in the range 192–223. Table 9.1 shows how IP addresses are broken down by the different network classes.

Table 9.1: IP Address Breakdown by Network

Class	Range within First Octet	Network ID	Host ID	Possible Networks	Possible Hosts per Network
A	1-126	a	b.c.d.	126	16,777,214
B	128-191	a.b	c.d	16,384	65,534
C	192-223	a.b.c	d	2,097,151	254

I would like to point out a couple of things about this table. First, the network address 127 represents the local computer, regardless of what network it is really on. This is helpful for testing as well as for many internal operations. Network addresses 224 and more are reserved for special purposes, such as multicast addresses. The "possible networks" and "possible hosts per network" are those that are calculated mathematically. In some cases, 0 and 255 are not acceptable values for either the network address or the host address.

Keep in mind that a class A address does not necessarily mean that there are 16 million hosts on a single network. This would be impossible to administrate and would overburden most network technologies. What normally happens is that a single entity, such as Hewlett-Packard, is given a class A address. They then break it down further into smaller *subnets*. I'll get into more details about this shortly.

A network host uses the network ID and host ID to determine which packets it should receive or ignore and to determine the scope of its transmissions (only nodes with the same network ID accept each other's IP-level broadcasts). Because the sender's IP address is included in every outgoing IP packet, it is useful for the receiving computer system to derive the originating network ID and host ID from the IP address field. This is done by using subnet masks, as I will describe in the following section (see Section 9.1.4, Subnet Masks).

In some cases, there is no need to have unique IP addresses because the network will *never* be connected to the rest of the world; for example, in a factory where the machines communicate with each other via TCP/IP. There is no reason for these machines to be accessible from the Internet. Therefore, there is no need for them to have an official IP address.

You could just randomly assign IP addresses to these machines and hope that your router is configured correctly not to route the packets from these machines. But one slip and you could potentially not only mess up your own network but someone else's as well.

The solution was provided in RFC-1918. Here, three sets of IP address were defined for use in "private" networks. These won't be routed and there is no need to coordinate their use with any of the registrations agencies. The IP addresses are

10.0.0.0 - 10.255.255.255
172.16.0.0 - 172.31.255.255
192.168.0.0 - 192.168.255.255

As you can see, there is just a single class A address but 16 class B and 255 class C networks. Therefore, no matter what size your network is, you can find a private network for your needs.

9.1.4 Subnet Masks

Subnet masks are 32-bit values that allow the recipient of IP packets to distinguish the network ID portion of the IP address from the host ID. As with an IP address, the value of a subnet mask is frequently represented in dotted-decimal notation. Subnet masks are determined by assigning 1s to bits that belong to the network ID and 0s to the bits that belong to the host ID. Once the bits are in place, the 32-bit value is converted to dotted-decimal notation, as shown in Table 9.2.

The result allows TCP/IP to determine the host and network IDs of the local computer. For example, when the IP address is 102.54.94.97 and the subnet mask is 255.255.0.0, the network ID is 102.54 and the host ID is 94.97.

Table 9.2: Default Subnet Masks for Standard IP Address Classes

Address Class	Bits for Subnet Mask	Subnet Mask
A	11111111 00000000 00000000 00000000	255.0.0.0
B	11111111 11111111 00000000 00000000	255.255.0.0
C	11111111 11111111 11111111 00000000	255.255.255.0

Keep in mind that all of this regarding subnet masks is the principle and not necessarily the practice. If you (meaning your company) have been assigned a class B address, the first two octants are assigned to you. You could then break down the class B net into class C nets. If you take a look at Table 9.1, you will see that there are 65,534 possible nodes in that network. That is really too many to manage.

However, if you considered each of the third octets to represent a subnet of our class B network, they would all have 254 possible nodes per subnet. This is basically what a class C net is, anyway. You can then assign each subnet to a department or building and then assign one person to manage each of the class C subnets, which is a little easier to do.

To keep the different class C subnets from interfering with each other, give each subnet a *class C* subnet mask, although the first octet is in the range for a class B network. That way, machines on this subnet are only concerned with packets for the subnet. You can also break down the subnets physically so that there is a gateway or router between the subnets. That way, the physical network is not overburdened with traffic from 65,534 machines.

Let's look at a example. Assume your company uses the class B address 172.16.0.0. The different departments within the company are assigned a class C address that might look like this: 172.16.144.0. Although the first octet (172) says that this is a class B address, it is really the subnet mask that makes that determination. In this case, our subnet mask would be: 255.255.255.0. Therefore, any packet destined for an address other than one starting 172.16.144.0 is not on this network.

It is the responsibility of IP to ensure that each packet goes to the right machine. This is accomplished, in part, by assigning a unique address to each machine. This address is referred to as the Internet address or IP address. Each network has a set of these IP addresses that are within a specific range. In general, packets that are destined for an IP address within that range will stay within the local network. Only when a packet is destined for somewhere outside of the local network is it "allowed" to pass.

In other words, IP is responsible for the delivery of the packet. It functions similar to the post office, whereby you have both a sending and receiving address. Often times, you have many more letters than a single mail bag can handle. The mail carrier (or someone else at the post office) will break down the number of letters into sets small enough to fit in a bag. This is what IP does.

Because many people use the line at once, IP will break down the TCP packets into units of a specific size. Although often also referred to as *packets*, the more correct terminology is to refer to IP packets as *datagrams*. Just as bags of mail need to go from one post office to the next to reach their final destination, IP datagrams must often go through different machines to reach their final destination.

Saying that IP routing can be accomplished completely in software isn't entirely accurate. Although no physical router is needed, IP can't send a packet to someplace where there is no physical connection. This is normally accomplished by an additional network card. With two (or more) network cards, a single machine can be connected to multiple networks. The IP layer on that one machine can then be used to route IP packets between the two networks.

Once configured (I'll talk about how that's done in Section 9.1.9, Your Own IP Address), IP maintains a table of routing information called a routing table. Every time the IP layer receives a packet, it checks the destination address.

9.1.5 Routing and IP Gateways

I mentioned a moment ago that IP is an unreliable, connectionless protocol. That is, it contains no provision to ensure that the packet arrives correctly at the destination, nor is there any guarantee that when packets arrive, they arrive in the correct order. Although IP is responsible to ensure that the packets get to the right machine, it has essentially no understanding of the physical connection between the two machines. IP will happily run on machines that are connected with something as simple as a telephone wire to something as complex as satellites. IP depends on some other means to "physically" carry it across the network.

This means that the system administrator (or network administrator) is responsible for laying the "map" that is used to define which network address goes with which sets of machines and what IP addresses are assigned to individual machines.

One important job that IP does is routing; that is, getting the packet to the right machine. If the source and destination machines are directly connected–that is, on the same network–then routing is easy. Essentially, there isn't any routing. IP sees this and simply hands the packets off to the data link layer. Otherwise, IP has to figure out how and where to send it.

Usually the "how" is over a *router*, which is some piece of hardware that acts like an air traffic controller, sending one packet one way and others a different way. Often routers are separate pieces of equipment that can be configured in very detailed ways. The disadvantage to this is that with power comes price. The ability to configure a router in many different ways usually means a high price tag. Fortunately, many operating systems, including Linux, allow IP to serve as router software, thereby avoiding the cost of router hardware.

In comparison to the router is the concept of a *gateway*. Like a router, a gateway has knowledge of other networks and how to reach them. In general, you can think of a router as a special piece of hardware that does the work for you. A gateway is more of a concept in that it is the means by which you go from one network to another. Today, the distinction between a router and a gateway is blurred. Originally, a gateway was a machine that converted from one protocol to another. However, in common usage today, routers can server as gateways, and gateways can serve as routers.

The path the packet takes from one machine to the next is called a *route*. Although each machine can maintain static routes for specific destinations, the default gateway is usually used to find remote destinations. (The default gateway is needed only for computers that are part of an internetwork.) If you have a gateway connected to several other networks, there will (probably) be route definitions for each of those other networks.

Let's look at this process as though you were sending a letter, as we did earlier in this section. Each letter you send has an envelope that contains a message. On the envelope, you write the source and destination addresses. When you mail the letter, it goes to the post office and the person sorting the mail checks the destination zip code. If it's the same as the local zip code, the envelope is sent to a carrier for deliver. If the zip code is different, it is sent to some other location. Perhaps all nonlocal mail is sent to the same place.

If you live across the country from me, the letter probably doesn't go directly from my local post office to yours (assuming I don't live in San Francisco and you don't live in New York). The same applies to IP packets. My letter first goes to my local post office; if it is destined for a local address, it is processed there. If not, it is sent along to a larger post office. If I sent a letter from Santa Cruz, California, destined for Annsville, Pennsylvania, it will probably go first to San Francisco and then to New York (or Philadelphia) before it is sent to Annsville.

Again, the same applies to IP packets. If I were communicating with a network on the other side of the country, my machine needs to know how to get to the other one. This is the concept of a gateway. A gateway is the first step in the path, or "route," to the remote machine. Just as there are a couple of post offices between Santa Cruz and Annsville, there can be multiple gateways between computers.

Because San Francisco is the closest "major" city to Santa Cruz, it is possible that all mail bound for points beyond must first go through there. What if I lived in Fresno, which is about halfway between San Francisco and Los Angeles? If I sent a letter to Annsville, it could go through Los Angeles or it could go through San Francisco. To make things easy, it might always be sent through San Francisco if it's not destined for a local address. What if the letter is bound for Los Angeles? It seems silly to go through San Francisco first when it is bound for Los Angeles. At the post office in Fresno, they might have a special procedure that says all remote mail goes through San Francisco, except for those with a zip code in a special range.

Here, too, the same applies to IP addresses. One machine may be defined as the "default" gateway, but if an IP packet was bound for a particular network, it could be told to use a completely different gateway. Which gateway to use to get to a particular machine or network is the concept of "routes." (This we see in Figure 9.4.) If I want all remotely bound packets to use a particular route, I add that route as a default to my machine. If packets bound for a particular network are to go via a different route, I can add that route as well.

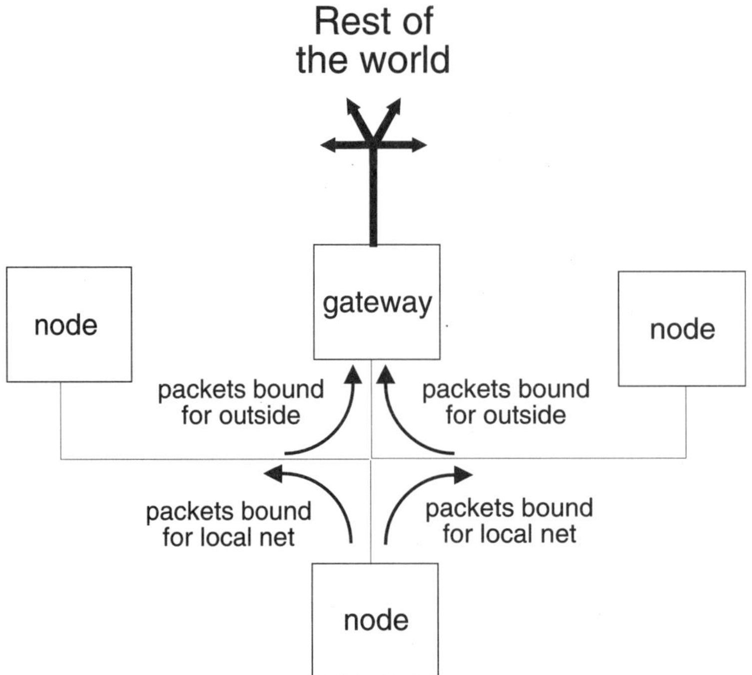

Figure 9.4: Network Gateway

When IP prepares to send a "message," it inserts the local (source) and destination address IP addresses in the IP header. It then checks whether the network ID of the destination and source match (the zip codes). If so, the packet is sent directly to the destination because it is on the local network. If the network IDs don't match, the routing table is examined for static routes. If none are found, the packet is forwarded to the default gateway.

The default gateway is a computer connected to the local subnet and other networks that has knowledge of the network IDs for other networks and how to reach them. Because the default gateway knows how to reach the other networks, it can forward the packet either to other gateways or directly to that machine if the gateway is on the same network as the destination. This process is routing.

If you only have a single network, there is no reason to have a gateway because each machine is directly connected to every other. It's possible that you only want certain machines within your network to go beyond the local net to the outside. In this case, these machines can have a default (or static) route default, while the others have none. However, users can add routes themselves, using the `route` command.

The `telnetd` daemon is a server that supports the Telnet program. Telnet is a terminal program that allows you to work interactively with remote machines, just as you would with the local machine. When `inetd` receives a incoming `telnet` request, it invokes `telnetd`.

What you then see is no different that if you had logged in locally to that machine (probably). You are presented with a `login:` prompt, you enter your logname and password. If these are correct, you then are given a shell in which you can enter commands, start applications, etc.

The way `telnetd` works is that it allocates a pseudo-terminal device for you. This pseudo-terminal has the same behavior as a "normal" terminal in that you input commands and see the results on your screen. Internally, the pseudo-terminal is broken down into two parts. The master portion is the side that you see. Because your side controls things, your side is the master. The master side accepts input from your Telnet program and passes it to `telnetd` on the remote side. As you might guess, the side that has to listen to the master is the slave. The slave side of the pseudo-terminal serves as `stdin`, `stdout`, and `stderr` for the remote application. What this looks like graphically you see in Figure 9.5.

Similar in functionality to `telnet` is `rlogin`. The server for `rlogin` is `rlogind`, which, like `telnetd`, is started by `inetd`. One primary difference is that, if configured, `rlogind` can provide a connection without the normal login procedures.

The functionality of `rlogind` is very similar to that of `telnetd`. Pseudo-terminals are allocated and the slave portion becomes the

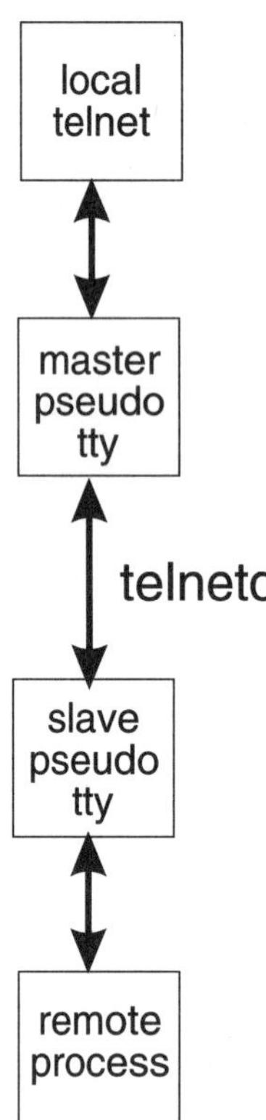

Figure 9.5: Pseudo ttys

stdin, stdout, and stderr. During login, rlogind uses an authentication procedure called host equivalence, which sets up remote machines as being "trusted." If rlogind on the destination machine authenticates the source machine, the user is automatically logged in. If the authentication fails, the user must go through the normal login procedure. I'll get to how to set up host equivalence later.

As I talked about earlier, TCP connections are not the only ones that inetd manages; inetd manages basically all network connections. You can better understand this if I go back to the telephone operator analogy. If the operator (inetd) is also the receptionist, you can then think of TCP connections as incoming telephone calls and UDP packets as incoming letters. Like incoming phone calls, the receptionist is responsible for routing the incoming mail to the right person. (This is a valid analogy because like regular mail, nothing guarantees the delivery of the message in the letter, although with TCP connections, you can ask your partner to resend the message.) Like TCP connections, UDP daemons are "listening" on specific ports. Also like TCP, connections these well-known ports are listed in /etc/services.

One common UDP connection is the routing daemon: routed. The routed daemon supplies (as you might have guessed) route information in the form of routing packets. If your system is serving as a router, routed periodically sends copies of its routing tables to other machines.

One key difference is that inetd does not actually start routed. Instead, routed normally starts through a script under /etc/rc.d as the system is booting. This actually calls the script /etc/sysconfig/network-scripts/ifcfg-routes.

When it starts, routed makes the assumption that it will forward packets between all interfaces on the system. This only includes those packets that are "up" and does not include the loopback driver. (The loopback driver is a special TCP/IP interface that simply loops the packets back to the local machine.) Then, routed transmits a REQUEST packet on each of these interfaces and waits for a RESPONSE packet for any other hosts. Other machines on the network are also potentially sending REQUESTS packets, so routed can also respond to them.

The response routed gives is based on information it has in its *routing tables*, which contains information about known routes, including how far away the destination machine is in terms of *hops*, or intermediary machines. When routed receives a RESPONSE packet, it uses the information contained in that packet to update its own routing tables. Look at the routed man-page for more information.

Routes are added to and removed from the system using the route command. The general syntax for route is

```
route <option> command destination gateway metric
```

The two commands used are add and delete. The destination is the IP address of the machine or network you want to reach. You can also use tokens for the network name by including entries in the /etc/networks file, which is an ASCII file containing two columns. The first column is the name of the network and the second column is the network address. You can then use that name in the route command.

The gateway is the IP address of the interface to which the packets need to be addressed. Keep in mind that the system must already know how to get to the gateway for this to work.

The metric is a value that normally indicates the number of intermediate machines (hops). The system uses this value to determine the shortest route to a particular machine.

For example, let's assume I have an entry in /etc/networks like this:

```
siemau   132.147
```

Let's also assume that the machine I need to use to access this route has an IP address of 199.142.147.1. I could then run the `route` command like this:

```
route add  siemau199.142.147.1 0
```

This says that any packet destined for the `siemau` network (as defined in `/etc/networks`) should go to the IP address 199.142.174.1 with a metric of 0. Normally, 0 is used when the IP address you specifiy is directly connected to your machine.

If you have a single machine that serves as your gateway to the rest of the world, you can specify `default` instead of a specific address or network as your destination. In the previous example, if I wanted to use the same machine for all networks instead of just *siemau*, the command would look like this:

```
route add default 199.142.147.1 0
```

As you move about the network, dynamic entries are created by the routing protocol that you use (`routed` being the most common). The routing protocol communicates with its counterpart on other machines and adds entries to the routing tables automatically.

When it starts, `routed` looks for the file `/etc/gateways`, which contains a list of gateways. The general format for this file is

```
<net|host> name gateway metric type
```

The first field specifies whether the gateway is to a specific machine or network. The name field is the name of the destination host or network, which can either be an IP address or a token. If the field is a token, then the host name must be located in `/etc/hosts` or can be determined through DNS. If it is determined through DNS, routed must start after `named`. If the entry is the name of a network, the name must be in `/etc/networks`.

The `gateway` field is the name or address of the gateway that is to be used. The `metric` is the same as that for routes and indicates the number of hops. The type can be either passive, active, or external. A passive gateway is one that is not expected to exchange routing information. Active gateways will exchange information and usually have `routed` running on them. External gateways are those managed by another system but on which alternate routes should not be installed.

9.1.6 DNS: Finding Other Machines

If you have TCP/IP installed, by default, your machine is set up to use the `/etc/hosts` file, which contains a list of IP addresses and the corresponding name of the machine. When you try to connect to another machine, you can do it with either the IP address or the name. If you use the name, the system will look in the `/etc/hosts` file and make the translation from name to IP address. The only real drawback with this scheme is that every time a machine is added or removed from the network, you have to change the `/etc/hosts` file on all the affected machines.

Those of you who have had to administer large networks know that updating every `/etc/hosts` file like this can be a real pain. There is always at least machine that you forget or you mistype the name or address and have to go back and change it on every machine. Fortunately, there is hope.

Provided with Linux is a hostname/IP address database called the Berkeley Internet Name Domain (BIND) service. Instead of updating every machine in the network, the Domain Name System (DNS) server maintains the database and provides the client machines with information about both addresses and names. If machines are added or removed, only one machine must be changed: the Name Server. (Note: Some documentation translates DNS as Domain Name Server; other references [most importantly, the RCFs] call it the Domain Name System. I have seen some references call it Domain Name Service. Because you know what it is, I'll just call it DNS.)

So, when do you use DNS rather than the `/etc/hosts` file? It's up to you. The first question I would ask is "Are you connecting to the Internet?" If you answer yes, maybe, or someday, definitely set up DNS. DNS functions somewhat like directory assistance from the phone company. If your local directory assistance doesn't have the number, you can contact one in the area in which you are looking. If your name server doesn't have the answer, it will *query* other name servers for that information (assuming you tell it to do so).

If you are never going to go into the Internet, then it is up to you. If you only have two machines in your network, the trouble to set up DNS is not worth it. On the other hand, if you have a dozen or more machines, setting it up makes life easier in the long run.

I must discuss several key concepts before I dive into DNS. The first is DNS, which, like so many other aspects of TCP/IP, is client-server oriented. You have the name server containing the IP addresses and names that serve information to the clients. Next, you need to think about DNS operating in an environment similar to a directory tree. All machines that fall under DNS can be considered as files in this directory tree structure. These machines are often referred to as nodes. Like directories and file names, there is a hierarchy of names within the tree, which is often referred to as the domain name space.

A branch of the DNS tree is referred to as a domain. A domain is simply a collection of computers that are managed by a single organization.

This organization can be a company, university, or even a government agency. The organization has a name that the outside world knows. In conjunction with the domains of the individual organizations are *top-level domains*, which are broken down by the function of the domains under it. The top level domains are

COM: Commercial
EDU: Educational
GOV: Government
NET: Network
MIL: Military
ORG: Nonprofit organizations

Each domain falls within one of these top-level domains. For example, the domain *prenhall* (for Prentice Hall) falls under the commercial top-level domain. It is thus designated as *prenhall.com*. The domain assigned to the White House is *whitehouse.gov*. The domain assigned to the University of California at Santa Cruz is *ucsc.edu*. (Note that the dot is used to separate the individual components in the machine's domain and name.)

Keep in mind that these domains are used primarily within the U.S. While a foreign subsidiary *might* belong to one of these top-level domains, for the most part, the top-level domain within most non-U.S. countries is the country code. For example, the geographical domain "Germany" is indicated by the domain abbreviation de (for Deutschland). I do know some German companies within the *com* domain, however. There are also geographic domains within the U.S., such as *ca.us* for California compared to just *.ca* for Canada. This is often for very small domains or non-organizations, such as individuals. You can see a few example domains in Figure 9.6.

In many places, international companies may use a combination of the upper-level domains used in the U.S. and their own country code. For example, the domain name of an Internet provider in Singapore is *singnet.com.sg*, where *sg* is the country code for Singapore.

Within each domain, there *may* be subdomains. However, there doesn't have to be. You usually find subdomains in larger domains in an effort to break down the administration into smaller units. For example, if your company had a subdomain for sales, it's domain might be *sales.yourdomain.com*.

Keep in mind that these are just the domain names, not the machine, or node name. Within a domain, there can be (in principle) any number of machines. A machine sitting on the desk in the Oval Office might be called *boss1*. Its full name, including domain, would be *boss1.pres.whitehouse.gov*. A machine in your sales department called *darkstar* would then be *darkstar.sales.yourdomain.com*.

Up to now, I have only seen a machine name with five components: the machine name, two subdomains, the company domain, and the top-

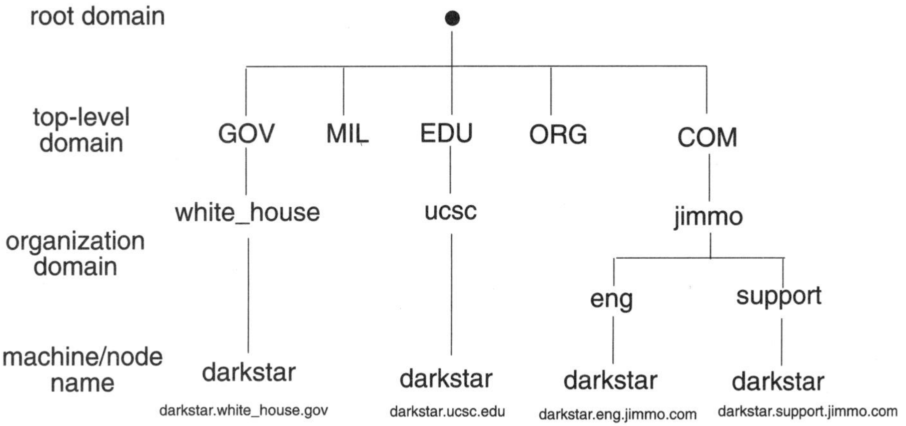

Figure 9.6: Internet Domains

level domain. On the other hand, if there was no sales subdomain and everything was under the *yourdomain.com* domain, the machine's name would be *darkstar.yourdomain.com.*

You may often see the fully qualified domain name (FQDN) of a machine listed like this

darkstar.yourdomain.com.

including the trailing dot(.). That dot indicates the root domain. This has no name other that root domain, or dot (.), which is very similar to the way the root directory has no name other than root or /. In some cases, this dot is optional. In some cases, however, it is required, and I'll get to those in the section on configuring DNS (see Section 9.1.7, Configuring the Domain Name System [DNS]).

As with files, two machines can have the same name. The only criteria for the files is that their full path is unique. The same applies to machines. For example, there might be a machine *darkstar* at the White House. Its FQDN would be *darkstar.whitehouse.gov.* This is obviously not the same machine as *darkstar.yourdomain.com* any more than 1033 Main Street in Santa Cruz is the same as 1033 Main Street in Annsville. Even something like *darkstar.support.yourdomain.com* is different from *darkstar.sales.yourdomain.com.*

A zone is a grouping of machines that may or may not be the same as a domain. This is the set of machines over which a particular name server has authority and maintains the data. In my previous example, there might be a zone for support *even though* there was no subdomain. On the other hand, there might be a *team.support.yourdomain.com* domain, but the zone is still *yourdomain.com.* Therefore, zones can be subordinate or superior to domains. Basically, zones are used to make the job of managing the name server easier. Therefore, what constitutes a zone depends on your specific circumstances.

In DNS, there are a couple different types of servers. A primary server is the master server for one or more DNS zones. Each server maintains the database files and is considered the authority for this zone. It may also periodically transfer data to a secondary server, if one exists for that zone.

DNS functions are carried out by the Internet domain name server, `named`. When it starts, `named` reads its configuration file to determine for which zones it is responsible and in which files the data are stored. By default, the configuration file is in `/etc/named.boot`. However, `named` can be started with the `-b` option to specify an alternate configuration file. Normally, `named` is started from a script in `/etc/rc.d`.

For example, the primary server for the *yourdomain.com* domain needs to know about the machines within the *support.yourdomain.com* domain. It could serve as a secondary server to the *support.yourdomain.com* domain, whereby it would maintain all the records for the machines within that subdomain. If, on the other hand, it serves as a subserver, the primary server for the *yourdomain.com* need only know how to get to the primary server for the *support.yourdomain.com* subdomain. Note that it *is* possible for a server to be primary in one zone and secondary in another.

By moving responsibility to the subzone, the administrator of the parent zone does not need to concern him or herself with changing the configuration files when a machine is added or removed within the subzone. As long as the address of subzone primary server matches the subserver entry, all is well.

A secondary server takes over for the primary, should the primary go down or be otherwise inaccessible. A secondary server maintains copies of the database files and refreshes them at predetermined intervals. If it cannot reach the primary to refresh its files, it will keep trying at predetermined intervals. If, after another predetermined time, the secondary server still cannot reach the primary, the secondary considers its data invalid and flushes it.

Caching-only servers save data in a cache file only until those data expire. The expiration time is based on a field within the data that is received from another server. This is called the time-to-live. Time-to-live is a regularly occurring concept within DNS.

A slave server can be a primary, secondary, or caching-only server. If it cannot satisfy the query locally, it will pass, or forward, the request to a fixed list of forwarders (forwarding server), rather than interacting directly with the primary name servers of other zones. These requests are recursive, which means that the forwarder must answer either with the requested information or a reply that it doesn't know. The requesting machine then asks the next server, and the next and the next, until it finally runs out of servers to check or it receives an answer. Slave servers never attempt to contact servers other than the forwarders.

The concept of recursive request is in contrast to iterative requests. In a recursive request, the queried server either gives an answer or tells the requesting machine where it should look next. For example, *darkstar* asks *iguana*, the primary server for *support.yourdomain.com*, for some information. In a recursive query, *iguana* asks *boomer*, the primary server for *yourdomain.com*, and passes the information back to *darkstar*. In an iterative query, *iguana* tells *darkstar* about *boomer*, and *darkstar* then goes to ask boomer. This process of asking name servers for information, whether recursive or iterative, is called *resolution*.

Keep in mind that client software is running on the server. When an application needs information, the client DNS server asks the server for the information, despite the fact that the server is running on the same machine. Applications don't access the server directly.

There is also the concept of a root server, which are servers located at the top of the domain tree and maintain information about the top-level zone. Root servers are positioned at the top, or root, of the DNS hierarchy, and maintain data about each of the top-level zones.

9.1.7 Configuring the Domain Name System (DNS)

In the first part of the chapter, I discussed DNS as being a means of centrally administering the files necessary for node-name-to-IP-address translation. Although the relationship of the files is pretty straightforward, they are rather intimidating to the uninitiated.

So, what do the DNS configuration files look like? Well, because the first file that named looks at is `/etc/named.boot`, that seems like a good place for me to start. Let's assume you wanted to set up a primary name server. You might have a file that looks like this:

```
;
; Boot file for Primary Master Name Server
;

;
; type     domain              source file or host
;

directory   /etc/named.d
primary     siemau.com              siemau.forward
primary     147.142.199.in-addr.arpa  siemau.rev
primary     0.0.127.in-addr.arpa   named.local
cache       .                 root.cache
```

Lines beginning with a semicolon are considered comments and blank lines are ignored. The first line with configuration information is

```
directory   /etc/named.d
```

This tells named that if no path is specified, it should look for the other configuration files in the specified directory–in this case, `/etc/named.d`. Because the `named.boot` file is read when `named` starts up, you could change it to anything you want.

The first primary line says that you are the primary name server for the domain *siemau.com*. This says that the information to resolve forward requests are found in the file *siemau.forward*. What are forward requests? Well, "forward requests" is my term. I use it for two reasons. First, the file containing the information often ends with `.forward`. Second, I think the primary function of a name server is to translate names to IP addresses. Therefore, this is going forward. Translating IP addresses to names is going in reverse.

Note that you will often see that the forward mapping file is referred to as `named.hosts` or `domain_name.host` and the reverse mapping as `named.rev` or `domain_name.rev`. I like to call one `.forward` and one `.rev` so I know by looking at them what their function is. It doesn't matter what you call them as long as they are pointed to in `named.boot`.

To be the primary server, you must say that you are. This is accomplished through the Start of Authority (SOA) record, which says you are the start of authority for the given domain. That is, when trying to find the answer to a query, the buck stops here. You have all the right answers when it comes to this domain. The SOA record is required and might look like this:

```
siemau.com. IN SOA  siemau.siemau.com. jimmo.siemau.com. (
             8675309 ; Serial
             10800     ; Refresh
             1800      ; Retry
             3600000   ; Expire
             259200 )   ; Minimum
```

The fields in the first line are domain, data class, type of record, primary name server, responsible individual. The data class will always be IN for Internet. Often you will see root or postmaster as the person responsible for this domain. Here, I picked myself. Note that the format is `jimmo.siemau.com` and not `jimmo@siemau.com`, as you might expect.

The Serial number is a way for secondary servers to keep track of the validity of their information. If the secondary has a serial number that is lower than that on the primary, it knows that the information is outdated. It then pulls over an updated copy.

The Refresh is how often (in seconds) the secondary servers should check the primary for updated information. In every implementation I have ever seen, this value is set to 10,800 seconds, or three hours. You can change it if your site requires it.

The Retry is how often (in seconds) the secondary server should retry to contact the primary. This value of 3,600 seconds (one hour) is also something I have seen in almost every case. Again, change it as you need to.

The Expire time is how long the secondary server will try before it gives up and declares the data it has are invalid. This is based on the attitude that no data are better than old data. Here you have 1,000 hours, or almost 42 days.

The Minimum is the value that other resource records should use as their time-to-live, if no other value is defined for them. The time-to-live is how long a given piece of information is considered valid.

At the end of each of these records is a semicolon, which is used in DNS database files as the start of a comment. Any text from the semicolon to the end of the line is considered part of the comment. You will also see that many lines have semicolons as their first character. In these cases, the whole line is a comment.

Note also that there is a dot after each *.com* entry, which indicates the end of the name. Remember that I mentioned that the trailing dot indicates the root domain? In these cases here, this dot is required. If you leave it off, the system will assume that it should tack the domain name onto the end. Therefore, you might end up with the domain name twice. This behavior can actually come in handy and I'll get to it shortly.

The SOA record is just one resource record that you find in DNS database files. I will get through several others during the course of this discussion. Resource records have the following general format:

```
name {ttl} data-class record-type record-specific-data
```

The name is simply something you are looking for. For example, you might have a machine name and want to find the IP address. You have the machine name; this is your value. On the far right is the record-specific-data or the IP address. The TTL value is the time-to-live, which is an optional value because you already defined a minimum in the SOA record. You could have also defined a TTL value for this SOA record if you had wanted. The data-class can be one of several values. However, only the IN for Internet class is commonly used, therefore, that is the only one I'll use here. The record-type tells you what kind of resource record you have. For example, SOA is one record type.

After the SOA record, there is usually an entry saying which machines are name servers, such as

```
siemau.com.IN   NS    siemau.siemau.com.
```

The value you have is *siemau.com.* For this record type, this value is the domain name. The domain is the same for the SOA record because you are defining this machine to be the name server as well. The dataclass, again, is IN for Internet. Because you are defining which machine is the name server, the record type is NS, for name server. Lastly, you get the FQDN of the machine (*siemau.siemau.com.*). Note that in both cases, you have the dot at the end of each name.

One thing that I should point out here is that a good choice for which machine is the name server is one that is on multiple networks; that is, one that serves as gateway. This kind of machine is a good choice because it already has to know about multiple networks to be the gateway. It is said to be *well connected*. This saves managing one machine as the gateway and the other as the name server.

Next, you have the name to address mappings. Let's assume for simplicity's sake that I only have two other machines in my network. The entries for all my machines might look like this:

```
siemau.siemau.de.IN    A    192.168.42.1
vesta.siemau.de. IN    A    192.168.42.2
jmohr.siemau.de. IN    A    192.168.42.3
```

The general format is

```
machine-namedata-type record-type   IP-address
```

Note that despite the fact that *siemau* is our name server, we still need to include it here, otherwise there would be no way to translate its name to an address. The new piece of information here is the A record-type. This simply says that this specific record is making the translation from machine name to IP address. Each entry is an address record, or address resource record. Note again the trailing dot (.).

You also need a mapping for the node "localhost," a special name for the local machine that is accessed using a special driver called the "loopback driver." Rather than accessing the card, the loopback driver knows that this is the local machine and that it does not need to go out to the network card. Certain functions on the system take advantage of the capabilities of this driver.

```
localhost              IN    A      127.0.0.1
```

One thing I need to point out is the dot (.) at the end of each FQDN. This dot says that the name stops here. Remember that the dot is also used to indicate the root domain. By putting the dot here, this says that you have reached the root domain, so it won't go any further.

You can omit the dot by mistake or intentionally. In these examples, it would be a mistake. In fact, in the time I was doing tech support, omitting the dot was (perhaps) the most common mistake made when users configured the name server. However, you can intentionally omit it in certain circumstances and it will still be correct. You can use abbreviations (shorten forms) to indicate the machine name. For example, you could have written the first entry like this:

```
siemau    IN    A    192.168.42.1
```

Because you already defined what the domain name is in the `named.boot` file, the system knows what to append. Therefore, you can try to contact either *siemau* or *siemau.siemau.de* and the name server will translate that correctly to 192.168.42.1.

You now need to make the translation from IP address to name. As I mentioned earlier, there are "reverse" translations. The data for these translations is in the file `siemau.rev`, as indicated by the line from `named.boot`:

```
primary     42.168.192.in-addr.arpa  siemau.rev
```

In general, the format of the entry is similar to that of the forward entries. For my three examples, the format would look like this:

```
1.42.168.192.in-addr.arpa.IN    PTR    siemau.siemau.de.
2.42.168.192.in-addr.arpa.IN    PTR    vesta.siemau.de.
3.42.168.192.in-addr.arpa.IN    PTR    jmohr.siemau.de.
```

There are a couple of new things here. First, is the record type. Here you have PTR for pointer records, which point to the machine name. The next is the `in-addr.arpa` after the IP address. To understand, I need to take a step back.

Assume you wanted to make the translation from machine name to IP address and you had no idea where that machine was. As I mentioned earlier, name servers for all of the top-level domains are aware of the name servers for all of the domains under it. For the *.com* domain, one such machine is *kava.nisc.sri.com*. So, if you had wanted to find the machine *vesta.siemau.de*, you could ask the name server that was responsible for the *.com* domain (*kava.nisc.sri.com*). Because *kava* knows about the *siemau* domain and knows that *siemau.siemau.de* is the name server for that domain, it tells you to go ask *siemau* yourself.

Now, let's go the other way. Is the domain with the first octet of the IP address 199 a *.com*, *.edu*, or *.gov* domain? How can you tell? The answer is that there is no way to tell. IP addresses are not arranged by the type of organization. You can guess that the network 199 is probably a class C network (because it is more than 192), but it can just as easily be *.com*, *.edu*, or anything else. So, rather than trying to find the name server for every single domain and asking "Are you the right one?" a quicker way had to be developed.

The solution was to create a portion of the Internet name space that used the addresses as a name. This portion is considered to be a separate domain and is referred to as the *in-addr.arpa* domain. The names of both machines and subdomains within the *in-addr.arpa* domain are simply the IP addresses. There are 256 subdomains of the *in-addr.arpa* domain, 256 subdomains of each of those domains, and so on.

If you look, the "names" listed in the *in-addr.arpa* domain have the IP address reversed from the way you are accustomed to seeing it. This is keeping with the idea that in the names, the more specific names are on the left and become more general as you move to the right. It also makes things easier to manage because you can say that the 42.168.192.*in-addr.arpa* domain is administered by one organization (because 192.168.42 is a separate class C network).

Note also that a dot is at the end of the reverse address. Here, too, this tells the name server where the end is. Because you already said what the *in-addr.arpa* domain was in the `named.boot` file, you can make a shortcut by listing only the host portion, just as you did with the FQDN. The entry for siemau would then look like this:

```
1 IN  PTR  siemau.siemau.de.
```

Note that here you have the dot at the end of the FQDN, though it wasn't at the end of the IP address in the address (A) record. This is because the dot comes at the end of a domain name. In *in-addr.arpa* notation, the IP address is part of a name–it just happens to look like an IP address, albeit a reversed one. Think of it this way: A period comes at the end of a sentence, which is a set of words. If you have a set of numbers, there is no period.

If you had a class B network, you could also make use of these abbreviations. For example, if *siemau* had an address of 159.144.147.1, its pointer (PTR) record could have been written like this:

```
1.147     IN    PTR    siemau.siemau.de.
```

This reminds me of the second most common error–using the abbreviations for the reverse address, but not reversing them! That is, using the preceding example, writing it as

```
147.1     IN    PTR     siemau.siemau.de.
```

Don't do that! A reverse domain has the IP address portion of the name reversed as well, no matter what part you include.

By writing the IP address reversed like this, you essentially create a new domain. The root domain is still dot (.), however, this time there is just the single top-level domain *in-addr.arpa*. This notation is often referred to as the *reverse domain*. Because you define a new domain in the `siemau.rev` file, you need a new Start of Authority record. You could copy the SOA record from the `siemau.forward` file, but the domain is wrong. The domain is now 147.144.199.*in-addr.arpa*. So, all you need to do is replace the old domain name with the new one and the entry would be identical. The first line would then look like this:

```
147.144.199.in-addr.arpa. IN SOA siemau.siemau.de jimmo.siemau.de (
```

You can now duplicate the remainder of the SOA record from the `siemau.rev` file. One thing I do to help keep things straight is to think of the NS record as part of the SOA record. In reality, they are separate records. If you think of them together, however, you won't forget and omit the NS record. Because you define a new domain, you also need the NS record for this new domain. Its NS record would look like this:

```
147.144.199.in-addr.arpa.IN NS   siemau.siemau.de.
```

However, I don't like the idea of two SOA records. There is the chance that I might update the database files but forget to update one of the SOA records with the new serial number. To eliminate that problem, you can give the name server a directive to include another file while it's reading the information. This is the $INCLUDE directive. To include a single SOA record, create a file, perhaps `siemau.soa`, and use the $INCLUDE directive in both the `siemau.forward` and `siemau.rev` files. The line would look like this:

```
$INCLUDE siemau.soa
```

Because you already defined the directory in the `named.boot` file, there is no need for a path here. However, you have a problem. The SOA record in `siemau.forward` is for a different domain (*siemau.com*) than in `siemau.rev` # (147.144.199.*in-addr.arpa*). You can take advantage of a magic character: @, which will be read as the domain name, provided the domain name is same as the origin (the origin is the machine that this data is on).

Let's create a single SOA file (i.e., `siemau.soa`) and make it identical to others with the exception of the domain name. Instead, replace it with @. Next, remove the SOA records from the `siemau.forward` and `siemau.rev` file and replace it with the $INCLUDE directive. When the name server reads the `siemau.forward` file, it gets to the $INCLUDE directive and sees that it needs to include the `siemau.soa` file. When it gets to @, the system translates it as `siemau.de`. Next, when the system reads the `siemau.rev` file, it sees the same directive and includes the same file, however, this time @ is interpreted as 147.144.199.*in-addr.arpa*.

I still haven't covered two lines in the `named.boot` file. The first sets up this server as primary for the "local" domain, a special domain that refers to this host only. Remember from our discussion of IP addresses (see Section 9.1.3, IP Addressing) that the IP address for the local host is 127.0.0.1. The "network" that this host is on is 127.0.0. You always need to be the primary name server for this domain, and there is the line in `named.boot`:

```
primary     0.0.127.in-addr.arpa       named.local
```

The `named.local` file could contain just two lines:

```
$INCLUDE named.soa 1      IN    PTR  localhost.
```

Note that here, too, you include the `named.soa` file. When the system reads `named.local`, it includes `named.soa` and @ is translated to 0.0.127.*in-addr.arpa* as it should.

The last line tells you to read the cache file:

```
cache        .                          root.cache
```

The `root.cache` file is the list of the root domain name servers. You can obtain the most current list of root name servers using anonymous ftp from the *machine ftp.rs.internic.net*. The file is `domain/named.root`.

Let's assume I want *vesta* to be the secondary name server for this domain. I would then create a `named.boot` file on *vesta* that might look like this:

```
directory   /etc/named.d
secondary   siemau.de  192.168.42.1  siemau.forward
secondary   42.168.192.in-addr.arpa   192.168.42.1 siemau.rev
primary     0.0.127.in-addr.arpa      named.local
cache       .                         root.cache
```

If you look carefully, you see that the only difference is that for the forward and reverse files, I changed "primary" to "secondary." Note that *vesta* is still the primary for the domain 0.0.127.*in-addr.arpa* (the local domain). The contents of the files are theoretically the same. This is where the concept of the serial number comes in. When the secondary server loads its file, it compares the serial number to what it reads from the primary server. Note also that the IP address, 192.168.42.1, is the address of the *primary* server; in this case, this is the machine *siemau*.

If you want a caching-only server, the `named.boot` file is a little simpler:

```
directory     /etc/named.d
primary       0.0.127.in-addr.arpa    named.local
cache         .                       root.cache
```

You still specify the directory and the `root.cache` file, but now you are the primary for just a single machine, yourself.

In any of the example `named.boot` files, you could have included a line that simply said:

```
slave
```

That would be a name server, regardless of what of type, that forwards all requests that it cannot satisfy to a list of predetermined forwarders. If this server does not have the answer, it will not interact with any other server, except for those listed as forwarders. Therefore, any time you have a slave server, you must also have a list of forwarders. The entry for the forwarders might look like this:

```
forwarders   199.145.146.1 199.145.148.1
```

The last kind of server is called a client. Its configuration is the simplest. Create a file called `/etc/resolv.conf` and include a line defining the domain, then a list of the name servers, or resolvers, because they resolve your queries. If I had *siemau* as the primary server for this domain and *vesta* as the secondary, my file might look like this:

```
domain siemau.de
nameserver 199.144.147.1
nameserver 199.144.147.2
```

Note that if this file doesn't exist, your system will expect to get its information from the `/etc/hosts` file. Therefore, you can say that on the client side, if `/etc/resolv.conf` doesn't exist, you are not using DNS.

If you have a larger network with many different departments, you might have already decided to have multiple name servers. As I mentioned earlier, it is a good idea to have your name server also be the gateway because they are well-connected. This also applies to the gateway you have to the Internet. To make life simpler for both you, trying to reach the outside world, and the people trying to get in, it is a good idea to have the Internet gateway as also the primary name server for your entire domain.

If your organization is large, then having the Internet gateway a name server for your entire organization would be difficult to manage. Because you already decided to break down your network by department, each department should have its own name server. One thing you could do is set up the domain name server as a secondary server for the subdomains. This is easy to set up (as I described earlier) and saves you from having to maintain a list of every machine within your organization.

I still haven't mentioned several record types, one of which is machine aliasing. For example, you might have a machine that acts as your ftp server, your mail server, and your World Wide Web server. Rather than requiring everyone accessing this machine to know that *vesta.siemau.de* is the server for all three of these functions, you can create an alias to make things easier with the CNAME (canonical name) record. Example entries would look like this:

```
ftp      IN    CNAME    vesta
mailserv IN    CNAME    vesta
www      IN    CNAME    vesta
```

Any reference to these three machines is translated to mean the machine *vesta*. Keep in mind that if you use such an alias, this should be the only reference in your name server database. You should not have PTR record that points from an IP address to one of these aliases; instead, use its canonical (real) name, *vesta*.

You can also use the name server database to store information about the machine itself. This is done through the HINFO (host information) resource record. I could have the entry for my machine, *siemau*, that looks like this:

```
siemau   IN    A   192.168.42.14
         IN  HINFO     Pentium  Linux
```

The record-specific data on the right is composed of two strings: The first is the hardware and the second is the operating system. The strings may contain spaces or tabs, but you need to include them within quotes or the system will see them as separate strings. Technically, these two strings should be "machine name" and "system name" and match one of the strings in RFC 1340, but this requirement is not enforced. There is also the problem that many newer machines won't be on the list.

One thing that seems to be missing is the machine name from the HINFO record. Well, this is another shortcut. By leaving the name field out of any record, it defaults to the same value as the previous entry. Here, the previous entry is the A record for *siemau*. Therefore, the name field of the HINFO record is also *siemau*.

You can also use the name server to manage certain aspects of your users. For example, you can have mail systems (such as MMDF) read the name server information to determine on what machine a particular user receives his or her mail. This is done with the MB (mailbox) resource record. An example might look like this:

```
jimmo    IN    MB    siemau.siemau.de.
```

In this domain, mail for the user `jimmo` should be sent to the machine *siemau.siemau.de*. Note that this only works if you have unique users within the domain. In addition, there must only be one MB record for each user.

You can make things easier by specifying a single machine, such as the mail server, with an MX (mail exchanger) resource record. The MX record can also be expanded to include subdomains. For example, the name server for the *siemau.de* domain has MX records for all the subdomains under it. The resource-specific information contains the presence, which is a numerical value used to determined the order in which mail is sent to different machines. The preference should be 0 unless you have multiple mail servers within the domain.

Let's assume that this is a large company and you have given each department its own domain (regardless of whether they have different IP subnets). You then decide that mail sent to anyone in a subdomain goes to the mail server for that subdomain but that any mail to the parent domain goes to a different server. Some entries might look like this:

```
siemau.de.                IN  MX  0  siemau.siemau.de.
finance.siemau.de.        IN  MX  0  cash.finance.siemau.de.
sales.siemau.de.          IN  MX  0  buyer.sales.siemau.de.
                          IN  MX  1  cash.finance.siemau.de.
market.siemau.de.         IN  MX  0  editdmon.market.siemau.de.
images.market.siemau.de.  IN  MX  0  images.market.siemau.de.
```

In this example, mail sent to a user in the domain *siemau.de* will go to *siemau.siemau.de*. Mail sent to either of the other three domains (*finance*, *sales*, and *market*) will be sent to a machine in that respective domain. Note that two MX records are listed for the *sales.siemau.de* domain: one has a preference of 0 and the other a preference of 1. Because the preference for *buyer.sales.siemau.de* (0) is lower than for *cash.finance.siemau.de* (1), the mail program will first try *buyer*. If *buyer* can't be reached, the mail program will try *cash*. Keep in mind that the numbers only mean the order in which to check. You could have given one a preference of 45 and the other a preference of 66, and they would still have been checked in the same order.

Let's assume that you feel mail to the sales department is so important that you want the program to try still another machine before it gives up. You could have a third MX record for *sales.siemau.de* that looks like this:

```
IN      MX  2   siemau.siemau.de.
```

In this case, the program will check *buyer* and, if the mail message cannot be delivered, will check *cash*. If *cash* cannot be reached, *siemau* is checked. If you changed the preference of *siemau* to 1, like the preference for *cash*, one of them will be chosen at random. You can use this if you want to spread the load across multiple machines.

I haven't discussed a few other resource records types. They are not as commonly used as the others, so I will forgo talking about them. If you would like to learn more, check the book *DNS and BIND* by Paul Albitz and Cricket Liu from O'Reilly and Associates.

As I mentioned earlier, you can use the $INCLUDE directive to include a file containing the SOA record. However, you can also use the $INCLUDE directive to include any file. This is very useful if your files have grown to unmanageable sizes and you need to break them apart. Assume your network contains 200 machines. There are A, PTR, and possibly MX records for each machine. You could create three separate files for each of these. (Normally, A and PTR are in separate files already.) You could then use the $INCLUDE directive to include the MX records in one of the other files.

9.1.8 Debugging the Name Server

Sorry, but you're going to have to do it: debug the name server. Unless you are a flawless typist and have every step written down exactly, one day you are going to forget something. As a result, the name server won't function the way you expect. I would hope that it's something simple (like forgetting a dot) and that you can quickly make the change.

The problem is what to do after you've made the change. Remember, `named` reads the configuration information when it starts. To get `named` to reread the configuration file, you could stop and restart TCP. However, this would not be taken too kindly by the users, whose connection would suddenly drop. The solution is to poke `named` in the ribs and tell it go reread the files, which is done by sending the `named` process a hang-up signal with "`kill -1 <pid>`," where `<pid>` is the PID of `named`. To find the PID, either `grep` through `ps -e` or look in `/etc/named.pid`. This also has the side effect of having secondary name servers check the serial numbers, which can be used to force updates.

If you want to have `named` dump its current database and cache, you can send `named` a interrupt signal (SIGINT, `kill -2`), which dumps the database into `/usr/tmp/named_dump.db`. Sending `named` SIGUSR1 (`kill -16`) you can turn on debugging, the output of which is sent to `/usr/tmp/named.run`. Subsequent SIGUSR1 signals sent to `named` will increase the debugging a level. Sending it SIGUSR2 (`kill -17`) turns off debugging completely.

You can also get `named` to trace all incoming queries, which is sent to `/usr/adm/syslog`, by sending SIGWINCH (`kill -20`). Be careful with this, however. Even on smaller networks, the amount of information logged in `syslog` can be fairly substantial. If you forget to turn it off, you can fill up your root file system. To turn of tracing, send SIGWINCH again. Note that you can enable all of these options from the start-up script in `/etc/rc2.d`.

Perhaps the most useful debugging tool is `nslookup` (name server lookup). The `nslookup` command can be used either interactively or non-interactively to obtain information from different servers. Depending on how it's set, you can input an IP address and get a name back or input the name and get the IP address back. If you are using the name server as either a server or a client, you can use `nslookup` to gather information.

To start it interactively, simply type `nslookup` at the command line. You are then brought into the `nslookup` shell, where you can issue commands and set the options needed to get the information you need. Using "set all," you can view the current options. By default, `nslookup` will return the IP address of the input machine name (a forward query). For example, if I ran `nslookup` on *vesta*, `nslookup` would respond with something like this:

```
Default Server:  siemau.siemau.de
Address:  192.168.42.1

>
```

This tells me what the default server is and shows that it is ready for the first command by displaying the > prompt.

Let's say I wanted to see the information the name server when I run `nslookup` on *siemau*. I type in *jmohr* and press `Enter`, which gives me

```
> siemau
Server:  localhost
Address:  127.0.0.1

Name:    siemau.siemau.de
Address:  192.168.42.1
```

As you can see, this is what I expected. Note that in the first case, the default server was *siemau*. However, when I run it on the name server itself, the server is "localhost."

One question that comes to my mind is does nslookup translate the IP address back to the host name correctly? Let's see. When I type in the IP address, I get

```
>  192.168.42.3

Server:  localhost
Address:  127.0.0.1

Name:    vesta.siemau.de
Address:  192.168.42.3
```

I can list all the available information for a domain with the ls command. The general syntax is

```
ls [ option ] domain
```

where domain is the name of the domain about which I would like the information. If I want, I can redirect the output to a file, using either type of output redirection (> or >>). If I want to see it on the screen, I get

```
>set all
Default Server:  localhost
Address:  127.0.0.1


Set options:
 nodebug         defname      search          recurse
 nod2            novc       noignoretc      port=53
 querytype=A      class=IN        timeout=5        retry=4
 root=ns.internic.net.
 domain=siemau.de
 srchlist=siemau.de
```

If you want to see everything there is about a domain, use the ls command. Keep in mind that by itself the system will think it is a machine name and try to resolve it. However, followed by the domain name, you get

```
> ls siemau.de
[localhost]
  siemau.de  server = siemau.siemau.de
  siemau     192.168.42.1
  jmohr      192.168.42.2
  localhost  127.0.0.1
  vesta      192.168.42.3
```

However, this does not tell you anything about the mail exchanger or canonical names that you may have defined. To get everything, use the -d option, like this:

```
> ls -d siemau.de
[localhost]
siemau.de.  SOA  siemau.siemau.de jimmo.siemau.de.
(60001 1080 0 1800 3600000 86400)
  siemau.de.   NS       siemau.siemau.de
  siemau.de.   MX   0   vesta.siemau.de
  jimmo        MB       siemau.siemau.de
  siemau       A        192.168.42.1
  jmohr        A        192.168.42.2
  siemau       HINFO    Pentium Linux
  localhost    A        127.0.0.1
  www          CNAME    vesta.siemau.de
  mailserv     CNAME    vesta.siemau.de
  ftp          CNAME    vesta.siemau.de
  vesta        A        192.168.42.3
```

As you can see, this gives me everything I can thing about, including mail boxes, HINFO lines, canonical names, the SOA records, and all of the address records. Note that only one MB record is here. In reality, I probably would have had MB records for all the users on this system. If this network had been even a little larger, this output would probably be too much to view. Therefore, you can use other options to limit what you see. For example, the `-t` option is used to specify a type of query. If you wanted to look for all the mail exchangers, you could use the command `ls -t MX siemau.de`, which gives you

```
siemau.de.                        0    vesta.siemau.de
```

giving you the domain, the preference of the mail-exchanger, and the name of the mail exchanger, which is all the information in the MX record.

You can also tell `nslookup` that you want to look for particular kind of record. Say I want to look for the MX record for a particular machine. I could set the query type to MX and look for that machine, like this:

```
> set type=MX
> siemau.siemau.de
Server:  localhost
Address:  127.0.0.1


siemau.siemau.de preference = 0, mail exchanger = vesta.siemau.de
siemau.siemau.de  Internet address = 192.168.42.3
```

This says that the mail exchanger for *siemau* is *vesta*. Is that right? What `nslookup` is actually telling me is that *vesta.siemau.de* is the mail exchanger for *siemau.siemau.de*. Why? Because I didn't put the dot at the end of the domain name. Like other aspects of the name server, `nslookup` tacked the domain name onto the end of *siemau.siemau.de* to give me *siemau.siemau.de*. If I just use a machine name, the domain name is tacked on as well, but it comes out differently:

```
> siemau
Server:  localhost
Address:  127.0.0.1

siemau.siemau.de preference = 0, mail exchanger = siemau.siemau.de
siemau.siemau.de Internet address = 192.168.42.1
```

The `nslookup` program also has a configuration file, the `.nslookuprc` file in your home directory, which can come in handy. Like the `.exrc` file for `vi`, the `.nslookuprc` is read every time you start `nslookup`. The format is also like `.exrc`, with one entry per line. Assuming I wanted to set the query time to PTR records and set the time out to five seconds, I could have these two lines in my `.nslookuprc` file, like this:

```
set querytype=ptr
set timeout=5
```

This would be the same as starting `nslookup` from the command line, like this:

```
nslookup -query=ptr -timeout=5
```

Setting parameters is not all you can do from the command line. In fact, almost anything you can do from inside of `nslookup` you can also do from the command. I could expand the above command to give me

```
nslookup -query=ptr -timeout=5 192.168.42.3
Server:  localhost
Address:  127.0.0.1

Name:    vesta.siemau.de
Address:  192.168.42.3
```

So what is this all good for? The most important thing is tracking down problems you might experience. For example, if a particular machine cannot be reached, `nslookup` might show you that there is no A record for that machine. Perhaps mail to a particular machine never ends up where it should. Checking the MX record for that machine would indicate that it goes to a completely different machine than you thought.

Unfortunately, I cannot list every problem that could arise and what `nslookup` would show. However, with the understanding of how DNS and `nslookup` work that you've gained in the last couple of sections, the best way to proceed is to look at what `nslookup` tells you. Based on the way you think DNS is configured, is what `nslookup` records correct? This may sound like an oversimplification, but isn't that what problem solving really is? Knowing what should happen and what would cause it to happen differently?

9.1.9 Your Own IP Address

If you have a network that is completely disconnected from the rest of the world, then there is no need for you to adhere to any of these conventions. You might be a commercial organization but still want to use the EDU domain. Nothing prevents you. There is also nothing preventing you from using IP addresses that are used by some other organization. However, once you decide to connect to another organization or the Internet at large, you need to ensure that both your names and IP addresses are unique.

To ensure that you use a unique name and network, the best thing is to contact the Network Information Center, or NIC. Via e-mail, you can contact them at *hostmaster@nic.ddn.mil*. The telephone is 1-800-365-3642 or 1-703-802-4535. By regular mail, use

DDN Network Information Center
14200 Park Meadow Drive, Suite 200
Chantilly, VA 22021

If you are not in the United States, the NIC can still provide you with a contact in your area. In addition, many ISPs will be able to register your domain for you.

If you would like to have one machine that connects to the Internet but have other machines that cannot, one solution is to use one of the IP addresses defined in RFC 1918. This RFC describes the need for "private" addresses and lists a range of class A, B, and C addresses that can be used internally within a company.

Some routers will filter out this address automatically, others require that they be so configured. This allows you to not only limit access to and from the Internet, but also limits the need for unique addresses. If you only have a handful of machines that need Internet access, some Internet providers will subnet a class C address and assign you a small block of addresses. See the RFC for more details.

In many cases, your Internet service provider (ISP) can apply for an IP address for you. Also, the ISP could provide you with a single IP address that is actually part of their network. Internally, you then use a private network as defined in RFC 1918. In other cases, when you have a dial-up connection to your ISP, you may have a dynamically assigned address, so it isn't always the same.

Table 9.3: Network Commands

File	Function
`/bin/netstat`	Shows network status
`/bin/hostname`	Delivers name of current host
`/bin/ping`	Sends ICMP ECHO_REQUEST packets to network hosts
`/etc/dig`	Sends domain name query packets to name servers
`/etc/ftpaccess`	Indicates FTP access configuration file
`/etc/ftphosts`	Indicates FTP individual host access file
`/etc/ftpusers`	Lists users automatically denied FTP access
`/etc/gated`	Indicates gateway routing daemon
`/etc/hosts`	Lists hosts on network
`/etc/hosts.equiv`	Lists trusted hosts
`/etc/http/conf/*`	Indicates HTTP configuration files
`/etc/inetd.conf`	Indicates `inetd` configuration file
`/etc/named.boot`	Indicates name server configuration file
`/etc/netconfig`	Configures networking products
`/etc/networks`	Lists known networks
`/etc/protocols`	Lists Internet protocols
`/etc/services`	Lists network services provided
`/etc/tcpd`	Accesses `control` daemon for Internet services
`/sbin/bin/arp`	Delivers ARP information
`/sbin/ifconfig`	Configures network interface parameters
`/usr/bin/finger`	Finds information about users
`/usr/bin/ftp`	Indicates network file transfer program
`/usr/bin/logger`	Makes entries in the system log
`/usr/bin/nslookup`	Queries name servers interactively
`/usr/bin/rdate`	Notifies time server that date has changed
`/usr/bin/rdist`	Indicates remote file distribution program
`/usr/bin/rlogin`	Indicates remote login program
`/usr/bin/route`	Manually manipulates routing tables
`/usr/bin/rwho`	Lists who is logged in on the local network
`/usr/bin/talk`	Talks to another user
`/usr/bin/telnet`	Indicates Telnet remote login program

File	Function
/usr/sbin/ftpshut	Shuts down ftp services
/usr/sbin/httpd	Indicates HTTP daemon
/usr/sbin/inetd	Indicates Internet "superserver"
/usr/sbin/routed	Indicates network routing daemon
/usr/sbin/in.ftpd	Indicates FTP daemon
/usr/sbin/in.rlogind	Indicates remote login (`rlogin`) daemon
/usr/sbin/in.rshd	Indicates remote shell (`rsh`) daemon
/usr/sbin/in.telnetq	Indicates Telnet daemon
/usr/sbin/in.tftpd	Indicates trivial ftp (TFTP) daemon
/usr/sbin/in.fingerd	Indicates `finger` daemon
/usr/sbin/traceroute	Traces packet routes to remote machines

9.2 NFS

The network file system (NFS) is an industry standard means of being able to share entire file systems among machines within a computer network. As with the other aspects of networking, the machines providing the service (in this case, the file system) are the servers. The machines utilizing the service are the clients. Files residing physically on the server appear as though they are local to the client, enabling file sharing without the hassle of copying the files and worrying about which one is the more current.

One difference that NFS file systems have over "conventional" file systems is that it is possible to allow access to a *portion* of a file system, rather than the entire one.

The term *exporting* is used to describe how NFS makes local directories available to remote systems. These directories are then *exported*. Therefore, an exported directory is a directory that has been made available for remote access. Sometimes the term *importing* is referred to the process of remotely mounting file systems, although *mounting* is more commonly used. We see Figure 9.7 in what this might look like graphically.

You can mount a remote file system in a couple of ways. The first is automatically mounting it when the system boots up by adding an entry into `/etc/fstab`. You could also add a line in some rc script that does a `mount` command.

If the remote mount is a one-time deal, the system administrator can also mount it manually. Potentially, the administrator could create an entry in `/etc/fstab` that does not mount the file system at boot time,

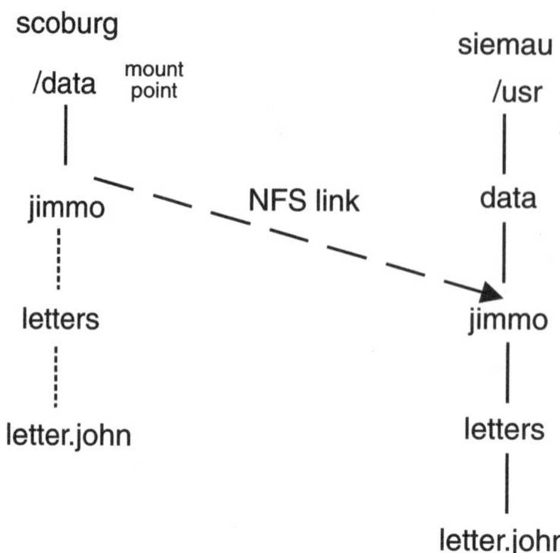

Figure 9.7: An NFS mount

but rather is mounted later. In either event, the system administrator would use the `mount` command. If necessary, the system administrator can also allow users to mount remote file systems.

A client machine can also be configured to mount remote file systems on an as-needed basis, rather than whenever the system boots up through the mechanism of the Automount program. I'll get into a lot of details about how Automount works later on (see Section 9.2.3, Automount).

The syntax for using the `mount` command to mount remote file systems is basically the same as for local file systems. The difference in the syntax is that you specify the remote host along with the exported path. For example, if I want to mount the man-pages from *jmohr*, I could do it like this:

```
mount -t nfs [-o options] jmohr:/usr/man /usr/man
```

Here I told the `mount` command that I was mounting a file system of type NFS and that the file system was on the machine *jmohr* under the name `/usr/man`. I then told it to mount it onto the local `/usr/man` directory. There are a couple of things to note here. First, I don't have to mount the file system on the same place from which is was exported. I could have just as easily exported it to `/usr/doc` or `/usr/local/man`. If I want, I can include other options like "normal file systems," such as read-only.

If you are a server, the primary configuration file is `/etc/exports`, which is a simple ASCII file to which you can make additions or changes with any text editor. This is a list of the directories that the server makes available for mounting along with who can mount them and what permissions they have. In addition, the server needs a way to find the client's address, therefore mount will fail if the name cannot be resolved either by DNS or /etc/hosts. Likewise, the client depends on name resolution to access the server.

The /etc/exports file has one line for each directory you want to export. The left side is the *full path* of the directory you want to export and the right side are the options you want to apply. For example, you can limit access to the directory to just one machine or make the directory read-only. On *junior*, the exports might look like this:

```
/pub             *
/                jmohr(rw)
/usr/jmohr_root jmohr(rw)
```

The first line in this example says that I am exporting the /pub directory to the entire world. Because there are no options, this means that the file system is also writable. I wouldn't normally do this if I were connected to the Internet, even if there wasn't anything sensitive here. It is a matter of practice that I know exactly what access I am giving to the world.

The next line says that I am exporting the entire root file system to the machine *jmohr*. Because this is a development environment, I have different versions and distributions of Linux on different machines. I often need to have access to different files to compare and contrast them. Here, the file system is also writable because I explicitly said rw.

The last line takes a little explaining. When I mount the root file system from *jmohr*, I mount it onto /usr/jmohr_root, which is the name of the directory that I am exporting here. This demonstrates the fact that I can export a file system to one machine and then re-exported it.

Keep in mind, however, that you cannot increase the permission during the re-export. That is, if the file system was originally made read-only, you could not make it writable when you re-export it. However, if it was writable, I could *export* it as read-only.

A solution that many systems provide is amd, which is an automatic mounting facility for NFS file systems. Once configured, any command or program that accesses a file or directory on the remote machine within the exported directory forces the mounting to occur. The exported directory remains mounted until it is no longer needed.

If you can access a file system under Linux, you can access it under NFS (including DOS file systems) because the access to the file is a multistep process. When you first access a file (say, open a text file to edit it), the local system first determines that this is an NFS-mounted file system. NFS on the local system then goes to NFS on the remote system to get the file. On the remote system, NFS tries to read the file that is physically on the disk. At this point, it needs to go through the file system drivers.

Therefore, if the file system is supported on the remote system, NFS should have no problem accessing it. Once a file system has been exported, the client sees the file system as an NFS file system and therefore what type it is *really* irrelevant.

There are a couple of limitations with NFS. First, though you might be able to see the device nodes on a remote machine, you cannot access the remote devices. Think back to the discussion on the kernel. The device node is a file that is opened by a device driver to gain access to the physical device. It has a major and minor number that points and passes flags to the device driver. If you open a device node on a remote system, the major and minor numbers for that device node point to drivers in the *local* kernel.

Remotely mounted file systems present a unique set of problems when you're dealing with user access rights. Because it can have adverse effects on your system, it is necessary to have both user and group IDs unique across the entire network. If you don't, access to files and directories can be limited, or you may end up giving someone access to a file who shouldn't have access. Although you could create each user on every system or copy the `passwd` files, the most effect method is using the Network Information Service (NIS).

9.2.1 The Flow of Things

Two daemon processes provide the NFS services on the server: `mountd` and `nfsd`. The first daemon, `mountd`, is responsible for checking access permissions to the exported file system. When a client tries to mount a file system, `mountd` returns a pointer to the file system if the client has permission to mount it.

The workhorse on the server side is the `nfsd` daemon, which has the responsibility of handling all file system requests from the clients. Once a file system has been mounted, all access to the data on that remote file system is made through `nfsd`. Remember that you could export directories and not just entire file systems. Therefore, it's better to say that access to the *mount point* and below is made through `nfsd`.

Also key to this whole process is the portmapper, `portmap`. The portmapper converts TCP/IP port numbers to RPC program numbers, which means that when the NFS starts up, it registers its port with the local portmap process. The clients access the server by asking the portmapper on the server for the port number of `nfsd` and `mountd`. The port number is then used on all subsequent RPC calls.

In principle, mounting a remote file system is like mounting a local one. The general syntax is

```
mount <options> <file system> <mountpoint>
```

One primary difference is that because you are an NFS file system, you have to explicitly tell this to `mount`, using the `-t nfs` option. You can also include other options such as `-r`, for read-only. Let's assume that you I have my two machines *jmohr* and *siemau*. On *siemau* is an NFS file system that I want to mount from *jmohr*. Assuming that the proper entries exist in the `/etc/exports` file on *siemau*, the command on *jmohr* might look like this:

```
mount -t nfs junior:/usr/data /data
```

Like other file systems, the local mount command parses the command into tokens and ensure that entries don't already exist in the mount table (`/etc/mnttab`) for either the file system or the directory. Realizing that this is a remote file system, `mount` gets the IP address for *siemau* (by whatever means are configured on the local machine) and gets the port number of `mountd` on *siemau*. The `mount` command then passes `mountd` the pathname of the requested directory (`/usr/data`).

Now it's the server's turn. To ensure that it can service the request, `mountd` must first check `/etc/exports` for the requested file system. In this case, it is `/usr/data`. If *jmohr* is permitted, `mountd` passes back what is called a file handle, or pointer. Now the `mount` back on *jmohr* uses that file handle and the mount point (`/data`) as arguments for the `mount()` system call. Finally, an entry is placed in the local mount table.

There are two primary NFS configuration files: `/etc/exports` and `/etc/fstab`. The `/etc/exports` file exists on the server and lists those files and directories that can accessed by remote hosts. It can also be configured to allow or deny access to specific hosts. Because these are file systems, you can manage anything mounted by NFS through `/etc/fstab`, allowing you to mount remote file systems at boot or in any way you can with a "normal" file system. One advantage NFS has over local file systems is that you can configure them to be mounted only when you need them. That is, if the files in the directories are not used, the connection is not made. However, if the files are needed, the connection is automatically made. This is the concept of automounting, which I will get into next.

9.2.2 When Things Go Wrong

You can use a couple of tools to specifically check NFS connections. Because NFS relies on the same mechanism as other programs that use TCP/IP, solving NFS problems start with understanding the tools used for TCP/IP. Rather than repeating myself, I will point you to the section on configuring TCP/IP and the various HOWTOs (see Section 9.1. TCP/IP).

If you want see all the programs using RPC on a specific machine, I would run it as

```
rpcinfo -p <hostname>
```

which might give me something like this:

```
program   vers   proto   port
100000    2      tcp     111    portmapper
100000    2      udp     111    portmapper
100068    2      udp     1027   cmsd
100068    3      udp     1027   cmsd
100068    4      udp     1027   cmsd
100068    5      udp     1027   cmsd
100083    1      tcp     1028   ttdbserver
100005    1      udp     692    mountd
100005    1      tcp     694    mountd
100003    2      udp     2049   nfs
100003    2      tcp     2049   nfs
```

The columns are

```
Program-numberversion-number protocol port program
```

The program number is the RPC number of that program. You can see what RPC number equates to what program number by looking in `/etc/rpc`. Here you see that all the NFS-related daemons are running. If you look carefully, you see that for each program (except `walld` and `rusersd`), there is a copy of the program using both UDP and TCP. If you find that one or more of these is not running, then stopping and restarting NFS might work. Otherwise, rebooting should correct the problem. Note that `portmapper`, `mountd`, `nfs`, and `status` are required.

If you want to check whether a particular program is running on the server, you can also do this with `rpcinfo`. The general syntax for this command is

```
rpcinfo -u <server_name> <program_name>
```

For example, if I wanted to check to see if `lockd` was running on *jmohr*, I would *not* run it as

```
rpcinfo -u jmohr nfsd
```

If I did, I would end up with the message

```
rpcinfo: nfsd is unknown service
```

because the name of the service in RPC's eye is `nfs`. Therefore, the correct syntax would be

```
rpcinfo -u jmohr nfs
```

which should give you the response

```
program 100003 version 2 ready and waiting
```

If you don't see this, run `rpcinfo -p` to find out what programs are registered.

If you want to find out which file systems are being mounted or can be mounted, you can use `showmount`. On the server, `showmount -a` will show you which file systems have been mounted and by whom. This will be in the form `host:file system`. If you want to find out what file systems are being exported and their permissions, use `showmount -e`. On *jmohr*, I get this

```
export list for jmohr.siemau.de:
/usr/man (everyone)
/usr/lib (everyone)
/u1      access=siemau
/u2      (everyone)
```

Each file system listed is accessible from every other system, with the exception of `/u1`, which is only accessible from *siemau*. This is essentially what is contained in `/etc/exports`.

If a client simply stops responding, it may be because the server is down and you have configured a hard mount. If so, the client may wait indefinitely for the server to come back up. Once it does, the processes can continue as before. If the mount is soft, you will (should) get an error after the number of retries specified (five, by default). You can find more tools in Table 9.4 on page 411.

9.2.3 Automount

To be able to mount a remote file system using Automount, you would first need to be able to mount it using normal NFS. That is, there are no flags that you can set on the remote side (where the file system is being exported) that says either to explicitly allow or deny access via Automount. The remote file system simply makes a resource available and you access it with whatever tool you see fit. Therefore, for the purpose of this discussion, I am simply going to assume that in each case, the remote host has given us permission to access that file system. For more details, see Section 9.2, NFS Configuration.

The amd program provides you with the ability to mount NFS file systems only when you need them, automatically. They are automatically mounted by Automount, hence the name. Actually, conventional NFS-mounted file systems can also be mounted automatically in the sense that you can configure them in /etc/fstab so they are automatically mounted as the system boots. Automount file systems, on the other hand, are mounted when a user tries to access files or directories under the mount point. Also, if the files or directories are not accessed within a specific time (five minutes, by default), they are unmounted, thereby saving network resources. When booting, you also save time because the system is waiting to connect to a remote machine that possibly could be down.

Keep in mind that the server side is oblivious to the fact that the request is coming from Automount. As far as it knows, it is just your normal every day NFS mount, therefore automounter can be used with systems that don't know about it.

The basic configuration unit with the automounter is one or more files called "maps." These files map the file systems you want to access to the directory where you want to mount them (the mount points). These map files are fairly easy to configure and can be edited with any text editor. All Automount connections are based on references in map file.

The amd program is command-line based, so you can specify the name of the map file directly. An example map file would look like this:

```
/defaultsopts:=rw;type=nfs
jmohr_homerhost:=jmohr;rfs:=/home
```

The first line specifies default parameters that are used during the mount. In this case, say that the file system should be read-write and of type nfs. The next line specify the directories to be mounted. The syntax for these lines is

```
directory rhost:=<remote_host>;rfs:=<remote_file system>
```

where directory is the name of the directory on the local machine where the file system should be mounted, <remote_host> is the name of the machine from which you are mounting the file system, and <remote_file system> is the name of the remote file system.

To start amd, the general syntax is

```
/usr/sbin/amd -a <temp_dir> -- /<real_dir> <map_file>
```

Here, <temp_dir> is the name of a temporary directory where the remote file systems are actually mounted. This directory is created by amd and should be removed if you start amd automatically through the rc scripts. A common convention is to define this directory as /amd. The two dash (--) is a common construct that tells amd that there are no more options to process. The /<real_dir> indicates the directory where the users will see the file systems mounted. Finally, <map_file> is the name of the map file where amd should get its configuration information.

To run amd using the example configuration file, I might start it like this:

```
/usr/sbin/amd -a /amd -- /usr/jmohr/homes /etc/amd.junior
```

Here I mount the remote file systems under /amd and the users see them under /usr/jmohr/homes. So, if my home directory on *junior* was /usr/jmohr/homes/jimmo, every time I log into *junior*, amd kicks in and mounts the /home directory from *jmohr*.

Don't think of Automount as your only means of mounting NFS file systems just because of its advantages. If you are constantly accessing certain file systems, you gain nothing by making them automounted. In fact, you might lose something because each time the connection is made, you need to wait. If the system is mounted in the conventional manner, you only need to wait once. If you have file systems that are accessed regularly but others that are accessed only on occasion, simply mount some at boot and the rest via Automount.

A common use of Automount is with NIS. NIS is used to distribute configuration files from the NIS server across the Internet to the NIS clients. Why not include the Automount maps in the set of files that is being distributed? This could be useful if you wanted to have all the documentation on a single machine to save space and access to the documentation is made through Automount. Because documentation is not being constantly accessed, this saves the problem of having the file system containing the doc be continually mounted.

Another use is when you want each user to have the same home directory no matter where they are, something similar to what I had in the previous example. If the system is mounted by Automount and distributed via NIS, every time your remote users logged in, no matter on what machine, they would have the same home directory. Granted, there is the problem of not being able to access their home directory if the server is down. However, that problem still applies when logging into a single machine.

In reality, Automount behaves very similarly to traditional NFS mounts. The system knows that the specified directory is an NFS mount point. When something is accessed on the other side of the mount point, the automount daemon reacts to the request basically the same way nfsd does with a normal NFS file system. The automount daemon then checks the mount table (`/etc/mnttab`) to see if the file system is already mounted and mounts it if it isn't. Once the file system is mounted, requests are handled normally.

Like other file systems, an entry is maintained in the system mount table (`/etc/mnttab`) for all file systems that have been mounted with Automount. When the timeout has expired (five minutes by default), Automount removes the entry from `/etc/mnttab` but still maintains a copy in its memory. This copy is updated whenever it mounts or unmounts a file system.

The version of `amd` that I installed with Caldera OpenLinux has some really nifty features. (These features may be available in other releases–I just didn't test them.) The most exciting feature for me required me to reconsider why `amd` was there.

I had always used `amd` (as well as the automounter of other UNIXs) to automatically mount file systems from other machines (that is, mounting them via NFS). On the surface, one thinks of UNIX system administrators as being lazy. They spend all day trying to get out of work. That is, they develop programs that save them work. Nevermind that the work they save is much less than the work in which they invested in trying to save that work.

This is not a bad thing, for two reasons. First, the mentality of most UNIX administrators is that this really isn't an attempt to get out work. There should be a better way of doing something, so they set out to find it. Just like the great inventors and explorers of the past, they try it because "it's there."

The reason that this is not a bad thing is because, like other kinds of inventions, the results are there for others. Once the program exists, other administrators can use it. In keeping with the Linux mentality, you create a program that *you* want to write, share it with others, and they share theirs with you. You now have an entire toolbox of utilities that didn't exist a year ago.

So, what does this have to do with `amd`? Well, how often have you wanted to access a floppy, CD-ROM, or DOS partition on your machine? First, you need to find the device that it's on, then find a place to mount it, and then finally you get around to mounting it. Wouldn't it be nice if you could access these file systems without having to go through all of this? You *can*!

That's the nice thing about `amd`. You can use it to mount all sorts of file systems, including those on floppies, CD-ROMS, and DOS partitions. In fact, that's what I did. I have a handful of applications that do not run under Wabi, so I am forced to switch to Windows 95 when I want to run them. Therefore, I cannot make my entire system Linux. Often, I need to transfer data from one system to other, which means finding the device that it's on, then finding a place to mount it, and then finally getting around to mounting it. What a waste of time!

I noticed that amd was running on my system, using the configuration file /etc/amd.localdev. Seeing that I thought, "localdev? Local devices? Hmmm...." Checking this file, I discovered that you can, in fact, mount local file system via amd. So, let's take a look at the file that had on my system:

```
# /etc/amd.localdev: automounter map for local devices

# Don't forget to unmount floppies with "amq -u /auto/floppy" before
# ejecting them, especially when they are mounted read-write !!!

/defaults  opts:=nodev,nosuid,ro;dev:=/dev/${key};type:=msdos;

# floppy      -dev:=/dev/fd0;type:=msdos opts:=rw opts:=ro
floppy        dev:=/dev/fd0;type:=msdos;

# floppy95    -dev:=/dev/fd0;type:=vfat; opts:=rw opts:=ro
floppy95      dev:=/dev/fd0;type:=vfat;

cdrom         type:=iso9660

c_drive       dev:=/dev/sda1;type:=vfat; opts=rw
d_drive       dev:=/dev/sda5;type:=vfat; opts=rw
e_drive       dev:=/dev/sdb1;type:=vfat; opts=rw
f_drive       dev:=/dev/sdb5;type:=vfat; opts=rw
g_drive       dev:=/dev/sdb6;type:=vfat; opts=rw
h_drive       dev:=/dev/sdb7;type:=vfat; opts=rw
*             dev:=/dev/${key}
```

In principle the options are the similar to those fstab and exports. I leave it to you to check the amd(8) man-page for the details.

The thing I want to first point out is the line

```
*              dev:=/dev/${key}
```

As you might guess from the asterisk, this is a wild card that represents every file system that I have not specified previously. The options used on those are in the /default line. The nifty part of this is the ${key} part of the device name, which is translated to mean the name of the subdirectory under /auto. For example, my c: drive is /dev/sda1. If I did cd /auto/sda1, amd would see the name of the subdirectory as *sda1*, then it would look for a matching device. Because it finds one, it can mount that device. Therefore, if you have mountable file system, you do *not* need to explicitly define them.

In this file are two lines for floppies (floppy and floppy95). The type of file system in the first line is MSDOS and this second is VFAT, which allows you to mount a floppy and still have access to the long filenames. The next line is one for CDROM. These were the lines that were originally in my `amd.localdev` file.

When you start `amd`, tell it the name of where it should mount these file systems. By default, on my system, this is the directory `/auto`. So, when I do `cd /auto/cdrom`, CDROM is automatically mounted and I find myself in the root directory of `cdrom` without going through the hassle of mounting it first.

Once I discovered this, I added the lines that look like this:

```
c_drive         dev:=/dev/sda1;type:=vfat; opts=rw
```

As you might guess, this automatically mounts my DOS file systems. I originally had them all in `/etc/fstab` so they would automatically mount at boot up. Because I only use them occasionally, this didn't make sense. I changed the entries so that they weren't mounted automatically, and all I had to do was run mount `/dev/sda1` (or whatever) and they were mounted.

Note in this case that the file system type is actually VFAT, and not the standard DOS FAT file system. Now, when I do `cd /auto/c_drive`, I find myself on the c: drive of my Windows 95 system (`/dev/sda1`). When I do `cd /auto/g_drive`, I am then on the g: drive.

Being a normal Linux system administrator, this was too much for me. Not that the work was too much–I had too many entries that were basically the same. In essence, the default behavior that I wanted was that I would `cd` into a directory under `/auto` and I would be on one of my Windows 95 drives. Therefore, I could change the `/default` line to look like this:

```
/defaults  opts:=nodev,nosuid;dev:=/dev/${key};type:=vfat;
```

Note that I not only changed the file system type to VFAT, but I also removed the options to say that this was a read-only file system (`ro`). Now when I do `cd /auto/sda1`, I am on the c: drive, or, when I do `cd /auto/sdb6`, I am on the g: drive.

Hmmm. How do I know that `/dev/sdb6` is the g: drive? Trying to figure that out each time is as much work as mounting it, manually. (Well, not quite.) To save me some work, I simply created a handful on links in `/dev` that look like this:

```
lrwxrwxrwx   1 root   root   4 Jan 26 10:46 /dev/c_drive -> sda1
lrwxrwxrwx   1 root   root   4 Jan 26 10:46 /dev/d_drive -> sda5
lrwxrwxrwx   1 root   root   4 Jan 26 10:46 /dev/e_drive -> sdb1
lrwxrwxrwx   1 root   root   4 Jan 26 10:46 /dev/f_drive -> sdb5
lrwxrwxrwx   1 root   root   4 Jan 26 10:46 /dev/g_drive -> sdb6
lrwxrwxrwx   1 root   root   4 Jan 26 10:46 /dev/h_drive -> sdb7
```


Now, I all need to do is `cd /auto/g_drive` and I end up on the right drive.

You might ask what advantage this has over traditional mounts via `/etc/fstab`. When you're dealing with NFS mounts across the network, there is the issue of bandwidth and the problems that occur when the server side goes down. Because you are accessing a local drive, there are no issues of bandwidth and, if the server goes down, the client goes with it.

Well, that last part is the point. If I only need to access the file system for a short time, it is safer to unmount when I am done. By using `amd`, I don't need to worry about forgetting it. After a specific period of time (default: 5 minutes), the system will unmount any unused file systems.

Table 9.4: Key NFS Files

File	Function
`/etc/amd.local`	Automount configuration file for local devices
`/etc/exports`	NFS files systems being exported
`/usr/sbin/rpc.portmap`	Portmapper; converts DARPA ports to RPC program number
`/usr/sbin/rpc.mountd`	NFS mount request server
`/usr/sbin/rpc.nfsd`	NFS daemon to handle client requests
`/usr/sbin/amd`	Automount program
`/usr/sbin/rpc.rusersd`	Network user name server
`/usr/sbin/rpc.rwalld`	Network wall server
`/usr/bin/rpcinfo`	Reports RPC information
`/usr/bin/rusers`	Reports information on network users
`/usr/bin/rwall`	Writes to all users on the network
`/usr/bin/showmount`	Shows information on remotely mounted file systems

9.3 SAMBA

Due to the incredibly large number of Microsoft applications, it is almost expected that a server is able to provide some kind of access to the Windows machines. If you have TCP/IP running on your machines, you have connectivity from your Windows machines to a Linux server through Telnet and ftp. However, you do have access to the file and print services provided by an NT server. Or do you?

Windows NT networks use the network protocol Session Message Block, or SMB. This is the same protocol that Microsoft has been using for years with their LAN Manager product. Therefore, anything that can access a LAN Manager server will be able to access an NT server.

Recently, Linux has been able to support SMBs through the SAMBA package. This not only means that a Linux machine can provide file and print service to Windows machines, but they can also provide the same services to a Linux machine.

Because Linux and Windows have a different understanding of security and approach it in a different way, you have to be careful in what you make available. However, in keeping with the UNIX tradition of configurability, you have a wide range of choices on how to configure your system. There are many different options to define your security as well as what you make available and how.

SAMBA has both a server and a client component and, as you might expect, the client side is fairly straightforward. Fortunately, to get the server side working, you don't have to do too much. On the other hand, there *are* a lot of options that you can use to configure the system to fit your needs.

SAMBA uses five primary files. The SMB daemon is `smbd`, which is the SMB server. This provides the services. The client side is the program `smbclient`. This allows you to access Windows machines from your Linux workstations and servers. The `nmbd` program is the NetBIOS name server daemon. Table 9.5 has a list of the key SAMBA files.

SAMBA's configuration file is `smb.conf`, which you should find in the `/etc` directory. This file has a format similar to Windows INI files in that it is broken up into sections. Each section has a particular function. For example, the section that describe the printer configuration would start like this:

```
[Printers]
```

Like the Windows `ini` files, `smb.conf` is line based, with one option per line. In general, the configuration options have the format:

```
option = value
```

Finally, there is the `testpararm` program, which is used to test the SAMBA configuration.

The first section of smb.conf sets up the global configuration and is called [global]. The default looks something like this:

```
[global]
  printing = bsd
  printcap name = /etc/printcap
  load printers = yes
; Uncomment this if you want a guest account
; guest account = pcguest
  log file = /var/log/samba-log.%m
  lock directory = /var/lock/samba
  share modes = yes
```

The printing option determines how the printer status information is interpreted. The default is bsd, which is most commonly used. For information on the others, see the smbd man-page.

The printcap name option defines the name of the printcap file. In this example, I am using the standard printcap file. If you use a different printing option, the printcap file could be different.

The load printers option determines whether or not all the printers listed in printcap are loaded for browsing.

The guest account is used for enabling access somewhat anonymously. By default, this is disabled, as in this example. To enable it, uncomment the lines by removing the semicolons. I'll get to the actual effects of this account later.

The log file option defines to what file to write diagnostic messages and other information. Note that there is %m at the end of the file. This variable is the NetBIOS name of the client machine. This can be used in other places as well. In this case, there will be one log file for each client.

The lock directory options define the directory where lock files are put. The share modes option is used to enable/disable the "share modes" when files are opened. This allows clients to get exclusive read or write of files. Because this is something not directly supported by Linux, smbd uses locks in the lock directory.

There are primarily two types of services that you access via SMB: file and print services. File services are directories that have been made available. Normally, all subdirectories under the exported or *shared* directory are accessible. Let's assume that you want to make the user's home directory available. To do this, you *share* them. The section might look like this:

```
[home_dirs]
   comment = Home Directories
   path=/home
   read only = no
```

Here the section name is [home_dirs], but you specify the path of /home. So when you are on Windows machine (e.g., Windows 95), you would see this directory as homes (because that is the share name). In this example, I specified the directory as not being read-only, which would be the same as specifying the directory as writable. (Note that the section [homes] is a special section, which I will get to shortly.)

We can also define access for specific users. For example, if I wanted to give each user access to his or her own home directory and no other, I could create shares for each directory. So, the share for jimmo's home directory might be

```
[jimmo]
   comment = Jimmo's Home Directories
   path=/home/jimmo
   valid users = jimmo
   writable  = yes
```

Here I added the valid users option, which, as you might expect, indicates which users can have access to this directory. Because the only user specified is jimmo, only I can access this directory. Note that if I were to add the option browseable = no and use the Windows browser (not the same as a Web browser), I would not be able to see the share, even though I could explicitly connect to it. If it were browseable but not on the list of valid users, I could see it but would then be asked for your password. Because I was not in the list of valid users, no password I entered would work (at least this is the behavior from Windows 95).

Setting up a printer is the same basic process. You define a resource that you share and specify what access is permitted. An example might look like this:

```
[deskjet]   comment = Deskjet on Junior
   path = /tmp
   printer = lp
   public = no
   writable = no   printable = yes
```

Here the path is not the path to the resource, but rather a world-writable directory that has the sticky-bit set. This is the spool directory and allows you to write to it, but no one can remove your files. In this example, I just used /tmp. However, you could create a special directory for this purpose, for example, /var/spool/public. You could also specify a list of valid users for this printer.

The [homes] section is used to connect to users' home directories on-the-fly without having to create individual shares as I previously suggested. When you try to connect to a service with the same name as a user, smbd will do one of two things. If there really is a service of that name, smbd will connect to it. If there is no such service, smbd will treat it as a user name and look for that user's home directory in the passwd file. Next, smbd will create a "virtual" share by making an internal copy of the [homes] section but using the user's name as the share name. An example [homes] section might look like this:

```
[homes]
   comment = Home Directories
   browseable = no
   read only = no
   create mode = 0750
```

Note that no path is specified in this example. This is because the path for the share is the home directory specified in /etc/passwd. However, you could have specified a path and although the name of the share would be that of the user, the path would be whatever you specified.

You could still specify the path using the %S variable, which is the name of the current service, which, in this case, is the name of the current user. This could be done like this:

```
path=/data/pcusers/%S
```

This might be useful if you give the users one home directory when they access from a PC and another when they directly login to the Linux machine.

The [printers] section behaves similarly to the [homes] section. If you try to connect to a service, smbd will first look for a service with the specific name. If it finds one, that's what it will connect to. If there is none, it will look through the printcap file. If there is a matching printer name in the printcap file, this is the one that will get used. Otherwise, an error is returned. An example, [printers] might look like this:

```
[printers]
  path = /var/spool/public
  writable = no
  public = yes
  printable = yes
```

Note that this service is defined as not writable. However, it is defined as being printable. This is necessary for correct operation.

To a limited extent, you can configured you Linux machine as an SMB client using the smbclient program. This program provides a functionality similar to ftp in that you can copy files from one machine to another. The general syntax would be

```
smbclient \\\\server\\service
```

Note that there are twice as many back-slashes as normal. This is because the shell will first try to interpret the slashes, so you have to escape each one with a back-slash. Alternatively, you could enclose the complete service name inside of single quotes, like this:

```
smbclient '\\server\service'
```

At this point, you have configured SAMBA to allow users to connect from a Windows machine or any other machine that understands SMB. The good news is that that's not all. SAMBA has many more configuration options. The bad news is that I don't have space to cover them all. The first place to start looking is the `smbd` and `smb.conf` man-pages. These both go into a lot of detail about how to configure SAMBA.

There are a few configuration options that I would like to address. The first have to do with security. SAMBA allows you to specify access based on both user (as described previously) and host with the `allow hosts` option. Like the `valid user` list, the list of authorized hosts are comma-delimited values; in this case, the IP address or host name. You can globally define access by including the list in the `[global]` section, or you can define it for specific services.

Using the IP address, you could specify entire networks by simply including just the network portion of the IP address. For example

```
hosts allow = 192.168
```

You could also exclude specific addresses. For example

```
hosts allow = 192.168 EXCEPT 192.168.42
```

This allows access from the class B network 192.168 but denies access from any machine on the class C network 192.168.42.

Supplemental to `hosts allow` is `hosts deny`, which, as you might guess, is used to specifically deny access. This has the same syntax as `hosts allow`. Note that access defined here is the first phase. If you deny access to a particular machine, that's it. It can't get any further. However, if you allow access, it can still be restricted at the user level.

You could also use a list of `invalid users` to restrict access. For example, you could define root as an invalid user. This would prevent root from accessing any service, which is helpful if you leave a security hole open. You can also include users that are part of Linux group by preceding the name with @ (at sign). For example, to keep root and members of the `adm` group out, the line might look like this:

```
invalid users = root,@adm
```

Note that you can use the @ construct to include group names any place that you have a list of users.

In some cases, you don't want users to have access to some directories, although you allow them access to their parent. This is first accomplished by setting the permissions on the directory. However, this is not always a valid alternative. For example, you may not want users to have access to the `/dev` directory, but you can't change the permissions. However, you can use the `dont descend` option to prevent them from accessing through SAMBA. This option takes a common separated list. For example

```
dont descend = /proc,/dev
```

The `guest ok` option (and its synonym, `public`) are used to give access to services without requiring a password. Once connected, access will be the same as the guest account. This is a Boolean option with a default of no.

Another useful option, the `config file` option, which appears in the global section, enables you to define a configuration file based on the user or machine that is connecting. Setting the configuration file based on the machine name might look like this:

```
config file = /etc/smb.conf.%m
```

When you connect, `smbd` will look for a matching configuration file. If it finds one, it will *reload* the new one. If there is no match, the original configuration stays in effect. This is useful for defining a configuration for some machines (or users) and not for others.

To make management easier, especially if you have a lot of shares for a lot of different machines, you can have one main configuration file and include the configuration files for specific machines and users by using the include option. By using variable substitution, you can create files based on machine or user name and then include them. For example, to include files based on machine name, the directive might look like this:

```
include /etc/smb.com.%m
```

Also helpful to manage your services is the copy option, which allows you to copy services. This way you can create services with different names but have the same basic configuration options. The syntax is simply

```
copy = service
```

where service is the name of the service that you want to copy.

Two things to note. First, the "original" must appear first in the configuration file. Second, you can change parameters in the copy and they will override anything in the original. This would be useful in creating a kind of template. The template could define the access permissions, but each service would define its own path.

The `guest account` option is used in conjunction with the `guest ok` and defines a user name that will be used during the connection. This user *must* exist in the password file, but it is safest if they don't have a valid login (i.e., have `/bin/false` as their shell).

You can limit access further by defining a service as `guest only`, which means that although a user has a valid password to access a particular service, he or she is limited to whatever the guest account has access to.

If you are working with UNIX and DOS/Windows machines at the same time, you probably have experienced something that is affectionately called file name *mangling*. This results from the fact that UNIX file names can be longer than the standard DOS 8.3 names.

You can configure SAMBA so that it will "mangling" the DOS names for you, so they are accessible by DOS and Windows. (Note that you don't need to do this with Win95 or WinNT.) Depending on what your needs are, you can mangle names in different ways.

One difference between UNIX and DOS file names that always gives me trouble is that DOS doesn't see a difference between upper a lowercase. Therefore, the files `LETTER.TXT` and `letter.txt` are the same in DOS's eye. The `mangled names` option (`yes/no`) is used to turn this functionality on and off. If enabled (`yes`), names are mangled according to the rules you define. Otherwise, they are invisible. (See the `sbm.conf` man-page for details on how names are mangled.)

To mangle the name correctly, you first need to define a `default case` with the default case option, which can either be `upper` or `lower`. Using the `mangle case` option (`yes/no`), you tell `smbd` to mangle the characters that are not the default case.

You can also set the `case sensitive` option (`yes/no`), which controls whether the names are case sensitive. If not (the default), `smbd` must do a name search to access the appropriate file. When you create a new file, the `preserve case` option (`yes/no`) defines how `smbd` will behave. The default is `no`.

The `mangled map` option allows you to define specific changes to files. This is useful when file name mangling is not the best choice. The classic example is Web pages. On UNIX machines, these normally have the extension `.html`. However, this does not fit with the 8.3 convention of DOS file names. Normally, DOS would come up with some weird, mangled name. You can keep the name somewhat normal by using a `mangled map`. For example

```
mangled map = (*.html *.htm)
```

This means that whenever `smbd` files a file with an extension of `.html`, it will automatically convert the extension to `.htm`.

The good and bad news is that that's not it. The `smb.conf` file contains dozens more options, many of which require a very strong imagination to come up with uses. However, this is in keeping with the Linux tradition that you are only limited by your imagination.

Table 9.5: Key SAMBA Files

Command	Function
/usr/sbin/smbd	SMB Daemon
/usr/sbin/nmbd	NetBIOS name server daemon
/usr/bin/smbclient	ftp-like SMB client
/usr/bin/testprns	Check printer name for use with SAMBA
/usr/bin/testparm	Check/test SAMBA configuration files

9.4 Serial Network Protocols

Because Ethernet cards have gotten so inexpensive, it no longer makes too much sense to connect two local machines using serial protocols. However, if you are spanning long distances (particularly at irregular intervals), then serial lines protocols are a good alternative as they can be used across standard telephone lines.

9.4.1 Serial Line Internet Protocol (SLIP)

The first protocol in the TCP family to be developed to run across a serial line was the aptly named Serial Line Internet Protocol (SLIP). One advantage that SLIP provides over PPP is simply its age. Many computers still are running comparatively old systems and some do not understand PPP. As a result, the only way to make a serial line TCP connection is SLIP.

Despite the fact that some machines cannot speak SLIP, I am going to leave the discussion of it for another time and place. PPP is becoming predominant enough that time would be better served learning how to configure it rather than SLIP.

9.4.2 Point-to-Point Protocol (PPP)

The Point-to-Point Protocol (PPP) allows computers to communicate with one another using IP over serial lines. Because of its point-to-point nature, both ends of the connection can be thought of as being equal. Although a machine at one end is a client in the traditional sense and the other is a server, from PPP's point of view, both sides are equal.

Although PPP looks superficially like the Serial Line Internet Protocol (SLIP) in that they both run across serial lines, PPP has many advantages over SLIP. However, one advantage that SLIP has over PPP is simply its age. Because it has been around a lot longer, there are may be more machines that are using SLIP than PPP. Despite this, the advantages that PPP provides makes it the serial protocol of choice for most Internet Service Providers. (As we shall soon see.)

One primary advantage is that PPP supports dynamic IP assignment, which means that every time a machine connects, it gets a new IP address. This is a major advantage for Internet Service Providers who may have fewer IP addresses than customers. For example, they may only have a class C network and therefore only 254 address but have 1,000 customers. Because not all 1,000 are going to login simultaneously, they assign IP addresses dynamically. This is, in my opinion, the reason why PPP will become the de facto standard.

To make the discussion a little easier, I am going to refer to the client machine as the one that does the calling and the server as the one that does the answering. However, just like Ethernet, either end can be client or server. Keep in mind, though, that either machine can be both a client *and* a server.

One problem that I face in this book is that PPP is not initialized in a "standard" way. RedHat and its offshoots, like Linux Pro, use the System V style initialization. Slackware and its offshoots use the BSD style. All this really means is `rc` scripts are different. BSD uses `/etc/rc`, `/etc/rc.local`, etc. System V uses `/etc/rc0.d`, `/etc/rc2.d`, etc.

At this point, I need to assume that you have PPP configured into your kernel. When you run `make config`, you are prompted to add PPP support. Note that the installation may not create enough PPP devices, so you may have to edit the source. PPP can be configured statically into your kernel or you can configure it as a loadable module. If you configure it as a module, you must also configure the kernel to support loadable modules. When prompted to add the PPP support, you then need to indicate that PPP is a loadable module. See Section 6.3.3, Disk Layout, for more details on relinking your kernel.

If you configure your machine as a gateway (that is, between two networks), you have to configure your kernel for IP forwarding. In addition, if you are connecting to the Internet, configuring your kernel to support IP firewalls is also a good idea.

Remember earlier when I talked about the IP address for private networks (see Section 9.1.3, IP Addressing)? If your internal network uses these IP addresses, you will need IP masquerading, which is where the gateway "converts" the internal IP addresses into something that the Internet can deal with. If so, you *must* have the IP firewalling configured in the kernel.

9.4.3 Testing the Configuration

Although I rarely see it, some systems will change the login prompt. They may have the time or even the device node on which you are connecting. Your PPP login script should look for only those parts that are static. Be careful that you check both the prompt asking for your user name and the prompt asking for your password.

It is probably a good idea to try to login once using a terminal program and watch the flow of things. My IPS, for example, gives me a single account for both PPP and interactive shell. If I want to start PPP, I need to start a special program once I have logged in.

To manipulate the routing tables and network device, PPP needs to have root privileges. Therefore, the `/usr/sbin/pppd` program needs to have an owner of root and be `suid`. I have yet to see a system in which the default is not `suid`, but it is something to watch.

PPP is initiated using the `ppp-on` and `ppp-off` scripts, which are usually in `/usr/sbin`. If you allow anyone to use these scripts (that is, initiate a PPP connection), these files should be world-readable and -executable. Otherwise, create a PPP group in `/etc/group` and make the scripts readable and executable by only the owner and group. (Make sure you add the appropriate users to the PPP group.)

Table 9.6: Key PPP files

File	Function
`/usr/sbin/pppd`	PPP binary
`usr/sbin/ppp-on`	Dialer/connection script
`usr/sbin/ppp-on-dialer`	Part 1 of the dialer script (not in PPP 2.1.2)
`usr/sbin/ppp-off`	Actual chat script
`/etc/ppp/options`	Options pppd uses for all connections
`/etc/ppp/options.ttyXX`	Option specific to a connection on this port

Note that I have also seen the scripts (`ppp-on`, etc) in `/etc/ppp/scripts`.

There may be a file, /etc/ppp/options.tpl, which is a template for the options file. This contains an explanation of the different PPP options that you can use. If you have options that are specific to a specific device, you would have a file /etc/ppp/options.ttyXX, where XX is the device number. For example, I have a Stallion EasyIO board with modem-control devices tty0A00-tty0A03. If I had a specific file for the first port, it would look like this: /etc/ppp/options.tty0A00. This is normally the case when you have a PPP server with several incoming PPP lines.

As a client, you can also configure your machine based on the systems you call. If you call several different sites, you can have an option file for each of them. The name would simply be option.site, where site is the name of the remote site. You then use the options file as an argument to pppd.

What options you use depends on a lot of things. If you are a client, talk to the system administrator of the server to find out which options to use. If you are setting up a server, I suggest limiting the options that you try, unless you are sure that they are necessary. Once the connection works, you can start making changes. The PPP HOWTO on the CD-ROM contains an example options file that will work in most cases.

Don't forget to add the appropriate entries for your ISP's name server in your resovle.conf file.

To prevent some evil hacker from masquerading as you, some IPSs will set up an authentication using one of two authentication schemes: Password Authentication Protocol (PAP) and Challenge-Handshake Authentication Protocol (CHAP). If authentication is enabled, the administrator can choose either of these methods (provided the other side also supports it). The authentication is on a per-link basis, so you can enable it for some, disable it for others, and choose the authentication method you want.

Authentication is done on a user-name basis and not a computer-name basis. You provide your name using the name entry in your pppd options file. The entry might look like this

```
name <username>
```

where <username> is your user name at the ISP. If your ISP is using PAP, you would then use the /etc/ppp/pap-secrets file. The format of each entry is

```
client server secret local_IP_addresses
```

The client field is the same as the name entry in your options file. The server is the name of the server for which this entry is valid. If you only have one ISP, you can use an asterisk as a wild card (assuming that you have the same username on each server). The secret field is your password on that server. Because this is written in clean text, you need to make sure that the secrets file is not world-readable. If you have a static IP address, you set the `local_IP_addresses` field to that IP address. However, if you use dynamic IP address, leave this field blank.

The `/etc/ppp/chap-secrets` file has the same syntax as that for PAP. The difference is that CHAP needs to authenticate *both* sides. Therefore, your ISP needs to have an entry in a CHAP-secrets file for you as well.

I would recommend that you test your PPP configuration by first trying to make a manual connection. If you have a communications package such as Minicom, you can use that. Otherwise, you can use `cu` to connect directly to the modem and then dial from there. Now end the communications program without hanging up the modem (`ALT+A+Q` in Minicom), then start the PPP connection on that port. For example, to start it on `/dev/cua0`, the command would be

```
pppd -d -detach /dev/cua0 &
```

(The `-detach` option says not to fork and become a background process.)

Because you are trying to see if the connection works, I recommend that you use the `-d` option here to turn on debugging. Because you will probably want to continue using the same terminal, it's best to put the process in the background (`&`). Note that every exchange the systems make between each other is recorded to your system log file. If you are not careful, you can quickly fill up your disk with PPP debugging information. Therefore, I suggest that you remove the debugging option once you are sure the configuration works.

It may take a minute or two for the negotiation to complete (the lights stop blinking on your modem). You can then check the connection using `ifconfig`, which should give you an output that looks like this:

```
ppp0    Link encap:Point-Point Protocol
        inet addr:192.168.42.10  P-t-P: 192.168.42.10
Mask:255.255.255.0
        UP POINTOPOINT RUNNING  MTU:552  Metric:1
        RX packets:0 errors:0 dropped:0 overruns:0
        TX packets:0 errors:0 dropped:0 overruns:0
```

If you don't see anything, this is the entry for your first PPP interface (`ppp0`). If you don't see any entry, more than likely the connection was not successful. Check your spelling in the configuration files (a *very* common mistake) and the output of the debugging.

You should also be able to see a route to the remote host (and beyond). To do this, issue the command `route -n`. You should see something like

```
Kernel routing table
Destination  Gateway       Genmask          Flags MSS  Window Use Iface
192.168.43.1 *             255.255.255.255  UH    1500 0      1   ppp0
127.0.0.0    *             255.0.0.0        U     3584 0      11  lo
192.168.42.1 *             255.0.0.0        U     1500 0      35  eth0
Default      192.168.42.1 *                 UG    1500 0      5   ppp0
```

Note that there are two entries for `ppp0` here, the first and the last one. In the FLAGS column, you will see that each interface is up (`U`). In the case of the first `ppp0` entry, there is also an `H`, which indicates that this is for the host itself. The last entry has a `G` in the flags column to indicate that it is a gateway.

Notice that in the first column are the respective IP addresses (host or network). For the last `ppp0` entry, this says default. When this system gets an IP packet that it doesn't know what to do with, it will send it through the default Interface. Because in this scenario, the `ppp0` interface is connected to the Internet, this is a logical choice.

At this point, you can test the connection further by trying to connect to a remote site. First try pinging a machine or two at your ISP. Then try to ping something a little more distant. I think it is better to do it this way because it may happen that your ISP has trouble connecting to its provider. If you try something past your ISP but can't reach it, your first thought should be that there is something wrong with *your* system. (Trust me, I know.)

Once you are sure that the connection is working, you can shut down your PPP link by running the `ppp-off` script. If you can't make a connection, run through the configuration files again to make sure that you haven't misspelled anything (one of my favorite mistakes). If you are sure they are all correct, check the PPP HOWTO on the CD-ROM for some trouble-shooting tips.

9.4.4 Automating the Login

Although you could run everything manually every time you wanted to start PPP, Linux is kind enough to allow you to do it automatically. The three primary files are: `ppp-on`, `ppp-off`, and `ppp-on-dialer` (all in `/usr/sbin`). The `ppp-on` script is somewhat of a configuration file and the information is passed to the `ppp-on-dialer` script. The one already on your system (assuming that you have installed PPP) will need to be edited to fit your system.

The script is referred to as a *chat* script and has the same basic function as a chat script in UUCP (if you are familiar with that). It consists of expect-send pairs in which the calling (client) machine "expects" the server to send a particular string. When that string is received, the client sends the other half of the pair.

The last line of the script will look something like this:

```
exec /usr/sbin/pppd debug /dev/ttySx 38400 \
      $LOCAL_IP:$REMOTE_IP \
      connect $DIALER_SCRIPT
```

The three variables (`$LOCAL_IP`, `$REMOTE_IP`, `$DIALER_SCRIPT`) are defined earlier in the `ppp-on` script. By using the `exec` at the front, the `ppp-on` script is "overwritten" with the `/usr/sbin/ppd` program. If you set the local and remote IP address in the options file, you must delete the line `$LOCAL_IP:$REMOTE_IP \` from here. Note that the dialer script is also a variable. A few lines before this, it was set like this:

```
DIALER_SCRIPT=/etc/ppp/ppp-on-dialer
```

This means that you could use a different `ppp-on` script and therefore a different dialer script for each system.

The dialer script (default: `ppp-on-dialer`) is actually a single line. As with many configuration files, a backslash (\) at the end of the line indicates that the line continues. Note that when you look for the login, there are two logins on the line

```
ogin:--ogin:    $ACCOUNT
```

and the word `login` is not complete. This is in case the first part of the word is lost in transmission or that the server uses `Login` instead of `login`. If you don't get the "ogin" within the timeout you specified (default 30 seconds), send a return and wait for "ogin" again.

The default `ppp-on-dailer` file on the CD-ROM should be sufficient to get you connected. If not (for example, you have a different login prompt), take a look at the `chat`(8) man-page.

9.4.5 Starting the Server

If PPP is automatically started on the server end (maybe it's your login shell), this process works fine. However, if you have to explicitly start the PPP server, you can simply add an extra line to your chat script. (Make sure to add a backslash to the line before it to make sure the system knows that the line continues). What you will probably have to look for is the prompt that your server gives. For example, my PPP server is called *jmohr*, which is part of the prompt. Therefore, the last line of my chat script might look like this:

```
jmohr -- jmohr ppp
```

This says to expect the string `cumulus` and, if it does not appear within the timeout, send a return and wait for `cumulus` again. When `cumulus` is received, send `ppp` to start up the PPP server. Note that here I included the entire string `cumulus`. Normally, if you get to this point, the entire string is being received.

Once PPP is running, it looks for the script `/etc/ppp/ip-up` and executes it. You can include any special routing commands here to make your PPP connection the default route (or whatever). One suggestion I have if your PPP connection is to the Internet and you use it for e-mail is that you flush your mail queues once the link is up. This, too, can be added to the IP up script. (See the `sendmail` man-page for more details.)

9.4.6 Setting up a PPP Server

If you are going to be a PPP provider, you will need to set up an options file as well. If you only have one dial-in line, you can use a single options file. However, if you have multiple modems, it is best to create an options file for each serial port. You can then assign a specific IP address to that port. This has the advantage that should someone call in with a problem, you can keep track of the IP address. If the same IP address repeatedly has problems, it may be related to the modem or serial port.

In his PPP HOWTO, Robert Hart suggests including the following entries in the options file:

```
asyncmap 0
proxyarp
lock
crtscts
modem
```

The `asyncmap` entry describes the control characters that cannot be received over the serial line. When such a character is received, it is mapped to a 2-byte escape sequence. In this example, you map the character ASCII 0. The `proxyarp` entry says to set up an proxy ARP entry in the *server's* ARP table. The means that all packets destined for the client are to go through this interface. Note that this only works if you are making a one-to-one connection and not trying to route two LANs through this interface. To specify a UUCP-style lock on the serial port, use the lock option, which ensures exclusive access to the serial port, as with UUCP.

The `crtscts` option specifies hardware flow control. To specify `XON/XOFF`, you could use either the `-crtscts` option or `xonxoff`. The `modem` option may not be fully implemented on your system. This says that the system should use the modem control lines, and therefore implies RTSCTS flow control.

The easiest thing is to not specify any options and test the connection. Using the debugging output and your observations, you should be able to figure out what you need to include.

9.5 Accessing the Web

It was difficult to decide where to put this topic. You can't have access to the Web without networking, however, it loses much of its impact unless you are using a graphical interface like X. Because the Web is a network of machines accessed in a common manner, I figured the networking chapter would be the best place to talk about it. I think this is a good choice because there are character-based programs that do not require X.

So what is the Web? Well, as I just mentioned, it is a network of machines. Not all machines on the Internet are part of the Web, but we can safely say that all machines on the Web are part of the Internet. The Web is the shortened version of World Wide Web, and as its name implies, it connects machines all over the world.

Created in 1989 at the internationally renowned CERN research lab in Switzerland, the Web was originally begun as a means of linking physicists from all over the world. Because it is easy to use and integrate into an existing network, the Web has grown to a community of tens of thousands of sites with millions of users accessing it. With the integration of Web access software, on-line services have opened the Web to millions of people who couldn't have used it before.

The Web really is a vast network of interlinked documents, or resources. These resources may be pure text but can include images, sound, and even videos. The links between resources are made through the use of the concept of *hypertext*. Hypertext is not something new. It has been used for years in on-line help systems, for example, those in MS Windows's programs. Certain words or phrases are presented in a different format (often a different color or maybe underlined). These words or phrases are linked to other resources. When you click them, the resource that is linked is called up. This resource could be the next page, a graphics image, or even video.

Resources are loaded from their source by means of the hypertext transfer protocol, HTTP. In principle, this is very much like ftp in that resources are files that are transferred to the requesting site. It is then up to the requesting application to make use of that resource, such as display an image or play animation. In many cases, files are actually retrieved using ftp instead of HTTP and the application simply saves the file on the local machine.

The application used to access the Web is called a Web browser. Web resources are provided by Web servers. A Web server is simply a machine running the HTTP daemon, `httpd`. Like other network daemons, `httpd` receives requests from a Web client (such as Mosaic) and sends it the requested resource.

Like the ftp daemon, `httpd` is a secure means of allowing anonymous access to your system. You can define a root directory that, like ftp, prevents users from going "above" the defined root directory. Access to files or directories can be defined on a machine basis and you can even provide password control over files.

When `httpd` starts, it reads its configuration files and begins listening for requests from a document viewer (one that uses the HTTP protocol). When a document is requested, `httpd` checks for the file relative to the `DocumentRoot` (defined in `srm.conf`).

Web pages are written in the hypertext Markup Language (HTML), a "plain-text" file that can edited by any editor, such as `vi`. Recently, as a result of the increasing popularity of the Web, several commercially available HTML editors have become available. The HTML commands are similar, and also simpler, that those used by troff. In addition to formatting commands, built-in commands tell the Web browser to go out and retrieve a document. You can also create links to specific locations (labels) within that document. Access to the document is by means of a Uniform Resource Locator (URL).

Several types of URLs perform different functions. Several different programs can be used to access these resources, such as ftp, http, gopher, or even Telnet. If you omit the program name, the Web browser assumes that it refers to a file on your local system; however, just like ftp or Telnet, you can specifically make references to the local machine. I encourage using absolute names like that as it makes transferring Web pages that much easier.

All that you need to access the Web is an Internet connection. If you can do ftp and Telnet, then you can probably use the Web. So, assuming you have a Web browser and an Internet connection, the question is, where do you go? The question is comparable to "Given a unlimited-value plane ticket, where do you go on vacation?" The sky is the limit.

As I mentioned, the convention is that the Web server's machine name is *www.domain.name*. To access its home page, the URL would be *http://www.domain.name*. For example, to get to your home page, the URL is *http://www.yourdomain.com*. To keep from typing so much, I will simply refer to the `domain.name` and you can expand it out the rest of the way.

In some cases where the convention is not followed, I'll give you the missing information.

I remember when comet Schumaker-Levy 9 was making history by plowing into the backside of Jupiter. The Jet Propulsion Laboratory has a Web site on which they regularly updated the images of Jupiter. I still remember my friends asking me if I had seen the "latest" images. If they were more than three hours old, I would shrug them off as ancient history.

If you are interested in *free* software (did I say the magic word?), check out *www.cdrom.com*. You can download gigabytes worth of games, utilities, GIFs, ray-traces, source code, and full-text copies of *Alice in Wonderland*. Most of these are available from sites spread out over the Internet. It's really nice to have them all it one place. The machine *www.cdrom.com* is the Web server for Walnut Creek CD-ROM. Although you could spend weeks downloading their archives, you don't need to–the CD-ROMs they offer are very reasonably priced. Use the Web site or you can even ftp to *ftp.cdrom.com* to get access to many of the CD-ROMs that they offer. I liked and found some of those so useful that I subscribed, which saves me about $10 per CD-ROM, and I get quarterly updates of many of them.

Another place that contains similar information is InfoMagic. Their offering is similar to Walnut Creek CD-ROM, but InfoMagic provides a few that Walnut Creek doesn't. One thing they do provide is a six CD package called the Linux Developers Resource, which contains several Linux versions, archive, tools and a lot more. They can be reached at *www.informagic.com*.

One CD-ROM that I found very useful was the Internet Info CD-ROM, which contains a wealth of information about the Internet, including standards that are applicable to the Internet, like IEEE and RFCs. There are also Frequently Asked Questions (FAQ) from some of the Usenet newsgroups.

The issue of Usenet *newsgroups* opens up a whole new can of worms. Without oversimplifying too much, I could say that Usenet was the first nationwide on-line bulletin board. Whereas the more commercial services like CompuServe store their messages in a central location, Usenet is based on the "store and forward" principle. That is, messages are stored on a message and forwarded to the next at regular intervals. If those intervals are not all that often, it may be hours or even days before messages are propagated to every site.

Messages are organized into a hierarchical tree structure, very much like many things in UNIX (although you don't have to be running a UNIX machine to access Usenet). Groups range from things like *rec.arts.startrek.fandom* to *alt.sex.bondage* to *comp.unix.admin*.

Although I would love to go into more detail, this really goes beyond the scope of this book. Instead, I would like to recommend *Using UUCP and Usenet* by Grace Todino and Dale Dougherty, and *Managing UUCP and Usenet* by Tim O'Reilly and Grace Todino, both from O'Reilly and Associates. In addition, there is a relatively new book that goes into more details about how Usenet is organized, what newsgroups are available, and some general information about behavior and interaction with other when participating in a Usenet sendmail: *Usenet Netnews for Everyone* by Jenny Fristrup, from Prentice Hall.

Note that the browser provided on the CD-ROM does not support many of the advanced features of some of the commercial ones, such as Netscape. Because a Netscape version runs on Linux, I would suggest that you get it before you get too involved in the Web. You can get the Netscape Navigator via anonymous ftp from `ftp.netscape.com/pub/navigator/3.01/unix/`. Note that the release number (3.01) will probably change.

9.6 Firewalls

If you are connecting yourself to the Internet at all, you need to consider protecting your internal network. If you set up an Internet server that has only one network interface, that being to the Internet, then your internal network is safe from intruders. This solution provides the ultimate in security (short of not connecting at all) but requires more work on your part to transfer data to and from that machine.

The alternative is to implement a system in which someone from the outside has the least chance of getting into your network but to which you have the ability to access and get through that gateway machine. This is the concept of a *firewall*.

Like a firewall in a building, a network firewall functions more or less as "damage control." Should a fire break out, the firewall prevents it from spreading further. With a network firewall, should an intruder break into the gateway machine, the potential for further damage is limited.

In the following section, I will be talking about the basic issues involved with implementing a firewall on your machine. Keep in mind that these are the *basics*. There is more to it if your want to make your system as safe as possible. In comparison to car security, this is analogous to telling you about locking your door or installing an anti-theft device like "The Club," but I won't go into details like electronic devices that cut the gas flow if the car is hot-wired.

First, let's briefly talk about the firewall itself. Your firewall is a machine that has routing capabilities. Technically, it does not need to be a computer but can be something as simple as a router. As its name implies, a router is a machine that routes packets. Most routers allow you to not only configure where packets are allowed to go to but also from where they are allowed to come. In addition, many can be even more finely tuned to limit the type of packets and to/from what ports.

If you use a computer as your router, it needs to have routing capabilities such as a Linux machine. Because of the features such as ftp and http services, a Linux machine is well-suited to the task. This explains why approximately 10 percent of all Internet servers are running Linux.

One way to make the firewall safe is to prevent all packets from going *through* it. This means that packets are not *forwarded*. Certain routers will allow you to configure them in such a way that incoming packets are blocked but outgoing packets are let through.

Note that this does not mean that you can only send packets to the outside but never hear them respond. Instead, that means that packets that *originate* on the outside are blocked. When you send a request from an internal machine, the packet that you receive is a response or acknowledgement. Such packets are allowed through, but those that are sending the initial request are not.

This has a slight danger in that acknowledgment packets can be intercepted and manipulated. This requests detailed knowledge of both the TCP/IP protocols and the application involved, so it is not something that the casual hacker is going to try. However, it is *possible*.

To increase the security of your system, turn off packet routing altogether, which means that no packet is let through. In such as system, you need to connect first to the firewall machine and *then* to the Internet. At this point, you now have two distinct networks. Although the firewall can see *both* of them, neither can see the other. Because nothing gets through, not even e-mail, your internal network is (fairly) safe.

This means that an intruder cannot reach your internal network. He or she must first reach the firewall and use it as a springboard to get inside. Unfortunately, this also means that people on the inside cannot reach the Internet without first getting to the gateway machine. If this is your choice, the security is more important than the slight inconvenience that the users encounter.

The alternative is what is called a *proxy server*. In essence, this functions like a translator. When packets reach the proxy server, they are redirected to another connection on the other side of the firewall. For example, `httpd` normally listens on port 80. However, this has been disabled. Instead, I connect to port 1080 (or something greater than 1024). The services that listen on that port make a connection to port 80 on the destination machine to complete the http connection. This middleman, or proxy, does the translation for my application. Other than knowing that I need to connect to the proxy server first, the functionality is the same as though there were no firewall.

There are a couple of ways of implementing the proxy under Linux, which I will get to shortly.

9.6.1 Securing the Server

A key aspect of a firewall is the security of the firewall itself. If it is not secure, it is comparable to locking all the doors to your house but leaving the key under the mat. Therefore, taking the key with you, or for that matter throwing it away, is a much safer alternative.

So what do I mean when I say throw away the key? Well, what I mean is that you eliminate all potential routes that an intruder can use to get through the firewall or from the firewall to the internal network. Granted, your security should be sufficient enough that the intruder cannot get into the firewall in the first place. However, you need to plan for that possibility.

The question is not whether I am too paranoid, but rather whether I am paranoid enough. To me, not making the firewall machine secure is comparable to locking all the doors but writing your safe combination on the wall next to it. The house is secure, but *should* someone break in, they have free run of all your valuables.

So, let's first talk about locking the doors.

The purpose of your Internet gateway is to provide a gateway to the Internet. Sounds simple enough, but what that means is not always clear. The question you need to answer is "What is the purpose of the Internet connection?" The answer will define what steps you take to secure the firewall.

For example, let's assume that you have a Internet connection so that your employees can connect to the Internet, but you do not provide any services yourself. In this case, you do not need to enable services *on the firewall* such as ftp or http. All that happens is packets are routed through the firewall. Therefore, you can remove the daemons themselves (i.e., `telnetd`, `ftpd`, `httpd`, etc.) and the programs (Telnet, ftpd, etc.). To simply disable them, place a pound sign in front of the appropriate entry in `/etc/services`.

This is where a lot of controversy occurs. In a article I wrote for SCO World, I describe the procedures as "throwing away the key," in that the programs and daemons were physically removed from the machine. Some people disagreed and said to move them to a place that the normal user would not have access to, their reason being the difficulty in administering the system should these programs be needed.

Despite the respect I have for their technical capabilities, I have to disagree with them on this point. Although they were correct in that it does make the administration more difficult, two important security issues are involved. First, it makes hacking more difficult. If these programs are not on the machine, they *cannot* be compromised. You have, in essence, thrown away the key.

The other issue is that hackers are *not* normal users. They are sneaky, plodding, and patient. Maybe you have hidden the file on the system, but a good hacker isn't thwarted by such simple tricks. I wouldn't be and I am not even a good hacker. If a program was not in its original location, the first thing I would do is to see whether it was anywhere on the system. I have seen administrators simply rename the file to something like `telnet.orig` so simply starting `telnet` does nothing.

My attitude is that it is better to err on the side of inconvenience than on that of security. If you discover that access is too inconvenient, you can always change it. However, if you discover that the security is too lack, it's too late.

I apply this same attitude when it comes to the services that I make available. If you remember from earlier in this chapter, the available services are defined in `/etc/services`. My suggestion is to first comment out *every* service. Then, one by one, uncomment those that you want. Yes, you may forget one and cause a certain amount of inconvenience. However, doing it this way, you know exactly what services you are enabling. If your forget to enable one, you have inconvenienced someone. If you do it the other way, by disabling the ones you do not want and forgetting to disable one, you may have let the would-be hacker into your system.

Another means of securing your system is to limit access to the machine. There is, of course, the issue of the physical security of the machine. If someone has physical access to your firewall, all the network security in the world is of little value.

What you turn on depends on your needs. For example, if you were providing ftp and http services, these two entries should be uncommented. (Note this assumes that `httpd` is running from `inetd` and is not stand-alone.) I would definitely say that on the firewall, you should *not* uncomment `netstat`, `systat`, `tftp`, `bootp`, `finger`, and `ntp`. There is no reason that I have ever heard of to make these services available across the Internet. Personally, I think you should also leave out `telnet` and `login` (for `rlogin`). The key is to only give want you *have* to.

To set this all up, there need to be a couple of changes in the kernel. Obviously, the basic networking functionality needs to be turned on, but you will find two other options useful. The first is `IP_FORWARDING`, which needs to be turned *off* so that packets are not passed through the firewall.

The next is `IP_FIREWALLING`, which is necessary for the basic firewall functionality. If you want to keep track of the IP packets, you need to turn on IP accounting. I recommend doing this because it allows you to keep track of from where the packets are coming and where they are going.

Another concept is the idea of IP masquerading. With this enabled, the internal network is "invisible" to the rest of the world. What happens is the firewall server converts the IP addresses so that machines on the Internet think they are communicating with the firewall and not an Internal machine. You can then assign IP addresses to your internal network that reside with the private ranges as defined by RFC 1918. Then you must enable `IP_FIREWALLING` for this to work.

If you plan to use your firewall as springboard, the configuration is basically complete. If you are planning to go from your workstations through the firewall, however, then there is more that you need to do. This is where the concept of a proxy comes in.

There are currently two well-known proxy packages available for Linux. The first is Socks, which operates as a full proxy and can work with any program. There is a single configuration file and a single daemon that need to be configured.

The other is the TIS Firewall Toolkit, which requires a new version of each daemon that will be going through the firewall. If you do not want users to have access to a particular service, just don't provide them with the necessary programs. However, with Socks, it is easier to unintentionally allow access.

Although not really a firewall, the TCP Wrapper program can be used to control access to and from a *specific* machine. That is, it must be installed on each machine individually. In contrast, a firewall works for all machines that are trying to get past it to the Internet.

The Socks proxy server is available on many of the newer distributions. If you don't have it, you can get as a gzipped tar archive from *ftp://sunsite.unc.edu/pub/Linux/system/Network/misc/socks-linux-src.tgz*.

Here you have come to the point where you have locked the door and put "The Club" into your steering wheel. The firewall HOWTO goes into detail of the actual configuration of the proxy server and the associated files.

9.6.2 Securing the Internal Network

How secure the Internal network should be is another issue about which I have had "heated discussions" with my co-workers. They argue that if we "make sure" that the firewall is secure, we don't need to worry about the security on the internal network. To me, this is the same issue as locking the front door but writing the safe combination on the wall. Based on my hacking experiences, I think that it is unwise to take anything for granted.

Here again, you need to weigh security with convenience. In most cases, the inconvenience of slightly slower connections or an extra two seconds to login is negligible compared to the damage cause by a malicious intruder. The best approach is to address those issues that I talked about earlier, including implementing the private IP address as defined in RFC 1918.

In addition, you should very much consider implementing the same security on the Internal machines as you would on your gateway. The reason is security. If any intruder breaks into the gateway and *if* they can then get into the internal, how safe are the other machines? If you left holes open on the gateway, the odds are the holes are on the internal machines as well.

9.7 Network Technologies

Depending on your needs,. There is a wide range of network technologies that you can choose from. Because Linux is developed by the people who need and use the technology, you will often find that there are drivers available for Linux before commerical operating systems. To be able to cover them all properly, we would need an entire book. Instead, I will focus on some of the more common technologies.

9.7.1 Ethernet

Linux supports two of the major network types: Ethernet and Token-Ring. Ethernet could be labeled as the great-grandfather of all the other network types. It was developed in the 1970s by Xerox for linking computers to printers. Although not very widespread at first, Ethernet has since expanded to be (perhaps) the most widely spread type of network.

The principle behind Ethernet is called Carrier Sensing, Multiple Access with Collision Detection (CSMA/CD), which means that every machine on the Internet sits quietly listening for messages. When one of the machines needs to talk, it waits for a pause and jumps in to send its message. What if two machines simultaneously see the pause and start to send? A collision occurs. This is detected by both machines, which wait a random amount of time before they try again. Although the random amount of time could be the same for both machines, it doesn't happen too often and each machine eventually gets to send its message. The one that didn't get its turn will see that the other one is talking and wait.

Because there is no guarantee that a specific machine will *ever* get a turn on the Internet, this type of mechanism is referred to as a probabilistic access system, because each machine will probably get access to the system someday. Keep in mind that the busier a network is, the greater the chance for collisions and the greater the likelihood that there will be more waiting. This does not mean that more machines mean more collisions. If I am sitting at my machine doing all of my work locally, then the traffic on the network caused by my machine is minimal. However, once I make a connection, the traffic increases.

Ethernet appears in several different forms, depending on its physical characteristics. Primarily, these fall into the IEEE specification 802.3, with an average speed of 10 MHz. One thing I need to point out is that the original specification developed at Xerox is not what most people think about when they think about Ethernet. Rather, it is the IEEE 802.3 standard.

The most popular ways Ethernet appears is 10Base5 (Thicknet), 10Base2 (Thinnet) and 10Base-T (Twisted-pair). The general format of these labels is *StypeL*, where *S* is the speed of the cable in megahertz, `type` is the transmission system (in this case baseband versus broadband), and *L* is the maximum length of the cable in 100 meters. I have also heard that the last number indicates the thickness of the cable in tenths of an inch. Thicknet, as you would guess, is thicker than thinnet, but both are coax cable. Twisted-pair is similar in format to normal phone cable, but may often have eight separate wires.

Often times, the topology (layout) of your network depends on what kind of cable you use. Because it requires a central hub, twisted-pair is usually laid out in a star, with the hub at the center. This is a star topology. Thin- and thicknet are usually spread out in a line, or linear topology. This is also called a bus topology.

9.7.2 Token-Ring Network

The Token-Ring Network, developed by IBM, is embodied in the IEEE standard 802.5. The key concept in this type of network is the idea of a token. This is similar to a baton in a relay race, when each machine must receive the token before it is allowed to go. If a particular machine has nothing to send, it simply passes the token on to the next machine. If it does have something to send, the message is "linked" with the token before it is sent. By seeing the token linked to the message, the other machines know that the token is in use and pass it along to the destination. When the destination machine gets the entire bundle, it puts the token back on the network with a tag to indicate that it received the packet. It is then passed to the originator as an acknowledgment. The originator then passes the token along to the next machine.

This scheme provides guaranteed access to the network because every machine will eventually get the token. Even if the originator of one packet has more to send, once it gets its acknowledgment back, it must pass the token along. If no others want to send anything, it can then come back to the first machine. However, the others were given the *chance* to send something. This method also provides reliability because the destination machine sends the packet back with an acknowledgment.

9.7.3 ATM

Although not provided in commercial distributions as of this writing, there are drivers for cards supporting the Asynchronous Transfer Mode (ATM). ATM functions like a never-ending train. When an empty car comes along, the data can jump into it. These cars, or *cells*, are fairly short (58 octets total, 48 data, 5 header).

The basic idea behind ATM is that mixed bandwidth systems (such as data and voice) can use the same cable without loss of efficiency. ATM is the layer directly above the physical hardware, with the ATM adaptation layer (AAL) serving as the interface to the higher-level protocols. The ATM layer is actually broken up into two sublayers: the transmission control (TC) is responsible for building the cells and the physical medium (PM) layer is the interface to the physical hardware.

As of this writing, ATM is supported in Linux but is not available in any of the standard distributions. An experimental (that is, pre-beta) driver is available from *lrcwww.epfl.ch*.

9.7.4 ISDN

For most of the life of electronic/electrical communication, the primary method of communication has been the telephone. As a result, a network of cables and connections exist throughout the world that dwarfs the Internet in both number of connections and in miles of wire. Wouldn't it be wonderful if you could take advantage of the already existing network? Well, you can. This comes in the form of a system called Integrated Services Digital Network, or ISDN.

ISDN is one of the fastest growing technologies, particularly in Europe. Local telephone companies are offering it as a replacement (or addition) to conventional telephone lines. Until recently, the German phone company offered cash incentives for businesses and private individuals to switch to ISDN. The primary benefit (at least to most end users) is that you can simultaneously send data across the same line as your phone. For example, while you are speaking to a customer, you can be faxing them the spec sheets on your latest product *across the same phone line*. Although such functionality for both partners requires ISDN connections on both ends, your phone could be talking to their conventional phone and your fax could be talking to their conventional fax. However, from your office to the phone company is a single telephone connection.

If both sides are using ISDN, they need to be communicating in a fashion similar to a network (as with TCP/IP or IPX/SPX) so both sides know who is calling. Imagine getting a call from a customer and having your database automatically call up the record on that customer, even before you pick up the phone! This ability to integrate all these different services from voice to fax to data communication gives ISDN its name.

The key concept in ISDN is the idea of a digital data pipe between the end device and the service provider. Note that I didn't say between the two participants. This allows the service provide (the phone company) to switch between the ISDN connection on one side to the analog connection on the other. At the receiving end (your office) will be something similar to a switch box. As the packets come in from the service provider, this switch box will route the packets to the appropriate device. Each device is set with a particular ID number. This works conceptually the same way as SCSI IDs.

As of this writing, three types of connections have been standardized. The first is often referred to as the "basic" rate because it provides the necessary service for basic users such as homes and small businesses. This provides two 64-kbps channels for voice or data and one channel for "out-of-band" signaling. In some cases, you could use these two channels simultaneously and get 128 kbps. However, this would be considered two phone calls.

The "primary" service provides 23 voices or data channels instead of just two. In Europe, this has increased to 30 channels. The third type provides a 4-KHz analog phone channel along with an 8- or 16-kbps data channel, which allows you to use your old analog phone along side the new ISDN device.

ISDN is not just for data communication. As I mentioned, the German phone company subsidized the transfer from the old analog system to ISDN. I have an ISDN connection at home. Using the same wires as my old phone line, the ISDN line comes into a telecommunications box that converts the signal so that my normal analog phones can work.

ISDN support is provided by `isdn4linux`, which is a set of kernel modules. The main module (`isdn`) communicates with the driver for the particular card. As of this writing, a limited number of cards are supported. However, many cards are supported that don't have "official" drivers for them. For example, the AVM A1 (Fritz) card is supported using the Teles driver. For more information, check out the `/pub/isdn4linux` directory on *ftp.franken.de*. This not only has many of the drivers but also a *very* extensive FAQ.

If you have a 2-0 or later kernel, you are in luck–ISDN support is included by default. When you run `make config`, you are prompted to include it along with several different options. Only a few cards are mentioned by name. However, I know that many other cards would mention those with the drivers that are included.

CHAPTER 10

INSTALLING AND UPGRADING

- Getting Linux up and running
- Adding hardware
- Choosing the right Linux

I am sure that you are wondering why the installation chapter appears at this point in the book. Well, it's something that I took a lot of time to think about, for two reasons. First, I'm betting that you already have an Linux system installed and you bought this book because you want to find out more. If you do need to install something at this point, it's less likely that it's the whole system, but rather something like new hardware or software. That's what the bulk of this chapter is all about. However, because you may (one day) want to install a system from scratch, I'm going to talk a little about that.

On the other hand, you have considered implementing a Linux solution and wanted to learn more about it before you jumped in. With this in mind, I feel it's necessary that you understand what your system is all about (in terms of both hardware and software), how things fits together, and what could happen on you system before you start your installation. By knowing what your system "could" be, you are in a better position to decide what to install and how to install it.

So, how does one go about installing Linux? This is not an easy question to answer because it's hard to define what Linux is. Just as there is no one operating system that you can define as the official UNIX, there is also no one version of Linux that is the official version. No single entity is responsible for Linux. No one organization is responsible for maintaining and distributing Linux. In fact, anyone can gather all the components and create and *sell* his or her own version as long as it adheres to the GNU Public License.

Because CD-ROMs have become so inexpensive, the distributions that are readily available contain not only the operating system and associated programs, but *massive* amounts of application software. Much of it is freeware, like Linux itself. However, this is often copies of commercial software. The licenses for these can range from 30-day full versions to unlimited versions with limited functionality. In some cases, complete versions of commercial products are bundled with Linux, so you are actually paying for the commercial product and are getting a free copy of Linux.

You can also obtain Linux from various sites across the Internet. The best-known site is perhaps *sunsite.unc.edu* in the `/pub/Linux/distributions` directory. If you have a DOS system, can take one of these distributions and copy disk images using the DOS `RAWRITE.EXE` program. Depending on what version you get and what you want to install, this will take a lot of time: 50 disks! Other versions allow you to install across a network. In any case, if you do download a version from the Internet, a README file should describe what to do with what you have.

Although this is a quick way to get a distribution, it may not be cheap. If you have a dial-up connection, it could take an hour or longer to download all of the associated files and, unless call is local, that can be expensive. Complete distributions are very inexpensive, ranging from $30 to $200 or more. The higher prices are for more complex systems that may contain add-on packages like Advanced X-Windows servers or application software (such as the Caldera Network Desktop).

Due to it's very nature, Linux has a lot of upgrades. New versions of programs, new drivers for the kernel, and patches to existing drivers are always being released. In many cases, it's often difficult to say just what release you are running.

One major problem that you will probably encounter is that there is no "installation guide," as with other operating systems. Granted, there is the *Linux Installation HOWTO*, written by Matt Welsh. It does a good job of detailing how to get and install Linux distributions. Plus, it covers some of the more common problems that people encounter. However, it does not cover every distribution and hardware configuration, so this guide must remain fairly generic and cannot give you the step-by-step instruction that you may need.

Many versions, such as RedHat, WGS, Craftworks, and DLD come with manuals that address their releases specifically. Even Slackware comes with a booklet that addresses the more pressing issues involved with installation. I suggest that you read them before you put the CD-ROM in the drive, although after my twentieth Linux installation, I became fairly proficient. However, when I install a distribution that I have never seen before, I always have the installation guide nearby.

Different distributions are installed in different ways. Perhaps the most common way is to provide a DOS/Windows-based program that creates a set of floppies that you use to boot your system. In most cases, there are dozens of different prebuilt kernels. You are taken through a series of menus from which you select the hardware configuration you have, and the program selects the appropriate kernel.

Other distributions have a DOS program that loads a Linux kernel. Once the Linux kernel is loaded, you have the same installation menu that you would have had you booted from the floppy.

During the install, you must keep your mind on your hardware. This is something that I forgot to do once. If you have an older release (with a kernel earlier than 2.0), then you probably don't have a driver for the Adaptec AHA-2940 host adapter. In some cases, you can't use the program to make floppies and have to do it manually. This is not difficult and doesn't take much longer than using the program (provided you don't have any other "exotic" hardware); you just need to be aware of it.

Here, I have to point out that being aware of this means more than just having to create the boot floppy manually. When I installed the program, I did not have my Ethernet card installed, so I couldn't add the networking components to the kernel. Later, when I added the card and rebuilt the kernel, I nearly had a heart attack. During the reboot, the system panicked because it couldn't access the root file system. Why? Because I have an AHA-2940 and when I rebuilt the kernel, the new kernel didn't have the right driver for the AHA2940.

This teaches two lessons. First, know what hardware you have on your system, what drivers are necessary, and, above all, whether those drivers are part of your kernel source tree. Second, configure LILO so that one of the options is for a good kernel. If you rebuild your kernel and it doesn't boot correctly, you can always get back in. I have three kernels: the current kernel, the previous kernel (before the most recent built), and a very generic kernel with the very minimum number of drivers (usually just the host adapter driver and no networking).

10.1 Preparing for the Installation

I have provided you with an "installation checklist" that you can print out before you start your installation. Try to refer to it as much as possible before you start the installation. Though a lot of the information won't be asked for the install, gathering this information can help you identify problems before you start. I suggest you include the complete checklist in your notebook.

You will notice that there are some very basic questions like keyboard language and time zone. It may seem almost too basic to include this type of information in your notebook. However, I speak from experience when I say that the more you write down, the less likely you are to make mistakes, even if the information is "basic."

Before you start, you need to check out your system. The very first thing you need to check is the hardware itself. The first question to ask yourself is whether the hardware is supported. I'm sure a few of you out there are groaning, thinking this is an attempt to blow you off. I talked with many customers while I was in tech support who go ballistic when I even bring up the question of whether the hardware is supported.

With Linux, the word "support" has a completely different tone than that for commercial operating systems. Companies that produce a commercial OS usually have a list of supported hardware and platforms. If your system doesn't conform, they have the right to "blow you off." On the other hand, "support" under Linux means that there is a driver for it. Whether there is a driver in the current kernel is almost secondary. Because there is a driver, someone took the time to write it and is anxious to hear about any problems.

Commercial distributions of Linux walk the razor's edge between Linux's philosophy and that of other OS vendors. So far, I have had nothing but good experiences with Linux vendors. If they don't have a driver themselves, they often know where to get one. However, the reaction you get from them will depend entirely on your attitude.

"It works under DOS!" is a common response when people learn that something is "not supported." However, as I have said many times, all it really means is that the hardware is probably not broken. I say "probably" because I have seen defective hardware work under DOS, but not on UNIX. Under DOS, a lot of hardware is accessed through the system BIOS. The BIOS is often built especially for that machine. It understands the hardware in a way that Linux doesn't. Because the Linux device drivers access the hardware directly, the hardware has to behave in a standard way. Otherwise, the device drivers don't know what to expect.

Users have also commented that the driver works under another version of Linux or even another dialect of UNIX. If it works under another dialect of UNIX, the driver for that piece of hardware was probably provided for you. If it works on another version of Linux, maybe that version has that latest kernel. Because the jump has just been made from 1.2 to 2.0, there are a lot of new drivers. Make sure that you have the correct release.

Does this mean that your no-name hardware won't work? Not at all. I have one machine that is running a fair bit of "unsupported" hardware. Much of it is clones of supported hardware (which causes a lot of grief). However, it works. When I tried to install something that wasn't supported and it didn't work, I wasn't frustrated because the unsupported hardware wasn't guaranteed to work. (Well, I was a little frustrated, but I knew to expect it.)

There is also the issue of conflicts. Linux is good about enabling you to install a wide number of cards at their default. The common place for conflict is with multiple cards of the same type, such as host adapters. However, with the list in front of you, you will be able to confirm this before you try to install and something goes wrong.

Once you have installed the operating system and it works diligently for six months, then the first problems may crop up. Now, what was the model of the hard disk? Rather than digging through a box of papers looking for the invoice, you will have it right in front of you in the checklist. Okay, knowing that you should fill out the installation checklist is easy, but knowing what to put in each entry is the hard part.

You can install Linux in several different ways, depending on the distribution you bought. If the Linux distribution on the CD-ROM does not have exactly what you need, knowing about the different versions available might help you decide which one is best for you. (Note that the version of the kernel that installs on your system will *not* be the latest, 2.0. However, you will find a copy of the 2.0 on the CD-ROM, as well as instructions on how to upgrade it.)

An important thing to consider for the installation is the installation media. If you want to install Linux on a laptop that has neither a CD-ROM drive nor a network connection, then you probably need to think about doing installing it from floppies. Many Linux versions will allow you to do a network install via PPP, so at the very least, you need a modem. However, not all versions allow it.

Normally, underneath the root directory is a subdirectory `dosutils`. Among other things, this subdirectory probably contains the program `rawrite.exe`, a DOS program used to write disk images onto your floppy. Also underneath the root directory, you will probably find a directory on the CD-ROM called images, which contains the images that are used to make the boot and root floppies, as well as to make floppy sets to install the rest of the packages.

In addition, at least one subdirectory contains the disk images for the various boot floppies. There is one file for any one of dozens of different hardware configurations. There is an index that you can use to select what boot disk is most appropriate. However, this is normally not necessary if there is a program to create the boot floppies for you. There is also a "bare" image that contains very few drivers.

You need to consider whether the version you have can install additional products with floppies once the initial installation was complete. I ran into this problem myself. I thought I would install the base product first and then install other components that I needed later on. However, once the installation was complete, I discovered that the only tool on the system that could read the package information on the floppies was the initial installation program. This meant that I had to either be satisfied with what I had or install again. (If the distribution supports rpm, then this is not so much of a problem.)

Even if you do have a CD-ROM drive, there are a couple of installation methods. With some products, you can install directly from the CD-ROM. That is, a DOS program will load the Linux kernel, which then starts the installation. In this case, you have to be able to boot under DOS and not just a DOS window. Others provide a DOS or Windows program that creates a boot floppy and, if necessary, a root file system floppy. Some distributions, such as Craftworks or Caldera, provide you with a boot disk so you don't have to make one yourself.

During the course of the installation, you may have the choice of several different installation types, from fully automatic to fully configurable, depending on the version. For the more advanced system administrators, the fully configurable enables you to control many different aspects of the install. Fully automatic basically does everything for you, that is, it evaluates your system and essential makes all the decisions itself. I recommend that if you are a novice administrator *and* there is nothing on the hard disk that you want to save, the fully automatic is your best choice.

Most versions will enable you to select the components that you want to install. In the case of Craftworks, you can select among several different "architectures" that have a set of predefined packages. If you want, you can choose a custom architecture in which you choose each package yourself. The Installation HOW-TO provides a list of the Slackware packages and what they contain.

Take notes during the entire process and include these in a notebook. Write down everything you input and what the prompt/question was. These notes will be helpful if things go wrong and you want to try a different approach. You know what you input the last time; this time, you can try something different.

To install Linux (or any other OS for that matter), a hard disk must be divided into partitions. Actually, it may be only one for a single OS, but it may be up to four (DOS logical partitions are actually subdivisions of extended partitions). The partition table (which tells how many partitions there are and where they are located) has been standard for years and it is essentially impossible to get away from it, so the limit is four partitions. Linux, unlike other UNIX dialects, can be installed on logical partitions, as well as the primary partitions.

Files are stored in file systems, as with other UNIX dialects. Under Linux, file systems take up the entire partition. File systems can be on different partitions or even different hard disks, or you can put all files on a single file system. Having different file systems can be safer: if one is trashed, the others are often safe; if everything is on one (root), then the whole system is gone.

The more activity there is on a file system, the greater the chance it will become corrupt if the system should crash. If your database application and the data are on the root file system, all of your activity is in one place. If the database and the data are on a separate file system, there is less activity on the root file system. If the system goes down, the root file system may be okay and you can use it to fix the other problems. However, I don't mean to scare you–disks are much more reliable today than a few years ago.

Traditionally, the way to break it up is to have `/usr` as a separate file system. Often, even directories under `/usr`, such as `home` are on separate file systems. This can make your backups even quicker. The root file system contains things that remain fairly constant and you need only back it up on occasion (once a week, for example). Daily backups need only be done for the file systems with data on them. Plus, if you have partitions on multiple disks, performance is increased.

On any one system using the NFS automounting facility, I had all the users on a single machine. The `/usr/home` directory was exported via NFS to other machines that mounted it on their `/usr/home` directory. The advantage was that the file system was only mounted when it was needed. Also, there is nothing to prevent statically mounting the `home` directory. No matter what machine a user logged into, he or she would have the same home directory. On many systems you might even find the home directory mounted under /.

When considering the partitions size, you must also consider the swap space size as well. I've seen references that say swap should be one-and-a-half to two times the amount of RAM. Personally, I think this is too much, unless you have a good reason. The swap space should be considered a safety net, not an integral part of your memory system. If you are swapping, performance will suffer. If you think you would need the extra swap space, consider buying more RAM. That way, you are less likely to swap in the first place.

However, you also need to consider growth. If you expect to increase your RAM in the future, you should consider that when you set how much space you are going to use for swap. RAM just slides into your system; increasing swap may require reinstalling the operating system. So, how much do you assign to swap? Good question. My suggestion is twice as much as RAM. The "good reason" I mentioned above is that it is easier to do it now and waste the space than to reinstall later. Another good reason is when you have more than one user running graphical applications. In this case, then even setting swap to two times RAM is reasonable. If all the space is taken up on the primary hard disk, you can add a hard disk and use the swap command to add additional swap space.

You also need to keep in mind that swapping takes up system resources. The time to access the hard disk is hundreds of times slower than the time to access RAM. Therefore, if speed is an important consideration, you should think about having enough RAM so you don't swap. More recent versions can have swap partitions that are as large as 128Mb and you can have as many as 16 different swap partitions.

The size of your partitions needs to be based on how much software or data you will have. You need to consider the growth of your system. If you put your data on a second disks, it would be easier to backup the data, add a larger disk, and then restore the data.

If you have a larger disk, you need to be aware of the 1,024 cylinder boundary. PC BIOSs are limited to 1,024 cylinders. Until Linux is loaded and has control of the system, the BIOS is accessed. You can run into problems if any part of your kernel is above this boundary. See the section on hard disks in the hardware chapter for details.

10.1.1 Hardware Requirements

Although Linux will install and run on something as small as a 386/16 with no hard disk (you boot from floppies), you can't really expect to run your business on it. To do useful work, you have to be installed on a hard disk and have at least 4Mb of RAM for text-based applications and 8Mb if you are running X-Windows.

However, this, too, is pushing things a bit, and you probably can only have one user working effectively. Consider an extra megabyte per user for text applications and 2Mb for X-Windows, or slightly less if the users will all be using the same applications (because the text segments will be shared).

The amount of hard disk space you need is a completely different matter. It's not as easy to come up with a rule of thumb because each site will want to have a different set of applications. The *basic* UNIX utilities and programs will fit in less than 20Mb. However, there is not much you can do with that. On the other end of the scale, I installed the Caldera Network Desktop with the Internet Office Suite onto a 500Mb partition containing a complete RedHat distribution. I then had to reinstall to make the partition larger because I ran out of space. In the middle is my laptop, on which I have a 100Mb partition and almost a complete Linux Pro installation (no X-Windows).

Most of the commercial distributions list a few example installations and how much hard disk space you will need. Every commercial product I have seen lists how much space you will need. The products that are bundled with a Linux distribution also tell you how much the OS will/can take. It is therefore fairly easy to get an *idea* of how much space you will need.

For the most part, if you have a standard PC, Linux will run on it. By "standard" I mean that the components are common brands and types–there are no clones and the hardware has been on the market for more than a week.

Linux is most commonly available for Intel machines. However, a few commercial versions are available for the DEC Alpha processor. There are also versions for the Motorola 680x0 as well as the PowerPC, SPARC, and MIPS (how many am I missing?). The best thing to do is check the Hardware HOWTO to see whether the hardware you have is supported.

10.1.2 Repartitioning

If you have an existing system that takes up the whole disk, you will have to backup and reinstall the existing system to make room for Linux. You need to be careful because you may make partition too small for all the files that were there before!

A couple of tools are available on the Internet that will reformat a DOS partition with an existing system (assuming there is enough free space). I have never used such a tool, although I have read messages on the Internet from people who have done it successfully.

During the installation, you will have a chance to either install on an existing partition or repartition the drive. As with other PC-based OSs, use the `fdisk` tool to partition the drive. Some distributions have full-screen, menu-driven versions, but they all perform the same functions, such as creating, deleting, and making partitions active.

However, the Linux `fdisk` can do much more than that. For example, it can change the partition type, which is helpful when you need to have a system with several different OSs. DOS can only create a single primary and a single extended partition. I have used Linux to create all of the necessary partitions and then used DOS to recognize them correctly.

Another useful thing is that the Linux `fdisk` will do what you tell it. I have wanted to delete an entire extended partition but couldn't because logical partitions were there. Linux will do that for you.

As with other operating systems, Linux `fdisk` will see that other partitions are there, even though it may not know what type they really are. Linux is very good at recognizing the type, although there are a few cases in which I have seen it off the mark (but not by much). The reason is that all `fdisk` versions just read the partition table, which is in a common format.

10.1.3 Installation Problems

Some possible problems could occur during the installation, one of which is that you have no free space. Many Linux distributions will allow you to install it on an existing DOS partition, so you need to be careful with this one. Fortunately, the system will tell what kind of file system it is.

If you are having trouble booting from floppies, there are a few reasons for this. The first, which I saw quite often while I was in tech support, happens on new machines when the CMOS setting for the floppy does not match what really is in the drive. Even today, CMOS are delivered in which the default A: floppy is 5.25" and 360K. If you have a 3.5" 1.44Mb, it won't work right. The kernel *might* load, because it is just reading one sector after the other. However, the first time you have to seek to a particular sector, you're hosed.

Another common problem is simply that it is defective media. If you can install directly from the CD-ROM, this problem is unlikely to happen. If your CD-ROM drive needs a caddy, I have seen sticky slots that don't open all the way. It might also be that the CD-ROM is just dirty. Wipe it off with a clean *dry*, nonstatic cloth. If you have to create a boot floppy set, it's best to have new floppies. The cost of a new box is worth the piece of mind.

If the system hangs during boot process, pay close attention to any messages that come up, particularly the last few. These messages might indicate what the problems are. Although it didn't cause a hang, I had an Ethernet card and multiport board that were both software configurable. Both configured to IRQ10. Because the multiport board was initialized first, my Ethernet card was inaccessible. Also check the Hardware HOWTO to make *sure* that your hardware is supported.

I have heard of out-of-memory errors. I have never experienced them myself because I have always installed my system with 32MB. The reason for this error is that you have very little RAM and a RAM disk is created during the install for the root file system. If the amount of RAM you have minus the ramdisk doesn't leave enough for Linux, you're in trouble. If you don't have enough RAM, get more. RAM is not prohibitively expensive, and you can't run a productive system without it anyway.

If you run into hardware problems, strip the system to just the devices you need for the install. Remove the parallel/serial ports, sound cards, network cards, mouse cards, and anything else you don't need for the installation. If the problem still continues, maybe one of the other cards is loose (like the SCSI host adapater). Remove and reseat all the cards. Check for conflicts of base address, IRW, DMA, and, obviously, check that your hardware is supported.

SCSI devices are good things to have, but they can also be a major headache. I must admit that at times I almost have a too-relaxed attitude when installing. (Hey, I know what I am doing, right?) I often take for granted that the hardware is configured in a particular way, especially when other hardware of the same type is configured that way. This leads to problems!

I have seen systems in which a SCSI device is detected at all IDs, though no devices are there and no manufacturer's ID is recognized. This happens when there is a device and HA at the same SCSI ID. The host adapter must be at ID 7. Every other device must be at a different, unique ID.

Maybe Linux detects errors on the disk, but the disk is known to be error free, which is often caused by either bad cables or incorrect termination. If your SCSI devices report timeouts, there may be a conflict with BA, DMA, or IRQ of the host adapter. I have also experienced timeouts when more than two devices on the bus are terminated. Remember that only the two devices at the physical end of the SCSI bus should be (must be) terminated.

If the SCSI devices report timeouts, this may also be due to bad connections or termination problems. However, it might also be due to conflicts with the I/O address or IRQ or DMA channels.

If you have obtained a version from the Internet, you can get read errors or "file not found" messages. I specifically mentioned the Internet because I have never seen it with commercial versions. This might be an indication of bad media (so instead, use new floppies) or that something went wrong with the transfer.

If you used ftp to copy the files from DOS/Windows machine, the transfer mode is normally ASCII by default. These files *must* be transferred in binary mode or they could result in messages like "tar: read error" or "gzip: not in gzip format."

After installing, you may have some problems booting. You may see something like "non-system disk in drive," "disk not bootable," "NO OS," etc., probably because your master boot block is corrupt. This can occur when installing onto machines with multiple operating systems. Some OSs have to install the on the active partition. I have experienced this once, when I installed a second OS on a system only to find that the second simply overwrote the first.

The `fdisk` program on all PC-based OSs can read the partition table. It may not see what kind of partition it is, but it will see that something is there. On the other hand, the Linux `fdisk` can read the partition table and recognize what kind of partitions they are.

Another cause of this kind of message is that LILO might not have been installed correctly. Therefore, you should boot from the boot/root floppy that you made for the installation. Once you get to the `boot:`, you can specify the root file system to be on the hard disk. Once there, check the `/etc/lilo.conf` file and install it again.

Here's one of my favorite problems I saw both with Linux and other UNIX dialects: When you boot, another OS starts instead of Linux, or Linux is installed first and after installing the other OS, Linux is no longer accessible. In the first case, LILO may not have been installed. If it was installed, maybe it was not installed in the master boot record; but Linux is not active, so the other OS boots. Maybe you simply configured LILO so that OS will boot by default. `Ctrl+Shift+Tab` and often just `Tab` gives you the LILO menu. (See man-page for more details.)

Depending on the distribution, you may be able to choose what type of file system on which you want to install. If you will remember from the section on file systems, Linux supports several different types of file systems, most of which you can install on. The newest Linux file system is the `ext2fs`, which is what most distributions install on by default. This is (in my opinion) the best choice, and unless there are some compatibility issues, there is no need to install on other filesystems. If you need the support later, you can always add it in.

If you are fortunate to have a system that understands the RedHat Package Manager Format (like the one on the CD-ROM), adding additional software is fairly easy. See the `rpm` man-page for more details.

10.1.4 Preparing for the Worst

One thing that many administrators don't plan for is the possibility that things will go wrong. Although good planning and preparation can prevent many disasters, the most devastating disasters are those that are you are not prepared for. When you're doing an upgrade, a point will come when backing out is no longer possible. If the new operating system doesn't book and you cannot go back to the old one, then you have problems.

One problem with which I have personal experience is device drivers for "newer" hardware. In most cases, the driver will list what operating systems under which it is supported and what specific releases. Unfortunately, in a few cases, the vendor says what versions of Linux under which it is supported because the vendor doesn't provide any support itself.

Another problem is that the driver is release-specific. If you have a driver that was written for the 1.2 kernel, there are no guarantees that it will work with the 2.0 kernel.

10.2 Upgrading an Existing System

The fact that your computer contains an existing Linux installation presents its own set of problems. I have yet to find a Linux product that does "upgrades" in the sense that other OSs do them. In every installation (so far), the root file system is overwritten (during which all data is lost). If your data is on a different file system, it is "probably" safe. However, all the configurations that you have done in the files on your root file system are gone.

However, that is more of a design than a problem. If you want to upgrade the kernel, that's all you have to do. Most programs do not depend on specific releases of the kernel, so upgrading presents few problems for them. Keep in mind that the newer kernel versions support ELF binaries. If you have an older program that is in `a.out` format, it will still run on the newer kernels. However, newer ELF binaries won't run on older kernels.

Also, upgrades to the kernel occur at fairly frequent intervals. These upgrades are not full copies of the newest kernel but rather patches to an existing one. Even if you do replace the entire kernel, you rarely have to do more than replace the `/usr/src` directory.

When programs or sets of programs (packages) are updated, you only need to upgrade what you want. You can find the latest versions of the packages in several places on the Internet. The most common format is RPM, so you can use the `rpm` program to install and upgrade your programs. Many distributions have `glint`, which is a graphical program with which you can remove and install each package.

One advantage of `glint` is that you can install sets of packages. For example, you have a set of editors, such as `emacs` and `vi`. Rather than first installing `emacs` and then `vi`, `glint` enables you to install them both at once.

If you don't have `glint`, running `rpm` from the command line is only slightly more complicated. Although there are a large number of options and arguments, it is fairly straightforward to install something.

10.3 Adding Hardware

No one really expects your system to remain stagnant. As your company grows, your computer should be able to grow with it. You can add more memory or a new printer with little or no changes to the operating system itself. However, if you need to add something like a hard disk or CD-ROM drive, you may need to tell the operating system about these changes, especially if the piece you are adding is the first of its kind.

You tell Linux that you have new hardware by linking in the appropriate drivers in the kernel. This is done when you run the `make conf` when you are asked a series of questions about your hardware. In newer distributions, you will find in your kernel source directory a subdirectory, Documentation, that contains some very detailed information about what to look out for.

As when you add any device to your system, I need to remind you to have everything planned out before you start. Know what hardware exists on your machine and what settings each card has. Look at the documentation to see what settings are possible in case you need to change them. If you are adding a new device of a particular type, the odds are that you are going to need to make some changes.

10.3.1 Preparation

As I have said before and will say a hundred times again, before you start to do anything, prepare yourself. Get everything together that you will need before you start. Gather the manuals and diagrams, get your notebook out, and have the settings of all the other cards in front of you. Also, before you start, read the manual(s) that came with your release, the installation HOWTO, and the hardware HOWTO.

Perhaps the most important thing to do before you add anything is to know how the hardware is *really* configured. I need to emphasize the word "really." Many customers have become arrogant with me, almost to the point of being angry because they insist that the hardware is set at the "defaults" and I insist that they check anyway.

Unfortunately for me, in most cases, the devices are set at the default. However, confirming this takes less time then trying to install something for a couple of hours and only then finding out the devices are not at the default. Therefore, I would insist that the customer check before we continued. I had one customer who made noises as though he was checking and "confirmed" that the device was at the default. After almost an hour of trying to get it to work, I asked him to change the settings to something other then the defaults, thinking maybe there was a conflict with some other device. Well, as you might have guessed, he didn't need to do anything to change the devices to nondefault because they already were nondefault! Lesson learned: *Don't lie to tech support* (or to people on the Internet).

One most important thing about installing hardware is knowing what you are doing. This may seem like an overly obvious thing to say, but there is a lot more to installing hardware than people think.

One most common problem I see is that cards are simply snapped into the bus slot with the expectation that whatever settings are made at the factory must be correct. This is true in many, if not most, cases. Unless you have multiple boards of the same type (not necessarily the same manufacturer), you can usually get away with leaving the board at the default. But what is the default?

Unless you are buying your hardware secondhand, some kind of documentation or manual ought to have come with it. For some hardware, like hard disks, this documentation may only be a single sheet. Others, like my host adapter, come with booklets of 50 pages or more. These manuals not only give you the default settings but tell you how to check and change the settings.

On ISA cards, settings are changed by either switches or jumpers. Switches, also called DIP switches, come in several varieties. Piano switches look just like piano keys and can be pressed down or popped up. Slide switches can be moved back and forth to adjust the settings. In most cases, the switches are labeled in one of three ways: on-off, 0-1, and closed-open. Do not assume that on, open, or 1 means that a particular functionality is active. Sometimes "on" means to turn on the disabling function. For example, to disable the floppy controller on my SCSI host adapter, I put the jumpers in the "on" position. Always check the documentation to be sure.

Jumpers are clips that slide over pairs of metal posts to make an electrical connection. In most cases, the posts are fairly thin (about the size of a sewing needle) and usually come in rows of pin pairs. Because you need both posts to make a connection, it is okay to store unused jumpers by connecting them to just one of the posts. You change the setting by moving the jumper from one pair of pins to another.

The most common thing that they jumpers configure are base address, IRQ, and DMA. However, they sometimes are used to enable or disable certain functionality. For example, jumpers are often used to determine whether an IDE hard disk is the master or the slave.

The other three bus types, MCA, EISA, and PCI bus cards, often do not have DIP switches or jumpers and are software controlled. They normally come with some kind of configuration information provided on a disk or in CMOS. Provided with the machine itself is a configuration program that reads the information from the diskettes and helps to ensure that there are no conflicts. Although hardware settings are configured through these programs, it is still possible in some cases to create conflicts yourself, though the configuration utility will (should) warn you.

If this configuration information is on a disk, then this disk is as important as the Linux installation media. If this disk gets trashed, there is no way you will even be able to add another piece of hardware, your kids will hate you, and your co-workers will think you are a geek. On the other hard, you could get a copy from the manufacturer, but that's a hassle. The real problem is that some machines, like the IBM PS/2 series, recognize when you add a new card to the system and won't let you boot until you feed it the configuration disk.

In some cases, the configuration program is part of the hardware (firmware) or resides in a normally inaccessible part of the hard disk. Check the machine documentation for details.

Knowing what kind of card you have is important not only to configure the card, but unless you know what kind of bus type you have, you may not be able to even put the card in the machine. This is because all the different cards are different sizes or shapes. As you would guess, the slots on the motherboard they go into also are different sizes and shapes.

Hopefully, you knew what kind of card to buy before you bought it. Often, however, the administrator will know what kind of slots are on the machine from reading the documentation but never opens the case up so has no idea what the slots look like. If this is a pure ISA or MCA machine, then this is not a problem because none of the cards for any other bus will fit into these slots.

Problems arise when you have mixed bus types. For example, it is very common today to have PCI or VLB included with ISA or EISA. I have also seen MCA machines with PCI slots, as well as both PCI and VLB in addition to the primary bus (usually ISA or EISA). If you've gotten confused reading this, imagine what will happen when you try to install one of these cards.

If you are using your Linux machine as a server, the computer you bought probably has at least six slots in it. There can be more slots if you have a tower case or PCI in addition to the primary bus. Due to the distinct size and shape of the cards, it is difficult to get them into slots in which they don't belong. Usually there is some mechanism (i.e., notches in the card) that prevents you from sticking them in the wrong slots.

On some motherboards, you will find a PCI slot right next to an ISA or EISA slot. By "right next to," I mean that the separation between the PCI slot and the other is much smaller than that between slots of the same type. This is to prevent you from using both slots. Note that the PCI electronics are on the opposite side of the board from ISA and EISA. Therefore, it's impossible to fill one slot and then use the other.

When installing the expansion cards, you need to make sure that the computer is disconnected from all power supplies. The safest thing is to shut down the system and pull the plug from the wall socket so that you ensure that no power is getting to the bus, even if it is turned off. Though the likelihood of you injuring yourself seriously is low, you have a good chance of frying some component of your motherboard or expansion card.

Another suggestion is to ground yourself before touching any of the electronic components. You can do this by either touching a grounded metal object (other than the computer itself) or wearing a grounding strap, which usually comes with a small instruction sheet that suggests where the best place to connect is.

When I first started in tech support, we had a machine that would reboot itself if someone who wasn't grounded so much as touched it. I have also cleared my CMOS a couple of times. Therefore, I can speak from experience when I say how important grounding yourself is.

When you open the case, you will see parallel rows of bus card slots. Near the outside/back end of the slot, there is a backing plate that is probably attached to the computer frame by a single screw. Because some connector, etc., sticks out of the slot in most cases, this plate will probably have to be removed. In addition, the card will have an attachment similar to the backing plate that is used to hold the card in place. I have seen cards that do not have any external connector, so you could insert them without first removing the backing plate. However, they are not secure because nothing holds them in place. See the hardware chapter for more details.

This plate has a lip at the top with the hole for the screw. To align the screw hole properly, insert the card correctly (provided it is in the right kind of slot). As you insert the card into the slot, make sure that is going in perpendicular to motherboard. That is, make sure that both ends are going into the slot evenly and that the card is not tilted. Be careful not to push too hard, but also keep in mind that the card must "snap" into place. Once the card is seated properly in the slot, you can make the necessary cable connection to the card.

After you connect the cables, your can reboot the machine. Many people recommend first closing the computer's case before turning on the power switch. Experience has taught me to first reboot the machine and test the card before putting the case back on. If, on the other hand, you know you have done everything correctly (just as you "know" the hardware is at the default, right?), go ahead and close things up.

Avoiding address, IRQ, and DMA conflicts is often difficult. If your system consists solely of non-ISA cards, it is easy to use the configuration utilities to do the work for you. However, the moment you add an ISA card, you must look at the card specifically to see how it is configured and to avoid conflicts.

If you have ISA and PCI cards, you can use the PCI setup program (which is usually built into the firmware) to tell you which interrupts the ISA bus cards are using. You can also reserve specific IRQs for ISA devices. If you don't, there may be interrupt conflicts between the ISA bus card and a PCI bus card, or even between two ISA cards.

Unlike DOS, every expansion card that you add to an Linux system requires a driver. Many, such as those for IDE hard disks, are already configured in your system. Even if the driver for a new piece of hardware exists on your system, it may not be linked into your kernel. Therefore, the piece of hardware it controls is inaccessible.

10.3.2 CPU

There isn't too much I can say about adding CPUs. There are no jumpers to set on the CPU. In some newer machines, a lever pops out of the old CPU and you pop in a new CPU. This is (as far as I have seen) possible only on 486 machines to enable you to add a Pentium. These levers are called Zero-Insertion-Force (ZIF) sockets because you use the lever to lock the CPU into place and it requires zero force to insert it.

One thing that you must consider is the speed of the CPU. You may want to increase the speed of the CPU by simply buying a faster one. From Linux's perspective, this is okay: you plug it in, and Linux can work with it. However, it might not be okay from the hardware's perspective. Motherboards are often sold with the same speed as the CPU because they cannot handle faster speeds. Therefore, in many cases, you cannot simply replace the CPU with a faster one.

In other cases, the motherboard is of higher quality and can handle even the fastest Pentium. However, if you only had a 50Mhz 486, then you might have to change jumpers to accommodate the slower CPU. Often these changes effect such things as the memory waits states. Here you need to check the motherboard documentation.

10.3.3 RAM

The day will probably come when you need to expand the RAM on your system. As more users are added and they do more work, the little RAM you have won't be enough. Once you have decided that you need more RAM, you still have most of your work ahead of you.

One key issue you need to consider is the kind of RAM. In almost all newer machines, RAM comes in the form of SIMM modules. As I mention in Chapter 12, these modules are about the size of a stick of chewing gun, with the chips mounted directly on the cards. These modules have almost entirely replaced the old RAM, which was composed on individual chips.

There are two primary type of SIMMs. The somewhat larger type is called a PS/2 SIMM because it was first used on PS/2 machines. This has 72 connectors on it and can be immediately distinguished by the small notch in the middle. The other kind is referred to as non-PS/2, normal, regular, etc. This has 30 pins and no notch. (There is also a 32-pin SIMM, but it is uncommon. I have never seen one, but someone who works in the chip manufacturing business told me about it.)

Two important aspects of RAM are the speed and whether it has parity. The speed of RAM is measured in nanoseconds (`ns`). Most RAM today is either 70 or 60ns, with a few machines still being sold with 80ns. The speed of RAM is a measure of how quickly you can read a particular memory location.

Although it is possible in many cases to mix RAM speeds, I advise against this. First, memory can only be accessed as quickly as the slowest chip. Therefore, you win nothing by adding faster RAM, and loose if you add slower RAM. I have also seen machines in which mixing speeds actually causes problems. Because the difference between 80ns and 70ns is more than 10 percent, the delay waiting for the slower (80ns) RAM makes the system think that there is a problem. This can result in kernel panics.

Another issue is the motherboard design. For example, in one of my machines, I have two banks of memory with four slots each. Because of the way the memory access logic is designed, I must fill a bank completely, otherwise, nothing in that bank with be recognized. On other machines, you can add single SIMMs. Check the documentation that came with the motherboard.

Another important issue is the fact that Linux uses only extended, not expanded, memory. Expanded memory dates back to the early days when the XT bus could only handle up to 1MB of RAM. To give programs access to more memory than the computer could handle, some memory board manufacturers came up with the concept of "bank switching." With bank switching, a 64K area between 640K and 1Mb is reserved and then portions above 1Mb are "switched" into this reserved block as needed.

When the AT bus was developed, the system could access more memory. To make it compatible with older peripherals, however, the area between 640K to 1MB was left "unused." Memory beyond 1MB is known as extended memory.

Some machines have a hardware limitation on the maximum amount of memory that can be installed. Because I use 30-pin SIMMs on one machine, the largest available (as of this writing) is 4Mb. Because of this, I max out at 32Mb when I fill all eight of my slots. If you have 72-pin memory, there are larger modules, such as 8, 16, and even 64Mb. Again, refer to your motherboard manual for details.

If you have a Pentium or Pentium Pro, you will need to add PS/2 memory in pairs because memory is read 64 bits at a time and PS/2 SIMMs provide only 32 data bits. If you have a Pentium machine that has the older SIMMs, they will have to be in groups of four.

If you experience repeated panics with parity errors, consider replacing your memory. Because of the way memory is accessed, you may have to remove or replace entire banks (like mine). I have also seen cases in which mixing memory types and speeds can cause panics. Panics may also be the result of improperly inserted SIMMs. That is, if the SIMM is loose, it may not make a good contact with the slot. If the machine gets jarred, the contact may be lost.

In some cases, you can simply add the memory and the machine will recognize it (like mine). However, I have some machines for which you have to set jumpers to enable each bank as you add memory. In other cases, when you have filled up all the slots on the motherboard, you can add a memory expansion card. If this is on a machine like a PS/2, it requires you to tell the system of the memory expansion card using the configuration disk.

10.3.4 SCSI Devices

If the SCSI is the first device you are adding to the host adapter, you need to configure that host adapter into the system. If you are adding a second host adapter (or anything after that), you will have to disable the BIOS on it. Remember from our discussion on SCSI in the chapter on hardware that the system will look for a bootable hard disk. If the BIOS on the second host adapter is enabled, the system may try to boot from this one. If it is the same model host adapter, it will probably have to change the base address, IRQ, and DMA as well.

Remember that every device on the SCSI bus, including the host adapter itself, is identified by a SCSI ID. SCSI IDs range from 0–7 on standard SCSI and 0–15 on a Wide SCSI bus. Regardless of what type it is, the host adapter is almost exclusively set to ID 7. It is this ID that is used to identify devices on the bus, not their location in relation to the host adapter.

Because there is no real need to configure a SCSI host adapter unless something is attached, the only "official" way to add a host adapter to the system is to go through the configure script. If the system recognizes that you do not have a configured host adapter, you will be prompted to add one.

If you are adding a device to an existing host adapter, the driver for that host adapter is already linked into the kernel. (At least we hope so.) If you are adding new kind of device onto the new host adapter, the driver may not be configured. Watch carefully as the system boots to see whether the device is recognized. If it is not, you will need to run the configure script.

Here is one example in which I have first hand experience about not paying attention to what is supported and what is not. The distribution you have may provide a disk image that has support for a particular host adapter (or any driver for that matter). However, this does not mean the kernel has the support.

10.3.5 Hard Disks

If you have trouble figuring out what kind of hard disk you have, either refer to the documentation that came with the drive, call the vendor, or re-read the chapter on hardware.

The key thing to keep in mind is to make sure how the disk is configured. Every drive should come with some kind of documentation, either a detailed, multipage manual, as is the case with many SCSI drives, or a single sheet, as is common with IDE drives. This documentation usually contains information about the default settings of the drive. Don't trust those default settings. Check them out yourself to ensure they are correct before you stick the drive in the machine. It is easier to check beforehand than it is after you've tried to install it and failed.

If it's an IDE drive, then one key issue is whether it is the master or slave. If you are adding a second drive to a system that only has one drive, you are adding the slave. If you already have two drives on the first IDE controller and this is the first one on the second controller, then it is the master.

Another key issue is making sure the cabling is right. In the section on hard disks earlier, I mentioned that the position on the cable is irrelevant for IDE drives; the jumpers determine which drive is which.

A problem often crops up when you connect the cable to the drive itself. Usually there is a small "key" on the connector on the cable that fits into a notch on the drive-side connector. If the key is missing or the drive-side connector is wide enough, it may be possible to fit the connectors together backward. Fortunately, you don't have to resort to "trial and error" to figure out which is which. On one side of the cable is a colored stripe (usually red), which is line 1 of the 40-line IDE cable. In fact, on almost all ribbon cables (such as SCSI), line 1 is marked in red.

On the drive side, things are a little more complicated. The IDE cable has 40 parallel lines, but the connectors (both on the cable and on the drive) are in two parallel rows. Usually the connector on the drive is either male (pins) or there is a small "card" sticking out that is similar to an expansion card. These alternate with the odd numbered lines on one side and the even numbered lines on the other.

On the drive near the connector, often on the circuit board itself, will be some small numbers that tell you which pin is which. Sometimes there will be a 1 and 2 on one end with 39 and 40 on the other. Other times there will be just a 1 and 39. (I have seen cases in which there is just a 2 and 40.)

SCSI drives may have jumpers to configure them, but they may also be configured in other ways such as with dials, DIP switches, or piano switches. Like IDE drives, SCSI usually has one set of jumpers, which will be for the SCSI ID of the drive. In some cases, there will be up to eight pairs of pins to indicate the SCSI ID. Others have three pins that operate in binary. (For more details on SCSI configuration, see the section on SCSI in the hardware chapter.)

Standard SCSI cable looks very similar to the IDE, except that the cable has 50 lines instead of just 40. However, the same issues with the key and slot and the number applies. On the other hand, I can't remember seeing a SCSI device in which the key and slot didn't match up correctly.

If you are not sure how the drive is configured, check the documentation that came with your drive. If you can't find that, most hard disk manufacturers have fax services and will fax you installation information on any of their drives.

Once you have added the support for the hard disk, you have to create a file system on the disk partition (assuming that you are not creating a swap partition). When you install, you tell the system what kind of file system you want and it will call the appropriate program. For example, `ext2` file systems are created using `mke2fs`.

I want to point out a couple of things. One thing that you can change when running `mke2fs` is the number of inodes on the files system. Normally, `mke2fs` will calculate a number based on the size of your partition. If you know that you will have a lot of small files (like for a mail or news server), you may run out of inodes because the average size of the file is less than what `mke2fs` expects.

You can also use `mke2fs` to create a file system on a floppy. You could use this for crash recovery by copying a lot of necessary tools onto the floppy. Keep in mind that you must first format the floppy before you can create a file system on it.

10.3.6 Other SCSI Devices

If you are adding a SCSI CD-ROM, then you must attach it to a supported host adapter to access it. Like a hard disk, if you are adding a CD-ROM and there is not already a SCSI device on your system, you will need to configure the kernel for the host adapter. Also, if you are adding it to a second host adapter, you may need to configure that as well. Before you rebuild the kernel, run `make config` to specify the option that you want. Here you have the opportunity to select the hardware.

If you are a good little system administrator, you have already bought yourself a tape drive and have configured it into your system. Therefore, I don't need to talk about adding one. On the other hand, a time may come when the tape drive you have is not sufficient for your needs (maybe not large or fast enough) and you have to add a new one.

Before you begin to install the tape drive, be sure that you have read your tape drive hardware manual. This manual will often contain information about the physical installation of the device, as well as configuration. Whenever I think about installing tape drives, I think of the first SCSI tape drive I had. There were three jumpers to set the SCSI ID. It didn't make sense that you could only set it to ID 0, 1, or 2. Had I read the manual first, I would have known that this was the *binary* representation of the number.

10.3.7 Serial Terminals

In general, installing a serial terminal is the same whether it is connected to a standard COM port or an intelligent multiport board. In either case, you obviously must ensure that the driver for that port is linked into the kernel, otherwise the terminal will not be able to talk to the system.

Often terminals are set up using 9600 baud, 8 data bits, 1 stop bit, no parity, full duplex, and XON/XOFF handshaking. If your terminal cannot handle these settings, then you can either change the line in `inittab` to reflect the appropriate `gettydefs` entry, or you can create your own `gettydefs` entry if none of these fit. See the section on starting your system or the `gettydefs` man-page.

Pay attention to which pins are on the terminal. You only need to worry about three: transmit, receive, and signal ground. The serial port will be set up (probably) with pin 2 as transmit, 3 as receive, and 7 as ground, if you have a DB25 (25-pin) connector. If you have a DB9 (9-pin) connector, pin 2 is receive, 3 is transmit, and 5 is ground. Make sure that the cabling is set up so that transmit on one side goes to receive on the other and that the two ground pins are connect. In some cases, you need a crossed cable when the pin numbering is the same on both sides (i.e., the same number of pins). If pins 2 and 3 are different, then you need a straight-through cable.

You must ensure that there is an entry for the terminal in `/etc/inittab`. It is the fact that there is a `respawn` in `inittab` that gives you the `login:` prompt when the system starts and gives you a new one when you log out. For more details, see the section on starting and stopping the system and the `inittab` man-page. When enabled, the corresponding entry might look like this:

```
S1:234:respawn:/etc/getty /dev/ttyS1 M19200
```

If the login prompt doesn't look right (i.e., garbage characters), the `gettydefs` entry probably is incorrect. As you remember from our discussion of starting and stopping the system, this is the last entry on the line, in this case, m. If the m entry in gettydefs does not match what the terminal is set for, you get incorrect behavior. See the gettydefs man-page for more details.

If you don't see a login on the terminal, it's possible that it was sent before the terminal was turned on. Therefore, the terminal cannot display it. If you press Enter a couple of times and no login prompt appears, maybe it's not really enabled or there is a hardware problem. Run telinit q again. You should also try simply sending the date to the file with

```
date > /dev/<tty_name>
```

If that still produces nothing, then you may have a hardware problem. If you have enabled the port, you can run

```
ps -t<tty_name>
```

to see if there is a getty or login running on that port. If not, there may be some serious software problems.

Often times the connector on the terminal is female. You can test the terminal by taking a paper clip and putting one end in hole 2 and the other end in hole 3. Press the keys on the keyboard so the data go out the transmit line (pin 2 or 3, it doesn't matter) and come back in on the other pin. If nothing appears, first make sure that the terminal is turned on (I've had my share of *those* calls). If it is turned on, check the brightness (I've had enough of those as well). If still nothing, the monitor is probably on vacation.

If you suspect the cable or serial port is at fault, you can try the terminal on a port that you know is working. Then switch parts one at a time until you isolate the part that's broken.

10.3.8 EIDE Drives

One limitation of the of the IDE drive is that it was limited to about 520Mb because the BIOS can only access cylinders less than 1,024 because it uses a 10-bit value. Because DOS accesses the hard disk through the BIOS, it, too, is limited to locations on the hard disk under this 1,024 cylinder limit.

The older IDE controllers accessed the hard disk through the combination of cylinders, heads, and sectors per track. The problem for the BIOS is when the hard disk has more than 1,023 cylinders. So, to make the BIOS happy, EIDE drives "lie" to the BIOS by saying that there are fewer than 1,024 cylinders and more heads. (Often, the cylinders are halved and the heads are doubled so that the number of blocks works out to be the same.)

If you have a hard disk that is used just for Linux, you can turn off this translation completely before you install and it's no longer an issue. However, if you have DOS on the disk, this is a problem. Linux still gets the geometry from the BIOS as it is booting. If the translation is on, it gets incorrect values for the physical layout on the hard disk.

However, until the kernel is loaded, LILO still uses the BIOS, therefore the Linux image must lie under this limit. The only way to ensure that this happens is to make the root partition lie under the 1,024 cylinder boundary.

Another alternative is to leave the translation on but pass the correct geometry to Linux at the boot/LILO prompt. You can even include them in `lilo.conf` so that you don't have to type them in every time.

10.3.9 CD-ROMs

CD-ROMs are configured into the kernel like the other devices: through the `make config`. If you have a SCSI CD-ROM, you obviously need to configure your host adapter as well. You can do this at the same time if your host adapter is not installed already.

For the SCSI CD-ROMs, it's just a matter of turning on the support. Non-SCSI CD-ROMs are different. There are options to turn on the support for several other specific types of CD-ROMs. Rather than listing them all here, I will point you to the CD-ROM HOWTO, which contains more up-to-date information.

10.4 A Treasure Chest of Choices

Getting a copy of Linux is obviously an important part of the install. Technically, Linux is the kernel, so it isn't all that big. You can download the latest kernel from many sites. However, if you want all the programs and utilities that go along with Linux, you will probably spend days downloading everything.

The alternative is to buy a copy. A dozen different versions are available in many more different configurations. Some are sold as a single CD-ROM, others come with CD-ROMs full of shareware or demos, still others are bundled with commercial products.

One argument against UNIX in general compared to Windows NT that I frequently encounter is that so many different versions compete with each other. With Windows NT, there is only one product. For me, that is an argument in favor of UNIX. No matter what your needs, no matter what your tastes, there is a UNIX version to suit you.

You need WWW Server and Web development tools? No problem. Development system? No problem. So, you *really* want to pay for all this? No problem. If you want, you could get it all for free if Linux wasn't what you wanted.

For me, the biggest problem with Linux really is the choice–not because there are so competing many versions but rather because there are so many good products, and I feel bad about having to choose one over the other. On the CD-ROM, you'll find a copy of Linux PRO from Work Group Solutions. Why this one? It's not just because Linux Pro is a good product; it's also because we feel comfortable with the company and its president, Mark Bolzern.

In the next few sections, we will take a quick look at a few of these distributions. This list is far from complete and represents only those versions I received and installed. For more information on these distributions and the others that I didn't install, the Linux Distribution HOWTO contains, among other things, contact and pricing information. There is also information on companies that provide other Linux-related products.

10.4.1 Caldera Open Linux (COL)

A key aspect of COL is to get it certified through the X/Open group. The result will be that Linux can call itself "UNIX." Although not necessary for us true-believers, the ability to call itself UNIX is very important for the business world.

Installing Caldera Open Linux was a real pleasure. Using the Linux Installation and System Administration tool (LISA), the installation went very easily and comfortably. LISA was developed by LST, a German company that is based in Erlangen, quite near to where I am. Being a German company, LST provides the option of running LISA in either German or English. (I chose English.)

One thing that Caldera finally learned was do ask for the keyboard type right up front. As I mentioned, this is helpful when you have a non-American keyboard, as I do.

Although LISA *could* have included a lot of configuration options, I found those that were included to be very useful. Depending on what options you install, you can configure everything from your mouse to your printer to what services should be started by default. When configuring the printer, I was even given the chance to specify what kind of printer I had, plus the size of the pages. This was great because I have DIN A4 printer and I do not use letter size.

I did run into problems configuring the X server, which caused me to hang the first two times that I installed. The third time, I postponed the X configuration until after I was done with everything else. That worked like a charm. One thing that really impressed me was the improvement to the `xf86config` program. There are many more options and more than twice as many video cards are supported.

Note that COL comes with the Metro-X server. I did not configure the system to use it. I have Wabi 2.2 for Linux and the release notes say that I can only use the Xfree86 servers. This did not appear to be a problem because I was finally able to configure my system at 1024x768 instead of 800x600 without getting a headache!

COL comes with a newer version of `fvwm`. That's sweet! After working with it for just a few minutes, I kept asking myself how people can work with MS-Windows when they could have something like this. The "Goodies" toolbar is improved and looks very professional, the pop-up menus are enhanced, and you can even set characteristics, such as the focus policy.

If you do a complete install, you will find the CD-ROM *loaded* with software. Note that the improvements to much of this is a result of the original developers. However, it is very nice to have this all in one place.

10.4.2 Craftworks Linux

Craftworks Linux is sort of a home-brew to me. Craftworks Solutions, Inc., is located just a few blocks from my high school. This was the first distribution I got that came with the new 2.0 kernel (actually, it was 2.0.14).

A small handbook came with the distribution and I felt that it could have covered more installation issues rather than going into the general usage of Linux. Craftworks uses their proprietary CRAFT (Computer Replacement and Fabrication Tool) to install. Craftworks also recognizes the RedHat Package Manager (`rpm`).

For most people, however, this is just a minor annoyance. The installation is one of the easiest I have seen. One thing that impressed me is that it not only recognized the partitions but also determined which of the handful of partitions I had was another version of Linux and asked specifically if I wanted to install there.

Also, you could select the layout of the file systems. I had several partitions on multiple drives and I could decide which of the "standard" file systems I wanted on what partition. For example, I could select to have different partitions for `/pub`, `/home`, and `/local`, or I could have had them all as subdirectories of /, or any combination I wanted.

Here I had to be very careful. I had an existing Linux installation (different vendor) and Craftworks wanted to install on that partition. Craftworks was on one partition and `/usr`, etc., were on the other. I missed it the first time through, so I ended up re-installing the first Linux. Because I wanted Craftworks as well, I reinstalled it, too. The next time I was careful.

Another nice touch is that almost all the necessary information is on one screen, not one screen after the other, as with many distributions. This relaxes me when I'm installing because I don't feel that I have to rush to answer. Plus, you can see how your answers relate to each other, rather than as separate entities.

One shortcoming with Craftworks is that this information is not complete. For example, does "workstation name" include the domain name? For me, that's not part of the of the workstation name. However, it might be for others.

Craftworks Linux also has some predefined sets of packages (called "architectures") that you can select to install. If you are a beginner, these architectures take the hassle out of deciding what packages to install. These architectures are:

- Minimal—Just the programs and files that are necessary for a basic installation
- X Workstation—Programs to configure your machine as a W workstation, including X-Windows and TCP/IP
- Developer—Programming and development tools
- Custom—Completely configurable

Craftworks also comes with "commercial test drives" with a couple of commercial Linux products, such as the BRU backup software and the Metro Enhanced X Server.

10.4.3 Deutsche Linux Distribution (DLD)

DLD is a German distribution of Linux from Delix Computer in Stuttgart, Germany. It comes with two handbooks, both in German, that provide more than enough information to get you up and running. The menus during the installation process, many man-pages, and some of the system messages are in German. For the most part this is good thing, but the documentation and menus appear to have been translated by someone who does not have much experience in UNIX. Many of the terms are simple word-for-word translations of English and are not commonly used German words. In addition, there is no consistency as to what is in German and what is in English.

With the package I received, there were two additional CD-ROMs that contain a larger number of applications, programs, and archives from various sites that I could install later. There were also two floppies that I could boot from so I didn't have to create them myself. A version with the Accelerated X-Windows server is also available.

One major advantage that I found in this distribution was that it not only recognized my existing Linux partition, but when I went to install on that partition, I was prompted to save the system configuration onto a floppy. I was also asked whether the previous configuration should be used to configure the DLD installation. Unfortunately, not all aspects of the configuration were saved.

Also, when I went to remote format this partition, I was reminded that a Linux system was already installed there and I was prompted to confirm the fact that I wanted to reformat the partition. Other distributions would simply go ahead without asking.

During the course of the installation, it automatically recognized that I had a DOS partition and asked me if I wanted to mount it at system startup. DLD went so far as to identify that it was really a Win 95 VFAT file system.

Selecting a kernel to load on the hard disk was rather confusing. Other distributions give you a menu from which you select the components you have. The installation script then picks the appropriate kernel. With DLD, you have a fixed list from which to choose and it is not very clear.

At this point, two annoying problems cropped up. First, when LILO was configured, it installed Linux under the name `linux1` and DOS under the name `dos2`. Afterward, you have to reboot to continue with the installation. Because I expected to be able to type `linux` to start up, I was unpleasantly surprised to find that only `linux1` worked.

One very exciting aspect of the installation was my ability to install the shadow password facility, which we talked about in the chapter on system administration. Some distributions don't even provide it, but here you can configure it automatically during the installation!

During DLD installation, you have two choices: standard and expert. The expert installation is similar to that of Craftworks in that you can choose from a couple of predefined installations or pick and choose features to suit your needs. The advantage of DLD over Craftworks is that even though you select a predefined set, you can still go in and add or remove packages from that set. Even after you install those packages, you can still go back and install others. Once the system is up, you can use the dldinst program to install additional components.

10.4.4 Linux PRO

The commercial version of Linux Pro, from WorkGroup Solutions, also comes with the Linux Encyclopedia, which contains hardcopy versions of various HOWTOs as well the User's Guide, Administrator's Guide, and the Network Administrator's Guide. The Administrator's Guide is the basis for *Running Linux* by Matt Welsh and Lar Kaufmann, available from O'Reilly & Associates. The Network Administrator's Guide is the basis for *Linux Network Administrator's Guide* by Olaf Kirch, also from O'Reilly.

Linux Pro from Workgroup Solutions comes in a six-CD-ROM package that not only contains the Linux Pro distributions but additional applications, archives, and even the Linux On-line Shopping Mall as well. Though Linux Pro is based on the RedHat distribution, it seems to be a somewhat smoother installation. However, it did *not* recognize the fact that I had an existing system. It *did* find my Linux partition, but simply asked whether it should format it without saving any of the configuration information.

During the installation, you are presented with a predefined set of packages to install. The choice seems to be somewhat random because the games package is selected but the network package is not, although I already spent a couple of minutes answering questions about by network configuration. However, even after you select the sets, you can choose individual packages to install.

In addition to Linux Pro, WGS also provides consulting services and complete Linux solutions. Simply by registering a purchased version of Linux Pro, you are entitled to two free 15-minute support calls. Additional 15-minute calls are available at $25 a piece, which is significantly less than most software vendors.

10.4.5 RedHat

On the commercial side of things, RedHat Linux is growing more popular. Both the original distribution of the Caldera Network Desktop and Applixware are provided with a complete RedHat distribution. In addition, many of the other distributions include the RedHat Package Manager, which is a easy-to-use tool that makes installing packages under Linux fairly straight forward.

RedHat enables you to install directly from CD-ROM or create floppies. To install from the CD-ROM, you must be able to boot into DOS. A DOS window in Win95 or WinNT doesn't cut it, though you can boot your Win95 machine in DOS mode and install from there.

You can also run one distribution directly from CD-ROM. However, my first attempt to install directly from the CD-ROM ended quickly because I have and Adaptec 2940 PCI host adapter. This was not part of the stable kernel at that time, so I had to create a set of boot floppies.

A major shortcoming I found was that the hardcopy documentation that was provided referred to a specific file on the CD-ROM that contained important information. The problem was that the file didn't exist. (Well, it did exist–it just wasn't where the documentation said it would be.)

Another shortcoming I find quite often with American software is that there is a certain amount of ethnocentrism, in that there is a certain expectation that every computer is like an American one. I don't have one. My keyboard is German. Because of the difference, installation is slower. I have to think about what letters and symbols are hidden behind my keys. I often had to erase things I wrote. Because of the necessity of inputting from the keyboard, the first question to ask is what kind of keyboard are you using, *not* the last.

RedHat also had the shortcoming among other distributions in that you couldn't install the networking components unless you had an Ethernet card in the machine. I actually did, but RedHat couldn't find it because it wasn't in that release of the kernel. Therefore, I couldn't install any of the networking components. What about installing it later? What about PPP?

What was nice was the ability to install on something other than the boot disk. Although this is slowly changing, RedHat was one of the first distributions I saw that allowed this. Some still don't. You can also create and delete partitions during the install to make the space you need.

10.4.6 Slackware

For a long time, Slackware seemed to be synonymous with commercial distributions of Linux. This was the first version of Linux I had. It, along with most subsequent versions I received from Walnut Creek CD-ROM (*www.cdrom.com*), provides regular updates. Aside from the various versions of Slackware, Walnut Creek also has a plethora of other CD-ROMs. I used several in the course of this project–GNU, Perl, X11R6, and their Internet Info CD-ROM, all of which fit well with my Linux system.

Slackware provides these various Linux programs in several sets. Most of the books that I have seen on Linux describe Slackware as being the distribution and these sets being the only way that programs are distributed. One advantage this has is when you want to install from floppies, particularly if you decide to install these sets after the initial installation. Some products I have seen enable you to create installation floppies, but you need to install them all at once. With the Slackware sets, it is easy to create floppy sets (although a couple of sets require a large handful of floppies).

The Slackware 96 package that I got from Walnut Creek CD-ROM is a four-CD-ROM set that contains a couple of different Linux archives. In addition, there is a 36-page installation guide, but this contains just the minimal amount of information for you to install system. If you have nonstandard hardware or trouble installing, you have to look elsewhere.

Monitoring your system means more than just watching the amount of free hard disk space or the number of users running a certain application. Many aspects of your system are static over fairly long periods of time, such as the layout of your hard disk. However, such information is as important to really knowing your system as how much free memory there is at any given time.

Linux provides a wide range of tools to not only monitor your system as it runs but to find out how it's configured. In this chapter, I am going to talk about the tools you need and the files you can look in to find out anything about your system that you need. In the next chapter, we will take some of these tools and see how you can use them to help you achieve the goal of administering your system.

11.1 Finding Out About Your System

One challenging aspect of tech support is that before you talk to the customer, you have no way of knowing what the problem will be. It can be anything from simple questions that are easily answered by reading the manual to long, drawn-out system crashes.

Late one Monday afternoon, when I had been idle the longest, my phone rang when the next customer came into the queue. The customer described the situation as simply that his computer would no longer boot. For some reason, the system rebooted itself and now it would not boot.

When I asked the customer how far the system got and what, if any, error messages were on the screen, his response indicated that the root file system was trashed. At that point, I knew it was going to be a five-minute call. In almost every case, there is no way to recover from this. On a few rare occasions, `fsck` can clean things up to be able to boot. Because the customer had already tried that, this was not one of those occasions.

We began discussing the options, which were very limited. He could reinstall the operating system and then the data, or he could send his hard disk to a data recovery service. Because this was a county government office, they had the work of dozens of people on the machine. They had backups from the night before, but all of that day's work would be lost.

Because no one else was waiting in the queue to talk to me, I decided to poke around a little longer. Maybe the messages we saw might indicate to us a way to recover. We booted from the emergency *boot/root* set again and started to look around. The `fdisk` utility reported the partition table as valid but it looked as though just the root file system was trashed, which is bad enough.

I was about ready to give up when the customer mentioned that the `fdisk` table didn't look right. Three entries in the table had starting and ending blocks. This didn't sound right because he only had two partitions: root and swap. So I checked `/etc/fstab` and discovered that another file system was being mounted.

Because the data was probably already trashed, there was no harm in continuing, so we decided to try running `fsck` on it. Amazingly enough, `fsck` ran though relatively quickly and reported just a few errors. We mounted the file system and, holding our breath, we did a listing of the directory. Lo and behold, *there* was his data. All the files appeared to be intact. Because this was all in a directory named `/data`, he simply assumed that there was no `/usr` or `/home` file system, which there wasn't. However, there was a *second* file system.

I suggested backing up the data just to be safe. Because it was an additional file system, however, reinstalling the OS could preserve it. Within a couple of hours, he could be up and running again. The lesson learned:

Make sure you know the configuration of your system! If at all possible, keep data away from the root file system and do a backup as often as you can afford to. The lesson for me was to have the customer read each entry one-by-one.

Being able to manage and administer your system requires that you know something about how your system is defined and configured. What values have been established for various parameters? What is the base address of your SCSI host adapters? What is the maximum UID that you can have on a system? All of these are questions that will eventually crop up, if they haven't already.

The nice thing is that the system can answer these questions for you, if you know what to ask and where to ask it. In this section, we are going to take a look at where the system keeps much of its important configuration information and what you can use to get at it.

As a user, much of the information that you can get will be useful only to satisfy your curiosity. Most files that I am going to talk about you can normally read. However, you won't be able to run a few of the utilities, such as `fdisk`. Therefore, what they have to say will be hidden from you.

If you are an administrator, there are probably many nooks and crannies of the system into which you never looked, many you probably never knew existed. After reading this section, I hope you will gain some new insight into where information is stored. For the more advanced system administrator, this may only serve as a refresher. Who knows? Maybe the gurus out there will learn a thing or two. Table 11.1 on page 483 gives you a good overview of the various files configuration files on your system.

11.1.1 Hardware and the Kernel

The first place we're going to look is that place that causes the most problems and results in the largest number of calls to support: hardware.

For those of you who have watched the system boot, you may already be familiar with what I call the hardware or boot screen (which actually consists of several screens). This gives you a good overview to what kind of hardware you have on your system and how it is configured. Because many hardware problems are the result of misconfigured hardware, knowing what the system thinks about your hardware configuration is very useful.

Fortunately, we don't need to boot every time we want access to this information. As the system boots (as well as at other times), the kernel writes to system log files. In the case of the messages you see at boot, this file might be `/var/log/messages`, `/usr/adm/messages`, or `/usr/var/messages`. You can also get a dump of these messages using the `mesg` command.

Supplementary to this are the files under `/proc`. If you look at your mount table (using the `mount` command), you will see that this is a mounted file system. However, you will also note that no physical device is associated with it. However, it behaves just like a normal file system, with a number of directories and files, even though none of the files actually exist. When someone accesses this "file system," the appropriate VFS structures are filled and the appropriate information is delivered.

You find two basic types of information via the files in `/proc`. First, you can get a lot of kernel information by reading the files in this directory. On many systems, the only way to access this information is to read the device `/dev/kmem` (the kernel memory device) directly. Here, all you need to do is run `cat <file_name>` to be able to read the various information.

In addition to these files, there is one subdirectory for each process on the system. The name of the directory is the process ID of the respective process.

- `cpuinfo`: Various information about the CPU, such as the manufacturer, model (SX/DX), integrated NPU, etc.
- `devices`: A list of block and character devices configured into the kernel, along with their major number.
- `dma`: Devices and their dma channels.
- `filesystem`: File system drivers in the kernel.
- `interrupts`: A list of interrupts and the total number of interrupts on that interrupt vector.
- `kcore`: The physical memory of the system. Same format as a core file. The size of this file is the same as physical memory, plus a 4Kb header to make it look like a core file.
- `kmsg`: Often used instead of the `syslog()` system call to log kernel messages. To access this file, a process must have root privileges. If the `syslog` process is running, this file should **not** be read.
- `ksysms`: A list of kernel symbols.
- `loadavg`: Load average. This is the same information produced by uptime.
- `meminfo`: Memory information in bytes including free memory, user memory, and swap.
- `module`: An ASCII list of kernel modules.
- `net`: Subdirectory containing information about the network layer.
- `self`: The process currently accessing the `/proc` FS and is linked to directory with the applicable PID.
- `stat`: Various statistics about the system, including time CPU spent in user mode, pages brought in and out from the disk, number of swap pages brought in and out, number of interrupts since boot, number of context switches and the boot time.

- `uptime`: Amount of time system has been up and time spent in the idle process.
- `version`: Version information.

In each process subdirectory are several files and one directory.

- `cmdline`: Complete command line for the process.
- `cwd`: Current working directory of the process.
- `environ`: Environment for the process.
- `exe`: A link to the executable that started that process.
- `fd`: A subdirectory that contains one entry for each file that the process has opened. Each entry is the file descriptor that the process is using.
- `maps`: Memory mappings the process uses.
- `mem`: Memory of the process.
- `root`: Pointer to the root directory of the process.
- `stat`: Status information about the process. This file is mostly just numbers (with the exception of the executable's name and the status). In general, this is the same information you would get from running `ps`, with various options:
  - `pid`: The process ID.
  - `comm`: The command's (executable's) filename.
  - `state`: Process state, such as R, running; S, sleeping in an interruptible wait; D, sleeping in an uninterruptible wait or swapping; Z, zombie; and T, traced or stopped (on a signal).
  - `ppid`: PID of the parent.
  - `pgrp`: Process group ID of the process.
  - `session`: Session ID of the process.
  - `tty`: The tty the process uses.
  - `tpgid`: Process group ID of the process that currently owns the tty to which the process is connected.
  - `flags`: Flags of the process.
  - `minflt`: Number of minor faults (i.e., those that have not required loading a memory page from disk).
  - `cminflt`: Number of minor faults that the process and its children have made.
  - `majflt`: Number of major faults (i.e., those that require loading a memory page from disk).
  - `cmajflt`: Number of major faults that the process and its children have made.
  - `utime`: Number of jiffies (10 milliseconds) that this process has been scheduled in user mode.

- `stime`: Number of jiffies that this process has been scheduled in kernel mode.
- `cutime`: Number of jiffies that this process and its children have been scheduled in user mode.
- `cstime`: Number of jiffies that this process and its children have been scheduled in kernel mode.
- `counter`: Current maximum size in jiffies of the process's next time slice, of what is currently left of its current time slice, if it is the currently running process.
- `priority`: Standard nice value, plus 15. The value is never negative in the kernel.
- `timeout`: Time in jiffies of the process's next timeout.
- `itrealvalue`: Time in jiffies before the next SIGALRM is sent to the process due to an interval timer.
- `starttime`: Time the process started in jiffies after system boot.
- `vsize`: Virtual memory size.
- `rss`: (Resident set size) Number of pages the process has in physical memory, minus three for administrative purposes.
- `rlim`: Current limit in bytes on the RSS of the process (usually 2,147,483,647).
- `startcode`: Address above which program text can run.
- `endcode`: Address below which program text can run.
- `startstack`: Address of the start of the stack.
- `kstkesp`: Current value of esp (32-bit stack pointer), as found in the kernel stack page for the process.
- `kstkeip`: Current EIP (32-bit instruction pointer).
- `signal`: Bitmap of pending signals.
- `blocked`: Bitmap of blocked signals (usually 0; 2 for shells).
- `sigignore`: Bitmap of ignored signals.
- `sigcatch`: Bitmap of signal with dhandling routines.
- `wchan`: The wait channel of the process.
- `statm`: Additional status information that takes longer to gather and is used less often.
- `size`: Total number of pages that the process has **mapped** in virtual memory (whether or not they are in physical memory).
- `resident`: Total number of pages the process has in memory; should equal the RSS field from the `stat` file.
- `shared`: Total number of pages that this process shares with at least one other process.
- `trs`: (Text Resident Size) Total number of text pages the process has in physical memory. (Does not include shared libraries.)

- `lrs`: (Library Resident Size) Total number of library pages the process has in physical memory.
- `drs`: (Data Resident Size) Total number of data pages the process has in memory.
- `dt`: Number of library pages that have been accessed.

Access to this information is useful when you run into problems on your system. System slowdowns, for example, are difficult to track down. Using `ps`, you can get a feel for what is on your system. Sometimes, `ps` will show you what process is running but not what it is doing. With a little practice, the files and directories in `/proc` can.

11.1.2 Terminals

Each line in `/etc/inittab` that refers to a terminal device points to an entry in the `/etc/gettydefs` file. The entry for the COM1 port (`/dev/ttyS1`) might look like this:

```
S1:234:respawn:/etc/getty  ttyS1  M19200
```

From our discussion of the `/etc/inittab` file in the section on starting and stopping the system, you see that this entry starts the `/etc/getty` command. Two arguments are passed to `getty`: the terminal on which it should run (*ttyS1*) and the `gettydefs` entry that should be used (m). The `/etc/gettydefs` file defines such characteristics as the default speed, parity, and the number of data bits. For example, the m entry, to which the previous `inittab` entry points, might look like this:

```
M19200 # B19200 CS8 CLOCAL # B19200 SANE -ISTRIP CLOCAL
#@S login: # M19200
```

The fields are

```
label # initial_flags # final_flags #login_prompt #
next_label
```

The `label` entry is what is being pointed to in the `inittab` file. The `initial_flags` are the default serial line characteristics that are set, unless a terminal type is passed to `getty`. Normally, the only characteristic that needs to be passed is the speed. However, we also set HUPCL (hang up on last close).

The `final_flags` are set just before `getty` executes `login`. Here again, set the speed and HUPCL. However, we also set the terminal to SANE, which is actually several characteristics. (Look at the `gettydefs`(F) man-page for more details.) We also set TAB3, which turns tabs into space; ECHOE, which echoes the erase character as a backspace-space-backspace combination; and IXANY, which enables any character to restart output if it is stopped by the XOFF character.

11.1.3 Hard Disks and File Systems

A common problem that has caused long calls to support is the layout of the hard disk. Many administrators are not even aware of the number of partitions and file systems they have. This is not always their fault, though, because they often inherit the system without any information on how it's configured.

The first aspect is the geometry, which includes such information as the cylinders, heads, and sectors per track. In most cases, the geometry of the hard disk is reported to you on the hardware screen when the system boots. You can also get this information from fdisk.

To find how your hard disk (or hard disks) is laid out, there are several useful programs. The first is fdisk, which is normally used to partition the disk. Using the -l option, you can get fdisk to print out just the partition table. On my system, I get output like this:

```
Disk /dev/sda: 64 heads, 32 sectors, 1170 cylinders
Units = cylinders of 2048 * 512 bytes

Device     Boot Begin Start End  Blocks Id System
/dev/sda1  *    1     1     364  372720 83 Linux native
/dev/sda2       396   396   649  260096 6  DOS 16-bit>=32M
/dev/sda3       650   650   1169 532480 63 GNU HURD
/dev/sda4       365   365   395  31744  82 Linux swap
```

As you can see, the first partition on this drive is the Linux partition and the last one is the Linux swap space.

The preceding information shows the parameters for the first SCSI hard disk on my system. Here I have four partitions, the first one (Linux) of which is active. Note that although the Linux swap partition is physically the second partition, it shows up as the fourth partition in the fdisk table. In addition, it accurately recognizes the fact that it is a 32-bit DOS partition. However, did not accurately reflect the fact that the third partition is actually SCO.

If you look carefully and compare the ending blocks with the starting blocks of the next physical partition, you see that, in this case, there are no gaps. Small gaps (just a few tracks) are nothing to have a heart attack over because you are only loosing a couple of kilobytes. However, larger gaps indicate that the whole hard disk was not partitioned, and you may be loosing some useful space.

If you have multiple hard disks on your system, your messages file (i.e., /var/log/messages) may show you this. Every version of Linux I have seen will report all the SCSI devices it sees, and because hard disks are all standard devices, they should all be reported.

If you have multiple hard disks, you can specify the devices as an argument to fdisk. For example, to print the partition table for the second SCSI hard disk, the commands would be

```
fdisk -l /dev/sdb
```

Unlike other dialects of UNIX, Linux cannot have multiple file systems in each partition. Therefore, you cannot have more file systems than you have partitions. (I'll ignore NFS, etc., for the time being.) To find out what file systems are on your disks, use the mount command. However, this command only tells you which file systems are currently mounted. Using this command on a running system is useful to determine whether a directory is part of one file system or another. Although the df command (more on that later) will tell you which file systems are mounted, it doesn't tell you what options were used, such as whether the file system is read-only. On a few occasions, I have had customers call in reporting file systems problems because they could write to them, but found out they were mounted as read-only.

What if you suspect that there are more file systems than are mounted? The first thing to do is check fdisk for all the hard disks on your system. If you have only one hard disk and it only has one partition, then only one file system can be mounted.

Maybe the file systems exist but aren't mounted. To check, first run the mount command to see what is currently mounted. Then check /etc/fstab to see what file systems are known and what the options are. A "noauto" in the options column means that file system should not be mounted automatically when the system boots.

11.1.4 User Files

The /etc directory contains the all-important passwd file, which gives important information about which users are configured on the system, what their user ID numbers are, what their default groups are, where their home directories are, and even what shells they use by default.

The default group is actually a group ID number rather than a name. However, you can easily match the group ID to the group name by looking at /etc/group. This also gives you a list of users broken down into the groups to which they belong. Note that "groups" is plural because a user can belong to more than one group.

11.1.5 Network Files

If you are running TCP/IP, you can look in a couple of places for information about your system. First, check out the file /etc/resolv.conf. If you don't find it and you know you are running TCP/IP, don't worry! The fact that it is missing tells you that you are not running a nameserver in your network. If it is not there, you can find a list of machines that your machine knows about and can contact by name in /etc/hosts. If you are running a nameserver, this information is kept on the nameserver itself.

The content of the /etc/hosts file is the IP address of a system followed by its fully qualified name, and then any aliases you might want to use. A common alias simply uses the node namz and omits the domain name. Each line in the /etc/resolv.conf file contains one of a couple different types of entries. The two most common entries are the domain entry, which is set to the local domain name, and the nameserver, which is followed by the IP address of the name "resolver." See the section on TCP/IP for more information on both of these files.

It's possible that your machine is the nameserver itself. To find this out, look at the file /etc/named.boot. If this exists, it is probably a nameserver. The /etc/named.boot file will tell you the directory where the nameserver database information is kept. For information about the meaning of these entries, check out the named(8) man-page, as well as the section on TCP/IP.

Another place to look is the start-up scripts in /etc/rc.d. Often, static routes are added there. One likely place is /etc/rc.d/init.d/network. If these static routes use tokens from either /etc/networks or /etc/gateways that are incorrect, then the routes will be incorrect. By using the -f option to the route command, you can flush all of the entries and start over.

Although not as often corrupted or otherwise goofed up, a couple other files require a quick peek. If you think back to our telephone switchboard analogy for TCP, you can think of the /etc/services file as the phone book that the operator uses to match names to phone numbers. Rather than names and phone numbers, /etc/services matches the service requested to the appropriate port. To determine the characteristics of the connection, inetd uses /etc/inetd.conf, which contains such information as whether to wait for the first process to finish before allowing new connections.

Other common places for confusion are incorrect entries and the inevitable calls to support deals with user equivalence. As I talked about in the section on TCP/IP, when user equivalence is set up between machines, many remote commands can be executed without the user having to produce a password. One more common misconception is the universality of the /etc/hosts.equiv file. Though this file determines what user equivalence should be established with what other machine, it does not apply to one user: root. To me, this is rightly so. Though it does annoy administrators who are not aware of this, it is nothing compared to the problems that might occur if it did apply to root, and this is not what you would expect.

To allow root access, you need to create a .rhosts file in root's home directory (usually /) that contains the same information as /etc/hosts.equiv but instead applies to the root account. The most common mistake made with this file is the permission. If the permission is such that any user other than root (as the owner of the file) can read it, the user-equivalent mechanism will fail. See /etc/hosts.equiv and $HOME/.rhosts to see which remote users have access to which user accounts.

Table 11.1: Configuration Files and Where to Find More Information

File	Purpose	Where to Find More Information
	User and Security Files	
/etc/group	User group information	group(5), chmod(1)
/etc/npasswd	npasswd configuration file	npasswd(1)
/etc/shadow	shadow password file	password(5), npasswd(1)
/etc/passwd	User account information	password(5), chmod(1)
	Networking Files	
/etc/bootptab	Internet Bootstrap Protocol server database	bootptab(5)
/etc/exports	Directories to export to NFS clients	exports(5)
/etc/gateways	List of gateways	routed(8)
/etc/hosts	Hostname to IP address mapping file	route(8)
/etc/hosts.equiv	Lists of trusted hosts and remote users	route(8)
/etc/inetd.conf	inetd configuration file	inetd(8)
/etc/named.boot	named default initialization file	named(8)
/etc/networks	Known networks	route(8)

Table 11.1: Configuration Files and Where to Find More Information (Continued)

File	Purpose	Where to Find More Information
	Networking Files	
/usr/lib/named or /etc/named.d	named configuration files	named
/etc/smb.conf	SAMBA configuration file	smb.conf(5)
/etc/snmpd.conf	SNMP daemon configuration file	snmpd.conf(5)
/etc/ftpaccess	FTP configuration file	ftpaccess(5)
/etc/httpd/conf/access.conf	HTTP access configuration file	
/etc/httpd/conf/httpd.conf	HTTP daemon configuration file	WWW HOWTO
/etc/httpd/conf/srm.conf	HTTP server resource management configuration file	WWW HOWTO
/etc/services	Network services list	services(5)
	X-Windows Files	
/etc/XF86Config or /etc/X11/XF86Config	X-Server configuration file	XF86Config(4/5), xf86config(1)
/etc/X11/xinit/xinitrc	xinit configuration file	xinit(1)
$HOME/.xinitrc	User-specific xinit configuration file	xinit(1)
$HOME/.fvwmrc	fvwm configuration file	fvwm(1.2),X(1)
/usr/lib/X11/system.fvwmrc	System default MWM configuration file	fvwm(1.2),X(1)
/usr/lib/X11/app-defaults	Application-specific defaults	X(1)
$HOME/.Xdefaults-hostname	Host-specific defaults	X(1)
	System Start-Up Files	
/etc/init	init configuration file	inittab(5)
/etc/lilo.conf	Lilo configuration file	lilo.conf(5), lilo(8)
/etc/rc	System start-up scripts	init(8), initscript(5)

Table 11.1: Configuration Files and Where to Find More Information (Continued)

File	Purpose	Where to Find More Information
	System Log Files	
/etc/syslog.conf	System login configuration file	syslog.conf(5)
/var/log/message	General system log file	syslogd(8)
	Miscellaneous Files	
/etc/profile /etc/bashrc /etc/cshrc	Systemwide shell configuration files	
$HOME/.bashrc $HOME/.chsrc $HOME/.kshrc	User-specifc shell configuration files	man-page for respective shell
/etc/sysconfig	Miscellaneous configuration files	man-page for respective shell

11.2 What the System Is Doing Now

At any given moment, there could be dozens, if not hundreds, of different things happening on your system. Each requires systems resources, which may not be sufficient for everything to have an equal share. As a result, resources must be shared. As different processes interact and go about their business, what resource a process has and the amount of that resource that it is allocated will vary. As a result, performance of different processes will vary as well. Sometimes the overall performance reaches a point that becomes unsatisfactory. The big question is, what is happening?

Users might be experiencing slow response times and tell you to buy a faster CPU. I have seen many instances in which this was the case, and afterward, the poor administrator is once again under pressure because the situation hasn't changed. Users still have slow response times. Sometimes the users tell the administrator to increase the speed on their terminal. Obviously 9600 isn't fast enough when they are doing large queries in the database, so a faster terminal will speed up the query, right?

Unfortunately, things are not that simple. Perhaps you, as the system administrator, understand that increasing the baud rate on the terminal or the CPU speed won't do much to speed up large database queries, but you have a hard time convincing users of this. On the other hard, you might be like many administrators who, because you were "unlucky" enough to have worked with a computer before, was thrown into the position, as often is the case. What many of us take as "common knowledge," you may have never experienced before.

The simplest solution is to hire a consultant who is familiar with your situation (hardware, software, usage, etc.) to evaluate your system and make changes. However, computer consultants can be like lawyers–they may charge enormous fees, talk in unfamiliar terms, and sometimes in the end, you still haven't gained anything.

Not all computer consultants or lawyers are like that. It's simply a matter of not understanding what they tell you. If you do not require that they speak in terms that you understand, you can end up getting taken to the cleaners.

If you feel you need a consultant, do two things. As with any other product, you must shop around. Keep in mind that the best consultant to get is not necessary the cheapest, just as the best one is not necessarily the most expensive. The second key aspect is to know enough about your system–at least, conceptually–to understand what the consultant is saying.

In this section, I am going to combine many of the topics and issues I discussed previously to find out exactly what your system is doing at this moment. By knowing what the system is doing, you are in a better position to judge if it is doing what you expect it to do, plus you can make decisions about what could and/or should be changed. This knowledge also has a side benefit of helping you if you should need to call a consultant.

So, where do we start? Well, rather than defining a particular scenario and saying what you should do if it happened, let's talk about the programs and utilities in terms of what they tell you. Therefore, I am going start with general user activity and proceed to the specifics.

11.2.1 Users

It's often useful to know just how many users are logged onto your system. As I mentioned earlier, each process requires resources to run. The more users who are logged on to your system, the more processes there are using your resources. In many cases, just seeing how many users are logged in rings bells and turns on lights in your head to say that something is not right.

The easy way to figure out how many users are logged in is with the who command. Without any options, who simply gives you a list of which users are logged in, the terminal into which each user is logged, and the time each user logged in. If you use the `-q` option (for "quick"), you get just a list of who is logged on and the user count. For example

```
root      root      root      jimmo
# users=4
```

For every user logged in, there is at least one process. If the user first gets to a shell and starts its application that way, it probably has two processes: the login shell and that application. Therefore, the minimum is the number of users times two (assuming the application isn't the login shell). Granted, the shell is sleeping, waiting for the application to finish, though it is still taking up system resources. Plus, dozens of system process are running, also taking up system resources.

Although I rarely use who with any option except `-q`, it does have several other options that I have used on occasion. One is the `-w` option, which tells you whether the user has the `mesg flag` set to yes or no. A + (plus sign) means you can contact him or her with `write`, for example, and a - (minus sign) means you can't. Another option, the `-i` option, tells you the user's idle time.

11.2.2 Processes

The `ps` command gives you a process status. Without any options, it gives you the process status for the terminal on which you are running the command. That is, if you are logged in several times, `ps` will only show you the processes on that terminal and none of the others. For example, I have four sessions logged in on the system console. When I switch to one and run `ps`, I get

```
PID    TTY     STAT    TIME    CMD
625    ttyp0   S <0    0:03    bash
991    ttyp0   R <     00:00   ps
```

This only shows those processes running on the terminal where I started the `ps` (in this case, `ttyp0`). Note that the output might be slightly different, depending on what version of Linux you are running.

If I am not on that terminal but still want to see what is running there, I can use the `-t` option. A nice aspect of the `-t` option is that you don't have to specify the full device name or even the "tty" portion–you can just give the `tty` number. For example, to get the same output as previously shown, I could enter (no matter where I was)

```
ps -tp0
```

Keep in mind that if I was on a pseudo-terminal, the terminal number also includes the p. If I have a console or serial terminal, then the p isn't used because it isn't part of the tty name. For example, if I wanted to check processes on tty4, I would enter the following:

```
ps  -t4
```

Note also that you do *not* specify the /dev/ portion of the device name, even if you specify the tty portion. For example, this works

```
ps -tttyp0
```

or

```
ps -t ttyp0
```

but this doesn't work:

```
ps -t /dev/ttyp0
```

Also be careful with spaces after the -f. Some versions require that there be no spaces.

If you are curious about what a particular user is running, use the -u option to find out every process that user owns.

Although running ps like this shows who is running what, it tells you little about the behavior of the process itself. In the section on processes, I showed you the -l option, which shows you much more information. If I add the -l (long) option, I might get output that looks like this:

```
F UID PID PPID PRI NI SIZE RSS WCHAN  STAT TTY TIME COMMAND
0 500 189 1    3   0  120  708 11a2f0 S <  v04 0:02 -bash
0 500 956 189  24  0  46   328 0      R <  v04 0:00 ps -l
```

When problems arise, I quite often use the TIME column, which tells me the total time that this process has been running. Note that the time for bash is only two seconds, though I actually logged into this terminal several hours before I issued the command. The reason for this is because the shell spends most of its time waiting either for you to input something or for the command that you entered to finish. Nothing out of the ordinary here.

Unless I knew specifically on which terminal the problem existed, I would probably have to show every process to get something of value. This would be done with the -e option (for "everything"). The problem is that I have to look at every single line to see what the total time is. So, to make my life easier, I can pipe it to `sort`. My `sort` field will be field 11 (TIME), so I use the `-k 11` option. Because I want to see the list in reverse order (largest value first), I also use the `-r` option. Because I probably only want the first few entries, piping it through `head` would not be a bad idea. So, the command would look like this:

```
ps -el | sort -r -k 11 | head -5
```

On my system, I get this:

```
USER PID %CPU %MEM SIZE RSS TTY STAT START TIME COMMAND
root 355 0.0  2.4  122  720 v01 S <  14:51 0:02 -bash
root 48  0.0  1.6  164  488 ?   S <  14:18 0:01 klogd
root 187 0.0  2.4  120  712 v02 S <  14:18 0:01 -bash
root 196 0.0  1.0  27   308 ?   S <  14:18 0:00 update (bdflush)
```

At the very top of the list is `bash`, the shell on which I have been typing all of my interactive commands since the system booted. It's no wonder it is so high. Keep in mind that this time is in seconds. Therefore, my `bash` has only been running for a total of two seconds, even though I actually booted the system several *hours* before I ran the `ps` command. Because I am the only one on the system at the moment, this value is actually low. A database that is running might have times that are several minutes, if not hours, long.

Figuring out what is a reasonable value is not always easy. The most effective method I have found is to monitor these values while they are behaving "correctly." You then have a rough estimate of the amount of time particular processes need, and you can quickly see when something is out of the ordinary.

Something else that I use regularly is the PID-PPID pair that occurs when I use the `-l` option. If I come across a process that doesn't look right, I can follow the PID-to-PPID chain until I find a process with a PPID of 1. Because process 1 is `init`, I know that this process is the starting point. Knowing this is often useful when I have to kill a process. Sometimes, the process is in an "unkillable" state, which happens in two cases. First, the process may be making the transition to becoming defunct, in which case I can ignore it. Second, it be stuck in some part of the code in kernel mode, in which case it won't receive my kill signal. In such cases, I have found it useful to kill one of its ancestors (such as a shell). The hung process is inherited by `init` and will eventually disappear. However, in the meantime, the user can get back to work. Afterward comes the task of figuring out what the problem was.

However, you don't need to follow the PID-PPID chain yourself. By using `-f`, you can get `ps` to print the output in "forest" modes, whereby the family tree of each process is shown. This might look like this:

```
PID  TTY  STAT  TIME  COMMAND
187  v02  S <   0:02  -bash
1095 v02  R <   0:00   \_ ps -f
188  v03  S <   0:00  /sbin/getty tty3 VC linux
190  v05  S <   0:00  -bash
191  v06  S <   0:00  /sbin/getty tty6 VC linux
355  v01  S <   0:02  -bash
189  v04  S <   0:00  -bash
1087 v04  S <   0:00   \_ vi trash
1090 v04  S <   0:00       \_ /bin/bash -c ls /etc/|more
1092 v04  S <   0:00           \_ more
```

Here you see two sets of processes that are related. The first set is the first two processes in the list. I was running a shell and issued the `ps -f` command to give me the output. The second set is at the bottom. Here, I started `vi` from the shell prompt. Within `vi`, I did a shell escape in which I took a listing of what was in `/etc` (`/bin/bash -c ls /etc/|more`). Finally, `more` is a separate process. (Note that `more` appears as part of the shell escape command and as a separate process.)

One nice thing is that `ps` has its own `sort` options, so you don't need to pipe it through sort.

11.2.3 Files and File Systems

Another thing you should monitor is how much space is left on your file systems. I have seen many instances in which the root file system gets so close to 100 percent full that nothing more can get done. Because the root file system is where unnamed pipes are created by default, many processes die terrible deaths if they cannot create a pipe. If the system does get that full, it can prevent further logins (because each login writes to log files). If root is not already logged in and can remove some files, you have problems.

Fortunately, by default, when `mke2fs` creates a file system, a little space is reserved for root. This prevents the system from becoming completely full, so you have a chance to do something about it.

So the solution is to monitor your file systems to ensure that none of them get too full, especially the root file system. A rule of thumb, whose origins are lost somewhere in UNIX mythology, is that you should make sure that there is at least 15 percent free on your root file system. Although 15 percent on a 200MB hard disk is one-tenth the amount of free space as 15 percent on 2Gb drive, it is a value that is easy to monitor.

Consider 10–15Mb as a danger sign, and you should be safe. However, you need to be aware of how much and how fast the system can change. If the system *could* change 15Mb in a matter of hours, then 15Mb may be too small a margin.

Use `df` to find out how much free space is on each mounted file system. Without any options, the output of df is one file system per line, showing how many blocks and how many inodes are free. Though this is interesting, I am really more concerned with percentages. Very few administrators know how long it takes to use 1,000 blocks, though most understand the significance if those 1,000 blocks mean that the file system is 95 percent full.

Because I am less concerned with how many inodes are free, the option I use most with `df` is `-v`, which shows the data block usage. On my system, I get something like this:

```
Filesystem  1024-blocks Used     Available Capacity Mounted on
/dev/sda2   987251      910262   25983     97%      /
/dev/sda3   261852      212100   10856     81%      /u
/dev/sdb7   247855      69241    165815    29%      /usr/data
```

You see that my root file system is getting pretty full. Although I have about 25MB free, I need to be aware of the situation. Note, however, that the `/u` file system is only 81 percent used but has less than half the free space as the root file system. Because this is where my data is, I am much more concerned with it being at 81 percent than I am with root being at 95 percent. Note that I can also monitor free space on my DOS partitions.

The shortcoming with `df` is that it tells you about the entire hard disk but can't really point to where the problems are located. A full file system can be caused by one of two things. First, there can be a few large files, which often happens when log files are not cleaned out regularly.

The other case is when you have a lot of little files. This is similar to ants at a picnic: individually, they are not very large, but hundreds swarming over your hotdog is not very appetizing. If the files are scattered all over your system, then you will have a hard time figuring out where they are. At the same time, if they are scattered across the system, the odds are that no single program created them, so you probably want (if not need) them all. Therefore, you simply need a bigger disk.

If, on the other hand, the files are concentrated in one directory, it is more likely that a single program is responsible. As with the large log files, a common culprit are the files in `/var/log`.

To detect either case, you can use a combination of two commands. First is `find`, which, you already know from previous encounters, is used to find files. Next is `du`, which is used to determine disk usage. Without any options, `du` gives you the disk usage for every file that you specify. If you don't specify any, it gives you the disk usage for every file from your current directory on down.

Note that this usage is in blocks because even if a block contains a single byte, that block is used and no longer available for any other file. However, if you look at a long listing of a file, you see the size in bytes. A 1 byte file still takes up one data block. The size indicated in a long directory listing will usually be less than what you get if you multiple the number of blocks by the size of the block (512 bytes). To get the sum of a directory without seeing the individual files, use the `-s` option.

To look for directories that are exceptionally large, you can find all the directories and use `du -s`. You also need to be sure that you don't count multiple links more than once, so include the `-u` option as well. Then, sort the output as numerical values and in reverse order (`-nr`) to see the larger directories first, like this:

```
find / -type d -exec du -us {} \; | sort -nr > /tmp/fileusage
```

I redirected the output into the file `/tmp/fileusage` for two reasons. First, I have a copy of the output that I can use later if I need to. Second, this command is going to take a very long time. Because I started in /, the command found this directory (/) first. Therefore, the disk usage for the entire system (including mounted file system) will be calculated. Only after it has calculated the disk usage for the entire system does it go on to the individual directories.

You can avoid this problem in a couple of ways. First, use `-print` instead of `-exec` in the `find` and then pipe it first to `grep -v`. This strips out /, and you can then pipe that output to `xargs`. This way, you avoid the root directory.

Personally, this is not very pretty, especially if I were going to be using the command again. I would much rather create a list of directories and use this as arguments to `du`. That way I can filter out those directories that I don't need to check or only include those that I do want to check. For example, I already know that `/var/log` might contain some large files.

On occasion, it's nice to figure out what files a process has open. Maybe the process is hung and you want some details before you decide to kill it.

11.2.4 Checking Other Things

UNIX performance tuning is often considered a black art. I've talked with many customers who call in to tech support, expecting that we will say a few magic words, wave our wizard's wand, and abracadabra, their systems will run better. This misconception is often compounded by the fact that support engineers often don't have the time to go into long, detailed explanations and instead quickly look over output from various system utilities and tell the customer to increase kernel parameter X or change setting Y. Miraculously, the system instantly runs better. From the customers stand point, this is "magic."

Well, not really. Some customers do express their frustration at not being able to improve the situation themselves. This is not because they aren't smart enough, but it is the same reason why many people take their cars to a mechanic for a tune-up. By comparison to replacing the block, a tune-up is a relatively simple procedure. However, many people don't have the skills to do it themselves.

This applies to system tuning as well. Because many customers do not have the skills, they turn to the mechanic to do it for them. I remember when I was about 18 and had a couple of friends who were real car enthusiasts. When their cars suddenly started making strange sounds, I can still remember them saying that the franistan had come loose from the rastulator. Well, at least that's what it sounded like to me at the time. The reason why I couldn't figure that out myself was that I didn't have the training or experience. However, they had the experience and could tell what the problem was just by listening to the car. My not being able to tell what was wrong with a car just by listening to it is the same as many system administrators, who don't have the training or experience, to tune an Linux system. However, you can.

Although a book like this one cannot provide the experience, it can provide some of the training. Keeping with the car analogy, I've talked about the transmissions, the breaks, the drive shaft, the electrical system, and even the principles of the internal combustion engine. With that knowledge, you can now understand why it is necessary to have clean spark plugs or the proper mixture of air and gasoline.

With a car's engine, you often get a "feeling" for its proper behavior. When it starts to misbehave, you know something is wrong, even though you may not know how to fix it. The same applies in principle to a Linux system, though many garages can afford the high-tech equipment that plugs your into you car and shows you what the car is doing. From there, it is a simple step for the mechanic to determine the proper course of action. What you need for a Linux system is a tool that does the same thing. Fortunately, you already have the tools. Using your eyes, your brain, and the utilities that Linux provides you can easily make the same kind of diagnoses on your system.

Using "Problem Solving" as the title for this chapter was a very conscious decision. I intentionally avoided calling it "Troubleshooting" for several reasons. First, troubleshooting has always seemed to me to be the process by which we look for the causes of problems. Although that seems like a noble task, so often finding the cause of the problem doesn't necessarily mean finding the means to correct it or understanding the problem.

The next reason is that so often I find books in which the troubleshooting section is just a list of problems and canned solutions. I find this comparable to the sign "In case of fire, break glass." When you break the glass an alarm goes off and the fire department comes and puts out your fire. You may never know what really happens.

The troubleshooting sections that I find most annoying list 100 problems and 100 solutions, but I usually have problem 101. Often I can find something that is similar to my situation, and, with enough digging through the manuals and poking and prodding the system, I eventually come up with the answer. Even if the answer is spelled out, it's usually a list of steps to follow to correct the problem. There are no details about what caused the problem in the first place or what the listed steps are actually doing.

12.1 Solving Problems Yourself

In this chapter, I am not going to give you list of known problems and their solutions. A lot of ideas in the HOWTOs do that for you. I am not going to give you details of the system in which you need to find the solution yourself. I hope I did that in the first part of the book. What I am going to do here is to talk about the techniques and tricks that I've learned over the years to track down the cause of problems. Also, I'll talk about what you can do to find out where the answer is, if you don't have the answer yourself.

12.1.1 Preparation

Problem-solving starts before you have even installed your system. Because a detailed knowledge of your system is important to figuring out what's causing problems, you need to keep track of your system from the very beginning. One most effective problem-solving tool costs about $2 and can be found in grocery stores, gas stations, and office supply stores. Interestingly enough, I can't remember ever seeing it in a store that specialized in either computer hardware or software. I am talking about a notebook. Although a bound notebook will do the job, I find a loose-leaf notebook to be more effective because I can add pages more easily as my system develops.

In the notebook I include all the configuration information from my system, the make and model of all my hardware, and every change that I make to my system. This is a running record of my system, so the information should include the date and time of the entry, as well as the person making the entry. Every time I make a change, from adding new software to changing kernel parameters, should be recorded in my log book.

In putting together your notebook, don't be terse with comments like, "Added SCSI patch and relinked." This should be detailed, like, "Added patch for Adaptec AIC-7xxx. Rebuild and reboot successful." Although it seems like busy work, I also believe things like adding users and making backups should be logged. If messages appear on your system, these, too, should be recorded with details of the circumstance. The installation guide should contain an "installation checklist." I recommend that you complete this before you install and keep a copy of this in the log book.

Something else that's very important to include in the notebook is problems that you have encountered and what steps were necessary to correct that problem. One support engineer with whom I worked told me he calls this his "solutions notebook."

As you assemble your system, write down everything you can about the hardware components. If you have access to the invoice, a copy of this can be useful for keeping track of the components. If you have any control over it, have your reseller include details about the make and model of all the components. I have seen enough cases in which the invoice or delivery slip contains generic terms like 486 CPU, cartridge tape drive, and 500MB hard disk. Often this doesn't even tell you whether the hard disk is SCSI, IDE, or what.

Next, write down all the settings of all the cards and other hardware in your machine. The jumpers or switches on hardware are almost universally labeled. This may be something as simple as J3 but as detailed as IRQ. Linux installs at the defaults on a wide range of cards, and generally there are few conflicts unless you have multiple cards of the same type. However, the world is not perfect and you may have a combination of hardware that neither I nor Linux developers has ever seen. Therefore, knowing what *all* the settings are can become an important issue.

One suggestion is to write this information on gummed labels or cards that you can attach to the machine. This way you have the information right in front of you every time you work on the machine.

Many companies have a "fax back" service in which you can call a number and have them fax you documentation of their products. For most hardware, this is rarely more than a page or two. For something like the settings on a hard disk, however, this is enough. Requesting faxed documentation has a couple of benefits. First, you have the phone number for the manufacturer of each of your hardware components. The time to go hunting for it is not when your system has crashed. Next, you have (fairly) complete documentation of your hardware. Last, by collecting the information on your hardware, you know what you have. I can't count the number of times I have talked with customers who don't even know what kind of hard disk they have, let alone what the settings are.

Another great place to get technical information is the World Wide Web. I recently bought a SCSI hard disk that did not have any documentation. A couple of years ago, that might have bothered me. However, when I got home, I quickly connected to the Web site of the driver manufacturer and got the full drive specs, as well as a diagram of where the jumpers are. If you are not sure of the company's name, take a guess, as I did. I tried *www.conner.com*, and it worked the first time.

When it comes time to install the operating system, the first step is to read the release notes and installation HOWTO and any documentation that comes with your distribution. I am not suggesting reading them cover to cover, but look through the table of contents completely to ensure that there is no mention of potential conflicts with your host adapter or the particular way your video card needs to be configured. The extra hour you spend doing that will save you several hours later, when you can't figure out why your system doesn't reboot when you finish the install.

As you are actually doing the installation, the process of documenting your system continues. Depending on what type of installation you choose, you may or may not have the opportunity to see many of the programs in action. If you choose an automatic installation, many of the programs run without your interaction, so you never have a chance to see and therefore document the information.

The information you need to document are the same kinds of things I talked about in the section on finding out how your system was configured. It includes the hard disk geometry and partitions (`fdisk`), file systems (`mount` and `/etc/fstab`), the hardware settings (`/var/log/messages`), and every patch you have ever installed. You can send the output to all of these commands to a file that you can print out and stick in the notebook.

I don't know how many times I have said it and how many articles (both mine and others') in which it has appeared–some people just don't want to listen. They often treat their computer systems like a new toy at Christmas. They first want to get everything installed that is visible to the outside world, such as terminals and printers. In this age of "'Net-in-a-box," often that extends to getting their system on the Internet as soon as possible.

Although being able to download the synopsis of the next Deep Space Nine episode is an honorable goal for some, Chief O'Brien is not going to come to your rescue when your system crashes. (I think even he would have trouble with the antiquated computer systems of today.)

Once you have finished installing the operating system, the very first device you need to install and configure correctly is your tape drive. If you don't have a tape drive, buy one! Stop reading right now and go out and buy one. It has been estimated that a "down" computer system costs a company, on the average, $5,000 an hour. You can certainly convince your boss that a tape drive that costs one-tenth as much is a good investment.

One of the first crash calls I received while I was in tech support was from the system administrator at a major airline. After about 20 minutes, it became clear that the situation was hopeless. I had discussed the issue with one of the more senior engineers who determined that the best course of action was to reinstall the OS and restore the data from backups.

I can still remember their system administrator saying, "What backups? There are no backups."

"Why not?" I asked.

"We don't have a tape drive."

"Why not?"

"My boss said it was too expensive."

At that point the only solution was data recovery service.

"You don't understand," he said. "There is more than $1,000,000 worth of flight information on that machine."

"Not any more."

What is that lost data worth to you? Even before I started writing my first book, I bought a tape drive for my home machine. For me it's not really a question of data but rather, time. I don't have that much data on my system. Most of it can fit on a half-dozen floppies. This includes all the configuration files that I have changed since my system was installed. However, if my system was to crash, the time I save restoring everything from tape compared to *reinstalling* from floppies is worth the money I spent.

The first thing to do once the tape drive is installed is to test it. The fact that it appears at boot says nothing about its functionality. It has happened enough that it appears to work fine, all the commands behave correctly, and it even looks as though it is writing to the tape. However, it is not until the system goes down and the data is needed that you realize you cannot read the tape.

I suggest first trying the tape drive by backing up a small subdirectory, such as `/etc`. There are enough files to give the tape drive a quick workout, but you don't have to wait for hours for it to finish. Once you have verified that the basic utilities work (like `tar` or `cpio`), then try backing up the entire system. If you don't have some third-party back-up software, I recommended that you use `cpio`. Although `tar` can back up most of your system, it cannot backup device nodes.

If the Linux commands are too cumbersome (and they are for many newcomers), a couple of commercial products are available. One such product is Lone-Tar from Cactus International. I have used Lone-Tar for years on a few systems and have found it very easy to use. The front end is mostly shell-scripts that you can modify to fit your needs.

In general, Lone-Tar takes a differential approach to making backups. You create one Master Backup and all subsequent backups contain those files that have changed since the master was created. I find this the best approach if your master backup takes more than one tape. However, if it all fits on one tape, you can configure Lone-Tar always to do masters.

Cactus also produces several other products for Linux, including Kermit, and some excellent DOS tools. I suggest you check them out. Demo versions are available from their Web site, *www.cactus.com*.

Like religion, it's a matter of personal preference. I use Lone-Tar for Linux along with their DOS Tar product because I have a good relationship with the company president, Jeff Hyman, who pops up regularly on CompuServe. Lone-Tar makes backups easy to make and easy to restore. There is even a Linux demo on the Lone-Tar Web site (*www.lone-tar.com*). The Craftworks distribution has a demo version of the BRU backup software.

After you are sure that the tape drive works correctly, you should create a `boot/root` floppy. A `boot/root` floppy is a pair of floppies that you use to boot your system. The first floppy contains the necessary files to boot and the root floppy contains the root file system.

Now that you are sure that your tape drive and your boot/root floppy set work, you can begin to install the rest of your software and hardware. My preference is to completely install the rest of the software first, before moving on to the hardware. There is less to go wrong with the software (at least, little that keeps the system from booting) and you can, therefore, install several products in succession. When installing hardware, you should install and test each component before you go on to the next one.

I think it is a good idea to make a copy of your kernel source (`/usr/src/linux`) before you make any changes to your hardware configuration or add any patches. That way, you can quickly restore the entire directory and don't have to worry about restoring from tape or the distribution CD-ROM.

I suggest that you use a name that is clearer than `/usr/src.BAK`. Six months after you create it, you'll have no idea how old it is or whether the contents are still valid. If you name it something like `/usr/src.06AUG95`, it is obvious when it was created.

Now, make the changes and test the new kernel. After you are sure that the new kernel works correctly, make a new copy of the kernel source and make more changes. Although this is a slow process, it does limit the potential for problems, plus if you do run into problems, you can easily back out of it by restoring the backup of the link kit.

As you make the changes, remember to record all the hardware and software settings for anything you install. Although you can quickly restore the previous copy of the kernel source if something goes wrong, writing down the changes can be helpful if you need to call tech support or post a message to the Internet.

Once the system is configured the way you want, make a backup of the entire installed system on a different tape than just the base operating system. I like to have the base operating system on a separate tape in case

I want to make some major revisions to my software and hardware configuration. That way, if something major goes wrong, I don't have to pull out pieces, hoping that I didn't forget something. I have a known starting point from which I can build.

At this point, you should come up with a back-up schedule. One of the first things to consider is that you should backup as often as necessary. If you can only afford to lose one day's worth of work, then backing up every night is fine. Some people back up once during lunch and once at the end of the day. More often than twice a day may be too great a load on the system. If you feel that you have to do it more often, you might want to consider disk mirroring or some other level of RAID.

The latest kernel versions support RAID 0 (disk striping), which, although it provides an improvement in performance, has no redundancy. Currently, I am not aware of any software RAID solutions, though some hardware solutions might work with Linux.

The type of backup you do depends on several factors. If it takes 10 tapes to do a backup, then doing a full backup of the system (that is, backing up *everything*) every night is difficult to swallow. You might consider getting a larger tape drive. In a case where a full backup every night is not possible, you have a few alternatives.

First, you can make a list of the directories that change, such as `/home` and `/etc`. You can then use `tar` just to backup those directories. This has the disadvantage that you must manually find the directories that change, and you might miss something or back up too much.

Next, there are incremental backups. These start with a master tape, which is a backup of the entire system. The next backup only records the things that have changed since the last incremental. This can be expanded to several levels. Each level backs up everything that has changed since the last backup of that or the next lower level.

For example, level 2 backs up everything since the last level 1 or the last level 0 (whichever is more recent). You might do a level 0 backup once a month (which is a *full* backup of everything), then a level 1 backup every Wednesday and Friday and a level 2 backup every other day of the week. Therefore, on Monday, the level 2 will back up everything that has changed since the level 1 backup on Friday. The level 2 backup on Tuesday will back up everything since the level 2 backup on Monday. Then on Wednesday, the level 1 backup backs up everything since the level 1 backup on the previous Friday.

At the end of the month, you do a level 0 backup that backs up everything. Let's assume this is on a Tuesday. This would normally be a level 2. The level 1 backup on Wednesday backs up everything since the level 0 backup (the day before) and not since the level 1 backup on the previous Friday.

A somewhat simpler scheme uses differential backups. Here, there is also a master. However, subsequent backups will record *everything* that has changed (is different) from the master. If you do a master once a week and differentials once a day, then something that is changed on the day after the master is recorded on every subsequent backup.

A modified version of the differential backup does a complete, level 0 backup on Friday. Then on each of the other days, a level 1 backup is done. Therefore, the backup Monday–Thursday will backup everything since the day before. This is easier to maintain, but you may have to go through five tapes.

The third type, the simplest method, is where you do a master backup every day and forget about increments and differences. This is the method I prefer if the whole system fits on one tape because you save time when you have to restore your system. With either of the other methods, you will probably need to go through at least two tapes to recover your data, unless the crash occurs on the day after the last master. If you do a full backup every night, then there is only one backup to load. If the backup fits on a single tape (or at most, two), then I highly recommend doing a full backup every night. Remember that the key issue is getting your people back to work as soon as possible. The average $5,000 per hour you stand to loose is much more than the cost of a large (8Gb) tape drive.

This brings up another issue, and that is rotating tapes. If you are making either incremental or differential backups, then you *must* have multiple tapes. It is illogical to make a master then make an incremental on the same tape. There is no way to get the information from the master.

If you make a master backup on the same tape very night, you can run into serious problems as well. What if the system crashes in the middle of the backup and trashes the tape? Your system is gone and so is the data. Also, if you discover after a couple of days that the information in a particular file is garbage and the master is only one day old, then it is worthless for getting the data back. Therefore, if you do full backups every night, use at least five tapes, one for each day of the week. (If you run seven days a week, then seven tapes is likewise a good idea.)

You don't necessarily always have to back up to tape. If the amount of data that changes is fairly small, you could backup to floppies. This is probably only valid if your system is acting as a Web server and the data change at irregular intervals. As with any backup, you need to weigh the time to recreate the data against the time to make the backup. If your data on the Web server is also stored elsewhere (like on the development machine), it may be easier to back up the Web server once after you get your configuration right, and then skip the backups. However, it's your call.

Other choices for backup media include WORM (Write Once–Read Many) drive and CD-Recordable. This is only effective if the data isn't going to change much. You could back up your Web server to one of these media and then quickly recovered it if your machine crashes. Copy the data to another machine on the network where a backup is done. (You could also mount the file system you want to back up via NFS.)

Although most people get this far in thinking about tapes, many forget about the physical safety of the tapes. If your computer room catches fire and the tapes melt, then the most efficient backup scheme is worthless. Some companies have fireproof safes in which they keep the tapes. In smaller operations, the system administrator can take the tape home from the night before. This is normally only effective when you do masters every night. If you have a lot of tapes, you might consider companies that provide off-site storage facilities.

Although some commercial products are available (which I will get into in a moment), you can use the tools on your system. For example, you can use `tar` or `cpio`. Although `tar` is a bit easier to use, `cpio` does have a little more functionality. The `tar` command has the following basic format:

```
tar options files
```

An example might be

```
tar cvf /dev/fd0 /home /etc
```

This example would back up `/home` and `/etc` and write them to the floppy tape device `/dev/fd0`. The `c` option says to create an archive, `v` is verbose mode in which all the files are output to `stdout`, and `f` says that `tar` should output to the following *file*. In this case, you are outputting to the device file `/dev/fd0`.

If you have a lot of directories, you can use the `T` option to specify a file, containing the directories to backup. For example, if you had file called `file_list` that contained the list of directories, the command might look like this:

```
tar cvfT /dev/rft0 file_list
```

To extract files, the syntax is essentially the same, except that you use the `x` option to extract. However, you can still use both the `f` and `T` options.

The GNU version of `tar` (which comes with most versions of Linux) has a very large number of options. One option I use is `z`, which I use to either compress or uncompress the archive (depending on which direction I am going). Because the archive is being filtered through `gzip`, you need to have `gzip` on your system. Although `gzip` is part of every Linux distribution, it may not be on your system. Also, if you want to copy the archive to another UNIX system, that system may not have `gzip`. Therefore, you can either skip the compression or use the `Z` (notice the uppercase) to use `compress` and `uncompress`.

Although I can imagine situations in which they might be useful, I have only used a few of them. The best place to look is the `tar` man-page.

If your backup media can handle more than one set of backups, you can use the `mt` command to manage your tape drive. Among the functions that the `mt` can do is to write a "file mark," which is simply a marker on the tape to indicate the end of an archive. To use this function, you must first back the backup to the no-rewind tape device (for example, `/dev/rft0`). When the drive has written all of the archive to the tape, write the file marker to indicate where the end is.

Normally, when `tar` is complete and the tape device is closed, it rewinds. When you use the no-rewind device, the `tar` process finishes, but the tape does not rewind. You can then use the `mt` command to write the file mark at the tape's current location, which is at the end of the `tar` archive. Even if there are multiple archives on the single tape, `mt` will find the specific location. Therefore, whenever you need to restore, you can access any of the archives. See the `mt` man-page for more detail.

12.1.2 Checking the Sanity of Your System

Have you ever tried to do something and it didn't behave the way you expected it to? You read the manual and typed in the example character for a character only to find it didn't work right. Your first assumption is that the manual is wrong, but rather than reporting a bug, you try the command on another machine and to your amazement, it behaves exactly as you expect. The only logical reason is that your machine has gone insane.

Well, at least that's the attitude I have had on numerous occasions. Although this personification of the system helps relieve stress sometimes, it does little to get to the heart of the problem. If you want, you could check every single file on your system (or at least those related to your problem) and ensure that permissions are correct, the size is right, and that all the support files are there. Although this works in many cases, often figuring out which programs and files are involved is not easy.

Fortunately, help is on the way. Linux provides several useful tools with which you can not only check the sanity of your system but return it to normal. I've already talked about the first set of tools–these are the monitoring tools such as `ps` and `vmstat`. Although these programs cannot correct your problems, they can indicate where problems lie.

If the problem is the result of a corrupt file (either the contents are corrupt or the permissions are wrong), the system monitoring tools cannot help much. However, several tools specifically address different aspects of your system.

Linux provides a utility to compute a checksum on a file, called `sum`. It provides three ways of determining the sum. The first is with no options at all, which reports a 16-bit sum. The next way uses the `-r` option, which again provides a 16-bit checksum but uses an older method to compute the sum. In my opinion, this method is more reliable because the byte order is important as well. Without the `-r`, a file containing the word "housecat" would have the same checksum if you changed that single word to "cathouse." Although both words have the exact same bytes, they are in a different order and give a different meaning.

On many systems, there is the `md5sum` command. Instead of creating a 16-bit sum, `md5sum` creates a 128-bit sum. This makes it substantially more difficult to hide the fact that a file has changed.

Because of the importance of the file's checksum, I created a shell-script while I was in tech support that would run on a freshly installed system. As it ran, it would store in a database all the information provided in the permissions lists, plus the size of the file (from an `ls -l` listing), the type of file (using the `file` command), and the checksum (using `sum -r`). If I was on the phone with a customer and things didn't appear right, I could do a quick `grep` of that file name and get the necessary information. If they didn't match, I knew something was out of whack.

Unfortunately for the customer, much of the information that my script and database provided was something to which they didn't have access. Now, each system administrator could write a similar script and call up that information. However, most administrators do not consider this issue until it's too late.

We now get to the "sanity checker" with which perhaps most people are familiar: `fsck`, the file system checker. Anyone who has lived through a system crash or had the system shut down improperly has seen `fsck`. One unfamiliar aspect of `fsck` is the fact that it is actually several programs, one for each of the different file systems. This is done because of the complexities of analyzing and correcting problems on each file system. As a result of these complexities, very little of the code can be shared. What can be shared is found within the `/sbin/fsck` program.

When it runs, `fsck` determines what type of file system you want to check and runs the appropriate command. For example, if you were checking an `ext2fs` file system, the program that would do the actually checking would be `/sbin/fsck.ext2`.

Another very useful sanity checker is the `rpm` package manager (assuming that your system uses the RPM file format) that is the RPM program itself. As I talked about earlier, the `rpm` program is used to install additional software. However, you can use many more options to test the integrity of your system.

When the system is installed, all of the file information is stored in several files located in /var/lib/rpm. These are hashed files that rpm can use but mean very little to us humans. Therefore, I am not going to go into more detail about these files.

Assuming you know what file is causing the problem, you can use rpm to determine the package to which this file belongs. The syntax would be

```
rpm -q -f <full_path_to_file>
```

The -q puts rpm into query mode and the -f tells it to query the following file and tell me to what package it belongs. Once you know to what package a file belongs, you can verify the package. For example, let's say that you believe that there is something wrong with the xv file viewer. Its full path is /usr/bin/X11R6/xv, so to find out to what package it belongs, the command would be

```
rpm -q -f   /usr/bin/X11R6/xv
```

This tells you that xv is part of the package

```
xv-3.10a-3
```

Now use the -V option to verify the package:

```
rpm -V xv-3.10a-3
```

If rpm returns with no response, the package is fine. What if the owner and group are wrong? You would end up with an output that looks like this:

```
...UG.   /usr/bin/X11R6/xv
```

Each dot represents a particular characteristic of the file. These characteristics are

5	MD5 checksum
S	File size
L	Symbolic link
T	Modification time
D	Device
U	User
G	Group
M	Mode (permissions and file type)

If any of these characteristics are incorrect, rpm will display the appropriate letter.

12.1.3 Problem Solving

System problems fall into several categories. The first category is difficult to describe and even more difficult to track down. For lack of a better word, I am going to use the word "glitch." Glitches are problems that occur infrequently and under circumstances that are not easily repeated. They can be caused by anything from users with fat fingers to power fluctuations that change the contents of memory.

Next are special circumstances in software that are detected by the CPU while it is in the process of executing a command. I discussed these briefly in the section on kernel internals. These problems are traps, faults, and exceptions, including such things as page faults. Many of these events are normal parts of system operation and are therefore expected. Other events, like following an invalid pointer, are unexpected and will usually cause the process to terminate.

KERNEL PANICS

What if the kernel causes a trap, fault, or exception? As I mentioned in the section on kernel internals, there are only a few cases when the kernel is allowed to do this. If this is not one of those cases, the situation is deemed so serious that the kernel must stop the system immediately to prevent any further damage. This is a panic.

When the system panics, using its last dying breath, the kernel runs a special routine that prints the contents of the internal registers onto the console. Despite the way it sounds, if your system is going to go down, this is the best way to do it. The rationale behind that statement is that when the system panics in this manner, at least there is a record of what happened.

If the power goes out on the system, it is not really a system problem, in the sense that it was caused by an outside influence, similar to someone pulling the plug or flipping the circuit breaker (which my father-in-law did to me once). Although this kind of problem can be remedied with a UPS, the first time the system goes down before the UPS is installed can make you question the stability of your system. There is no record of what happened and unless you know the cause was a power outage, it could have been anything.

Another annoying situation is when the system just "hangs." That is, it stops completely and does not react to any input. This could be the result of a bad hard disk controller, bad RAM, or an improperly written or corrupt device driver. Because there is no record of what was happening, trying to figure out what went wrong is extremely difficult, especially if this happens sporadically.

Because a system panic is really the only time you can easily track down the problem, I will start there. The first thing to think about is that as the system goes down, it does two things: writes the registers to the console screen and writes a memory image to the dump device. The fact that it does this as it's dying makes me think that this is something important, which it is.

The first thing to look at is the instruction pointer. This is actually composed of two registers: the CS (code segment) and EIP (instruction pointer) registers. This is the instruction that the kernel was executing at the time of the panic. By comparing the EIP of several different panics, you can make some assumptions about the problem. For example, if the EIP is consistent across several different panics, this indicates a software problem. The assumption is made because the system was executing the same piece of code every time it panicked. This *usually* indicates a software problem.

On the other hand, if the EIP consistently changes, this indicates that probably no one piece of code is the problem and it is therefore a hardware problem. This could be bad RAM or something else. Keep in mind, however, that a hardware problem could cause repeated EIP values, so this is not a hard-coded rule.

The problem with this approach is that the kernel is generally loaded the same way all the time. That is, unless you change something, it will occupy the same area of memory. Therefore, it's possible that bad RAM makes it look as though there is a bad driver. The way to verify this is to change where the kernel is physically loaded. You can do this by rearranging the order of your memory chips.

Keep in mind that this technique probably may not tell you what SIMM is bad, but only indicate that you may have a bad SIMM. The only sure-fire test is to swap out the memory. If the problem goes away with new RAM and returns with the old RAM, you have a bad SIMM.

Getting to the Heart of the Problem

Okay, so we know what types of problems can occur. How do we correct them? If you have a contract with a consultant, this might be part of that contract. Take a look at it and read it. Sometimes the consultant is not even aware of what is in his or her own contract. I have talked to customers who have had consultant charge them for maintenance or repair of hardware, insisting that it was an extra service. However, the customer could whip out the contract and show the contractor that these services were included.

If you are not fortunate to have such an expensive contract, you will obviously have to do the detective work yourself. If the printer catches fire, it is pretty obvious where the problem is. However, if the printer just stops working, figuring out what is wrong is often difficult. Well, I like to think of problem solving the way Sherlock Holmes described it in *The Seven Percent Solution* (and maybe other places):

"Eliminate the impossible and whatever is left over, no matter how improbable, must be the truth."

Although this sounds like a basic enough statement, it is often difficult to know where to begin to eliminate things. In simple cases, you can begin by eliminating almost everything. For example, suppose your system was hanging every time you used the tape drive. It would be safe at this point to eliminate everything but the tape drive. So, the next big question is whether it is hardware problem or not.

Potentially, that portion of the kernel containing the tape driver was corrupt. In this case, simply rebuilding the kernel is enough to correct the problem. Therefore, when you relink, link in a new copy of the driver. If that is not sufficient, then restoring the driver from the distribution media is the next step. However, based on your situation, checking the hardware might be easier, depending on your access to the media.

If this tape drive requires its own controller and you have access to another controller or tape drive, you can swap components to see whether the behavior changes. However, just as you don't want to install multiple pieces of hardware at the same time, you don't want to swap multiple pieces. If you do and the problem goes away, how do you know whether it was the controller or the tape drive? If you swap out the tape drive and the problem goes away, that would indicate that the problem was in the tape drive. However, does the first controller work with a different tape drive? You may have two problems at once.

If you don't have access to other equipment that you can swap, there is little that you can do other than verify that it is not a software problem. I have had at least one case while in tech support in which a customer called in, insisting that our driver was broken because he couldn't access the tape drive. Because the tape drive worked under DOS and the tape drive was listed as supported, either the documentation was wrong or something else was. Relinking the kernel and replacing the driver had no effect. We checked the hardware settings to make sure there were no conflicts, but everything looked fine.

Well, we had been testing it using `tar` the whole time because `tar` is quick and easy when you are trying to do tests. When we ran a quick test using `cpio`, the tape drive worked like a champ. When we tried outputting `tar` to a file, it failed. Once we replaced the `tar` binary, everything worked correctly.

If the software behaves correctly, there is potential for conflicts. This only occurs when you add something to the system. If you have been running for some time and suddenly the tape drive stops working, then it is unlikely that there are conflicts; unless, of course, you just added some other piece of hardware. If problems arise after you add hardware, remove it from the kernel and see whether the problem goes away. If it doesn't go away, remove the hardware physically from the system.

Another issue that people often forget is cabling. I have done it myself when I had a new piece of hardware and after relinking and rebooting, something else didn't work. After removing it again, the other piece still didn't work. What happened? When I added the hardware, I loosened the cable on the other piece. Needless to say, pushing the cable back in fixed my problem.

I have also seen cases in which the cable itself is bad. One support engineer reported a case to me in which just pin 8 on a serial cable was bad. Depending on what was being done, the cable might work. Needless to say, this problem was not easy to track down.

Potentially, the connector on the cable is bad. If you have something like SCSI, on which you can change the order on the SCSI cable without much hassle, this is a good test. If you switch hardware and the problem moves from one device to the other, this could indicate one of two things: either the termination or the connector is bad.

If you do have a hardware problem, often times it is the result of a conflict. If your system has been running for a while and you just added something, it is fairly obvious what is causing the conflict. If you have trouble installing, it is not always as clear. In such cases, the best thing is to remove everything from your system that is not needed for the install. In other words, strip your machine to the "bare bones" and see how far you get. Then add one piece at a time so that once the problem reoccurs, you know you have the right piece.

When trying to track down a problem yourself, remain calm. Keep in mind that if the hardware or software is as buggy as you now think it is, the company would be out of business. It's probably one small point in the doc that you skipped over (if you even read the doc) or something else in the system is conflicting. Getting upset does nothing for you. In fact (speaking from experience), getting upset can cause you to miss some of the details for which you're looking.

As you try to track down the problem yourself, examine the problem carefully. Can you tell whether there is a pattern to when and/or where the problem occurs? Is the problem related to a particular piece of hardware? Is it related to a particular software package? Is it related to the load that is on the system? Is it related to the length of time the system has been up? Even if you can't tell what the pattern means, the support representative probably has one or more pieces of information to help track down the problem. Did you just add a new piece of hardware or SW? Does removing it correct the problem? Did you check to see whether there are any hardware conflicts such as base address, interrupt vectors, and DMA channels?

I have talked to customers who were having trouble with one particular command. They insist that it does not work correctly and therefore there is a bug in either the software or the doc. Because they were reporting a bug, we allowed them to speak with a support engineer even though they did not have the valid support contract. They kept saying that the documation is bad because the software did not work the way it was described in the manual. After pulling some teeth, I discovered that the doc the customers used is for a product that was several years old. In fact, there had been three releases since then. They were using the latest software, but the doc was from the older release. No wonder the doc didn't match the software.

12.1.4 Crash Recovery

If your system crashes, the most important thing is to prevent further damage. Hopefully, the messages that you see on your screen will give you some indication of what the problem is so that you can correct it. (For example, timeout errors on your hard disk might mean it's time to buy a new hard disk.)

Emergency Floppies

It may happen that the system crash you just experienced no longer allows you to boot your system. What then? The easiest solution (at least the easiest in terms of figuring out what to do) is reinstalling. If you have a recent backup and your tape drive is fairly fast, this is a valid alternative, provided there is no hardware problem causing the crash.

In an article I wrote for SCO's DiSCOver magazine, I compared a system crash to an earthquake. The people who did well after the 1989 earthquake in Santa Cruz were those who were most prepared. The people who do well after a system crash are also those who are best prepared. As with an earthquake, the first few minutes after a system crash are crucial. The steps you take can make the difference between a quick, easy recovery and a forced re-install.

In previous sections, I talked about the different kinds of problems that can happen on your system, so there is no need to go over them again here. Instead, I will concentrate on the steps to take after you reboot your system and find that something is wrong. It's possible that when you reboot all is well and it will be another six months before that exact same set of circumstances occurs. On the other hand, your screen may be full of messages as it tries to bring itself up again.

Because of the urgent nature of system crashes and the potential loss of income, I decided that this was one troubleshooting topic through which I would hold your hand. There is a set of common problems that occur after a system crashes that need to be addressed. Although the cause of the crash can be a wide range of different events, the result of the crash is small by comparison. With this and the importance of getting your system running again in mind, I am going to forget what I said about giving you cookbook answers to specific questions for this one instance.

Let's first talk about those cases in which you can no longer boot at all. Think back to our discussion of starting and stopping the system and consider the steps the system goes through when it boot. I talked about them in detail before, so I will only review them here as necessary to describe the problems.

As I mentioned, when you turn on a computer, the first thing is the Power-On Self-Test, or POST. If something is amiss during the POST, you will usually hear a series of beeps. Hopefully, there will be some indication on your monitor of what the problem is. It can be anything from incorrect entries in your CMOS to bad RAM. If not, maybe the hardware documentation mentions something about what the beeps mean.

When finished with the POST, the computer executes code that looks for a device from which it can boot. On a Linux system, this boot device will more than likely be the hard disk. However, it could also be a floppy or even a CD-ROM. The built-in code finds the active partition on the hard disk and begins to execute the code at the beginning of the disk. What happens if the computer cannot find a drive from which to boot depends on your hardware. Often a message will indicate that there is no bootable floppy in drive A. It is also possible that the system will simply hang.

If your hard disk is installed and it *should* contain valid data, your master boot block is potentially corrupt. If you created the boot/root floppy set as I told you to do, you can use `fdisk` from it to recreate the partition table using the values from your notebook. Load the system from your boot/root floppy set and run `fdisk`.

This is done from the hard disk. With the floppy in the drive, you boot your system. When you get to the `Boot:` prompt, simply press `Enter`. After loading the kernel, it prompts you to insert the root file system floppy. Do that and press `Enter`. A short time later, you are brought to a # prompt from which you can begin to issue commands.

When you run `fdisk`, you will probably see an empty table. Because you made a copy of your partition table in your notebook as I told you to do, simply fill in the values exactly as they were before. Be sure that you make the partition active as it was previously. Otherwise, you won't be able to boot, or you could still boot but you will corrupt your file system. When you exit `fdisk`, it will write out a copy of the master boot block to the beginning of the disk. When you reboot, things will be back to normal.

(I've talked to at least one customer who literally laughed at me when I told him to do this. He insisted that it wouldn't work and that I didn't know what I was talking about. Fortunately for me, each time I suggested it, it did work. However, I *have* worked on many machines where it didn't work. With a success rate of more than 90 percent, it's obviously worth a try.)

Table 12.1 will give you a good overview of the tools available to solve problems on your own. If not, the next section will be of use to you.

Table 12.1: Files Used in Problem Solving

Command	Description
/bin/pstat	Reports system information
/bin/who	Lists who is on the system
/bin/whodo	Determines what process each user is running
/etc/badtrk	Checks for bad spots on your hard disk
/etc/crash	Examines the running kernel
/etc/custom	Displays information about install packages (also used to install and remove software)
/etc/dfspace	Calculates available disk space on all mount-mounted file systems (front end to df)
/etc/divvy	Creates and administers divisions
/etc/fdisk	Creates and administers disk partitions
/etc/fsck	Checks and cleans file systems
/etc/fuser	Indicates which users are using particular files and file systems
/etc/ifconfig	Configures network interface parameters
/etc/ps	Reports information on all processes
/usr/adm/hwconfig	Contains the hardware configuration log
/usr/adm/lastlog	Contains information on each user's last login
/usr/bin/cpio	Creates archives of files
/usr/bin/last	Indicates last logins of users and teletypes
/usr/bin/llistat	Administers network interfaces
/usr/bin/lpstat	Prints information about status of print service
/usr/bin/netstat	Administers network interfaces
/usr/bin/sar	Reports on system activity
/usr/bin/swconfig	Reports on software changes to the system
/usr/bin/tar	Creates archives of files
/usr/bin/w	Reports who is on the system and what they are doing
/usr/lib/acct/lastlogin	Keeps record of date user last logged in
/usr/spool/lp/pstatus	Contains printer status information

12.2 Getting Help

If you're like me, you think the manual is for cowards. Any good computer hacker should not be afraid to open up the box and start feeding in disks without any regard for the consequences. You tear open the box, yank out the floppies, pop the first one in the drive, and start up the Software Manger or custom and happily go through the thankless task of installing the software. After everything has been installed and your desktop icons have been created, you double-click the icon and start your new multimedia Web viewer. But wait! It doesn't work right. No matter how much you point and click and click again, nothing happens. In frustration, you get on the phone and frantically dial the 800-number from the back of the manual (making this the first time you opened it).

When you finally get through to support after waiting for two hours (it was actually only five minutes), you lash out at the poor tech support representative who was unlucky enough to get your call. You spend more time ranting about poorly written software than you spent on hold. When you finally finish insulting this person's ancestry, he or she calmly points out that on page 2 in the manual, where it describes the installation procedure, it says that to get the Web to work correctly, you have to have a network installed. Because you decided not to install TCP/IP when you first loaded the system, there is no way for the Web viewer to work. You're embarrassed and the whole situation is not a happy thing.

The obvious solution is to read the HOWTOs and other documentation before, during, and after the installation. Doing so tends to limit the embarrassing calls to tech support, but the world is not perfect and eventually something will go wrong. Programs are (still) written by human beings who can make mistakes, which we users call bugs. Perhaps the QA technician who was checking your SCSI host adapter sneezed at the very moment the monitor program reported an incorrect voltage. Maybe the manufacturer never tested that one, rare set of circumstances that causes the program to freeze the way it did on your machine. The end result is that you've read the manual, checked and rechecked the hardware, and it still does not behave the way it is supposed to. You can't solve the problem yourself, so you need help.

12.2.1 Calling Support

The most commonly known source of help is the company's tech support department. With Linux, however, there is no one to call. At least, there is no one single company or organization to call. If you bought Linux as part of a complete system or from an established distributor, they will probably be able to help you. Many have free e-mail support for those who can't afford the phone support. Many also will charge you a certain amount per minute or a flat fee per call. However, even if you are left with other sources, such as USENET newsgroups or the mailing lists, going through "tech support" has the same basic principles, so I will address this as though you were getting help directly from the company.

Tech support is like any system. You put garbage in and you're likely to get garbage out. Calling in and demanding immediate results or blaming the support representative for the problem will probably get you one of a few responses. They'll tell you that it's a hardware problem if you've called a software company, a software problem if you've called a hardware company, or they'll say there is "something" else on the machine conflicting with their product, but it's your job to figure it out. You may even get an answer that, yes, that board is bad, and you can return it to the place of purchase to get a refund or exchange. In other words, they blow you off.

If the board was bad, getting a replacement solves the problem. If there is a conflict, however, you will probably spend even more time trying to track it down. If the problem is caused by some program problem (conflicts or whatever), reinstalling may not fix the problem.

Rather than spending hours trying to track down the conflict or swapping out boards, you decide to call tech support. The question is, "Which one?" If there is only one program or one board, it's pretty obvious which tech support department to call. If the problem starts immediately after you add a board or software package, the odds are that this has something to do with whatever you just installed. If, however, the problem starts after you've been running for a while, tracking down the offender is not that easy. That's why you're going to call tech support, right? So grab that phone and start dialing.

Stop! Put that phone down! You're not ready to call yet. There's something you need to do first. In fact, you need to do several things before you call.

Calling tech support is not as easy as picking up the phone and dialing. Many people who are having trouble with their systems tend to think that it is. In many cases, this is true. The problem is basic enough that the tech support representative can answer it within a few minutes. However, if it's not, your lack of preparation can turn a two-minute call into a two-hour call.

Preparation for calling tech support begins long before that first phone call or the first news post. In fact, preparation actually begins before you install anything on your system. I mean *anything*–before you install your first program, before you make the change to `.profile` to change your prompt, even before you install the operating system.

In previous chapters, I talked about purchasing a notebook and detailing your system configuration. This kind of information is especially important when you call a hardware vendor to help track down a conflict or when the software *should* work. You may never use most of this information. When you do need it, however, you save yourself a great deal of time by having it in front of you. This is also important when you post a message to a newsgroup and someone asks for the details of your configuration.

By knowing what product and what release you have before you call, you save yourself time when you do call. First, you don't have to hunt through notes or manuals while the clock is ticking on your phone bill. Even if you can't find the release, don't guess or say "the latest." Though you can get the release number from the installation media, this may not be exactly what was used to install. The best source is to run `uname -a`. This tells you exactly what release the system is currently running.

The problem with Linux is that there is no one "official" release. There are "official" releases of the kernel, but that doesn't necessarily tell you everything about your system. If you purchase a complete Linux system (either just the software or with hardware), you should have some documentation that not only lists the kernel version but also that distributor's version as well.

If you guess, the support technical might have to guess, too. This is important because fixes are almost always release-specific. If you say "the latest" and it isn't and the "bug" you have was corrected in the latest release, the analyst is not going to give you the fix because he or she thinks you already have it. This wastes the analyst's time, wastes your time, and in the end, you don't get the correct solution. More than likely, if you guess and say "the latest" when posting to a newsgroup, you will get some "friendly" reminders that you should provide more specific details.

Should it be necessary to contact a support organization, at the very minimum, you should have the following information:

- Operating system(s) and versions
- Machine type: 486/DX 50, P6/133, etc.
- Make and model of all hardware (rarely is just the brand sufficient)
- Controller make, model, and type
- Symptoms of problem: noises, messages, previous problems
- An exact description of the error message you received and the context in which you received it
- Drive organization: partition sizes, special drivers
- Special devices/drivers, such as disk array hardware and software
- What the machine was doing when the problem occurred
- What the sequence of events was that preceded the problem
- Whether this problem has occurred more than once and if so, how often
- Whether you recently installed any device drivers or additional hardware
- What the last thing you changed was
- When you changed it
- Whether this a production machine and whether you are down now
- If this is related to a software product you have installed, what the exact version is
- What distribution of Linux your are running, whether and from where you downloaded it, copied it, or purchased it

- What version of the kernel you are running and what options you are using
- Whether any additional packages are not part of the standard distribution
- How urgent the problem is

The last question is essential to getting you the service you need. If you are not clear to tech support about the urgency of the situation, you may end up waiting for the available support analyst or you might get the "try this and call back later answer." By explaining the urgency to everyone you contact, you are likely to get your answer more quickly.

On the other hand, most tech support is based on an honor system. The support organizations with which I have dealt will believe you when you call in and say your system is down. (This was also the case when I worked in support.) Many customer service people are not in a position to judge the severity of the problem. However, the support analyst is. Saying that your company is down because you can't figure out the syntax for a shell-script is unfair to other people who have problems that are really more severe than yours. Simply turn the situation around when you are the one waiting for support on a system crash and someone else is tying up the lines because he or she can't install a printer.

Once you have all the details about the problem, you are ready to call, right? Well, not yet. Before you actually start dialing, you must make every effort to track down the problem yourself. The first reason is pretty obvious. If you find it yourself, there is no need to call tech support.

This doesn't apply as much to newsgroups, but you do save time by listing the things that you have tried. If there is no specific solution to your problem, other newsgroup readers will probably make suggestions. If you list what you have tried, no one will suggest doing something that you have already tried. Telling them what you have tried applies to tech support as well.

Many vendors have bulletin boards containing answers to commonly asked questions. There may even be a WWW page for the bulletin board to make access even easier. Unless your system won't boot at all, this is usually a good place to look before you call support. Again, it's an issue of time. It is generally much easier to get into a bulletin board than to a support engineer. You may have to spend a little time becoming familiar with the particular interface that this company uses, but once you have learned your way around, you can not only find answers to your questions, but you often find treasures such as additional programs that are not part of the base distribution. Even if you don't find the solution, knowing that you did look on the bulletin board saves the support engineer a step. In addition, access a Web page or a bulletin board can keep you up-to-date on patch releases.

I mentioned that some companies have fax-back services. Often, answers to common questions are available this way. If you try the fax-back service, as well as newsgroups or on-line services like CompuServe, you have saved time if you need to call into support. Even if you don't get the solution to your problem, you may have gotten some of the suggestions that the tech support representative would have given you. Because you already know that something doesn't work, you have saved yourself the problem of getting a "try this and call back" answer.

From the tech support perspective, this is very helpful. First, there is the matter of saving time. If it takes 20 minutes just to get through the basic "sanity" checks, then that is 20 minutes that could have been used to service someone else. Why do you care if someone else gets help instead of you? Well, if you happen to be the one waiting to talk to the support representative, you want him or her to be done with the other customer as soon as possible to be able to get to you more quickly. The bottom line is that the more quickly they're done with one customer, the quicker it is for everyone.

Make sure that any hardware you have added is supported before you call to support. If not, getting effective support is difficult at best. Tech support may have to guess at what the problem is and possibly give you erroneous information. In many cases, you may be referred to the hardware vendor and simply told they can't help you. Not that they won't try. The issue is usually that they don't have any information about that product, so the best they can do is go from knowledge about similar products. If the product you want to use deviates from the norm, generic information is of little value.

If this is a software problem, make sure that the release you have is supported on this release of Linux. One common problem is that the software may be ELF, but your kernel only supports `a.out`, in which case, you have a problem.

If a piece of equipment is not "officially" supported, the support representative or people on the newsgroup may never have seen this before and may be unaware of quirks that it has. A printer may claim to be HP LaserJet-compatible, but the driver may send commands to the printer that the clone does not have. Many people will insist that this is a problem with the operating system. No one never claimed that the hardware was going to work. So, if the hardware vendor claims it is 100 percent compatible, it is up to them to prove it.

On the other hand, because of the nature of the job in tech support and the nature of people using Linux, the representatives probably have encountered hardware that is not officially supported. If they try to get it to work and they succeed, then they are in a position to try it the next time. If they have successfully installed something similar, then many of the same concepts and issues apply.

This same thing applies to software. Make sure the software is supported by the OS. It may be that the particular release of the application is only supported with a kernel after a particular release. In that case, neither the people on the newsgroup, the Linux distributor, nor the application vendor will be able to help. They know that it will not work. I remember one call into tech support in which the customer was having trouble with a version of our spreadsheet product that has been discontinued for more than two years. To make things more interesting, the customer was trying to get it to work not on our OS, but someone else's.

Also try to determine whether it is really an operating system problem and not specific to just one application. If you call your Linux distributor with a problem in an application that you got somewhere else, make sure the problem also occurs outside of that application. For example, if you can print from the command line but can't print from WordPerfect, it's not an operating system problem. However, if the OS and WordPerfect both have trouble printing, then it is probably not an issue with WordPerfect. The reverse is also true.

If the problem is with the software and deals with configuration, make sure that all of the associated files are configured correctly. Don't expect the distributor or the people on a newsgroup to check your spelling. I had one customer who had problems configuring his mail system. He spent several minutes ranting about how the manuals were wrong because he followed them *exactly* and it still didn't work. Well, all the files were set up correctly except for that he had made something plural though the manual showed it as being singular.

Even after you have gathered all the information about your system and software, looked for conflicts and tried to track down the problem yourself, you are still not quite ready to call. Preparing for the call itself is another part of getting the answer you need.

One of the first questions you need to ask yourself is "Why am I calling tech support?" What do you expect? What kind of answer are you looking for? In most cases, the people answering the phones are not the people who wrote the code, although you will find them by subscribing to mailing lists. Due to the nature of Linux enthusiasts, many *have* spent hours digging through the source code, looking for answers or creating a patch. However, this is not the same as writing the SCSI hard disk driver. Therefore, they may not be in a position to tell you why the program behaves in a certain way, only how to correct it. Despite this, Linux users may have a better overall knowledge of the product than many of the developers because they deal with more diverse issues. Therefore, they may not be in a position to tell you why the program behaves the way it does, only how to correct it.

If you are contacting the support representatives via fax, e-mail, or any other "written" media, be sure that there are no typos. Especially when relating error messages, always make sure that you have written the text *exactly* as it appears. I have dealt with customers who have asked for help and the error message they report is half of one release and half of another. The change required is different depending on the release you are running. This is also important to know when calling. Telling the support representative that the message was "something like" may not do any good. If there are several possible errors, all with similar content, the exact phrasing of the message is important.

This is also a problem with two systems when one is having the problem and the other is not. It is not uncommon for a customer to describe the machines as "basically the same." This kind of description has little value when the representatives trying to track down a problem. I get annoyed with people who use the term when trying to describe a problem. I don't want the basics of the problem, I want the details. Often customers will use it as a filler word. That is, they say "basically," but still go into a lot of detail.

Many customers insist that the two systems are identical. If they were *identical*, then they both would be behaving the same way. The fact that one works and the other doesn't indicates that the machines are *not* identical. By trying to determine where the machines differ, you narrow down the problem to the point at which tracking down the problem is much easier. You can even find the problem yourself, thus avoiding the call to support.

Once you get tech support on the phone, don't have them read the manual to you. This is a waste of time for both you and the support representative, especially if you are paying for it. Keep in mind that although there may be no charge for the support itself, you may be calling a toll number. If this is during the normal business day (which it probably is), the call could still cost $20–$30. However, this also depends on your support contract. Many customers will pay tens of thousands of dollars a year for support so that the can have the manual read to them. They don't have the time to go searching for the answer, so they pay someone else to do it for them. If you want a premium service, you have to pay a premium price.

The same applies to newsgroups. Don't waste bandwidth by asking someone to give you the option to a command. RTFM! (Read The Friendly Manual) Every version I have seen comes with manual-pages, as well as dozens of documents detailing how to run your system.

If you do read the manual and your problem still does not work out the way you expect it to or you are having problems relating the doc to the software, ensure that the doc matches the SW. One customer was having trouble changing his system name. He said the documentation was worthless because the software did not work as it was described in the manual. It turned out that the doc he was using was for a release that was two years old, and he never got the latest doc! No wonder the doc did not match the software.

If you don't know the answer to the question, tell the support representative "I don't know." Do not make up an answer. Above all, don't lie outright. I had a customer who was having problems running some commands on his system. They were behaving in a manner I had never seen before, even on older releases. To track down the problem I had him check the release his was on. None of the normal tools and files were there. After poking around a while, I discovered that it was not our OS. When confronted with this, the customer's response was that their contract for the other operating system had run out.

Getting information from some customers is like pulling teeth. They won't give it up without a fight. To get the right answer, you must tell the analyst everything. Sometimes it may be too much, but it is much better to get too much than not enough.

When talking to support, have everything in front of you. Have your notebook open, the system running if possible, and be ready to run any command the support representative asks you. If you have a hardware problem, try to have everything else out of the machine that is not absolutely necessary to your issue. It is also helpful to try to reinstall the software before you call. Reinstalling is often useful and several companies seem to use this method as their primary solution to any problem. If you have done it before calling and the problem still persists, the tech support representative won't get off with that easy answer. I am not professing this as the standard way of approaching things, though if you believe reinstalling would correct the problem and you have the opportunity, doing so either solves the problem or forces support to come up with a different solution.

Another common complaint is customers calling in and simply saying that a particular program doesn't work right. Although this may be true, it doesn't give much information to the technician. Depending on its complexity, a program may generate hundreds of different error messages, all of which have different causes and solutions. Regardless of what the cause really is, it is almost impossible for the technician to be able to determine the cause of the problem simply by hearing you say that the program doesn't work.

A much more effective and successful method would be to simply state what program you were trying to use, then describe the way it behaved and how you expect that it should behave. You don't even need to comment on it not working right. By describing the behavior, the technician will be able to determine one of two things. Either you have misunderstood the functionality of the program, you are using it incorrectly or there really is a bug in the program.

People who call into tech support very commonly have the attitude that they are the only customers in the world with a problem. Many have the attitude that all other work by the entire company (or at least, tech support) needs to stop until their problem is resolved. Most tech support organizations are on schedules. Some have phone shifts scattered throughout the day and can only work on "research" problems during specific times of the day. Other organizations have special groups of people whose responsibility it is to do such research. In any event, if the problem requires special hardware or a search through the source code, you may have to wait several hours or even days for your solution. For the individual, this may be rather annoying, but it does work out better for everyone in the long run.

The attitude that the analyst needs to stop what he or she is doing and work on this one customer's problem becomes a major issue when problems are caused by unique circumstances. The software or hardware company may not have that exact combination of hardware available. Although the combination ought to work, no one that has not tested it can guarantee there will be no problems. As a result, the support representative may have to wait until he or she is not working on the phone to gather that combination of hardware. It may also happen that the representative must pass the problem to someone else who is responsible for problems of this type. As a result, the answer may not come for several hours, days, weeks, or even *months*, depending on the priority level of the contract.

In addition to the priority of the contract, there is also the urgency of the problem. If you have a situation in which data is disappearing from your hard disk, you will be given a higher priority than your contract would imply.

While I was working in support, I talked with many other support representatives. Often a customer would have a support contract with his or her vendor and the vendor would have the contract with us. The vendor would call us if they could not solve the problem. I had a chance to ask many of them some of the more common problems.

There are several common complaints among tech support representatives. Although it may seem obvious, many people who call in are not in front of their machines. It's possible that the solution is easy enough that the support representative can help even without you at the machine. However, I talked to a customer who had printer problems and wanted me to help him fix things while he was driving down the freeway talking on his car phone.

Another very common issue that support representatives bring up is customers who come off as thinking they know more than tech support. When they are given suggestions, their response is usually "That won't work." Maybe not. However, the behavior exhibited by the failure often does give an indication of where the problem lies. If you are going to take the time to call support, you must be willing to try everything that is suggested. You have to be receptive to the support representative's suggestion and willing to work with him or her. If necessary, you must be willing to start the problem from scratch and go over the "basics." The customers who get the best response from tech support are usually those who remain calm and are willing to try whatever is suggested.

People have called computer manufacturers to be told how to install batteries in laptops. When the support representative explains how to do this and that the directions are on the first page of the manual, one person replied angrily, "I just paid $2,000 for this damn thing, and I'm not going to read a book."

At first glance, this response sounds reasonable. A computer is a substantial investment and costs a fair bit of money. Why shouldn't tech support tell you how to do something? Think about a car. A car costs more. So, after spending $20,000 for a new car, you're not going to read the book to figure out how to start it? Imagine what the car dealer would say if you called in to ask how to start the car.

The computer industry is the only one that goes to this level to support its products. Sometimes you get very naive customers. At least, they are naive when it comes to computers. In attempting to solve a customer's problem, it is often essential that tech support know what release of the operating system the customer is using.

Some customers are missing some basic knowledge about computers. One customer was having trouble when we needed to know the release. Although he could boot, he was having so much trouble typing in basic commands, like `uname`. We told him to type `uname` then press `Enter` and it responded "`dave: command not found`."

We then asked him to get the N1 floppy and read the release number off the floppy. He couldn't find it. Not the floppy, the release number. So after 10 minutes of frustration, we decided to have him photocopy the floppy and fax it to us.

"Wow!" he said. "You can get information from the floppy that way?"

"Sure," we said. "No problem." (What's so hard about reading a label?)

A few minutes later a fax arrived from this customer. It consisted of a single sheet of paper with a large black ring in the center of it. We immediately called him back and asked him what the fax was.

"It's the floppy," he said. "I'm still amazed that you can get information from the floppy like that. I must tell you, I had a heck of a time getting the floppy out of the case. After trying to get it out of that little hole, I had to take a pair of scissors to it." (The case he mentioned was actually the plastic jacket.)

Many of us laugh at this because this is "common knowledge" in the computer industry. However, computers are the only piece of equipment about which the consumer is not expected to have common knowledge.

If you drive a car, you are expected to know not to fill it with diesel when it takes regular gasoline. However, trying to load a DOS program onto an UNIX system is not expected knowledge.

One customer I had was having trouble installing a network card. The documentation was of little help to him because it was using a lot of "techno-babble" that most "normal" people couldn't understand. The customer could not even answer the basic questions about how his hardware was configured. He insisted that it was our responsibility to know that because we wrote the operating system and he's not a computer person. Well, I said that it's like having a car that won't start. You call the car dealership and tell them it won't start. The service department asks you what model you have. You say that they should know that. They then ask if you have the key in the ignition. You say that you are not a "car person" and don't know this technical stuff.

In the past few years, many software vendors have gone from giving away their support to charging for it. Support charges range anywhere from $25 a call for application software to $300 for operating systems like UNIX. As an end user, $300 can be a bit hard to swallow. However, in defense of the software industry, it really is not their fault. As more and more computers are being bought by people who have never used one, the number of calls to support organizations have gone up considerably. People treat computers differently than any other piece of equipment. Rather than reading the manual themselves, they much prefer to call support.

Would you ever call a car manufacturer to ask how to open the trunk? Would you ever call a refrigerator manufacturer to ask how to increase the temperature in the freezer? I hope not. However, computer tech support phones are often flooded with calls at this level, especially if their support is free or free for a specific warranty period.

The only way for a company to recover the cost of the support is either to include it with the cost of the product or to charge extra for it. The bottom line is that there is no such thing as a free lunch, nor is there free tech support. If you aren't paying for the call itself, the company will have to recover the cost by increasing the sales price of the product. The result is still money out of your pocket. To make the situation fairest for everyone involved, companies are charging those people who use the tech support system.

I remember watching a television program a couple of years ago on air plane accidents and how safe planes really are. The technology exists today to decrease the number of accidents and near accidents almost to zero. Improvement to both airplane operations, air traffic control, and positioning could virtually eliminate accidents. However, this would result in increasing the cost of airline tickets by a factor of 10! People won't pay that much for safety. The risk is too low.

The same thing applies to software. It is possible to write code that is bug-free. The professor who taught my software engineering class insisted that with the right kind of planning and testing, all bugs could be eliminated. The question is, "At what cost?" Are you willing to pay 10 times as much for your software just to make it bug-free? One support representative put it like this: "How can you ask us to hold up the entire product for an unknown length of time, to fix a single problem that affects few users and is not fatal? Would you expect Ford to ship their next year's model of Escort three months late because they found out that the placement of the passenger door lock was inconvenient for people taller than 6'9"?" As ridiculous as this seems, calls reporting bugs are often at this level.

Because of the nature of Linux and software in general, it is going to be released with bugs in it. Although no one organization is responsible for it, Linux has as good a track record as any commercial OS. One key difference is that you don't have a huge bureaucracy causing Linux 96 to come out in 98. New versions of the kernel come out every few months and it is literally only a matter of days for patches to appear when bugs are detected.

After years of tech support, I am convinced that the statement "The customer is always right" was not coined by some businessman trying to install a customer service attitude in his employees. It must have been an irate user of some product who didn't bother to read the manual, tried to use the product in some unique way, or just generally messed things up. When this user couldn't figure out how to use whatever he or she bought, he or she decided it was the fault of the vendor and called support.

You as the customer are not always right. Granted, it is the responsibility of the company to ensure that you are satisfied. This job usually falls on the shoulders of tech support because they are usually the only human contact customers have with hardware and software vendors. However, by expecting tech support to pull you out of every hole you dig yourself into or coming across to representatives as a "know-it-all" or "I-am-right," you run the risk of not getting your question answered. Isn't that the reason for calling support in the first place?

12.2.2 Consultants

You may someday find yourself in a position where you cannot continue to try to solve problems over the phone. You need someone to come to your office to look at the problem first hand. This is where the computer consultant comes in. Sometimes consultants are called in to evaluate and analyze the current situations and make recommendations and sometimes even implement these recommendations.

Computer consultants are like lawyers. They often charge outrageous fees (several hundred dollars an hour) and rely on the fact that you know little or nothing about the subject. They have a service that you need and want you to pay as much as you are willing to pay. Fortunately, all you need to do to see whether a lawyer is qualified is to look on his or her wall. If the diploma is from Joe's Law School and Barber College, you'll probably go somewhere else. However, there are few laws governing who can call himself a computer consultant. Therefore, you need to be extra careful in choosing a consultant.

I had one consultant call for a customer of his who was having trouble with a SCSI tape drive. The consultant almost got upset when I started talking about the technical issues involved such as termination, proper cabling, etc. You see, he had a master's degree in electrical engineering and therefore was fully aware of the technical issues at hand. I asked him how much RAM his system had. He responded, "Do you mean memory? Well, there is, uh, 32, uh, what do you call them, megabytes." (No, I'm not making this up.)

Another time a customer was having a similar problem getting a network card working. Again, it was the issue of the customer not having the basic computer knowledge to know about base addresses and interrupts. The difference between thin-net and twisted pair was foreign to him. He had worked for many years on mainframes and had never had to deal with this level of problem. After more than half-an-hour of trying to help him, it became apparent that this was really beyond what tech support is there for. I suggested he hire himself a consultant. In the long run, that would ensure he got the attention and service he need. There was a long pause, and then he said, "I am the consultant."

One of my favorites is a consultant in Texas who was trying to do long-distance hardware troubleshooting for a site in Alaska. Despite the fact that they had a modem connection, it is often quite difficult to check hardware settings and cabling through a modem.

My auto mechanic has a PC running a DOS application written specifically for automobile workshops. Aside from the fact that the consultant has them start Windows and then click on an icon to start this *DOS* application, it does its job (it's the only thing the machine is used for). Recently they discovered that they were running out of hard disk space and needed a larger drive. So, the consultant came in put in a larger hard drive and things looked better. Because it was not part of their contract, he charged them for two hours labor to replace the drive, plus 10 percent more than the average market price for the hard disk. Now, so far, this seems like an acceptable practice. However, they took the smaller drive with them, although they charged full price for the larger drive. It wasn't defective, just too small.

These stories represent four basic problems with computer consultants. First, you don't have to have studied computer science or even a related field to open shop as a computer consultant. Although electrical engineering is a related field and the person may know about the computer at the transistor level, this is comparable to saying that a chemist who knows what goes on at the molecular level inside an internal combustion engine is competent to fix your brakes.

The next issue is that although the person had worked with computers for years, he or she knew little about PCs or operating systems. I have seen enough times consultants who assume that all computer systems are the same. They worked for years on Windows so they are qualified to install and support UNIX, right?

There is also the issue of the consultant not making house calls. They have to. They have to be willing to come to your site and check the situation themselves. You cannot be expected to shut down operations to bring a computer to their office, nor should you tolerate them trying to do remote support (i.e., across a modem).

Lastly, if you do need to hire a consultant, make sure you know what you are paying for. When you do decide on a consultant, make sure that you know specifically what services are being provided and what obligations the consultant has. These services include not only hardware and software, but what work the consultant is going to provide. If the consultant needs to replace a defective hard disk, the cost of the disk is included but the time to replace it may not be included.

The best solution is to ask your friends and other companies. If you have a good relationship with another company of similar size and product, maybe they can recommend a consultant to you. Another source is the Internet and on-line services like CompuServe. Ask people there what their experiences have been. Web search engines, like Yahoo or Alta Vista, can give you names of companies that specialize in Linux as well.

How to Get the Most for Your Money

Deciding that you need a consultant doesn't mean that you are throwing yourself to the wolves. With a little preparation, you can be ready and ensure that you don't make any costly mistakes. There a four basic steps to follow when deciding which consultant to go with:

- Define the project.
- Find the right person for the job.
- Agree **in writing exactly** what the job entails and what is expected from both sides.
- Makes sure the job gets done correctly and on time.

When you think you have found the right consultant, you must treat them like a telephone company: Get it in writing! This, along with finding the right person, are the two essential factors in deciding which consultant to choose.

Let's look at the right person first. There are several ways to go about choosing a consultant. First, you can pick up the telephone book and find the one with the fanciest ad. Personal referrals are also a way, but this can cause a lot of problems. If the consultant is a friend or family member of the person making the recommendation, you can get yourself into an awkward position when you either find he or she is not the right person for the job, or he or she is not really competent and you have get rid of him or her. Personally, I think recommendations from other companies are best. They have had real experiences with the consultant and (should) know their capabilities.

Part of choosing the right person is making sure that he or she has the skills necessary to get the job done. Never hire a consultant who doesn't know the product or issue at hand but insists can learn it. You are paying for an expert, so that's what you should get, not someone still in training. The process is basically the same as hiring an employee. You can request a resume and references and then call those references. Things to ask the references should include the following:

- What did you think of this consultant in general?
- What did you think of the consultant's technical abilities?
- Did he or she interact well with your employees?
- Did he or she follow through with commitments? Finish on time?
- When the project was finished, were there any points of dispute? How well did the consultant react?
- Did you understand what the consultant did?

When you have your first meeting with the consultant, there is nothing wrong with having your expert present to "test" the consultant's knowledge. This is the same thing as an interview–you are trying to determine whether to hire this person. Therefore, you have the right to ask about his or her technical abilities.

In one company for which I worked, we had a very bad experience with a consultant. The company ran mostly PCs with Windows for Workgroups, but there were several UNIX servers and workstations. We found a consulting firm that were "experts" with Microsoft's Exchange because we were planning to implement this on the company's intranet. We explicitly told the consulting firm that one of our goals was to get connected to the Internet. We scheduled a three-day workshop during which the consultant would go through the details of configuration and give us guidance on how to implement it.

When the consultant arrived, we were pleasantly surprised that it was one of the owners of the firm. However, the pleasure was short-lived when we discovered that he had no understanding of Internet mail and therefore could provide us no guidance on how to configure MS-

Exchange for the Internet. We also later discovered that he was no expert with MS-Exchange because he spent the entire afternoon on the last day trying to get a basic configuration issue to work.

This taught us two things. First, just because someone is the owner of a consulting firm does not mean he or she knows what he or she is talking about. Unlike with doctors, few laws govern who can call him- or herself a consultant. Second, we were not clear with what our expectations were or what the consultant was to provide. Nothing was in writing other than that the consultant would give us a "workshop." It was obviously up to the consultant to decide whether he had achieved this goal.

There are many areas in which a consultant is necessary. You cannot hire experts in every area. It would just be too expensive. Even if you do have people in your organization who are experts, it is often useful to have someone come in with a fresh perspective. As an employee, you often have emotional responses involving your system or company that a consultant doesn't have. This is helpful to get to the core of the issue.

Another aspect is the specialization. A consultant has a particular skill set in which he or she knows almost everything (at least that's what you're hoping). Being really good at this one subject means that he or she may not be as useful to a company to hire full time. However, if the company is involved in a project that requires that skill, it is cost-efficient to hire the expert and get the job done more quickly. I think of setting up an Internet server as the primary example. After I had done it a few times, it became a lot easier. However, once I have done it a dozen or so times, it might become easy. Potentially, I could hire myself as a consultant to develop Internet servers. (But then again, maybe not.)

When you hire a consultant, you must know what you what out of him or her. What information do you expect the consultant to impart on you or what project do you expect the consultant to complete? What does "complete" really mean? If the project is configuring a Web server and all the consultant does is hook you up to the Internet, then the job is not done. If the project will take a long time and you expect regular status reports, have the consultant define when these reports are due. If he or she says every other Friday, then handing it to you on Monday is not acceptable.

You may not be able to use the correct "buzzwords" to define what you want, but you can come up with a clear idea of what you want.

Once you have the concept of what you want, you should work with the consultant to define the project in the correct terminology. However, don't let the consultant confuse you. If you don't understand, say so. There is nothing wrong with not understanding something. If you were an expert on this subject, you wouldn't need a consultant. One thing that our MS-Exchange consultant did a lot of was talk in techno-babble. He would throw out a technical word to make him sound like an expert. The problem was that he really didn't know much about the subject and often used the words in the wrong context. If you get the feeling that the consultant is trying to baffle you with buzzwords and techno-babble, it's time to get another consultant.

When dealing with a consultant, you are bound to face concepts and vocabulary that are foreign. What about the other way around? Will the consultant know everything about your business? If the consultant specializes in your area, you would hope so. However, you are probably hiring a computer specialist, not a legal specialist or medical specialist or wholesale distribution specialist. Therefore, there is a lot that you will have to explain to your consultant.

Do not assume that the consultant knows your business at all. Specify *every* aspect of the project. One example is a wholesale soft drink distribution company. When people buy large quantities of soda, they are most familiar with buying by the case. A consultant you hire to develop a tracking system may take this for granted and write the program to deal only in cases. What if you distribute containers of cola syrup as well? These are not measured in cases. If you assume that the consultant knows this and don't tell him or her and he or she programs for cases, who is responsible for paying for the changes? You said you wanted a tracking system and you got one. The project description didn't mention the kind of units.

Don't let the consultant get away with estimates on anything. If he or she estimates anything, it can be off. Just like the estimate on car repairs. The more vague the job description, the easier it is for the consultant to postpone or claim that something was never agreed on, in terms of time as well as money.

If the job will take a while and you have said you want status reports, you can use these reports for the basis of payment. For example, the project is to take 10 weeks with five bi-weekly status reports. Each time you get a status report, the consultant gets one-fifth of the total fee. Another way would be to set "milestones." Each phase of the project is to be done by a certain date. At each milestone, the consultant gets a certain percentage of the total. The idea of completion-based payment is important if you have deadlines to meet yourself. The consultant must be made aware of these as well. It is not unreasonable to make completion within the time specified be part of the contract. However, you need to be clear in the contract what is to be done and by when.

The consultant may not be working solely on your project during the time you contracted him or her. This is acceptable, provided he or she meets all his or her commitments. Explaining to you that he or she couldn't meet the deadline because of a problem at another site should tell you that the other customer is more important. They might be, so find a consultant who will consider you most important.

Do You Get What You Pay For?

Well, that depends. Just because a consultant asks for a high rate does not mean he or she is good. I consider Ferrari or Jaguar as examples. These are very expensive cars. They have a "performance" comparable to their price in that they go fast. If you buy a Ferrari consultant, he or she might be done with the job in a short time. However, as with the Ferrari, you might spend as much on repairs as on the cost of the car.

On the other hand, a consultant's rates will get higher as he or she gets better. Not only does he or she have more technical ability, but he or she has the ability to do a better job more quickly. As a result, you pay a higher rate for his or her time, but you pay for less time. Therefore it comes out cheaper in the long run. Even if it is not cheaper on your checkbook, having the project done faster may save you money.

Some consultants are paid $200 an hour, some are paid $1,000 a day. Those are reasonable prices. Your employees (probably) don't get paid that much, so why should you pay a consultant like that? Well, first, a consultant may not be "on the job" when he or she is at your site. Depending on the project, there maybe hours, days, or even weeks of preparation. Plus, there are all the administrative costs for the consultant's office. You have to pay for the people in your IS/IT department out of your own budget, but for not the company receptionist. The consultant does.

Legal Issues

Remember that the consultant may have complete access to all of your data. Though I am not saying he or she is likely to be a spy for your competition, you need to be careful. Even if the consultant doesn't have access to your more precious trade secrets, having him or her sign a nondisclosure agreement is a wise decision. This could be as simple as stating that the consultant is not to disclose any aspect of the job to anyone, or it may go into detail about what is and is not to be kept secret. Talk to your lawyers about this one.

When the consultant finishes the project, who owns the project? Well, you do as far as the project within your company is concerned. The consultant is not going to charge a license fee to use the program you paid him or her to develop. (We hope.) However, what about the code itself? This was done on your time, so like the code a regular employee writes, it's yours, right? Well, it may be the case that the consultant does keep the right to the code he or she has written, although the compiled, running program is yours. Make this clear in your contract. If you want the right to everything written by the consultant, make sure that part is written in the contract as well.

One important aspect of the contact is the default terms, that is, what happens if the consultant defaults on the agreement. This is especially important if you have deadlines and by not meeting them you loose money. It is not unreasonable to deduct a specific amount from the total for going past the deadline. Not only does the consultant not get paid for those days past the deadline, but money is deducted from what is owed him or her for the other days. I have seen consultants who intentionally overextend themselves just to get a contract. They can promise to have it within a certain time, but have no pressing need to unless they will be losing money.

You have to be careful with this one. If the project is a feasibility study and it turns out that the project is not feasible, did the consultant do his job? Sure, he or she determined whether the project was feasible. Therefore, he or she did his or her job. Also, what happens if the cause of the delay is not the consultant's fault? If you promised him or her certain resources that were not available, you are at fault.

You might even get a consultant who has an attitude of all or nothing. That is, if he or she doesn't deliver on time and what is promised, you don't pay him or her. However, you can guarantee that this consultant will probably have you spell out everything you want done so there is no room for discussion.

POINTS TO REMEMBER

When dealing with consultants, remember these general issues that will help make things easier:

- A consultant is not one of your employees. Don't insist that he or she arrive at a certain time or work until a certain hour. Maybe part of what he or she is doing can be done at his or her office. You're concerned with him or her getting the project done on time and not being physically present at your site.
- Judge the price you pay by what it would take you to do the job without the consultant. How many hours would it take? How much money might you lose? If you would end up paying more than a "high-priced" consultant, the consultant is cheap. However, comparison shopping is also valid for consultant. Get a second or even third estimate.
- Insist on some kind of proof that the consultant knows what he or she is talking about. A resume is fine, but references are better.
- Make sure the consultant communicates well. Can he or she express himself? Does he or she understand your needs and requirements?
- Be comfortable with the consultant. If there is something about him or her that you don't like, you don't need to hire him or her, just as it would be for a normal employee.
- Don't judge the consultant by personal appearance. Then again, I wouldn't hire a slob. It's okay to expect him or her to be clean, but don't expect a suit.

It may sound like I was try to bash all computer consultants. This is not the case. Instead, I tried to give you a few tips in case you happened to get a consultant that really was not looking out for your best interest.

If you decide to implement Linux in your business, you are not destined to try to find a general UNIX consultant who may have some experience with Linux. Instead, you can go directly to a large number of consultant who specialize in Linux. The Consultants HOWTO (*consult.cyrius.com/mohr.html*), maintained by Martin Michlmayr is a list of over 150 consultants world-wide who provide Linux consulting. Although these are mostly in the USA and Germany, there are consultants in places like Argentina, Cambodia, Japan and many places in between. You can request the newest version of the listing by sending a message with the subject "request" to *consult+mohr@howto.cyrius.com*.

12.2.3 Other Sources

Although, as I said, there is no such thing as a free lunch, you can get pretty close sometimes. For about less than a $30 start-up fee and about $10–$20 a month, you can get support that is comparable to the tech support of a software vendor. The only problem is that it might be several hours (rarely longer) before you get an answers. I am talking here about the various forums on CompuServe.

Although I haven't found a forum yet that's specific to Linux, a few others deal with generic UNIX and some deal with specific dialects like SCO. If your problem is general, such as getting DNS to work, or you need help with a shell-script, this is not a bad place to start. Despite the delays that are caused by the very nature of this media, responses are fairly quick. Unless your system has crashed and you are losing thousands of dollars an hour, this is an excellent source of information.

You can reach CompuServe customer service at (800) 848-8990 or (617) 718-2800. In addition, there are offices all over the world. The CompuServe "starter-kit" that is available through many computer software sources contains a list of phone numbers.

Another valuable source are the USENET newsgroups. To gain access, however, you need a "news feed," that is, some other site that will provide you with the newsgroups, because USENET uses "store and forward." Turn around time can be days, depending on where you get your feed. CompuServe, on the other hand, stores all of its messages in a central location. The minute your message is posted, it is available for everyone. Talk to your ISP about finding a news server.

Mailing lists are another way of getting information. The difference between lists and newsgroups is that you receive *all* of the messages posted to the list. Therefore, you need to be careful about what you subscribe to. I subscribe to just a few and I have *hundreds* of messages a day to wade through. You can subscribe directly from the Internet by going to *summer.snu.ac.kr/~djshin/linux/mail-list/index.shtm.*

Throughout this book, I made references to several other works that I feel would be very helpful if you want to learn more about a particular subject. Aside from books, many magazines provide useful information. Although it's geared more toward DOS and Windows, *BYTE* magazine often provides good technical articles about both new and existing technologies.

Not to be outdone by the commercial UNIX dialects, Linux has its own monthly magazine, called *Linux Journal.* It includes articles for almost all skill levels. You can reach the *Linux Journal* at *subs@ssc.com,* (206) 782-7733.

Another place to check is the Internet. Unfortunately, it's hard to be more specific than that. Thousands of resources are out there for every conceivable topic. Most major computer companies have a Web site. Often all you need is to add "www." to the company name to get access to the Web page. I have done this to get to Intel (*www.intel.com*), Conner (*www.conner.com*), and even CNN (*www.cnn.com*). Here you can get product information, as well as press releases. Many of these sites have links to other sites, so it's easy to bounce from site to site.

Also, several search engines have already done a lot of research for you. The one I use most frequently is Yahoo (*www.yahoo.com*), which also links to other search engines. Web sites are broken down by category, which makes browsing easy. You can also input search strings to help you find what you are looking for. If you input a phrase that's fairly common, you can end up with thousands of matches.

CHAPTER 13

LINUX IN YOUR BUSINESS

- Making it work for users
- Securing your system
- Commercial software

If you've gotten this far, you have probably already made the decision to implement Linux in your business. In the introduction, I talked a lot about the reasons why you should use Linux and why Linux is a valid business choice. What I am going to talk about here is just a few things you must consider when implementing Linux (or, for that matter, any operating system).

13.1 Supporting Your Users

Unless you are configuring your system to be just an Internet server, you'll have users on it. As with their desks, users want to be able to create a work environment on their computer that is easy for them to use and with which they are comfortable. Configurability is a primary philosophy of all UNIX-like systems. Despite occasion difficulties in fitting things to your needs, there is very little that you cannot do.

Also, every program that a user will encounter has a configuration file for it. Knowing what these configuration files are and what they can do for you is an important part of administering your system. By making your users aware of this functionality, you can help increase their efficiency either by making the program easier to use or by simply making them happier to use it.

In previous chapters, I talked about a wide range of programs and what you can do to configure them. In this section, I am not going to repeat everything, but rather give you an overview of some of the more common programs and files.

13.1.1 Configuring the System

Even as the system administrator, you can use a large number of files to configure your system. For example, the start-up script under `/etc/rc.d` is almost always modified to fit the needs of your system. Then there are the files that are used to configure mail, DNS, NIS, and a whole range of things.

One first thing that a user may encounter is a shell. Each shell has its own set of configuration files, which I discussed in the section on shells. Here you can set environment variables, as well as define aliases and functions. In most cases, users can modify these files themselves. In addition, you (as the system administrator) can make changes to the files `/etc/skel/` so that each of these modifications are valid for any subsequent users.

The problem with this solution is that any time you want to make additions, you need to change the `rc` file for each user. Some shells have files in `/etc`, but not all do. The answer is to have a line in one of the start-up files that "sources" a systemwide file. This is a single file that would be valid for all users. Note that the syntax of the shells is different, so you would need a different file for each type of shell. For example, one for `sh`-like shells and one for `csh`-like shells.

When you source a file, you prevent the system from creating a new shell. Therefore, all changes remain. Otherwise, a subshell is started and, when that shell exits, the changes are lost.

Let's assume that you have a file called `/etc/user.config`. To source the file under a `sh`-like shell, the command would look like this:

```
. /etc/user.config
```

For a csh-like shell, the command would look like this:

```
source /etc/user.config
```

One shortcoming of Linux occurs when you install new software. Problems arise when the software requires that you define specific environment variables and you need to change it for all users. Some installation scripts will change the shell configuration files for the system, but you cannot always depend on it. It is therefore a good idea to place these kinds of environment variables in your local configuration file.

If you have any local programs that you created and to which you want to give your users access, you can either place them somewhere to which everyone has access (such as /usr/bin) or you can add the location of the files into each user's path. I suggest placing all local programs into /usr/local/bin. This keeps everything in one place and makes changing them easier. You can then add an entry into the PATH environment variable (assuming that it is not already there).

One thing that you need to be careful with is the order of the directories in the PATH variable. I mentioned a case in which a user created a program called sort that appeared in the path before the default version. This resulted in the user not being able to run certain software. However, if you are not careful, the consequences could be worse.

Take, for example, a situation in which the current directory (.) is listed in your path before the standard directories like /bin and /usr/bin. Now imagine that some nefarious user creates a program called ls and places it in /tmp. Any user who is in /tmp and runs ls will run this program first. Your local users won't usually do this, but this is just the kind of trap that an intruder would set. You "know" your network is safe, so why take the risk?

Another useful variable to set is the prompt. For your first shell, this is the PS1 variable. If you start a subshell, this will be the PS2 variable, and so on. It is very common to set your prompt to the current directory. Depending on your shell, this might be done like this:

```
export PS1='$PWD->   '
```

Note that you are doing a couple of things to get this right. First, you are using the PWD environment variable, which shows you your current working directory. Next, you include the whole thing in single quotes, which is necessary to ensure that the PWD variable is not expanded by the shell until it is used. (Note that some shells use CWD instead.)

Some shells do not have the ability; that is, you set the PWD variable and it is not dynamic. That means that once it is set, it keeps that value. The solution is to create an alias for the cd command:

```
alias cd=(cd $1; PS1=$PWD)
```

If you have a large number of aliases, functions, or environment variables, you might want to consider having a separate file for each type of file. For example:

```
user.alias
user.function
user.variables
```

Both of the primary editors (vi and emacs) have their own configuration files, which I covered in their respective sections (see Section 4.1, Interactively Editing Files with vi, and Section 4.2, Interactively Editing Files with emacs, respectively).

If you have a network, you can configure several files to suit your needs. The .netrc is used when connecting to a site via ftp and enables you to connect automatically. This file contains a single line for each system to which you want to connect and includes the user name and password. The syntax of each line is

```
machine <machine_name> login <login_name> password <password>
```

where machine <machine_name> is the fully qualified name of the system to which you want to connect, <login_name> is the logname under which you want to login, and <password> is the password for that account. For example, if I wanted to login to my own account on my own machine, the line might look like this:

```
machine ftp.mydomain.com login jimmo password  MyPasswd
```

One problem with this file is that the password is in clear-text. You can eliminate some of the problem by making it readable only by you. However, should someone break into your account, they then have your password on other machines. Therefore, I only use this for machines to which I connect via anonymous ftp.

Another file that makes your life easier is .rhosts. This file enables you to remotely execute commands on another system as well as login without a password. (See Chapter 9, Talking to Other Machines.) I highly recommend limiting the number of systems in this file. If someone can read this file, they know what other machines can access this one. It is then a short jump to conclude that the other machines are accessible from this one.

The `.forward` file is useful for redirecting mail. You must use this file with care. If you are on vacation, it might not be a bad idea to use the `.forward` file to send a copy of the message to someone taking your place. However, I think it is a serious security breach if mail is ever forwarded outside of the company.

13.1.2 Accessing Information

As I have said before and will say again, and as many other people will say over and over, a very significant benefit of Linux is that it is extensible. That is, you can make changes, additions, variations, etc., all day long. However, this brings up a problem when other people try to make sense of your changes or additions.

If you add a new program to your system, it is of little use to people when they can't figure it out. If it is a simple problem that does one thing (for example, figures out the square root of the number that you input), there may be no reason to document it. However, if the tool is something complicated (for example, it searches for specific files based on the content then processes them into different archives), you may need some documentation to tell the user how to use that program.

Proper documentation has two equally important aspects: accessibility and content. An easily accessible document that does not describe the solution in sufficient detail for someone else to use is of little value. Conversely, a solution with the necessarily detail but information that no one can find is also of little value.

If a call number is necessary, then documenting the problem is as important as documenting the solution. Properly documenting the problem enables other help desk members to more easily find solutions that are relevant to the problem. Also, they can more easily find other similar problems that may be related. This helps them either disregard potential solutions or try to apply them. If the problem description is not detailed enough or does not accurately reflect the problem, relating it to other problems and finding solutions is difficult, at best.

What is documented in terms of solutions is a matter of policy. Each department or section should decide what should be documented. I don't recommend spending time defining what shouldn't be documented, other than to say that there is no *need* to document something if it does not fall within specific guidelines. However, unless a great deal of time is invested, there is no such thing as too much documentation.

You can document solutions in several ways. If you have Windows PCs, you can create windows help files (`*.hlp`) by using any number of programs and macro packages. You can then compiled these into the `*.hlp` files. Alternatively, you can store all your information as HTML so that even UNIX workstations can use them. Caldera provides a Linux version of Netscape Navigator Gold with a built in HTML editor. Also, Applixware has a built-in HTML authoring program.

In many of the TeX word processing packages is a program called `html2latex`, which will convert HTML documents to LaTeX. This can then be filtered through other programs to create hard-copy documentation.

DOCUMENTATION

Traditionally, UNIX systems have had on-line documentation describing the various programs and utilities called manual-pages, or man-pages, because they represent a single page from a larger "manual." As I talked about earlier, where each man-pages ends up depends what function it serves.

Being able to use a program is important not only for programs and utilities provided on your Linux system but also for those that you create yourself. In addition, documentation is not only valid for programs and utilities but for every aspect of your business.

For example, does every one of your employees know how to request a vacation? Who is the appropriate contact person for medical claims for your dependents? How do you get office supplies? Who is responsible for your phones? All of these questions are important, and the bigger the operation, the less likely people are going to know the answers. The solution is to document it.

If you need to know how to request a vacation, you simply type

```
man vacation
```

You will then see the steps necessary to submit a request for vacation.

At first, much of this kind of documentation might seem silly. Why not simply ask your supervisor? Well, if asking your supervisor is all you need to do, then you may not need to document it. However, if there is a particular form that you need to fill out *correctly* that you then have to take to your supervisor for approval and then send to the personnel department, having the form on-line saves time. It may take longer to write a description than it takes for a single person to ask how to do it, but what about 10 people? If it takes three minutes per person to write, the tenth person means that the company has spent half an hour repeating something that would have taken half that time to write. Your company will decide whether this issue needs to be documented.

You need to consider several characteristics of documentation. One thing that often falls between the cracks is that documentation needs to be accessible. It does little good if no one can find it. Creating man-pages is one sure way of making it available. However, users need to know it's there. One suggestion would be to tell everyone about a single man-page that points to the root of your documentation. For example:

```
man company
```

This could list all the subjects that are covered by the documentation: administration, finance, personnel, cafeteria, phones, etc. The user then types in

```
man admin
```

and gets a list of the administration subjects available, which he or she then uses to type

```
man vacation
```

to figure out how to submit a vacation request.

The documentation you provide must also be accurate. You get upset when a man-page gives syntax to a command that is either not valid in the newest version or is just plain wrong. This also goes for the vacation documentation that forgets to mention that the request must be signed by the supervisor *before* it goes to personnel.

If you are creating documentation for tools you created yourself (or maybe even for administrative stuff), a couple of other programs are useful. The first program is actually a supplement to the `man` command. It's called `whatis` and takes the name of a command as an argument. Normally, it shows you a one-line description of what that command is. For example, if you run `whatis vacation`, you might get

```
vacation(1) - Something only management gets
```

The `whatis` command reads the `whatis` database, which is composed of all description lines from all your man-pages. Therefore, you need to have a man-page before you can have a `whatis` entry. Because you don't get anything more than this one line, `whatis` is mostly useful to figure just what a command does rather than testing it out and having it overwrite your hard disk.

Another program that searches the `whatis` database is `apropos`. Rather than searching on the command name, `apropos` searches on the description. This is useful if you know that there is a command on the system that has a certain functionality. For example, if you run `apropos archive`, you might get the entry for `tar`, `cpio`, and `ar`.

Although you could put your man-pages anywhere and configure your system to find them, you can use a few conventions to make things easier. Man-pages are normally grouped by function. If a particular entry fits more than one category, you might find it in more than one place. The best example is `passwd`. There is a entry in section 1 for the command passwd (`/usr/bin/passwd`) and an entry in section 5 for the data file (`/etc/passwd/`). The more common man-page sections are

Section

1: User commands
2: System calls
3: Library functions
4: Devices files
5: File format descriptions
6: Games
7: Miscellaneous
8: System administration tools and programs
9: Kernel routine documentation (Linux-specific)
n: New documentation that hasn't been moved to the correct section
o: Old documentation that's being kept around, just it case
l: Documentation for the local system

The convention is for the name of the file containing the man-page to be

```
command.section
```

Therefore, you would have the two files `passwd.1` and `passwd.5`. Potentially, the file name might have some kind of extension based on how it was stored on the disk. Recently, it has been common to store the files as zipped files to save space. These files have `.gz` tacked onto the end.

If you decide to add new programs to your system, please, please, please don't use the same name as existing programs. Once while in tech support, I had a customer who could no longer install any software. After looking through the source code, I found out that the error he was getting came when the system installation program ran the sort command. When I checked his system, he had a `sort` command in `/usr/local/bin` that ran before the command that should have run. Therefore, you should not only give the program a unique name to be able to locate the information, but also so other programs don't die.

Another aspect of accessing the data is making sure that the reader can actually read it. You must put the document in a format that the users can use. Making it a PostScript file might be very useful when the user prints it out, but not everyone has the ability to look at it directly on his or her terminal. So, what format do you use?

The obvious answer is to store your file as preformatted ASCII text. That is, put spaces and new lines and other formats on the page. You see in the editor (like `vi`) what comes out on the screen. This is actually the safest mechanism because you know exactly how it will come out on each system. The problem is that you have to make sure all the spacing is right, and so on.

Another alternative is to use `*roff` formatting. I say `*roff` because there are several different variations of the text processing system and you may be familiar with only one or two. Common examples are `troff`, `nroff`, and `groff`, `groff` being the most common on Linux systems. By passing the appropriate options to man, man will call the necessary pre-processors to format your man-page for you. If you copy this man-page onto another system that does not have the name text processing system, you might end up with some goofy looking man-pages.

You could also format all the pages as HTML. This makes it difficult to view them with the normal manual viewer without some major preprocessing, which is possible by writing a `sed` or `perl` script that strips out the HTML format and adds the correct number of line feeds, etc. One thing that you need to watch with HTML is that the browser formats the pages for you. Man will just send them out to `stdout`.

I like having documentation in HTML because it is then available all over your network. Granted, this functionality might be provided with NFS, where all the man-pages are all in one shared directory. However, not every machine can have NFS, especially if you are running PCs as well. If they have a browser, they can read it.

By convention, man-pages are laid out in a specific formation. In general, this is the header, body, and supplemental information. At the top of the header is the NAME section. This is usually a one-line description that names the subject of the man-page. This is the *exact* same information that you get when you use the `whatis` command because `makewhatis` exacts this information. That's one reason why this section is important.

Next is the SYNOPSIS section. This section gives an overview of the program options, arguments, or perhaps syntax variants that you can use. A more detailed description is found in the DESCRIPTION section. (Where else?) This gives you all the whys and wherefores. Here you explain in detail what the program is used for, what is done as a result of each option, and what the effects on each argument are. If this were a description of a data file, for example, the DESCRIPTION section might describe the contents of this file and tell what programs it uses and how.

The OPTIONS section is used for just that. Here you go into details about what each option is, what arguments might come after the option, and what effects are generated as a result of these options and arguments. More than likely if you a describing a data file, there is no options section. That's okay.

Should the program or command interact with some datafile, this datafile might be listed in the FILES section. One example would be the `passwd(1)` man-page, which describes how to use the `passwd` program to change your password. Because the `/etc/passwd/` file is what is changed, the `passwd(1)` man-page has a reference to it.

The ENVIRONMENT section lists the environment variables that either are affected by or affect your program. For example, the `man(1)` man-page lists (among other things) the MANPATH environment variable environment variable, which tells `man` where to look for the man-pages.

If the program can generate error messages, you might find some information in the DIAGNOSTICS section.

If there are any limitations, you will find them in the LIMITATIONS sections. Some people call this the BUGS section, and it is even listed on the man-page as such. In that there are no real rules here, you could call it what you like. For example, if your program can only process 65,535 files at a time, this might be a limitation. If the program inexplicably crashes when you input a file name with `%` (percent sign), that may be a bug. If you want, you could even have both sections.

The SEE ALSO section lists other man-pages related to this one. This is usually other commands with similar functionality or that support the program in some fashion. For example, the `man` man-page has both apropos and `whatis` in its SEE ALSO section.

Last but not least is the AUTHOR section. You won't find this in most commercial versions of UNIX because it is the "vendor" who wrote this man-page. For Linux, the person who contributed this program usually wrote this man-page, so you need to contact him or her if you have suggestions about the program or the man-page.

Put all together, a man-page may look like this:

```
VACATION(1)        Company Procedures        VACATION(1)


NAME
vacation - time off from work

SYNOPSIS

Submissions procedures for vacation.
```

```
DESCRIPTION
   Vacation is time off from work that is normally paid.
   Each employee starts off with 10 days paid vacation
   each calendar year. New employees will have their vaca-
   tion prorated from the day employment starts. Departing
   employees (except for retirees) will also have their
   vacation prorated and will have pay deducted for all
   vacation days more than what is calculated. Extra days
   will be paid out. Each employee will be given one extra
   vacation day for each two full years of service.

   Requests for vacation will be submitted by the employee
   on company form PERS-12 at least ten working days
   before the start of the vacation. Departments may
   require more time if the employee requires scheduling
   (e.g., Telesales).
OPTIONS
   Should an employee not have enough vacation days
   remaining, he or she has the option of either going
   into the new year with a negative number of days or
   taking unpaid vacation. Negative days are limited to no
   more than a total of five and three, consecutively.
   Departments can limit either of these numbers based on
   any criteria, including staffing.
FILES
    /usr/local/lib/calendar The company calendar listing
   all company holidays.
AUTHOR
   Human Resources Department

   Company                MARCH 1995                     1
```

So, once you've created a new utility and written a man-page, where do you put it? Man-pages are normally found under `/usr/man`. However, the system will actually search in the directories listed in the MANPATH environment variable environment variable, which has the same format as the MAN environment variable.

As I talked about previously, there is a subdirectory for each set of man-pages. The system will search each subdirectory, so you can put your man-page anywhere and the system will find it. Therefore, you can create a subdirectory for each different set of man-pages you create. On the other hand, if you only have a few pages, you could keep them in a single directory.

Using straight ASCII text has the advantage that you can easily convert your man-pages to HTML. This then enables you to leave your man-pages on one machine and make them accessible anywhere on the network. You could also then access them from Windows, as well as other Linux machines.

The only disadvantage is that you can't use of any of the formatting that you see in the standard Linux man-pages. If you do, converting to HTML is a little more difficult. However, you can create a `perl` script that converts them for you.

No matter what format you decide to use, you need to consider a couple of things. First, proofread your man-pages and all other documentation. Spelling mistakes have fewer consequences on internal documentation than documentation that is shipped with a product. On the other hand, internal documentation that has technical errors has as great an effect as any other kind. Even if you can tell what the document is supposed to mean, all mistakes decrease the effectiveness of the documentation.

You should have someone, other than the person who wrote it, proofread the documentation. I know from experience that you often make mistakes that you overlook when you proofread it yourself. After all, you know what you wrote, right?

One aspect of checking your documentation is to make sure that you describe reality. I have seen so many products for which the documentation describes characteristics of the product that behave differently that what the product really does. I have also seen "screen shots" in documentation that don't match the product. This makes it very difficult to use the product.

When you document your business, the same thing applies. If you document a procedure that has mistakes, your employees cannot follow the procedures correctly. Therefore, you need to make sure that

- The documentation is easily accessible
- There are no spelling or grammar mistakes
- References to all forms are accurate, including the form number (if any) and what the form actually says
- Department names and phone numbers are correct
- Current procedures are accurately reflected

Additionally, you must have one person who is responsible for each document. (In this context, a document could be a single page or an entire volume, depending on what makes sense.) This person must ensure that the information is correct and up-to-date and should be responsible for checking the document at periodic, *predefined* intervals to ensure the accuracy of the documentation.

If you decided to install the development package, there are a couple tools that are very useful in areas other than just program development. This first is the Revision Control System, RCS. As its name implies, it is used to manage revisions. Best known for its use in managing program source code revisions, RCS can be used to manage documents as well.

If your company provides documentation for its employees, you may need a way to manage different versions and changes that are made. This is where RCS can come in handy. Many peoples' first impression of RCS is that it is cumbersome. However, in the simplest case, there are really only two commands that you need to learn:

`ci` - Check in a file into RCS

`co` - Check out a file from RCS

By themselves, these two files do a fairly efficient job of maintaining your documents. RCS has several advantages over simply making backup copies of older versions. One most obvious advantage is in terms of space. When you make a backup copy, there are (at least) two versions of your file on the system. If you want to save several versions, you need several copies. RCS keeps the changes in the same file as your text (only the changes are stored), and when you "check out" a file, all you see is the current state. However, if necessary, RCS can revert back to previous versions.

Another key advantage of RCS is that it automatically logs the changes. You could *insist* that your writers keep a change log, but this process is built into RCS. Each time you make a change to a file and check it in, you are prompted to include details about the change you made. In addition, RCS automatically stores information about who made the change (the author) and the date/time the change was made. This makes tracking the changes very easy.

Another key advantage is that RCS can help prevent conflicts. First, RCS enables you to maintain multiple "trees." That is, you can start with one document and make changes that are independent of each other. For example, with source code, you could try to implement a new module while continuing developing on the original source. You can later merge the two branches if you need to. If there are conflicts between the two branches, RCS will identify them and enable you to correct it.

Another way that RCS helps prevent conflicts is through its ability to lock files. By locking a file when you check it out, you prevent someone else from checking it out him- or herself and making changes that conflict with yours. RCS also enables you to set access permissions so that people only access the files that they should access.

RCS can only handle ASCII texts. It keeps a log of the changes simply as the differences between one version and the next. You can take a look at these files with a text editor (or ever more) and see that how the file is laid out.

Starting the RCS process is simply a matter of checking in each file with the command: `ci file_name`. This will create the RCS file in your current directory. This will have the ending `,v`, so the file would be `file_name,v`. You will be prompted to input some text to indicate the change you made.

If this is the first time, you can simply make a statement to that effect or put a period (`.`) on a line by itself to indicate "No comment."

The convention is to have a directory called `RCS`, where all the files are stored. If this directory exists, then files will be moved into it when you check them in. Files will be *copied* into your current directory when you check *out* a file so you can simply throw out changes without affecting your base file. If you check out a file, the `co` command first looks in the `RCS` directory and then in the current directory.

RCS enables you to manage files in the same directory structure in which you currently store files. For example, assume that you have a directory called `manual`, with subdirectories `CHAP1`, `CHAP2`, etc. You could leave all the files in these directories if you want, or you could use the convention of putting all files in the `RCS` directory.

However, you need to be careful with this when you have multiple directories. Let's say I *don't* want to have an `RCS` directory. As I mentioned earlier, when you check out a file, `co` looks in the current directory. If you have files in a subdirectory, you can specify the path. For example, if I were in the root directory of my document tree, I could check out a file like this:

```
co Manual/CHAP01/section1.txt
```

This will make a copy of the `section1.txt` in `Manual/CHAP01`. So far, so good. Now let's assume that I do want to use an `R` have files in `CS` directory. I can create a directory RCS that contains the subdirectory Manual. I can then check it out with

```
co RCS/Manual/CHAP01/section1.txt
```

On the other hand, if there were individual `RCS` subdirectories for each of the chapters (i.e., `Manual/CHAPO1/RCS`), the command would look like this:

```
co Manual/CHAP01/section1.txt
```

This because both the `co` and `ci` command will add the `RCS` to the end of the directory name, unless it is already present in pathname. If you look in the `Manual/CHAPO1/RCS` directory, you will see a file called `section1.txt,v`. This is the RCS version of your file containing all of the text *and* changes. Each file that you administer using RCS will have the `,v` ending.

Whenever you check out a document, what you see is the current state of the document. All the changes are in place, but you have none of the RCS information indicating what changes were made.

There is much more to RCS than this. However, going into more detail is beyond the scope of this book. The best places to check for more information are the `rcs(1)` and `rcsintro(1)` man-pages.

The next development tool that you can use in documentations is make. The basic unit of the make program is the "`makefile`." Most of the time, I see the file itself capitalized, as in "`Makefile`," while references to it are in lowercase. The `makefile` is often referred to as the descriptions file because it contains a description of what make should do. I also like to think of it as a script, because like a movie script, `make` describes the action that will be taken. One thing that a lot of people do not know is that the `descriptions` file (or `make` file) is simply a list of shell commands that are executed in a prescribed order.

Each entry in the `make` file has three components: a target, dependants, and actions. The simplest form would look something like this:

```
target: dependants
      actions
```

The target is what you are trying to make and, in the case of source code, this is usually the complete executable or object modules. However, it doesn't have to be that at all. In fact, a target is really just a label within the `makefile`; by itself, it does not create any files.

As its name implies, the dependants are something on which the target is dependent. This means that before the actions for that entry can be taken, make must first process the dependents. Let's look at an example. Assume you have a file called `Makefile`, which looks like this:

```
program: module1.o module2.o
     gcc -o program module1.o module2.o

module1.o:
     gcc -c  module1.c

module2.o:
     gcc -c  module2.c
```

Keep in mind that a dependent doesn't have to be an object module. It could be another target, in which case `make` would complete that target first. It could also be a file, like a header (`.h`) file. If a header is made a dependent of a target, changes to the header will force `make` to remake the target. Otherwise, `make` would report that the target was "up to date."

In many cases, the actions taken are compiling, linking, or some other action related to creating an executable. Here again, it doesn't have to be. The `makefile` used to compile the Linux kernel (`/usr/src/linux/`

Makefile) has a lot of targets that do nothing but remove files from various directories and other "housekeeping" chores.

I often have makefiles that have a label called clean. The line might look like this:

```
clean:   rm -f *.o
```

By running make clean, I remove all the object files in the current directory. I have seen other make files that have an additional entry, realclean, which is dependant on the clean target:

```
clean:
      rm -f *.o
realclean: clean
      rm program
```

By running make realclean, make sees that realclean is dependant on clean, so it is run first and all of the object modules are removed. The file program is removed as well. Notice that these are not compiler directives but rather normal UNIX commands. In fact, these can be any command. For example, I have an entry in one of my files that looks like this:

```
install:
       chown root program
       chmod u+s program
       cp program /usr/local/bin
```

So when I have a successful relink and am happy with the result, I enter

```
make install
```

and my program is set with the necessary permission and copied to the appropriate directory.

If you call make without any options, it searches for a file named makefile; Makefile; makefile,v; Makefile,v; RCS/makefile,v; or RCS/Makefile,v. As you can see, make automatically looks for makefiles that you may already be administering with RCS. If you want to use a alternate makefile, you can use the -f option to make.

In this example, our makefile is called Makefile, so we can start make without any arguments. By default, make starts on the first line and works its way through the file. (This behavior can be changed, which I will get to shortly.) The first line it finds is

```
program: module1.o module.o
```

The target here is program, which has two dependants: module1.o and module2.o. Therefore, make must first process these two before it can execute the command in the next line. make searches for the first dependant and finds module1.o. This has no dependants of its own, so the command can be executed, in this case gcc -c module1.c, which compiles the source code module1.c (using the gcc compiler) and creates the object module, module1.o.

Note that in this example, the target is the same name as the object module that gcc creates. However, this does not need to be the case. The target could have been called module1 or even banana and it wouldn't have mattered. As long as make processes the targets in the correct order and the commands create the correct files, it doesn't matter what the targets are called. However, the convention is often to use the name of the object module.

After completing the first dependent (module1.o), make looks for more dependants. In this case, there is module2.o, which is processed like the first. If there are no more dependents to process, make can now execute the command for the target program:

```
gcc -o program module1.o module2.o
```

This uses the gcc compiler again, this time to compile the two object modules into an executable program. In this case, the executable program has the same name as the target, but this is not always the case.

So what does this have to do with documentation? Well, let's forget about using make to compile source code and use to execute other programs instead. Let's say our makefile now looks like this:

```
one:
      date
      echo "One"

two: one
      ps
      echo "Two"

three: two
```

If we were to simply run make, the first target found has no dependants, so the commands are executed. You end up with an output that looks like this:

```
date
Wed Jan  8 15:45:44 MET 1997
echo "One"
One
```

Note that in each case, the line executed was echoed to stdout.

One thing that make will let us do is specify a target yourself, without having it run through the defaults. We could say

```
make two
```

which would cause make to run through target two. If target two has a dependant (one, in this case), that target must be made first. So, target one is made, then target two. We then get an output like this:

```
date
Wed Jan  8 15:51:23 MET 1997
echo "One"
One
ps
 PID TTY      S          TIME COMMAND
28121 ttyp1    I        0:00.38 - (ksh)
28156 ttyp2    I        0:00.37 - (ksh)
28330 ttyp3    S        0:05.77 - (ksh)
29969 ttyp3    S  +     0:00.11 make two
16924 ttyp5    I  +     0:01.15 rlogin dec016
28816 ttyp5    I  +     0:00.64 rlogin dec016
echo "TWO"
TWO
```

We have the output from target one and then from target two. What if you decide to run make three? Well, if target three has target two as a dependent, it must be made first. The result is the same output as above. If target three does not have a command, there is nothing to do once make is finished with target two.

Let's assume that you have written all of your documentation using TeX. You now change one of your targets, so it looks like this:

```
chapter1:
     tex chapter1.tex
     dvi2ps chapter1.dvi
```

When you run make on this target, there is no dependant so the command is executed. This target uses the tex command (part of the TeX text processing system), which processes the file chapter.tex. This creates the output file chapter.dvi (the dvi extension means that this is a device-independent file). The next command is executed, using the dvi2ps command to convert the file chapter1.dvi to chapter1.ps, which is the postscript version of the original file, chapter1.tex. This can now be output to a postscript printer to get a good look (at least of chapter one).

Let's now assume that there are corresponding targets for the remaining chapters. Assuming you have four chapters, you then have a target that looks like this:

```
manual: chapter1 chapter2 chapter3 chapter4
    cat chapter1.ps chapter2.ps chapter3.ps chapter4.ps > /dev/lp1
```

When you run `make manual`, each chapter is a dependant and must be made in turn. When the last chapter is made, you have four postscript files that you then output to your printer to create a nice-looking manual.

Note that dependents are not just for targets that you want to make first. If a dependant is not a target, there is nothing for make to do to that file. However, when creating the target, `make` will compare the date of the target file with the date of the dependant files. If any of the dependant files are newer than the target, the target is made.

This is commonly used in source code compilation. Let's take your previous source code example and change it slightly:

```
module1.o: module1.c
    cc -c module1.c
```

Here you are saying that the file `module1.o` is dependant on the file `module1.c`. When you run make, the date of `module1.o` and `module1.c` are compared. If `module1.o` is older, you know that `module1.c` has *not* been changed since the last time the target was made. Therefore, there is no need to make the target again, so it is just skipped.

In this example, you could change the target line to read

```
chapter1.ps: chapter1.tex
```

Therefore, if `chapter1.tex` had not been changed since the last time `chapter1.ps` was made, there would be no need to run the commands. You then change the manual target to look like this:

```
manual: manual.ps
    cat manual.ps > /dev/lp1

manual.ps: chapter1.ps chapter2.ps chapter3.ps chapter4.ps
    cat chapter1.ps chapter2.ps chapter3.ps chapter4.ps > manual.ps
```

If you run `make manual`, the dependant `manual.ps` is made. This compares the dates on the files `chapter1.ps`, etc., against the date of `manual.ps`. If any date is newer, that target is made. When all dependants are checked, each of the postscript files is output using `cat` to the file `manual.ps` and that target is complete.

`make` then returns to the target manual and `cats` the file `manual.ps` to the printer.

I previously made a reference to the file `html2latex`, which converts HTML files to LaTeX (a variant of TeX). You could conceivably have your source files in HTML, to make them available on-line, then, using a `makefile` similar to the one we have here, use `html2latex` to create the LaTeX files, use LaTeX to create the DVI files, and then `dvi2ps` to create the PostScript files that are passed on to the printer. This is one way to ensure that your on-line documentation matches the hard copy version.

This is not all that you can use make for. Think back to the chapter on monitoring your system (see Chapter 11, System Monitoring). You could create a shell-script that monitored every aspect of your system. It could run `mount` to check what file systems are mounted, run `df` to see how full they were, run `netstat` to check your network connections, and so on.

What if you didn't want to check every aspect but rather just specific aspects, like file systems or hardware? You could create a menu in the shell-script so you could select the parts you wanted. If you included it in an infinite loop, you could repeatedly input different components. The other alternative is to use a `makefile`. By entering something like

```
make filesystem
```

you can get `make` to run the necessary commands to check our file systems. Maybe the file system section is dependant on the partitions section, so you could have an entry like this:

```
filesystems: partitions
    df -v
    df -i

partitions:
       fdisk -l
```

So, when you want information, enter `make filesystem` and `make` first gives you the information on the hard disks and then on the file systems.

Like other `makefiles`, you can define variables and use them in various sections. In fact, you can get quite complex `makefiles`. I would suggest first looking through the Linux kernel `makefile` (`/usr/src/linux/Makefile`) and the book *Managing Projects with Make* by Steve Talbot and Andrew Oram, published by O'Reilly & Associates.

13.2 Security

Linux, like any computer system, has a set of security issues that need to be considered. Regardless of what mechanisms are in place, the basic concepts are the same. In fact, the security of a computer system is very much like the security of your house, just as running a computer system is like running a household. You only want to let those people in who should be let in and you only want people accessing resources that they should. (Do you *really* want your three-year-old playing with your collection of Dresden porcelain?)

The term *security* is common enough. On a personal basis, we think of it as freedom from risk or danger; being safe. We might also think of this as the methods we undertake to prevent someone from breaking into our house. In computer science terms, both of these ideas are applicable, depending on what you are referring to.

If we talk about being safe from risk when working with computers, we are often talking about things like regular backups and reliable hardware. Although these are very important issues, these are not what is generally meant when referring to security. On computer systems, security is more along the lines of preventing someone from breaking in. The definition can be expanded by saying computer security is preventing someone from doing something that they are not allowed to do. This could be anything from reading other people's mail to stopping the printers.

In this section, I'm going to be talking about what mechanisms exist to keep people from poking around and doing things they shouldn't. I'll talk about what tools Linux provides to control access, change what users can access, and how to make sure users are not even trying to do things they shouldn't.

13.2.1 Real Threats

One thing that I enjoyed most about one job I had was that I was one of the few people that most of the end users felt comfortable talking to. One day I was approached about how we required passwords to be changed every couple of months. Computers are to be used, not to keep people out. Many people were annoyed that they even had passwords, let alone had to change them regularly. The biggest problem is not that the users were right, but that users, as well as many system administrators, don't understand the dangers involved without the protection of passwords.

The stereotypical image of a pair of teenage computer enthusiasts breaking into a military computer and almost starting a war may be good for Hollywood, but the times have changed. Yes, there are still those kind of hackers running around, but they are not likely to break into systems with the more advanced security techniques employed today, because most of the security is good enough. But then again, it may not be.

Hacking has become an almost cult phenomenon with newsgroups, magazines, and even their own language. The people who belong to this culture are not only equipped with the latest technology, they also have an almost never-ending list of new security holes that they can use to break into a system. Because they spend much of their free time trying to break into systems, they may have found some of the security holes themselves. However, the techniques they use go beyond just the list of known holes (though these are probably things that they try first). Instead, there is a methodology to the attack.

More and more, hackers are not just randomly trying systems across the country. Instead, there is usually some motivation for attacking a particular site. It may be just the notoriety of being the first to break into the crystal palace that is some major corporation. In some cases, this is what these people do for a living. The ability to break into a competitor's computer system and look over the shoulder of its research and development people may be worth the investment of hiring a hacker.

As we all know from many of the detective shows we see on TV, criminals are caught because of the clues they leave behind. This also applies to the computer hacker. Hackers breaking into a computer are less likely to leave evidence that can trace directly back to them. Instead, it is usually a case in which the perpetrator is caught in the act during a subsequent break-in. Then there is the added problem of criminal jurisdiction because the hacker could just as easily be on the other side of the world as on the other side of town.

Just knowing that you should lock your front door or buckle your seat belts is enough for many people to do it. However, I am not one of those people. Understanding that someone could walk away with my TV or that my head could go flying through the windshield is what motivates me to do what I should do. I am also less likely to forget or not to do it one time because it's inconvenient. I take the same approach to computer security.

Most system administrators are aware that there needs to be "security" on their systems. I put it in quotes because it is often just a phrase brought up at staff meetings. When addressed, security often just means forcing users to change their password at regular intervals or making sure that users were logged out when they went home. One company at which I worked forced users to change their passwords every six weeks, but the root password was only changed when someone left the company (it was too inconvenient). Added to that, the root password for all the machines were variations on a single theme, so once you figured out one, it was easy to figure out the rest.

With all the talk of the Internet, the kind of security most often in peoples' minds is the attack from outside. Although this is a very real threat, it is not the only one. Personal experience has taught me that inside attacks can be just as devastating.

In this same MIS shop, everyone had the root password to every machine (also the administrator password on our NT machines). There were people who only administered the UNIX machines and others who only administered the NT machines. However, they had the passwords to all machines. One employee was not satisfied with the speed with which the hardware vendor was reacting to a problem he was having with one of the NT machines. Because they were the same vendor for the UNIX machines, he decided to "motivate" them to make a personal call.

On several irregular occasions, this employee killed the Oracle database process. Because almost everyone used that database, the company was brought to a standstill for the couple of hours it took to discover the problem, reboot the system, and clean up. Eventually he was caught, but not after causing tens (if not hundreds) of thousands of dollars worth of damage.

Keeping the UNIX root password from him would have probably prevented him from doing this exact thing. However, he could have done other things to damage the company if that was his intent. Nothing can prevent this kind of act. However, if passwords are limited and something goes wrong, it is not so easy for the guilty party to deny it.

In the beginning, I was a firm believer that information about security holes should be kept secret (security by obscurity). I had an obligation as the all-knowing UNIX guru to protect the innocent system administrators in the world. Therefore, I felt it was improper to discuss these issues publicly.

As I began to read more about security, I discovered that I was one of the few people that shared this belief. Most of the books and articles that I read presented the material as "Here's the threat and here's what you can do about it." By not only knowing that there is a threat but why it is a threat, you can correct the problem as well as identify other potential problems that may not have been discussed.

On any computer system, there is always the danger that something can be compromised. Now the word "danger" can span a whole spectrum of meaning and it all depends on what you are talking about. It might be dangerous to leave a bowl of sugar on the counter where your two-year-old can reach it, just as it might be dangerous to walk through Chernobyl without a radiation suit. It's purely a matter of scale.

The dangers involved with an insecure computer system are like that. If someone else found out the password of another user on our system, the danger of damage is low. On the other hand, if someone found out a password for a computer at the CIA, the danger is greater.

The damage caused can also span the entire spectrum. Sometimes there is no real damage. Someone who breaks into a system might simply be curious and want to look around. This is comparable to having someone wandering through your living room.

The "worm" that Robert Morris let loose on the Internet in 1988 was such an event. Although little real damage was done, it "infected" 2,100 to 2,600 computers. Many machines were brought to a standstill as file systems filled up and systems could no longer write their log files and were busy running the processes that the worm started. In the end, it has been estimated that between $1 million and $100 million was lost due to time spent cleaning up and the loss in productivity when the systems were down. Even with the lowest estimates, the loss was stunning.

On the other end of the of the spectrum is the case that was documented by Cliff Stoll in his book *The Cuckoo's Egg*. The information that these intruders from West Germany had gathered from more than 450 government and military computers was sold to the Soviet KGB. There were a few convictions and one of the prime suspects was found burned to death in a wooded area near his home.

Computer intruders also have the ability to cause physical damage. A virus that's introduced to a system acting as a file server for DOS PCs could change the scan rate of the monitor, which can cause it to explode. One computer that Cliff Stoll was monitoring that was broken into was used to regulate the radiation doses given to cancer patients. If the computer behaved unexpectedly as a result of the hackers actions, it could have meant the death of a patient.

In any information system, whether it is a computer or filing cabinet, there are some basic security issues that need to be considered. First, there is one aspect of security that no operating system can help you with: the physical security of your system. You might have implemented all the security that Linux provides, but if someone can walk off with your computer, even the highest levels of operating system security won't do any good. Just as a security policy in an office has no effect if someone can just walk away with sensitive files.

One of the easiest and most effective types of physical security is simply a locked door. This prevents the "crime of opportunity" from ever happening, such as someone who just walks away with pieces of equipment, or the whole machine, for that matter. The only thing that can prevent this kind of theft is more elaborate security measures that are beyond the scope of this book. However, it is something to which you must give serious thought. Locking the door to the computer can also prevent people from breaking into the system. Anyone who has a set of installation disks or an emergency boot disk set can gain access to your system if they have access to the computer itself.

Another aspect of physical security is access to the machine itself. It may be impractical for someone to walk off with your computer. However, a knowledgeable user with root access to a another Linux system can gain access to your system if he or she has physical access. Even without access to another system, if that user has access to the installation floppies, he or she can get into your system. Once in, it doesn't matter what kind of security has been configured on the hard disk because the only security the system knows is what it has been told by the floppy.

The next issue is privacy. This can be the company's or individuals' privacy. You don't want unauthorized users to have access to payroll records, just as you don't want to have access to other employees' personal files.

One most commonly ignored aspect of privacy is the power of small pieces of information. As individual items, these pieces may have no significance at all. However, when taken in context, they can have far-reaching implications. Police use this same concept to investigate crimes, and intelligence agencies like the CIA use it as well. Extending this to the business world, such techniques are useful for corporate spies.

There are other cases in which security is important in business. What if someone came along and changed an important piece of information, for example, an employee who thinks he is underpaid may want to change it? Whether this information is on paper or in a computer, the integrity of the data is an important part of security. Along the same lines is the consistency of the data. You want the same behavior from the system in identical situations. For example, if salary is based on position, inconsistent data could mean that the night watchman suddenly gets paid as much as the company president.

Another aspect is the concept of auditing. Like an audit of a company's books, auditing in a computer security sense is a record of the *transactions* or *events* that occurred on the system. This enables the system administrator to follow the tracks of suspected perpetrators and maybe catch them in the act. It was a combination of auditing and accounting for time on the system that led Cliff Stoll to discover his hackers.

When preparing one company for connection to the Internet, I checked the security on the system. I found dozens of holes in the system. Keep in mind that this was actually my first attempt at being a hacker. Added to that, I exploited no real bug in the software; instead, I just took advantage of "features" that were not considered in a security context. By using just the tools and programs that the system provides, I was able to gain complete access to the system. Once the system is compromised, the danger of further compromise grows steady. The only safe thing to do is to reinstall from scratch.

I do not mean to scare you when I say that every system has the potential for being broken into. In the end, every security-related decision and every function in the program was written by a human. The security could be mathematically tested, but who is to say that the mathematical test is not flawed?

The first step in stopping the would-be intruder is to keep him or her from getting to your system in the first place. This is similar to having a lock on your front door. You could go to the extreme of fencing off your property, hiring full-time guards, and installing video cameras and alarms, but this is too extreme for most people. First, they probably can't afford it. Second, the threat is not that great, compared to the costs.

But what about your business? The potential loss from someone breaking in can be devastating. Corporate spies can clean out your sensitive data or a disgruntled former (or current) employee can wipe out your entire system.

With regard to the Internet, the only way to ensure that no one can break in is to completely cut yourself off from the rest of the world. This also means no modems, ISDN lines, or any other device that can be used to call in and out. For some companies, this may be the only way to go. However, because of the fantastic market potential on the Internet, it may not be a wise decision.

If there is a physical connection to the outside, there is the *potential* that someone could break in. However, once you have made the decision to connect to the Internet (and you really should), you need to be much more aware of security than when you network was isolated.

When an attacker improperly accesses a system, her or she may not necessarily continue with the attack immediately after gaining access. Instead, he or she might create backdoors to gain access to the system at a later time. He or she can add entries to `.rhost` files to give him or her access later. For example, putting the line + + would give him or her access from any machine with any account. New accounts can be created to give him or her access. He or she can also use one machine to gain information about other machines and the network in general.

An unauthorized user gains access to a system and is able to determine which files and directories this account has access to. He or she then places `.rhosts` and `.forward` files in every home directory he or she has `write` permission on. He or she now has unlimited access to all of those accounts, even though he or she never knew their passwords.

In the `.forward` file is a pipe to a script that copies `/bin/sh` in `/tmp` and makes it SUID to that user. Whenever `/tmp/sh` is started, the UID is the new user. Now access can be obtained to other machines with the appropriate entries in `.rhosts` or `host.equiv`.

RESTRICTING ACCESS

Regardless of what security issue you are talking about, any breach in security can be prevented by not allowing access to the system. Now, this can be taken to extremes by not letting *anyone* have access. However, by limiting access to the system to only authorized users, you substantially lower the risk of breaches in security. Keep in mind that there is no such thing as a secure system. This is especially important when you consider that the most serious threat comes from people who already have an account on that system.

Access control has been a part of UNIX for a long time. It is a fundamental aspect of any multiuser system. The most basic form of access control is in the form of user accounts. The only way you should be able to gain access to a Linux system is through an account. Users usually gain access to the system when they have an account set up for them. Each user is assigned an individual password that allows the access. Access to files is determined by the permissions that are set.

Passwords. In some cases, passwords may be blank, meaning you only need to press Enter. In other cases, it can be removed all together so you are never even prompted to input your password. Removing the password may not always be a good idea. Because you have the source code, Linux gives you the option to prevent users from either having no password or having to just press Enter. Because I am talking here about security and accounts without passwords that are not very secure, I'll restrict myself to talking about accounts that have passwords.

On many systems (including many Linux versions), you cannot force users to use (or not use) specific passwords. As a system administrator, it is your responsibility to not only enforce a strong password policy, but to educate your users as to why this is important. Later, we'll go over some examples of what happens when users are not aware of the issues involved with password security.

If you write your password on a Post-It® and stick it on your monitor, no operating system in the world can do anything about it. But what about cases in which you inadvertently give someone your password? This happens when users choose passwords that are easily guessed by someone trying to break in. Often users will choose passwords that are easy to remember, such as their license plate number or spouse's birthday. Linux cannot do anything to keep you from using your license plate number as a password. However, some features can be easily built-in to limit what you can use as a password.

File Access. Although this password protection stops most attempts to gain unauthorized access to the system, many security issues involve users who already have accounts. Unchecked, curious users could access payroll information and find out what their boss is paid. Corporate spies could steal company secrets. Disgruntled workers could wreak havoc by destroying data or slowing down the system.

Once logged in, Linux (among other UNIX dialects) provides a means of limiting the access of "authorized" users. This is in the form of file permissions, which I already talked about (see Section 3.1.1, The Search Path). File permissions are one aspect of security with which most people are familiar in regard to UNIX security. In many cases this is the only kind of security other than user accounts.

As we talked about earlier, each file has an owner (whether or not a user explicitly went out there and "claimed" ownership). It's a basic characteristic of each file that is imposed on them by the operating system. The owner of the file is stored, along with other information, in the `inode` table in the form of a number. This number corresponds the User ID (`UID`) number from `/etc/passwd`.

Normally, files are initially owned by the user who creates them. However, many circumstances could change the ownership. One obvious way is that the ownership is intentionally changed. Only the owner of the file and root can change its ownership. If you are the owner of a file, you can, in essence, "transfer ownership" of the file to someone else. Once you do, you are no longer the owner (obviously) and have no more control over that file.

Another characteristic a file is its *group*. Like the owner, the file's group is an intrinsic part of the file's characteristics. The file's group is also stored in the `inode` as a number. The translation from this number to the group name is made from the `/etc/group` file. As I talked about in the section on users (see Section 5.2, Users and User Accounts), the concept of a group has only real meaning in terms of security; that is, who can access which files.

What this means is that only "authorized" users can access files in any of three manners: read, write, and execute. It makes sense that normal users cannot run the `fdisk` utility, otherwise they would have the ability to repartition the hard disk, potentially destroying data. It also makes sense that normal users do not have write permission on the `/etc/passwd` file, otherwise they could change it so that they would have access to the root account. Because I talked about it in the section on shell basics (see Chapter 3, Shells and Basic Utilities) and on users (see Section 5.2, Users and User Accounts), there is no need to go into more detail here.

The Root Account. There is also access to the all-powerful root account. On a Linux system, root can do anything. Although it is possible to restrict root's access to certain functions, a knowledgeable user with root privileges can overcome that restriction. In many instances, you may have several people administering some aspect of the system, such as printers or the physical network. I have heard myself when someone says, "Well, he has root access. Why can't I?"

Access to the root account should be limited for a couple of reasons. First, the more people with root access, the more people who have *complete* control over the system. This makes access control difficult.

Also, the more people who have root access, the more fingers get pointed (that is, the more blame is placed). I know from experience that people will deny having done something wrong. Often this results in a corrupt system because everyone has the power to do everything, someone did something that somehow messed up the system, and no one will admit it. Sound familiar?

The fewer people who have root, the fewer fingers must be pointed and fewer people can pass the buck. Not that what they did was malicious; mistakes do happen. If there are fewer people with root access and something goes wrong, tracking down the cause is much easier.

Rather than giving several users the root password password, some people think that it is safer to create several users all with the UID of root. Their belief is that because there are several lognames, it's easier to keep track of things. Well, the problem in that is that the system keeps of track of users by the UID. There is no way to keep these users separate once they log in.

My suggestion is that if several users need root powers, make it company policy that no one logs in as root. Instead, grant each required user the `su` system privilege. The users then login with their own account and do an `su` to root. Although everything is still done as root, a record of who did the `su` can be written to `/var/adm/syslog`.

Once an intruder gains root access, your entire system is compromised. It is therefore important not only to limit who has access to root but to record who uses the root account. One way to do this is to implement a policy that no one logs in as `root` but must first login with their own account and then do `su` to gain access to `root`.

Another security precaution is to define secure terminals. These are the only terminals from which the root user can login. In my opinion, it is best to only consider directly connected terminals as "secure." That is, the root user can log into the system console but not across the network. To get access as root across the network, a user must first login under its own account and then use `su`. This also provides a record of who used the root account and when.

The Network. If you have a stand-alone Linux system or one that is connected on an internal network with *no* connection to the outside world, security is much less an issue. (Though it does *not* go away.) However, if you connect to the Internet, such as for an HTTP or FTP server, security is a primary consideration.

One way to avoid compromising your system is to have your WWW server connected to the Internet but not to your internal network. Should someone be able to break into the WWW server, the worst that can happen is that your WWW server is down for a day or so while you reload from backups. If the intruder had access to the internal network, your livelihood could be threatened.

By its very nature, UNIX is not very security oriented. When it was first designed and implemented, UNIX was created by programmers for programmers. The environment was of cooperation, not privacy. As UNIX moved into universities and businesses, that changed. Security was an issue. Because security was not built into the original concept, it had to be included "after the fact." Therefore, security solutions were not as far-reaching as for later systems.

13.2.2 Real World Examples

The severity of this problem can be demonstrated by what I found at one company for which I was working. In preparing for connecting the company to the Internet, I conducted a security check of the internal network. I wanted to see just how far I could get. One of the first steps that a burglar takes before he breaks in is to case the joint. He may observe it for several days or weeks before making his move. To make his presence less conspicuous, he may watch several scattered locations and then choose the easiest target (or may choose all of them in turn). A computer break-in is basically the same. The only difference is the tools the burglar uses and the information that is collected. In both cases, however, the more careless you are as the potential victim, the easier time the burglar has in gathering the information and breaking in.

Because you are not trying to keep someone from breaking into your house, let's talk about the tools that a hacker would use to break into your computer system. One most innocuous and most dangerous tool is `finger`. In the many papers and books that have been written recently about computer security and break-ins, `finger` is always mentioned. I have used it myself on our internal network and have collected a great amount of information. What information is provided depends on the operating system and the version of `finger`. However, at the very least, it can provide information about who is logged in, where they logged in from, and so on.

One common tactic used works on the belief that an account that is not used too often will have an easily guessed password. Based on my experience, this seems to be true. Usually people who don't use their computer accounts are not as aware of the security issues and are more than likely to choose a password that is easy to remember and therefore easy to guess. What are good passwords and what are not is something I'll get into in a minute.

You need to be careful since `finger` often delivers information stored in the `.plan` file in a user's home directory. This file may contain personal information that a hacker can use to try to guess the password. If the password is not easy to guess, the information obtained from `finger` can be combined with other information that may be useful. However, one thing that `finger` quite often delivers is a user's home directory. If that home directory is exported through NFS, an attacker may be able to mount that directory, copy an `.rhosts` file into the directory, and access the system without even supplying a password.

At the same company, there was a very arrogant system administrator who would simply not accept the fact that *his* system was insecure. However, one of the home directories that was exported via NFS was his. Because I had root access on my machine, I could import his home directory. His `.rhosts` file was writable, so I could give myself permission to use `rlogin` to his account from any machine as any user on the network. Once in, I planted a Trojan horse version of `su` because I knew he would eventually use it to get access to the root account. Even if I wasn't root, that he had a writable `.rhosts` file enabled me to gain access.

One very common attack is the dictionary attack. Here the hacker uses common words, encrypts them using the same word as the password taken from the password file, and then compares the two. Remember that everyone can read the `/etc/passwd` file and the seed is contained within the encrypted password. Once I have access to the system, I can bring a copy of this to another system and, using that seed, I can encrypt the words from my "dictionary." In addition to just words in a dictionary, the hacker could use place names and other proper nouns related to the target.

With just my first attempt at cracking passwords, I was able to crack almost 200 on one system alone. In fact, this was the first time I tried to hack a system at all. Among the passwords I was able to gather were those belonging to the head of purchasing, the head of sales, and the company president! This list only contained about 30 words, including the name of the town and state we were in, the day of the week, the month, and a few words related to the company. Plus the program only had to run about half an hour. What kind of luck would a serious hacker have with 30,000 words running the program for a week?

Although this seems to be a major security hole, it is very effective if you use passwords that are not easy to guess because the encryption goes only one way. You take a word, use the seed to encrypt it, then compare it to the encrypted password. However, there is no way to take the encrypted password and use the seed to figure out the unencrypted password.

Keep in mind that snatching the `/etc/passwd` file does not necessarily mean you have to break into the system first. I was able to get it on one system using the "guest" account that had a *very* easy password. With just a single password, I could then log into the system. Once in, the potential for more serious and directed attacks is much greater. I could continue to use these accounts or edit the `.rhost` files in various home directories to continue to gain access even after the passwords were changed. Remember, here I cracked almost 200 hundred on my first attempt!

It was once common to find UNIX machines that had an account *guest*. This stems from the time when people were not so worried about security and computer resources were freely shared. Often the password for such accounts was very easy to guess. Considering this, I though about the first word one might say to a guest: welcome. Sure enough, that's what the password was. So, on my very first try as a computer hacker I was able to break in.

When you export file systems or directories, you must watch several things. First, I recommend against *ever* exporting a file system to the whole world, especially one that is writable. There is generally no need to make this information available outside of your company and if there is, there are probably just a few trusted hosts. See if the same result can be reached by making the information available via ftp or the Web.

If there is a + in the `/etc/hosts.equiv` file, this is a wildcard that says any nonroot user can login without a password. If an attacker gets into a machine as root that has an entry in the `hosts.equiv`, they could do `su` to the user bin or `sys`. Then they could use `rlogin` to gain access to the other system and then have access to many key files and directories. Permissions could then be changed to set the user ID on executables to root and, once the program is started, the user is root.

One way I got the `/etc/passwd` file was through ftp. Anonymous ftp was disabled on this system, but I simply used the "guest" account, which had a password that was easy to guess. The most obvious solution is to disable ftp. However, if it is a necessary service, you can limit the potential for damage. You need a `passwd` file when using ftp, but it doesn't have to be the same one that you use when logging in normally. In fact, you can do many things to configure ftp to enable people access to your system without open it up for them. I'll get into configuring anonymous ftp shortly.

Once in, I could copy the password file to my home machine and begin to crack it. Not just try to crack it. I knew going in that the odds were in my favor. Once I had the `passwd` file, I was statistically guaranteed that I would crack at least one password. People are people and will tend to choose passwords that are easy to guess.

Within about 20 minutes, I was able to create a password cracking program on my own. Because I had never done this before, it took that long. Because the program was only a couple dozen lines (without the enhancements I later made), it was easy to do. I discovered subsequently that password cracking programs are already available on the Internet that are much more powerful.

I then created a "dictionary" of words to try. I encrypted each word using the seed/salt that was in the password file and then compared this encrypted word with what was in the password file. If the words matched, I had found a password.

The dictionary that I had created contained only about 50 words, including the name of the company, the city and state where it was located, the generic term for the product that the company produced, and a few other words related to the company and the area where we were.

Because there were only 50 words to compare, the program ran relatively quickly. Within half an hour, I had found almost 200 passwords out of about 850 users! Most of these still had the original, start-up password, *welcome.*

I then went back to the original system and did a search of the word "phone" in any file or directory name. Soon, I had a copy of the company's telephone book, which I used to crack more passwords. In the end, I had 235 passwords.

An analysis of the passwords showed some interesting things. One person chose as a password the geographic area for which he was responsible. His girlfriend, the personal secretary of the company president, chose his name as her password. Other people chose their first name, their spouse's first name, and other easy-to-guess passwords. One even chose *123456.*

One thing bothered me about the system in general. Of all the passwords on the system, more than 400 (almost half) had the same seed. I could have sped things up by encrypting all the words in the dictionary with this one seed and I would have still cracked more than 100 passwords within about five minutes!

Because I use the same password on many different machines, I went on the assumption that other people did the same. As you might expect, several people used the same password elsewhere. The reason I only cracked about 10 passwords on other machines was that very few people actually had accounts on other machines.

I then tried some of these passwords in our bookkeeping and management software. Here, too, I was able to crack "only" about 20 passwords, including those of the head of the purchasing department and the head of sales.

For a real hacker, the speeds of machines have become an advantage. Whereas checking a single password on a Microvax several years ago would have taken hours, the same password can now be cracked within a matter of minutes. It has been estimated that to encrypt a dictionary with 250,000 words using all 4,096 seeds and several machines networked together, you would need just a few hours.

On several machines, I was able to list what file systems were being exported. Also using finger information, I could tell what file systems were used for home directories. I mounted one of these file systems and discovered that because I had root access on my machine, I had root access on the mounted file system. I could now write my own `.rhost` files to give me complete access to any of these users' accounts.

The first thing was to check to see which machines were "personal workstations." Often there is an entry in the `/etc/hosts` or HINFO DNS-record to describe to whom the machine belongs. If there are a lot of PCs and only a few workstations, these workstations probably belong to the system administration group. However, if everyone has a workstation, this trick doesn't work.

Because I could now look in the `/etc/passwd` file, I found out who were the system administrators, as this was written in clear text in the GEOS field. I then found out what file system their home directories were on and mounted those via NFS. I could then edit their `.rhosts` files to give me access to their accounts.

Using the same information, this told me who the system administrators were and for what areas they were responsible. I could then concentrate my attacks on their accounts. As the system administrator, you should know who the other administrators are. There is no need for users to know this. In my opinion, there should be nothing in the password to identify the user. If you need this information regularly, put it in a file somewhere that is not world-readable.

Having access to their accounts doesn't necessarily mean I have root access. However, it does mean that I have access to an account that sooner or later will want to get root access. More than likely, this will be with the `su` command. With write permission to that user's directory, I could trick it into giving me the root password. I could create a Trojan horse version of `su` that comes first in the user's path (maybe changing the path, if necessary). The next time the user uses `su`, I will have the root password password.

13.3 What You Can Do about the Danger

If you are the system administrator of a Linux system and security is even a minor issue, you definitely need to read *The Cuckoo's Egg* by Cliff Stoll and *Internet Security and Firewalls* by Cheswick and Bellovin. Although I have covered some of the issues that they confronted and the techniques they used to monitor their intruders, there's nothing like reading it yourself. Plus, if you hear the true stories, they sink in better than hearing just the theory.

The Cuckoo's Egg reads like a spy novel and, even though I knew the outcome before I started reading it, is difficult to put down. I say "is" because I am in the middle of it reading it as I write this.

13.3.1 Watching Your System

In the preceding paragraphs, I detailed many of the holes that are used to break into a system. I also addressed the methods that hackers use to gain information about your system to exploit these holes. In this section, I am going to talk about specific methods people (including myself) have used to circumvent normal security.

One aspect of watching your system that can cause the most problem is what to do when you see that someone is hacking your system. Remember that in many places, the mere fact that someone has gained unauthorized access to your system means that that person has committed a crime. Like any criminal, he or she will want to cover his or her tracks. If you let the hacker know you have caught him or her, he or she might end up removing all the files on your hard disk (`rm -rf /`) and then disappear.

Take a look at the holes we talked about previously. Use those as a guideline for determining what security measure you want to implement on your system.

ACCOUNTS

User accounts should be monitored and inactive user accounts should either be removed or disabled. "Inactive" should be defined by the company's security policy (e.g., three months). Users should be contacted by telephone and told that they need to come *in person* to have their accounts reactivated. All accounts must have passwords on them. If possible, configure the system to disallow null passwords.

User account areas (home directories, etc.) should be monitored regularly to check for possible compromise, which includes removing or monitoring the contents of `.rhosts` and `.forward` files. These files must be owned by the account for which they are in the home directory and permissions must be set to readable by the owner only (permissions 600).

Require that the person's supervisor or someone else known to the system administrators request new user accounts. You don't want someone calling up and saying that he or she is new in the accounting department and needs a new account. The request can be made via e-mail but confirmation of the request should be made over the phone in cases in which the supervisor's account was compromised. All accounts, as well as changes to groups and permissions, must be requested by the supervisors.

The root/administrator account should be the only shared account on the system. Only users who have a specific need should be given access to this account. Because the root password password should be different for all machines, is then possible to give root access only to those machines that are necessary.

All guest accounts should be removed from the system. There is no need for a guest account. You should know in advance that someone will be using the system and you can create an account for that person. This limits access to the system as well as provides a record of activity.

Monitor accounts that are no longer "active" because break-ins are less likely to be noticed. The hacker in *The Cuckoo's Egg* used an account from someone who was on an extended leave. Because Cliff Stoll was aware of this, he knew that whoever was using the account was doing so "improperly." One alternative would be simply to remove the account. When the user returns, a new account can be generated. If the person leaves the company, the account should be disabled or removed.

Know who is on vacation and consider disabling that person's account. Depending on the system, you could set up an at job that turns the account off the last day before that person goes and turns it back on the day that person returns. If that is not an option, occasionally checking the system to see whether one of these people is logged in might provide clues to a break-in.

Many software products will create their own users. Be careful of these. Make sure you are aware of exactly what the purpose of those users is. If deleting them is not possible, make sure that they have limited access to the system. If there are guest accounts on your system that are not needed, delete them.

Make sure that all accounts have passwords. If the system allows null passwords or simply hitting `Enter`, run your password cracker at least once a day to make sure.

Avoid group accounts, other than root/administrator. You can accomplish the same goal by placing everyone in a group and giving access permissions to that group.

Depending on how sensitive your data is, you might consider setting alarms on system accounts for when they are accessed at "inappropriate" times. What these times are and who can access the system should be specified in your company's security policy (see Section 13.3.2, The Official Word).

You can also have users monitor their own accounts. By using the last command, you can show the last time a user was logged in. By having the users check this themselves, you save yourself the trouble and they know better when they logged in. Fortunately, this information is provided for you each time you log in. Therefore, you can have your users check this and report any inconsistencies.

PASSWORDS

Words that can be found in a dictionary are not good choices for passwords. With just a few lines of code, you could write a simple program that searched through a list of words and tried them all as passwords. However, if any words are activated, Linux will prevent you from choosing any of them as your passwords. It also prevents you from making simple changes to the password like rotating (*strawberry* becomes *awberrystr*) or reversing (*yrrebwarts*).

The `passwd` program source is relatively easy to modify to add all of the features I discussed. When checking the validity of the password, the program could first check to see whether the input was something very obvious, like the user's name. Next, a dictionary containing common words could be scanned. The input password could also be rotated and reversed to see whether they match anything on the "no-no" list.

Some systems have added the ability for the system to generate a password. This could be anything from generating random characters, like *rY3h%n0&*, to combining random syllables like *bofandi*.

If your system doesn't allow you to select passwords for your users, you could regularly run a password cracking program. If you are successful in cracking a password, that password *must* be changed immediately. Simply mail a message to the user saying that the system has determined that the password selected is unacceptable and must be changed. Never include that password in a message.

Password attacks are perhaps the most common way of getting into a system and not bugs in the system. Studies have shown that unless the system stops "bad" passwords, password guessing *will* eventually succeed. The hackers in *The Cuckoo's Egg* used the same techniques I did to crack passwords and gain access. As Stoll showed, known or assumed account names and guesses at passwords succeed amazingly often.

Here are some guidelines when you're dealing with passwords.

Don'ts

- Don't use your login name in any form (as-is, reversed, capitalized, doubled, etc.).
- Don't use your first or last name in any form.
- Don't use your spouse's or child's name.
- Don't use other information easily obtained about you, including license plate numbers, telephone numbers, social security numbers, the brand of your automobile, the name of the street on which you live, etc.
- Don't use a password of all digits, all the same letter, or keyboard patterns like qwerty. This significantly decreases the search time for a cracker.
- Don't use a word contained in (English or foreign language) dictionaries, spelling lists, or other lists of words.
- Don't use a password shorter than six characters.

- Don't use the same password on multiple machines.
- Don't use a password that has appeared in any published work as being a "good" password.
- Don't ever use your password again if it is discovered.

Dos

- Do use a password with mixed-case alphabetics.
- Do use a password with nonalphabetic characters, e.g., digits or punctuation.
- Do use a password that is easy to remember so you don't have to write it down.
- Do use a password that you can type quickly without having to look at the keyboard. This makes it harder for someone to steal your password by watching over your shoulder.
- Do change your password often.
- Do choose a phrase and use the first letters of that phrase. You could also use a line from a song. For example, the first line of "Yellow Submarine" is "In the town where I was born," which would become Ittwiwb.
- Do use some nonsensical word like slewblue.
- Do combine words with some punctuation in the middle: rain;drain, lemon?curry.

If you are a system administrator, consider running something a password cracking program at regular intervals. This will show you whether users are actually using good passwords or not. Do not allow users to use the passwords by replacing the password program on those machines where possible.

Keep Your Eyes Open

A prefect crime is more than one in which the perpetrator gets away clean. It is one where the crime is not even detected. If an intruder can access a system *undetected*, he is safe. If you do detect an intruder, your company security policy (see Section 13.3.2, The Official Word) should detail what to do. If you are monitoring his activity to see what other machines he is trying to break into, don't let him know you are there. If he is clever enough, he might have built-in a backdoor, like one of those I discussed earlier (see Section 13.2.1, Real Threats).

Certain auditing packages like COPS will monitor and report changes to key files. Even a shell-script that simply compares values is sufficient to catch these kind of changes. Because hackers are aware of these kinds of tools, it is not a good idea to run them automatically from `cron` jobs.

A hacker could look in the `cron` tabs and see what programs are being executed and either disable them or work around them.

Another thing you can use is SATAN (System Administration Tool for Analyzing Networks). This is an interactive, complex application that checks a wide range of security "issues." Although it didn't find any more security holes than I did manually (in fact, I found more), it doesn't matter. SATAN is based on HTML and `perl`. You have all the source code and you can quickly expand it to exploit other holes that you know about. The problem is that as of this writing, certain browsers give it problems. You may have to change the way the browser reacts to the `perl` scripts. It's available at a lot of places, such as *ftp://ftp.win.tue.nl/pub/security*.

Know your system. Know what kind of activity is normal for every hour of the day. Imagine it's late Friday night and you know no one is still working, though one computer is busily working on some process. Is it an `at` job that someone started? Or is it a crack program that's going through a password file? This is how one system administrator *was* able to detect a person trying to crack passwords.

What processes are normal? If suddenly a new program appears on your system and you are the only one who has access to a compiler or can install software, where did it come from? What processes run with UID of 1? If someone's shell suddenly starts running with a UID of 1, you know you have a problem.

Excessive processes can result in a *denial of service*. That is, the system is so busy doing work for the hacking that it doesn't have time to do other things. Although you can limit the number of processes each user has, if those processes are disk-intensive, a hacker could bring the system to a standstill. If the hacker were to keep writing to the file system, you could run out of space or inodes, which might cause the system to panic. Even if the system doesn't panic, cleaning up after this will cost a great deal of time and money.

FILE SYSTEM SECURITY

Knowing what the permissions should be is useful in detecting intruders or other improper activity. If the permissions on files (particularly programs) is changed, you should know why. This is especially important if the files are SUID. If a program is owned by root and changed to be SUID, this could allow someone improper access to the system.

Fortunately, the `rpm` database has much of the necessary information. Among the information stored is the permissions of the files, owner, group, and a checksum. I'll go into details on using `rpm` to check this later on in this chapter.

You should also check the write permissions on all system directories and files. If an intruder has write permissions on a system directory, he can change log files or add his own version of system programs. While you're at it, check the ownership of system directories as well. It does little good if no one but the owner can write to a file though the owner is a normal user.

In principle, no one should have write permission to a user's home directory other than that user. If someone else has write permission, that person can overwrite that user's `.rhosts` file. Even if the file is write-protected, `write` permission on the directory means the file can be erased and a new one can be put in its place. You should also check the existence and content of `.rhosts` files to ensure that they do not give too much access. Obviously, if `.rhosts` are not allowed at all, they should be removed.

I also recommend that you be aware of every SUID or SGID program on your system. Know why it is there and why it should be SUID/SGID. If you know that you won't need it, consider removing it or changing the permissions. Also, check ownership of all system directories and files. Some files on the system must be writeable by everyone. Make sure you know which files they are so you can see whether there have been any changes.

Look for files without owners. That is, the owner in the `inode` does not have an entry in `/etc/passwd`. This could be innocent, when a user has one UID on one machine and another UID on other machine. Using `cpio` or `tar` to copy files, copy the UID of the source to the new machines. This happened to me once, but maybe there was something else behind it. Both `-nouser` and `-nogroup` are options to `find`, so it's easy to hunt for these files.

Check *specifically* for "weird" filenames like "..." (three dots) or "..(space)" or "..(backspace)" or anything that might be unusual. It is possible that these files were created by accident, but they are also common ways of hiding files on a system. Someone could also create filenames with control characters in them. This could help mask them. On most systems, the `ls` command has an option (e.g., `-q`) that will print out the directory list with a `?` instead of the control characters.

If your system does not have RPM-compatible packages, you should create a list of important information before you add any users. Make a complete list of your entire system. Include the owner, group, and permissions. For binaries and other nonwritable files, get sizes and creation dates. Include the sums, using the `sum` command, or create M5D checksums using a tool available on the Internet. These should never change. Maybe the `inode` number itself is important as well. If the `inode` is different, that means the file was copied.

Once you have your checklist, move it someplace away from that machine. It should *not* be stored on the local machine. If a clever hacker gets into the machine and finds this list, what's to prevent him or her from changing it so it matches the modifications he or she made to your system?

Devices nodes are one group of files that are often overlooked. Check access permissions on device nodes like `mem`, `kmem`, hard disks, tape drives. If the intruder has write permission on `/dev/kmem` or the hard disk, he or she can change things directly without using the standard tools. In addition, there is rarely a reason why device nodes should exist anywhere other than in `/dev`. If you find one, find out why it's there. Check the major and minor number to see what kind of device it is.

The Network

If you provide access to the Internet or any network services, you should monitor these as well. Remember that threats do not need to come from outside. Disgruntled employees or someone who has been bribed your competition can compromise security just as much as someone from outside. Good security does not mean pulling the plug on all network connections, but it does mean taking a few simple precautions.

Trusted Hosts. Trusting other computers is a double-edged sword. Many systems that did not allow trusted hosts did well against the Internet worm, compared to other sites that did not. You need to specify in your company's security policy just what kind of access is allowed. Maybe it's the extreme in which everyone trusts everyone else–maybe it's the extreme that no one trusts anyone. The middle ground would be to say that the database server trusts no one, although the database server is trusted by the others. That way, if one machine is compromised, the database server is safe.

You need to weigh convenience with security. When I was able to crack the account of one system administrator, he already had an `.rhosts` file that allowed access to his account on every machine from every other machine by both his own account and root. Therefore, once I had broken into one machine using his account, I could break into all of them.

If you are setting a system for the first time, you need to define your access policy before you hook up the machine to the rest of the network. Once on a network where security "can" be broken, the new system is no longer secure.

If you are taking over a system, you need to check it to make sure that it adheres to both the security policy and common sense. Check `/etc/hosts.equiv` to see who is given access and *every* `.rhosts` file on the system. Make sure that they are what you want. Never allow wildcards of any kind. Make sure that you specifically define who has access and from what machines.

One common mistake is that the `.rhosts` file is world-readable. No one should be able to figure out what access another account gives. Just because someone knows what other machines can reach this one does not mean that he or she can access that account. However, the more information an intruder has, the more directed the attack and the greater the chances of success.

FTP. Anonymous FTP should *not* be made available on every host on the network. Choose one machine (preferably a server or stand-alone host) that is protected from your internal network. This can be same machine as the mail or WWW server. This makes monitoring for security violations much easier. In the section on configuring an Internet server (see Section 14.2, Building the Server), I go into detail about securing your ftp server. Here, I'll just cover some basic issues.

Incoming transfers to this server should be in a separate directory (i.e., incoming). This is the *only* directory on which the user ftp can write. However, they cannot read this directory. This is to keep your site from becoming a repository for pornography, pirated software, and other nasty stuff. Check often the contents of the directories into which ftp is allowed to write. Any suspicious files you find should be deleted.

Although the ftp directory should not be writeable by the ftp user, you should still check for "hidden" directories or files. Review what is being abused to take appropriate action, based on what your security policy says. If you can determine where the stuff is coming from, notify CERT (Computer Emergency Response Team) and/or that site. If you can't find a phone number for that site, do not send the system administrator e-mail. If the other site is compromised, the intruder may check through the e-mail files.

NFS. NFS, by it's very nature, is insecure. One of it's basic premises is that you are a trusted machine to begin with. A major flaw in NFS security is that it is name-based and not based on IP address. Hostnames can be easily changed, which is an even bigger problem when access is granted to machines without domain names.

If it's not properly secured, NFS can be used to gain access to a system. You need to be sure that the file systems that you are exporting do not allow extra permissions and that you allow access to only those machines that need it. Be specific about who has what access.

I don't recommend that any file system be accessible by the world unless it's completely harmless and read-only. Even then, you could still provide the files via anonymous ftp and limit the potential for compromise. An example would be your man-pages and other documentation. It might be a good idea to share this directory to every system in an effort to keep things consistent and to save space.

Even if you do implement such a system, you should not export it to the world. By making the file system(s) accessible to only specific machines, you limit the potential for compromise. You know exactly the consequences of what you did. By using wildcards and making the systems available to everyone, you can't be sure of what can happen.

Even if you set up your NFS "correctly," you should check the configuration at regular intervals. If your system has been compromised, it would be a simple matter for someone to add an entry or change on to get access. The `showmount` command will show you a list of machines that are currently mounting your file systems. You should use this to check to see just who is accessing your system.

Check the `/etc/exports` file at regular intervals to ensure that you exporting only those directories that you think you are exporting. Although it really depends your company, the safest thing is to export only directories and file systems to machines within your local domain. If you have machines outside of your domain, implementing a firewall that allows NFS is more difficult. Besides, I have yet to hear a convincing argument why it should be done at all.

The `showmount` command shows machines currently remotely mounting your file systems. Only local machines should appear here. Monitor this. Only "normal," nonsystem directories should be mounted and they should be read-only, if possible.

Modems. Is access to your machine possible by modem? I had worked for one company for more than year before I found out that there was a modem on the system. It was connected to a terminal server that has its own password, so you actually needed two passwords to get into the system. However, this is important for every system administrator to know.

What are the characteristics of the modem and the port? Is hang-up forced when the user logs out? If the connection is broken, does the system log the user out? What are the permissions on the port? Can it be used by normal users to dial out? Are the answers to these questions in keeping with your company security policy?

BACKUPS

Your system backups are an integral part of your security policy. Not only are they useful when the system goes down, but they can be helpful in an investigation (see Section 13.3.2, The Official Word). One thing to consider is how long to keep your backups. If an intruder gains access to the system and does nothing for a month, do you have a clean backup from *before* the break-in? Do you have a copy of a clean system?

In one company I was in, we had five tapes for each machine, one for each day of the work week. We then got a tape loader that could hold enough for two weeks. However, each August the company shut down for three weeks. Several people from the IS department as well as some people in sales and customer service continued to work through the vacation. Therefore, regular backups were done. What would happen if someone came back from the three-week vacation to find a file missing? There is no backup old enough to find the file!

13.3.2 The Official Word

Several organizations and agencies deal with computer security issues. Perhaps the most widely know is the Computer Emergency Response Team (CERT) at Carnegie-Mellon University. They serve as a clearinghouse for known security problems for most common operating systems. They regularly issue CERT Advisories that detail the steps necessary to correct security problems without revealing too much about how to use the problem to break in. For details, check their Web site at *www.cert.org.*

One organization that is vital for the security of your system is your own management. They have to take an active, if not pro-active stance, in promoting security on your system. It is up to them to define what security means for the company and how important it is. In addition, they must give you, as system administrator, all the tools necessary to put these goals into effect.

Security and Network Policies

A security policy is a set of decisions that collectively determines an organization's posture toward security. This not only includes what is and what is not acceptable behavior, it also defines what actions are taken when the policy is violated. A network policy defines what is acceptable when using the Internet. These policies cover different areas but are very much intertwined.

Before you define a security policy, you must define your security stance. This is more or less decided by your company's attitude on security. If you believe that everyone should have access to everything and nothing will be limited, your security policy will be significantly different than if you want security above all, no matter how inconvenient it is for your users.

It's often difficult to define what is considered an "acceptable" behavior. Some companies give their employees the freedom to hang themselves; that is, they have complete access to the Internet, including e-mail, WWW, ftp, and so on. If the company discovers that the employees spent all their time downloading games and not working, the employees get a warning, a reprimand, and finally termination. On the other end of the scale, some companies say that a computer is for company business and will not be use *at all* for personal use, even if it means you can't get e-mail from your brother.

One thing I feel should be in there, no matter what end you are on, is that you must clearly state that employees' activity on the Internet should present the "proper" image for the company. I had to put the word "proper" in quotes because this will obviously be different from company to company.

I worked in two places that were very similar on the surface: father-son businesses, both with about 1,500 people worldwide. One was very rigid and formal ("Good morning, Mr. Smith") and the other was very laid back ("Mornin' Tom, how's it going?"). What was proper in one place was not so in the other. On a business trip to Australia while at the second company, I was told that when you call someone Mr. or Mrs., you are angry or upset or want to be sarcastic.

The first step in defining either your security or Internet policy is to *define* what is and is not permitted. Spell it out in clear text so that everyone knows what it means. To make things easier and perhaps the list smaller, you could simply define the "don'ts": define what is *not* permitted. This could include the hours during which Internet activity is not allowed and the types of material that cannot be brought into the company (i.e., pornography, pirated software).

Also part of the security policy should be what protocols and programs you will allow. If you are only going to allow outbound connections, then the policy should state this. If inbound connections are okay, what protocols can be used? Are incoming ftp and http connections okay, but not incoming Telnet? If so, this needs to be spelled out in the security policy.

A key aspect of your security policy is your stance on passwords. If you have decided that passwords are to be of a specific length and cannot have specific contents (such as the user's first name or spouse's name), this needs to be spelled out.

The policy should also define the system administrator's responsibility. On a Linux system, it's a simply matter of changing the source code to the `passwd` program to check a list of unauthorized passwords or of manipulating the password so not to use unauthorized passwords but spell them backward. If necessary, the security policy can state that it is the system administrator's responsibility to ensure that such password *cannot* be used. This can be easily accomplished by using the `npasswd` program.

Have your company management sign a password security policy and make all employees sign it as well. This policy should specifically define what is unacceptable behavior when dealing with passwords. Make sure that the employee is aware of the consequences of violating this policy, such letters of reprimand and even immediate termination. Users must be told that they will be held accountable for action taken by anyone using their account.

At first, termination might seem a little harsh for someone who gives his or her password to someone else in the same department, for example. However, there is no need to. If that other person really needs access to the data, either the permissions on the file should be set or the file should be copied to a common area. If access to the account is necessary, that person's supervisor or someone else known to the system administrators should call. The system administrators will either copy the file, change permissions, or change the password to something known (in accordance with the company password policy). This password will then be changed again when the account is no longer needed.

Users must keep their passwords to themselves and must never write them down anywhere, including blotters, calendars, Post-Its®, and especially in files on the computer. The hacker in *The Cuckoo's Egg* scanned e-mail files and found one in which the user told a coworker his password.

Users must change their passwords from time to time. Certain dialects of UNIX can force users to change their passwords. If the version of Linux you have cannot force users to change their passwords, you could implement a program that checks for specific dates and then notifies users. One possibility is to send mail to half the employees one month and the other half the next month.

However, users must know to never reset passwords to *specific* values based on e-mail they have received. This would prevent a hacker from compromising the mail system and send a message to an unsuspecting user. Would your users be able to recognize mail if it didn't come from a real administrator? All your mail should do is say that the password time has expired and that it should be changed. If the user gets a message to change his or her password to a specific password, it didn't come from an administrator.

CHANGING USER'S ATTITUDES

Although your company has a security policy, you need to concentrate more on changing people's attitudes. Perhaps a violation of the policy leads to someone's termination, but does that recover the millions of dollars of research that was lost?

If a user chooses an easily guessed password, it will be cracked using a dictionary attack. No question. Even if the hacker only has access to a small, low-powered PC, he or she can quickly crack the password. Many users believe that if a password is not in the traditional UNIX dictionary file (`/usr/dict/words`), it can't easily be broken. However, dozens of dictionary files spread out all over the Internet contain lists that are much longer. In addition, the words are not limited to just English anymore–there are dictionary files for several other languages as well.

In his paper "Foiling the Cracker: A Survey of, and Improvement to, Password Security," Daniel Klein of Carnegie Mellon University reported that during tests he conducted, 2.8 percent of all passwords were "guessed" within 15 minutes. He further states that on a machine with 50 accounts, at least one will be cracked within the first two minutes! Without user support the number will be a lot higher.

As system administrator or IS manager, you have to educate your users. Explain the general need for the passwords and security. Make them aware of the real cases in which lax security had detrimental effects. Be sure that that they know that they dangers are real.

One thing I found useful was making comparisons that the user understands. For example, compare the inconvenience of having a difficult password to the inconvenience when the system crashes. It might take five seconds longer a day to type in the correct password, but if the database is down for two hours, then the user could have typed his or her password 1,440 times–in other words, once a day for almost four years.

Another comparison that works well is that of car keys. No one would think of leaving his or her car unlocked, let alone change the car so that an ignition key is no longer needed. It is just as inconvenient to have to use keys for a car as it is to use a password on a computer account. It's just a necessary evil.

Finally, you can use threats. I don't mean holding a gun to the users' heads to force them to use good passwords and follow good security practices. Your security policy should state the consequences of giving out passwords or letting others gain access to your account. Users should be aware that they *could* be held legally responsible for anything done on the system with their account, especially if they are negligent.

For example, check TFTP (Trivial File Transfer Protocol), which is often used to transfer files automatically. I suggest that you disable it completely. There is nothing that can't be done with other means, and the risks are too great. If not, there is the potential that someone can access files on your system without any password at all.

One significant file is `/etc/passwd`. Because is it is world-readable, if TFTP is enabled, someone could easily download this file without a password. Once he or she has it, he or she can use a dictionary attack to try to crack some of the passwords. Another way would be to copy `.rhosts` files into users' home directories to gain access to the system.

Another useful tool is `rpcinfo`. This communicates with the portmapper daemon and provides information about what kind of services are being run. One very dangerous service is NIS. Although NIS is useful in propagating passwords to other machines, a clever hacker can "persuade" NIS to give him a copy, thus making the system vulnerable to dictionary attacks (among other things). Though you must know the NIS domain name, it is much easier to guess than users' passwords because it is more than likely some variant of the company name or the Internet domain.

There is no way to make a computer completely secure other than to lock the room and turn the computer off. Systems can be made impregnable to the casual intruder, as well as made more difficult for the experienced cracker. However, there are no guarantees.

SYSTEM SECURITY

In early versions of UNIX, account passwords and file permissions were the only types of security implemented. As computers became more widespread and those who wanted to gain unauthorized access became more devious, it became apparent that this was not enough. Because the U.S. government was steadily increasing the number of agencies that had computers, the level of system security needed to be increased as well.

In 1985, the National Security Agency's National Computer Security Center (NCSC) created a set of computer security standards for the Defense Department, titled *Trusted Computer Systems Evaluation Criteria.* This is commonly known as the "Orange Book" because it was published with an orange cover. (This is part of a series of documents by the DOD related to computer security, all with different colored covers.)

Within the Orange Book are four broad classes of security levels for computers:

- D: Minimal security
- C: Discretionary protection
- B: Mandatory protection
- A: Verified protection

The C class contains two sublevels, C1 and C2, C2 offering slightly more security than C1. Class B offers three sublevels: B1, B2, and B3.

Traditional PC-based operating systems, like DOS and Windows, fall within Class D. This minimal protection does not mean there is no security, just that it is not as high as the C class. You can buy add-on products to add passwords to your system or change the file attributes to prevent accidental erasure. There are even products available with which you can add passwords to DOS and Windows systems, but that's about it.

Class C systems include the features and functions to employ *discretionary protection*, which means that it is up to the system administrator's discretion to decide how much access people have. Class C1 systems offer enough security to let users keep their data private from other users and prevent it from being accidentally read or destroyed. As I've already talked about, standard UNIX already provides this level of security in the form of user passwords and file permissions. Class C2 demands tighter login procedures, auditing of security related events, and isolation of system resources.

B-class systems implement *mandatory protection*, that is, the system administrator *cannot* turn it off if he or she likes. Class B1 systems have *labeled protection*, which means that security procedures and *sensitivity labels* (basically security classifications) are required for each file. Class B2 adds the requirement that the system must be able to account for every code in the system. This helps to prevent security holes such as Trojan horses.

Class B3 deals with the security of data access in terms of prevention of tampering and notification of security-relevant events.

The most secure class, Class A1, requires *verified* designs. Although they are functionally the same as B3 systems, A1 systems have also been formally defined as well as *proven* by tests.

For years, the Orange Book was seen as the bible for computer security. Often, people would see a system that followed the guidelines specified for a C2 level of trust and call the machine C2 "secure." This is a misnomer. The machine is *trusted* to provide a certain level of security, but it is not "secure."

Recently, groups in several countries have gotten together to update the guidelines defined by the Orange Book. They have developed the "Common Criteria," which is a standard for security *criteria*. These countries are Canada, France, Great Britain, the Netherlands, Germany, and the U.S. Acceptance by these countries has made the Common Criteria, more or less, the de facto standard for information technology security worldwide.

Two of the more important basis documents for the Common Criteria (CC) is the Orange Book and the Information Technology Security Evaluation Criteria from the Commission of the European Community (ITSEC). However, the CC is not just a synopsis of other documents, but rather it is planned that the CC will replace these other documents.

Two key concepts in the CC are the *protection profile* and the *security target*. The protection profile is not product-specific, but after being reviewed, it becomes part of the CC. It documents a particular IT-security problem and the appropriate solution. For this problem and solution, the requirements for specific product types can be developed.

Security targets enable protection profiles to be fit to a specific product; in other words, the product as a particular goal, regarding security. With this, the security target forms the basis of the evaluation. A product evaluation determines whether a particular product has properly identified and addressed a particular IT-security problem.

The CC will be expanded as needed. The version planned as of this writing will contain requirements for cryptology. Cryptology solves problems of confidentiality, data integrity, and verification. The first version already addresses the issues of data protection and secure communication, even over open networks.

The evaluation process has several stages. First, a product manufacturer identifies an IT-security problem and decides to develop a solution and wants to have it evaluated. If a protection profile exists for this problem, the manufacturer can fit the profile to the product through the security profile.

If there is no security profile, a new one can be developed and a standard can be established to measure similar products. However, a security target can be defined without reference to a protection profile.

First, the security target is evaluated according to the CC. Then the product itself is evaluated according to the security target. If the product passes the evaluation, it is given an Evaluation Assurance Level (EAL). The evaluation, which is conducted by an organization *independent* of the manufacturer, confirms that there are no obvious security errors. In the case of a higher EAL, the evaluation confirms that there are no hidden errors. Also, the evaluation confirms that there is user documentation.

One advantage that the CC brings is that it is flexible and provides a clear concept of security. Products that have been evaluated and certified by the CC will gain significance and acceptance. The costs resulting from the evaluation process will be compensated by the improvements to security as well as the increase in market demand for certified products. As of this writing, most of the protection profiles deal with network issues. However, because of its flexibility, the CC can be implemented in other areas.

For the current version of the CC, check out the Nation Institute of Standards and Technology's Web site at *http://csrc.nist.gov/nistpubs/cc/*.

Security and the Law

The laws governing computer break-ins will differ from state to state and from country to country. Although there are now federal laws covering break-ins, they only apply to the United States. What about hackers who come in from other countries? Cliff Stoll can tell you horror stories of the problems he had.

One thing Stoll did was take very careful notes of the intruder's activities and keep print-outs of the hacker's activity on his system. What made this useful in court in many aspects is that he was very careful about how he handled the evidence.

There are several guidelines to follow if someone breaks into your system. The first thing is to contact CERT and your local law enforcement agency. Both will give you guidelines on what to do.

One thing that the law enforcement agency will do is to determine whether a crime has been committed. Although federal law says that the mere fact someone has gained unauthorized access to your system means that they have committed a crime, other issues may be involved, such as theft of trade secrets, loss in work, etc.

Because of the federal laws involved, the FBI *might* have jurisdiction or, at least, want to be involved. However, I recommend contacting your local authorities first and let them determine whether the FBI should be involved. Additionally, the local authorities can provide you with information on how to proceed.

One thing that the law enforcement authorities will help you with is evidence collection. Maybe you know your system inside and out and have monitored the intruder's activities, but that does not mean what you have would be considered valid evidence in court. Your local authorities can tell you how to handle things properly.

If information has been stolen, you will want to find out what that information was. This is important in estimating the financial losses for unauthorized disclosure. As an extreme example, let's take a case in which an intruder steals plans for a new machine. You had planned to patent it, but because your system crashed, you are delayed. Although it would be foolish for a competitor to try and patent it themselves, they could publicize your research to destroy your competitive advantage. Therefore, it would be much more difficult to obtain a patent yourself. The amount you lost in royalties are *real* damages.

If you decide to pursue the issue and press both civil and criminal charges, you have to be willing to make a commitment. The police (or whatever agency is involved) cannot do it alone. They need your help in terms of both time and resources. They need someone to show them the logs, identify the data that have been stolen, as well as identify any evidence found in the hands of the intruder. Even after the intruder is caught, you will still have to spend time to support the investigation, such as identifying data or appearing in court.

Unless you live in a large metropolitan area, there is a good chance that your local authorities may not understand the technical aspects of the crime. Basic concepts like data and networks are something they probably heard about, but understanding them is something else. There are just too many kinds of crimes for them to be experts in them all. Even if they have one computer crime a year, they just don't have the experience. Therefore, you may have to explain just what root access is and what the extent of the access/damage could be for someone with root privileges. In other areas in which crimes are reported regularly, there are special units that deal with these types of crimes.

Obviously, if you can't prove "who dunnit," there is no way to collect any compensation. That is why it is vital that the rules of evidence be followed. Although the police can give you specific guidelines, you should consider a few points while you are waiting for the police to arrive.

However, do not let this discourage you. In most places, there is a difference between criminal and civil charges. In a criminal case, the prosecution must prove its case *beyond a reasonable doubt*. In a civil case, the plaintiff must prove *preponderance of evidence*, which means that someone can be declared "not guilty" in a criminal trial but still be held liable in civil case. Look at the O.J. Simpson case as an example.

First, if the only evidence you have is based on on-line information such as files in the user's directory or e-mail messages, you are on thin ice. Just as an intruder can steal files, he can also plant evidence. Though this kind of "evidence" might be sufficient to get a warrant to search the suspect's house, it might not be enough to prove the person's guilt.

It might be sufficient for you to use this information as grounds for termination of an employee. But you must also be careful. Is there a reasonable expectation of privacy when you send e-mail or store files? If it is company policy that *anything* on the computers is company property, then you may have a case. I have worked for companies that have said e-mail will not be read by *anyone*. There is a reasonable expectation of privacy and the company could be sued if they looked through someone's e-mail. Here again, talk to the law enforcement agencies.

Speed is also important when you are gathering evidence. Maybe an intruder has used one machine as a storage house for information that he or she has collected from other machines. Copy all the files and try to maintain the directory structure. This *might* be useful as evidence because the likelihood that two people have the same directory structure is low (sort of like dental X-rays). If the intruder deletes all the files, your evidence is gone. There are repeated cases in which password files from other machines have been found along with password cracking programs.

As I mentioned before, don't let the intruder know you are watching. The best (least bad?) thing he or she could do is simply disappear, maybe breaking out through some other hole that you don't know about. The worst that could happen is that the intruder reformats your hard disk in an effort to cover his or her tracks.

Another aspect of evidence is "chain of possession." This means that it can be proven in court where the evidence was the whole time. Who obtained it, who secured it, and who handed it to the police are all aspects of chain of possession. Once you have a piece of evidence, you should mark it with your initials and then seal it in a container so no one else can get access to it.

In *The Cuckoo's Egg* case, the logs of the hacker's activity proved to be a vital piece of evidence. Stoll was able to prove that certain actions on the system were made by hackers other than the one he was tracking. There were patterns to his behavior that Stoll recognized and could separate from those people who were just having a look around.

Although what I have just talked about provides the foundation for a security investigation, don't take it as gospel. Laws are different from state to state and from country to country. Talk to your law enforcement agencies *now*, before the first attack. Find out what services they can offer in case of a break-in. Most importantly, find out what the law is governing break-ins, rules of evidence, and especially privacy because you don't want to lose the case and be sued yourself.

13.4 User Software

One most dramatic advantage of Linux over commercial UNIX versions is the availability of free software. In many cases, free means the traditional no cost (gratis) and in others, it means free to configure the way you want (libres). Dozens of sites all over the Internet have both types of software. Many of the distributions that I talked about come with additional CD-ROMs with (somewhat) complete copies of these archives.

Even if the distribution you receive doesn't have any of the archives, they are available from many sources, most notably Walnut Creek CD-ROM (*www.cdrom.com*) and InfoMagic (*www.infomagic.com*).

Many of the commercial distributions come with different applications programs. Many are freeware or fall under the GNU public license. Others are limited versions of commercial products.

If you wanted to run a business using Linux, you could use `vi` or `emacs` to write your business letter and access an ASCII database with `perl` scripts. Because you have the `gcc` compiler, you could write your own applications to do your job. However, your business is not to develop and program business applications. It really doesn't make sense to install Linux in your business without having the applications you use to make your business work.

The great thing is that you don't have to. Dozens of products available provide the necessary functionality. Some are freeware, falling within the GNU Public License, which include a Wordstar-like word processor (see Figure 13.1), a spreadsheet (see Figure 13.2), and a database (see Figure 13.14).

Others are full blown commercial packages that rival the functionality and features of their better-known counterparts. Still others *are* the better-known counterparts, as more and more vendors realize that Linux is a valid operating system and have already ported their applications.

In the next section, I'm going to talk about *some* of the commercial products and noncommercial application software available for Linux. This is *far* from complete. I intend to show you that software is out there, and what's out there is good. Most distributions come with a very extensive list of products that range from spreadsheets to drawing programs to CD players. These are almost exclusively freeware.

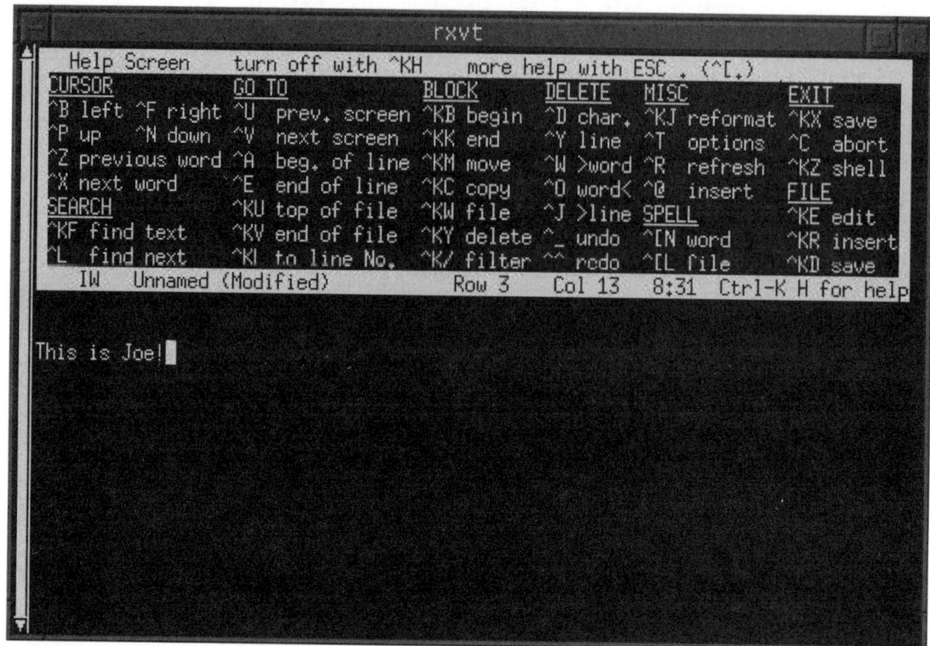

Figure 13.1: The Joe Editor

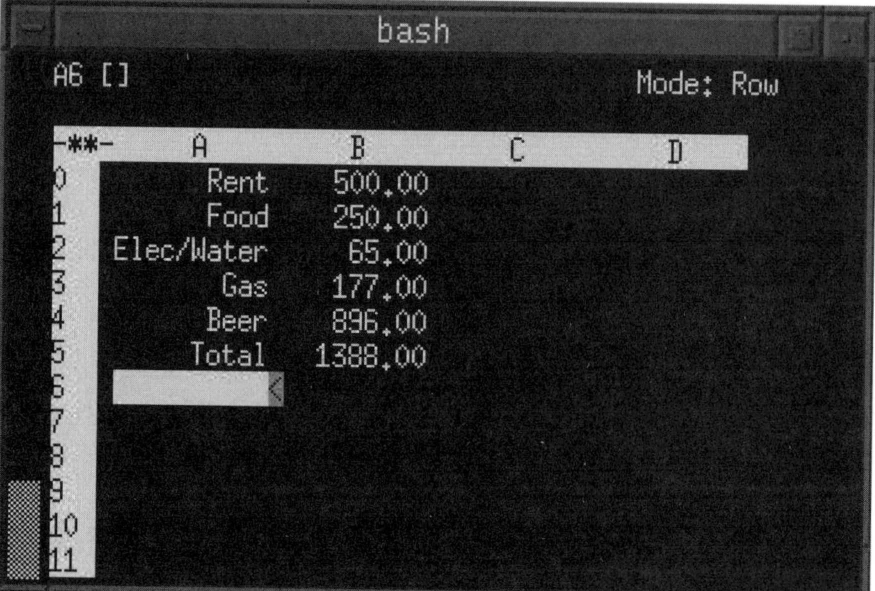

Figure 13.2: The SLSC Spreadsheet

Another place you can look is the Commercial HOWTO that you will find on the CD-ROM. This is probably not the most up-to-date version, but it does give you a very extensive list of available products. You should check out *www.sypher.com/tbm/Commercial-HOWTO* for the latest version. This is well worth a visit because unlike the version on the CD-ROM, this one has links to all the companies in question. (It can also be downloaded via FTP from *ftp://ftp.sypher.com/tbm/HOWTO*.)

The only "non-good" thing I can say about this list is that as of this writing, only one company is listed with commercial hardware: Stallion Technologies (*www.stallion.com*). They produce very good multiport boards (I have one myself) and the entire organization is very enthusiastic about Linux.

There is also the list maintained by the Linux.org.uk site at *www.linux.org.uk/LxCommercial.html*. This list contains many of the same companies, but some are listed at one and not the other. This means that to get everything, you will have to look at both sites.

If you are looking to buy, then check out the All Linux Mall at *www.all-linux.com*, which is sponsored by WorkGroup Solutions. Although this is far less complete than the other two lists, this site provides you the opportunity to order a wide range of products directly on-line.

The Linux Journal (*www.ssc.com*) has come out with a buyers' guide for Linux products. In the guide, you will find an amazing list of software, hardware, and companies. Much of the software listed is freeware that you find on many of the CD-ROM distributions. However, there are loads of commercial products, many of which I mention throughout this chapter. The companies that are listed not only include vendors of Linux products but also provide Linux support and consulting services.

13.4.1 Desktops

Caldera Network Desktop

The Caldera Network Desktop (CND), Figure 13.3, provides the kind of interface to which people using MS Windows have grown accustomed. The appearance may be different from Windows's, but the CND does an excellent job of fitting the "desktop metaphor" that people expect.

The copy of CND 1.0 that I had was very easy to install. You use two disks to install both the operating system (RedHat Linux) and the desktop. What do you do if you want to install the desktop on an existing system? There is no easy way. Perhaps the CND is limited to a specific version of Linux. However, this was not mentioned in the manual.

Like other desktops, you can configure the CND as you would your "real" desk. Commonly accessed applications and tools can be laid out on the desktop itself for easy access. You can also change the behavior of

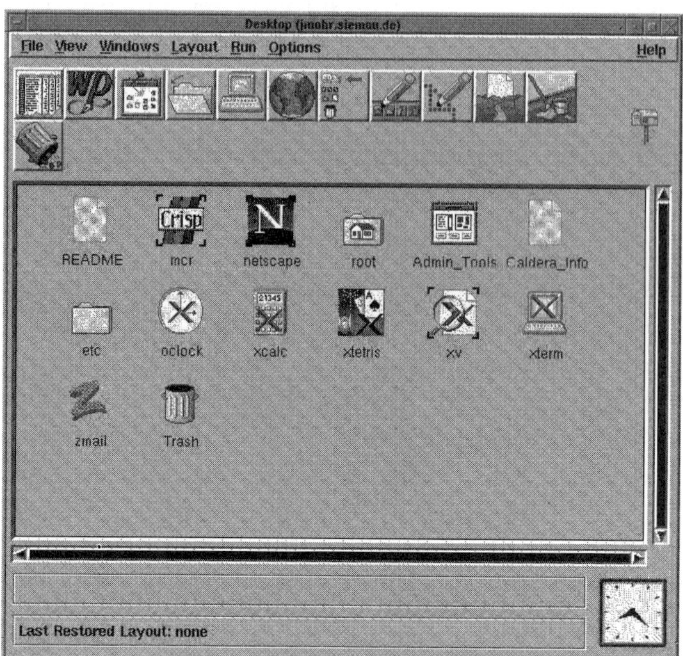

Figure 13.3: Caldera Network Desktop

the system based on the file you are accessing. Similar to the "associations" made in other windowing systems, CND enables you to click a file and have a specific application or other function start up. When I installed WABI, a script modified the configuration files so that when I click a file ending in `.EXE` (like any windows program), WABI will automatically start that application.

Desktops, and therefore their behavior, is defined by preconfigured desktops, which you can copy and modify to suit your needs. Therefore, all this configuring can be done on a per-user basis. You can configure the desktop as well as the toolbar. I haven't been able to figure out how to configure the menus, if that is even possible. Despite that limitation, if it is one, the configuration is very straightforward.

The major drawback of the CND is the documentation. This is not to say that the documentation is bad–I have seen worse–it's just incomplete. Much too much time was spent on describing common UNIX functionality and not enough on the CND. In addition, there are some problems with the order of things in the manual. For example, I feel you should first learn how to use something before you start talking about configuring it. How else do you know what you should be configuring?

Most of the configuration I tried was by trial and error. As I mentioned, the basic configuration was straightforward, but it was very difficult to go beyond that. For example, to create new associations, you edit several files. The documentation said to take an existing entry and modify it to suit your needs. However, the entries do not clearly identify what each option does. Still, once I figured it out, I quickly had a new icon displayed for my own files that started a specific application.

Despite the problems with the documentation, I am very impressed with the product. It provides a single interface to almost all of the system functions. With the point-and-click configurability, it's easy to add the missing components, including access to products provided in the Internet Office Suite and other applications.

Along with the Caldera desktop, you'll find the "lite" version of the crisp editor. Even the "lite" version is sufficient for most tasks. I wrote the text that I am writing now with the X version of `crisp`. In addition, there is also a character-based version, as shown in Figure 13.4.

Figure 13.4: The crisp Editor

Despite that it is a "lite" version, the crisp editor comes with a wide range of features that makes it an excellent tool for users and administrators. One feature that I grabbed the first time I used it was the ability to change colors. Although the lite versions only allow you to change the foreground and background colors, for me, this is enough.

I've been looking for a simple text editor along the lines of Microsoft's Notepad or Write, and crisp does the job. It has enough features to make editing worthwhile but not so many that you are overwhelmed. Another useful feature is the ability to edit multiple files. You can then cut and paste between files. The crisp editor also has a very complex search and replacement mechanism. Not only can you search for words and phrases, but both the search and replacement patterns can be the same regular expressions that we can use in `grep`, `sed`, or `vi`. (However, there are a couple of exceptions.)

In their most recent product, Caldera OpenLinux, you will also find a copy of the Caldera Network Desktop. This time, instead of paying for the desktop and getting the operating system free, you pay for the operating system and get the desktop free.

THE COMMON DESKTOP ENVIRONMENT

The Common Desktop Environment (CDE), shown in Figure 13.5, is an attempt to provide a common interface to the system across multiple platforms. CDE is very easy to use and includes most of the tools that one expects from a desktop.

Figure 13.5: The Common Desktop Environment

The version of CDE that I installed was the Accelerated-X CDE version 1.0.10 from X Inside. The installation was fairly easy, but it does not conform to the RPM standard. Instead you do the installation manually in that you change into the appropriate directory and then extract the files using `tar`.

Among the CDR's features is a login manager, which is used to manage user access to the system. A session manager is used to maintain a "snapshot" of the work space. When the same user logs back into the system, he or she is given the chance to get back the same desktop that he or she had when he or she was last working. Part of the "common" aspect of the CDE is an API that can be used when developing applications. Any applications that follow this API can communicate with each other.

Unfortunately, I was not able to get much beyond that. The manual that was provided is best suited for people who have already worked with CDE or for those who love to flip through manuals. Repeatedly, terms and phrases were used that were not yet defined. In many cases, I couldn't even find the definition of the term.

When I finally figured out how to start the desktop itself, I was stuck once again. The desktop looked great, consisting primarily of an icon bar at the bottom of the screen. Unfortunately, there was no indication of what each of the icons were for. The manual had no diagram for the toolbar, so all I could do was click the icons to see what they would do.

Unfortunately for me, there was an on-line help that starts automatically when the desktop starts. I can't stand on-line help, unless I am trying to search for something. I want a hard copy so I don't have to flip back and forth between windows. I want that window for which I am looking at the help on the screen. What I like least than on-line help is when the on-line help doesn't match the hard copy, as in this case. Despite my complaints, the on-line tutorial that accompanies the document was very helpful in getting me started.

I also found that there was a touch of Microsoft in the product. When I started the desktop once I got a window labeled "Action Required." Inside the window was a message that said "! Message" and a single button that said okay. This must have been the "Mission: Impossible" button, because when I clicked it (the only thing I could do), the entire desktop self-destructed. Afterward, the three subsequent times that I started the desktop, I got the same message. Finally, I did get an indication of the problem and was able to continue.

Like the CND, the CDE is very configurable. In fact, based on the documentation, it *seems* as though there is more that you can do with it.

However, it is less intuitive than the CND. This was compounded by the fact that the documentation was not only poorly laid out, but it was often unclear. (As I mentioned, I had a feeling that you had to have used to CND before.)

Another drawback that I encountered is that CDE "requires" the Accelerated-X server. Although this was provided in the package, it does not support either of my video cards. On one machine, it came fairly close, but not exactly. As a result, I ended up having "afterimages" of my windows and had to constantly refresh my screen. When I switched back to the X server that I had been using before, things were noticeably slower. Therefore, I would recommend that you call X Inside before you by it, just to make sure that the video card you have is support. Their URL is *www.xinside.com*.

One thing that really impressed me with the CDE is the support for many different languages. Although not every one of the worlds languages are supported, the CDE provides support for the "big ones" such as German, Spanish, and French, and some not-so-common languages such as Swedish and Korean. The problem is that this version is supposed to support Linux. So what language is missing? Finnish!

Don't get me wrong. I am impressed with what the desktop does. It's nicely laid out and you can configure it in many different ways. There are many easy-to-use applications, so it is not just a window/program manager.

As one would expect, a wide range of tools is available from the desktop, including a graphical interface to mail, a calendar/scheduling tool, and several graphical administration tools, including one to manage the configurations.

13.4.2 Office Suites

Not to be outdone by Windows, Linux provides complete office solutions in several forms. The best known is the Caldera Internet Office Suite (CIOS), which includes Flagship (a Clipper clone), the NExS spreadsheet (see Figure 13.7), and MS-Word's arch rival, WordPerfect (see Figure 13.6) In addition, the CIOS also contains a copy of Zmail, a very easy to use e-mail interface.

The "Internet" aspect of the office suite is that all applications are network aware and can pull in data from other sources across the Internet. NExS is "network extensible" in that it can send and receive messages from other X applications, even those on other computers.

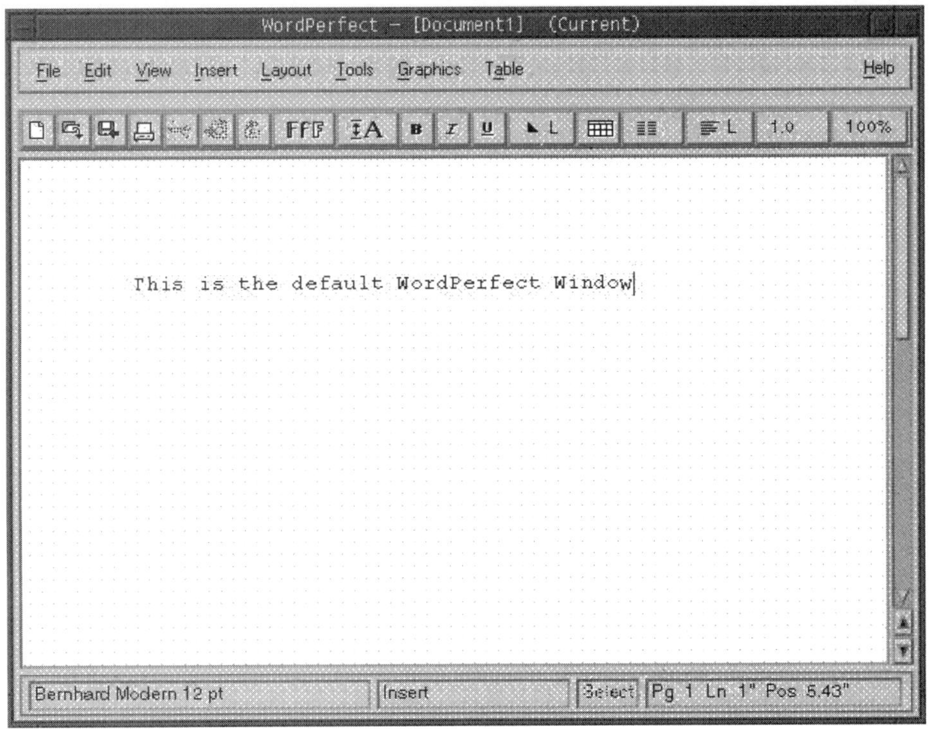

Figure 13.6: WordPefect for Linux

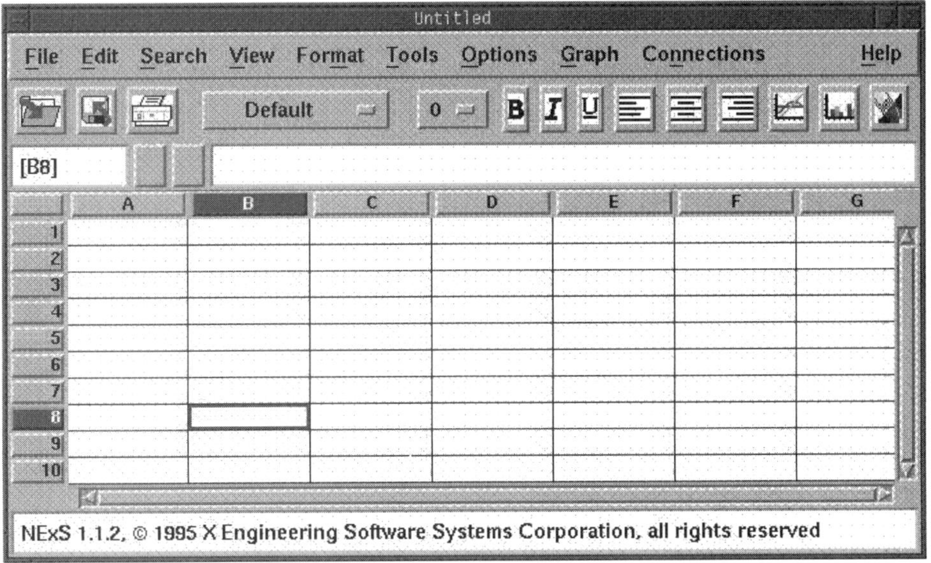

Figure 13.7: NExS Spreadsheet

Caldera has also released their Solutions CD-ROM, which contains the same products as the CIOS, plus many others. Check out the Caldera Solutions CD-ROM and other Caldera products at *www.caldera.com*. The products include:

- ADABAS D (database)
- ASWedit (HTML editor)
- CorelDraw 3 (graphics package)
- Crisp (text editor)
- EditTable and ChartObject (graphics development tools)
- Labtam X-WinPro (enables Windows-based PCs to become fully functional remote/networked Caldera Workstations that can run CND and many host-based applications simultaneously)
- MetaCard 2.0 (GUI development and multimedia authoring tool)
- Metro-X (accelerated X-Server)
- Motif (full Motif development libraries)
- NetCat Product Suite (Interactive Inter/intranet catalog ordering and uotation system)
- PartitionMagic (hard-disk manager)
- Starter Kit (Web site builder for commerce and information exchange on Inter/intranets)
- Stronghold - The Apache Secure Socket Layer Web server
- Synchronize (scheduling and task management)
- X11 PrintManager (printing for X11 environment) Ematek

Keep in mind that the Solutions CD-ROM is not a product, per se. That is, you don't buy the CD-ROM–you buy the products on it. Recently, Caldera has provided a copy of the CD-ROM in many of their products. To use them, however, you must first unlock them. By calling the number included on the CD-ROM, you can quickly gain access to any of the products.

The Caldera representative guides you through the unlocking process, which gives you a decrypted RPM file that you install like any other file. Because this RPM file is the only medium you get, you need to back it up and keep it safe. Some of the RPM files are a dozen megabytes or more, so backing them up to tape is a good idea.'

One problem I found with the Solutions CD-ROM is that it was a mix-match of products from several vendors. Though I like the products, each has its own interface, keyboard accelerators, and feel, so you have to adjust yourself to each product. This in itself is a strong argument in favor of MS Windows office suites (at least for the novice user).

Caldera solved this problem with an agreement with StarDivision, known for their StarWriter product. Caldera will be the official distributor for StarOffice on Linux. Included in the Start Office product are both dynamic libraries (if you already have Motif installed) and static libraries (if you do not).

In addition to the Solutions CD, Caldera has also brought out several versions of it's OpenLinux product. OpenLinux Lite, is a good entry level product. This should be available for downloading by the time this book is in print. It comes with the standard version of the Netscape Navigator for Linux, a graphical text editor, and all of the standard tools that you expect. The OpenLinux Base product contains everything that the Lite version has, plus a the Java Development Kit from Sun, a full, non-commercial version of StarDivision's StarOffice Suite for Linux, and the Caldera Desktop.

Next up the line is the Caldera Open Linux Standard. This has the same feature as the Base product, you would expect. However, it also includes the Netscape FastTrack Server, Netscape Navagator Gold (with a built-in HTML Editor), a commericial version of StarOffice and Software AG's Adabas D Personal Edition, SQL database. Finally, there is the Deluxe version. This includes Novell GroupWise and a full Netware NDS client.

With the addition of this wide range of commerical software, Caldera has provided a complete business and Internet solutions for Linux. When coupled with add-on products like WABI or existing parts of Linux like SAMBA, the Caldera line of products can provide exactly what you are looking for from the desktop to the enterprise server.

StarOffice has some powerful characteristics that put it one step ahead of MS Office. First, there are versions for several UNIX and UNIX-like platforms, plus MS Windows. At the CeBIT in March 1997, I had the chance to look at the StarOffice 4.0 for Windows. The most amazing thing about it was that it is a *single* application. That is, you have access to all of the functions of StarWriter, StarCalc, and the others from the *same* interface. This does not mean that they are separate programs and that all look the same. Instead, there is one small program that calls the functions you need.

The Windows version also had other features, such a integrated mail, discussion forums, and HTML publishing. The HTML publishing gives you WYSIWYG and the ability to design frames directly on the screen, as well as Java and Java-Script. Also, the features of Microsoft Explorer (available in Windows 95 and NT 4.0) is built into the office interface, allowing you to perform all your work from a single interface.

For Linux users, there is still StarOffice 3.1, a full-featured office package. Many of these features are available, but it is not as complete as the version for Windows. However, the Linux 4.0 version is expected to be available by late 1997. (Don't take this as an announcement of a release date–it may need to be pushed back.) For Linux users, there is another plus–you can download the StarOffice product from the StarDivision Web site (*www.stardivision.de*) for *free* and use it for noncommercial purposes.

RedHat distributes ApplixWare, which is another well-rounded office suite. Applixware is one of the most popular and complete office automation suites for UNIX systems. The version that I installed on my system has proven it to be a useful product. Applixware for Linux includes the easy-to-use fully graphical and integrated word processor, spreadsheet, presentation graphics, mail, and object-oriented application development tool (Applix Builder). See Figures 13.8 and 13.9.

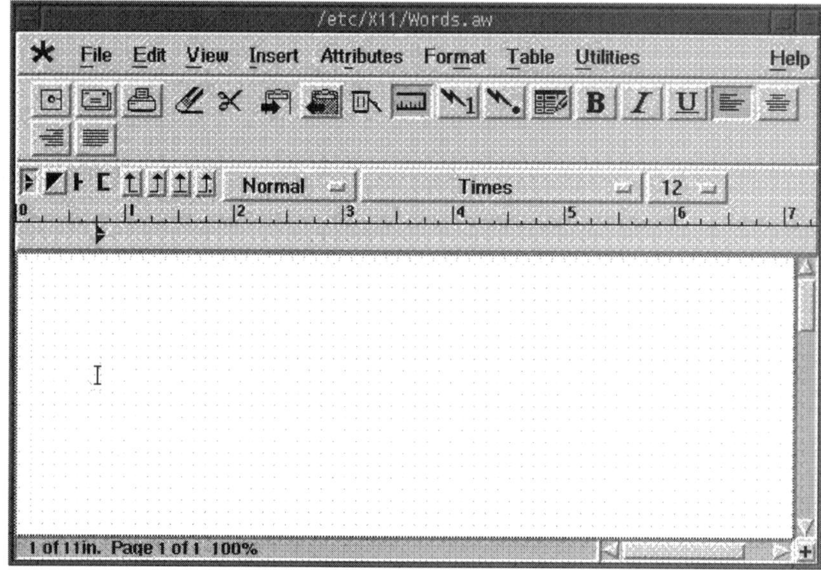

Figure 13.8: Applix Words

Also present is an HTML editor. This is not as extensive or as easy to use as a product like Microsoft's Frontpage, but once you get the hang of it (in about 30 minutes), you can quickly create fairly complicated Web pages.

A very appealing part of both StarOffice and Applixware is that they offer versions that run on both Windows and Linux. Because they are completely compatible, there is no need to have different applications on each type of machine, or provide users with two different machines, one for each OS. Instead, each user can use the appropriate operating system to run the special applications necessary, and the office product each users gets will be the same.

13.4.3 Development Software

If you can't find anything that suites your needs, then you have to create your own. All Linux distributions come with a complete development environment. You have all the tools necessary to build the applications

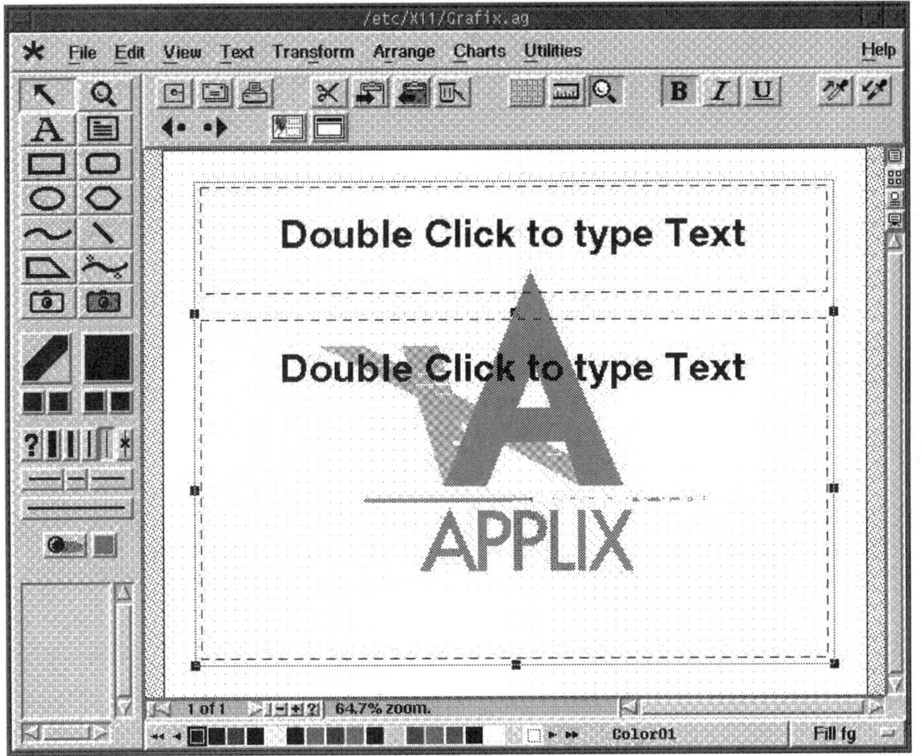

Figure 13.9: Applix Presentation Graphics

that you need. Even if you don't like to or can't program in C, there are other tools available for you, such as `perl` or `tcl`.

`Xxgdb` is a GUI front end for the `gdb` debugger. It allows you to control the program flow as well as examine variables, structures, and even the stack.

XWPE in the X-Window Programming Environment has a feel to it like the Integrated Development Environment that comes with Borland development products (see Figure 13.10). The menus have a similar structure and you can change the colors of code elements like in the Borland IDE (for example, comments are blue and constants are red).

One major difference is that XWPE is just the development environment. When you compile or make the program, you can choose which compiler you want to use (along with any options). These means that a single development environment can be used for C, Pascal, or Fortran.

There are also commercial development products. You can use something like Flagship or the tool builder in Applixware. There are also development packages such as ScriptEase from Nombas, Inc. (*www.nombas.com*). As its name implies, ScriptEase is a scripting language but has all the power of C. The advantage over C is that their is automatic variable declaration and the pointer syntax of C is gone.

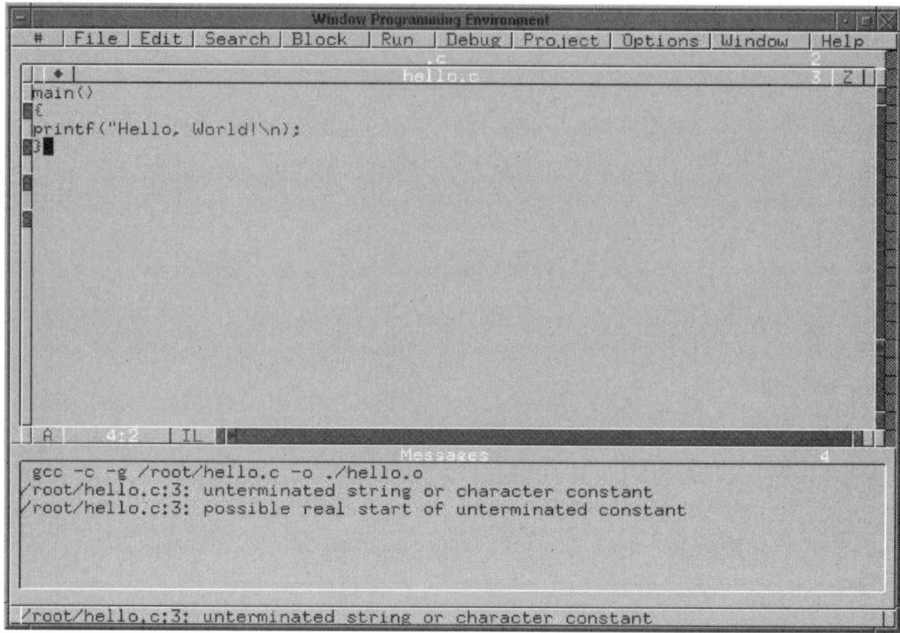

Figure 13.10: X-Window Programming Environment

ScriptEase is available in a couple of different products to suit your needs. One is the WebServer edition, which gives you all the Web server variables as ScriptEase variables and remote debugging, which makes it a valuable tool for Web site development.

Another company that provides development tools for Linux is Parasoft Corporation (*www.parasoft.com*). Parasoft provides two tools to help your software development. CodeWizard is a program that aids programmers by looking for such things as poor designs and mistakes that compilers overlook or consider trivial. CodeWizard can also do adaptive, context-sensitive error suppression. (Note that as of this writing, CodeWizard is not yet available for Linux, but they *are* working on it.)

Insure++ is a comprehensive tool for error detection in C/C++ programs that will detect "standard" errors like incompatible variable declarations, mismatched argument types, and unreachable code. In addition, it can detect memory leaks, string manipulation errors, and mismatched variable types in `printf` and `scanf` argument lists. (Where was it when I was learning?) If the error is caused by third-party libraries, Insure++ also determines whether the error is caused by the user or the library.

Actually, Insure++ is a set of tools/modules that helps your development efforts. One, called INSRA for Insight Reporting Analyzer, is a GUI reporting tool. This makes reacting to the messages much easier. The Total Coverage Analysis (TCA) module is used to monitor the flow of the program and, among other things, test each block of your program. The Insure module "visualizes" the run-time memory use of your program, giving you a better understanding of how your program actually uses memory.

13.4.5 Back-up Software

You may like using `tar` or `cpio` manually, but you don't have to do so. As I talked about earlier (see Section 12.1.1, Preparation), the Lone-Tar product is an easy to use tool to backup your system. If you are familiar with the version for other UNIX dialects, then you should have no problem switching to the Linux version. Lone-Tar is available from Cactus International (*www.cactus.com*). Also, Cactus has one of the best tech support organizations around. Although they may not have the answer to every question, you get the feeling that they genuinely care about your problem and you.

On the Craftworks CD-ROM, there is a limited version of the BRU backup software. At least the two versions I installed had one. This, too, is a good product. Backup software is like text editors. Both have their pluses and minuses and it is usually an emotional choice the determines which one you use.

13.4.6 Text and Publishing

For me, the most surprising tool was Lyx. Lyx, simply put, is a text editor/word processor. But that's not doing it justice. Lyx is fairly straightforward in that the formatting on the screen is "almost" what you see in the document. This means that uninteresting things like like-breaks and page-breaks are not shown as they would in a word processor (see Figure 13.11).

What makes Lyx so special is that rather than saving text as some proprietary, unintelligible format, it saves everything as LaTex. LaTex, and its predecessor TeX, are perhaps the most commonly used text processors on UNIX machines. A large number of Linux documents are available *only* as TeX or LaTex. One key difference is that the writer is no longer concerned with formatting problems and can therefore spend more effort on the content.

One nice touch is printing. By default, Lyx will pass the file straight through LaTex and then `dvi2ps` to create a PostScript file that can then be sent to any PostScript printer. In addition, you can start PostScript viewers (such as ghostview, which is also on the CD-ROM) directly from Lyx to see exactly how your document will appear on paper.

As a nice addition to Lyx, there is `xwpick`, a screen capture program. Aside from standard graphics formats like GIF and PCX, `xwpick` can also save them as `EPS` (Encapsulated PostScript) files that can be inserted into the documents that you create with Lyx.

`Xfig` (see Figure 13.12) is an X-based "figure" drawing tool. It is somewhat along the lines of CorelDraw in that you draw and manipulate objects, not pixels. This tool is also and nice addition to Lyx as you can save the drawings as EPS or directly in LaTeX format.

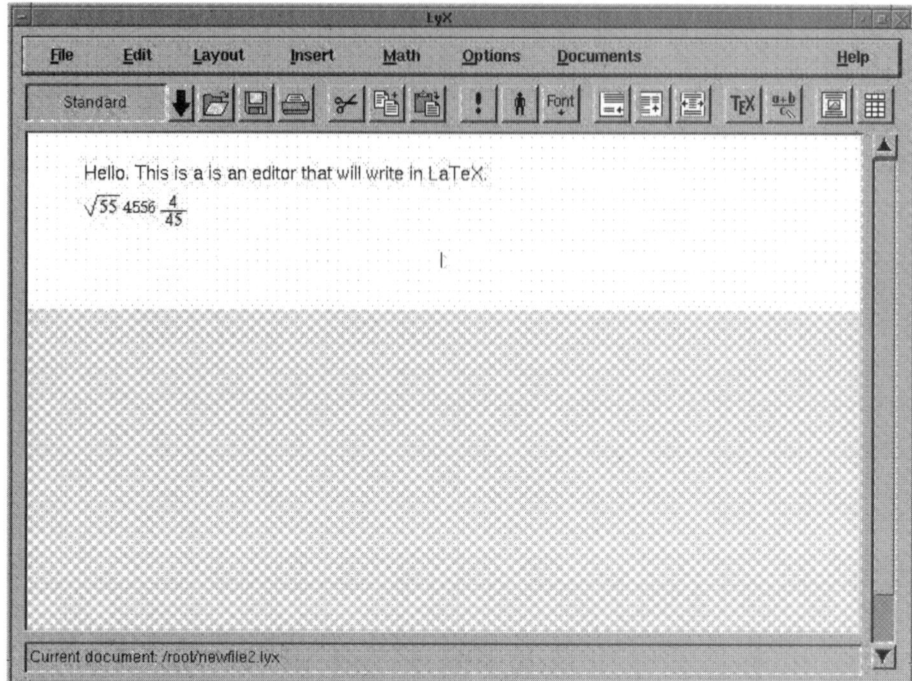

Figure 13.11: Lyx LaTeX Editor

`Xpaint` is a drawing tool á la Windows PaintBrush. It enables you to store your images (pictures) in a wide range of formats, including JPEG, PPM, and XBM, which makes it a good tool to create your own icons. Unlike PaintBrush, `Xpaint` is split into two components, the "canvas" and the toolbar, as shown in Figure 13.13.

Perhaps the most well-know UNIX graphics tool is `xv`. This has been around for years and is available (that is, has been ported) to almost every UNIX dialect. The `xv` program can save to the standard formats like GIF and JPEG, but also PPM, XPM, and PostScript (among others). Although I use it mostly as a viewing tool, `xv` can also convert between formats as well as change the image itself, through cropping, rotation, and other processes.

13.4.7 Databases

The `grok` is a rather nice database that that not only stores your information but enables you to display it in a number of ways. There are several predefined "applications," such as a phone book, checkbook, and book library. When you select a particular database, the display and the menus change accordingly. A GUI build is also provided to enable you to create your own database and forms. See Figure 13.14 for a look at it.

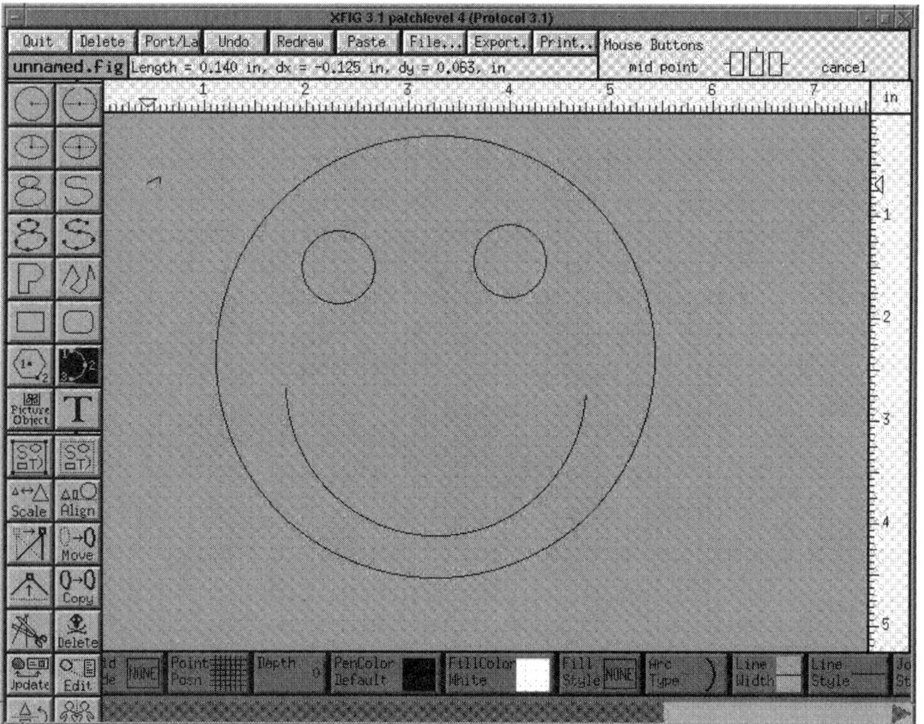

Figure 13.12: XFig

On the commercial side of things is `/rdb`, available from Revolutionary Software (*www.rsw.com*). This is a command line tool that is perfect for Internet sites or incorporation into shell-scripts or tools that you build with other products.

FlagShip is a Clipper clone that is available on the LinuxPro CD-ROM. Internet FlagShip is a superset of Clipper 5.3 that is fully source- and data-compatible to it. As a result, code written for versions of Clipper can access the FlagShip data, and vice versa. Your source code can also be converted to C code, which is then compilable. If you have one of the other versions (Personal or Pro), you can then distribute the executable programs.

This is a trial version, but has most of the same functionality as the full versions. One difference is that you cannot distribute the code that your create. See the `license.doc` on the CD-ROM for more details. You can get the full versions through WorkGroup Solutions (*www.wgs.com*).

13.4.8 Wabi

Sunsoft's Windows Application Binary Interface (Wabi) is a program that enables you to run Microsoft Windows applications directly from

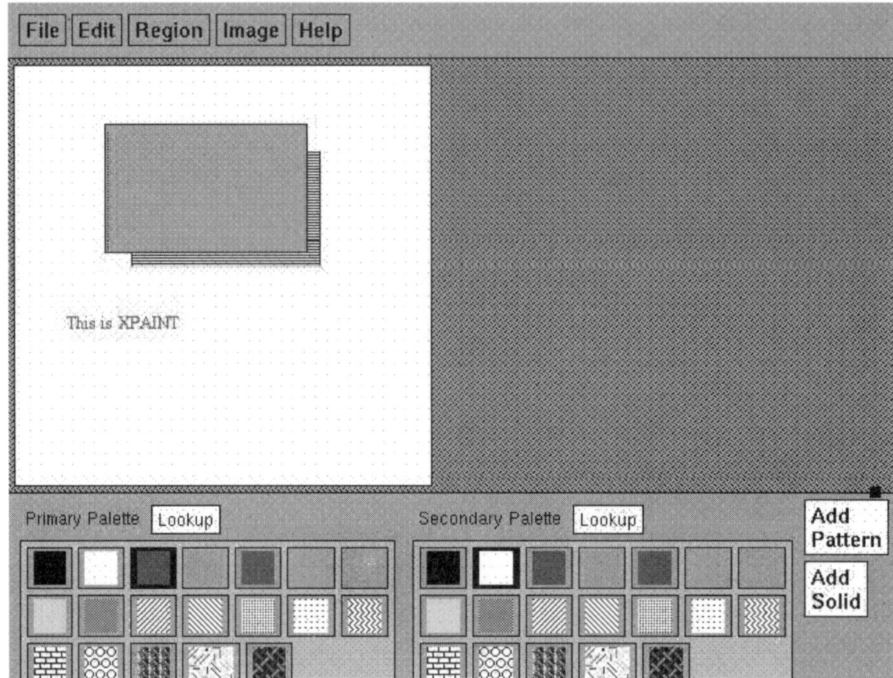

Figure 13.13: XPaint

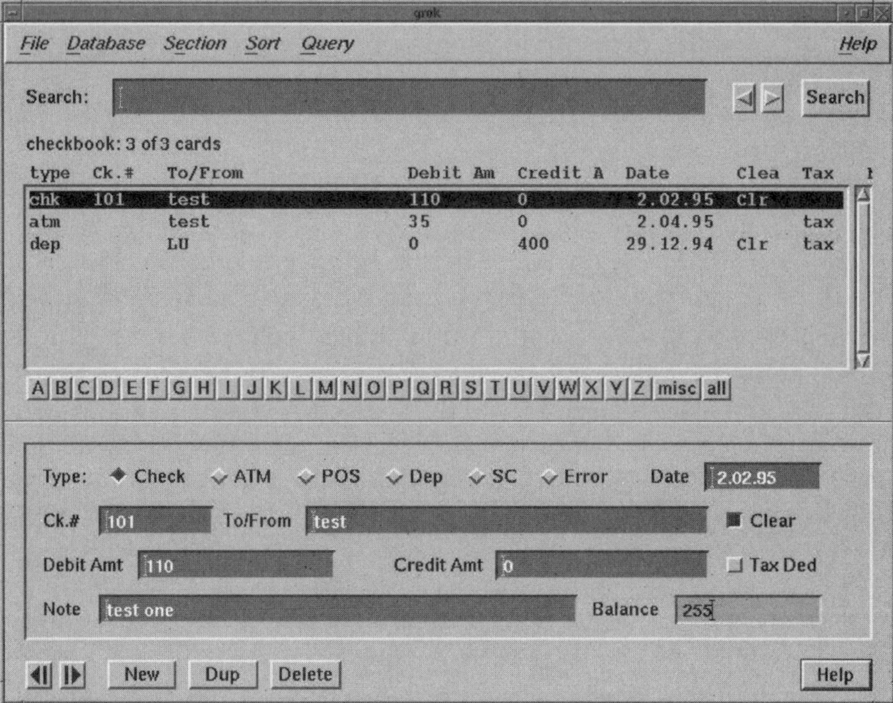

Figure 13.14: The grok Database Applications

your Linux machine, provided you are running the X Windowing System. This enables you to take advantage of applications that are not currently available for your Linux machine.

One of Wabi's advantages is that it translates Windows calls to the equivalent X-Window and UNIX calls. This is different from the "virtual machine" that needs to be created and at which calls are translated at a much lower level. The result is much faster performance. Figure 13.15 shows what this looks like graphically.

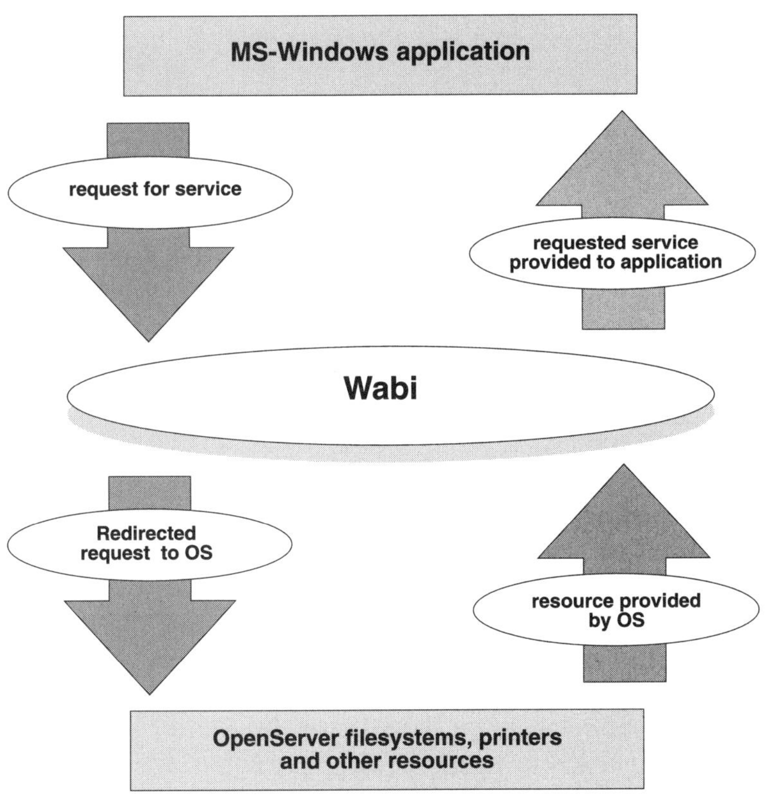

Figure 13.15: The Flow of Wabi

Perhaps the major drawback of Wabi is its inability to run 32-bit applications, including those specifically designed for Windows NT, Windows 95, and win32s. Despite this limitation, there is a wide range of software available that does run.

For example, the entire Microsoft Office Suite 4.3, which includes Word 6.0 and Excel 5.0, run without problems. CorelDraw 3 and 4, as well as Harvard Graphics, are two more programs that run. I have installed other lesser-known applications that have run wonderfully under Wabi.

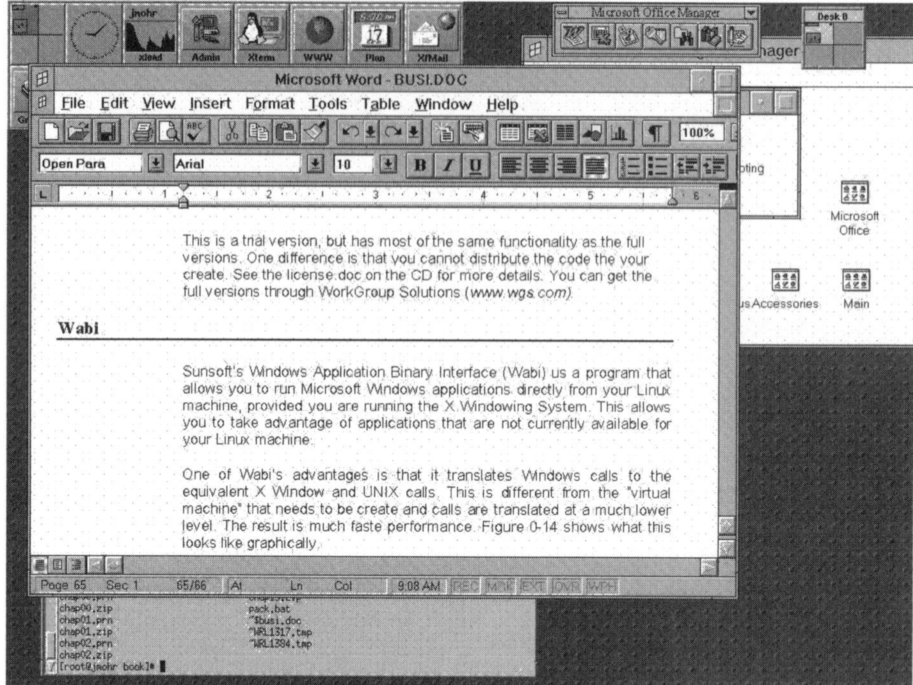

Figure 13.16: MS Office under Wabi

I installed MS Office 4.3 on my Caldera OpenLinux (see Figure 13.16) system. Because of the easy configuration of my drive mappings (Linux directories to DOS driver letters), I was able to install MS Office so that it would run from the CD-ROM. Even the File Manager showed it as CD-ROM.

With the exception of a few predefined drive letters, you have the whole alphabet to choose from. I was able to mount all of my DOS/Windows drives and then map them to the same drive letter that I had under Windows. Many of the programs started without a glitch, not realizing that they were not running under a better operating system.

The major shortcoming is that I cannot run 32-bit applications. Not that I really need the extra functionality of these applications. The problem is with the file names. I have grown used to being able to give my file an intelligent name (including spaces). These get mangled in the process. Though there might be a way of fixing this because the names are accurately recognized from a `xterm`, I couldn't find it in the documentation.

One of the biggest benefits is that Linux really multitasks. If a Windows program running under Wabi becomes unstable and "locks up," no problem. The worst case is that you have to kill the Wabi process and restart it. This is what happened the first time I tried to install MS Office, although it went flawlessly the second time. How many times have I rebooted as a result of an errant Windows program?

Keep in mind that Wabi does not provide you with a license for Microsoft Windows. Either Windows 3.1, 3.11, or Windows for Workgroups must be purchased separately. In addition, you will need one copy for each user running Wabi.

CHAPTER 14

BUILDING AN INTERNET SERVER

- Setting up your web server
- Configuring anonymous ftp
- Writing web pages
- Creating CGI scripts with `perl`

In this chapter, I'm going to talk about (as the title suggests) building your Internet server. Although you could build the server without actually connecting it to the Internet, I am going to make the assumption that you will want to share it with the rest of the world.

In the first part, I will talk a little bit about actually getting hooked up. Next, I'll go through the basics of putting together a useful (but maybe not perfect) Internet site.

Keep in mind that you don't really have to connect to the Internet to build an "Internet" server. You could use the same basic features to create an intranet server (in other words, a server for your own internal network). This would enable you to centralize information while still making it available to the entire company.

14.1 Connecting to the Internet

You can get connected to the Internet in two ways. The first is by connecting yourself directly. You become a *point-of-presence* on the Internet. Everyone else can reach at least one of your machines. The alternative is to have your site sit on someone else's machine. You create the pages, but someone else manages the connections. Each way has its own advantages and disadvantages that I will get into as I move along.

14.1.1 Web Services

An Internet Service Provider (ISP) provides Internet services. Up until recently, this meant providing you with a connection to the Internet either through a leased line or a dial-up connection.

When you have a leased line, you are normally on the Internet 24 hours a day. Visitors (i.e., potential customers) can reach you any time of the day or night. In fact, they might be connecting to you in the middle of the night your time though it is the middle of the day their time.

The leased line usually requires a connection through your telephone company because it is the only service with the network of connections all over. The costs depend on the area and the kind of connection you want. The number of ISPs grows every day, so it doesn't make sense to talk about prices and the connections here.

When you get a dial-up connection, you have to make the connection to your ISP every time you want to connect to the Internet. Your system may be configured so that every time you send a mail message to the Internet, it makes a connection, or it may be configured to make the connections only once an hour or only when you tell it to connect.

If you are going to provide services on the Internet, whether they are sales services or just information, you should really consider getting a leased line. In today's market, customers will not accept a CLOSED sign. They expect to reach your site any time of the day or night.

If you think that the costs are prohibitive, compare the amount of the leased line to what you would spend on some other form of advertising. For that price, it is worth it to get a commercial that runs 24 hours a day, and it is more entertaining and more valuable than anything you have ever seen on TV or in a magazine.

One major advantage of this kind of system is the Internet presence. You are accessible through the machine *www.your_company.com*. No other company has this address. It belongs to you. This is often easier to remember that a phone number because both the *www* and *com* elements remain constant. Just the company portion of the domain name needs to be remembered. Additionally, there is a certain amount of prestige in having your domain as compared to just having a page with someone else's domain.

If you only want to be a passive participant on the Internet, then getting a leased line is not the best thing. With a passive connection, you get the information you want but normally don't provide anything yourself. If you are constantly on the Internet looking for information, maybe it would be worth getting a leased line. Otherwise, the costs would be prohibitive.

What kind of physical connection you decide to get (e.g., modem, ISDN) will depend on your needs and the amount of money you want to spend. To determine what kind of connection to get, take a look at the chapter on networking (see Chapter 9, Talking to Other Machines).

I would recommend that you consider what kind of connection you need before you start looking for an ISP. Although you may really need something else, make a "guess" about what you *think* you will need. If you wait until you talk with an ISP, they may say that you need the service that they provide.

For example, they may only offer dial-up connections and therefore "recommend" that you set up your pages on their server. Their reason could be anything from security to cost. However, if you feel that you *should* have the site on your own server, then that is the service that you should get.

You need to consider both the cost and the bandwidth. You might think that you can only afford an ISDN connection, but what will the effect be if your customers have to wait too long to access the information? This is almost as bad as not having a site at all.

14.1.2 Web Service Providers

Instead of maintaining their own sites, some businesses set up pages through an ISP. The ISP provides you with space on their Internet server for your pages and connectivity to the Internet.

Some ISPs have many companies for which they provide space. As a result, their Web site becomes a sort of "Internet Mall" where you can buy anything to suit your needs.

Another service that the ISP might provide is managing your site themselves. Your Internet server may be physically located at their site. You may provide the pages, but the ISP provides the hardware, the Internet connection, and the administration. As a result, this might be substantially less expensive than administering it yourself.

Other services that ISPs provide include

- General advice about using WWW as a marketing tool
- Assistance in Web services purchases
- Marketing research
- Document/page development
- Document/page conversion
- Image manipulation
- Consultants who may not offer these services but consult you about them

My advice, in any event, is to see for yourself. Look at that company's Web site. If they have a bogus Web site that doesn't look professional, you can't expect them to put something worthwhile together for you.

Putting "your" site on someone else's machine has a couple of advantages. First, it can be cheaper than a leased line but still provide your customers with 24-hour access. Second, because you are not connected directly to the Internet, there is no danger that someone will break into your system.

The disadvantage is the prestige. You are not a presence on the Internet yourself. You are accessed though a URL, for example

http://www.other_company.net/your_company/home_page.html

In my mind, this diminishes your value. You are secondary to the ISP. If you have your own Web site, you are an equal to companies like IBM and Microsoft.

One important thing to consider is the fact that the Internet is already the marketing tool. No longer do you see 800-numbers in advertisements but rather, the company's URL.

When you do decide which direction to head, there are some things you should consider. First, does the ISP provide any kind of initial and ongoing market research/assessment? This is important when you determine what to offer on your site and whether you are achieving your goals. Part of this also includes tracking and analyzing site traffic: how many people are accessing your site, where are they located, and in what are they interested?

Next is the integration of the Web site information into your overall Internet presence as well as your corporate image. Does the company understand your market well enough to integrate the pages into your market strategy? These cannot appear like disjointed or confused efforts because then your company will appear confused.

Does the company provide services to develop your pages? Some will simply put your pages on their site and it will be up to you to make sure they work and are connected. Other companies will create and manage the pages for you.

Will the company register your site for you? This is important so that people know that you are out there. What's the point of having the greatest Web site if no one knows you are there? You can get your Web site registered at several places and the ISP should know the correct procedures.

Of course, a very important aspect of all of this is what it will cost. This will obviously depend on what the ISP is providing. If you are managing your site, you may only need to pay for the connection charges. Some will provide DNS registration services as well as have pointers to your machine from their DNS server. If the pages are on the ISP's machine, you may need to pay a monthly "rental" fee for the hard disk space. Although some sites will actually charge a fee for each megabyte transferred, this appears to be generally a European phenomenon.

If you have the ISP do more of the work, you will probably pay for the creation of the pages themselves, either on a per-page or per-job basis. If you want your site to be completely interactive, such as with forms, you can expect the fees to be substantially higher.

When deciding on an ISP, you need to consider the hardware they have. If you are just using them as your connection to the Internet, you will be primarily concerned with the type of connection to the Internet that they have. It is unlikely that the ISP has a dial-up line. However, it would not be surprising if they had an ISDN. Though this is sufficient for low-traffic sites, it can get overburdened quickly.

What kind of security does the ISP have? This means preventing people from getting unauthorized access to their site as well as protecting the site in case of an emergency. Are their machines connected to a UPS? What kind of backup and restore procedures do they have? Is there a guaranteed recovery time?

14.2 Building the Server

One nice thing about the Linux Web server is that it runs pretty much out of the box. All you need to do is copy your Web pages into the right directory and you're up and running. If you are not interested in all the fancy features or security that your Web server can provide, then the default configuration might be enough. However, there are many interesting and useful features that can improve the usefulness and security of your site.

14.2.1 Browsing the Web

So what is the Web? It is a network of machines. Not all machines on the Internet are part of the Web, but you can safely say that all machines on the Web are part of the Internet. The Web is the shortened version of World Wide Web, and, as its name implies, it connects machines all over the world.

Created in 1989 at the internationally renowned CERN research lab, the Web was originally begun as a means of linking physicists from all over the world. Because it is easy to use and integrate into an existing network, the Web has grown to a community of tens of thousands of sites with millions of users accessing it. With the integration of Web access software, on-line services have opened the Web to millions of people who couldn't have used it before.

The Web really is a vast network of inter-linked documents, or resources. These resources may be pure text but can include images, sound, and even videos. The links between resources are made through the use of the concept of *hypertext*. Hypertext is not something new–it has been used for years in on-line help systems, for example, like those in Microsoft Windows's programs. Certain words or phrases are presented in a different format (often a different color or maybe underlined) and are linked to other resources. When you click them, the resource that is linked is called up.

Resources are loaded from their source by means of the hypertext transfer protocol, *http*. In principle, this is very much like ftp in that resources are files that are transferred to the requesting site. It is then up to the requesting application to make use of that resource, such as display an image or play an animation. In many cases, files are actually retrieved using ftp and the application simply saves the file on the local machine.

The application used to access the Web is called a Web browser, or simply, browser. The first commonly used browser was Mosaic, from the National Center for Supercomputing Applications (NCSA). Currently, Netscape is the most commonly used browser, with the Internet Explorer from Microsoft second. Although a Linux version of MS Explorer is not available, I have worked primarily with Netscape on my Linux machine. You can obtain this from the Netscape Web site (*www.netscape.com*). On the CD-ROM, you will find a copy of the Arena Web browser.

14.2.2 Configuring the Web

Web resources are provided by Web servers. A Web server is simply a machine running the http daemon, `httpd`. Like other network daemons, `httpd` receives requests from a Web client (such as Mosaic or Netscape) and sends it the requested resource.

The most common Web server provided with Linux is the Apache server. Therefore, in the following sections, I will be addressing issues involved in configuring this particular server. Although the concepts are generally the same among all servers, the specific entries and file names may be different.

Like the ftp daemon, `httpd` is a secure means of allowing anonymous access to your system. You can define a root directory that, like ftp, prevents users from going "above" the defined root directory. Access to files or directories can be defined on a per-machine basis and you can even provided password control over files.

When `httpd` starts, it reads its configuration files and begins listening for requests from a document viewer (one that uses the http protocol). When a document is requested, `httpd` checks for the file relative to the `DocumentRoot` (defined in `/etc/httpd/conf/srm.conf`). By default, this is set to `/etc/httpd/htdocs`. If you want to make references to your documents, you can use symbolic links to point to places other than the `DocumentRoot`.

Unless you are running an old version of Linux, the odds are that you have an `httpd` daemon that is plug-and-play. By that I mean that all you have to do is install it and it works. You can create documents and immediately begin to access them.

Where the configuration files end up depends on your distribution. In some distributions, like Linux Pro, this will be in `/etc/httpd`. With others, it is `/usr/local/etc/httpd`. Here are the default directories that the `httpd` daemon accesses. This is the ServerRoot, which you can define in the `httpd` configuration file. Note that the daemon will be looking for the configuration file relative to this root. If you change it, you must specify the configuration file when you start `httpd`.

You can use two primary options to `httpd`. The `-d` option specifies a different ServerRoot directory than the default. The `-f` option specifies a different server configuration file than the default. The default file is normally the `httpd.conf` file in the `conf` subdirectory under your server root directory.

The directory `conf` contains the configuration information for various aspects of the `httpd` daemon. In many cases, the files here appear twice, once with the ending `-dist`. This is the distribution version of the file, which means that this the default state of the file. Because the `httpd` daemon is looking for the file without this ending, you may need to copy them first if there is only one copy. For example, the primary configuration file is `httpd.conf`. You would find the file `http.conf-dist` and then copy it `httpd.conf`. If this file is ever tampered with so badly that you cannot fix it, you can revert to the default file. The files here are

`httpd.conf`:	Main server configuration file
`access.conf`:	Access control file
`srm.conf`:	Server resource management file
`mime.types`:	MIME types description file

The behavior of httpd is defined by the httpd.conf file. First, decide whether httpd runs standalone or through inetd. The big difference is one of performance. If you run httpd through inetd, each time you make a request, inetd needs to start a new process, which means loading the httpd daemon binary. If a copy is already running, the system should be able to copy the pages in memory without having to load the binary from the hard disk.

If httpd is running as standalone, a copy is *always* in memory. When a connection request is made, httpd can easily make a copy of itself without needing to go to the hard disk. Set the server type with the ServerType directive. For example, to set it up as standalone, the entry would look like this:

```
ServerType standalone
```

The next entries to look at are the User and Group entries. These entries determine under what user and group the server runs when answering requests. This in turn determines what access the server has. The default user is nobody, so this user must have access to the files. I have also seen some systems in which the default user is -1. To specify a user ID instead of the user name, precede it with a pound sign (i.e., #-1). The default group is often -1. I have experienced some problems on some machines when specifying -1 as a UID or GID. The problem is that httpd changes the UID and GID. Because -1 does not exist, httpd can't change.

You might want to consider creating a user and a group specifically for your Web server. I find it easier to monitor and control access when I specifically assign access in this way. Because the only place you give the http user access is in the documents directory, there is less risk of giving it more access than necessary. The same applies to the group.

The next directive to look at, which does not really need to be changed to get the system working, is the ServerAdmin directive, which specifies the e-mail address where problem reports should go. Often, when the server detects a problem, it will send this address to the browser. This enables visitors to send you e-mail when problems occur.

I would suggest that you create a user called "webmaster," which seems to be a convention on other sites. This user is the contact point for people visiting your sites. You then define the ServerAdmin to be webmaster.

Lastly is the ServerName directive, which is the hostname that the server will send back to the clients. The most common thing to put in here is *www.domain*, as www is the most common name for the Web server. This name doesn't have to exist, but I do advise that you have a DNS alias, even if the machine is not really called www.

Once you make these changes, your Web server should be up and running. To test it, create a small document in the `htdocs` directory, for example, `test.html`. You can connect from the server itself by simply inputting *http://www/test.html* (assuming that you have a DNS entry to www; otherwise, give the real name of the machine).

If you cannot connect, some kind of message may display to the client to indicate what went wrong. Otherwise, check in the logs directory under your ServerRoot.

RESTRICTING ACCESS: THE `access.conf` FILE

If you are setting up your server to allow access to all the documents, then you are pretty much set. However, if you want to restrict access to specific directories, you can do this through the `access.conf` file. When you look in the `acces.conf` file, you see that it is broken down into several sections. The sections are delimited by the `<Directory>` and `</Directory>` directives, which is very similar to the formatting in HTML. Each section is delimited by a directive that specifies what the access is in regard to. For example, on many systems, you would have an entry that looks like this:

```
<Directory /etc/httpd/cgi-bin>
Options Indexes FollowSymLinks
</Directory>
```

This section relates to the directory `/etc/httpd/cgi-bin`. In this case, it is saying that from within `/etc/httpd/cgi-bin` directory, the `Options` are `Indexes` (users can retrieve indexes created by the service) and `FollowSymLinks` (`httpd` will follow symbolic links).

A subsection within each `<Directory>` section is the `<Limit>` directive, which essentially describes the limit of the access. It needs a specific access method after it. For example:

```
<Limit GET>
```

(Note that as of this writing, the only access method support is `GET`.)

Because the `<Limit>` directive needs to be defined for a specific directory, you end up with something similar to this:

```
<Directory  directory_path> list of options
<Limit GET>
    access restrictions
</Limit>
</Directory>
```

In its simplest form, the <Limit> direct can allow or deny access to specific directories. This might be useful if you want to allow users from within your own domain to have access to specific directories but not make the files world-accessible. Let's assume that you have already defined a directory and want to restrict access to just your domain. You might have an entry that looks like this:

```
<Limit>
order allow,deny
allow from your.domain
deny from all
</Limit>
```

The first line determines the order in which the access rights will be evaluated. Here you said that you first check who is allowed before you check who is denied. If you are from the domain that is specified with *your.domain*, you get in. Otherwise, you are denied access.

It may be possible that your company is broken down into smaller domains, for example, into individual departments. It may be necessary to restrict access to every domain except those departments. For example, finance documents may be restricted to the *finance* and *admin* domains. You could then have something that looks like this:

```
<Limit>
order allow,deny
allow from finance.your.domain admin.your.domain
deny from all
</Limit>
```

In this configuration, someone from the marketing subdomain would not have any access to this directory. Note that the names you specify on the access and deny lines need only be separated by white spaces. Therefore, it could have looked like this:

```
allow from finance.your.domain
admin.your.domain
```

There are also many sites on the Internet that restrict access to everyone, except those who have an account. Having an account also means that you have a password. Although you can take the system `passwd` file, you have to edit it a bit to get it to work. In addition, the user names and passwords that `httpd` uses are completely independent of the system accounts. Therefore, you can have users who do not have system accounts who still access files via `httpd`, in the same way a user can have a system account but can't access the Web pages.

To add this functionality, you have to make some changes to the `access.conf` file. The new entry might look like this:

```
<Directory /etc/httpd/html/secret>
AllowOverride None
AuthName Secret Stuff
AuthType Basic
AuthUserFile /etc/httpd/conf/htpasswd
AuthGroupFile /etc/httpd/conf/htgroup
    <Limit GET>
    require valid-user
    </Limit>
</Directory>
```

At the top and bottom of this section, you will see the directive that defines the directory for which this is valid. This is case `/etc/httpd/html/secret`. At the top of the section, you define the access you want to allow. The first line

```
AllowOverride None
```

says that you do not want access control lists in specific directories to override the accesses you define here. If you did want to do this, you would create an access control list (ACL) in the file `.htaccess` in each directory you want to change. This has a similar format to the `passwd` file that you might specify in `srm.conf`.

The `AuthName` entry is a label for the directory to which you are defining access. Although this label does not effect the access, it is required. When you try to access one of the restricted directories, this label will appear along with the password prompt.

The `AuthType` entry specifies the type of authorization used for this directory. As of this writing, only `Basic` is supported.

The `AuthUserFile` is the full path to the user password file. This is not the system password file (`/etc/passwd`) but rather, the password file specifying access to directories. The `AuthGroupFile` list users who are part of specific groups. You can restrict access to files either on a per-user basis or a per-group basis, as you will see in a moment.

Inside the `Limit` section is the require directive. Generically, this has the syntax

```
require entity
```

In this case, the entity is "valid-user," which means any user listed in AuthUserFile. If you wanted to specify just a single user, the entry would look like this

```
require user <user_name>
```

where <user_name> is the name of the user, as specified in AuthUserFile, to whom you want to give access. If you want to specify a group, the entry would look like this

```
require group <group_name>
```

where <group_name> is the group name defined in AuthGroupFile. Keep in mind that just because a user is listed in AuthGroupFile does not mean that that user has access. The system has no way of identifying the users, so they still need a user name and password in AuthUserFile. If they are listed in AuthUserFile but not in AuthGroupFile, they will still be denied access.

When you test the behavior of httpd by making changes to these files, you have to tell it to re-read the files. Despite what some books say, you *don't* have to reboot your machine. Instead, all you need to do is send a hang-up signal (SIGHUP) to the inetd process (kill -HUP <pid_of_inetd>).

I mentioned a moment ago a case in which you might want to have a set of permissions on a specific directory tree but want to have different accesses for specific subdirectories. This is accomplished with the .htaccess file. However, to enable it, you have to set the AllowOverride directive to All in access.conf.

There are other ways to configure the .htaccess file. For example, setting AllowOverride to AuthConfig enables you to change the AuthName, AuthType, AuthUserFile, and AuthGroupFile directives. With this, you can then change the label for this directory or the paths to the password and group files. Note that all the other values, including what entity is required (user, group), is still in effect.

You can also set AllowOverride to Limit so that you can change whatever you had in the access.conf file. For example, if you wanted to restrict access to this directory to a single person, you could change .htaccess to

```
<Limit GET>
require user UserName
</Limit>
```

where UserName is the name of the user who should have access. Needless to say, you could have also changed the requirement to be a specific group. As this point, I'll mention that the AllowOverride directive can take more than one argument, so if you wanted to specify a new AuthName as well as a new Limit, it might look like this:

```
AllowOverride AuthConfig Limit
```

WEB RESOURCES: THE srm.conf FILE

Earlier (see Section 14.2.2, Configuring the Web), I talked about the server resource management file (srm.conf). Although the configuration that you currently have would be sufficient to run a decent Web server, the srm.conf file has a few things that warrant taking a quick look.

The first, the AccessFileName directive, defines the name of access file that you would copy into a directory to override the accesses defined in access.conf (assuming this is allowed at all). By default, this is the file .htaccess, about which I have been talking all along.

The Alias directive is used to assign an alias to a specific path. This directive is useful in keeping a specific file structure while still being able to move the tree with limited problems. By default, often one Alias is defined:

```
Alias /icons/ /etc/httpd/icons/
```

Another Alias directive, ScriptAlias, defines where script files are located. The default is

```
ScriptAlias /cgi-bin/ /etc/httpd/cgi-bin/
```

This alias is used when you have CGI scripts (more on those later) that you want to execute. You specify an alias here so you don't need to specify the whole path.

The DocumentRoot specifies the root directory for your documents. For example, let's assume DocumentRoot is set to /etc/httpd/html. When you specify a URL as *http://www.your.domain/file.html*, the file file.html would be physically located in the directory /etc/httpd/html. If you specified the URL *http://www.your.domain/data/file.html*, this file would be physically in /etc/httpd/html/data.

There are several indexing directives, which I will discuss next.

INDEXING

The DirectoryIndex directive in the srm.conf file determines the default file the server should deliver if none is specified by the client. For example, if you input *http://www.your.domain* in the browser, the server would try to deliver a file in the DocumentRoot (because no path was specified). The file delivered is what is specified in `srm.conf` as the `DirectoryIndex` directive, which is `index.html`, by default. So, if there was a file called `index.html`, the URL *http://www.your.domain* would be the same as *http://www.your.domain/index.html.*

If the file specified by `DirectoryIndex` (`index.html`, in your case) does not exist, what the server does depends on whether indexing is allowed or not. Remember that in the `httpd.conf` file, you specify configurations on a per-directory basis. One option you can specify is indexing. If indexing is turned on, the server will deliver an index (directory listing) of that directory. For example, assume you have an entry in `httpd.conf` that looks like this:

```
<Directory /etc/httpd/html>
Options Indexes
</Directory>
```

This means that for the directory `/etc/httpd/html`, indexing is enabled. So, if `index.html` was not in `/etc/httpd/html`, you would just get a listing of the files in that directory. Note that this is a dynamic list–you do not need to create it yourself. When a visitor inputs the appropriate URL or clicks a link, the directory listing is created for them on-the-fly.

Supplemental to this is the `FancyIndexing`, which adds icons, file names, and other "fancy" things to the directory listing (index). This is a Boolean value, so it is turned on with `FancyIndexing On` and off with `FancyIndexing Off`.

When `FancyIndexing` is on, you get a header at the top of the list. In addition, each entry will be proceeded by an icon. I recommend that you only turn this on if you have CPU cycles to burn. For each file in the directory, an icon needs to be sent as well as the information, such as modification time. Without `FancyIndexing`, you get just a listing of the files, which should be sufficient.

You can also turn on `FancyIndexing` using the IndexOptions directive. This has the syntax

```
IndexOptions option1 option2
```

Some useful options in the `srm.conf` file are

`FancyIndexing`	Turns `FancyIndexing` on.
`IconsAreLinks`	Makes the icon part of the anchor for the link. Normally the icon just sits there and does nothing. (Only valid when `FancyIndexing` is on)
`ScanHTMLTitles`	Scans the information in the HTML `<TITLE>` section to include it as a description. (Only valid for those files without a predefined description. See the following discussion.)

`SuppressLastModified`	Does not print the last modified date. (Only valid when `FancyIndexing` is on.)
`SuppressSize`	Does not print the size of the file. (Only valid when `FancyIndexing` is on.)
`SuppressDescription`	Does not print the file description. (Only valid when `FancyIndexing` is on.)

Add descriptions using the AddDescription directive. The syntax is

```
AddDescription "description" filename
```

Here you can specify full names for files or use a wild card. For example, if you wanted to provide the description "WWW Pages" for all HTML documents, the entry would look like this:

```
AddDescription " WWW Pages" *.html
```

Which icons are used for what kind of documents is also configured through the `srm.conf` file. You can do this in two ways. The easiest way is via the `AddIcon` directive, with which you have one-to-one mapping between a file extension and the icon that is used. The syntax for this directive is

```
AddIcon /virtual/path .ext1 .ext2 ...
```

The `/virtual/path` is the path relative to the server root, so if you have a subdirectory of your server-root-named icons, the reference to the icon `text.gif` would be `/icons/text.gif`. In most distributions, this is also aliased with

```
alias /icons /etc/httpd/icons/
```

This alias then replaces anywhere `/icons` appears.

The extensions for which these icons should be used follow the path to the icons. Note that in many, if I wanted to use this icon for all files ending in `.txt` and `.doc`, the whole line would look like this:

```
AddIcon /icons/text.gif .txt .doc
```

There are three additional types of directories for which you can use icons:

..	For the parent directory
^^DIRECTORY^^	For any directory
^^BLANKICON^^	Used to format the list

The next way to configure which icons are used for what kind of documents through the `srm.conf` file does not directly depend on the file types. Here, you use the MIME types to determine what icons to use. Granted, the MIME types depend on the file types, but using this mechanism enables a consistent configuration. The syntax for this is

```
AddIconByType icon type1 type2 ...
```

An example of the simplest form would be

```
AddIconByType /icons/text.gif text/*
```

Here the type is defined as `text/*`, so this is valid for any MIME type of text (e.g., HTML, txt), which would then have the `text.gif` icon. You can make this a little more complicated by defining a text string to display for nongraphic clients. An example would then look like this:

```
AddIconByType (TEXT,/icons/text.gif) text/*
```

This will display the word "TEXT" for all text files. In some cases, you don't want to display an icon. To avoid this, use the `IndexIgnore` directive.

14.2.3. Anonymous ftp

If you are going to set up an Internet server, you should definitely consider allowing access via ftp. If you are providing specific documents, such as white papers, source code, and even compiled programs, visitors may not want to deal with clicking through the Web site or waiting for the graphics to download. Having the documents available through FTP means that visitors can go right where the documents are stored. The only thing sent across the line is the commands, output, then the document, once they have found it.

This doesn't meant that these documents are unavailable via the Web. You could have links on your Web pages that point to them as well. You could either have links connecting with http or with ftp. If you have links that access the file via ftp, a lot of browsers will be able to handle this and actually show the same directory structure you would have if you logged directly with ftp. If the browser can't handle it, the visitor can still access the file using ftp directly.

What happens during all this is that the browser simply logs you as the user anonymous itself. The browser doesn't have any special privileges, and if anonymous ftp isn't working correctly, you you can't get in using a browser.

Setting up anonymous is fairly straightforward, but setting it up correctly is not. A lot of security issues are involved, which I talked about in the chapter on networking (see Chapter 9, Talking to Other Machines). Here I'll get into what you need to do to address those security issues. Fortunately, the later versions of Linux have made anonymous ftp easier. The system is already preconfigured (in most cases) to allow anonymous ftp and there are configuration files that enable you to specifically define what access can and cannot be made. First I'll talk a little bit about doing this all manually and then I'll talk about how this problem has been solved in the newer versions.

First, if you are going to configure an ftp server, you should really get one of the newer releases. Let's forget all other wonderful features that you have now. The ease at which you can configure your ftp server makes it worth the few dollars to get a new version.

Access with ftp is controlled by several files in your `/etc` directory (at least it is for most versions of Linux I have seen). Even if you have the older 1.2 kernel, these files should be present.

The primary file is `ftpaccess`. As its name implies, it controls access with ftp. Here you not only define who has access but also what kind of access they have and even how many people can log in and when they can login. In addition, this file enables you to define the behavior of the system. For example, when a user logs in for the first time or changes to a particular directory, you can have the system display messages.

Through this file, each user is assigned to a specific group. Groups do not necessarily mean individual users but can mean complete sites. That is, you can assign an entire site to a group (based on its IP address) and control its access this way. For example, you might have documents that only people from within your company can access. Rather than having to give everyone his or her own account, define their group, and therefore their access, based on their IP address.

This can be even more finely defined, for example, by saying that if a user has an account on the local machine *and* comes from a particular IP address they belong to one class. If the same user comes from a different IP address they belongs to a different class. In this way, you can define a single account and password and still limit the user's access. Note that in the cases of the IP addresses, you don't have to define each individual host address, but you can defined networks as well.

Before you go into the other capabilities, let's go over some examples of class. All definitions take the following form:

```
keyword definition
```

One keyword is class, and a class entry takes the following form

```
class <class_name> <typelist> <address> [<address> ...]
```

where <class_name> is the name you have given for this class of machines, <typelist> is the type of users, and <address> is the IP addresses to which this class should be applied. By default, the first line of the ftpaccess file probably looks like this:

```
class all real,guest,anonymous  *
```

This defines the group all for the user types real, guest, and anonymous (all the types there are). ADDR can also be a domain name, but it's easier to spoof. Because the IP address is * (asterisk), it will be valid for all IP addresses. You might think that an anonymous user is a guest, but there is a difference that I will get into in a moment. Let's now define a group of anonymous users who come from your local network: 192.168.42. It might look like this:

```
class local anonymous 192.168.42.*
```

If you simply added this line to the `ftpaccess` file after the first class definition, things would not behave as you might think. What you must keep in mind is that once a match as been made, it sticks. Because every user from every machine is a member of the all group, no matter who logs in, that's the group to which the user is assigned. Because this is the broadest reaching group, I would suggest putting it last (assuming you keep it at all). That way, if a user doesn't fit into any of the other groups, they will fit into this one.

So what can you do with this? Let's make things easy and define a message file that will be different for members of your local domain. Maybe you want to tell them more about what your site has to offer and where things reside. Your completed `ftpaccess` file might look like this:

```
class local real,guest,anonymous 192.168.42.*
class all real,guest,anonymous *
message /local.msg login local
message /welcome.msg login all
```

You've define the local group and then defined the group for anyone who does not come from your local domain. Next, you define the message capability, which has the following general form:

```
message <message_path> [<action> <class>,<class>,...].
```

The first entry says to show the message `local.msg` that is in the root directory. Note that if a user logs in as a real user, that user's home directory is the same as when they log in with Telnet or anything else. Therefore, no message will show in this case unless there really is a file called local.msg in the / directory. The solution I came up with is to have all system messages in a single directory. (Note that some sources refer to the "action" as "when.")

For example, you create a directory in ftp's home directory called usr/messages. This is then symbolically linked to /usr/messages. All messages are then placed in this directory. If you log in as a real user, the messages are read out of /usr/messages. If you login as an anonymous user, the messages are read from ~ftp/usr/messages. Any directory-related messages (more on those shortly), you just keep in that directory.

One entry would then look like this:

```
message /usr/messages/local.msg login   local
```

If I were to login as a user from the local domain who actually did have an account on this machine, /usr/messages/local.msg would be read. If I logged in as an anonymous user from within the domain, the ~ftp/usr/messages/local.msg file would be read. Because the directories are symbolically linked, the same file is read whether you are logged in as a real user, anonymous, or guest.

You could also configure the system so that whenever you changed directories to somewhere specific, a message is displayed. For example, you might have software that hasn't been thoroughly tested but that you still want to make available. Let's say this software is located in ~ftp/pub/software/beta. You would then have a line that looked like this:

```
message /usr/messages/beta.msg cwd=/pub/software/beta
```

In this case, the action was that you changed directories into /pub/software/beta. Therefore, the message /usr/messages/beta.msg was displayed. If you logged in as anonymous user, this would be ~ftp/usr/messages/beta.msg.

There may be some cases in which you want to restrict the access of real users. (Why have a real user other than to have individual accounts for each user?) To do this, use the guestgroup capability, which has the following syntax:

```
guestgroup <groupname> [ <groupname> ... ]
```

where <groupname> is the name of a system group as defined in /etc/group. So, if you had a system group called noftp, the entry would look like this:

```
guestgroup noftp
```

Anytime a real user who was a member of this group logged in, the system behaved just as though this were anonymous ftp. However, you must configure this account, which might look like this:

```
guest1:<passwd>:100:92:Guest Account:/ftp/./incoming:/etc/ftponly
```

Next is the concept of a `README` file, a file that you should read. With software, this is usually the file that has vital information about how to install the software and prevent problems, which most people ignore. On ftp sites, these files usually have specific information about what's in the directories. If the directory contains downloadable software, this would probably contain information about how to install the software.

The difference between a `README` file and a message file is that a `README` file simply exists in the directory, whereas a message file is actually displayed. Otherwise, the principle is the same. Each time an event occurs (login or changing directories), the file is accessed. For the `README` file, that access means that its existence is displayed to the visitor, along with the date that the file was last changed. First this serves as a marker to a visitor. If the visitor sees that the `README` file hasn't been changed, there's no need for him or her to download it.

When a visitor logs in, they might see something like this:

```
230-Please read the file README
230-it was last modified on Sat Oct 12 18:21:35 1996 -
1 day ago
```

This says that the file was last modified one day ago. If the visitor hadn't been to the site for a month, they probably hasn't seen this file before, so it might be worthwhile to download the file.

Note that a `README` file doesn't need to be called "readme." In fact, you can call it anything you want. The general format for the `README` file capability is

```
readme <file_path> [<action> [<class>]]
```

As you can see, because you have both action and class fields, `README` files can be set up to be shown each time a user logs in or when they changes directories. In addition, you can have different `README` files for different classes of users. I could have entry that looks like this:

```
readme /usr/messages/README*  login
```

The file referenced is in `/usr/messages` and the appropriate information is displayed whenever a visitor logs in. Note that because you did not include a class of users, this is valid for everyone. Also note the asterisk following the file name. This does not mean that the file is really called "README*" but rather, any file that starts with README will be shown.

For example, another way to use this file is to have a list of changes. You could have a file called /usr/messages/README.general that contains general information and one called README.changes that lists the changes to the site. The information about both of these files will be displayed when a user logs in.

Another entry I created looks like this:

```
readme  README*  login
```

This displays any file starting with "README" that is in the current directory when the user logs in. If it's an anonymous user, this would be ~ftp/. If this is a real user (who wasn't mapped to the guest group), this would be that user's home directory. If you create a file ~jimmo/README.jimmo, I will see references to this file every time I log in with ftp. This is a useful way of sending messages to users without giving them an interactive account.

Something nice that you can do with the contents of your message files (not the READMEs) is display certain kinds of information dynamically.

%T	Local time (in the form Thu Nov 15 17:12:42 1990)
%F	Free space in partition of CWD (in KB; not supported on all systems)
%C	Current working directory
%E	E-mail address of the person who maintains the site, as defined in ftpaccess
%R	Remote host name
%L	Local host name
%u	Username as determined via RFC 931 authentification
%U	Username given at login time
%M	Maximum allowed number of users in this class
%N	Current number of users in this class

So far, you have grouped users into classes and decided what messages they see, but you haven't done anything to control their access. The files and directories created for them are configured in such a way as to greatly limit access. Several directories contain the necessary files and programs. However, you might want to limit access to a few programs in the bin directory.

The first capability to limit access that I'll talk about is deny. The general syntax for it is

```
deny <address> <message_file>
```

where <address> is the IP address or hostname/domain to which you want to deny access. The <message_file> is any file that you might want to display instead of simply saying that access is denied. One way you can use this capability is if you have a site that is overburdening your server. Maybe other users are downloading all of your files and the strain on the server and network is making life for the other users miserable. To figure out who is taking up all the bandwidth, you can enable logging. You can log both the commands issued or the transfers that are done. The syntax to log commands is

```
log commands <typelist>
```

where <typelist> is any of your standard user types: real, anonymous, and guest. To log transfers, the syntax is

```
log transfers <typelist> <directions>
```

where <typelist> is again your user types and <directions> is the direction you want to log, using the key words "inbound" and "outbound."

The shortcoming of this scheme is that you cannot enable logging for classes of users (at least I have tried on several different versions). In addition, transfers are logged in /var/log/xferlog, whereas the commands are logged in /var/log/messages (or the equivalent). Because every command is logged, the messages file can grow rather quickly. To login listings takes four lines, and each time a directory list is shown, it takes another two lines.

Even commands that cannot be executed are logged. For example, if I want to change to the pub directory, make a typo, and say "cd pub," the command is logged, although no action was taken. If transfer login is enabled, an entry is made for both the command, and the actual transfer is logged in xferlog. If you have a busy site, you need to be careful that your message files don't grow too large.

Part of the logging process is the ability to know just who is accessing the system. Most UNIX-like ftp programs know the user login name of whoever initiated the connection as well as the machine's name on which the user logged in. This can be used to enable more detailed login. Using the passwd-check capability, you can force the user to input his or her logname and machine name as a password to get in.

Actually, this can be set at several levels, depending on your needs. For example, if you have a very trusted site, you don't even need to enable the `passwd-check` capability and everyone can get in, even if the logname/machine name the user enters is completely bogus (e.g., just typing random keys). If you have a slightly less trusting site, you can require that the password contain at least `@` (at sign). At the highest level, you can require that the password is a fully RFC 822-compliant address, like *company.domain.*

So what do you do if the password doesn't match your requirements? You can simply issue a warning and let the user in anyway, or you can issue the warning and toss the user out. The syntax of the `passwd-check` capability is

```
passwd-check <none|trivial|rfc822> (<enforce|warn>)
```

An example of this would be

```
passwd-check trivial warn
```

With this, the visitor is required to have `@` in the password. If it isn't a valid password, a warning is generated, but the user is still admitted. If the entry looked like this

```
passwd-check rfc822 enforce
```

the visitor would be required to input an RFC 822-compliant address and, if the visitor did not, he or she would be tossed out. Remember that I mentioned that the system can tell who you are and where you come from. Therefore, it's not sufficient to make up a name and use it as a password.

You can also deny access to specific files with the `noretrieve` capability. The syntax is

```
noretrieve <filename> <filename> ....
```

where `<filename>` is either a path or a filename. For example, if you wanted to keep users from downloading the `/etc/passwd` file, the line would look like this:

```
noretrieve /etc/passwd
```

However, if you wanted to deny access to core files, no matter where they were, the entry would look like this:

```
noretrieve core
```

Aside from setting the permissions, you can control where files can be uploaded by using the `upload` capability. The syntax for this command is

```
upload   <root-dir>  <directory> <yes|no> <owner>
<group> <mode> ["dirs"|"nodirs"]
```

where `<root-dir>` is the root directory of where the following conditions are applied. This is relative to the system root and not the root of the ftp directory. The `<directory>` is the path (relative to the root you just gave) and `<yes|no>` determines specifically whether download is allowed. Permissions on the file are set by `<owner>`, `<group>`, and `<mode>`. These have the same meaning as for other kinds of files. For example, you might have something like this:

```
upload /home/ftp /incoming yes root root 0600
```

This says the uploads are allowed into the ftp user's home directory and that all files will have an owner and group of root. The permissions for these files will be 0600 (read-only for the owner).

I recommend that if you do have an incoming directory, do not allow the files to be readable by others. If the files are readable, it might happen that your site becomes a drop for pirated software or pornography, possibly making you legally responsible. In some cases, people have copied such files into an incoming directory and the files were later picked up by someone else. This maintains the anonymity of both the sender and the receiver. If no one can read these files, the user can copy a new file to you, but will only be able to read the files that you specify. This prevents your site from becoming a drop.

Access is controlled by three other files: `ftpgroups`, `ftphosts`, and `ftpusers`. The `ftpgroups` file is used in conjunction with the private capability defined in `ftpaccess`. By setting the private capability to `yes`, visitors have the ability to get greater access through a special group password.

I have noticed some weird behavior in terms of how ftp behaves regarding symbolic links. Let's say you create the directory `~ftp/pub/software/beta`. To maintain the directory structure, you create a symbolic link from `~ftp/pub` to `/pub`. When you log in as a real user who has ftp access, you end up in your home directory. To get into the `beta` directory, you reference the absolute path `/pub/software/beta`.

On at least one version of Linux, when I issue the command `cd /pub/software/beta`, I get a message saying that the directory does not exist! However, if I first do `cd /pub` and then `cd software/beta`, it works correctly. In other cases, when I want to display a message when I enter that directory, the entry might look like this:

```
message /usr/messages/beta.msg cwd=/pub/software/beta
local
```

When I log in as an anonymous user, this message is displayed. However, when I log in as a real user and change to this directory, I don't see the message. It's not until I put the full path `/home/ftp/pub/software/beta` that I see the message.

Even if you have an older Linux version without all the ftp configuration files, you can still create a fairly secure ftp server. The most important point to consider is that all access should be denied unless it is explicitly needed.

The first step is creating an ftp user, which depends on the system you have. At the very least, I would suggest creating a specific group for the ftp user. Call it ftp, for example. That way you can more clearly determine which files can be accessed and by whom. Don't give the ftp user a valid password; this prevents them from logging in to an interactive shell. You should also consider giving the user something like `/bin/true` as its shell just in case it does get a valid password.

The ftp user's home directory does not need to be anyplace special. You could simply create it where all the other home directories are (e.g., `/home`) or put it in its own file system (which could then be mounted under `/home/ftp`). Make the directory owned by root and not by ftp to prevent the ftp user from changing the permissions. However, make the group of the directory the same as ftp so that you can still give ftp access. Set the permissions to read and execute, but not write (555) so that anonymous ftp users can read files and access directories but cannot write anything.

You may want to allow visitors to send files to you. Therefore, you need to have at least one writable directory. Consider creating an incoming directory for which the ftp user has write but *not* read permission–that is, the user can copy files in but not out. This prevents your site from becoming a repository for undesired files (pirated software, pornography). The best thing to do is set the permission at 1733, making the directory writable but not readable by the ftp user. The first "1" is the same as `chmod +t` and, for a directory, this prevents other people from deleting files that they don't own.

You'll probably want to have visitors look at the files, so you need to give them the `ls` command. Create a directory under ftp's home called `bin`. Here the permissions should be 111 so that your visitors can only execute (search) this directory. Copy ls and any other program to which the visitor should have access into the bin directory. The permissions on these files should be 111 as well.

Next, create an etc directory and put in it a password and group file. These should not be exact copies of the system files in /etc but rather, should only contain the necessary entries. The password files should contain the entries for root, daemon, UUCP, and ftp, and the group file should only contain the entry for ftp. In both cases, the file should be world-readable but not writable by anyone.

Keep in mind that the entries in these files are only used by the ls command. Therefore, you really don't need to have "real" entries in there. At any rate, do not include the real passwords because someone could view this file then run it through a password cracking program.

Although the ~ftp should not be writable at this point, to increase security, you should create empty .rhosts and .forward files. This is done as root with

```
touch ~ftp/.rhosts
touch ~ftp/.forward
chmod 400 ~ftp/.rhosts
chmod 400 ~ftp/.forward
```

Once you have gotten it configured to this point, I would suggest you try to do some of the things that you wouldn't want visitors to do. I have found this useful in finding security holes.

14.3 Building Your Pages

In this section, I will talk about the basics of putting together Web pages. Entire books have been published on this subject, which go into more detail than I do here. However, as with perl scripts, I feel that the best way to create a good Web page is to practice. I can give you the tools, but it is up to you to become good at using them.

14.3.1 HTML: The Language of the Web

Web pages are written in the Hyptertext Markup Language (HTML), a "plain-text" file that can be edited by any editor, like vi. Recently, as a result of the increasing popularity of the Web, several commercially available HTML editors have become available, such as the Caldera Solutions CD-ROM, which comes with a GUI-based HTML editor.

The HTML commands are similar, and also simpler, that those used by troff. In addition to formatting commands, built-in commands tell the Web browser to go out and retrieve a document. You can also create links to specific locations (labels) within that document. Access to the document is made by means of a Uniform Resource Locator (URL).

Several types of URLs perform different functions. You can use several different programs to access these resources, such as ftp, http, `gopher`, or even `telnet`. If you leave off the program name, the Web browser may assume that it refers to a file on your local system (depending on the browser). However, just like with `ftp` or `telnet`, you can specifically make references to the local machine. I encourage using absolute names because it makes transferring Web pages that much easier.

As with any document with special formatting, you have to be able to tell the medium that there is something special. When you print something, you may have to tell the printer. When a word processor displays something on the screen, you have to tell the screen. When the `man` command is supposed to display something in bold, you have to tell it as well. Each medium has its own language, and this applies to the medium of the World Wide Web. The language that the Web uses is the Hypertext Markup Language (HTML). HTML is what is used to format all those headings, the bold fonts, and even the links themselves.

Like other languages, HTML has its own syntax and vocabulary. It shouldn't be surprising that there are even "dialects" of HTML. What does the interpretation of this language is your Web Browser, or simply browser. Like the word processor or the `man` command, the browser sees the formatting information and converts it into to the visual images that you see on the screen. If the browser doesn't understand the dialect of the document you are trying to read, you might end up with garbage or maybe even nothing at all. Therefore, it is important to understand these dialects.

HTML is like other formatting languages in that it is used to define the structure of the document. However, it is the viewer (in this case, the browser) that gives that structure its form.

Most browsers support the HTML 2 standard, though the newest standard is HTML 3.2. Some vendors have specific additions (such as Netscape) that make pages designed for them sometimes unreadable. However, as of this writing, Netscape has become pretty much the standard. Many sites that have Web pages designed specifically for Netscape have links back to Netscape, where you can download the latest version.

The Web is a client server system in its truest sense. From the user's perspective, however, there is a single client (the browser) and tens of thousands of servers spread out all over the world. Keep in mind that the server doesn't have to be at some other location. In fact, the server doesn't even need to be at another machine. Your own machine can serve documents locally, even though they are loaded with `httpd`.

As with any server, it sits and waits for requests. In this case, the requests are for documents. When the server gets the request, it looks for the appropriate document and passes it back to the client. To be able to communicate, the client and server need to speak the same language. This language is the hypertext transfer protocol or http.

In the next section, I am going to give you a crash course on the basics of HTML. This is not an in-depth tutorial nor am I going to cover every aspect of the language. However, you should cover enough information to get you on your way to creating fairly interesting Web pages.

HTML uses *tags* (formatting markers) to tell the Web browser how to display the text. These consists of pairs of < > (angle brackets) with the tag name inside. Following this is the text to be formatted. Formatting is turned off using the same tag, but the tag name is preceded by a slash (/). For example, the tag to create a level 1 header is <H1>, therefore to turn off the level 1 header, the tag is </H1>. In a document, it might look like this:

```
<H1>Welcome to My Home Page</H1>
```

HTML documents are usually broken into two sections: a header and a body. Each has its own tag: `<HEAD>` and `<BODY>`. The header usually contains information that may not actually be displayed on the screen but is still part of the document and is copied to the client machine. If both of these tags are omitted, all of the text belongs to the body.

By convention, every HTML document has a title, which is primarily used to identify the document and is, by convention, the same as the first heading. The title is not displayed on the screen but rather at the top of the window.

While browsing on the Web, you have certainly clicked some text or an image and had some other document appear on the screen. As I talked about earlier, this is the concept of a hypertext link. Links are defined by two HTML tags. The first one is `<A>` tag, which stands for anchor. Like a heading or any other formatting tag, the anchor is started using the tag and closed by the same tag with a leading slash (`</A>`).

The text or image will then appear somewhat highlighted. When you click it, nothing happens, because you haven't yet told the server what to do. This is where the `<HREF>` tag comes in. This is a reference to what document should be loaded. It doesn't have to be another HTML page, but it does have to be something that the Web server and browser understand, like a CGI script (more on those later).

If the document is another HTML page, it will be loaded just like the first and will probably have its own links. If the link points to an image, that image is loaded into the browser. It is also possible that the link points to something like a tar archive or a pkzipped file. Clicking it could cause the browser to start a particular program, such as PKUNZIP.EXE, or simply to ask you whether you want to save the file. This depends on how your browser is configured.

Many browsers have an option, "View as source," with which you can see the HTML source for the document you are currently viewing. This way, you can see what each reference is anchored to. In general, these links have the following format:

```
HREF="http://[machine_name]/[document_name]"
```

The line pointing to your home page may look like this in a document:

```
<H1><A HREF="http://www.your.domain/index.html">Jimmo's
WWW Home Page</A> </H1>
```

When you look at the document, you don't see any of the tags–just a line that looks like this:

```
Jimmo's WWW Home Page
```

When you click this link, the browser loads the document specified by HREF. In this case, the browser will load *www.your.domain/index.html.*

Often times the link is identified by a different color than the other text, and links that you haven't visited are underlined. When you click a link and later return to that same page, the link will have a different color and the underline will be gone. I have seen in some cases in which there is no underline and the link just changes color. This is normally configurable by the browser.

The <H1> entry says that this line is to be formatted as header level 1. The anchor is indicated by the <A> entry and refers to the page index.html on the machine *www.your.domain*. Remember from your previous discussion that using the file index.html is a convention. If you had defined the DirectoryIndex to be some other file, this would replace index.html.

There are six levels of headings, numbered 1 through 6, H1 being the largest and most prominent. Headings are generally displayed in larger or bolder fonts than the normal text. Normal text is simply anything not enclosed within tags. Like `troff` and similar editing languages, HTML does not care about formatting carriage returns and other white spaces. Therefore, you can include a carriage return anywhere in the text, and it will be displayed according to the rules of the tags as well as the width of the viewing window. This allows smaller windows to display the same text without altering the text.

With lower resolutions, the level one header (`<H1>`) is too large. I cannot remember ever seeing a site in which a level 1 header really looked good. In most cases, unless you have a 17-inch or larger monitor and at a high resolution, just a couple words in a level 1 header can take up the whole width of the screen and is overwhelming. (I'll get more into some tips and techniques later.) The best way to see what it looks like is to try different browsers at different resolutions. You can see in Figure 14.1 how the headers relate to each other in size.

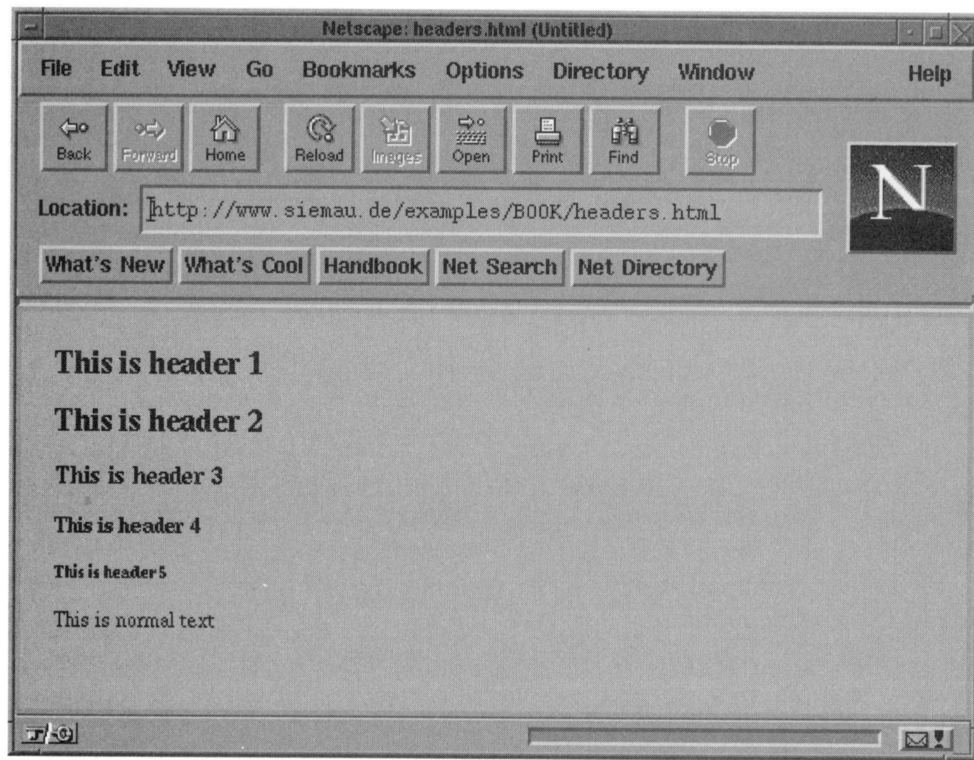

Figure 14.1: Examples of Headers

HTML also provides explicit changes to the physical style, such as `<B>` for bold, `<UL>` for creating lists, and `<PRE>` for forcing the Web browsers not to do any formatting. Some the more common tags are listed in Table 14.1.

Table 14.1: Basic HTML Tags

Tag	Expansion	Definition
<TITLE>	TITLE	Describes the content of the document
<H1>-<H6>	HEADING	Creates headings with the specific level (1–6)
<P>	PARAGRAPH	Starts a new paragraph
<EM	EMPHASIS	Logical tag that displays emphasis, defaults to italics
<STRONG>	STRONG	Logical tag that displays something of significance, defaults to bold
<DT	DEFINED ITEM	Specifies the item you define
<DL>	DEFINITION LIST	Starts a list of definitions
<DD>	DEFINITION	Gives a definition of the term
<B>	BOLD	Physical tag that enables bold text
<U>	UNDERLINE	Physical tag that enables underlined text
<I>	ITALICS	Physical tag that enables italic text
<PRE>	PREFORMATTED	Disables formatting by Web browser
 	LINE BREAK	Forces a line break
<A>	ANCHOR	Logical tag that encloses a link, normally used with HREF attribute
<UL>	UNNUMBERED LIST	Indicates the beginning of an unnumbered list
<OL>	ORDERED LIST	Indicates the beginning of a numbered or ordered list
<HR>	HORIZONTAL RULE	Draws a line across the page
<HEAD>	TEXT HEADER	Indicates the document header
<BODY>	TEXT BODY	Indicates the document body
<LI>	LIST ITEM	Indicates an item within a list
<IMG SRC=>	IMAGE SOURCE	Defines the source/path of an image to be displayed

Here, too, when you want to stop the formatting, use the same tag but precede the tag with a slash. For example, to turn on bold, the syntax would look like this:

```
<B>
```

To turn bold off, the syntax would look like this:

```
</B>
```

You could also include multiple formatting on the same line:

```
<H3><I>Welcome to <U><B>Jim's</B> Wonderful</U> Web
Site</I> </H3>
```

This HTML coding would look like this:

*Welcome to **Jim's** Wonderful Web Site*

In this example are several different tags that are laid inside each other. You don't have to match the pairs exactly like this. For example, the `<U><B>` or the `</I> </H3>` at the end of the line could have been reversed. You could also have had something like this:

```
<H3><I>Welcome to <U><B>Jim's</B> Wonder</I> Web Site
</U> </H3>
```

This would stop the italic formatting before it stopped the underline, though you had started these in the other order. The result would then look like this:

*Welcome to **Jim's** Wonderful* Web Site

Here, the underline continues under "Web Site," but the italics now stop at the word "Wonderful."

As I mentioned earlier, the convention is that the Web server's machine name is *www.domain.name*. To access the home page, the URL would be *http://ww.domain.name*. For example, to get to SCO's home page, the URL is *http://www.sco.com*.

THE PAGE ITSELF

Using HTML, you have the ability to control the overall appearance of the page. One simple way of doing this is to specify a color to use as the background by using the `BGCOLOR` option within the `<BODY>` tag, like this:

```
<BODY BGCOLOR =#rrggbb >
```

The color is specified as a red-green-blue (RGB) triplet. The value of the color is a hexidecimal value between 00 and FF, which specifies the intensity of each color. The higher the intensity, the closer it is to white. So, if you set all three colors to FF, you end up with a pure white background. Setting them all to 00 gives you a black background.

By default, the text is black. So, if you were to specify a black background, the text would be invisible. To get around this problem, use the `TEXT` option within the `<BODY>` tag. This, too, is an RBG triplet. So, to specify white text on a black background, the line might look like this:

```
<BODY BGCOLOR =#000000 TEXT=#FFFFFF >
```

You have undoubtedly seen Web sites in which an image is the background rather than a single color. This is simply done with the `BACKGROUND` option. Note that if you specify a background image, this will overwrite the background color. Also, you must pay attention to the text color. Sometimes the default color (black) doesn't come out right, but slightly modifying it does. An example of using a background image and setting the text color to red would look like this:

```
<BODY BACKGROUND="background.gif" TEXT="#FF0000">
```

On the CD-ROM, you will find several images in the `backgrounds` directory. Although these images were all taken from a CD-ROM where they were listed as background images, I think many of them are just too "loud" to be used. However, what you use will depend on what message you are trying to give the visitor.

Also within the `<BODY>` tag, you can define the color of the links. The `LINK` option is the color of a link before anything happens. The `ALINK` (`A` for active) option defines the color of the link when you click it. The `VLINK` (`V` for visited) option defines the color of links that you have gone to already (visited). All three of these are RGB triplets.

LISTS

As I mentioned in the previous section, you can create two types of lists: ordered and unordered. An unordered list is often called a *bullet list* because some symbol, called a bullet, is at the beginning of each line. You can use three types of bullets: `DISC`, `CIRCLE`, and `SQUARE`.

For example, to specify an unordered list using circles, the line would look like this:

```
<UL TYPE=CIRCLE>
```

Ordered lists can also be different types. The type indicates what symbols are used to identify each entry. Possible symbols are

1: Numbers (the default)

a: Lowercase letters

A: Uppercase letters

I: Large roman numbers

i: Small roman numbers

To specify an ordered list using small roman numbers, the syntax would look like this:

```
<OL TYPE=I>
```

If you use the TYPE attribute within the list tag, the type is valid for all list items. If you use the TYPE attribute within the list item tag, it changes the type for all *subsequent* items.

An interesting thing is that with an ordered list, the system keeps track of the numbers, even if you change types. For example, you could start off with uppercase letters, switch to lowercase letters, and then finish with numbers. You can see some examples in Figure 14.2, Figure 14.3, and Figure 14.4.

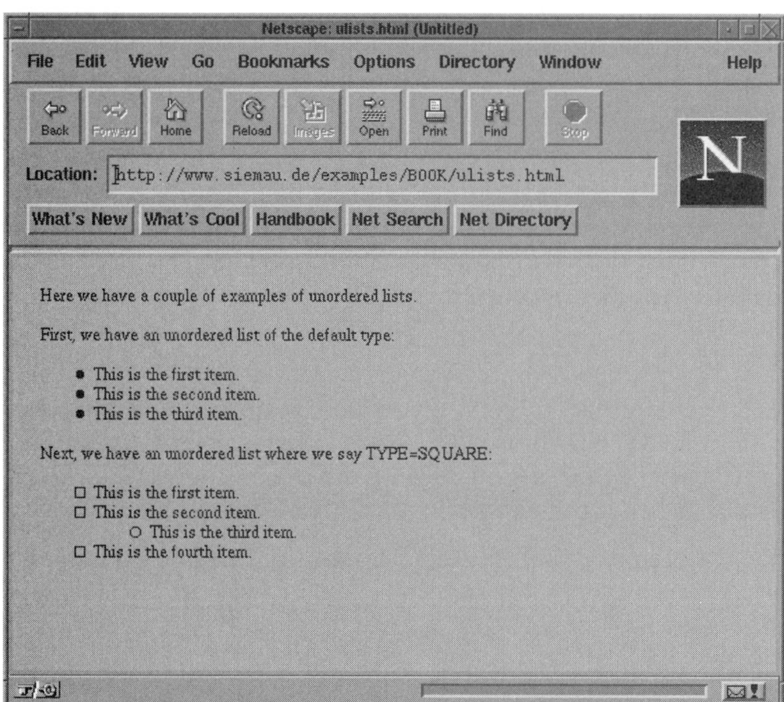

Figure 14.2: An Example of Unordered Lists

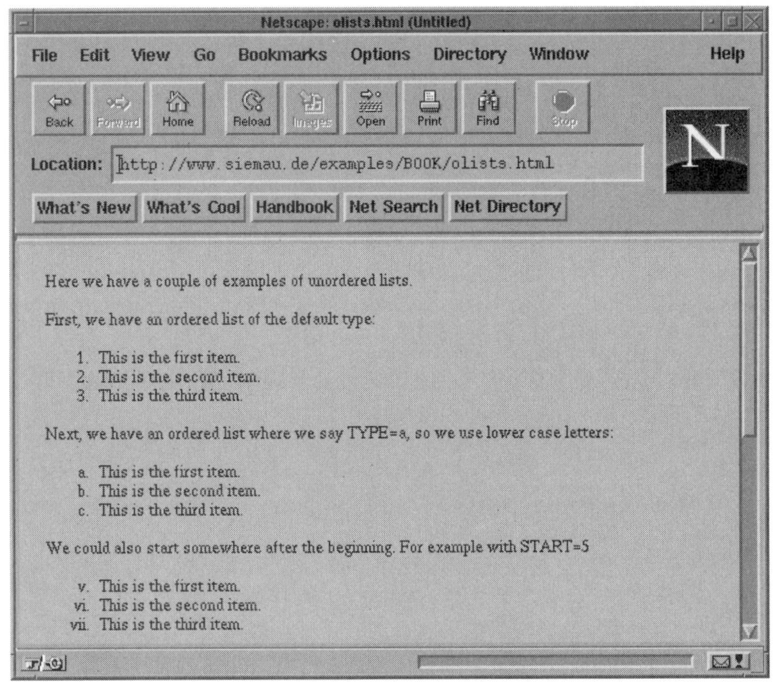

Figure 14.3: An Example of Ordered Lists

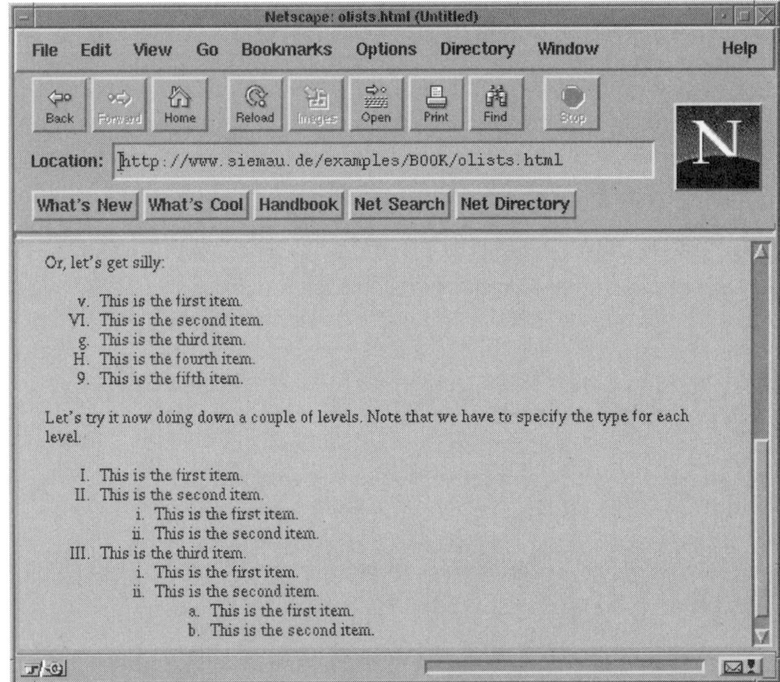

Figure 14.4: Another Example of Ordered Lists

Tables can also be created using HTML. The `<TABLE>` tag starts the table and each row and each cell must be defined as well. The tag `<TR>` marks the table row and `<TD>` is used for the cells. In addition, you can create borders around the table, change the alignment, and even specify that certain columns span multiple rows or rows span multiple columns.

Within the table cell tag, you can also use several attributes. Each has the syntax

```
attribute = value
```

For example, to set the horizontal alignment to center, you would use

```
<TD align=center>
```

The attributes that you can use are

- `align`: Specifies the *horizontal* alignment. Possible values are left, center, justify, right, and decimal (which aligns on the decimal point).
- `valign`: Specifies the *vertical* alignment. Possible values are top, middle, bottom, and baseline (which ensures all cells share a common baseline).
- `colspan`: Specifies the number of columns that a cell will span.
- `rowspan`: Specifies the number of rows that a cell will span.

The following syntax is a table describing the technical specification for a theoretical compressor. As you can see, in many cases, I specified both vertical and horizontal alignment, and in some cases, I specified spanning multiple rows or columns.

```
<TABLE border>
<TR><TD rowspan=2 align=center valign=middle>Typ<TD
rowspan=2 align=center valign=middle>Air Volume
<TD rowspan=2 valign=middle align=center>Highest
Pressure
<TD rowspan=2 valign=middle align=center>Tank Vol.
<TD COLSPAN=2 align=center>Motor performance
<TD COLSPAN=2 align=center>Fuse Amperage
<TD  valign=middle align=center>Measurements
<TD rowspan=2 valign=middle align=center>weight kg</TR>
<TR><TD align=center valign=middle>230V AC
<TD align=center valign=middle>400V DC
<TD align=center valign=middle>230V AC
<TD align=center valign=middle>400V DC

<TD align=center valign=middle>L x W x H mm<TD
```

```
align=center valign=middle></TR>
  <TR><TD valign=middle align=center>TNG L/42
  <TD valign=middle align=center>260
  <TD valign=middle align=center>10
  <TD valign=middle align=center>40
  <TD valign=middle align=center>1,3
  <TD valign=middle align=center>1,2
  <TD valign=middle align=center>16
  <TD valign=middle align=center>6
  <TD valign=middle align=center>920x410x700
  <TD valign=middle align=center>40
  </TR>
  </TABLE>
```

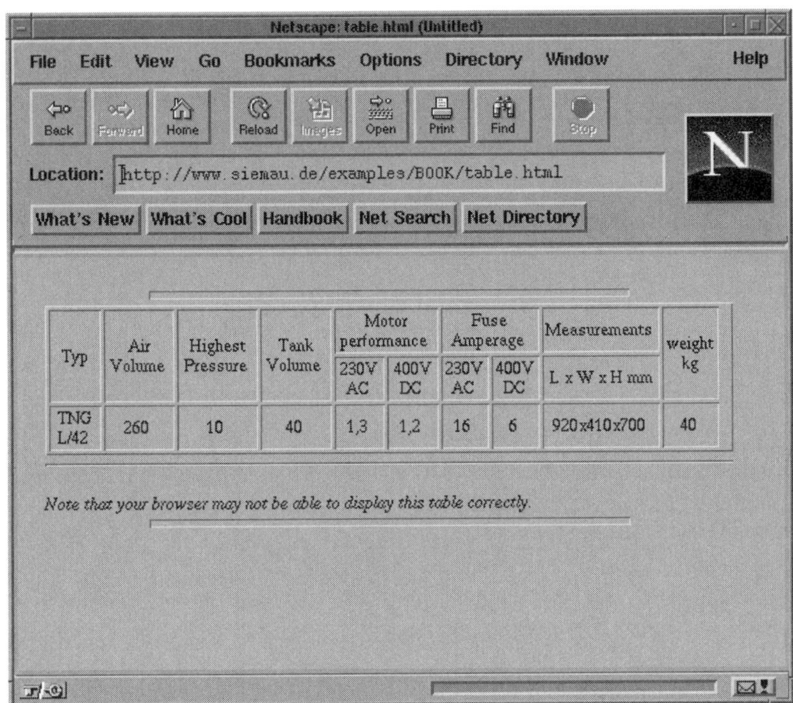

Figure 14.5: Example HTML Table

Be careful with tables–not every browser can handle them. For example, some browsers do not display the table in Figure 14.5 correctly. Even if the browser can't handle creating a table correctly, the table may still be usable. The best thing is to test it with different browsers.

BOOKMARKS

What I call bookmarks, a lot of other documentation calls anchors. Because you specify them within an anchor tag and give them names, I guess "anchor" is the correct term. However, I find that calling them bookmarks is more descriptive of the function they serve. However, this also is confusing since many browsers use the term "bookmark" to describe the process by which you mark a page in your list of favorite site to get back to it quicker.

To use a named anchor, you first have to name the anchor. The name is an attribute given to that anchor. Although you don't have to use headers or any special formatting, specifying a named anchor might look like this:

```
<h1><a name="bm1">Here is bookmark 1</h1></a>
```

In the document that has the link, the reference might look like this:

```
<a href="doc.html#bm1">Jump to bookmark 1</a><br>
```

When you click the text

Jump to bookmark 1

you are brought to the label `name=bm1`. Because you jumped to an anchor, you could have another reference, so the line might look like this:

```
<h1><a name="bm1" HREF="bookmark.html">Here is bookmark
1</h1></a>
```

The text "Here is bookmark 1" would now be a link and when you clicked it, you would jump to the document `bookmark.html`.

Let's look at an example consisting of two files. One file contains the links to the other document and the other document contains the name anchors. The first file looks like this:

```
  <H1>Here is an example of jumping to specific places
within a document.</H1>
  <a href="doc.html#bm1">Jump to bookmark 1</a><br>
  <a href="doc.html#bm2">Jump to bookmark 2</a><br>
  <a href="doc.html#bm3">Jump to bookmark 3</a><br>
  <a href="doc.html#bm4">Jump to bookmark 4</a><br>
  <a href="doc.html#bm5">Jump to bookmark 5</a><br>
```

The document to which you jump looks like this:

```
  <h1><a name="bm1" HREF="bookmark.htm">Here is bookmark
1</h1></a>
  <a HREF="bookmark.htm">Back to bookmark.html</A>

  <HR><BR><BR><BR><BR><BR><BR><BR><BR><BR><BR><BR><BR><BR>

  <h1><a name="bm2">Here is bookmark 2</h1></a>
```

```
<a HREF="bookmark.htm">Back to bookmark.html</A>

<HR><BR><BR><BR><BR><BR><BR><BR><BR><BR><BR><BR><BR><BR>

<h1><a name="bm3">Here is bookmark 3</h1></a>
<a HREF="bookmark.htm">Back to bookmark.html</A>

<HR><BR><BR><BR><BR><BR><BR><BR><BR><BR><BR><BR><BR><BR>

<h1><a name="bm4">Here is bookmark 4</h1></a>
<a HREF="bookmark.htm">Back to bookmark.html</A>

<HR><BR><BR><BR><BR><BR><BR><BR><BR><BR><BR><BR><BR><BR>

<h1><a name="bm5">Here is bookmark 5</h1></a>
<a HREF="bookmark.htm">Back to bookmark.html</A>
```

In this example, I included the lines with the horizontal rule and the breaks to demonstrate the effect. If all of the bookmarks are visible on one page, you don't see the fact that you are jumping to a different spot in the text.

MENUS

Menus are not actually built into HTML, but you can create some very interesting and useful menus on your own. Unfortunately, you cannot create the pull-down and pop-up menus that you know in other applications, but you can design something that allows easy navigation through the Web site.

The simplest form of a menu is simply text on the screen; for example:

- Products
- History
- Customer Service
- Sales

When you click one line, it brings you to another document. For example, if you clicked the link "Products," you would be taken to the products page, which has another menu of its own. The HTML source for this would look like this:

```
  <UL>
  <LI><A HREF="http://www.your.domain/products>Products
</A>
  <LI><A HREF="http://www.your.domain/history>History</A>
  <LI><A HREF="http://www.your.domain/custserv>Customer
Service</A>
  <LI><A HREF="http://www.your.domain/Sales>Sales</A>
  </UL>
```

This is nothing more than a series of links that happen to be included in an unordered list. In this example, I did not specify a file to load, just a directory. Therefore, the server would look for a file with the name specified in the `DirectoryIndex` directive.

MAPS

Maps, another very effective means of moving around a Web site, are images that are linked to a map file. You can click the image to be taken to another document. These files don't need to be "maps" in the conventional sense; they can be images of any kind. The location at which you click determines where you will go.

Maps consist of two parts: an image and a map file. The image can be anything that you want to display and the map file is a text file that gives coordinates and the document that should be loaded when that area of the image is clicked.

Let's assume that you have a site with a picture of the company's building. You would like to include a map so that when someone clicks a particular part of the building, he or she is brought to a page that describes the department situated within that part of the building. You might then have a link on the page that looks like this:

```
<A HREF="/maps/dept.map"> <IMG SRC="/images/
company1.gif" ismap></A>
```

Here the entire line is an anchor, but you are showing just an image (`/images/company1.gif`) and no text. There are two things to note here. First, the link that you are referencing (`/maps/dept.map`) is a map file and not a HTML page. Next is the reference to the image. Notice the `ismap` reference at the end. This tells the server that this is a map image. It is then able to process the map file correctly.

Let's now take a look at the map file:

```
default /dept/management.htm
rect (49,186) (178,196) /dept/export.htm
rect (250,195) (417,203) /dept/is_it.htm
rect (309,183) (415,194) /dept/marketing.htm
rect (181,190) (250,200) /dept/finance.htm
rect (48,197) (180,209) /dept/service.htm
rect (50,211) (177,222) /dept/purchasing.htm
rect (250,205) (416,217) /dept/sales.htm
```

The first line indicates what file should be accessed if you click a location that is not defined (in other words, the default document). The other lines have the following format

```
shape (upper_left) (lower_right) document
```

where `shape` is the shape of the area that is being referenced. To define a rectangle, all you need is two corners. Here you specify the upper left and lower right corner.

If you wanted, you could also define a polygon, which needs to be defined by all of its corners. In this way, you can define any common shape, like a triangle or pentagon, and even an irregular shape.

Circles are possible but are not as intuitively obvious as rectangles or polygons. Here you have two coordinates, which are obviously not the corners. Instead

```
circle survey.htm 249,170 180,173
circle survey.htm 180,173 249,170
```

When you click the image, the coordinates are passed by the client to the server, which then parses the map file to deliver to you the appropriate document.

There are actually two different map types: CERN and NCSA. These preceding examples are for a CERN map file because the document names come at the end. The NCSA maps come between the shape and the coordinates. The same map in both formats would look like this:

NCSA:

```
circle survey.html 224,104 224,166
rect survey.html 406,67 495,168
poly survey.html 74,91 47,162 105,167 149,115 136,76
72,91
```

CERN:

```
circle (224,104) 62 survey.htm
rect (406,67) (495,168) survey.htm
poly (74,91) (47,162) (105,167) (149,115) (136,76)
(72,91) survey.htm
```

Aside from the order of the information, another difference between these two map types is the way circles are defined. An NCSA circle is defined with the center and a point on the edge of the circle. CERN circles are defined by the center and the radius. Also, CERN maps have parentheses around the coordinates, and NCSA maps do not.

You can use these image maps in a lot of different ways. Some sites have fancy graphics that, when clicked, take you to different pages. These maps behave like menus. Maybe you have technical information on the product, such as a compressor. By clicking an image of a compressor, you will get the details about that component.

One thing I have to mention is that maps are easily identifiable as maps and image are images. I have been to some sites where you click something that looks like a map and nothing happens while clicking the images that look like decorations loads new documents.

You will find that most of the sample pages have a tool map that is actually a map image. Pressing a "button" takes you to a different page.

IMAGES

Images require two tags to be displayed. The first tag is the image tag itself (`<IMG>`) and the source or path of the image. For example:

```
<IMG SRC="/images/pictures.gif">
```

Because these tags always go together, I usually think of them as a single tag.

You can do several different things with images. Some techniques are newer and may not work with specific browsers. The possible attributes are

`texttop`	Aligns the image with the top of the "tallest" text on the line
`absmiddle`	Aligns the middle of the current *line* with the middle of the image
`baseline`	Aligns the bottom of the image with the baseline of the current line
`bottom`	Does the same as the baselineleft; Aligns image with the left margin; text will wrap to the right
	right Aligns image with the right margin; text will wrap to the left

You can also change the appearance of the image with a couple of other attributes. For example, the `HEIGHT` and `WIDTH` attributes are used to change the physical size of the image. Normally, the browser will display the image on the screen based on the resolution and the image itself. With these two attributes, you can define how large the image should be.

This is useful when you have a "hole" to fill in your page. If you use the default size, this hole might be the wrong size for the image and the text will look weird. When you specify the width and height, you can have the image fill the hole exactly.

You can also use the `VSPACE` and `HSPACE` attributes to leave some space around images. Normally, the text is right up against the image. These attributes change the vertical and horizontal space, respectively, to put a "buffer" between the text and image.

The `BORDER` attribute is used to place a border around the image. Although this looks good in some cases, I would use this carefully. Depending on what the browser does and how wide the border is, this might make it appear as though the image is a link. I can remember a couple of instances in which I clicked an image and nothing happened. I then looked at the source and discovered the image was *not* a link.

One thing I need to point out with images is that they don't behave as other elements of the documentation. For example, you might have:

```
Here is some text <BR>
<HR>
```

This would cause the horizontal line to be completely under the text. However, if you had an image, like this:

```
<IMG SRC="/images/pictures.gif"><BR>
<HR>
```

the horizontal line might stick out from the side of the image if you align to one side or the other. To avoid this, use the CLEAR attribute to the break tag (<B>), which takes the values ALL, LEFT, or RIGHT.

It's best to use the attribute that matches the alignment of the image. For example, if you aligned the image to the right (ALIGN=RIGHT), then also clear to the right (CLEAR=RIGHT).

Text Attributes

When you use the <P> (paragraph) tag, you start a new paragraph. Normally, this means you start a new line as well. You could use the
 (break) tag to start a new paragraph, but the convention is to use the paragraph tag if you are really starting a new paragraph.

Each type of text uses a particular font size, such as heading and normal text. However, you can specify different fonts without making them a specific header type. In the table at the beginning of this section, I mentioned using bold, italic, strong, etc. You can use these to change the characteristics of specific words or even individual letters. However, you can also change the size of each letter using the <FONT> tag.

The <FONT> tag's attribute is the "size" of the font. For example, to specify font size 6, the line might look like this:

```
<FONT SIZE=6>Here is some text in font size 6.
```

There is also a default font size that to which you can use to make other font sizes relative. This is called the *base* size for the fonts. By default, the base size is 3. If you wanted a font size larger than this, you could specify this with a font size of 4, or

```
<FONT SIZE=+1>Here is some text in font size 4.
```

You could also specify a font smaller than the base, like this:

```
<FONT SIZE=-1>Here is some text in font size 2.
```

You can also define the base font with the `<BASEFONT>` tag. To set the base font size to 6, the line would look like this:

```
<BASEFONT SIZE=6>Here is some text in font size 6.
<FONT SIZE=+1>Here is some text in font size 7.
```

You set the line following the change to a font that is one size larger. Now one size larger is no longer 4, but 7.

Depending on the browser, you can also change the color of the text. For example, if I wanted red text, the line might look like this:

```
<FONT SIZE=66 COLOR="FF0000">Here is some text that
would be in red.
```

The colors are specified in the same manner as the color for the background; that is, RRGGBB.

14.3.2 Connecting Your Pages

You can have links that point to other things than just HTML pages or images. For example, you could have compressed files or `tar` archives. Based on how the browser is configured, these links could then be copied to the local machine and even uncompressed.

You will often see a link pointing to an e-mail address (e.g., *webmaster@www.your.domain*). When you click this link, it starts any mail program that is connected to the browser.

It is very common to point links to forms, HTML documents that have input fields. The input is then passed to a program that parses the information.

At this point, I am going to assume that you are familiar with the basic constructs of HTML and `perl`. I hope that you have already created a few pages and some `perl` scripts. Now is the time to combine these two to create some really interactive Web pages.

Information is passed from a Web page to the Web server through the Common Gateway Interface (CGI). "Common" means that the information is passed in the same way no matter what is on the receiving end. If you want, you can write CGI programs in a compiled language such as C, or even as a `bash` shell-script. However, `perl` is quicker to use than a compiled language and is much more powerful than shell-scripts. Because you have a `perl` interpreter on the system and you are already a `perl` expert, there should be no problem.

To get the Web server to pass the information, you have to tell it that it's a good thing to do. In other words, you have to create an environment in which the server knows that it should pass this information. Do this by creating a form. A form is simply another section of a document. A form can take up the whole document, but it doesn't have to. As with other sections, forms are started with `<FORM>` and ended with `</FORM>`.

Passing information to the CGI program is done from an HTML form using a process called a *method*, which can either be the `POST` or the `GET` method. Each has its own way of handing the data off to the CGI program. Knowing which way the data is coming is important for the program to process it, and this is specified when you define the form. Here, too, you also specify what action is to be taken (that is, what script).

The `GET` method passes the data via the environment variable `QUERY_STRING`. This string is then parsed to be able to access the individual variables. The `POST` method passes the data as an input stream to the program, which comes in via `stdin`. In both cases, the format is the same, so once you have the string, parsing it is the same no matter what method was used.

In many books, magazines, and other sources, this string is referred to as a *query string*. This comes from the fact that in many (most) cases, this string is passed to the CGI program and is used to query a database. However, this does not need to be the case because the information can simply pass along without any kind of query.

One nice thing about CGI (okay, it was designed that way) is that the information comes across in a known form. Looking at the query string, you (as a human) can easily see that there are patterns to the way data is grouped in the string. The variable name and its value are separated by an equal sign (=), which is equivalent to saying, "This variable equals this value." The variable-value pairs are separated with an ampersand (&), which says, "I have this pair AND this pair AND this pair, etc." Should one of the values have a literal space it in, that space is replaced by a plus sign (+). When the variable-name pair is read, this plus sign needs to be considered.

The four primary types of form elements are

- text: the input is any text you want
- checkbox: can select any number of these options
- radio button: can select one button
- multiple: can select one of a list of options

Each form element can be used as often as you want. That is, you can have several different text variables, checkboxes, or whatever. Although you can have multiple instances of the same element, you should have each with a different variable name. (How are you going to keep track of which is which?) However, you could have a dozen text elements as long as they have different names.

One gotcha (at least, it got me) is that every checked checkbox will be passed to the CGI program. In the example form shown in Figure 14.6, you have four checkboxes all with the name, USAGE. Obviously, this is one case in which you *can* use the same name over and over. You could label each checkbox with a different name (usage1, usage2, usage3, etc.), but you don't need to. While parsing the query string, you can read each one in turn and (for example) set flags based on its value.

The gotcha is that if you decide to use the same name for each checkbox, each box that is checked will be passed along as a separate variable, *even though they have the same name.* It is up to you to parse them. If you only check for the existence of that variable (i.e., if `$variable_name eq usage`) and don't look for individual values, you'll lose all but the first (or last) value.

One thing I like to do with radio buttons is to preset one with the `CHECKED` attribute. This is done when you *should* have one of the values checked.

Keep in mind that unlike text, checkboxes and radio buttons can only take on discrete values. That is, there is only a limited number of values they can have. In fact, they either are set or are not set. In contrast, text variables can be *anything* you want. You can then check for each of the possible values. For example

```
if ( $value eq "fun" )
{
        for_fun = 1
}
if ( $value eq "work" )
{
        for_work = 1
}
*
*
*
```

It makes sense to assign radio buttons and checkboxes to a string of the same name because it is easier to keep track of which variable in the CGI program is associated with which field in the form. You can easily assign the value to the appropriate value:

```
  @data = split(/&/,$query_string); foreach  $line (
@data)  {
     ($field_name,$value) = split (/=/, $line);
     $$field_name = $value;
  }
```

The line `$$field_name = $value` says to expand the variable `$field_name` and, with the other `$` in front of it, it now becomes a new variable with the name of whatever it was expanded to. For example, if `$field_name = "lastname"`, then this line is equivalent to saying:

```
$lastname = $value;
```

You could do this to ensure the readability of the script and to ensure that the variable names are what the script expects. However, IMHO forcing the variable names in the CGI program to be the same as from the form ensures that there is no confusion.

Note that this assumes that you do not have any multiple variables with the same name, as with checkboxes. The solution, in this case, would be to either check specifically for these variables or give each box a unique name.

For names, keep them as two or three separate elements. Although you could parse the string, it's much more efficient to have them as separate fields to begin with. By this, I mean that you shouldn't have a single field "name" but rather one field "last_name" and one field "first_name." This is much easier to parse than the single variable "name."

Also, someone might add an extra space to the end of a name, which, unfortunately, appears automatically as a plus-sign (+). Therefore, it might be a good idea to strip out all the plus signs from people's names. (I have yet to see someone with a plus sign in his or her name. Besides, the + is changed to `%2B`, anyway [the hexadecimal value of +].)

Another good idea would be to set all variables you use to a default value within the CGI script before they are first referenced. That way you do not have to worry about any unexpected values if the form does not pass that variable. By setting it to NULL (`$variable = ""`), you could check to make sure all "required" fields have been filled out; that is, that they are not NULL. If you don't set them to anything and the user doesn't fill in the field, the CGI script does not send the variables. When you access that variable, you end up with an unreferenced variable.

If the information that a user inputs should be saved (i.e., in a customer database). I strongly recommend that you first check this information with the user to verify it (i.e., create a new page with this information and display it to the user). You can also check the validity of the values, such as names with numbers in them. (Note: I first thought about limiting zip codes to only numbers, but countries like Canada and England have letters in their "postal codes.")

So, let's look at your first form. This is a very simple form that searches a text file for an input value. The source for the form looks like this:

```
<HTML>
<HEAD>
<TITLE>FORM TEST</TITLE>
</HEAD>

<BODY>
<FORM METHOD=POST action="http://www/Scripts/phone.pl">


<B>Name: </B></I></I>
<BR>

<INPUT NAME="name" type=text maxlength=50 size=50 >
<BR><BR>
<input TYPE=submit>
<input TYPE=reset>
</FORM>
</BODY>

</HTML>
```

When you load the page in a browser, the page looks like Figure 14.6. Here you are prompted to input a single value, NAME. This is accomplished with the line:

```
<INPUT NAME="name" type=text maxlength=50 size=50 >
```

This line says that the variable's name is "name," it is of type "text" (as compared to radio button or checkbox), has a maximum length of 50 characters, and the input field displayed on the form has a size of 50 characters. Show a two button with the lines:

```
<input TYPE=submit>
<input TYPE=reset>
```

When you press the "submit" button, the information that you input into the form is passed to the script specified by the form action line–in other words, what action is to be taken when the button is pressed. In the preceding form, it looks like this:

```
<FORM METHOD=POST action="http://www/cgi-bin/phone.pl">
```

This is passed to the script `phone.pl` using the POST method. The `POST` method passes the string to the script via `stdin` and not through the environment variable `QUERY_STRING`, as the `GET` method would. The script then passes `stdin`. In your example script, which I'll get to shortly, input using either method is possible–check for which method is used and act accordingly.

The other button is a reset button. Rather than sending information to the script, the reset button tells the system to present a form in its default state. This normally means that all the text fields are blank.

The following script searches through a data file looking for the values you put into the form. In this example, the data file is a company phone book. The `perl` script looks like this:

```
# Here you set things up
srand(time|$$);
$random=int(rand(1000))+1;
$last_name == "";
$title = "";
$dept = "";

DocumentRoot="/var/httpd/html/";

# here you get the information passed through the CGI
# interface and
# Load it into the variable form_info
$request_method = $ENV{'REQUEST_METHOD'};

if ( $request_method eq "GET" ) {
       $form_info = $ENV{'QUERY_STRING'};
} else {
       $size_of_info = $ENV{'CONTENT_LENGTH'};
       read (STDIN, $form_info, $size_of_info);
}

# Here you define the output files. Note that the
# directories must already exist
$TEMPFILE="/temp/".$random.".htm";
$LOCATION="Location: http://www".$TEMPFILE."\n\n";
$OUT="> ".$DocumentRoot.$TEMPFILE;

# You open your input file 'telbook.txt' and die
# if you can't.
# You also open your output file.
open (INPUT, $DocumentRoot."telbook.txt") || die
"ooops: $! \n";
open (PAGE, $OUT);

# This creates standard header information for the HTML
# page that is created.
print PAGE "<HTML>\n";
print PAGE "<HEAD>\n";
print PAGE "<TITLE>Search results</TITLE>\n";
print PAGE "</HEAD>\n";
```

```
# Here you are splitting the for_info variable  (i.e.
# the QUERY_STRING) and loading
# it into the array 'data'.
@data = split (/&/, $form_info) ;

# The 'foreach' loop reads each entry in the array
# 'data' and then one
# at a time assigns the entry to the two variables
# field_name and value
foreach $line ( @data ){
($field_name, $value ) = split (/=/, $line) ;

# here you convert everything to lower case.
$value =~ tr/A-Z/a-z/ ;
}

# Read you read the input file a line at a time and
# after converting the line to all
# lowercase you determine if the string from the form
# is a sub-set of the input line.
while ( $line = <INPUT> ){
      $line =~ s/;/ /g;
      $line =~ tr/A-Z/a-z/ ;
      if ( index($line,$value) != -1)
      {
                 print PAGE $line,"<BR>\n" ;
      }
}

print PAGE "<BR>\n";

print PAGE "</HTML>\n";
close PAGE;
close INPUT;
print $LOCATION;
```

The first two lines of the script generate a random number for which the seed for the random number is based on the time and the process ID ($$). This random number will then be used to name the file where the script outputs its information, though this normally results in a unique random and therefore unique file name.

This section actually reads the information passed from the form to the CGI script:

```
$request_method = $ENV{'REQUEST_METHOD'};

if ( $request_method eq "GET" ) {
      $form_info = $ENV{'QUERY_STRING'};
```

```
} else {
        $size_of_info = $ENV{'CONTENT_LENGTH'};
        read (STDIN, $form_info, $size_of_info);
}
```

First, check for the method that is used to pass the information (`$request_method = $ENV{'REQUEST_METHOD'};`). Based on the method, you read the information in a different way. If the information was passed using the `GET` method, you must parse the `QUERY_STRING`. If you used the `PUT` method (specified by the `else` block), the input comes via `stdin`. In both cases, you assign the information from the form to the varaible `$form_info`, which you parse as you move along.

Next set up the input and output and write the header into output file. Then split the input line into fields of the array data, which are then parsed one field at a time. If the field name is "name," change the value to lowercase to ensure that the input value and the data are both in the same case.

In the `while` loop, you read each line from the data file (`telbook.txt`) one at a time. Your data file consists of a simple ASCII file in which each record is on a single line and the fields are separated by a semicolon. Change the semicolon to a space (`$line =~ s/;/ /g;`) then convert it to all lowercase (`$line =~ tr/A-Z/a-z/;`) so that everything is in the same case.

If the value you received from the form is a substring of the line you read from the input file (`if ( index($line,$value) != -1)`), write that line into the output file.

The `index` function delivers you an offset into a string. In your example, index would deliver the starting position of the `$value` string within the `$line` string. If a value other than `-1` is returned, then `$value` is a substring of `$line`. This enables you to input the department name or other piece of information, though the field name is "`last_name`" because you can see whether the telephone number, department, etc., are substrings of the line you read in.

If you find what you are looking for (i.e., `$value` is a substring of `$line`), the line you read in is written to the output file. Once you have completed the input file, finish up the output and tell the browser the location of the output file (`print $LOCATION;`).

You could actually output everything to the `stdout` rather than to a file. I prefer this method because you have a kind of buffer between the script and the page. I can prepare everything before I send it to the user.

One expansion of this script is to search for individual fields. In this current state, you look for a string *anywhere* in the record. You could search in just specific fields–for example, for departments–by having a radio button then switching which field is searched based on what button is active.

Another expansion would be checkboxes that determine which fields are displayed. You may only want to see just the name and phone number, for example.

Remember that you can execute system commands from within a `perl` script. If you wanted, you could execute a program that read information from a database. Provided that the output of the database query was in a form that the CGI interface understood, you could use the query program directly.

My opinion is that you should create some kind of "wrapper" around the database query, such as a shell-script so you can parse all input and make sure that the input is valid. This helps prevent instances in which input is passed along to the database program, which ends up unintentionally executing something.

The next example is a bit more complicated. The HTML for the form looks like this:

```
<HTML>

<HEAD>
<TITLE> Pick-a-Car</TITLE>
</HEAD>

<BODY>
<left>
<H1>Pick-a-Car</H1>
</left>
<FORM METHOD=POST action="http://www/cgi-bin/pick.pl">

<BR>
Where do you work?
<input NAME="work" VALUE="Admin" type=radio checked>
Administration
<input NAME="work" VALUE="Personnel" type=radio>
Personnel
<input NAME="work" VALUE="IS/IT" type=radio>IS/IT
<BR>
What is your form of address?
<input NAME="title" VALUE="Mr." type=radio checked >Mr.
<input NAME="title" VALUE="Mrs." type=radio>Mrs.
<input NAME="title" VALUE="Ms." type=radio>Ms.
<input NAME="title" VALUE="Miss" type=radio>Miss
<BR>
<BR>
<Select multiple name="occupation">
```

```
  <OPTION>Clerical
  <OPTION>Consultant
  <OPTION>Corporate Executive
  <OPTION>Educator
  <OPTION>Lawyer
  <OPTION>Manager
  <OPTION>Physician
  <OPTION>Student
  <OPTION>Technical Specialist
  <OPTION>Unemployed
  <OPTION DEFAULT>Other
  </SELECT><P>
  <BR>
  I use my car for
  <input NAME="use" VALUE="fun" type=checkbox>fun
  <input NAME="use" VALUE="work" type=checkbox>work
  <input NAME="use" VALUE="education" type=checkbox>
  education
  <BR>

  <B>
  First Name:
  <INPUT NAME="firstname" type=text maxlength=50 size=50 >
  <BR>
  Last Name:
  <INPUT NAME="lastname" type=text maxlength=50 size=50 >
  <BR>
  I would like a car that seats:
  <BR>
  <input NAME="size" VALUE="tiny" type=radio checked >
  2<BR>
  <input NAME="size" VALUE="small" type=radio>4<BR>
  <input NAME="size" VALUE="medium" type=radio>6<BR>
  <input NAME="size" VALUE="large" type=radio>8 or
more<BR>
  <HR>
  <input TYPE=submit>
  </FORM>
  </BODY>

  </HTML>
```

You might use the form in Figure 14.6 to get information about a car. You input the necessary criteria and the form finds you the right car (well, sort of). Here you introduce the input types `radio` and `checkbox`. A radio button is so named because it behaves like the buttons on a car radio. You can only press one at a time. If you press one, the other is popped out.

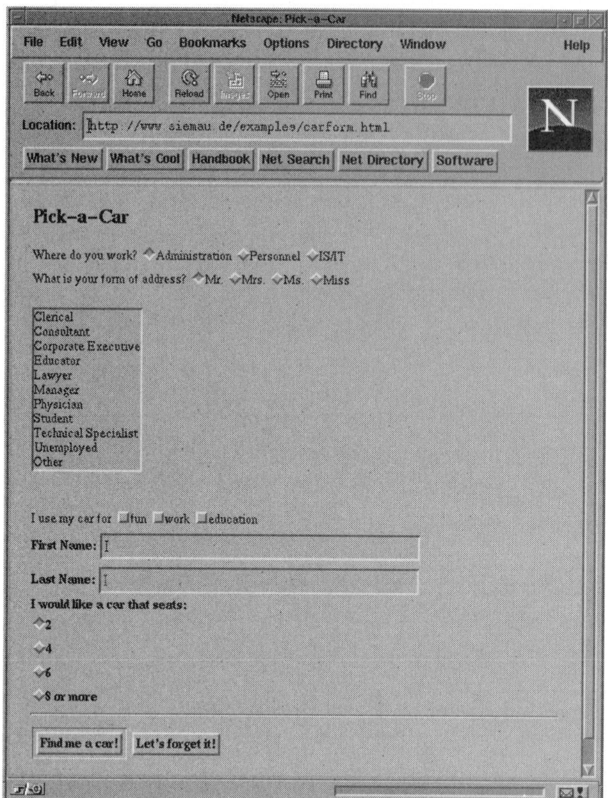

Figure 14.6: Example Form

Here, when you select one button, the other button is de-selected. In this example, several variables are defined via radio buttons, such as the form of address and the department. Normally, you are called by a single form of address and belong to a single department. Additionally, when looking for a car, you have an expectation of how many people it can seat. This, too, is a radio button.

On the other hand, what you use the car for could be several different things. For example, you might use it for fun and business, so that option is a checkbox instead of a radio button. In this example, you see again that each field is split out of the `QUERY_STRING` by the line

```
@data = split (/&/, $form_info) ;
```

This is the further split into the field name and value in the loop:

```
foreach $line ( @data ){ ($field_name, $value ) = split (/=/, $line) ;
```

Each time through the loop, you check for various field names, such as `firstname`, `lastname`, and so on. The `split` line separates each entry in the array `data` one at a time into the two variables `$field_name` and

$value. You then check each field name to see whether it is one of the fields for which you are looking. Here I used an interesting trick that perl allows you to use. For example, the block that I used to get the first name looks like this:

```
if ( $field_name eq "firstname" )
{
      $$field_name = $value;
}
```

In this example, if the $field_name variable has the value "firstname," I enter that block. I then assign the value of that variable to a new variable, $$field_name. There are two dollar signs ($$) here on purpose, which as you talked about earlier allows you to create a variable with the name that $field_name expands to. The variable $field_name is expanded to be the name of the field that is passed through the QUERY_STRING–in this case, "firstname." Because there is a second dollar sign, I now have the variable $firstname, which I assign the appropriate value. In this way, I have a variable that has the same name as the variable that was passed from the form.

At the end of the script, output a few lines to the output file that create a link to the appropriate HTML page. Output a simple greeting, using some of the values you got from the form and write them to the output file. These lines look like this:

```
  print PAGE "<B>Hello ".$title." ".$firstname." ".$last-
name." of the ".$dept." Department</B><BR>\n";
  print PAGE "<BR>\n";
  print PAGE "You requested information on a car that
seats  ";
```

Then output the URL to the file containing the information for the car that you selected. For example, if you had chosen a car that seated two, you would want the page tiny.htm. The block would look like this:

```
  if ( $deliver eq "tiny" )
  {
      print PAGE "2<BR>\n";
      print PAGE "That would be the  <A HREF=\"http://www/
produkt/tiny.htm\">
      Tiny Series</A><BR>\n";
  }
```

Note that you need to escape the double quotes (using \") to keep them from being interpreted by perl. When the page is finished, click the words “Tiny Series” and to be taken to the right page. Finally, at the end, tell the CGI interface the location of the URL with

```
print $LOCATION;
```

Adding all the components together, you get a perl script that looks like this:

```
srand(time|$$);
$random=int(rand(1000))+1;
$last_name == "";
$title = "";
$dept = "";

$request_method = $ENV{'REQUEST_METHOD'};

if ( $request_method eq "GET" ) {
       $form_info = $ENV{'QUERY_STRING'};
} else {
      $size_of_info = $ENV{'CONTENT_LENGTH'};
      read (STDIN, $form_info, $size_of_info);
}

$TEMPFILE="/temp/".$random.".htm";
$LOCATION="Location: http://www.our.domain".$TEMP-
FILE."\n\n";
$OUT="> "."//www.your.domain/".$TEMPFILE;

open (PAGE, $OUT);
print PAGE "<HTML>\n";
print PAGE "<HEAD>\n";
print PAGE "<TITLE>Just a third Test</TITLE>\n";
print PAGE "</HEAD>\n";

print PAGE "Your Query String is: ".$form_info."<BR>\n";

@data = split (/&/, $form_info) ;

foreach $line ( @data ){
($field_name, $value ) = split (/=/, $line) ;

if ( $field_name eq "firstname" )
{
               $$field_name = $value;
}
if ( $field_name eq "lastname" )
{
               $$field_name = $value;
```

```
  }

  if  ( $field_name eq "title" )
  {
                 $$field_name = $value;

  }
  if  ( $field_name eq "work" )
  {
         $value =~ s/\%2F/\//;
          if ( $value eq "" ) {
                   $dept = "Unknown";
         } else {
                   $dept = $value;
         }
  }
  if  ( $field_name eq "size" )
  {
         $size = $value;
  }
  }

  if ( $last_name eq "" ){

         $last_name = "Man without a name";
  }
  if ( $title eq "" ) {
                   $title = "Mr.";
  }
  if ( $dept eq "" ) {
        $dept = "Kitchen"
  }

  print PAGE "<B>Hello ".$title." ".$firstname." ".$last-
name." of the ".$dept." Department</B><BR>\n";
  print PAGE "<BR>\n";
  print PAGE "You requested information on a car that
seats  ";

  if ( $size eq "tiny" )
  {
         print PAGE "2<BR>\n";
         print PAGE "That would be the <A HREF=\"http://
www/Products/tiny.htm\">Tiny Series</A><BR>\n";
  }
  elsif ( $size eq "small" )
  {
         print PAGE "4<BR>\n";
         print PAGE "That would be the <A HREF=\"http://
```

```
www/Products/compact.htm\">Compact Series</A><BR>\n";

  }
  elsif ( $size eq "medium" )
  {
         print PAGE "6<BR>\n";
         print PAGE "That would be the <A HREF=\"http://
www/Products/medium.htm\">Medium Series</A><BR>\n";
  }
  elsif ( $size eq "large" )
  {
         print PAGE "more than 8<BR>\n";
         print PAGE "That would be the <A HREF=\"http://
www/Products/large.htm\">Large Series</A><BR>\n";
  }
  else
         { print PAGE "Sorry no car like that.<BR>\n"; }


  print PAGE "</HTML>\n";
  close PAGE;
  print $LOCATION;
```

The result returned from this form is shown in Figure 14.7.

Think back to the section on writing `perl` scripts (see Section 4.6, Perl: The Language of the Web). Remember that there was a script that would search through a list of books looking for specific information. You could even tell the script what field it should look in for the information you were searching for.

Well, imagine that you are a bookstore that sells many (if not all) of your books through mail order. You decide to start selling books on the Internet as well. Because you are an exclusive bookstore, you only sell a small list of selected titles, so the `bookdata.txt` file that you used earlier by coincidence happens to be your complete list of titles.

Wouldn't it be nice if you could let your customers search through your database for books? Once they found the books they were looking for, they could click a link and order that book. Fortunately, it's not too hard. Many businesses are doing it, not just bookstores.

You can create a very simple form and then modify your `perl` script to access the input from the form.

Depending on how large and complex the database is, using a `perl` script may not be the answer. Instead, you might want a more powerful database tool. One tool that is idea for this purpose is `/rdb` from Revolutionary Software (*www.rsw.com*). With this suite of programs, you can

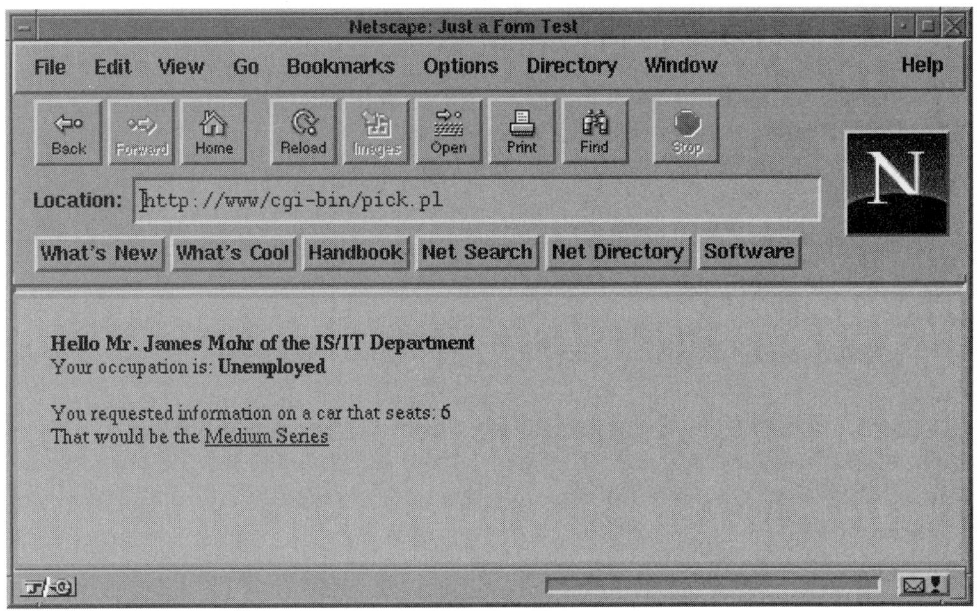

Figure 14.7: Results of CGI Script

build, manage, and access a relational database. `/rdb` does not have the fancy GUI that comes with many databases; instead, it was designed to run from the command-line. To me, it just follows the UNIX mentality of giving you the tools to create things the way you want. (And I wouldn't have mentioned it if there wasn't already a Linux version.)

14.3.3 Tips and Techniques

As you create the Web site, you must keep in mind how different Web browsers will to present the pages. Although there is a standard (HTML) that defines specific aspects of the formatting, how it *really* looks on the page will be different from browser to browser. Be careful to format so that the page can be used on all browsers.

You must test all your pages with more than one browser and from more than one system. I have experienced many times when a Web site developer *assumes* that I have the latest version of Netscape or Microsoft Explorer and the page looks terrible without it. One common problem is the use of frames. Newer versions of Netscape and MS Explorer can handle then, but few Linux browsers can, even the Netscape versions available for Linux.

Another problem is the resolution of the video card and monitor. I have written pages myself and have come up with a great-looking graphics only to find it looks terrible on another system with a lower resolution. Here again, it is an issue of testing the Web page.

Every browser can display any ASCII text files. However, the only formatting ASCII knows is spaces, carriage returns, etc. It is the browser that does word wrap if the line gets too long.

Always include a date of the latest version of the site. It may be sufficient to have a date on your home page to indicate the date the site was updated. It doesn't take much work to do it for every page, but it will depend on the layout of each page and how the date looks.

Remember that the page may be viewed by an international audience. Dates are not written in the same format everywhere. What does the date 01/09/96 mean to you? Is it September 1 or January 9? In the U.S., it means January 9, 1996. In Germany, however, this is September 1, 1996. It would be clear if you said Sep. 9, 1996, or 9 Jan. 1996, or something else that spells out the month. No matter what order it's in, it will be clear.

Always include some way to send comments to the Webmaster, either as a form or simply as a link to an e-mail address. In most Web pages, there is a link to *webmaster@company.com*. If you outsourced the pages, this e-mail address is normally someone at the developer's site who can make the changes.

Consider an interactive form that has a spot for the person's e-mail address, but don't make it required. Having an e-mail address on the page is an obvious way to notify users of the address, but you may get more responses with a form with checkboxes and fill-in boxes.

Icons are small pictures or graphics that are used to represent something, like buttons on a toolbar or bullets in a list. A set of icons with a similar appearance gives the pages a consistent look and feel. Icons should be small (less than 1Kb) so that they load quickly. So that each image must be loaded only once, use the same icon repeatedly. Most browsers will store the image locally and then re-use the same image each time a page calls, rather than load from the server each time.

Use the `<TITLE>` tag so that the title of page shows at the top of the browser. This helps to remind users where they are.

Be careful about the `<PRE>` preformatting tag. It may look right on your machine with its specific resolutions, but it may come out weird on another machine. Test it with several resolutions and several browsers.

Writing Styles

Writing for Web pages is not the same as writing brochures or data sheets. The Web is meant to be accessed in a non-linear fashion, that is, bouncing around. That's part of why it's called a Web. Like a spider's web, there is no top or start. The flow of access is in the hands of the reader, not the writer. You must write with this in mind.

Start with summaries, overviews, or the "big picture," and then go into details later from links or images. Let the reader decide how much to read and when. The information that you present to visitors must be downloaded fairly quickly. If something on the site is exceptionally large, you might consider summarizing the document and then placing a link to download the entire document. Consider compressing the document using `PKZIP.EXE` if you are a DOS-head or `gzip` if the site will be accessed by UNIX people. Even if the site is running Linux, you need to consider who the audience is.

By having summaries rather than full text, you can get more info into the hands of your visitors more quickly. This style also enables you to have summaries as the "start" of the document, putting all the choices and options before the visitor quickly.

Document Size Considerations

There is no rule to how big the site should be. However, you need to consider that larger documents take longer to load. If you have a relatively slow dial-up connection (14.4 modem or less), waiting for the page to materialize can be irritating if a home page is too large. Visitors might get upset and stop downloading the page even before it's finished. I know I have. If the page is too small, there might not be enough to tempt the visitor to look further.

I suggest that "main" pages are one or two screens. This gives a quick introduction to what the rest of the site offers. Later, when you have captured the visitor's interest and get into more detailed information, the pages can be longer.

If the document is large, consider placing bookmarks at the top and bottom to different sections *within* the page. Maybe include links at regular intervals throughout the document that jump to the top of the document. You could also have links at top and bottom, such as "Up to (`section_name`)" or "Down to (`section_name`)."

I have seen many pages that have links to within the same page. There might be technical terms defined elsewhere on the page or other information related to the current document. This is very effective if done correctly.

If a browser cannot show the image, it will normally replace the image with a symbol. Although the symbol tells the visitor that an image could not be loaded, it doesn't say which one. You can tell the browser to display specific text if the image cannot be loaded with the `<ALT>` tag:

```
<ALT="image description">
```

Be careful with the size of the images. They may look good and you may think that you *need* that particular image. However, the size might be overwhelming. For example, when preparing a Web site for one company, I included an aerial view of the factory. Although this was a very impressive shot, it was more than 300 Kilobytes. On my machine it was no problem because I was connected via Ethernet to the Web server in another room. However, if customers were to try to view that page across even a 14.4 modem, they would immediately lose interest.

There is probably little you can do about the size of a lot of images. However, you can change the resolution. Even on the best monitors, I have found that a resolution of as low as 75dpi provides the necessary clarity.

In my opinion, a link that says "click here" looks silly. There is no need to tell the visitor where to click. Take an elevator button as an example. It would look silly if one button was labeled

```
press here if you want to go up
```

and the other was labeled

```
press here if you want to go down
```

Instead, the buttons are labeled with just "up" and "down" or maybe even with just arrows. You *know* to press the button to go up. The same applies to links on a Web page. You *know* that clicking the link performs some action. Therefore, it would be better to have something like this:

```
Download a 1200dpi picture of your company president (4.6Mb)
```

The visitor knows that clicking this link will download the image. It may be via ftp or http, but that doesn't matter. It's the result that's important.

14.3.4 The Next Step

I've said it a couple of times already, but the only way to get good is to practice. The best thing is to create a bunch of pages on the local machine and get a feeling for how they look. Make changes and notice how the changes to the source change the appearance in the browser. Because you will do all this locally, you don't have to wait for the long transfers across the Internet.

14.4 Java

I'm sorry to disappoint you, but I am not going to talk about Java. Well, at least I am not going to go into detail. The reason I decided not to go into detail is simply that Java is a programming language. Like C, Fortran, Pascal, or any other programming language, talking about it really goes beyond the scope of this book. However, unlike other programming languages, Java is very new, so many people are unfamiliar with it. Therefore, I decided to give you a little background to help you decide whether it something into which you should look further.

If you already know C, you have a head start in learning Java. Java is similar to C in that it shares some of the syntax. Though both Java and C programs are compiled, Java programs are run from within Web browsers. These programs are given the name *applet*.

A key difference between Java applets and traditional programs is that Java is limited in what it can do. You can create programs in C or another language that directly accesses the hard disk or arbitrary locations in memory, but this is not possible in Java because many of the features of C and C++ have been removed from Java.

Perhaps the most significant benefit of Java is that it is platform-independant, which means that I can write my Java applet on a Linux machine and you can still access it from a Windows 95 machine (provided the browser supports Java). This is because although Java is compiled, it is compiled into an intermediate form called *byte* code. On the local machine, the Java interpreter reads the byte code and executes the instructions appropriate for the local architecture.

For you, the Web site developer, all of this may be interesting information, but does little to help you decide whether Java is right for you. Up to now, I've talked about making your Web site interactive. You get responses from your visitors and the site changes accordingly. Java helps you make a Web site that changes *dynamically*, without intervention from the visitor. Rather than pressing a link to get the page to change, it changes as you watch.

Another key advantage is that you are no longer limited to content types that the client understands. For example, you can have videos running on your Web pages without the client needing to have an extra viewer. With Java, you send both the video and the viewer.

This can actually be expanded to include any type of program, such as a spreadsheet or database. Instead of having the client application on your machine, it will be carried across the network to your machine. Because of its design, Java must only load those parts of the program that you need, so it's a lot faster than loading the entire application from a file server. In contrast to GUI frontends in other applications, the program is local, so you don't need to wait for the request to be sent to the server, evaluated, and sent back.

So, is Java right for you? Well, that depends. Although it does make for an exciting Web site, it isn't necessary to get your business up and running on the Internet. As with other Web page components, you could try creating a couple of Java applets and see what they can do for you.

CHAPTER 15

BUSINESS ON THE INTERNET

- Your company presence
- Developing your website
- Providing services

Without a doubt, the Internet is and will be the medium of the next several decades. Whether the goal is just to disseminate information or to actually conduct business, people all over the world are turning to the Internet and the World Wide Web.

Just what makes this medium so attractive is as varied as the message. This is something that I will *try* to address in this chapter. Unfortunately, I could dedicate an entire book to this (as some have) and still not cover everything. Instead, I am going to just going to give you as taste of the wondrous possibilities that the Web can provide.

To see the extent that the Internet has grown, just turn on the TV. I remember the presidential election in 1992. Many candidates and parties had 800-numbers. In the 1996 election, they had URLs to Web sites. Even as late as 1995, I remember CNN having to explain what the Internet was. Six months later, newscasters were using the term as matter-of-factly as cable TV and faxes.

As coincidence would have it, I am watching the tail end of the Flipper movie as I write this. In the trailing credits, there is a URL for the record company that produced the soundtrack. Magazines no longer have phone numbers and you even find URLs on soda cans.

15.1 Why Do Companies Do Business on the Internet?

Although both the Internet and the World Wide Web started out as non-commercial projects, there is no doubt that business has taken a hold and won't let go. With 100 million potential customers expected by the end of the decade, it's no wonder.

For business, the Internet is not just a new technology–it's a new medium that enables them to both advertise their services and sell them as well. Once the initial investment has been made, you can reach millions of people with almost no extra effort. When you consider how much it costs to send mailers out to just a few thousand people, this is a businessman's dream come true: virtually free advertising.

Well, not quite. There has been a recent change in the way businesses deal with the public. This started when faxes were the new technology. Once an advertiser got hold of your fax number, you were often flooded with advertisements that you didn't want and certainly did not ask for. It seemed unimportant to the advertisers that they were forcing you to pay for their ads. Granted, it was probably no more than a few cents, considering they were making the call, but you were still being forced to pay.

So, if you want to do business on the Internet, my first word of advice is not to force anything on people. Specifically, do not mail your advertisements to people. It is unethical, bad for your karma, and I will hate you! In fact, a lot of people will hate you.

If you don't believe me, check out the Blacklist of Internet Advertisers. This contains not only a list of advertisers that have been blacklisted, but also what other people can do to get back at you. The most gentle methods are filling up your Internet server with so much worthless junk that you will spend days cleaning up. At worst, people can start at legal action against you (and people are winning), and it gets worse. (See Section 15.7.1, Legal Issues.)

In 1995, $2.2 billion was made as a result of the Internet and 2.5 million people made purchases across the Internet. And it is increasing every day. It has been estimated that by the end of the decade, more than $40 billion will be invested each year in Internet-related business, more than 95 percent of business will advertise on the Internet, and the commercial transaction on the Internet will be close to $7 billion.

It makes sense to develop a marketing strategy that includes the Internet. Every conceivable area of interest is covered, so even if you have a niche market, the market is there. Because almost every business will be present on the Internet, the key will be customer service, content, and image.

Services, such as consulting or research, are good products to sell on the Internet because there is no "stock" that you need to keep in a warehouse. However, other businesses that do offer physical goods are just as capable of making their mark on the Internet. I have seen sites from which you can order flowers, books, music CDs, rent-a-cars, groceries, airline tickets, even pizza. Where once your market was the local neighborhood, it is now the world. If you market it right.

One business that has decided to make a business of business on the Internet is Internet Direct. Among its services are Web site development consulting, programming, design, and hosting services, in which they administer your Internet site for you. One of their projects is the GoSite Internet Server, which they developed to make that first step into the Internet much easier, including a domain name service.

The Web has a number of considerable differences from conventional advertising media. For example, you have the potential for 24-hour marketing. Once you go live, users can access your site at any time of the day or night. There is no such thing as prime-time. Your costs are the same whether the site is accessed at 2 p.m. or 2 a.m. This offers an advantage to the people visiting your site in that they can visit when they want to. They decide what they want to see, when they want to see it, and for how long they want to see it.

For the advertiser, your commercials can be longer and provide much more detail than you could do in a TV commercial. Even those half-hour-long "infomercials" are nothing compared to the Web. You could have hours' worth of multimedia presentations that cover your entire product line. The Web can also be interactive, in which what's on the screen is determined by what the user selects. This does not just mean the video the user sees, but the video could be created on-the-fly based on input from the user.

The Web can also be used as a sales tool. On-line forms can be created to enable customers to order from you. These forms could even check your database to see the availability of the product. One site that lists availability of products are the Computer Literacy Bookstores (*www.clbooks.com*). The visitor can also use these forms to ask for more detailed information or even request a visit from a salesperson.

One very useful aspect is access to customer feedback. You can create forms that the visitor can use to tell you exactly what he or she thinks about your site. This can be immediately send to the right department or person without the wait you have with mail-in questionnaires.

Another aspect is that for the people managing your Web site, it is also interactive. To have an effective Web site that keeps people coming back, it has to be dynamic. That means it needs to change often. Although keeping it up to date is not always easy, implementing the changes is. Because Web pages are text files, you can use any text editor to quickly and easily update your page for new products, additions, corrections, and so on.

For most people, not just businesses, the Internet is too new to fully understand the customs and culture. All the interconnected machines have created a community that exists no where else in the world. This is because it is the world. America was once called the world's melting pot because people from all over were "melted" into American society. The society of the Internet is significantly different in that the pieces are not melted together, but rather maintain their uniqueness.

Interacting on the Internet is not the same as when you talk on the phone to a long-time friend or when someone walks into your store. Both the expectations and the behavior are different. In a business where someone just walks in from off the street, it is expected that a salesperson will come up and ask "May I help you?" Although you may be "just browsing," the mere fact that you have physically come into the store means that you have a least a small interest in the product. On the Web, people might browse your store just to see what your Web site is like, without any real interest in the product.

Another difference the Web provides is that it enables you to compete with companies that are many times larger than yours. Perhaps the bigger companies have the budget to get the most powerful machines with the fastest Internet connections, but that doesn't mean they can create an interesting Web site. For example, I can give a box of paints to my two-year-old or to a professional painter. The professional painter may have dozens of graphic artists trying to develop the perfect Web site, but that doesn't necessarily mean they can. I remember something from my class on discrete mathematics when we were talking about permutations and combinations. The instructor said that if you place an infinite number of chimpanzees in front of an infinite number of typewriters, one will eventually type Hamlet. *Eventually.*

If your Web site looks professional, eye-catching, and functional, you *can* compete with large companies. If your pages look good, so do you. I have found many "professional" looking Web pages for companies that I was sure were multinational corporations with hundreds of employees, only to find out that they were just a "mom n' pop shop." Where just "major organizations" (companies, universities, institutes) were the only ones with Web sites a few years ago, now even individuals have pages.

Broadcast advertising, whether it is on TV, in magazines, or in bulk mailings, is the attempt to throw out as much information as possible to as many people as possible. You hope that enough people will find it interesting enough to make the expenses worth it. The Web is different. You tell the people that you have something interesting to show them and hope that they will come by for a visit. You hope that they feel so comfortable and enjoy it so much that they will stay longer and come back again.

What else can the Web offer you? It can save you time and money. My brother-in-law works for Hewlett-Packard and his "team" consists of people spread out all over the world who connect via the Internet to work on their projects. There's no need for him to fly to Europe from his office in Colorado to work with his team. Obviously, my brother-in-law has no extra travel costs.

A few years ago, being on the Internet was as much a status symbol as a means of conducting business. With the possibility that every business and even individuals can get on the Internet, the status has gone. However, it does not change its importance.

15.1.1 Corporate Identity and Your Web Site

Most companies want the same kinds of things. One is a leading edge corporate image. You are out there in the forefront of both business and technology. You are taking advantage of the latest advances to bring the best products to your customers. The Web can help you demonstrate that you can improve a service for customers as well as increase visibility to attract new customers.

One reason many companies get on the Internet is merely to be on the Internet. Simply having a site on the Internet is enough of a prestige issue today that many companies are making the investment for no other reason. In reality, many of these companies would be foolish to do otherwise. Although the Internet was leading-edge a few years ago, today it's standard. If you aren't on the Internet, there must be something wrong with your company.

Despite my recommendation that you get on now, the timing of creating a Web site is a double-edged sword. If you wait too long to get the "perfect" site, your competitor beats you to it. If you create one too fast, you run the risk of making something uninteresting and your customers never come back.

By creating a web site and making information available, you demonstrate that your company cares about its customers and you are willing to explore new technologies. By taking chances, you show that you are also financially sound enough to take the risk. This shows that your company takes advantage of all the available technology to get the resources it needs and doesn't just rely on "old-fashioned" methods. Your company then makes the information available to your customers using the available technology.

This last point is important enough to look at more closely. If you are willing to take chances, then you have the financial stability to take the risk. That is, if your investment is a failure, you can afford the loss. This is the mark of a financially sound company. If your competitor has the on-line tech support, fax-back service, and Web sites, your customers or potential customers may think you can't afford the effort and are not worth their risking investment.

By making these new technologies available to your customers, you demonstrate that you are willing to take on new projects that emphasize customer service, not just profits. People who visit your site will see that it took a lot of time and effort, neither of which can be recovered by the Web site (assuming that your business is not just the Web site, like a mail-order business). For companies that have a product that they aren't selling across the Web, the Web is not an obvious profit center. It is purely for customer service. A company that emphasizes customer service is more likely to get repeat customers and praises from them on the Internet.

Getting positive recognition on the Internet is the key to success in your Web efforts. You can register your site so that people know how to find it if they look for it, but word-of-mouth is one of the best forms of advertising on the Internet. If someone in the *biz.compressors.misc* group mentioned that your site was a great source of information on compressed air technology, people *will* want to check it out. If you're known for bad service, you are likely to be flamed on the Internet.

If your clients aren't on the Internet, you *might* get away with not being there yourself, but that depends on your business. Think about fast food restaurants. Many of their customers *are* on the Internet, but many of these restaurants aren't. Again, it depends on your product. However, you can order sandwiches and pizza on the Internet, so why not industrial compressors?

Maybe your customers are CEOs of companies who have a connection to the Internet for the prestige they get with *their* customers. As more and more operating systems that are "Internet Ready" are being delivered, the number of CEOs and purchasing officers with Internet access is growing. This is expected with new versions of MS Windows and it is certainly the case with Linux and many other dialects of UNIX.

If your customer were connected to the Internet, the help files for your software could contain a link back to your hardware for the latest bug fixes. The information (manuals, data sheets) that is delivered with your products could contain all the necessary information to get more up-to-date information from your Web site. Many browsers are available as freeware for a limited time or for people who do not use them in a business. One alternative would be to provide the browser to your customers. Rather than giving your customer a 50¢ lighter with the company's name on it, you could give them a 50¢ disk that provides them access to a treasure chest of information.

Once, even being on the Internet was newsworthy, but today you have to be first. You have to have the first site in your industry, the first to use a new technology, or the first to provide a unique service. Because the Internet itself is leading-edge, you need to create an image that's *cutting* edge. You want to show to your customers that you break new ground and that you are not afraid to take chances *in the interest of your customers*.

A leading-edge company naturally attracts leading-edge people. You can use this in two ways for your company. First, by demonstrating that your company is innovative and technologically modern, you demonstrate the quality of your product or service. You can expand on this with an "employee of the month" section that highlights the activities of that employee and why he or she became employee of the month. Should you have someone "famous" at your company (someone who developed a special process in your industry, wrote a book, etc.), it might be a good idea to highlight him or her as well. You have experts working at your company, and experts mean a quality product.

Another way the leading-edge nature of a Web site can help your business is through "career opportunities." Many companies post job openings on their Web sites. Because the company is leading-edge, a leading-edge person will want to get in on that and will naturally apply. You might get a lot of people who just think they are leading-edge, but you have a larger pool from which to pick. Also, job postings on the Internet give the impression that you are a vital, expanding company. If your weren't, why would you need to hire new people? If you aren't hiring, maybe you are stagnant.

15.1.2 The "World Wide" Web

When doing business in the Web, you have to be aware that people from anywhere in the world can look at your site and may decide to buy something. One issue that deals with the global aspects of the Internet is pricing. You can sell something for a higher price in Beverly Hills because people will pay more. However, price on the Internet is international. The price you offer a customer via the Web has to be valid for everyone. You may be able to get away with charging more when there are more shipping and processing fees involved, but you must be careful when publishing price lists in this way.

One company for which I worked was a major European manufacturer of industrial machinery. Not only did the prices differ from country to country (even after calculating the exchange rate, import fees, etc.), but the data in the product sheets was different. In certain countries, it was customary to measure the rate of air flow at the start of the cycle, in other countries, at the end. As a result, there were different values. Both were correct, but if they were published without further explanation, people in one country might be confused.

There is also the issue of international trade laws. What is legal in one country may not be in another. Consider the issue of pornography. Not that I am recommending you sell it on the Internet, but it is a good example of this kind of problem. The openness and legality ranges from countries like the Netherlands and Germany to countries like Iran, where you are likely to have a death squad sent after you. There are also strict U.S. laws for exporting certain technologies. Do you know what the laws are governing sending your products abroad and to what countries?

Due to the Internet's very nature, you are going to run into the problem of different cultures. First are issues like pornography or even politics. Criticism of the government is not only legal in the U.S., it is almost expected. In Iraq, it's a capital offense. Then there are language issues. There are a few classic examples in marketing that resulted in major problems. For example, Rolls Royce had a model called "The Silver Mist." No problem, except that "mist" means "manure" in German. Chevrolet tried to market their Nova is South America. Here again, no problem, except when one breaks apart the word into "no va," it means "doesn't go" in Spanish. My mother told me about a detergent that was advertised many years ago called "Dreck." On the one hand, this sounds like a detergent. However, you can't convince people that it can clean clothes when you consider it means "dirt" in German.

15.2 First Things First

The very first thing to do before you start doing business on the Internet is establish your goals. You must specify what you want to accomplish with your Web site. Remember these goals, which, like any business goals, must be realistic. You need to determine *exactly* what you hope to accomplish with your advertisement or Web site. You may spend days getting the right combination of fonts and colors for your magazine ad, so why should you spend less time on a Web page? One advantage of a Web site is that the basic format of each Web page is the same, but you still need to think about it. In fact, deciding how your Web site will look is more important because it has the potential to be seen by *millions* of people.

15.2.1 Plan

Start with the end of the process and work backward. The end result is the sale of one of your products. Start here and work back up through each the step. Examine your current sales process. Where can you integrate the Web into the process? Consider not just how to make sales using the Web, but also how your sales force can use your site and the Web in general. Examine your current marketing strategy. Where can you integrate the Web into this? Here again, consider both sides. How do you market on the Web and how do you integrate the Web into other marketing aspects?

Before you even start writing your first page, you need to plan what you are going to do. Don't just jump in. After defining your goals, determine how you are going to accomplish these goals. Lay out the structure of your Web site *in detail*. Decide what information you want to present and where it should be in your Web. Start collecting information and organize it. From experience, I know that you will soon be overwhelmed with all the information available.

Because you are running your server on Linux, you can take advantage of links to store the information in a Web structure. For example, you have a directory named `images` that contains all of your images. Both the product information and the technical manuals need a picture of the BN56 compressor. You don't need to copy the picture into both these products and technical directories; just make links (symbolic or hard links, depending on the way your system is configured). That way, when the picture is updated, both directories are updated as well. In addition, you don't have to go hunting for all the images to update them, because they are all together in one directory.

Also, define what links you will have, from where and to where. Remember this is a Web, not a tree. You have to learn to stop thinking hierarchically. If you come from a DOS or Windows environment, this is often difficult. Example of links would be product literature that can point to both the sales and technical manuals. Technical manuals can point back to the home page and sales manual and also to tech support.

As you develop your site, the planning continues. You need to prepare to go live. Determine who needs to know that you now have a Web site. Are there trade magazines that you should tell? On what newsgroups can you make an announcement? However, don't make announcement ahead of schedule. Take a lesson from Microsoft. How often did they announce the follow-up product to Windows 3.1 and how often did they keep pushing back the date? When someone tries to access your site, make sure that the site is available. Although you should monitor in advance where you will make the announcement, you *must* be ready.

Brochures give a taste of your quality, a picture of your product or facilities. Equipment manufactures or service providers may have large concept or facility guides. Without clear goals, however, you will never know whether you are successful in reaching those goals. If your goal is merely to have an Internet presence, that's fine. You must know before hand why you want to invest in Internet resources. What do you want to achieve?

Visiting your Web site is the electronic version of visiting the company. Do you present the right company image? Are your people professional? Do you provide the right information/services? The same care needs to be taken as with brochures, press releases, TV commercials, and any other thing you make public.

15.2.2 Forming Your Team

Marketing on the Internet is not a one-person show, unless that's all there is in your business. You need people from all over your company to be part of it. The two most obvious groups are your marketing and technical people, so I will discuss them first. However, because the process of providing your product from start to end involves the entire company, the entire company should be represented in the development of your Web site.

TECHNICAL

Your technical department (such as IT/IS) is responsible for–what else?–the technology. They need to know, among other things

- What are the available technologies?
- What are the current standards? What are future standards in the industry and what does the company want as standards?
- What hardware is available in the company? What needs to be purchased? (The same questions apply to software.)
- What has to be obtained versus what is "nice to have"?

Your technical staff is also responsible for the Web server management. They are responsible for making sure that everything runs efficiently. Part of this includes Internet connectivity. They need to know who the providers are and what they provide. If your Internet gateway is connected to the Internet, there are also issues involved with supporting your intranet and getting it connected to the Internet.

One responsibility of the technical staff that I often see ignored is training. You shouldn't use the "sink or swim" philosophy by throwing new technology at your users and expecting them to use it efficiently. One company for which I worked had people using their word processing program to do spreadsheet calculations and keeping a database in a spreadsheet. This was the fault of the MIS department for not teaching them how to use the technology.

Your technical people won't write up the HTML code any more than they will write up orders using the word processor. However, they are responsible for training the people who do use it. Designate someone to be responsible for the training and the training materials. However, creating the interface between the on-line ordering system and the database would be something for which your technical staff would be responsible.

MARKETING

The marketing department is responsible for developing the overall marketing strategy and managing the marketing programs. In general, they would also be responsible for the overall design of the Web site. They might decide the image of the company they want to present, which probably includes actually writing the text that will appear on many of the pages. Because market research is part of their responsibility, they will need to work closely with the technical staff to decide what questions are asked in the surveys and how the information is to be stored and processed.

CUSTOMER SERVICE

Depending on your organization, this department may also include sales. Customer Service helps define what services can/should be provided via the Web. These might include tech support. If so, Customer Service might help define how the support will be handled, what levels of support will be offered, and so on.

Sales needs to define what information should be monitored to aide in the sales efforts. Because your sales force knows the kind of questions that customers ask before making a purchase, this kind of information can be made available on the Web.

OTHER DEPARTMENTS

Above all, you need the participation of company management. You need their complete support of your activity on the Web. They are the ones who will make or break this effort. If you do not get enough funds to make an effective Web site, you might as well not start. As Yoda said in *The Empire Strikes Back*, "Do or do not. There is no 'try'."

You will also need a bit of legal support. Your legal staff must help you determine what you *can* put on the Internet. Are there any liabilities for making this information public? Was the information provided to you as a result of a non-disclosure agreement? You also need to keep international issues in mind. You can get sued in the U.S. for not displaying a notice that your microwave products should not be used to dry a pet poodle. In Germany, however, adult consumers are expected to have a certain amount of intelligence and should know this is something you don't do. Propagating pro-Nazi material is a guaranteed right in the U.S., but criminal in Germany. The laws are not yet clearly defined, so you must be extra careful.

15.2.3 Establish Ownership

Ownership in regard to a Web site has two aspects. First, you must establish who in your company has the overall say about the way the site is designed and what information is presented: Marketing? MIS? Management? Your company must make this decision, not me. I say, keep MIS out of it. They will tell you what technology is available, but it is up to marketing or management to decide how to use it.

In your company, different people could decide different things. Maybe Management decides the overall format, as this more or less defines the company image. Marketing and Sales then determine the content. You want a single format/style throughout the Web site. Maybe the background for the tech support page is different from that of the marketing page. However, the "feel" needs to be the same. On example of how the departments interact is deciding on how the visitor is to navigate through your site. Navigation needs to be the same or each page, so marketing decides that MIS should create a "toolbar" that works on every page.

For one company, I developed a style guide in which I defined not only what elements should be common on each page but also defined some of the content. For example, part of what we made available online to employees was solutions to common computer problems. The information that was required to be included was who this problem effected (user, administrators, just people in the production halls), what area this problem effected (network to printers to laser jet), and who was responsible for the page (i.e., if errors were found or the procedure was changed). This ensured us that pages would not be orphaned and end up out of date.

Here, too, we defined what standards we would use on our Web site. At the time, HTML 3.0 was not yet finalized, so we decided to use elements available only in HTML 2.0 to ensure that most of the visitors could use the pages. When 3.2 was finalized, we switched the standard.

Content ownership doesn't have to be for the whole site. You could/should have different branches with different ownership. One branch we had was for the technical documentation. We had the entire set of technical documents for all of our products on-line. This branch was the responsibility of our Technical Publications (Techpubs) department, not MIS or Marketing. However, the branches on company history and "What's new" were Marketing's responsibility.

When you define the content ownership, you also must define the procedures. Should everyone/anyone have the right to simply overwrite a page with a newer version? Can you be sure that the pages are checked to ensure all the links are correct? Better have an in-box in which pages are placed and one person/department is responsible for putting them where they belong.

I now get to the aspect of "legal ownership," which is especially important when you outsource the creation of your pages. If you pay someone to create a program for you, you should have the rights to the source code as well as the finished product. The same applies to the Web site. If you pay someone to develop the pages, everything about the pages should be yours. I have seen Web pages in which the "responsibility" for the content belonged the company for whom the site was developed, but the copyright on the pages belonged to the advertising agency.

Think about consultants. I have seen sites for companies that are very impressive and contain a lot of information. However, the copyright is held by the designer! If you pay for it, you should keep the copyright. This is *extremely* important if you put company information on the page, such as technical data. I can imagine a persuasive lawyer telling a jury that the Web page says the information is copyrighted by the consultant and, because the company didn't object for three months, it is the property of the consultant. Even if the lawyer wasn't persuasive enough, you will spend lots of money defending your rights to your property. You must make it clear from the beginning! Therefore, each page should have a statement saying that you have the copyright. For more detail on all this, see Section 12.2.2, Consultants.

If you surf the Web, you will often see a "webmaster" link. The Webmaster is the person who has overall responsibility for Web. When you click the link, you can send e-mail to the Webmaster. Just like a postmaster, a Webmaster does not need to be a real user, but someone should monitor the account for incoming messages.

When developing your site, you must keep in mind that every document used for marketing has its own purpose and longevity. Ads in a newspaper, flyer passed out at a conference, and technical data sheets all have a particular audience and goal. Sometimes these two elements overlap, but despite the different format, each has the goal of "hooking" the reader into wanting more information. If your ad makes it to the papers after the sale is over, it is of little value. If you change the specs on a piece of equipment and the data sheet doesn't reflect this, customers lose confidence in you.

15.2.4 Wait Until You Are Ready

Don't announce the Web site until it is already on the Internet. Don't bring it on the Internet until it is *complete*, and I mean complete! I have been involved in many discussions about this. It is no longer enough to have an Internet "presence." By that, I mean it is no longer just enough to be on the Internet. You must have something to offer.

People will check out a Web site literally within seconds after hearing about it. Imagine the frustration of excitedly typing in a URL about your favorite pastime only to find the entire site is "under construction." That is, a few tidbits are there, but there's nothing new. You wouldn't think of publishing a brochure on a product that is still on the drawing board (maybe you might, but it is not a good idea). How many years did Microsoft promise up the successor to Window 3.1? How annoyed were we when they kept saying "soon"?

There will be a flurry of interest at first and it will taper off (research indicates this is the first two weeks). There has to be something there to keep them coming back!

You should think about announcing in the appropriate news group, but do not advertise. Another key aspect is the word *appropriate*. There may be people in *rec.arts.star-trek* who need a compressor, but announcing your new Web site there will likely cause you to be flamed and to have people avoid your site!

Although some groups "tolerate" advertisements, they are few and far between (as far as I can tell). Internet people do not want to be forced to read anything. They choose specific newsgroups because they are interested, but this is also a choice; they are not forced.

Therefore, it's a good idea to look at the group first before you post anything. You can make your presence known by answering questions about technical problems and help people in other ways. By your presence and the existence of the *@company.com address*, your company is connected with helpfulness and technical expertise.

15.3 Developing Your Web Site

If you are moving documents from one machine to another, you must be careful of filename difference. Remember that Linux can have file names that are a lot longer than permitted under DOS. (DOS has what is called a "8.3" file name.) Also, Web pages conventionally have an extension of `.html` on UNIX machines and `.htm` on DOS and Windows machines. If you develop files on one type of machine and move your completed files to another type of machine, you must be aware of these differences.

You should decide on a standard appearance for your pages. Each page or set of pages should have the same basic layout. It is both confusing and annoying when you have to readjust how you look at each page as you move around a Web site. It is confusing if you put the menu/toolbar on the top on one page and then use a totally different one on the next page. Have a single background and toolbar. Maybe it's at the top and bottom of each page, but make sure it's the same.

Some Web sites break their pages into multiple sets. There might be pages that deal with new developments in the industry and another set of pages that deal with the technical details of the products. It's okay have different styles in each of these sets, provided the style remains consistent with the set and does not stray too far from each other.

Developing Your Web

To develop your Web, you must get the right tools. A couple of Linux tools can help you develop Web sites. If you really want, you can develop the sites on a Windows machine and port them. Although there are some really fancy tools out there, you don't need them. Linux provides enough tools to do a fairly comfortable job. Both `vi` and `emacs` have the capabilities you need. Besides, the Windows-based tools do a lot to hide the actual structure from you. If you get used to not knowing how your Web is really structured, you will have trouble when the tools start to break or you want to expand.

One suggestion is to have two Webs, one for development and one to be live. Changes are first made to the development Web before they go live. Consider also using a revision control system like RCS for your Web pages. RCS is part of the development tools and is very easy to use. Most people I know who use it do so for program source code management, but you can easily use it for HTML source as well.

Establish test procedures for your site. With test procedures and development procedures, you can easily avoid problems in which your site looks "broken." A broken Web site implies a broken product.

One thing to consider is who will test the site. Just like all the other aspects of your Web development, you have to designate who is responsible for the testing *and* who does the actual testing.

You also need to decide what is tested. What is tested will depend on your company and your site. You most definitely need to test all of the aspects of the site that you defined as being a requirement. For example, if you have decided that a toolbar is required on each page, you'll need to test whether it is there. Do all the links work? You could create a `perl` script that searches through the pages for IMG SRC= entries, HREF= entries, etc. and looks for the links and ensures they are there. If not, an error will display.

You need to have someone (maybe several people) test every page and every link. I don't know how many times I have been annoyed when I click a link and get an error message saying the link does not exist.

I also suggest you check the source for each page to discover whether anything is spelled incorrectly (like the name of your own company!).

Test it, and test it again. Test boundary conditions in your forms (0, 1, and infinity). Can you move around freely and easily? Do the links take you where you expect to go and then back again? Are the forms behaving correctly? What happens when someone puts in garbage? Have someone not involved in the development test the site: have Marketing test the techpubs pages and Techpubs test the marketing pages. Look for anything that is bothersome, cumbersome, or just plain annoying. If any department created something that bothers someone else in the company, you can bet that customers may be bothered, too.

HOME PAGES

Your home page is analogous to your company's reception area, where you are greeted by the receptionist and given directions to reach specific offices. Often, you will find a rack of newsletters, brochures, and other material related to the company. Often, you'll find something that tells you what's new in the company.

Your Web site is no different, other than the fact that that it's available 24-hours a day, 365 days a year. The impression your reception area gives customers provides them with a first impression of your company. If it's dark and dirty with brochures scattered all over a table, customers will get a bad impression of the company. If your home page is cluttered, disorganized, and the links don't work, that's what people will think about your company.

What I find most effective in a home page is a quick introduction to the company and its products or services. A toolbar or menu (list of links) then brings you to different parts of the Web site, depending on what you are interested in. One thing that I find to be very useful is a note on the front page telling the visitor when the site was last updated. This is useful for two reasons. It demonstrates that your site is dynamic, that it changes as the needs of the customer change. Also, it is one more service that you provide for your customer. If someone has visited the site before and has seen all there is to see, it'll be clear when he or she comes back two months later whether there is anything new to see.

I can't count the times in which I went to a site and spent 10 or 15 minutes looking to see if there was something new only to find there wasn't. Even if the site isn't updated, if the date is on the home page, I can quickly check and spend my time somewhere else if it hasn't been updated.

Please don't be sly and consider correcting typos an update of your pages. People get annoyed when a new version of software is just bug fixes and will get annoyed in the same way for your Web site. Bug fixes should be for free. The same applies to your Web site. A good technique is simply to put a link on the home page to "What's New." This can then be a page full of links pointing to all the other pages or brief descriptions along with the links. What you put here will depend what you are offering and what's new.

Along with including what's new, you should also include pointers to all your press releases, or at least the newer ones. Some sites provide the same full text versions they would provide to news services. This is fine, but you should also consider having a brief synopsis with a pointer to the full text. Here again, don't force more on your visitors than they want.

Other things that your home page could point to include the following.

- Events
  - Company events (personnel changes, new offices)
  - Industry events (technological advances, conferences, etc.)
- About the company
  - History
  - Current accomplishments
  - Upper management
  - Organization, branch offices
- About the industry
  - White papers
  - Copies of articles (with the authors' permissions)
  - Bibliography
  - Special information/knowledge
- Products
  - Overview
  - Specific lines
  - Order information
- What's new
  - The company
  - The industry
  - The Web site
- Customer Service/Tech Support
- FAQs
- Contact information

You could consider building a menu or toolbar with pointers to each of the main points and then adding an additional menu on each of these pages. For example, Events, About the Company, About the Industry, etc. would all be on the first page. When you click the link to Events, you have a menu that points to Company Events and Industry Events.

You need to keep your home page simple. Make sure it's clear why the page is there and for whom it's there. You want to grab the visitors, either with a "cool" graphic or compelling information. This information could be something right out of your ad campaign ("The most compressed air for the least amount of money") or a description of the contents ("The most complete technical information on compressed air anywhere on the Web"). If you don't grab them, they'll get away.

Paying Attention to the Web Visitor

As you design and write your pages, consider how it will look to your visitor, including includes both novice and expert surfers. Do you take things for granted that only an expert would know? There are certain visual clues that only people familiar with the Web with catch. Often, I find a site in which there is a toolbar, though it doesn't look like one. Because I know what to expect, I know that it is one. Other people who are new to the Web might have trouble.

Think about who will be visiting your site. The expectations of people visiting a manufacturing company site are different from those of people visiting a book publisher's site. Spending $30 on a book only to find it is not worth the paper on which it was printed is annoying. Spending $30,000 on a compressor that is not worth the metal out of which it is made can be devastating. Visiting the Web site of a industrial manufacturer, you would expect much more technical information.

As you develop your pages, consider the different paths that visitors will take. If the visitor is new to the site, he or she will probably move from top to bottom, in order. More advanced users or those who have visited before will probably jump to the links that they know or interest them. Visitors may jump in from anywhere to anywhere.

Multimedia

Multimedia and the Web are becoming almost synonymous. It's hard to find a Web site that doesn't have some kind of graphics, sound, or other multimedia components. The most common components are graphics or images because they are typically easier to produce than videos and are generally smaller than both videos or sound.

In-line images are those within the document that download as you load the document. These form an integral part of the page itself. Without them, the page would lose much of its impact and information. It is important to keep in mind what the image's intention is. Don't use fancy images just to have them. Be clear about what you want to accomplish. I have often encountered sites in which a large image is on the home page. When I use my 14.4 modem to access the Web, it might take 10 minutes or longer to download a single image on a page. Even with my ISDN connection, sometimes the wait is just too long, and I go elsewhere. Just because you have a 45Mbit T3 line does not mean everyone has. Even with my 56k ISDN line, I get annoyed when a Web site has a huge in-line graphics.

You may want to make the image available in its highest resolution, but you shouldn't force this on your visitors. Give them a quick, low-resolution image (a *thumbnail*) and then give them the opportunity to get the full version. In-line pictures can be anchors to any other kind of document (sound, pictures, text). If these other documents are other images, they are referred to as *external images*, as they are external to the original document.

Don't worry about the quality of the thumbnail image. Most monitors cannot handle the resolution necessary for photo-quality images. Besides, it will take quite a long time to download something like that. However, you can still get fairly good quality even at a low resolution.

I recommend that you test your images within the context of the page with several different browsers and at different resolutions. It may look good on your machine when you develop it, but for someone on a different machine with a different browser, it might look bad. You definitely need to try it in VGA mode as well.

Different browsers will support different graphics formats, so you must be careful. The two most commonly supported are GIF and JPG. If your images are either of these formats, you are in good shape. I have never seen a browser that can't handle them (assuming the browser can handle graphics at all). I recommend that you stick with one standard so you know that if your development tools can handle one format, they can handle the other. I recommend that you stick with JPG. You will probably lose some of the resolution compared to GIF, but the images are compressed, and you can have larger images in a smaller space.

Another possibility is a "text-only" page. Many sites have a very simple home page and a link to a set of pages without graphics. These contain the same information as the other pages, but there are no graphics. IBM, for example, has decided that speed is greater than beauty (*www.ibm.com*). As of this writing, they have several links, one to a text-only page and others to HTML 2.0 and HTML 3.0 pages.

I had a whole list of pages to which I wanted to make references. When I went back, however, I found that they had all changed. To get a feeling for what looks good, therefore, start with one site and go from there.

Don't use true-color images. They may look good on your machine, but most people can't display them. Besides, the size of the image will probably be too large for most people to wait for, and they will quickly lose interest. Best to stick with 256 colors, despite the limitations in displaying "lifelike" images. Do you really need pictures with that kind of detail? If you have to do so, use links to the true color images and give people the choice.

15.3.1 Accessing the Information

Even if you have the web site with the most extensive library of technical information in your field, it does little good if no one can find their way around. You therefore have to make sure that you can easily move around the site.

MENUS

Perhaps the most common way to navigate through a Web site is to use a series of menus. Menus are incredibly easy to create–just use links to new pages. In fact, if you have a list of key parts of your site, you can create a menu simply by turning them into links.

You can use a couple of menu types. If you use just a top-level menu, each entry points to just a few key pages. If you have top- and middle-level menus, each key area has its own menu pointing to pages that have even more detail. You could expand this even further so that there is a menu at every level.

Information is useless if you can't find it. Along the same lines, a Web site that provides "The most complete technical information on compressed air anywhere on the Web" is worthless if people can't find the information. You need to make it easy for them.

You can make accessing the information easy in several ways. The simplest way is with a menu system, as I talked about in the section on your home page (see Section 15.3, Developing Your Web Site, Home Pages). You don't need any special graphics, just a few lines of text with the appropriate links. This leads the customer to the right page.

One nice modification that you can make is turn your menu into a "toolbar." You can then put one on every page to make navigation through the site very easy. The simplest way is to have small images as your hot spots. The problem with this is the way the images might look with different viewers or different resolutions. For example, you might develop them to appear in a straight line across the top of the screen. If you suddenly have a lower resolution, the images are spread across multiple lines.

Another nice effect is to create a single image that looks like the toolbar. You must also be careful about different resolutions, but you don't have to worry about images splitting up. Each part of the image is a link to a different page. To do this, use the maps I talked about in Section 14.3.1, HTML: The Language of the Web, Maps.

You can create toolbars in a couple of ways, just as with menus. You can have a single toolbar that is the same on every page, such as

```
Home page - Products - What's New - Customer Server
```

or you could have different toolbars on different pages. One way is like in Intel, where one of the buttons is "disabled." Another way to do it is to use the toolbar, instead of menus expanding out. For example, on the home page, the syntax would be

```
Products - What's New - Customer Server
```

On the products page, you would write

```
Home - Compressors - Dryers - Blowers
```

On the compressors page, write

```
Home - Products - Industrial - Home - Mobile
```

And on the industrial page, write

```
Home - Compressors - Manuals - Ordering
```

Another alternative is to have a toolbar at the top of page related to the page you are currently on, such as the example preceding. Then at the bottom of each page is a toolbar that's the same on each page (i.e., a table of contents). Or you could have the opposite, in which the table of contents is on the top and the specific toolbar is on the bottom.

Your pages should be designed to look good on smaller screens as well as larger ones. Part of ensuring this is to limit the amount of scrolling. A couple of screens is okay, but not more. That's why they are called pages. They should contain as much information as a page in a book. Personally, I feel that pages that require you to scroll only once are more effective than those that require you to scroll more often. However, you need to be careful and see how it works on different monitors with different resolutions and with different browsers.

Please design pages so you don't have to scroll horizontally (i.e., use a very wide image). The browser should take care of wrapping the text properly, but I have found some sites that have images that could only look good on a 20-inch or larger monitor.

Searching for Information

Another way of navigating through a Web site is to search for information. Some sites are just search engines, such as Yahoo, AltaVista, Lycos, WebCrawler, etc. However, many sites have search mechanisms themselves with which you can search for particular documents or pieces of information.

You can create indexes that perform the same function as those in books. That is, they are static. You as the Web developer build an index that you then make available to your visitors. This is easy to program because you don't have to watch for things like capitalization, tense, singular/plural, and so on. You decide what entries to make available.

However, this does not take full advantage of what a Linux system can provide for you. You can create indexes dynamically with a `perl` script in which you search for the text that the user input. If a page is found containing this information, you can dynamically create a Web page that points to this information. How complex you want to get is entirely up to you. The advantage is that whenever a new page is added, you don't need to change the index.

Another advantage is from the visitor's point of view. A site with a dynamic index is an active site. The site reacts to input from the visitor and doesn't just sit there. The visitor has control over what the site does.

If you decide to use a dynamic search, I suggest including a list of words to ignore. These are words that will more than likely appear on every page. These shouldn't be searched for. Examples of such words are "is," "are," "and," "the," "or," "not."

Although it makes programming more complicated, consider having a radio button that switches between Boolean AND and OR. Some sites have very complicated search mechanisms, such as "a AND b NOT c."

Another way of improving user friendliness is to parse the input and specifically look for "and," "or," and "not." This enables the user to input somewhat complicated statements. However, it does require a little bit of programming on your part.

Hewlett-Packard (*www.hp.com*) has a page that helps you find the right printer. The normal consumer may not know the name of the model for which he or she is looking. HP has an index that you can use to search as well as an alphabetical list in which you can click the letter to get to that part of the index.

If you have information from different departments, you need to consider what other people might call a specific department. For example, your company might call the department responsible for new hires and other personnel issues the Personnel department. However, in certain politically correct companies, this is called the Human Resource department. Some more examples of this

Personnel: Human Resources

Marketing: Publicity, Public Relations

Support: Customer Service

15.3.2 Engage the Visitor

You have to be able to catch and keep your visitors. Someone "stopping by" your Web site for the first time is like a shopper who walks into a store to look around. If the first impression is bad, that shopper is not likely to stay or ever come back.

The sides of the Web site have two different perspectives. Customers who are looking for products are task-oriented while sales people tend to be product-oriented. For example, the customer asks, "Do you have something in your product line that can do X?" The salesperson, on the other hand, says, "Here is our product, Y, which can do X."

Because you are the salesperson, you want to tell the visitor (customer) about the wonderful qualities of your products. However, the visitor is interested in achieving a particular goal. Your goal is to tell the customer what your product can do to help him or her achieve his or her goal. This is a basic part of marketing that applies to all media, including the Web.

Advertisements, whether on TV, in magazines, or on the Web, have to get the customer involved. On one dimensional media like TV or magazines, the interactivity is more emotional or intellectual. There is no participation from the visitor. This has changed with the Web. The visitor can interact with your advertisement. The visitor's being able to do so effectively is a primary reason for the success of your Web site.

Much of the appeal of the Internet is *interactivity*–you push a button and something happens. Maybe it is just as simple as going to another page, or it could be more complicated, as when the visitor inputs values into a form and searches through a database or makes calculations to find the optimal airflow of a compressor.

Even the simple action of clicking links is interactive. Visitors can follow "threads" of interest throughout your Web site. This nurtures their interest in your company and gives them a reason to browse for a while as well as come back again.

Like a brochure, a Web site can be read at any time. So, why is the WWW so captivating? For those with some computer skills and a little familiarity with the Internet, there is the thrill of reading a page that is actually sitting on machine on the other side of the world. I still feel the thrill of clicking a link and knowing that somewhere in Finland, a hard disk is spinning to find the right page, the CPU (still in Finland) is copying the individual bits from the hard disk to the network interface card, through the network connections, through two dozen other machines until it gets to my ISP, and then through the telephone lines, into my ISDN card, and into my machine.

Part of the captivation with the Web is that you become involved. You control the action. Therefore, you Web page is not something to read. It is something to do!

Remember, if you read something, you become aware of it. If you see something, you can understand it. If you do something, you know it. With just text, your Web page is just read in a passive manner. However, a Web page in which the visitor makes choices, decides, and takes action is *interactive*–it is something that will make the visitor "know" your site. The result is longer participation.

15.4 Content: Service to Your Customer

So now that you have decided to use the Internet, what next? What can you offer to your customers? Well, you can offer a wide range of things on the Internet. The most obvious is marketing. For commercial organizations, this is most common. Although using the Web cannot replace the other forms of marketing (at least, not yet), it can provide a valuable compliment to your existing marketing strategies.

A key part of developing a good Web site is what you provide. There might be a lot of interaction with the site, but if the information it provides is worthless, why stick around? It is therefore important to make sure that what you give the visitor is something he or she is looking for.

The Internet mentality is one of support. In the beginning, the Internet was not easy to use and old-timers were always ready to help the newcomers. Programmers came up with utilities to help people accomplish specific tasks, which were then made available to everyone. The people who used the programs then made their programs available to others. Originally, the Internet and WWW were used by research and educational institutions who made their information freely available.

Today, providing information on the Internet for a fee is not unheard of. In fact, many businesses that run on the Internet only provide the service of information. Regardless of whether it is for free or for a fee, they still maintain the spirit of the Internet of giving something back.

One key aspect to marketing on the Internet and WWW is to provide "value-added marketing." By offering "something of value" for free, you are "proving your worth" as a vendor, delivering a valuable service or product *before* making the sale. What you make available is unique to your business. It could be research information or detailed technical information about your field. Even if you do charge for most of your information, you could provide enough for free to "tempt" others to come back.

15.4.1 Information

The Internet has a tradition of "giving back to the Internet." You can do a lot for your company's image if you create a Web site that gives something back to the Internet. This makes a value-added Web site. Depending on your type of business or company, you could provide a lot of information. Trusted Information Systems, Inc. (TIS), is a consulting firm that specializes in network security (*www.tis.com*). They have many things related to security on their Web site, all of which are free to everyone. This is the value that they give back to the Internet.

You may not want to publish trade secrets on the Internet, but you should make available things like the information that appears in brochures or on data sheets. One suggestion is to use a glossary of terms related to the business. This would keep customers coming back and establishing name recognition. How about a glossary in 16 different languages?

To find out what you should put on your Web site, ask your customers. Because the market keeps changing, ask them again and again. Use surveys to make additions/changes to the Web site. Look at other Web sites in your industry; find out what other people are doing. You may find interesting things, but make sure you don't copy their pages.

You can ask newsgroups related to the industry, but don't give away your marketing strategies. Ask your business partners, distributors, vendors. Maybe they have ideas, suggestions, or even resources for you, which would make your site valuable to customers as well. Ask your sales, customer service, and support departments: Customer Service knows frequently-asked questions, Sales knows what people look for in marketing the products, and Support knows the problems

Maybe you have information that you don't want give away to just anyone, let alone for free. Therefore, you could split up the information on your site. Some is available for anyone, and some is available for "members only" or only after visitors answer questions in a survey. What about the information that people are willing to pay for? Why not charge? If you spend money/time to gather this information, why not charge? This is easily accomplished by your Web server, so take a look at Section 14.2.2, Configuring the Web, to set up your Web server.

Once someone finds your Web site, you need to give them a reason to stay and then come back. Why would a visitor stay or come back? Curiosity, for one thing. If there is a lot of *interesting* information and there's too much to see during one visit, they will come back. I have been to the TIS site a few times. Although I download a lot of the information to which I want quick access, I don't need to copy it all.

Keep in mind that accessing the information must not be confusing and finding the information must not be difficult. If it is, the visitor may think that information is not worth the effort.

You also need to consider *item turnover*. In other words, it is a good idea to provide information that changes frequently or maybe even every time the person visits. Maybe include a "What's new" section that contains news items related to your company specifically or even your business or industry in general. Here you could also include press releases. You could keep older press releases in an accessible archive so a visitor can get a feeling for the history of the company.

One key to keeping customers coming back is to make your site an indispensable tool or resource. Not only do you have your own *extensive* database of industry-related information, but you also have links to other databases, archives, repositories, or other Web sites. As the springboard to information about the industry, your Web page will draw people in and keep them coming back.

There is also the aspect of the interactivity and "up-to-date" character of the Internet. A friend of mine has a site that shows his pet iguana. This is updated every few minutes, so you have almost "live" pictures of the Iguana. (This is the now famous IguanaCam.) KPIX TV has a splendid view of San Francisco that they update at regular intervals. I also know of sites that show me pictures of a Berlin subway station or downtown Santa Cruz, California. SCO had a camera at CeBit in 1996 that recorded the show every couple of minutes. These are features that attract the visitor in the first place. The rest of the content keeps them coming back.

You could have an "ask the expert" feature that enables the visitors to submit questions through forms or e-mail. This is slightly different than tech support as the emphasis is on industry-related issues and not just your products ("Are air-cooled or oil-cooled compressors better?"). You can then go into the technical aspects of the answer and lean toward your own products, making sure that you don't just spout company marketing propaganda. By giving customers the technical aspects of the answer, they draw the conclusion themselves that your product is better.

If you have specialty information, you may require an account with password. There we enter the area of security. There is the issue of how to get them a password by a secure means. One way is to have them provide an e-mail account to which to send the account information and password. However, no matter for what service or information you charge, you should always provide something for free before you have the users register. If you were to enter a department store and were immediately asked for your name and address and were told you couldn't come in until you were registered, you probably wouldn't even give your name and end up going to another store.

The only exception to this, I think, are sites that offer "adult" material, which should always ask for *verifiable* identification. I don't see this as a violation of free speech, no more than censoring profanity on TV is. Identification is required when you go to a liqueur store to buy alcohol or when ordering "adult" material through the mail. The business owner who requires identification is acting responsibly, whether conducting business through the mail or the Web.

One important aspect is to be customer-oriented, *not* company-oriented. You need to tell visitors what they want to hear, not what just you want to tell them. Tell them opposing sides, including your competition's, to show that you are fair and honest. If you have valid reasons for doing something different than the way your competitor does it, here is your chance to convince potential customers of this. If they then go to the competition who tells them that the other way is better but has no valid argument for it, you probably have a new customer.

Provide information that will be useful for making the decisions. White papers and research papers about your industry/business and not just your company are excellent ways of providing a service to your customers and showing them that you have the necessary know-how and expertise.

Consider a searchable index for other resources in your business; not just other Web sites, but addresses of research institutions or places to get hard copy documents.

If you have “famous” people (such as authors, inventors) in your company, it’s good to highlight them. This adds credibility to your company (even if they are not directly related to the business). For example, I worked in one company where the head of the press office wrote books about local history. Although this person’s special ability did not directly associate with the business, it demonstrated the quality of people who are associated with the company.

Be careful of what you make available. We had an information seminar consisting of dozens of slides contained in several files that people wanted on the Internet. In total, it was more than 35Mb. You don’t want people downloading this every time they need it. Alternatively, we could have broken it down into one file for each slide and had our people download only what had been changed.

By designing the presentation as HTML, you can make the presentation available to anyone on the Internet as well as your sales force. You can include presentations, proposals, schedules, and product information. However, you need a balance between what you want to say and what the visitor wants to see.

Even if something is freely available from another site (no copyright), there is no need to make a copy of it on your local machine; just have a link to another site.

15.4.2 Marketing

The first part of Web marketing is getting visitors to your site. There are several ways of doing this. The first way is to tell them. There are several sites where you can register your site. These serve as directories that others can access. There are other search engines with which you can search for not only Web sites, but also most any type of Internet resource related to your search criteria.

Another alternative is to use cross-links. If one of your customers already has a Web site, it would be in both your interest to refer people to the other’s site. You could have a company profile that describes the success of a company that uses your products, and they can have a link saying that they only use the “best components.” In one company where I developed an Internet site, we had cross-links to both our computer hardware and software vendors.

Another very successful way is to print your e-mail address and Web URL on all of your printed material, including not only business cards but anything else you print up, including·

- letterhead
- all stationary
- flyers
- brochures
- fax coversheets
- press releases
- notebooks
- folders
- report covers
- promotional gifts
- newsletters
- bulk mailing items
- ads in magazines, newspapers, TV, billboards, product labels, etc.
- anywhere your name appears

If your customers are on the Internet, they will understand what it means and will be curious to see what you have. If they don't understand, seeing the URL will prompt them to ask you what it means. This opens the opportunity for you to explain the additional services you can now provide.

I remember, during the primaries and elections, that almost everywhere you looked were URLs for the various candidates or parties. Even during the last election, there were 800-numbers to call. Now, the Web seems to be the media of choice. I have also seen TV ads containing URLs for non-computer-related companies. Some have even gone so far as to include their URL on their product labels.

To be successful, Web-based marketing must be integrated into your overall marketing strategy. You can't present one face in your magazine ads and another on your Web site. Therefore, you need to integrate your Web presence with other on-line activities and your existing "traditional" advertising and marketing.

You can also use the Web for marketing research. If you provide information for which the visitor has to pay or register to access, you will automatically get information when the customer opens an account or registers. Additionally, part of the registration process could be a customer survey. However, *never* force a survey on your customers. I have been to sites that have an interesting home page and one "What's Inside" button. This takes you to a marketing survey and the only way to get to the meat of the site is to answer their questions. Was it worth it? I don't know because I moved on before I even answered the first question.

The surveys you provide can cover many different aspects. You could have product interest or reaction surveys that address people's attitudes toward existing products as well as their interest in having you add products to your line. You could also have some general demographic questions such as gender, occupation, geographical area, etc. One suggestion is to have a contest in which the visitor needs to provide certain information in order to register.

You may be thinking that marketing isn't really a service that you are offering your customers. However, I support the position taken by commercials that I see repeatedly on CNN International. Advertising is your right to choose. Without it, we would be limited to the number of products available in our local store. If the local store chose to sell only one brand, that might be the only brand we know about. With advertising, we learn about alternatives. It is in this regard that marketing is a service.

In advertising research, you try to evaluate the effectiveness of your advertising expenditures. Did you earn more as a result of an advertising campaign than you spent? Based on what you find out, you use this information as a guide for future efforts.

Market analysis and forecasting is the attempt to identify and measure the market for specific products. You estimate the sales possibilities for particular products and in particular areas. Performance analysis helps you evaluate how well the marketing is meeting its objectives. For example, one objective might be to increase your share of the market by 10 percent. You analyze the market to determine if you have, in fact, increased your share by that 10 percent.

Product research is identifying the needs of the consumer and well as their characteristics. If you can identify what types of people use your product, it is easier to mold your marketing strategy to fit them. Part of this includes testing your product and its design. Keep in mind that this is not exact. Market research indicates conditions and trends. There is always a level of uncertainty.

Market research begins with the preliminary analysis. Here you need to identify factors that influence your analysis, including not only the factors that could influence the purchase of your product, but also the factors that could influence the data that you collect. For example, if you sell bathing suits, the time of year influences the purchase. If you are gathering some of your data through a survey, you need to be aware of what groups are more or less likely to take part in the survey. Also, you must consider variable factors. For example, if you have an international market, the exchange rate between U.S. dollars and the foreign currency is a variable factor.

Next, you need to define the problem or question. What are your trying to learn? Is it a trend? A particular value? Once you have defined your objective, you can begin to plan the research. Here you determine what information is important and how it will be collected. Do you yourself count sales over the last year or do you conduct a survey? How will you then organize the data to allow proper analysis?

The next step is collecting the data. Using the method or methods you chose previously, you gather as much raw data as possible through experimentation, surveys, or even external sources such as government reports. Then, once you have the data, you can begin to analyze it. After you analyze the data and draw your conclusion, you can present the result to the proper people (usually management).

There are several other aspects of market research that I did not address here, but they go beyond the scope of this book.

Advertising is an attempt to elicit a particular response. When a political candidate advertises, the desired response is that you vote for him or her. In business, the desired response is that you buy a particular product. Until recently, advertising was distinguished from other forms of communication in that the advertiser pays the media to deliver the message. An advertiser pays for TV time or space in a newspaper. Recently this has changed. Some advertisers are forcing the consumer to pay for the advertisement. On the Web, this comes in the form of junk e-mail.

Let's think about traditional advertising such as bulk mailings. Imagine the customer's reaction if the mail carrier came to the door and demanded 32¢ for a letter. You could see who it was from, but often the return address is just a post office box that doesn't give you a clue about the content. You pay the 32¢ only to find it is an advertisement for something in which you have no interest at all. What would your reaction to the advertiser be?

Sound far-fetched? Well, it isn't. In the past few months, I have had more than 100 such letters. Often, the case is such that I don't even know I am paying for the advertisement until after the money is already gone. The way it happens is this: I have a private e-mail account through an on-line service. Somehow, someway, an advertising company got my e-mail address and has been sending me junk e-mail. Although I can reply with "remove" in the body of the message, they have several e-mail accounts. So, when I mail one to say I want off the mailing list, I never hear from that account again. However, two days later, the next account sends me another set of junk e-mail. I ask to be removed, and two days later, the next sends me something. I am currently up to number 7.

When I get my e-mail, I have to dial up to my on-line service. Unfortunately, this is not a local call for me. When there is junk mail, I have to pay more because the connection is longer. I could get a summary of my mail first and delete those from any accounts at *cyberpromo.com*, but then I still have to make an extra phone call. Maybe it's only an extra 20¢ each time, but this company is forcing me to spend it. If they do a bulk e-mail of the 1 million people that many bulk emails claim to do, that means that Cyber Promotions would have forced people to spend $200,000! Although the company doesn't see any of it, they are still forcing people to spend money. Do you want your name connected to this behavior?

Another difference with advertising is that the advertiser controls the message and, within reason, controls when the message is presented. With the right money, an advertiser determines in what issue of a magazine the ad appears or during what TV program. I remember hearing several years ago that one fast food restaurant would pay networks a substantial sum to determine not only during what show, but exactly what minute the ad would appear. During the most suspenseful moment in the movie, you cut to a commercial of this fast food chain. There is then the association of relief from stress with this restaurant.

On the Internet, this goes even further. You have complete control over the message, including content length and availability. You can have a two-line message or a 2,000-line message. You can make your message available only during the weekends or change it just after the end of the Super Bowl.

What the message is depends not only on the product, but the business that is trying to influence the consumer. A retailer with a wide range of products presents to you a selection of what he is offering. A manufacturer, on the other hand, tries to create brand name recognition so that you will develop a preference for a particular brand. Groups of businesses might join forces to try to sell a generic product. For example, no single company tells you that "It does a body good."

Regardless of the differences, an advertiser needs to know who he or she is trying to influence. In other words, your market and message have to match. You don't place a cigarette ad in Sesame Street Magazine (at least I hope you don't), and you don't try to advertise your Christian bookstore on the Web with pictures of scantly clothed women.

In all forms of advertising, the basic principles are the same. First, you have to define who you are addressing–in other words, your audience. This is your "market." Next, figure out exactly what you want to say. You are not just trying to say "Buy our detergent." Instead, you are trying to say "Our detergent gets clothes whiter than clean and cleaner than white." It is then up to the consumer to say, "Well, if their detergent can do that, I should buy it."

But how do you tell the consumer that the detergent gets the clothes cleaner than white? How should you present your message? What should that message contain? These issues go hand-in-hand. Often the method you use to present the message depends on the message itself. This could be a blatant as very muscular, macho-looking man telling you how manly a particular deodorant is or it could be something as subtle as your choice of colors.

Lastly, you must consider your budget. Potentially, the actual dollar amount in your budget has been predetermined and all you can do is decide where to spend it. But that's enough. Using the amount you have, you determine exactly where to give it out for the mediums and messages you have chosen. Perhaps you want to do both TV and magazine ads, so the amount you spend on each is less. Or you may want to "blitz" all of the magazines and forget TV. Advertising on the Web is similar. You may want just text messages and a few simple graphics. On the other hand, you may want to develop some awe-inspiring 3D graphics. Which you choose will determine how much you will have to give out.

When you advertise on TV, you have the advantage of almost every form of advertising. You have the whole spectrum of multimedia, including video and audio elements. However, like magazine ads, you can use text as well. I have seen some very good TV ads that have just used still pictures and words and some terrible ones that use high-tech graphics. If you chose a purely written media like newspapers or magazine, each has its advantages. If you want something up-to-the-minute or repeated over several weeks, then you probably want to advertise in a newspaper. If brilliant colors are more important, then a magazine would be your choice.

The nice thing about advertising on the Internet is that it can be every one of these or none at all. You can produce high-tech graphics or have pages that consist solely of text with no images at all. Though you probably don't have the budget for a full-time TV production crew, you can create some fantastic Web pages even with a modest budget. It is this aspect that allows even the smallest businesses to compete with the "big guys."

In addition, with other media forms, the big guys can afford more exposure. They can afford more ads in more magazines or on more TV stations. Small firms cannot compete with this. All of that has changed with the Internet. You can afford to put together an advertising and marketing strategy that levels the playing field.

As with other forms of advertising, Web sites are most effective if they do something to make you remember them (hopefully in a positive light). Can you name the product advertised in a series of TV commercials involving a man and a woman in the same apartment building who became romantically involved? (It worked kind of like a soap opera.) Do you know the name of the product that had a series of billboards along the interstate? Even though the billboards are no longer there, we still know the name of the product.

To keep your visitors from flipping channels or surfing to another Web site, your advertisements have to communicate quickly. By this I don't necessarily mean that you have to have short messages, but you have to communicate quickly that your product is better. For example, if you can quickly convey the belief to your visitors that you are experts in your field, then you obviously have a better product. You can do this by showing the visitor just how much information is available on your Web site.

You must attract attention in some way. You must give a favorable impression of your product and your company. I remember a series of ads for a jewelry store chain. The owner came across as an obnoxious jerk. I could not imagine that this guy knew jewelry well enough to sell me anything.

Although most advertisements are more effective for consumer goods, they can work for industrial goods. Remember that most industrial goods are either shopping goods or specialty goods. Someone is looking for the right information to determine what to buy and from whom. By presenting a site with a library full of technical information about your field, you not only present yourself as an expert in the field but also make your site a resource for customers. Your name is now associated with knowledge and information in the field. Like consumer goods, brand names are just as important to industrial goods. You have to get consumers to associate your "brand" with quality and expertise.

One key difference in Internet marketing is that the customer actually goes looking for the advertisement, in contrast to other "in-your-face" advertisements in which the customer comes across it by "accident." Maybe a potential customer is watching a movie or sports event when suddenly there is a commercial break and the message blasts at him or her. It is important not to be blatant with what you are trying to say. You can tell the viewer that you are the best without using those exact words.

When you advertise on a Web site, everyone knows what you are doing. You don't need to be as subtle as in other media. You can get away with saying "We are the best because...." However, you don't need to. Advertising on the Web has the same principles as advertising elsewhere. You can list all the reasons why your product is good and let the visitor make the "logical" conclusion that you are the best.

Intrusive advertising, or forcing your advertising down someone's throat, is frowned upon by the Internet community. When someone reads a newsgroup about genealogy, he or she doesn't want to read ads for discount trips to the Bahamas. The same applies to e-mail. Some people may want this, but the people who don't are a lot louder. By sending out junk e-mail or posting to inappropriate newsgroups, you run the risk of annoying the users of the Internet. In other words, your customers.

On the other hand, with marketing on the Web, you need to attract the attention of your customers, get them to your site. You can't just advertise because you are likely to only get those people who are specifically looking for your product. You have to offer something to get the customer to your site in the first place as well as to stay there. It is important to offer something that will satisfy the need for both quality and service, quality in the product itself and quality in your business as a whole. By using the Web, you can demonstrate both very easily.

Your Web site serves as your storefront or corporate headquarters. It is often more important to make a good impression here because more people will see it. Your Web site and all your Internet activity gives you the ability to not only market your product but spread your reputation (good or bad) as well. "Unacceptable" practices such as junk e-mail and publicizing "questionable" political views can annoy people, causing you to get flamed and damaging your reputation.

Remember that it is more likely that people with a negative reaction to your action will react the loudest. When was the last time you sent a letter of praise to company? If you are like most people, it was probably less recently than you sent a letter of complaint. A key difference is that when you write a letter to a company to complain, usually only the people within the company see it. If someone on the Internet is annoyed by your actions and posts to a newsgroup (or several), there is the potential that *millions* of people will see the post within just a few hours, if not minutes! Remember that it is a lot harder to build your reputation back up once it has been damaged than it is to destroy it in the first place.

WWW marketing is not really though of a mass market, despite the enormously large numbers of users that you can reach. Instead, there is one person using his or her browser to access your Web site. Therefore, much of the approach you take has to be oriented as one-to-one.

15.4.3 Customer Service and Technical Support

Customer service is another area that is increasing in popularity on the Web. In many cases, customer service was the first thing for which companies used the Web, not marketing. This is in keeping with the original intent of the Web as a means of sharing information.

The term "customer service" covers a wide range of areas. It depends on your perspective and company philosophy. I have worked for companies in which there was a blanket term "services." This covered sales, tech support, and traditional customer service. Because there is no limitation to what you can have on your Web site, I am going to first talk about service in general and then get to specific issues related to each of these different areas.

Among the things that you can make available on your Web site are:

- updates
- patches
- documentation
- publications
- technical data of products

These could be the questions that your customer service people hear regularly and for which the answers are simple enough to explain in just a few lines.

One company, the Santa Cruz Operation (*www.sco.com*), has dramatically reduced the number of calls to tech support by providing its complete list of problems-solutions (technical articles) on-line via the Web. This is the same information that is available to the support engineers, and, for the non-novice, answers to common questions are quickly found. SCO realized that it was more efficient to have the customer look for the "canned" answers themselves and made them available. In addition, SCO make most of their patches available via the Web. If you want, you can even get SCO baseball caps and T-shirts via their Web site.

Another way you could provide tech support is to give users the opportunity to post questions. Users can input their questions using simple forms that they can then e-mail to the right person or that can be written to a file. If the question is in the database, give the user the answer by sending the article and telling them how to access it in the future.

Also, consider providing answers by different means. The first method is e-mail, so you need an entry in the form for the user's e-mail address. However, some people might not want the answer by e-mail, but rather by fax. You should then consider having the ability to give your answer by fax. Even if you do provide phone support, you have to be flexible enough to give the answer in the way the customer wants.

For example, I have repeatedly told one support organization that when I fax in question, I want an answer back by fax. I do this for two reasons. First, I don't want to have to explain the question more than once. If I include all the details in the fax, I don't have to tell both the person answering the phone and the technicians. Second, I often want a written record of what they said because I have often gotten answers that contradicted what *I know* or what is in the manual. With a fax, I can hold them to their answer. I have *never* had an answer sent by fax.

For tech support, the disadvantage of providing support like this is that if the question is not formulated properly, you have to contact the customer to get more details. With phone support, there is an immediate response when customer service or tech support isn't clear as to what the question is. When I was in support, I had calls that dragged on for more than a week when the customer would only give half of the answer each time.

If you do answer questions directly on the phone, your support people cannot just repeat canned answers. You have to have people who understand the technical background of the solution as well as the problem.

You need to be careful with this, however. Free technical support is a dangerous thing. First, it isn't free. You have to pay for staff and resources to provide it to your customers. Unless you charge for it (therefore making it not free), there are only expenses and no *visible* income. The income might be seen in the form of more repeat customers or a good public image of your company, but these are hard to measure. (I'll go into this a little more in the section on feedback (see Section 15.5, Measuring Your Success).

If you do provide free technical support, your customers need to be aware of the limitations. For example, let's assume you have a business that provides Linux integration. I would not recommend that you provide step-by-step installation instructions for free unless you have a single document that covers this. However, doing it on the phone or having someone post 30 questions to your Web site would cost a lot of time and money. Instead, free support *should* be limited to quick answers to quick questions. For example

***Q**: I want to make a backup of a small directory to a floppy. How do I do it?*

***A**: Look at the `cpio` or `tar` man-pages by typing `man tar` or `man cpio`.*

This gives the caller a push in the right direction and does not take up a lot of time.

You also need to consider those people who have trouble finding the answer on your Web site or don't have the time. Don't be pulled into the just-one-more-quick-question trap. Give them a gentle nudge in the right direction.

If you have any connection to the Internet, you *have* to have e-mail. Using e-mail is a good way to reach customers and have the customer reach you. It is generally quicker than postal mail and you spend no money on paper or envelopes. If you are already connected to the Internet or connected to set up a Web site, e-mail doesn't cost anything extra. You can read the message and respond all on the same screen. You can even configure you e-mail system to automatically respond if you are out or a customer sends a message to some generic address like *info@company.com*. `sendmail` is complex enough to process the message itself to determine who should get the e-mail.

If your customer service department has a connection to the outside world, they have one more way of providing a service to your customers. You must make clear to both customer service and your customers that, in essence, you provide customer service when it is convenient for the customer. That is, they will e-mail you when they have the time and can read your response when they have the time. Obviously, they can call if that's what is convenient for *them*. In addition, both you and the customer have an automatic record of the message and in some cases you can even get a receipt when the message was delivered.

Communication with customers via e-mail requires more care than communication by phone. You don't have inflection or tone of voice to get part of the message. Your use of sayings or expressions that might be common in your company or region may be misunderstood by the reader. Granted, this is a problem in verbal communication, but you don't have the other clues like tone of voice or emphasis on specific words in the sentence. The entire content of the message is contained in the words.

In addition, because e-mail is a record of the conversation, you need to ensure that you send the correct information. Of course, you need to be sure that what you say over the phone is correct, but you have to be more exact when there is a record. You can't afford a slip of the tongue or slip of the fingers.

I have also seen that people become less formal with e-mail than with phones. You need to be careful with this. This is particularly important in an international setting. I work in Germany for a German company. There are strict rules of address in Germany that are reflected in their language (almost like saying "you" and "thou"). It would almost be an insult to say "you" to my boss instead of "thou," just as it would almost be an insult to call him by his first name. I know people who have worked together for *decades* and they still refer to each other as "Mister So-and-so." When people communicate via e-mail, I have seen people automatically jump into a more familiar relationship and start calling people by their first name. This is acceptable in the U.S., but not in other countries. Therefore you need to be careful.

One key advantage of e-mail is that it is fast. You can configure your system to tell you whenever an e-mail message arrives, but you can read it and respond to it at your leisure.

To avoid an e-mail *faux pas*, you should create a company policy about e-mail usage. This could also be expanded to cover and electronic communication with customers (such as fax). Among the things to stress are clarity and professionalism. You also need to help employees understand that the casual nature of e-mail can be misleading and to be aware of the difference in culture. (This is often difficult for many Americans.)

You need to weigh the cost (both in time and money) by allowing your employees to use their office e-mail accounts for personal use to befit morale. Some companies have a firm policy that company e-mail run on company equipment is only for company business. Others allow private communication. My attitude is that it should be treated the same way as you treat your phone (even though the phone costs money). However, if it's already there, I think of e-mail as the person's desk. It, too, is company equipment, so you shouldn't have picture of your family on it, right?

One company for which I worked had free coffee, a soda dispenser, and regular social events for the employees. When my boss asked me to stay later to work, I was glad to. The next day when I told my boss I had to leave early for an appointment, he said, "Thanks for telling me." Another company took 1.33 minutes off your timecard if you punched your card less than a minute before you were *supposed* to start work (1.33 minutes was the estimated average time it would take to get to your desk, and why should the company pay for that?). Therefore, when I worked 10 minutes into my lunch because of an emergency in a branch office, I made sure that those 10 minutes were added to my timecard.

This attitude extends to other aspects of work. When I have to pay for phone calls to my wife when I am work (it's just a local call), I do not feel any desire to do anything related to work once I walk out the door. If I am given free access to the Internet and am allowed to demonstrate responsible behavior, my responsibility to the job does not end when I walk out the door.

I think about the question asked by the town pastor in the movie *Footloose*: "If we do not trust our children, how can they grow up to be trustworthy?" Therefore, I say let your employees use every aspect of your Internet connection for person business until they prove themselves untrustworthy. However, you *must* be clear that even if they are using the account for personal reasons, the *company_name.com* is still there.

Customer service on the Web is basically the same as through other media. First, you need to think like a customer. Does your competition offer something different than you do? Not necessarily better, just different. Better is arbitrary. For some, better is a lower price. For others, better is more service for the price. When I bought one of my computers, I intentionally went to a place I knew was a little more expensive. I called the company first and said that I had two hard disks from my old system with a version of UNIX on them. I was going to place an order for a complete system, minus the hard disks. If I plugged in the hard disks and the operating system didn't run, I wouldn't buy the machine. They said, "Fine. No problem." I made the order by fax and went in three days later.

Their technicians not only helped me install the hard disks, but the CD-ROM and tape drive as well (which I had bought somewhere else!). After an hour, the system was running perfectly and both UNIX and Windows on the hard disks recognized all of the hardware. When I wanted to give the technician a $10 tip for all the work he did, he said it was part of the job! Even though I could have done all of the work myself, the assistance provided was worth the extra money. How many of your customers have the same attitude?

One of my favorite stories about good customer relations concerns Knowledge Adventures (KA). These folks put out some of the best "edutainment" products on the market (not just one of the best, some of the best). I bought one product and was so thrilled, I bought three more.

Some months later, I saw a new product in the stores and bought it as well. Six weeks later, I got a flyer directly from KA saying that I could buy it directly from them for $20 less than I paid for it in the store. This annoyed me and made me feel as though they had already cleaned out the retail market and were trying to get in as many "last-chance" sales as possible. When I called customer service, their response was that they weren't responsible and could do nothing about it. Rather than playing phone bill, I decided to drop the issue.

Well, I forgot about the issue for several months until I saw a new product on the shelf. Rather than buying it, I decided to see if I was going to get a flyer to buy it cheaper a few weeks later. Sure enough, there it was. This really ticked me off. Once I could see as a mistake; a second time means that someone isn't thinking.

The nice thing was that they had a phone system on which you should "spell" the person's name to get their extension. Well, the president had signed the letter included with the software saying how important customer satisfaction was. So I called him.

Unfortunately, I got his voice mail. So, I just laid into him and told him that he had lost a loyal customer. The next day, I got voice mail from the director of marketing. I blew it off as a just an attempt to quickly put out a fire. Well, this was the Wednesday before Thanksgiving and by Tuesday of the next week, I had five (!) voice mail message from him, saying that he wanted to talk to me. With that many messages, I figured he *really* wanted to talk to me, so I called him.

He was very apologetic and, in my opinion, was sincere about it. He admitted that part of the problem was that they grew faster than expected and were just not prepared for that growth. While trying to keep up with demand, they had let one thing fall through the cracks: the flyers to registered customers. So, what does that do for me? I am out $20 for the first product and was almost out another $20 for the second. To prove to me that they really appreciated all of their customers, he offered to send me a copy of that product that I had decided not to buy.

Needless to say, they next flyer I got announced a upcoming product and allowed me to buy it *before* it appeared in the stores. I now have more than 10 of their products and regularly check their Web site (*www.adventure.com*) for more goodies.

How does this relate to marketing on the Internet? Well, most of the products I bought from KA were *after* this. KA showed me that they did value what I though about their products. Many of my friends were impressed with KA's behavior and admitted that they would feel the same as I had. By recognizing their mistake, making amends for it, *and* correcting it, KA kept a customer coming back and kept a good reputation.

This is especially important with the extent of the Internet today. If I were to post a flame of KA to, let's say, a newsgroup about children, hundreds if not thousands of people would see it. These people would tell others and eventually all of KA's potential customers would think that they were only concerned with making money. Instead, I am sitting here telling you how wonderful I think their products are and how you should go buy some even if you don't have children and the products don't run on Linux (at least, not yet).

Sometime customers *will* want to talk with a real person. Therefore, I think it is a good idea to have an interactive form so that your customers can leave messages for someone to call or e-mail them. Although your Internet site could provide all the same information, it lacks the personal contact that many people are looking for. That's all part of giving people what they want.

15.4.4 Discussion Lists/Forums

You can make your presence on the Internet in other places: discussion lists, newsgroups, and forums. All of these can be defined as methods by which individuals "network" with each other on focused topics. By joining these groups, you can gain visibility for your company.

Discussion lists are distributed via e-mail. There is normally one location that serves as the clearing house for subscription.

One thing I would recommend for everyone of these is that you "lurk" before you join in. Lurking is the term that describes when you simply read the messages and do not actively participate. While lurking, you can get a "feeling" for the way the members of the group interact and what is considered appropriate behavior.

Many groups have a list of frequently asked questions (FAQ) that are posted at regular intervals. This list contains important information not only on the subject being discussed but about participating in the group in general. FAQs were developed so readers who have not seen the answers can also get the information. You can expect that people new to the group will read it when it is posted at regular intervals.

Sometimes FAQs are also stored at one "archive" that might also contain other information related to the group. If you choose an on-line service like CompuServe, there might be a file (sometimes called `advice.txt`) that gives you tips on appropriate behavior.

One thing that is generally not acceptable is advertising in group. This applies primary to unsolicited ads that just pop-up. However, some groups do not allow advertising of any kind. These generally tolerate things like `.sig` files that list your company name, contact information, and a one-liner about your service or product ("Serving the Linux system integration needs of the Bratislava area since 1993"). Even if someone asks about a product, ads are not permitted. Instead, you respond with something like:

"Our company provides a product that might suit your needs: The Flizmo Glopdoober. Check out *www.flizmo.com* for details."

This answers the person's question without advertising. The group members who are curious can check out the Web site, where you can do all the advertising you want. It is also acceptable to mention that you could e-mail them some information or post it to the newsgroup *if more people were interested.* The key is that you don't force your advertising on anyone. At the very least, put your URL in your `.sig`. Again, those who are curious will check it out.

On the other hand, announcements and press releases are more acceptable than straight ads. Here you have to be careful because one person's press release is another person's ad. If you keep it to the facts and eliminate the propaganda, it's safer. Here again, it depends on the newsgroup. Lurk before you leap! Also, some groups are specifically for announcements related to that subject (for example, *comp.sys.linux.announce*).

15.4.5 The Frequently Asked Questions List

A list of frequently asked questions (FAQ) is an excellent way of reducing calls. Make access to this list as easy as possible. For example, it could be a menu item in the very top-most menu (i.e., the one on your home page.) Depending on how many questions there are, you could break it down into different areas, like one for sales and customer service, another for technical information, and other for problems and solutions.

Your customer service FAQ could contain answers to questions like this:

- How long is the warranty?
- How long will you guarantee the spare parts?
- What do I do if I decide I want a larger model?
- What number do I call if I want tech support?
- How do I arrange a tour of your facilities?

Your sales FAQ could contain answers to questions like this:

- Can I get a bulk discount?
- Are there distributors in my area?
- What do I do if I decide I want a larger model?

These are only examples of the kinds of things you can put into a FAQ. Note that there are questions that can be answered in both the customer service and sales FAQs. Actually, you could have the some of the same questions in every FAQ. It all depends on how you want to present your information and how much information you want to present. The information that you make available obviously depends on your business.

So, what kind of information can you give? If you sell computer components (hardware or software), your customer will probably want to see technical specifications, compatibility charts, release dates for new versions, benchmarks, pricing, and so on. If you sell industrial compressors, your customers will want to see delivery rates, pressure, size of the storage tanks, power consumption, etc. If you are a travel agency that books trips through your site, customers will want to see schedules, descriptions of the accommodations, flight information, prices, etc. Ask your sales and customer service people what kinds of questions are asked most frequently. This is the kind of information you want.

15.4.6 Public Relations

There is a small window of opportunity to become the first at something. As with many great discoveries in history, the time was ripe for that discovery. If the person we know hadn't discovered it, someone else might have. A good example was Einstein's theories of relativity. It wasn't that he was so unique in his theories, much of it was already known and understood. He was just the first to combine many of the existing theories of the day into something cohesive. The Internet is like that, too.

If you are the first with a major announcement or product, you may not necessarily make the cover of *Time* with your Web site, but it may be enough to make the cover of a trade magazine. This is enough to substantially increase your reputation. How many compressor companies provide their complete technical documentation on-line or provide complex calculation to determine the required airflow?

Let the journals in your branch know that the site exists and keep them coming back with new information. Provide them (via your Web site) with information on the company (history, personnel, description of products and technologies, a galley of senior executives and their accomplishments).

The easier it is for journalists to get information, the more often they will write about you. You could write to them in advance to tell them about your site.

15.4.7 Sales

Everything is being sold on the Internet. Well, a lot is. Some things do not lend themselves to being sold via direct sales like this. It may not work for big things like compressors because people want to see it in action. They need to know how it will fit into their current business. However, with something like an industrial compressor, they can get an idea of what's available, maybe even gather enough information about your company and products to decide to buy from you even before they know which model is necessary.

As with printed material, your Web site can contain product information and data sheets. In shopping for the right product, a potential customer is drawn to your site by the large assortment of information about your products, the industry as a whole, plus related subjects. You might have short "flyers" as well as long product descriptions. There may be interactive calculations of the necessary compressor volume for the work the customer is doing. The customer inputs range of values and has the Web page select the right compressor for his or her need. You then dynamically create a new page:

```
Personal Compressor Calculations for the Hooterton
Pillow Company:
Tank size: 500 liters
Air flow: 10 liters/minute
Pressure: 1.3 bar
The best compressor for you would be our CK44.
Because you are in 408 area code, your customer service
representative is John Richards.
```

Take a look at this example. The text "CK44" is a hypertext link to the data sheet on the CK44 compressor. Also, "John Richards" is a link that lets you send e-mail to John so you can have him give you a call or e-mail you himself. Keep in mind that a page like this could be made on-the-fly based on input from a form.

If you decide to have price lists on-line, there are a couple of things to consider. First, remember the difference between convenience, shopping, and specialty goods and how much people are willing to pay. Depending on your product and pricing strategy, on-line prices might not be a good idea. In many cases, prices are based on who is buying it. A company that buys a thousands of your products every month might automatically get a 15 percent mark-off. To get pricing information, a visitor would have to input a company name or ID number (or, if the visitor is a new customer, he or she could simply check a box labeled "New"). The form would then make calculations based on quality and any rebates.

You should also be able to go in the reverse direction as well .That is, to go to your order forms from the pages with the technical data. One thing I would suggest is that you have link to the detailed product information any time you mention pricing.

Maybe selling compressors on the Internet is not the best thing, but you can give your customers a great deal of information before the salesman even makes the first call. On the other hand, your service or product *might* lend itself perfectly to Internet commerce. If so, your site should provide all the options that a salesman would: color, size, pattern, shipping method, payment method and terms, etc. If people can/do buy services/goods from your Internet site, keep that confidential–not just the transaction itself, but *everything*.

Do *not* sell your customers'/visitors' names to another company that will then sell a huge list to an advertiser. It is a betrayal of trust. I do not like companies that do this. I am bothered by those who say "We'll do it unless you tell us otherwise," but I can live with that. By doing so without telling me, however, I can no longer trust anything that company does. It is obviously more interested in making money than keeping me as a customer.

Ordering On-line

Ordering on-line may not make sense for your business. In some cases, you *have* to talk to the customer. You can come up with a guess about the right compressor based on what the customer inputs. However, a compressor can cost tens of thousands of dollars. This is not something that people should order "off the rack." If your business makes ordering on-line viable, you can even go so far as to exchange money on-line, which you can do in different ways.

The simplest way that usually works on any kind of server is a membership-based ordering system. To be able to order anything, a customer has to first create an account. Credit card or other billing information is sent via some means other than the Internet. Then, to be able to order, the customer must input an account name and password.

It's true that the account name and password could be intercepted because they are normally sent without encryption. You can increase the safety by confirming the order by e-mail and only sending it out when your confirmation is confirmed via e-mail.

Identification and Verification

If you are providing a fee-based service or conducting business transactions on the Web, you need to address both identification and verification. How do you know that the person/site connecting to you is who they say they are? You don't want to give out your 100-page research paper to someone just because he or she says he or she is allowed to have it. Maybe the user doesn't want to pay for something someone else gets for free. Instead, you must ask for some kind of identification.

Experience has taught me that people are annoyed with passwords. First, it is cumbersome and they will forget them. Therefore, if you do implement a password scheme, you have to let your visitors choose their passwords themselves.

OpenMarket (*www.openmarket.com*) has a unique approach by allowing you to create your own challenge-response. If you exceed your predefined limit on purchases, you are asked one of a set questions that you have previously defined. This could be something that no one would ever guess ("What's the first name of your favorite Australian football player?") or something that makes no sense at all ("What is your wife's name if you are single?").

Some systems provide information like the hostname/IP address of the client machine. You can store the information from when the user logged in and created the account. If they say they will never log in from anywhere else, you can prevent access when the hostname is different, then present a message such as "Access attempted from an unauthorized location."

Verification is the process by which you make sure that what they are ordering is really what they want. It's possible that the order was input incorrectly or was somehow changed. For example, a customer actually orders one T-shirt, but a extra bit could mean that 129 are registered by the on-line order processing system. It would be very embarrassing for you if you sent 129 T-shirts. Or, what if a football team did order 129 and one bit got dropped and you only sent one?

Even if you have a page that comes up after the customer presses a "Submit Order" button, he or she may not see that he or she ordered 20 instead of 2. I experience this same phenomena when I proofread what I wrote myself. One possibility is an e-mail confirmation, which does two things. First it verifies that, yes, the customer did order 2 Winzding Fandoogles and not 20. Second, it tells the customer that the order was received. When the customer sees the order in a different context, he or she is more likely to catch the mistake.

I recently ordered books from two publishers on the same day. One sent me an e-mail confirmation within *minutes* and the book was delivered within a week. The other one never sent me anything to confirm it and the books took three weeks. Because of the time delay with credit card bills, I may not know that someone charged to my account for several weeks after the charge was made. By getting an e-mail confirmation of the order, I can quickly put a stop to erroneous orders.

One thing I want to ad in terms of validation is a "plausibility check." Does it make sense for someone to order 10,000 copies of a single book? Well, maybe. It's possible but not plausible, and most people know that if you were to order that many you could probably get a volume discount and wouldn't be ordering this way.

MONEY OVER THE INTERNET

Many Web sites allow you to input your credit card information to make a purchase. Some have a secure server that, coupled with your browser, encrypts the data before it is sent. This makes it virtually impossible to get credit card information. Older browsers do not have this luxury, therefore there is the danger of credit card theft.

In his book *World Wide Web Marketing*, Jim Sterne casually brushes off the danger of credit card theft from unsecured servers. He mentions the difficulty of analyzing the billions of billions of bits speeding around the Internet. True, this is difficult, but that's not the way it's done. You monitor those sites in which you *know* credit card numbers are being passed. You know what pages are accessed just before sending the credit card information (just by looking at the site yourself). You can then look for packets sending these pages and it is much easier to figure it out credit card numbers. Also, the person's name will probably be on the form. So looking for names is another way of finding the right page.

Because of the fleeting nature of information exchange on the Internet, security is an important aspect. Sterne's assertion is that the reason there needs to be a solution is that the "issue is prevalent and the attention high." I say that the reason that a solution needs to be found is that it is a problem. Sterne mentions the danger of low-paid workers at restaurants "duplicating" your card. Well, that danger does exists. However, you are relying on the integrity of the employees and the restaurant to maintain the security of the cards and their numbers. So there is a certain amount of control there.

The Internet is different. The packets bounce around the Internet and have the potential of being intercepted at any of dozens of places. One problem is that you don't even know whether someone was eavesdropping on your connection. Who is responsible for ensuring the safety of the connection? Unlike the restaurant, no single agency controls the flow of packets–it is too difficult. If someone saw that low-paid worker rummaging through the credit card receipts or writing the number down, you would hope that someone would notice it. However, there is no way to notice someone rummaging through your Internet connection looking for credit card information.

The First Virtual Holding Company (*www.fv.com*) was one of the first companies to address the issue of security when conducting business on the Internet. Part of the safety mechanism is that credit card information is not passed across the Internet. You apply for an account and First Virtual sends you account information and an application number via e-mail. You then call their 800-number to activate the account. It is here that you give your credit card information (via a touch-tone phone).

This process caused me a couple of problems. First, I live in Germany and you can't get 800 numbers in the U.S. from there. I had to e-mail back to ask for a number that I could call. Second, the default on many German phones is pulse signal, not tone. I then had to open my phone to make the switch.

After First Virtual confirms your credit card information, you get another e-mail with confirmation of your account and password. When you go to a site and make a purchase, you are prompted for your account name and password. Some time later, you get e-mail from First Virtual indicating that the vendor says you made the purchase. At that point, you can either accept the change, say that you changed your mind, or indicate that you have no idea what's going on. Because no credit card information is being transferred via then Internet, a system like this could be implemented on a Linux system.

DigiCash (*www.digicash.nl/home.html*) has a way to not only securely transfer money but also maintain the anonymity of the buyer. You have the equivalent of a virtual "wallet" on your local computer. When you purchase something, you pay for the purchase from your "wallet." Security is provided by public key digital signatures. Both users and vendors have accounts at the First Digital Bank and the money in the account is converted to e-cash, which you keep in your "wallet." On the DigiCash Web page, you will find a lot of information to help you get e-cash working on your Linux system.

Another alternative that is available no matter what kind of system you have is to create a customer account. Your customer would set up an account over the phone, by fax, e-mail, or some other means by which you can verify their identity. The credit card information is never sent over the Internet. In fact, if you establish customer accounts, there may be no need to ever send credit card information because you can simply bill the customer.

Authentication and Secure Transactions

As with business anywhere else, business on the Internet involves the authentication of data, people, products, and transactions. If you order something over the phone, the dealer needs to be sure of your credit card number (data), who you are (people), what you ordered (products), and whether the dealer is going to get the right amount of money (transactions).

Just as with other types of transactions (phone, mail, even in-person), those on the Internet will never be 100 percent safe. As with other types of transactions, a few precautions can reduce the risk. Both you *and* the customer should exercise caution when conducting business on the Internet. As a customer, you should check the claims and the products offered by companies on the Internet.

In some cases where the information is just services, such as information or access to a virtual mall of sorts, companies will charge you for something that is nowhere near what you expect. Because of the nature of the Internet, you will more than likely have to pay for it in advance and you will be sent an "access code" through your e-mail account. By the time you realize it is not what you expected, your card has already been charged.

Caldera (*www.Caldera.com*) has made a deal with Netscape to provide a copy of the Netscape Fast Track commercial Web Server with several of it's products. Caldera also provides the Netscape Navigator Gold, which includes a built-in HTML editor.

15.5 Measuring Your Success

Internet business is too new to have enough hard data to do anything other than guess as to where it is headed and how well your business is going. In addition, getting hard data is more difficult than in other fields due to the fleeting nature of Internet connections. Build your base-line of information. What is the state now? You can then compare this to the state in three months, six months, etc. to get an idea of how things are developing. Because you have invested substantial amounts of time and money in creating and maintaining your Web site, you want to know whether it was worth it and whether you should continue to maintain it.

Each time someone accesses a page, it is a "hit." By counting the number of hits, you get an idea of how many people are accessing your page and therefore how successful it is. Well, sort of. Just because your site was visited doesn't mean that they read or even cared about the information. A hit tells you only the number of times someone looked at the information, much like the number of copies a magazine that included your ad sold tells you how many people had access to the information. There is no way to demonstrate how many people actually read it.

Another problem is that pages are cached, which means that the pages are stored in one location to save time by not getting them from the source. Though the Web server might cache the recently used pages in memory, your browser has a cache of its own. Especially with the local browser cache, a user could potential view a page dozens of times and only see the cached copy; it is never loaded from your site. Some firewalls can also cache the pages so you register only one hit, although a thousand people have seen it.

If you have a magazine ad, you might get phone calls. If you do a bulk mailing, there are probably return cards. At a trade show, you get a stack of business cards. These can be measured. Likewise, there are tools to measure the accessing of your pages. You can count people who interacted with your survey. Hits of your home page have little value as you have know way of knowing whether they looked at the page for 30 seconds and moved on or whether they saw the whole site. Interactive surveys just say who was surveyed, not who spent time at rummaging through your pages (unless you count access to every page).

As with any kind of marketing, knowing what customers think about you, your product, and your Web site is an important aspect of marketing research. If you make the effort to create a Web site, you should solicit feedback, regardless of whether you solicit feedback for other aspects of your company or marketing strategy. Why not? You have the perfect medium. Use the same medium as you use to present your message.

Remember that the cost of surveys or other types of marketing research is expensive, especially when compared to the Web. However, learning what your customers think about your products is important to your being able to provide the right kinds of services or improve products/services. The question is how much is it worth to you? WWW is an excellent opportunity to get this information for "free." If the survey is done correctly, you can find out what your customers want and don't want, like and don't like, etc.

Consider how much a customer survey would cost if you sent it out through a bulk mailing. Companies sometimes rely on your good will or loyalty to answer questions in their survey. Others offer a contest to entice people to fill in the survey.

On your web site, you might say "All you need to do is register to win by answering these few questions." The translation of this would be:

"Register to win one-tenth the cost of a customer survey by completing our on-line customer survey. In other words, you spend one-tenth of the money and get the same information."

Jim Sterne, in his book *World Wide Web Marketing*, tells the story of getting a five-dollar bill with a survey. Despite the fact that the survey came from a company with which he enjoys doing business, it was three pages long in very small type. He put it in his in-basket until he could get to it. By the time he got around to it, the deadline had passed.

I got a survey with a one-dollar bill, but it consisted of a single-sided page of very specific questions. In my case, the fact that I could fill out the survey in about five minutes was enough to get me to fill it out. If my survey had been as long as Sterne's, I would have probably put it in *my* in-basket until it was too late.

The reason my company got its survey back is that I didn't loose interest and I was not overwhelmed. The desire to express my opinion and obligation for the dollar was not outweighed by the size of the task. Your goal is not just to get as much information from your customers as possible. Rather, you want to get as much *important* information as possible. If you ask for too much, the effort won't be worth the compensation. Similar to the incentive of the five-dollar bill, offer a contest for a free "whatever." To enter, the visitor must first read the rules and then fill out a survey.

Let's look at a couple of quick examples. If you are selling only through mail order from a central warehouse, knowing what state your customer is in is interesting, but how important is it? You may be more concerned with what new products your customer might want you to offer. If you are planning to open up new warehouse to cut down on transportation costs, new products are of less interest, but you may want to know what state your customer is in. Six months later when business has increased because of the new warehouse, you might have another contest. This time, the questions you ask are about new products and not about where the consumer lives.

Think back to the section on marketing (see Section 15.2.2, Forming Your Team, Marketing). You need to determine how you are going to get feedback from all of this and how you are going to evaluate it. Forms are an excellent way to get the data via the Web and you can use something as simple as a `perl` script to process the data. One cute trick would be to present the visitor with a graph or graphs that show the total responses. You could write a `perl` script to take their input, add it to the data pool and create a graph that is immediately presented to the visitor. This confirms to the user that the information was recorded, plus it adds a level of interactivity to your site. That is, the site changes based on the action of the visitor.

At the beginning of your market research, you defined your goals, so you now need to evaluate this information in terms of your goals.

If the feedback you are asking for is more than just a survey, you definitely need to react to the feedback. Above all, respond quickly. A survey sent through normal mail may have a turn-around time of two weeks or more. However, this is unacceptable on a Web site survey. A form on a Web site is immediate. Therefore, your response should be (within reason) immediate. Sending a "thank you" within 24 hours is fine. You need to have a plan for response. You need to have guidelines for what to do when people send in comments. If someone flames you or your site, you need to have the appropriate response. If someone praises you, you need to respond as well.

I recommend that you don't use some boilerplate responses. For example

```
Dear Mr. User@company.com,
Thank you very much for your comment about "Exact text
from the subject line of the message." We appreciate
your comments.
Sincerely ,
The obviously automatic response system from The
Wizbang-Doodle Company.
```

Make it obvious from the response that someone real read the message; just a few words about the comment are enough. You could consider autoresponders that operate during non-business hours (after 6 p.m. on weekends/holidays). This at least lets your customer know that the message was received. However, always follow it up by a message from a real person.

If a customer (or employee, for that matter) makes a valuable suggestion that is implemented, give that person the recognition the suggestion deserves. Many companies have programs in which employees can get cash rewards for suggestions. If the suggestions saves/makes the company $10,000, is it worth a $100 premium? I say yes. I would stay away from gift certificates unless it is substantially more than what you would pay in cash. Even if your cost of the product is as much 50 percent of your sales price (not unreasonable in the manufacturing industry), when you give gift certificates as premiums, you reduce their value by 50 percent. Therefore, if you would give $100 in cash, consider a $200 gift certificate (or more). You should not only send him or her a check, but announce it on your home page:

```
Thanks to Jane Jones of the Hooterton Pillow Company in
Fallsville, Idaho. Jane receives a $100 prize for her
suggestion on ways to improve the Ukelblat filter in
our Ecoline products. Thanks again Jane!"
```

Predicting what the user will want next week is a tricky thing. You can spends tons of money on market analysis to make a guess, but that's all it is: a guess. You could be wrong and have wasted a lot of money. In the Sunday paper, there is often a pull-out section with dozens of coupons, one of which might be for something you use. Here, advertisers are simply guessing/hoping that you will find something of interest.

On the other hand, at the checkout counter at grocery stores, you often get a coupon for something that you just bought. Why do they give you this coupon? They know you bought a particular product and therefore you are likely to buy it again. Often, the coupon is for another brand, but they know that this type of product is something you do buy. This is the first step in "demassifying" the market. You are now advertising on a one-on-one basis and are finding out what the customer uses.

You can create forms to let your users take a survey on-line. Although the kind of information that you can gather is essentially unlimited, you don't want to bog your visitors down with dozens of questions. Plus, you don't want to force them to do the survey. A few questions are okay on a membership form, but if you leave a bad taste in the visitors' mouth, they may never come back.

There are a couple of things to consider. First, always check the sanity of the input. Checkboxes or radio buttons are good because their value is clear cut.

Text fields are a different matter. There are obviously no checkboxes that you can use for someone's name, so the easiest way to check the validity of the information is to ask the visitor. I normally output the information to a new page and allow the user to view the information in a new context. I know from experience that you often miss mistakes that you input yourself. However, you can catch them if you see them in a different context.

Multiple surveys is another possibility. You can get feedback for different areas of your business and give the customer a chance to "win one of several products; enter as many times as you like." However, be sure that the customer has to fill out every field *before* he or she is allowed to continue.

On the one hand, many people consider allowing a customer to "register to win" more than once distorts the data. I disagree. If someone is willing to make the effort to enter more than once, then there is either a strong attraction to the prize or the company. *Something* is motivating the customer to make the effort. This, in itself, is useful data.

You could ask in your survey "If you could choose your own prize, what product would you choose and why?" The answer could give insight into product preferences as well as attitudes toward the products. For example, "I would buy product X, but it's too expensive for my budget." Would it be worth lowering the price by 10 percent if that meant a sales increase of 20 percent?

In some cases, I have seen surveys that consisted of a few related questions on each of about five pages. Once the visitor has filled out all of the questions, he or she clicks "Continue" to go on to the next set of questions. The user has more of a feeling of participating in the process and, because it is spread out over several pages, you can get away with asking more questions (within reason).

You could also "mask" the survey to find the right product for the customer. For example:

- Are you using this product for home or work?
- If both, what percentage are you using it for each?
- If you are using it at work, do you have a similar product at home?
- If you are using it at home, do you have it at work?

Probably 50 such questions make it obvious that you are more interested in survey data and not helping the user find the right product. However, carefully spacing such questions throughout the form, you can gather a lot of information without annoying the visitor.

Some companies make a living by buying and selling personal information. I don't like these companies. I especially don't like a company that sells my name and address to someone else without asking me.

Some places, like many magazines when you apply for a subscription, tell you that "unless you say otherwise" they will "make your name available" to another company. Although I am not a fan of this "negative option," it is an acceptable practice. Actually, selling customers' names without asking them is an acceptable practice.

If one person gets annoyed at you for making his or her name available, he or she can potentially flame you to *millions* of potential customers. Is it worth the risk? My opinion is that if you ask for someone's name and address for the contest/survey, you should use it *only* in connection with the survey. I would recommend not even using the customer's name for your own advertisements unless you explicitly tell them.

For example, you get a customer's e-mail address by having them subscribe to your free electronic newsletter that contains coupons for hundred of dollars in savings, etc. You could also have giveaways to subscribers. Hot-Wired is a Web site that is an on-line magazine. To read it, you must become a member, so they now have your name and address. They also sell advertising space on their Web site.

15.6 Attracting Attention

Although your Web page is a painless and comfortable way to get information, it's useless if your customers don't know it's out there. You have to advertise it somehow. Unlike cable TV where people "channel surf," people are not going to try every possible IP address to see whether there is a Web server there. They are only going to try those sites that they know about. You can announce your presence in several ways on the Internet, which will probably cause a flurry after the first time you make the announcement. It's a good investment to periodically update and announce the change.

One common way to get people to your site is to reciprocate links. Someone provides a link to your site and you, in turn, provide a link to their site. Let's look at our ongoing example of a compressor company. Manufacturing compressors requires computers to manage the sales and administration. You could have reciprocating links with your computer supplier. To manufacture compressors, you also need office furniture. You could have reciprocating links with your furniture supplier.

Another idea is to create a company profile of someone who uses your products. This gives your customer exposure to other potential customers while demonstrating that someone is satisfied with *your* products.

Your Web site should be a resource to your customers, so it's okay to point them to a different site if they will get some benefit from them. Avoid politics or other issues that might upset customers. You might feel the need to point to Amnesty International's page on the death penalty, but it might annoy some of your customers.

You can also register your home page with many different sites. One is BizWeb, which you can find at *www.bizweb.com*. This is simply a directory of links to companies with information about the products and services they offer. To find a company you are looking for, you can either do a keyword search or browse the various categories. As of this writing, this service is provided free of charge.

Another is IndustryNet, at *www.industry.net*, which has thousands of listings for companies of every imaginable business.

NetPost (*www.netpost.com*) is a service that will publicize your WWW site. This service is not like a magazine ad that will take anyone. Eric Ward, the owner of NetPost, will only take one client in a particular field.

15.7 Things to Consider

There is more to running your Web site than simply creating interesting pages and making the accessible. Even if you are not offering services or products for profit, there are many other issues to consider. Recently Viacom, the parent company of Paramount Pictures, who own the rights to Star Trek® had several Star Trek® related Internet sites closed down. Therefore, before you make your site available, here are a few things to consider.

15.7.1 Legal Issues

You must consider the legal issues involved because they can be considerable problems. Take copyrighting, for example. You might like someone else's page and want to include it on your site. Because the document is being transferred as you see it, most viewers have a copy of it on your local machine. This does not mean you *own* it. It may look free, but the minute you write it, you have a copyright on it. To keep your information safe, it's best to include a copyright statement on each page, maybe in the header or in an included file.

When you purchase something, usually the physical transfer is accompanied by the legal transfer. When you buy a Dr. Pepper or package of feta cheese, you own it. In this age of information technology, things are different. When I buy I book, I buy the paper that the words are printed on and the rights to use the information in it. However, the words themselves (the information) still belongs to someone else. When I buy a software program, I buy the rights to use the software. I do not own it.

The same thing applies to stuff on the Internet. You may find something of interest on the Web that you would like to incorporate on your own Web site. However, it may be copyrighted and you could run into serious trouble if you don't get permission to use it.

15.7.2 Intellectual Property

We are all aware of the ease with which programs can be copied with a computer. Often, people don't think about the fact that duplicating a disk of a copyrighted a program and giving it to a friend is illegal, though someone would think twice about sitting in front of a copier and copying a book to give to a friend. Most of this is the time involved. However, because less time is involved in copying disks, people often copy disks matter-of-factly and do not have the time to consider that someone spent months, if not years, developing what is on the disk.

The situation is similar with Web pages. Within seconds (or minutes, depending on your connection), you have a copy of some document. It was made freely available to you, so it must be free, right? No, it's not. Even though someone has forgotten to put a copyright notice on a page, it does not mean that that person has given up his or her copyright. The mere fact that he or she wrote it gives him or her the copyright. If you copy a page and use it somewhere else, you are guilty of violating that copyright. If you want details about the legal issues, check out *www.web-com/~lewrose/home.html*. This page contains a lot of the legal aspects of advertising on the Internet.

15.8 Odds and Ends

Get a connection to the Internet: If you can't convince your boss to get one, get one yourself at home. The price is no longer an issue and it will be an educational processes as well. (Imagine sitting in a staff meeting and presenting some significant, up-to-date information. The other people in the meeting ask you in amazement, "Where did you get that?" You answer, matter-of-factly, "On the Web.")

Start designing a Web site. Learn HTML and look at other sites to get an idea of what is possible and what looks good. Most browsers allow you to look at the HTML source of the pages you display. Don't copy them into your Web site, just get ideas. Look into the capabilities of different Web browsers. Some browsers are free but don't have all of the functionality of the commercial products. Become familiar with the terms used in the browser and how to move around the Web efficiently.

Find our what "netiquette" is all about (what can you do/say on the Internet and what you can't). Keep up with trends and technologies in the Internet community as well as in the computer business in general. You may develop an Internet strategy that takes several months to implement but that is outdated before you even go on-line.

Surf the Web! That's the best place to learn about it. Know who your competition is. Visit their sites and see what they have to offer.

One thing to consider is a profile-driven page. Here, the appearance and behavior of the Web site is based on the user who logs in. This is only valid if you require membership because that is where you gather the information about your user. The next time your user logs in, the right site presents a unique creation or something similar.

Profile-driven pages are usually effective when the visitor needs an account (i.e., to order) and you can check your database for last time that visitor ordered and what he or she ordered and make some suggestions for possible future purchases.

If your customer is on the Internet, you can be sure that he or she uses a computer. If your product or service is related to computers in some way, everyone has at least a passing interest in your product. If your product is not related to computers, your customers may not necessarily have an interest in computers or even use one. Let's take the compressors example I have been using all along. A small three-person painting business may still do all of its accounting with a calculator and its word processing on a typewriter. However, they may still need a compressor. It might then be necessary to spark their interest in the Internet by having your URL or e-mail address on your letterhead or business cards. The fact that you are on the Internet might give them motivation to get on it themselves. One way to find out how many customers have Internet access is to ask them.

If part of your concern is whether you should connect, I would say at least get a dial-up connection. Your MIS department could well use it. Then put your e-mail address on your business cards. If customers are on the Internet, they will understand the e-mail address; if not, they will ask about it. Although it could be fairly expensive, you might consider *giving* your customers Internet access. Some on-line-services, such as CompuServe, regularly offer free connections for a limited time (usually 10 hours of connection time). Maybe your ISP could provide them with a free connection for a specific time (30 days).

One thing that is becoming common is "personal" Web pages. These are provided by companies with their own domains. They will sell you space on their machines so that you can put up your own Web pages. You end up with a URL that looks like *www.somecompany.com/jimmo.html*. For example, one company that does this is Design System Laboratories (DSL), at *www.dsl.org*. In addition, DSL can create pages for you.

An alternative is something that Internet Images Worldwide (IIW) (*www.inet-images.com*) does, which is provide you a "virtual" domain. With this, you get your own Internet domain, such as *www.jimmo.com* (which actually does exist, by the way). However, rather than you having to put up the hardware and money, some other company (like Internet Images) will do it for you.

Some such companies are reasonably priced, like both DSL and IIW. However, others try to take advantage of the fact that everyone is trying to get on the Internet bandwagon. Therefore, I recommend that you shop around for the best deal.

Keep in mind that this isn't like looking for a mechanic. You don't need one in your local area. Although you might like to keep the business in town, you don't have to. That's the great part of the Internet. I'm living in Germany, but my domain is sitting on one of IIW's machines in New Jersey. Because the difference in connection time between sites is negligible, you can have your site anywhere that you get the best deal.

This glossary contains a list of commonly used terms and expressions. In many cases, I wrote something in bold in the definition as a flag that it is important, though this does not necessarily mean it has its own glossary entry. I just felt you needed to pay attention to it.

absolute mode	A mode in which file permissions are changed using the three-digit octal numbers instead of the letters.
absolute pathname	A pathname for a file or directory beginning at the root directory and including the leading slash (/).

accelerator keys — Keystrokes that select menu options of functions without explicitly pressing the button or selecting the menu.

access control — See **security**.

account — The environment that a user accesses to log into the system.

active partition — The **partition** from which the hardware will normally try to boot. However, **LILO** does not need to boot from the active partition.

active window — The window currently accepting input.

ACU — Automatic Call Unit. The term used in UUCP files to refer to a modem.

address — 1) A memory location. 2) The user and machine name used to send an electronic mail message.

ADF — Adapter Description File. A file provided with **MCA** devices on the **options disk** that contains configuration information for that device.

administrator — The person who manages your computer system or network. Also see **root**.

alias — 1) A name that is more commonly used or is easier to remember that represents something else. If your shell supports aliases, an alias can be a command that represents another command. 2) In mail, this is an address that represents another address.

alias tracks — Tracks used to store data contained in bad tracks.

anchors — Hypertext links. An anchor or hypertext link is a link from one document to another.

ANSI — American National Standards Institute. Organization responsible for defining many American standards.

anti-caching — Occurs when adding more memory makes the machine go more slowly. Sometimes the CPU cannot cache everything, so it caches nothing, thereby making the whole system run more slowly.

application — A computer program that performs a particular task, such as word processing or managing a database.

arbitration A process to determine which device has access to a particular resource, such as the system bus.

argument See **command argument**.

ARP address resolution protocol.

ASCII American Standard Code for Information Interchange. This code includes only 128 character and does not contain non-English characters.

AT command set See **Hayes command set**.

attribute See **permissions**.

authorization The ability to access a particular system function.

auto answer Setting your modem to automatically pick up when an incoming call is received.

automounter The process that automatically mounts an NFS file system when a file or directory under the mount point is accessed.

awk A programming language on many UNIX systems.

background process A process that does not require interaction with the user to run. While a background process runs, the user can continue using other programs or commands.

back-slash A slash that goes from the upper left to lower right (\). Also called a descending slash. Used to "escape" the special meaning of certain characters.

back-ticks Similar to an apostrophe except that it slants from upper right to lower left (`). Used to "hold" the output of a command.

backup A copy of files, directories, or file systems normally used as protection against accidental deletion but also used to maintain a copy of an object in a known state. Also the process of making a backup.

bad track A track on the hard disk that can no longer be read from or written to properly. Bad tracks are listed in a **bad track table** that points to good **alias tracks**.

bandwidth	Refers to the maximum I/O throughput of a system. Although this normally refers to communications channels such as Ethernet or serial lines, it is often used to refer to any system.
base address	The setting used to access expansion cards.
basename	The file name component of a path. This can also refer to the "primary" portion of a file name. For example, the base name of the file `program.c` could be considered `program`. This is also the name of the command used to extract the basename. Compare this to directory name, or **dirname**.
baud	One change in the electrical state of a signal.
baud rate	The number of electrical state changes per second.
bdflush	The buffer flushing daemon, which writes the contents of dirty buffers from the buffer cache to disk.
binary	The numerical system of counting with only two digits: 0 and 1. Also called "base 2."
binding	The process of joining two components. Networking programs are often bound to a port or key presses in the X-Windows system are bound to a specific function.
BIOS	Basis Input/Output Services. Special chip set on the computer that is used to access the hardware. Mainly used during boot-up and shutdown, although operating systems such as DOS use it as the primary means of accessing the hardware. The term BIOS is used for both the chip itself and the routines contained within the chip.
bit	A binary digit, either 0 or 1.
bitmap	A representation such as a picture or table that is stored as a series of 0s and 1s. Each character represents a single dot in the image or a particular value in the table.
block device	A hardware device that is accessed with buffering within the operating system. Although such a device can be read by an application a character at a time, input and output is buffered within the system's **buffer cache**. Compare this to a **character device**.

blocking I/O — **I/O** in which the process is forced to wait until the operation is complete. Also known as synchronous I/O.

boot — The process by which the computer is powered and goes through the necessary steps to load and start the operating system. Also refers to the program in the root directory that loads and starts the operating system.

boot device — The device (usually a floppy or a hard disk) from which the system is booted.

bootstring — The string passed to the **boot** program that it uses to determine what operating system to load and execute as well as how to do so.

bottleneck — When demand for a particular resource is beyond the capacity of that resource or beyond the ability of the operating system to provide that resource.

bps — bits-per-second.

bridge — A computer or other network device used to connect two networks. Bridges are often considered to connect similar systems, such as two Ethernet networks. Compare this to a **gateway**.

buffer — An area of computer memory on the hardware that is used to temporarily store information.

buffer cache — The system buffer that stores the most recently accessed blocks. Note this is only used when accessing block devices.

bus — A set of lines (such as wires or leads) used to transfer data or control information. See also **expansion bus**.

bus arbitration — The process of deciding which device has control of the bus.

bus mastering devices — Also **bus masters**. Devices that are capable of taking control of the system bus.

bus topology — A network that is laid out in a line, such as with a thin-wire network. Each node is connected to the next. Compare this with **star topology**.

byte — Eight **bits**. (Abbreviated B or b)

caret — A character (^) often used to represent the beginning of a line or a negation.

cache memory Also called **cache**. High-speed memory usually placed between a CPU and main memory. Cache memory holds recently accessed memory because it is more likely that this memory will be accessed again. See also **level-one (L1) cache** and **level-two (L2) cache**.

carriage return The keyboard key usually labeled `<Return>` or `<Enter>`. When you type at the command line, sending a carriage return indicates to the system that you are ready for the system to process the command. The term comes from typewriters on which pressing the carriage return actually returned the carriage of the typewriter to its starting position.

carrier The signal used as a reference point from which frequency changes are measured. These frequency changes are the actual data.

CCITT Comité Consultatif International de Télégraphique et Téléphoneique. One of the members of the Internation Telecommunications Union (**ITU**) that coordinates telephone and data communication standards.

CD-ROM A read-only optical storage media that uses the same technology as music CDs.

Centronics connector The official name of the printer side of a parallel cable connection.

CGA Color graphics adapter. A very old video card.

CGI Common gateway interface. Interface by which Web pages communicate with programs on the server.

chain Term used to describe the connection between different layers in a network.

character device A hardware device accessed with no buffering within the operating system. Although such a device can be read by an application block, input and output is *not* buffered within the system's **buffer cache**. Compare this to a **block device**.

chat script A set of Expect-Reply pairs that UUCP uses to log into a remote system.

checksum A value that is calculated based on the bites within a file. Some checksums depend on the order of the bytes within a file, whereas others are not. Two files with *identical* content must have the same checksum.

child process The process created when one process (the **parent**) calls the `fork()` system call.

class The description given to computer networks depending on what portion of their **IP address** is the network and what portion is the host.

clean The state of a data object when it has not had its contents altered. "Dirty" buffers or pages can be marked clean when the data is written to disk. File systems are marked as clean when the control structures are written to the disk.

client A process or machine that is using a particular resource provided by a **server**. In X-Windows, a client is usually an application that creates a display on the screen. In a network, a client is a machine that accesses a remote file system or other resource.

client-server model A model in which some components act as servers, providing resources or services, and other components are clients that use those resources or services.

clock tick The term used for an interrupt received at regular intervals from the programmable interrupt timer or clock. Clock ticks are signals to the kernel to enable it to initiate actions that need to be taken at regular intervals.

CMOS Complementary Metal-Oxide Semiconductor. Technically any chip that uses the CMOS technology, but more commonly used to refer to a special chip that retains the basic configuration information about your machine.

COM port Common term for a serial port. Although this is actually a DOS term, it is used often indiscriminately. The term comes from "communications port."

command A set of words or characters that is interpreted by the operating system as a request for action on the part of the system.

command alias An alternative name for a command. See also **alias**.

command argument Subsequent information passed to a command. This normally refers to information (such as the name of a file) that needs to be acted on. Normally arguments that change a command's behavior are called **flags** or **options**.

command flags See **command options**.

command line A place on your screen where you input commands. The command line is usually indicated by a **prompt**. Also refers to the string of characters that form your command.

command line interpreter The program that accepts your command line and reacts to it. See also **shell**.

command options Arguments passed to a command that change its behavior.

command substitution When using a command, the output of the command (enclosed in **back-ticks**) is substituted into the command line before the command is executed.

compile The process of taking the **source code** for a program and converting it into machine-readable instructions.

contention When two devices, processes, etc., request a system resource at the same time. For example, when two devices want to use the **bus** at the same time.

context The set of data, including the CPU register values and **uarea** that describe the state of a process.

context switch The process through which the system goes to change one process being the current/active process to another.

control character A character that has an ASCII value less than 32. These are often created by pressing the `<Ctrl>` key (see **control key**) and another key. Programs can also generate control characters, which get their names from the fact that they are often used to control certain function of an applications.

control key The key marked CTRL on most keyboards used to modify the value sent by another key that is pressed at the same time.

CPU Central Processing Unit. The primary chip or processor in a computer. The CPU is what reads and executes the machine's instructions and makes the computer go.

CPU privilege level The level of access a process has while running. This essentially determines what memory and hardware can be accessed.

crash An abnormal shutdown of the computer. Often this exhibits itself as the system "freezing," but it can also be that the system reboots itself or **panics**.

cross-over cable A serial cable in which the transmit pin on one end of the cable goes to the receive pin on the other end, and vice versa.

current working directory The directory that the system accesses when no paths are given. The current directory can also be specified as "`.`" or "`./`" depending on the context. This directory is taken as the starting point of all relative pathnames.

cursor The symbolic indicator of where input is being taken. This is usually in the form of a box, underline, I-shaped character, or other shape that may or may not blink.

cylinder The set of all **tracks** on a hard disk that are equidistant from the center of the disk.

DAC Digital to Analog Converter. A chip (usually) on a video card that converts the digital signals from the operating system to analog signals that the monitor uses.

daemon A process that performs a service for the system. Normally, daemon processes are in the **background** and wait for something to occur to which they must react.

DAT Digital Audio Tape. A form of backup (tape) media.

data mode The mode a modem is in when it transfers data.

DCE Data Communication Equipment.

decimal The numerical system of counting with ten digits: 0123456789. Also called "base 10."

decode To convert date from an encoded format into a format that the appropriate process (human, program, etc.) can read. See also **encode**.

default The standard configuration or values for a program, field, or any other aspect of the system.

defunct process A process that has made the `exit()` system call. This process does not use any system resources (including memory) except that it takes up a slot in the process table.

descriptor Pointers to specific memory locations that the kernel uses. These are stored in **descriptor tables**.

device Any peripheral hardware attached to the system. These are accessed by **device drivers** through **device nodes**.

device driver A set of routines internal to the kernel that performs I/O with a peripheral device. Although normally a user's process wishes to access that peripheral device, the kernel is actually doing the work.

device nodes Special files that are the entry points into the **device drivers**. Also referred to as **device files**.

digitalus enormus The technical term for making mistakes while typing. This translates as "fat fingers."

DIN connector Deutsche Industrie Norm connector. A small nine-pin connector used to attach peripheral devices such as mice and keyboards.

DIPP Dual In-line Pin Package. Usually refers to memory chips that are connected via two rows of parallel pins.

directory A file in a particular format that the system reads as a an inode and filename pair. The files contained within a directory can also be other directories.

directory name Also referred to simply as **directory**. This is the name of the directory path used to access a file. The directory component can be accessed with the **dirname** command.

dirty
The state of a buffer or memory page that has had its contents changed.

disk mirroring
The process by which the entire contents of a hard disk are duplicated on another disk.

disk/diskette
Also called a **floppy disk** or **floppy**. A thin, flexible data disk within a protective jacket. Data is stored on the floppy and accessed through the **media access hole**.

DMA
Direct Memory Access. The means by which devices can access memory directly without the intervention of the **CPU**. DMA is controlled by the **DMA controller**.

DNS
Domain Name System. Also called Domain Name Service and Domain Name Server. The system by which information about a computer network is stored on specific machines rather than spread out on every machine. Information is obtained by making a **query** that is then **resolved** by the **domain name server** or name server.

domain
A set of machines on a network that is controlled by a single administrative authority.

domain name
The name by which a domain is known. See also **FQDN** and **host name**.

DOS
A sort of operating system. Although the term refers to several different operating systems, it is most commonly associated with Microsoft's DOS, **MS-DOS**.

dot file
A UNIX file that has a period (dot) as its first character. With the exception of the root users, dot files are normally not visible. Because they are only visible with specific options to certain commands, they are often equated to DOS "hidden files."

dotted-decimal notation
The notation used to indicate **IP addresses** as decimal numbers.

double-quotes
(") Quotation marks used to partially remove the special significance of certain characters. Characters such as the $, **single-quotes** (') and **back-ticks** (`) retain their special significance.

DPI
dots per inch.

DRAM Dynamic Random Access Memory. Must be refreshed regularly with electric signals. Compare this to **SRAM**.

DTE Data Terminal Equipment.

Dual In-Line Pin Package See **DIPP**.

dump device The device to which the system will write (if it can) when the system **panics**.

Dynamic Link Libraries (DLLs) Libraries of functions that are linked into the program as needed (at **run-time**) and not when the program is compiled.

ECC Error Checking and Correcting.

edge-triggered interrupts Interrupts that are activated by the rising edge of the signal, which is when the signal makes the transition from low to high. Compare this to **level-triggered interrupts**.

EGA Enhanced Graphics Adapter. An old, old video adapter.

EIDE Enhanced Integrated Digital Electronics. A newer device interface most often used in hard disks that can overcome size limitations of **IDE** drives.

EIP Extended Instruction Pointer. The register containing the memory location that the CPU is currently executing.

EISA Extended Industry Standard Architecture. Enhanced version of the **ISA** that provides advantages over ISA. Developed by a consortium of companies.

ELF Executable and Linking Format. A new executable program format used by Linux.

encapsulation The process by which one data format is enclosed inside another. This technique is used in networking to pass data between various layers.

encode Converting data from one form to another. The newer form is generally more easily handled than the original. For example, 8-bit data converted to 7-bit data to send via mail is encoded.

encrypt Encoding something so that humans or other processes can no longer read it.

encrypted password The user's password that is stored in encoded form in the file `/etc/passwd` or `/etc/shadow`.

end user See **user**.

environment The settings and values that control the way you work on the system, including the shell you use, your home and current directories, and your user and group IDs. Also, a set of variables called **environment variables** contain many of these settings and values.

environment variable Variables that modify the behavior of your login shell as well as other programs.

error message A message indicating a problem. This can appear when something simple happens, such as inputting incorrect syntax to a command, or something more significant happens, like a needed file is missing. Usually the messages indicates the nature of the problem.

escape character Decimal 27, octal 033, and hexadecimal 1b. Characters used in many cases as a flag to indicating that the following sequence of characters has special meaning.

escape key The key marked ESC on most keyboards. This key is used to generate an escape character that is often used to remove the special significance of certain other characters.

escape sequences A sequence of characters preceded by an **escape character**. This usually changes the behavior of something. For example, escape sequences to printers might turn on bold printing.

escaping characters The process by which you remove the special significance of characters, often accomplished by preceding the special character by a **backslash**.

ESDI Enhanced Small Device Interface. An older hard disk interface.

Ethernet A local area network standard developed by the Xerox corporation.

event An occurrence on the system. For the kernel, this might be a device that is ready to provide requested data. For X-Windows this can be keystrokes, mouse movement, or windows resizing.

exception An unexpected event.

exception handlers Special functions within the kernel that are used to deal with exceptions.

executable file A file containing a program or set of commands. To be executable, these files must also have set the execute **permission bit**.

exitcode The value returned by a process as it is completed.

expanded memory In DOS-based computers, this is a means of getting around the 640KB base memory problem. With this technique, blocks of 64KB are shuffled in and out of "accessible" memory.

expansion bus The **bus** in a computer into which **expansion cards** are inserted.

expansion card A card inserted into the **expansion bus** that expands the functionality of the system such as a hard disk controller or a serial port.

export The process by which a file system or directory is made available to be remotely **mounted**.

extended memory Additional memory more than 1Mb. This memory is not switched in as with **expanded memory** but is treated as a single, linear unit.

fault An **exception** that occurs before the instruction is executed (e.g., **page faults**).

FAQ Frequently Asked Questions (List). A list of questions often posted to a newsgroup, mailing list, or Web site that provides answers to frequently asked questions.

field separator A special character used to delimit fields within a file or input.

file A named collection of information stored on a hard disk, floppy, or other media. Although a file is normally considered to contain data or executable instructions, hardware in UNIX is accessed through files. These have no size and therefore contain no data; their mere existence contains the information.

file creation mask See **umask**.

file descriptor A number associated with an open file used to refer to file during I/O operations.

file permissions The access permissions on a specific file.

file table A table internal to the kernel that maintains the relationship between the **file descriptors** and the physical file on the hard disk.

file system A hierarchical organization of directories and files.

first level cache The cache contained with the **CPU**.

flags See **command options**.

flow control The process by which data transfer is regulated so that it does not arrive too quickly for the receiving process.

focus The term used to describe the active window, to which keyput and other input is sent. A window is said to "have the focus."

foreground A process is said to be in the foreground when it interacts with the user.

fork The process and system call by which new processes are created.

format The process by which a disk is prepared for use.

forward slash A slash that goes from the upper right to lower left corner (/). Also called an ascending slash. Used as the path separator.

forwarder A name server that simply forwards requests to another name server.

FQDN Fully Qualified Domain Name. A machine name that contains both the **host name** and the **domain name**. This name is used to uniquely identify a computer.

fragmentation A term to describe when parts of a file are spread out across different parts of a hard disk. Although the term is also used to refer to memory, accessing memory from different locations has no effect on the process. However, when the hard disk reads a file and is forced to go to different locations, the physical movement of the hard disk's components slow down the access.

freelist	A linked list of unallocated (free) data structures.
ftp	A file transfer program that enables you to copy files to and from a remote computer in a network.
full path	See **absolute pathname**.
gateway	A computer or other network device that is used to connect one system to another. Gateways are often considered as connecting dissimilar systems, such as one network running TPC/IP and the other running NetWare.
Gb	See gigabyte.
GDT	Global Descriptor Table.
GID	Group ID.
gigabyte	2^{30} bytes. Often (erroneously) considered to be one billion bytes. (Aabbreviation Gb)
group	A set of users. These users are listed under a group name within the `/etc/group` file. The group name is associated with a GROUP ID (**GID**). Each file on the system has a group associated with it. This is indicated by the GID of the file.
GUI	Graphical User Interface. A graphic-oriented interface such as X-Windows.
hard link	A file with a different full path name but the same inode number. Compare this to a **symbolic link**.
hardware flow control	Controlling the flow of data across a serial cable by using line signals rather than control characters.
hardware-mediated bus	A bus to which the access is determined by special hardware and not software.
Hayes command set	A standard set of modem commands.
header	Information included at the beginning (head) of transmitted data. A header will identify the information being sent and may contain other information. For example, a mail header would contain the recipient, and an IP header would contain the source and destination **IP addresses**.

hexadecimal The numerical system of counting with sixteen digits: 023456789ABCDEF. Also called "base 16."

hit ratio The ratio of times that information was available to the number of times it was requested. For example, if data is requested from **cache memory** and is available, this is a **cache hit**. If the data is not available, this is a **cache miss**.

home directory The directory defined by your $HOME environment variable. This is normally the same directory you end up in after you log into the system.

hops The number of connections that need to be made to reach a destination. For example, if you want to go from machine A to machine B but first need to go to machine C, this is two hops (A to C then C to B).

host Any computer. Normally used when the computer is on a network.

host adapter An expansion card that serves as the interface between the system's **expansion bus** and a **SCSI** bus. This is often (erroneously) called a **SCSI** controller.

host equivalence The state whereby two machines are considered equal in terms of user access rights. This is normally accomplished through the `/etc/hosts.equiv` file.

host name Also **node name**. The name by which a **host** is known. See also **FQDN** and **domain name**.

hostname The system name or machine name.

HTML HyperText Markup Language. Text formatting language used in **WWW** documents.

http HyperText Transfer Protocol. Protocol used to transfer **WWW** documents.

I/O (Input/Output) A term that refers to the transfer of data to and from peripheral devices.

ICMP Internet Control Message Protocol.

icon A graphical representation of something.

IDE	Integrated Drive Electronics. Common hard disk interface.
IDT	Interrupt Descriptor Table. Table containing pointers to the interrupt handling routines.
init	The process "spawner" that is created at system start up.
inode	Index or Information Node. This is a structure containing the basic information about a file such as owner, type, access permissions, and pointers to the actual data on the disk. Inodes are stored in the **inode table** (one for each filesystem)and are referenced through **inode numbers**. See also **file**.
interrupt	A signal from a hardware device that indicates that the devices wants "attention." This signal can include an indicator that requested data is available or that an error has occurred.
interrupt handler	Special routines within the kernel that handle interrupts.
Interrupt Service Routine	See **interrupt handler**.
I/O	Input/Ouput.
IP	Internet Protocol. Standard by which packets of information are sent to the appropriate location within a network.
IP address	Unique address within a network that uses the **Internet Protocol**.
IRQ	interrupt vector. The hardware setting that indicates on what line a device will generate an interrupt.
ISA	Industry Standard Architecture.
ISDN	Integrated Services Digital Network.
ISO	International Standards Organization.
ISP	Internet Service Provider.
ISR	Interrupt Service Routine. See **interrupt handler**.
ITU	International Telecommunications Union.
K or **Kb**	See **Kilobyte**.

kernel The primary part of the operating system that manages all system functions, such as memory, task scheduling, how devices are accessed, etc.

kernel mode See **system mode**.

kernel parameter A value defined that controls the configuration of the kernel.

Kilobyte 2^{10} bytes.

LAN Local Area Network.

LDT Local descriptor table.

level-one (L1) cache Cache memory within the CPU.

level-triggered interrupts Interrupts that are indicated by them electrical signal being level but at the state opposite from what it normally is.

level-two (L2) cache Cache memory external to, but directly accessed by, the CPU.

library call A call to a library function. **Library functions** are collections of **system calls**.

lilo The Linux loader.

link 1) **hard link**. 2) **soft** or **symbolic link**.

link count The number of file names that point to a particular set of data.

locale The set of values that indicate your location such as language, keyboard type, etc.

localhost The special name given to the machine on which you are currently working.

locality principle Principle that the computer instructions that are executed are generally within the same area of memory (**spatial locality**) and that the same instructions are likely to be executed again (**temporal locality**).

logical block addressing (LBA) The means by which blocks on the hard disk are accessed based on a logical address and not the absolute address on the hard disk. The logical address is what the hard disk controller presents to the operating system.

login The process of gaining access to the system. Here you enter your login name (**logname**) and **password**.

login group — The **GID** that you are assigned by default.

logname — The name you use to gain access to the system.

logout — The process of disconnecting yourself from the system.

LUN — Logical Unit Number. The number used to identify a device controller by a single **SCSI host adapter**. Compare this to **SCSI ID**.

MAC address — Media Access Control address. The unique identifier given to a network interface card (**NIC**).

magic number — A number at the beginning of a file used to indicate what type of file it is.

maintenance mode — See **system maintenance mode**.

major number — A number that indicates which **device driver** should be used to access a particular device. See also **minor number**.

man-page — A reference page that contains useful information about a specific topic.

mask — A series of bits that "cover up" existing settings. For example, the **umask** masks out file permissions and the **netmask** masks out network addresss.

maskable interrupts — Interrupts that can be "ignored."

master boot record — The first block of your hard disk (or floppy) containing information necessary to find the **active partition** and boot your operating system.

Mb — See **megabyte**.

MBR — Master Boot Record. See **master boot record**.

MCA — Micro-Channel Architecture. A computer bus architecture developed by IBM that provides many advantages over the **ISA** architecture.

megabyte — 2^{20} bytes. (Abbreviation Mb)

metacharacter — A special character that the shell replaces with character strings.

MIME — Multipurpose Internet Mail Extensions. A standard for mail exchange that supports graphical, audio, video, and other binary data.

minor number A number that serves as a flag to a **device driver**. See also **major number**.

mirroring See **disk mirroring**.

MO drives Magneto-Optical drives. A storage medium that uses both magnetic properties and lasers to store data.

modem control port A serial port that reacts to the carrier signal.

modem Modulator/Demodulator. An electronic device attached to your computer that converts digital signals from the computer to analog signals (modulation) to be transmitted across telephone cable. When receiving the analog signals, a modem converts them back into digital signals (demodulation).

mount The process by which a **file system** is made available.

mount point The directory through which the mounted **file system** is accessed.

mount table The table containing all of the mounted **file systems**.

mouse A pointing device used to move a pointer on the screen.

MTA Mail Transfer Agent. The collection of programs used to transfer mail from one system to another. Most Linux systems provide the sendmail MTA.

MTU Maximum Transmission Unit. Maximum size of a transmitted piece of data.

MUA Mail User Agent. The program that you use to access the mail system, including reading and composing mail.

multitasking The process by which a computer system is able to maintain multiple programs (tasks) in memory and to switch fast enough to appear as though all programs are running simultaneously.

multiuser The process by which a computer system is able to maintain multiple programs (tasks) in memory and to ensure that they do not interfere with each other. Normally each task is associated with a specific user.

multiuser mode	The run state of the system in which access is allowed on terminals other than the system console.
multiprocessor system	A computer system with more than one CPU.
multiscreen	One of 12 console "terminals."
name server	A program running on a network that provides a centralized database of information on the names and **IP addresses** of machines on that network.
name cache	A data structure within the kernel that stores the most recently accessed translations of pathnames to inode numbers.
netmask	A binary mask used to mask out the network portion on an **IP address**.
network	A group of computers that are linked together.
NFS	Network File system. The set of programs and the protocol used to make file systems and directories available across a network.
nice value	A weighting factor that is used to calculate a processes **priority**.
NIS	Network Information System. System by which files and user information can be automatically spread across a network.
NMI	non-maskable interrupt. An interrupt that cannot be ignored.
octal	The numerical system of counting with eight digits: 01234567. Also called "base 8."
operating system	A group of programs and functions that provide basic functionality on a computer. Also, software that manages access to a system's hardware and other resources.
options disk	A disk provided with MCA devices that contains an **ADF** for that device.
owner	1) The user who created a file or directory. 2) The user who started a process.
package	A collection of related programs that perform a common function.

packet A unit of data sent across a serial line or network.

page A 4KB block of memory. The primary unit of memory.

page directory A structure in memory that the kernel uses to access **page tables**.

page fault A hardware event that occurs when a process tries to access a virtual address that is not in physical memory.

page table A structure in memory that the kernel uses to access **pages**.

paging The process by which **pages** are moved between the hard disk and main memory. Note that the hard disk can mean the file system from which the **text** is copied or the **swap device** to which data is copied.

panic The process the kernel goes through when an unexpected event occurs that it cannot deal with.

parallel The process by which data is sent one byte at a time. Compare this to **serial**.

parent directory The directory that contains the directory to which you refer. For example, if you refer to the `/etc/http` directory, the parent directory is `/etc`. If your current directory is `/home/jimmo`, the parent directory is `/home`.

parent process The process that executed a `fork()` system call to create a new, **child process**.

parity An error detection mechanism in which the number of bits is counted and an extra bit is added to make the total number of bits set even for **even parity** or odd for **odd parity**.

parity bit The extra bit used for parity.

partition A section of a hard disk that can be the entire hard disk. The starting location and size of each partition is stored in a **partition table**.

password A string of characters used to confirm your identity when you log in. See **encrypted password**.

path 1) The set of directories needed to reach a specific file. Also referred to as the **pathname**. 2) The list of directories through which the shell searches to find the commands you type.

PCI Peripheral Component Interconnect. One of the newer bus types.

PCL Printer Control Language.

peer Another computer at the same "level" as your computer. You can provide services to them and they to you. Computers in this situation use a **peer-to-peer model**. Compare this to a **client-server model**.

permissions The settings associated with each file or directory that determines who can access the file and directory and what types of access are permitted. Also called properties or attributes.

physical memory RAM.

PIC Programmable Interrupt Controller. A chip on the motherboard that manages hardware interrupts.

PID Process ID. A unique identifier for a process. This is simply the process's slot number in the **process table**.

pipe A way of joining commands on the command line in which the output of the first command provides the input for the next. The term also refers to the symbol used to create the pipe (|).

polling The process by which a device driver queries a device for a response rather than waiting for the device to generate an interrupt.

POST Power-On Self-Test. The self-test that the computer goes through when you first turn it on.

PPID Parent Process ID.

PPP Point-to-Point Protocol. A networking protocol used across serial lines.

pre-initialized data Variables and other structures within a program that already have their value set before the program is run.

pre-emption What occurs when a process that was running on a CPU is replaced by a process with a higher priority.

print queue A queue (waiting line) in which print requests are stored while they wait to be sent to the printer.

print spooler The term used to described the files and programs used to manage files to be printed.

printer class Multiple printers that are treated as one destination to spread the load more equally.

printer interface scripts Shell-scripts that actually send the file to the printer.

priority The value that the scheduler calculates to determine which process should next run on the CPU. This is calculated from its **nice value** and its recent CPU usage.

process An instance of a program that is being executed. Each process has a unique **PID**, which is that process's entry in the kernel's **process table**.

process table A data structure within the kernel that stores information about all the current processes.

prompt One or more characters or symbols that identify that the system is ready to accept a command.

protected mode A CPU mode in which mechanisms are implemented to allow or deny access to particular areas of memory. In other words, memory is *protected*.

protocol A set of rules and procedures used to establish and maintain communication between hardware or software.

protocol stack A set of protocols that appear to be stacked as one protocol hands off information to another.

protocol suite A collection of related **protocols**.

pseudo-terminal Also called a **pseudo-tty**. A device driver that allows one process to communicate with another as though it were a physical terminal.

queue A list. A waiting line.

quoting The mechanism used to control the substitution of special characters. See **single-quotes**, **double-quotes**, and **back-ticks**.

RAID Redundant Array of Inexpensive Disks. Combining multiple disks to improve reliability or performance.

RAM Random access or main memory.

raw device See **character device**.

redirection The process by which one of the three base file descriptors (stdin, stout, and stderr) reference something other than the default.

region An area of memory grouped by function. For example, text, data, and stack.

region descriptor A descriptor that points to a **region**.

region table A structure within the kernel that points to the currently active regions.

regular expression A notation for matching sequences of characters without having to specify all possible combinations. Regular expressions are composed of literal characters as well as **metacharacters**.

relative path A pathname that shows a **path** in relation to the current **working directory**.

relink The process by which a new **kernel** is generated.

remote host A computer in a network other than the one to which you originally logged in.

RFC request for comments. A specific document that relates to networking standards and activity.

ROM Read Only Memory.

root 1) The top directory of a UNIX file system, represented as a slash (/). Also called the **root directory**. 2) The login name of the super user.

root file system The file system onto which all the other file systems are mounted and that usually contains most of the system files.

route A path to a particular computer. The set of other computers needed to reach that destination.

router A device used to redirect network connections to the proper machine.

RPC Remote Procedure Call. A **system call** that is executed on a remote machine.

RPM RedHat Package Manager. A form used to manage and install program packages.

RTS/CTS flow control A form of flow control using the two signals **Request-to-Send** and **Clear-to-Send**.

run-level Also called **run-state**. An abstract term used to determine which process should be run or started.

SAMBA A **SMB**-based network suite for UNIX.

SATAN System Administration Tool for Analyzing Networks. An HTML-based application used to test the security of computers on a network.

scatter-gather The process by which requests for data from a hard disk are spread out across the disk (scattered) and are ordered into a more efficient list (gathered) to minimize the total access time.

SCSI Small Computer System Interface. An expansion bus that is controlled by a **host adapter** and supports several different device types.

second level cache See **level-two cache**.

security The mechanisms and policies used to prevent unauthorized access to system resources.

sector The smallest administrative unit on a hard disk. It contains 512 bytes of data.

sed Stream Editor. A stream/file manipulation program. The term is also used to refer to the language used to program the sed program.

segment See **region**.

serial The process by which data are sent one bit at a time. Compare this to **parallel**.

serial ports A device port that supports serial communication.

shared data region A data region that can be accessed by multiple processes.

shared libraries Sets of common library routines that are not part of a program but exist as separate files on the disk and can be accessed by different processes.

shell The program that controls the user interaction to the operating system.

shell escape A command or character you type from inside an interactive program to escape to the shell.

shell-script A text file containing written UNIX commands, shell built-in commands, and shell programming syntax. Shell-scripts must be made executable by setting the execute permission bit.

shell variable A variable associated with a shell script.

signal A flag sent to a process indicating a certain event has occurred.

SIMM Single In-Line Memory Module.

single-quotes (') Quotation marks that remove the special significance of all other characters. See **double-quotes** and **back-ticks**.

single-user mode See **system maintenance mode**.

SLIP Serial Line Internet Protocol. A networking protocol used on serial lines.

SMB Session Message Block. Protocol used by LAN Manager (i.e., MS Windows) networks.

smart host A computer that has more complete information about the mail network, including information on both users and other machines.

SMTP Simple Mail Transfer Protocol. A mail transfer protocol used over TCP/IP and the Internet.

SNEAKER-Net A old method of transferring data between two machines using sneakers.

SNMP Simple Network Management Protocol. A protocol used to manage information within a network.

SOA Start of Authority. A record with **DNS** used to determine which machine is the authoritative source of information.

soft link See **symbolic link**.

software flow control Flow control using the XON and XOFF characters. Compare this to **hardware flow control**.

software interrupts Interrupts generated by software, not by hardware.

spooler Although this term refers to any process that routes requests to a file or memory for later processing, it is normally used for the print spooler.

SRAM Static RAM.

stack A list of temporary data that a process uses when it makes function calls.

stack region The area of a process's virtual memory that contains its stack.

standard error The place where a process usually writes error messages (the screen, by default). Also called stderr.

standard input The place where a process usually takes its input (the keyboard, by default). Also called stdin.

standard output The place where a process usually writes its output (the screen, by default). Also called stdout.

star topology A network that is laid out like a star, such as with a twisted pair. Each node is connected to a central point or **hub**. Compare this with **bus topology**.

start bit The bit indicating the beginning of a byte being transmitted.

stop bit(s) The bit(s) indicating the end of a byte being transmitted.

streams A mechanism for implementing a layered interface between applications and a device driver. Most often used to implement network protocol stacks and X-Windows.

stripe width The number of physical drives in a striped disk. See **disk striping**.

subshell A **shell** that was started by another process.

subsystem Access to specific, but varied, parts of the sys-

authorizations tem, such as printing, backups, and memory.

subdirectory A directory residing within another directory.

subdomain A name that describes a smaller organization unit within a domain. An example would be the wgs subdomain within the COM domain (i.e., *www.wgs.com*).

subnet A logical portion of a network.

SUID Set User ID. The permissions bit that enables the process to run under a different user ID.

superblock An area at the beginning of a file system that contains information about that file system. In the Linux **EXT2** file system, copies of the superblock are stored are regular intervals within the file system.

superuser The user who has the special privileges needed to administer and maintain the system. The superuser logs in as root.

SVGA Super VGA. A newer video standard.

swap device An area on the disk reserved for swapping out portions of processes when the physical memory available becomes too small.

swapping The action taken by the operating system when the system is short of physical memory. The changeable portion (data) of a process is moved from physical memory to the **swap device**. Note that traditionally, swapping is referred to moving *entire* processes to the swap device. Linux does not swap, but moves **pages** to the swap device.

symbolic link A file that contains the path to another file or directory. Because this is just a path, symbolic links can cross mount points. Depending on the length of the path specified and the file system, symbolic links can also be stored within a file's **inode**.

symbolic mode Changing file permissions using key letters to specify the set of permissions to change and how to change them. Compare this to **absolute mode**.

system call A low-level system function. Compare this to a **library call**.

system maintenance mode The **run-level** in which access is only allowed through the system console. Used for maintenance, hence the name.

system mode The state of a CPU in which the kernel needs to ensure that it has privileged access to data and physical devices. Also called kernel mode.

Tb See **terabyte**.

TCP Transmission Control Protocol. A reliable protocol that is used transmit data from one process to another across a network.

terabyte 2^{40} bytes. (Abbreviation Tb)

terminal Video display unit with a keyboard and a monitor.

terminating resistors Resistors at the end of a thin-wire network connect or **SCSI** bus that absorbs the signals and prevents them from bouncing back, potentially interfering with other signals.

text The executable machine portion of a program. That is, the part of a program containing the instructions that a CPU can interpret and act on.

text file A file containing text.

text region Also called **text segment**.

thrashing The term for when the system spends all of its time **swapping** and not performing any real work.

throughput The amount of work that a part of the system can process in a specified time. This can be anything from the number of bytes sent to the number of jobs completed.

tilda The symbol (~) used by several shells and other programs to represent a user's **home directory**.

time slice The maximum amount of time a process can run without being pre-empted.

TLB Translation Lookaside Buffer. Buffer within the CPU that contains pointers to **pages**.

token Portions of a command line that need to be evaluated individually.

toggle — To switch between any two conditions. For example, to toggle from OFF to ON.

track — The set of sectors on a hard disk at the same distance from the center and on the same surface.

transaction intent logging — A new feature in OpenServer and one of the functions of the `htepi_daemon`. It is the process by which the intention to change file system control data is written to a log file on disk.

transport layer — The layer of a network protocol stack responsible for getting the data from one machine to another.

trap — An exception that is processed immediately after executing the instruction that generates the exception.

TSS — Task State Segment. Contains the contents of all registers when a process's context switched out.

type — The category that describes whether the file is a regular file, a directory, or other type of file.

uarea — The area of a process (user area) that contains the *private* data about the process that only the kernel may access. Also called **ublock**. This is defined in Linux by the task structure.

UART — Universal Asynchronous Receiver-Transmitter.

ublock — See **uarea**.

UDP — User Datagram Protocol. An unreliable protocol that is used transmit data from one process to another across a network.

UID — User ID.

umask — A mask that controls the permissions assigned to new files as they are created.

UNIX — An operating system originally developed at Bell Laboratories.

UPS — Uninterrupted power supply.

URL Uniform Resource Locator. A "network extension" to the standard filename concept that allows access to files and directories on remote machines, to which you may not have a constant connection, such as NFS. URLs can also point to resources on the local machine and provide a means of transporting the base files without having to change paths.

user account 1) The environment under which a user gains access to the system. This includes the **logname**, **shell**, **home directory**, etc. 2) The records and other information a UNIX system keeps for each user on the system.

user equivalence The process by which accounts on two systems are considered equal and authentication is no longer required for certain network operations.

user mode The state of a CPU when it is executing the code for a user program that is accessing its own data space.

user name See **logname**.

utilities Any command that performs more than simply just a function. An example would be `fdisk` because you can use it to create, delete, and make partitions active.

UUCP Unix-to-Unix copy. A set of programs and protocols used to transfer files across serial lines as well as to remotely execute commands.

variable An object known to a process that stores a particular value. Shell variables are known to a particular shell process and environment variables (generally) are known to all of a particular user's processes.

VGA Video Graphics Array.

VESA Video Electronics Standards Association.

viewport The portion of the virtual display that is currently being displayed on the monitor.

virtual address An **address** that exists within a process's **virtual memory** space.

virtual memory	A method of being able to access more memory than is physically available on your system. This combines physical RAM with the **swap space** as well as takes advantage of the fact that the entire program is not accessed at once and does not need to all be in memory.
VLB	Video Electronics Standards Association Local Bus.
Wabi	Windows Application Binary Interface.
wait channel	The addresss of an event on which a particular process is waiting.
WCHAN	see **wait channel**.
well-connected host	A host that is connected to many machines or networks.
white space	A space, tab, or carriage return.
wild card	Any character (such as ? or *) that substitutes for another character or a group of characters. See also **metacharacter**.
write policy	The process by which cache memory writes its contents to main memory.
write-back	The **write policy** when cache memory is written to main memory at regular intervals.
write-dirty	The **write policy** when cache memory is written to main memory only when it has been changed.
write-through	The **write policy** when cache memory is written to at the same time as main memory.
WWW	World Wide Web. A collection of machines on the **Internet** that contain **documents**. These documents contain hypertext links to other documents that may or may not be on the same machine.
X	See **X-Windows system**.
X client	A process that communicates with an X server to request that it displays information on a screen or receives input events from the keyboard or a pointing device such as a mouse.
X server	The software that controls the screen, keyboard, and pointing device under X.

X-Window System A windowing system based on the client-server model.

XON/XOFF flow control Flow controlling using the XON (`Ctrl+Q`) and XOFF(`Ctrl+S`) characters. Also called software flow control.

ZIF Zero Insertion Force. A special socket with a lever that locks the chip (normally the CPU) with no force required.

zombie process An entry in the process table that corresponds to a process that no longer exists. This is used to hold the **exitcode** of that process.

APPENDIX B SUGGESTED READING

This is a list of books that I think you will find both helpful and enjoyable. Many of these I have used as specific source for this book and may have mentioned them in the text. This is not a bibliography, but as the heading says, "suggested reading." The list is intended as a starting place to look for more information on the subjects we talked about. There are definitely more out there. These are just the ones I have personal experience with.

Linux specific:

BARKAKATI, NABA, *Linux Secrets*, IDG Books, Foster City, CA: 1996.

Despite the name, there is not much in this book that you cannot get from the existing Linux documentation. However, this does synthesis the more important aspects, so it is worth taking a look at.

BECH; M.; BöHME, H.; DZIADZKA, M.; KUNITZ, U.; MAGNUS, R.; AND VERWORNER, D., *Linux Kernel Internals*. Essex, England: Addison-Wesley, 1996.

The books goes into a lot of detail about the kernel. To really get the most out of it you need a basic understanding of C and operating system principles.

BENTSON, RANDALPH, *Inside Linux*, Seattle, Washington: Specialized System Consultants, 1996.

This is a good intro to both operating systems and the Linux implementations. I would suggested you read this one first, before you get to Linux Kernel Internals.

KIRCH, OLAF, *Linux Network Administrator's Guide,* O'Reilly & Associates, Sebastapol, CA: 1995.

This is not as up-to-date as it could be. However, for the most part it is valid. It addresses the basics and details of network configuration. It covers issues that I didn't in this book, such as `sendmail` and `netnews`, but skips FTP and WWW.

KOMARINSKI, MARK, *Linux Companion,* Upper Saddle River, NJ: Prentice Hall, 1996.

Mark is a columnist for the Linux Journal. This book addresses a lot of key issues that a Linux system administrator faces.

HUSAIN, KAMRAN; PARKER, TIMOTHY, et. Al., *Linux Unleashed.* SAMS Publishing: Indianapolis, IN, 1996.

This is 1200 pages long and covers every conceivable topic that you can image about Linux. That is both its advantage and disadvantage. It tries to cover too much and, as a result, doesn't cover anything in much detail. Despite this, it is worth a look if you want a quick look into everything about Linux.

WALSH, MATT and KAUFMAN, LAR, *Running Linux*, O'Reilly & Associates: Sebastapol, CA, 1995.

Again, this is outdated, but still covers the essentials for running your system. This stems from the time where commercial Linux meant Slackware, so some of what is in here is not valid for other distributions.

UNIX GENERAL

RUSSEL, CHARLIE and CRAWFORD, SHARON, *Voodoo UNIX*, Chapel Hill, NC: Ventana Press,1992.

My first reaction to this book was not another one of those "...for Dummies" books. Although the book is writing for fairly beginning UNIX users, I recommend it highly.

CURRY, DAVID A., *Using C on the UNIX System,* Sebastapol, CA: O'Reilly & Associates, 1998.

If you want to learn more about programming on a UNIX system, this is a good starting point. Knowing C is important to being able to poke around the kernel, making changes as needed.

DOUGHERTY, DALE, *sed & awk,* Sebastapol, CA: O'Reilly & Associates, 1990.

You can learn a lot of tricks about both sed and awk from this one.

KERNIGHAN, BRIAN W. and PIKE, ROB, *The UNIX Programming Environment.* Englewood Cliffs, NJ: Prentice Hall, 1990.

A more in-depth coverage of programming under UNIX.

KOCHAN, STEPHEN G. and WOOD, PATRICK H., *UNIX Shell Programming,* Carmel, IN: Hayden Book Co., 1985

A very good tutorial if you want to learn more about shell programming. It may looked "dated" but the basic shell concepts haven't changed.

LAMB, LINDA, *Learning the* vi *Editor,* Sebastapol, CA: O'Reilly & Associates, 1990.

Another place to learn a lot of tricks.

ROSENBLATT, BILL, *Learning the Korn Shell,* Sebastapol, CA: O'Reilly & Associates, 1993.

Everyone should learn the Korn Shell and this is a good place to go

WALL, LARRY and SCHWARTZ, RANDALL, Programming Perl, O'Reilly & Associates: Sebastapol, CA, 1991.

The definitive book on programming in `perl`. A good intro and then the details of the various functions.

CAMERON, DIRK and ROSENBLATT, BILL, *Learning GNU Emacs,* O'Reilly & Associates: Sebastapol, CA, 1992.

Operating Systems:

BACH, MAURICE, *The Design of the UNIX Operating System,* Englewood Cliffs, NJ: Prentice Hall, 1986.

This is THE book about UNIX internals. It may seen out of date, but it address the foundations of UNIX and is an invaluable tool. This is also not for the beginner. You need to have some understand of the principles to get the most out of this one.

MIKES, STEVEN, *UNIX for MS-DOS Programmers*, Reading, MA: Addison-Wesley, 1989.

If you are coming from the DOS world then this is a good place to go. Don't be scared off by the implication that this is for programmers. It presents a good comparison/contrast between the two.

SILBERSACHATZ, ABRAHAM, PETERSEN, JAMES L. and GALVIN, PETER B., *Operating System Concepts, 3rd Edition,* Reading, MA: Addison-Wesley, 1991.

Good intro to operating systems. A lot of historical stuff that may no longer apply. However, it is filled with a lot of background information.

TANENBAUM, ANDREW S., *Modern Operating System,* Englewood Cliffs, NJ: Prentice Hall, 1992.

Another good intro to operating systems. It also covers in detail some real OSs like UNIX and DOS.

VAHALIA, URESH, *Unix Internals: The New Frontiers,* Upper Saddle River, NJ: Prentice Hall, 1996.

Nicely written and a fair bit easier to read than the Bach book.

SYSTEM ADMINISTRATION

DOUD, KEVIN, *High Performance Computing,* Sebastapol, CA: O'Reilly & Associates, 1993.

This has some excellent coverage of the concepts involved with system performance and tuning.

FIEDLER, DAVID and HUNTER, BRUCE H., revised by BEN SMITH, *UNIX System V, Release 4 Administration, 2nd Edition* Carmel, IN: Hayden Book Co., 1991.

FRISCH, AELEEN, *Essential System Administration,* Sebastapol, CA: O'Reilly & Associates, 1991.

The concepts are easily applied to Linux systems.

LOUKIDES, MIKE, *System Performance Tuning,* Sebastapol, CA: O'Reilly & Associates, 1991.

Goes into the concepts as well as the practical side of system tuning. There is quite a bit of stuff that's applicable to Linux.

NEMETH, EVI, SNYDER, GARTH, and SEEBASS, SCOTT, UNIX System Administration Handbook, Englewood Cliffs, NJ: Prentice Hall, 1989.

This is a friendly approach and contains a lot of information.

PEEK, JERRY, O'REILLY, TIM, and LOUKIDES, MIKE, *UNIX Power Tools,* Sebastapol, CA: O'Reilly & Associates, 1993.

This book comes with a CD and is loaded with goodies to use on your system.

STRANG, JOHN, MUI, LINDA and O'REILLY, TIM, *Termcap and Terminfo,* Sebastapol, CA: O'Reilly & Associates, 1991.

If you have a lot of different terminals or have application problems, then this is a good source.

SECURITY

AMOROSO, EDWARD and SHARP, RONALD, *Intranet and Internet Firewall Strategies*, Emeryville, CA: Ziff-Davis Press, 1996.

This is an excellent introduction to computer security. Easy to read and covers the necessary topics.

GARFINKEL, SIMSON and SPAFFORD, GENE, *Practical UNIX Security,* Sebastapol, CA: O'Reilly & Associates, 1991

The concepts are applicable to every system.

RUSSELL, DEBORAH, and GANGEMI, G.T., Sr., *Computer Security Basics,* Sebastapol, CA: O'Reilly & Associates, 1991.

Not just for administrators, this presents some valid information for anyone using any kind of computer.

WOOD, PATRICK H. and KOCHAN, STEPHEN G., *UNIX System Security*, Carmel, IN: Hayden Book Co., 1985.

A good approach and loaded with information.

STOLLS, CLIFF, *The Cuckoo's Egg*, New York: Pocket Books, 1990.

Whether you like spy stories, computers or are interested in learning about security, this book is a **must**. It reads live a novel, but it is all true.

HARDWARE

Intel Pentium Microprocessor Data Book, Intel Corporation, 1994.

Intel486 DX Microprocessor Data Book, Intel Corporation, 1992.

Both of these require some hardware or operating system background to get much from them. There is a lot that is not applicable to Linux, but you can also learn a lot about what the CPU does to help out the OS.

MUELLER, SCOTT, *QUE's Guide to Data Recovery,* Carmel, IN: QUE Corporation, 1991.

This has some great information on the physical characteristics of floppies and hard disks.

ROSCH, WINN L., *The Winn L. Rosch Hardware Bible, 3rd Edition* Indianapolis, IN: Brady Books, 1994.

This contains over 1000 pages of information. Although there is a lot that is not necessarily useful (do you still have a CGA card in your machine?), this is an invaluable reference. I had the first edition and got the 3rd edition when it came out. I will buy the next one.

STANLEY, TOM and ANDERSON, DON, *ISA System Architecture*, Mindshare Press, 1993.

STANLEY, TOM and ANDERSON, DON, *PCI System Architecture*, Mindshare Press, 1994.

STANLEY, TOM, *80486 System Architecture,* Mindshare Press, 1994.

STANLEY, TOM, *EISA System Architecture,* Mindshare Press, 1993.

These four are part of the PC System Architecture Series. They are a much more friendly approach that the Intel data books. Well written and very understandable.

TANENBAUM, ANDREW S., *Structured Computer Organization, 3rd Edition*, Englewood Cliffs, NJ: Prentice Hall, 1990.

Tanenbaum covers a lot of the hardware concepts that you may be missing. This was used as the text book for my intro to computer hardware course at the university. I still go back to it as a reference.

WORAM, JOHN, *The PC Configuration Handbook,* New York: Bantam Books, 1990.

Another basic PC hardware book. A good approach and easy to read.

Networking

ALBITZ, PAUL and LIU, CRICKET, *DNS and BIND,* Sebastapol, CA: O'Reilly & Associates, 1992.

If you are setting up a name server of any size, this is the book to have. However, you need to have some TCP/IP background to understand it well.

BANKS, MICHAEL A., *The Modem Reference,* New York: Brady Books, 1991.

Although this goes into a lot about on-line services and other things you can do with a modem, it does go into details about the technical aspects of modems.

CHESWICK, WILLIAM R. and BELLOVIN, STEVEN M., *Firewalls and Internet Security*, Reading, MA: Addison-Wesley, 1994.

This is a very friendly and often humorous approach to network security. In some places it even reads like a spy novel. The first computer book I felt I could read in bed.

COMER, DOUGLAS E., *Internetworking with TCP/IP, Volume 1: Principle, Protocols and Architecture*, Englewood Cliffs, NJ: Prentice Hall, 1991.

Hard core stuff. Descriptions are quick and to the point. Not for the faint of heart, but very much worth it if you want to go into details about the TCP/IP protocol suite. A good reference.

HUNT, CRAIG, *TCP/IP Network Administration,* Sebastapol, CA: O'Reilly & Associates, 1992.

Great intro to TCP/IP. Very informative (like all the O'Reilly books) and enjoyable. This was what I used as my introduction to TCP/IP. I was even a reviewer for it!

KROL, ED, *The Whole Internet,* Sebastapol, CA: O'Reilly & Associates, 1992.

One of the first books to tell you what's out there on the Internet. Loaded with goodies.

O'REILLY, TIM and TODINO, GRACE, *Managing UUCP and Usenet,* Sebastapol, CA: O'Reilly & Associates, 1990.

Goes into a lot of details on setting up and administering UUCP and Usenet. Frequently recommend while I was in SCO support for those wanting to get more out of UUCP.

STERN, HAL, *Managing NFS and NIS,* Sebastapol, CA: O'Reilly & Associates, 1991.

A must if you want to go beyond the basics of NFS and NIS. There are a lot of neat tricks to both that I learned from this book.

STEVENS, W. RICHARD, *TCP/IP Illustrated, Volume 1: The Protocols*, Reading, MA: Addison-Wesley, 1994.

This is another hard core TCP/IP book, but is a little more friendly than the Comer book. This would be a good text book (it include exercises at the end of each chapter). However, not optimal as a "quick reference."

STEVENS, W. RICHARD, *UNIX Network Programming*, Englewood Cliffs, NJ: Prentice Hall, 1990.

This is a good book to learn about both programming and networking in a UNIX environment. However, I would really recommend knowing a little about both before you jump into this one.

TANENBAUM, ANDREW S., *Computer Networks, 2nd Edition*, Englewood Cliffs, NJ: Prentice Hall, 1989.

This covers loads of different aspects of networking. In comparison to other books, there isn't much that is directly related to Linux. However, I like Tanenbaum's style and you learn a lot.

TODINO, GRACE and DOUGHERTY, DALE, *Using UUCP and Usenet,* Sebastapol, CA: O'Reilly & Associates, 1991.

A good one for going beyond the basics.

USER SUPPORT

CZEGEL, BARBARA, *Running an Effective Help Desk,* New York: John Wiley & Sons, 1994.

An excellent resource for planning and implement a help desk. Addresses issues for both internal and external customers.

HARRIS, ELAINE, *Customer Service: A Practical Approach,* Upper Saddle River, NJ: Prentice Hall, 1996.

A good supplement to the Czegel book. This additions the human interaction aspects necessary to run an effective help desk

MICROSOFT PRESS, *Microsoft Sourcebook for the Help Desk,* Redmond, Wash: Microsoft Press, 1995.

Despite the source, an excellent overview. This reads much dryer than the Czegel book, but does speak from the experiences that Microsoft has running a help desk. There is a huge list with vendors of products that would be helpful in supporting users.

PFEIFFER, WILLIAM. *Technical Writing: A Practical Approach,* Upper Saddle River, NJ: Prentice Hall, 1997.

If your are going to support users you need to be able to communicate with them. This book is a good place to get the necessary start on writing good documentation.

TALBOT, STEVEN and OREM, ANDREW, *Managing Projects with make.,* Sebastapol, CA: O'Reilly & Associates,1991.

You'll need this as you implement the documentation source control scheme that I discussed.

WORLD WIDE WEB

ELLSWORTH, JILL and ELLSWORTH, MATTHEW, *The New Internet Business Book,* New York: John Wiley & Sons, 1996.

Similar in scope to the Sterne book. Lacks the technical background. It does have a good list of resources. This is still a good starting point.

ELLSWORTH, JILL and ELLSWORTH, MATTHEW, *Marketing on the Internet,* New York: John Wiley & Sons, 1996.

Not much different than the previous book.

STERNE, JIM, *World Wide Web Marketing,* New York: John Wiley & Sons, 1995.

A good overview of the subject. However, Sterne seems to lack some of the technological background necessary to address all the issues correctly.

GUNDAVARAM, SHISHIR, *CGI Programming on the World Wide Web.,* Sebastapol, CA: O'Reilly & Associates, 1995.

Nicely done. Not only a good review of `perl`, but it covers a wide range of topics that you can/should implement on your web site. Highly recommended.

NEOU, VIVIAN and RECKER, MIMI, *HTML CD for Windows*, Upper Saddle River, NJ: Prentice Hall, 1996.

Don't let the title scare you. Despite the fact that the programs on the CD run under Windows, the book covers the basics of HTML. There is a nice map editing program on the CD.

HAROLD, ELLIOTE RUSTY, *JAVA Developer's Resource,* Upper Saddle River, NJ: Prentice Hall, 1996.

Another good overview. You will quickly get your web pages livened up.

X-WINDOWS

MUI, LINDA and PEARCE, ERIC, *X Window System Administrator's Guide,* Sebastapol, CA: O'Reilly & Associates, 1992.

A little more for the administrator as it goes most into administration issue like security, font servers, etc.

QUERCIA, VALERIE and O'REILLY, TIM, *X Window System User's Guide,* Sebastapol, CA: O'Reilly & Associates, 1990

Good introduction to what X is all about. It is loaded with information on how to configure X to your tastes.

INDEX

Symbols 27, 55, 205, 206, 212, 220, 229, 237

$ 50
$HOME/.cshrc 73
$HOME/.forward 539
$HOME/.forward, security and 560
$HOME/.fvwmrc 255, 268, 269, 270, 272, 273, 484
$HOME/.hushlogin 183
$HOME/.login 72
$HOME/.netrc 538
$HOME/.profile 61, 94
$HOME/.rhosts 483
$HOME/.sh_history 65
$HOME/.twmrc 269
$HOME/.Xdefaults-hostname 484
$HOME/.xinitrc 484
$INCLUDE 387, 388, 392
% in vi 112
& 10
* 46
. 40
.. 40
.fvwmrc 484
.login 182
.nslookuprc 396
.profile 182
.startxrc 253, 266
.twmrc 269
.Xdefaults 261, 266
.zlogin 182
.zshrc 182
/ 23
/bin 23, 26, 28
/boot 24, 233
/dev 24
/dev/hda1 43
/dev/kmem 476
/dev/ttySn 236
/dev/zero 237
/ect/lilo.conf 484
/etc 24
/etc/amd.local 409
/etc/bootptab 483
/etc/cshrc. 72
/etc/default/filesys 403
/etc/dig 398
/etc/exports 403, 411

/etc/fstab 239, 498
/etc/ftpaccess 484, 625, 626, 629, 632
/etc/ftphosts 398
/etc/ftpusers 398
/etc/gated 398
/etc/gateways 482, 483
/etc/getty 172, 479
/etc/gettydefs 182, 463, 464, 479
/etc/group 177, 421, 481, 483, 562
/etc/hosts 376, 377, 389, 401, 482, 483
/etc/hosts.equiv 201, 398, 484, 566, 575
/etc/hosts.lpd 201
/etc/httpd 615, 617, 619, 621, 622, 623
/etc/httpd/conf/access.conf 484, 615, 617, 619, 620, 621
/etc/httpd/conf/httpd.conf 484, 615, 616
/etc/httpd/conf/mime.types 615
/etc/httpd/conf/srm.conf 615, 621, 623
/etc/inetd 363, 364
/etc/inetd.conf 363, 364, 398, 482, 483
/etc/inittab 169, 170, 172, 173, 210, 463, 479, 484
/etc/issue 181, 182, 183
/etc/lilo 24
/etc/lilo.conf 231, 452
/etc/magic 11, 102
/etc/motd 182, 183
/etc/msgs 24
/etc/named.boot 380, 381, 482, 484
/etc/named.d 381, 382, 388, 389
/etc/named.pid 392
/etc/netconfig 398
/etc/networks 375, 376, 398, 482, 483
/etc/nologin 170
/etc/npasswd 483
/etc/passwd 172, 176, 177, 178, 179, 180, 481, 483, 542, 544, 562, 565, 566, 568, 574, 581
/etc/ppp/options.tpl 422
/etc/printcap 195, 196, 200
/etc/profile 182
/etc/protocols 398
/etc/rc directory 24
/etc/rc.d 170, 171, 195
/etc/rc.d/init.d/network 482
/etc/rc2.d 393
/etc/resolv.conf 389, 482
/etc/rpc 404
/etc/securetty 184
/etc/services 362, 374, 398, 482, 484
/etc/shadow 483
/etc/skel 25, 183, 536
/etc/smb.conf 484
/etc/snmpd.conf 484
/etc/sysconfig 25, 485
/etc/sysconfig/network-scripts/ifcfg-routes 375
/etc/syslog.conf 169, 485
/etc/tcpd 398
/etc/X11/XF86Config 249
/etc/X11/xinit/xinitrc 484
/etc/XF86Config 249, 484
/lib 25
/lost+found 25, 246
/proc 25, 476, 479
/root 26
/sbin 24, 26, 28
/sbin/bin/arp 398
/sbin/ifconfig 398
/sbin/lilo 24
/usr 26, 28
/usr/adm 26, 29
/usr/adm/syslog 393
/usr/bin 26
/usr/bin/finger 398
/usr/bin/ftp 398
/usr/bin/logger 398
/usr/bin/nslookup 398
/usr/bin/rdate 398
/usr/bin/rdist 398
/usr/bin/rlogin 398
/usr/bin/route 398
/usr/bin/rpcinfo 411
/usr/bin/rusers 411
/usr/bin/rwall 411
/usr/bin/rwho 398
/usr/bin/showmount 411
/usr/bin/smbclient 419
/usr/bin/talk 398
/usr/bin/telnet 398
/usr/bin/testparm 419
/usr/bin/testprns 419

/usr/bin/X11 28
/usr/include 26
/usr/lib 27, 28
/usr/lib/kbd 27
/usr/lib/npasswd ì 27
/usr/lib/terminfo 27, 188
/usr/lib/uucp 27
/usr/lib/X11 28
/usr/lib/X11/app-defaults 259, 261, 484
/usr/lib/X11/fs/config 267
/usr/lib/X11/sys.startxrc 253
/usr/lib/X11/system.fvwmrc 269, 484
/usr/lib/X11/system.twmrc 269
/usr/local 28
/usr/local/bin 28
/usr/local/etc/httpd 615
/usr/man 28
/usr/sbin/amd 406, 407, 411
/usr/sbin/crond 188
/usr/sbin/ftpshut 399
/usr/sbin/httpd 399
/usr/sbin/in.ftpd 399
/usr/sbin/in.rshd 399
/usr/sbin/in.tftpd 399
/usr/sbin/inetd 399
/usr/sbin/nmbd 419
/usr/sbin/pppd 421, 425
/usr/sbin/routed 399
/usr/sbin/rpc.mountd 411
/usr/sbin/rpc.nfsd 411
/usr/sbin/rpc.portmap 411
/usr/sbin/rpc.rusersd 411
/usr/sbin/rpc.rwalld 411
/usr/sbin/smbd 419
/usr/sbin/traceroute 399
/usr/spool 28, 64
/usr/spool/cron 29
/usr/spool/lp 29
/usr/src/linux 226, 229
/usr/src/linux/include 27
/usr/tmp/named_dump.db 392
/usr/X11R6 28
/usr/X11R6/bin 28
/usr/X11R6/lib 28
/var/adm 29
/var/adm/syslog 563
/var/lock 29
/var/log 29
/var/log/message 475, 481, 485
/var/spool 28, 64
/var/spool/cron/crontab 188
/vmlinuz 23, 204, 210
> 55
? 46
^ 51
| 54
} 89
~ 61

Numerics

1-way set associative cache 307
32-bit bus 288, 289, 290, 291
386 305
486 305
4-mm tapes 332
4-way set associative cache 308
8.3 naming convention 12
802.3 standard 365
80286 281, 310, 311
80386 211, 281, 290, 305, 309, 310, 311, 318, 319
80486 290, 305, 306, 311, 318, 458
8-1-N, default modem settings 336, 345
8237, DMA Controller 282
8259 283
8259, Programmable Interrupt Controller 283

A

A record 384, 385, 386, 387, 390, 392, 393, 394, 395, 396, 400
abbreviations in vi 117
accelerator keys 268, 271
accessed bit 317
acknowledge line 340
active partition 167, 512
Adapter Description File 286, 287
adding devices
  CDROM 465
  CPU 457
  EIDE 464
  hard disk 460
  RAM 458
  SCSI 460
  terminals 463

address record 384
addresses in sed 131
ADF 286
aliases 58, 70
Alpha 319
anonymous ftp 624
application header 359
application layer 359
arbitration bus priority level 286
argument 38, 39
ARP 361, 366
asterisk delimiter 260
asynchronous transfer 345
AT command set 347
ATDP 347
ATDT 347
Athena Widget set 255
auto answer 347
automatic spell checking in vi 117
automatically creating sub-directories with mkdir 98
AutoRaise 255
awk 134, 142
  BEGIN- END 140
  field separator 135
  FS 135
  NF variable 138
  NR variable 138
  number of fields 138
  number of records 138
  printing lines 136, 138
  scripts 135
  string coomparisons 136

B

background, processes in 59
background, putting processes in 10
backing plate 457
back-quote 52
back-slash 40
back-tick 52, 54
backup levels 501
backups 33, 499, 501
banked memory 303
base address 455, 460, 475
base address conflicts 457
bash 62
Basis Input/Output Services 277
baud 345, 346
bdflush 210
BEGIN- END in awk 140
Bell 212A standard 346
Bell Labs 3
Berkeley Internet Name Domain 377
Berkeley Software Distribution 3
BIND 377
binding 269
BIOS 277, 326, 327, 444, 460
blanking 342
block device 43
book
  sed & awk 130
  Winn Rosch Hardware Bible 276
books
  DNS and BIND 392
  Inside Linux 2
  Learning GNU Emacs 124
  Linux Network Administratorís Guide 470
  Managing UUCP and Usenet 430
  Modem Reference 346
  Modern Operating Systems 2
  Operating ystem Concepts 2
  Running Linux 470
  The Cuckoo's Egg 568, 580
  Usenet Netnews for Everyone 430
  Using UUCP and Usenet 430
  Winn L. Rosch Hardware Bible 346
  World Wide Web Marketing 718
boot device 166
boot/root floppy set 328, 474, 500, 512
BORDER HTML text attribute 650
Bourne Again Shell 63
Bourne-Shell 62
branch prediction logic 319
BSD 3
buffer cache 8, 210
buffer flushing daemon 210
buffers in vi 113
building your web site 680
  customer service 683
  establish ownership 684
  form your team 682
  plan 681
    IS/technical 682
    marketing 683

bus 279
bus arbitration 286, 288, 289
bus architecture 280, 281, 285, 288
bus mastering devices 289
bus masters 289
bus mouse 352
bus topology 436
busy line 340
busy loop 7
by-36 RAM 303
by-9 RAM 303

C

C2 security
  C2
CAC unit 289
cache 305
  1-way set associative 307
  2-way set associative 307
  4-way set associative 308
  direct mapped 307
  first level 306
  fully associative 307
  parity 308
  pre-fetch 310
  second level 306
  write policy 307
  Write-Back 307
  Write-Dirty 307
  Write-Through 307
cache hits 306
cache memory 305
caching-only servers 380
calculating hard disk space 324
Caldera 200, 442, 446, 448, 466, 470, 591, 596, 634
Caldera Internet Office Suite 448
Caldera Network Desktop 442, 448, 470
Caldera OpenLinux 200, 592
Caldera Solutions CD 540
call gate 221
called Integrated Services Digital Network 437
canonical name record 390
caret 51
carrier 344, 345, 347
Carrier Detect 337
Carrier Sense, Multiple Sense with Collision Detection 365
Carrier Sensing, Multiple Access with Collision Detection 435
case-esac 94
cathode ray tube 341
CCITT 346
CD 298, 337, 338, 348
cdpath variable, csh 75
CD-ROM 333
cdspell variable, csh 76
cellulose acetate 330
Central Processing Unit 7, 309
Centralized Arbitration Control unit 289
Centronics cable 339
Centronics connector 339
CERT 578, 584
CGA 279, 341
CGI 621, 637, 652, 653, 654, 655, 657, 658, 660, 664
chain printer 348, 350
changing text in vi 109
changing window size 254
character device 43
character set 264
character-mapped mode 351
chassis ground 338
checkbox 653, 654, 655, 656, 660, 661, 662, 668
child process 73, 208, 215, 224
choices in shell scripts 94
Clear Interrupt Enable 283
Clear to send 337
CLI 283
click 252, 253, 254, 255, 269, 273
ClickToFocus 255
client 257, 259, 268
client geometry 256, 257, 258, 259
clients in the background 257
client-server model 362
clipboard 256
CMOS 166, 167, 286, 308, 325, 456, 512
CNAME record 390, 395
coercivity 329

COL 466
color graphics adapter 341
COM ports 234
combining variables 89
Comite Consultatif International
Telegraphique et Telephoneique 346
command argument 38, 39
command flags 38
command line completion 65
command line interpreter 5, 38
command mode in vi 107, 110
command options 38, 39
command substitution 52
commands
adduser 32, 175
apropos 39
at 33, 191
awk 134
batch 33, 191, 192
bind 65
cat 55, 85
chmod 86
cpio 49, 177, 499, 509
cpkgtool 30
crash 502, 505
crontab 188, 189, 190, 191
date 40, 41
df 481, 491
du 491, 492
e2fsck 245
emacs 123
fdisk 325, 449, 450, 451, 452, 474, 475, 480, 481, 512
file 133
find 81, 480, 481, 482, 491, 492
finger 563, 564, 565, 567
fontserv 267
fsck 170, 474, 505
ftp 427, 428, 429
grep 51, 79, 80, 89
gzip 503, 504
halt 174
head 87
html2latex 540, 554
kill 214, 220
lpc 195, 196, 197
lpq 198
lpr 195, 198
ls 12, 17, 77, 176
ls with multiple directories 78
ls with wildcards 78
mail 194
make menuconfig 229
md5sum 505
mkdir 38, 97, 98, 176
automatically creating sub-directories 98
mke2fs 462, 490
mkfs 244
mkswap 223
mount 403, 473, 474, 476, 481, 485, 489, 490
mt 504, 532
nice 215
nslookup 393, 394, 395, 396, 397
perl 142
pkgtool 30
popd 75
ppp-off 421, 424
ppp-on 421, 424, 425
ppp-on-dialer 424
pr 198
ps 53, 57, 223, 487, 488, 504
psupdate 225
pushd 75
rawrite.exe 445
reboot 172, 174
rpm 446, 452, 453, 467, 505, 506
sed 130
sh 62
smbclient 412, 415, 416
startx 250, 267
stty 184, 185, 186, 187
sum 505
swapon 223
syslogd 169
tail 88
talk 193
tar 177, 499, 500, 501, 503, 504, 509, 513, 514, 515, 517, 523, 524, 526, 533
telnet 356, 359, 362, 366, 373, 428, 433
test 92
testpararm 412
trap 96
tune2fs 245
umask 100
vi 106
vmstat 504
wc 52

whatis 39, 541, 544
who 486, 487
write 192
xargs 84
xfontsel 263
xlsfont 263
xset 265, 266, 267
Common Criteria 583
Common Gateway Interface 653
Complementary Metal Oxide Semiconductor 166
Computer Literacy Bookstores 675
configuring vi 122
conflicts with card settings 445
connectionless 360
connectionless protocol 370
constant linear velocity 334
context 9, 13
context switch 205, 214, 217, 219, 221
control characters 350
COPS 572
cpio 49, 50
CPU 3, 7, 8, 9, 10, 309
cpu privilege level 211, 219, 221
CPU privilege levels 211
CR0 314
CR3 316, 318
Craftworks 443, 446, 468, 500
crash recovery 511
crashed 2
Cron 33
cron 33, 188
crontabs 33
cross-over cable 339
CRT 341
CS 508
csh 72
CSMA/CD 365, 435
CTRL-Q 339
CTRL-S 339
CTS 337, 338, 340, 348
Cuckoos Egg, Stoll, Cliff
curly brackets 89
current directory 41
current directory in path 41
current task structure 206
current working directory 13, 14
cylinder 322, 324, 480

D

DAC 341
daemon 10
daemon process 10
daemons 210
/usr/sbin/lpd 198
bdflush 210
crond 188
httpd 614, 615, 616, 617, 618, 619, 620, 621, 622, 623, 636, 657
inetd 363, 364, 373, 374, 375, 433
kerneld 231
lpd 195, 196, 200, 201
smbd 412, 413, 414, 415, 416, 417, 418, 419
syslogd 29, 169
update 210
daisy-wheel printer 348, 350
DARPA 357
DAT 332, 333
data bits 345
data region 209
data segment 211
Data Set Ready 337
Data Terminal Ready 337
DB25 337, 338, 463
DB9 337, 463
DC300 331
DC600 331
DC6150 331
DCE 337, 338
dclock,X-client 258
DDS 332
DEC Alpha 9
DEC Alpha processor 319
Defense Advanced Research Projects Agency 357
demodulation 344
denial of service 573
descriptor table 206
developing your web site
FAQ 713
legal issues 726
technical support 706
device directory 24
device drivers 11, 17, 206, 233

device files 11, 16
device major number 233
device minor number 233
device nodes 11, 16, 24, 233
devices 233
differential backups 502
Digital Audio Tape 332
Digital Data Storage 332
Digital to Analog Converter 341
DIP switches 455
DIPP 301
direct data blocks 243
direct mapped cache 307
directory 12, 43
    child 13
    current 40
    current working 13
    parent 13
    permissions 44
    relative path 41, 48, 97
    stack, csh 75
directory listings with realtive paths 77
directory path, csh 75
dirty bit 317
DiSCOver magazine 511
display, X-Windows 252, 253, 256, 263, 266
Distribution
    Caldera OpenLinux 466
distribution
    Craftworks 467, 468, 469, 601
    DLD 468, 469
    Linux Pro 469, 470
    Red Hat 470
    Slackware 471
Divide-by-Zero exception 216
DLD 443
DMA 278, 279, 281, 282, 283, 289, 311, 455, 457, 460
DMA conflicts 457
DNS 376, 381
do_timer(), kernel function 215
do-done pair 85, 89
dollar-sign 50
domain 377, 378, 379, 380, 381, 428
Domain Name Server 381
Domain Name Service 381
Domain Name System 377
DOS three-letter extension 12
DOS -vs- UNIX file names 12
dosemu 35
dot 40, 41
dot-dot 40
dotted-decimal notation 366
dotting a shell script 95
double-click 254, 269
double-conversion UPS 353
double-quote 52
double-quotes 54
doubly-indirect data blocks 243
DPI 264
DRAM 301, 303, 305
D-shell connector 339
DSR 337, 338, 339, 347
DTE 337, 338, 339
DTR 337, 338, 339, 347
Dual In-Line Pin Package 301
dump device 508
dynamic execution 319
Dynamic RAM 301

E

ECC RAM 308
ECHOE 479
edge-sensitive interrupts 287
edge-triggered interrupts 285, 287, 290
EDITOR environment variable 65
EDORAM 304, 305
EGA 279, 341
EIDE 327
EIP 508
EISA 280, 288, 290, 291, 292, 455, 456
EISA Configuration Utility 290
emacs 123
emergency boot 328
encapsulation 359
encrypted password 176
end of file character 86
enhanced graphics adapter 341
Enhanced Small Device Interface 325
environment variables 44, 45, 62, 63
Epson 350
escape character 350

escape sequences 350, 351
escaping characters 50
ESDI 294
Ethernet 355, 356, 357, 359, 361, 365, 435, 436
Ethernet frame 359
even parity 336
event 213, 214, 216, 218, 219, 223, 224, 225
event binding 269
events 559
events, X-windows 252, 269
exception 507
exception handlers 217
exceptions 216
execute permission 42
execute permissions 43
ex-mode in vi 111
expanded memory 459
expansion bus 279
expansion of wildcards 49
explicit focus 254
ext2fs 240, 241, 244, 245
Extended Industry Standard Architecture 280
extended memory 459

F

f.exec 271
FAQ 713
fault 507
Faults 216
fdisk 498, 512, 513
field separator 135
file 11
file creation mask 100
file group 562
file name limits 12
filesystems 15, 480, 490, 505
- configuration 490

firewalls 430
first level cache 306
flags 38
floppy drives 4, 328
- head 329

focus 254, 268
focus policy 254
font
- alias 265
- server 266, 267, 268

fonts 263
- families 263
- font server 266
- foundary 263
- monospaced 264
- proportional 264
- resolution 263
- set width 264
- slant 264
- spacing 264
- weight 264

formatted storage capacity 323
forward slash 40
forwarder 380, 389
forwarding server 380
four layer network model 361
FPM RAM 304
FQDN 379, 384, 385, 386
frequency shift keying 345
Frequently Asked Questions list 689, 712, 713, 714
FS in awk 135
FSK 345
ftp 388, 390, 395
- anonymous 624

full-screen mode in vi 107
fully associative cache 307
fully-qualified domain name 379
functions 58, 67
fvwm 253, 268, 269, 270

G

gateway 361, 369, 370, 371, 372, 373, 375, 376, 384, 389, 390, 420, 421, 424
GDT 206
geometry, X-Windows 256
GET method (CGI) 653, 656, 659
gettydefs 182
GID 176, 177, 178
gigabyte 323
Global Descriptor Table 206
GND 337, 338
GUI 35

H

hard disk 2, 4, 8, 9, 11, 12, 13, 14, 15, 16, 17, 321
- calculating space 324
- configuration 480
- cylinder 322
- EIDE 325, 327
- ESDI 294, 325
- ESDI cable 325
- formatted storage capacity 323
- head 321, 322, 324, 337, 349
- IDE 326
- platter 321
- sectors per track 323
- tracks 322
- unformatted storage capacity 323

harddisk
- IDE 327

hard-disk ESDI 326
hardware conflicts 510
hardware flow control 338
hardware handshaking 338
hardware-mediated bus arbitration 286
Hayes command set 347
head 321, 322, 324, 329, 337, 349, 480
HEIGHT HTML text attribute 650
Hewlett-Packard Laser Jet 348
hidden files 12
HINFO record 390, 395
HISTFILE environment variable 65
hold space in sed 133
home directory 182
Honeydanber UUCP 356
horizontal retrace 342
host adapter 293, 327
host equivalence 374
host information record 390
HP JetDirect cards 348
HSPACE HTML text attribute 650
HTML 622, 636, 637, 638, 639, 640, 641, 646, 647, 651, 656, 657, 658, 660, 661, 663, 664, 665, 666, 668
- BGCOLOR 640, 641
- bookmarks 645
- forms 652
- HREF 636, 637, 639, 646, 647, 648, 663, 665, 666
- images 650
- lists 641
- maps 648
- menus 647
- tables 644
- Tags 634
- text attributes 651

HTTP configuration 614
HTTP server type 616
httpd 428, 431, 432, 433
httpd.conf 622
HUPCL 479
hushlogin 183
HyperText Markup Language 634
HZ system variable 216, 217

I

I/O bottleneck 291
IBM Proprinter 350
ICMP 361
icon 254, 268, 269
icon box 268, 269
iconify button 254
IDE 294, 324, 325, 326, 455, 457, 461, 462
- space loss when formatting 324

IDT 217, 218
if-then-else-fi 91
IguanaCam 64
image I/O addresses 278
images in HTML 650
images maps in HTML 648
IN record 382, 383, 384, 385, 386, 387, 388, 390, 391, 392, 394
in-addr.arpa 381, 385, 386, 387, 388, 389
incremental backups 501
indexing (HTTP server) 621
indirect data blocks 243
industrial goods 705
Industry Standard Architecture 280
inetd 363, 616, 620
InfoMagic 163
information node 12
inheriting from parent processes 60
init 170, 171, 172, 173, 210, 213, 214
initdefault, inittab entry 170, 172

ink jet printer 349
inline images 690
inode 12, 14, 15, 16, 239, 242, 244
inode table 14, 239, 244
input mode in vi 107
input redirection 56
input/output redirection 58
inserting command output in vi 119
installation checklist 444, 445
instance of a resource 259, 260, 261
Integrated Drive Electronics 326
Intel processors 310
intelligent serial boards 337
interlaced 342
interleaved memory 303
International Telecommunications Union 346
Internet 357, 361, 363, 364, 365, 366, 369, 377, 380, 382, 383, 384, 386, 389, 390, 419, 427, 428, 429, 437
Internet Control Message Protocol 361
Internet gateway 390
Internet Protocol 357
Internet record 382
Internet Service Provider 610
interpreting commands 58
interrupt 9, 17, 216, 217, 283
interrupt controller 217
Interrupt Descriptor Table 217
interrupt handlers 217
interrupt key 95
interrupt request lines 283
Interrupt Service Routine 283
interrupt sharing 287, 290
interrupt vector 218
interrupt vector table 278
invalid SHELL value 73
IO.SYS 167
IP 360, 366, 508
IP address 256, 361, 366, 367, 368, 369, 376, 377, 383, 385, 386, 387, 388, 390, 393, 394, 403
IP Addressing 366
IP datagrams 365, 366, 370
IP header 359, 373
IP packet 368, 372
IP_FORWARDING 433
IRQ 218, 455, 460
IRQ conflicts 457
ISA 280, 291, 292, 455, 456, 457
ISDN 361, 437, 560
iso8859-1 264
ISP 610, 611, 612, 613
ISR 283
ITSEC 583
ITU 346
IXANY 480

J

J.M.E 345
JAVA 670
job control 68

K

kernel 22, 23, 25, 26, 29, 204
    function
        wake_up() 221
    make menuconfig 229
    makeconfigî 229, 231
    memory 25
    modules 231
    rebuild 226
kernel function 215
kernel mode 219, 220
kernel parameters 496
    NR_TASKS 207
key modifiers, X-Windows 271, 272
keyboard mouse 352
Knowledge Adventures 711
Korn Shell 64
ksh 64

L

labeled protection 583
laser printer 349, 350, 351
LBA 327
LDP 35
LDT 206
Learning Perl 162
level-sensitive interrupts 287
level-triggered interrupts 287, 290
library calls 206, 220
library calls vs system calls 206
LILO 231, 232, 443, 452, 465

lilo 24
lilo.conf 231, 232
linear topology 436
link 14, 22
  hard 14
  symbolic 14, 43, 64, 98
link count 98
link layer 361
Linux Documentation Project 35
Linux Installation and System Administration tool 466
Linux Journal 534
linux loader 24
Linux Pro 449, 466
linux/sched.h 207
LISA 466
Local Descriptor Table 206
localhost 384, 388, 393, 394, 395, 396
locality, principle of
  spacial 222, 305, 306, 316, 317
  temporal 222, 305, 306, 316, 317
logging in 180
logical block addressing 327
logical unit number 297
login group 176
logname 44
LOGNAME environment variable 44, 50
Lone-Tar 499
long term memory 301
loopback driver 375, 384
loose binding 260, 261
low-level format 323, 326
LUN 297

M

M/IO# line 278
MAC address 360, 361
magic number 11
magic number, 750
magic with vi 107
magnetic deflection yoke 341
mail exchanger record 392
main system bus 280
maintenance mode 170
major number 233
man-pages 36, 39
man-pages, 750
man-pages, creating 540
MANPATH environment variable 544, 545
maps in vi 117
Mark Bolzern 466
maskable interrupts 217
master backups 502
master boot block 167, 168
master boot record 232
master pseudo-terminal 373
master tape 501
masterboot block 167, 512
maximize button 254
MBR 167
MCA 285, 290, 291, 292, 455, 456
Media Access Control 360
memory 301
menu, X-Windows 252, 254, 255, 263, 268, 269, 270, 271
metacharacters 10, 46, 47, 82, 121
mezzanine bus 292
MFM 323, 324, 328, 332
Micro-Channel Architecture 280, 285
Microcom Networking Protocol 346
Microsoft Windows 7
MIN_TASKS_LEFT_FOR_ROOT 207
minor number 233
MIT 248
MNP 346
modem standards 346
modems 344
  security 577
modified frequency modulation 332
modulation 344
Modulator/Demodulator 344
monitors 341
monospaced font 264
Motif 255, 256
Motif Toolkit 256
Motorola 68000 278
mount 502, 503, 513, 514
mounting filesystems 239
mounting filesystems, 751
mountpoint 239
MSDOS.SYS 167
MS-Office under Wabi 606

multi-tasking 4, 292, 310, 311, 318
multi-user 4
multi-user mode 170, 171
MX record 391, 392, 395, 396

N

name resolution 381
name server 381
named 482, 483, 484
named buffers in vi 115
named pipe 43
netmask 366
Network File System 399
network layer 359
network mask 366
NF variable in awk 138
NFS 34, 399
NFS and security 565
nfsd 402, 407
NMI 217, 308
non-maskable interrupt 217
non-volatile memory 301
nowait 364
npasswd 27
NR variable in awk 138
NR_TASKS 207
ntp 362
null-modem 339
number of fields in awk 138
number of records in awk 138
numbered buffers in vi 115

O

oclock, X-client 257, 258
octet 367, 369
odd parity 336, 345
OLDPWD environment variable 62
onion skin model 16
options disk 286
orange book 582
output redirection 56
oxide media 321

P

p_sig 220
package 30
package, 753
packet 358, 359, 360, 366, 368, 369, 370, 371, 372, 374, 375, 438
paddle board 326
page 221, 303, 312, 313, 314, 315, 316, 317, 318
Page Cache Disable 318
page directory 313, 314, 315, 316, 318
Page Directory Base Register 314
page fault 216, 313, 315, 316, 317
page table 223, 313, 314, 315, 316, 317, 318
Page Write Through 318
paging 221
Paging Unit 314, 315
Panasonic 350
panic 219, 507
paper empty line 340
parallel ports 339
parent directory 40
parent process 208, 214
parent process ID 214
parity 304, 308, 336, 345, 346
parity bit 308, 336, 345
partition 15, 238, 239, 474, 480
partition table 167, 239, 324, 474, 480
path 40, 42
PATH environment variable 45
path, UNIX -vs- DOS 41
pattern matching 46
pattern space in sed 131
PCI 280, 291, 455, 456, 457
PDBR 314
peer-to-peer model 362
Pentium 7, 290, 310, 311, 319, 458
PentiumPro 319, 320
Peripheral Component Interconnect 280, 291
perl 142
permission bits 11
permissions 11, 14, 42, 43, 86, 101
permissions lists 505
phosphors 342
physical address 303, 316
physical security 558
PIC 278, 279, 283, 284, 287
PID 207, 208, 210, 214, 224, 487, 489

pipe 11, 57, 58, 59
pipes 54, 80
pitch 341, 342, 344
pixel 341, 342, 343
pkgtool 30
platter 321
pointer focus 254
pointer record 385
pop-up menu 255
port 362
POS 286
positional parameter 0, special meaning of 93
positional parameters 89, 90, 91
POST 512
POST (Power-On Self Test) 166
POST method 653, 656
POST method (CGI) 653, 656, 660
POST(Power-On Self Test) 166
PostScript 198, 199
postscript 351
Power-On Self-Test (POST) 166
PPID 214, 224, 489
precedence of bindings 261
precedence of class and instance 261
pre-fetch cache 310
pre-initialized data 209
primary server 380, 381
principle of locality 305
printers 32, 348
printing lines in awk 136, 138
printing lines in sed 132
priorities 215
privacy 559
privilege levels 211
process 4, 5, 6, 7, 8, 9, 10, 11, 13, 17, 204
    child 5, 59, 215
    context 9, 205
    context switch 205, 211
    current task structure 206
    parent 5, 216
    scheduling 215
    scheduling priorities 215
    task structure 205, 206
    UID 205
Programmable Interrupt Controller 283
programmable interrupt controller 285
Programmable Option Select 286
programmed exceptions 216
Programming Perl 162
proportional font 264
protected mode 311, 312, 317, 318
protocol 357
protocol stack 358
protocol, 756
proxy server 431, 434
PS/2 configuration disk 455, 460
PS/2 SIMM 458
PS3 62
PTR 385, 386, 388, 390, 392, 396
pull-down menu 252, 255
punch cards 2
PWD environment varariable 537, 538

Q

QIC 330, 331, 332, 333
QIC-02 331
QIC-320 331
QIC-40 332
QIC-525 331
QIC-80 332
quarter inch cartridge 330
QUERY_STRING 653, 656, 657, 658, 659, 662, 663, 664
quotes 52

R

radio buttom 653, 654, 656, 660, 661, 662
RAID 501
RAM 301
Random Access Memory 301
RARP 366
raster scanning 342
rc.d 170
rc.sysinit 170
RCS 546
Read Only Memory 301
read permission 42, 43
read/write bit 318
real mode 312
rebuild
    kernel 226
Receive pin 337
Red Hat 443, 448, 452, 470, 471

redirection 54, 55
reference disk 286, 290
refresh rate 341
region 206
region descriptors, 756
regular expressions 46
regular expressions in vi 112
regular file 43
relative path 40
reliable connection 360
replacing text in vi 110
resetting your environment 60
resistor packs 295
resolution 341, 342, 343, 344, 349, 350, 352, 381
resolver 389
resource classes 259, 260
resource instance 259, 260, 261
resources, X-Windows 258
restricting access to HTTP server 617
Reverse Address Resolution Protocol 366
RFC 364, 365, 429
RGB 341, 342, 343
RI 337
ribbon cable 461
Ring Indicator 337
RLL 323, 324
rlogin 373
rlogind 373
ROM 301
root
  security 562
root directory 23, 40
root menu 269
root window 252, 255, 269
round-robin scheduling algorithm 215
routed 375
router 369, 370, 371, 375
routing 370
routing tables 375
rpm 574
RS-232 337, 339, 347, 361
RTS 337, 338, 340, 348
RTS/CTS flow control 338
run-level 170, 171, 172, 173
run-level, 757
run-levels 171
runnable process 223
run-states 171
RX 337, 338, 339, 347

S

SAMBA 412
SANE 479
SATAN 573
schedule() 215
scheduler 225
SCO XENIX 311
scope of substitution in vi 112
SCSI 280, 293, 294, 326, 327, 460
  adding devices 460
  bus termination 295
  cable 294, 296, 462
  Fast 298
  Fast-SCSI 294
  Fast-Wide SCSI 294
  hard disk 325, 326, 327, 461, 519
  host adapter 293, 294, 297, 327, 460
  host adapter BIOS 327
  ID 295, 297, 460, 461, 463
    binary representation 296
    labling 296, 297
  LUN 297, 298
  SCSI-1 298
  SCSI-2 298
  terminating resistors 295
  termination 300
  Ultra-Wide 298
  Wide 294, 298, 299
  Wide-SCSI 297, 460
searching your path 45
secondary prompt 84, 86
secondary server 380
sectors per track 323, 324, 325, 327, 328, 329, 334, 480
security 555
  $HOME/.forward 569
  .forward 560
  .plan 564
  .rhosts 560
  C2 582
  chain of possession 586
  class A 583
  class B 583
  class C 582

security 555 (*cont.*)
- Common Criteria 583
- filesystem 573
- finger 564
- passwords 561
- policy 558, 569, 570, 575, 576, 577, 579, 580, 581
- protection profile 583
- root account 562
- root password 556, 557, 563, 568, 569
- rpcinfo 581
- trusted hosts 575

sed 130
- addresses 131
- hold space 133
- pattern space 131
- pipes 131
- printing lines 132
- search and replace 130
- substitution 132
- writing lines 133

segment 206, 209
serial mouse 352
serial ports 335
serial terminals
- adding 463

server, X-Windows 252, 253, 256, 263, 266, 267, 268
Set Interrupt Enable 283
set the focus 254
setting variables in csh 73
seven layer (OSI) model 361
Seven Percent Solution, The 508
SGID 574
sh 62
shadow mask 341, 344
shared data segment 209
shared interrupts 218, 285, 287
shared library, 758
shell 5, 10, 11, 13, 16, 17, 37, 38
SHELL environment variable 73
shell escape 73
shell escape, 758
shell expansion 49, 53
shell functions 58, 67
shell history, csh 74
shell history, ksh 65
shell scripts, writing 88
shell variables 44, 50, 89
shells 62
Sherlock Holmes 508
shifting positional parameters 90, 91
short term memory 301
shutdown 173
SIGKILL 220
signal 9 220
Signal Ground 337
signals 220
SIMM 302, 303, 304, 458, 459
Single In-Line Memory Modules 302
single-quote 52, 53, 82
Slackware 30, 31, 443, 446, 471
slave name server 380, 389
slave pseudo-terminal 373
Small Computer System Interface 280
Small Computer Systems Interface 293
smb.conf 412, 413, 416, 417, 419
SNEAKER-Net 355
SOA 382, 383, 384, 387, 392, 395
socket 363
socks 434
soft link 14
soft select 332
software
- ApplixWare 597
- Applixware 540, 597, 599
- ASWedit 540, 596
- BRU 500
- Caldera Network Desktop 589, 590, 593, 594
- Common Desktop Environment 593
- FlagShip 603
- Lone-Tar 601
- ScriptEase 599, 600

software flow control 339
software interrupts 216
spatial locality, principle of 305
specialty good 705, 715
square brackets 47
SRAM 301, 305
srm.conf 428, 615
ST412 325
ST506/412 325
stack 206
stack segment 209

standard error 16, 55
standard in 16
standard input 54, 55, 56, 57
standard out 16
standard output 54, 55
star topology 436
start bit 345
Start of Authority 382
startx 253
Static RAM 301
stderr 16, 55, 56, 57, 58, 97
stdin 16, 55, 56, 86
stdout 16
stepping motor 322
STI 283
stobe line 340
Stoll, Cliff 558, 559, 568, 570
stop bit(s) 345
stream editor 130
stub server 380
sub-directory 13
sub-domain 378, 386, 390, 391
subnet masks 368
sub-shells 73
SUID 560, 573, 574
Super VGA 341
superblock 239
surface mount technology 285
SVGA 291, 341, 344
swap device 222, 223
swap space 222, 447, 448
swap space, selecting during install 447
swapping 221, 312
symbolic link 14
symbolic links
  shell behavior with 64
system calls 206, 211, 220
  exec() 59, 208, 209, 213, 224
  exit() 213
  fork() 59, 207, 208, 209, 212, 213, 224
  mount() 403
  seteuid() 224
  setuid() 224
system calls vs library calls 206
system mode 211, 212, 213, 219
system services 17
system stack 211, 219

T

TAB3 479
tape drives 330
Task Register 318
Task State Descriptor 318
Task State Segment 206, 318
task structure 207, 211, 219
TASK_INTERRUPTABLE 212
TASK_RUNNING 212, 223
TASK_STOPPED 212
TASK_SWAPPING 212
TASK_UNINTERRUPTABLE 212
TASK_ZOMBIE 212
TCP 359
TCP checksum 359
TCP header 359
TCP segment 359
TCP/IP 34, 252, 267, 357, 358, 362, 363, 365, 368, 375, 376, 377, 402, 438, 482
TCP/IP protocol suite 357
TCP/IP protocol suite, 756
Technology Security Evaluation Criteria from the Comission of the European Community ITSEC
telnetd 373
temporal locality, principle of 305
TERM environment variable 44
terminating resistors 294
termination, SCSI 300
terminfo 27
TeX 198
text attributes in HTML 651
text mode 343
text region 209
text segment 211
TFTP and security 581
thin film media 321
third-level prompt 62
thrashing 222
thumbnail 690
tight binding 260, 261
tilde 61
time-slice 7, 8, 9
time-to-live 383
title bar 253

TLB 316, 317
token 58, 59, 88
token-ring 361
toner 349
top-level domains 378, 385
topology 436
TR 318
tracks 322, 324, 325, 326, 328, 329, 331, 334
transactions 559
Translation Lookaside Buffer 316
Transmission Control Protocol 357
Transmit pin 337
trap 216, 507
trap gate 219
traps in shell scripts 96
triplets 243
triply-indirect data blocks 243
Trusted Computer Systems Evaluation Criteria 582
TSD 318
TSS 206, 318
TSSî 218
twm 253
TX 337, 338, 339, 347

U

uarea, 762
UART 336, 337
UDP 360, 364, 374, 375
UID 176, 177, 178, 562
UMASK 100, 101, 102
umask 100
unformatted storage capacity 323
Universal Asynchronous Receiver-Transmitter 336
Universal Resource Locator 612, 621, 622, 635, 640, 663, 664
UNIX -vs- DOS file names 12
unreliable protocol 360
UPS 352, 353
URL 635
usage message 39
USENET 35
Usenet 429
user accounts 32, 175
User Datagram Protocol 360
user documentation, creating 540
user mode 170, 171, 211, 212, 213, 219, 220, 221
user/supervisor bit 317
UUCP 34, 356

V

V.32 346
V.32.bis 346
V.34 346
V.42 346
variable operator 54
variables 59
verical retrace 342
VESA 290, 344
VESA Local Bus 290
VFS 240
VGA 279, 309, 341, 342, 343, 344
vi 17, 106
    $ 108
    % 112, 114
    * 112
    ^ 108, 111, 114
    abbreviations 117
    addresses 112
    asterisk 112
    automatic spell checking 117
    buffers 113
    caret 111
    changing text 109
    combining movement and editing 109
    configuring 122
    editing 108
    ex-mode 111, 113
    inserting command output 119
    inserting files 119
    inserting text 109
    magic 116
    maps 117
    movement 108
    movement keys 108
    named buffers 115
    numbered buffers 115
    replacing text 110
    scope of substitution 112
    searching 110
vi as EDITOR environment variable 65

video cards 341
Video Electronics Standards Association 344
Video Electronics Standards Association Local Bus 280
viewfinder 273
viewport 273
virtual address 316
virtual console 33
Virtual File System 240
virtual memory 221, 310, 312, 314
virtual mode 312
virtual workspace 273
viruses 167
VLB 280, 290, 456
VL-Bus 290
vmlinuz 204
voice-coil motor 322
volatile memory 301
VSPACE HTML text attribute 650

W

wait 364
wait channel 214, 225
wait channel, 764
Walnut Creek CD-ROM 587
Walnut Creek CDROM 163
WCHAN 214, 225
Web Servers 428
Web Service Provider 611
well connected host 384, 389
well-known ports 363, 374
WGS 443
WIDTH HTML text attribute 650
window manager 268
Window Menu 253, 255
window stacking 268
Windows 7
Windows Application Binary Interface 603
WorkGroup Solutions 443, 469, 470, 603
working directory 40
working set 222
workspace 273
World Wide Web 390
write 43
write permission 42
write permissions 43, 44
write policy 306, 307, 308, 318
Write-Back 307
Write-Dirty 307
Write-Through 307
WWW 517

X

X 247
X Toolkit 255
X Toolkit Intrinsics 255
X Windows System 247
Xaw 255
Xemacs 125
XENVIRONMENT environment variable 259
Xerox 356, 435, 436
xf86config 248, 249, 250, 252
XFILESEARCHPATH environment variable 259
XFONTS environement variable 266
xinit 253
XOFF 339, 463, 480
XON 339, 463
XON/XOFF flow control 339
X-resources 258
Xt 255
Xterm 260
xterm 252, 253, 261, 263
X-Windows 35
X-windows 247

Z

Zero-Insertion-Force 458
ZIF 458
zombie process 212, 214
zone 379, 380, 381
zsh 62

The Linux Shopping Mall

WORKGROUP SOLUTIONS, INC.

Linux is habit forming.

Archived treasures: Linux libraries and archives on CD-ROM

The Internet contains mountains of information that's available free—*if* you have the time to sort through it all and download the data you want. Instead, you can buy gigabytes of Linux-related data already downloaded and conveniently stored on CD-ROMs.

Treasure chest for developers: InfoMagic Linux Developer's Resource

Superb for application development and research, this distribution packs six CDs with the Metro-X servers from MetroLink, several different distributions of Linux, archives, How-Tos, and a collection of commercial demos.

00104 .....1 lb......US$ 27

Red Hat Linux Archives

These four CDs include the Official Red Hat Linux along with compilers, networking software, source code, on-line documentation, and 2.5 gigabytes of tools, utilities, applications and games.

00120 ....1 lb ....US$ 29

Searchable text for instant answers: Red Hat Linux Library

This single CD contains all texts and how-to's of the Linux Documentation Project, Internet Engineering RFCs, GNU docs, Usenet FAQ's, and much more.

00121 ....1 lb ....US$ 29

Eight disks of software from the Internet: Linux Internet Archives

Yggdrasil has compiled eight CDs' worth of software, including nine ready-to-install Linux distributions, the SunSite and TSX-11 archives, GNU, X11R6, and Internet RFC archives.

00122 ....1 lb ....US$ 22

Want to resell our products, or have us sell yours?

Visit our web site to find out how!

Linux does everything but make coffee and empty the wastebaskets.

As the popularity of Linux grows, software companies are realizing that they need to provide office applications for busy users. Whether they create them just for Linux, port them from their original operating system, or emulate their native OS, you'll find these applications more than equal to most office needs!

You won't even miss your MS Office: ApplixWare

This is the complete GUI office suite for Linux. It includes a Word Processor, Spreadsheet, Presentation Graphics, and E-Mail to help you stay productive. ApplixWare can access most file formats including HTML, Microsoft Word, PowerPoint, WordPerfect and more. ApplixWare was ported specifically for Red Hat Linux, and has been successfully tested by WGS on Linux Pro.

00078...........4 lbs..........US$ 199

More on ApplixWare on the next page!

WorkGroup Solutions, inc.

Secure online ordering too!

Linux is great in the office.

Send us proof of your status as a full-time student or faculty member, and you will be eligible for the **Educational Edition of ApplixWare:** not stripped-down, just priced for education.

00079 ....4 lbs ....US$ 79

For the technically minded, the **Developer's Version of ApplixWare** provides development tools and an extension language facility to let you add your own features.

00138 ....4 lbs ....US$ 495

All your favorites in one package: Caldera Internet Office Suite

Caldera Internet Office Suite is a complete bundle of familiar business applications that include WordPerfect, Z-mail, NExS Spreadsheet, and Metrolink's Executive Motif Libraries. With word processing, email, spreadsheet and more, this single suite can keep your whole office running smoothly.

00099 ....2 lbs.........US$ 325

Graphical word processing: Caldera WordPerfect & Motif Bundle

Caldera combines the graphical word processor WordPerfect with Metrolink's Executive Motif run-time libraries. You can publish HTML documents directly to the Internet, while Motif makes the best use of your hardware investment.

00098 ....2 lbs ....US$ 225

Windows without the pane: Wabi for Linux

If the thought of losing all your favorite 16-bit Windows applications has held you back from trying Linux, you've just run out of excuses! Wabi, Caldera's Microsoft Windows emulator, allows you to install and run those familiar programs just as you would on a native Windows system, but with all the added benefits of Linux! Wabi runs as a Linux program, giving you a multi-tasking, secure, Internet-aware platform to run your favorite personal productivity applications. In fact, you may even find those apps running faster—up to *ten times faster*—than they did under Windows 3.x! A 200-page User Guide is included with the CD-ROM.

Sorry, support for Windows 95 applications is still under development.

00094.................1 lb...................US$ 199

Prices and availability are always subject to change. For the latest information on any product, see our web site: **www.wgs.com**

Mac fans can use Linux too: Executor 2

ARDI started from scratch and rewrote the system services that are present on 68000-series Macintoshes. The resulting Mac emulator for Intel-compatible machines boasts unparalleled speed and versatility. Not only does it read and write Macintosh format files on floppies and hard drives, but it also runs many (not all) Macintosh applications flawlessly. In fact, Executor 2 on a Pentium will run many Mac-native applications up to one and a half times *faster* than the same application on a Quadra. Sorry, support for PowerPC applications is still under development. For limitations, see our web site.

00129 ....1 lb $249

To order:
1-800-234-7813
or 303-693-3321
Mention Offer

WGS The Linux Shopping Mall

WorkGroup Solutions, Inc.

Read all about it.

Keep them on your desk for reference... read them in your spare time... or both!
We offer a growing collection of books that will guide you in your understanding and use of Linux.

Claim your stretch of the Information Highway: ***Building a Linux Internet Server***
This single volume is the only book you need to successfully set up, configure and connect your Linux server and establish a presence on the Internet. It not only explains *how* to build your site, but *why* it is important to get connected as a host and what benefits you can expect when you do so.
00003......................2 lbs ....US$ 39

Internet tools and techniques: ***The UNIX Web Server Book***

Members of the famed SunSite development team present everything you need to build and maintain your own Internet information site, including a CD full of software tucked into the back cover. The text explains HTML, search engines, forms and more. The CD includes Red Hat Linux, Apache, graphics and audio utilities, among other highly useful software.
00131 ....3 lbs ....US$ 49

More books about Linux become available every day. If you don't see the one you want here, check our web site for the latest offerings.

What is it and where did it come from? ***Inside Linux: A Look at Operating System Development***

After eighteen years' combined experience with the UNIX system® and Linux, Dr. Randolph Bentsen shares his understanding of UNIX systems in general, and Linux in particular, in this SSC print publication. The book discusses the history, theory and practice of Linux. As a computer professional, you'll come away with a new, deeper understanding of operating system design and implementation considerations.
00061 ....2 lbs ....US$ 22

Faster than a speeding laser printer: ***Linux Man***

This collection of the essential man-pages for Linux is a complete reference to Linux and/or UNIX system commands, nicely formatted, indexed, printed and bound, for less than it would cost to print them out yourself. Neat, tidy, and super convenient!
00004 ....3 lbs ....US$ 29

Secure online ordering too!

And then read some more.

A comprehensive daily reference:

Linux In A Nutshell

O'Reilly—you know, the publisher with the animals on the cover—provides this complete reference to Linux commands, shell syntax, options and more. Users will want it on their desks every day.

00118 ....1 lb ....US$ 19

Both concise and complete: *The Linux Commands and Resources Directory*

This handy reference starts from the whatis database, then expands upon it. The result is a fully cross-referenced collection of one-line definitions of Linux user commands, options, system administration tools, programming calls and subroutines, all in an easy-to-use format.

00107......................1 lb $19

The latest developments at your door: *Linux Journal* Subscription

Now you can have the monthly magazine of the Linux Community delivered right to your home or office! The *Linux Journal* keeps you up to date on the latest developments in Linux and tells you what you need to know to make Linux work for you. Enjoy articles and features on how Linux is being used in the business world, on the Internet, and on the cutting edge of technology.

Also included each month are book reviews and tips & tricks columns. Shipping weight is not applicable for this item.

One year, U.S.A.: 00127...............................US$ 22
Two years, U.S.A.: 00133 ....US$ 39
One year, Canada: 00134 ....US$ 27
Two years, Canada: 00135............................US$ 49
One year, other countries: 00136..................US$ 32
Two years, other countries: 00137 ....US$ 54

The best of the *Journal*:
The Linux Sampler

240 pages of selected articles from past issues of the Linux Journal. Readers who weren't able to order the sold-out back issues of the Journal will appreciate finding articles from as far back as Issue 1.

00130.................1 lb ....US$ 14

You wouldn't believe the stuff we give away! Watch our web site for contests and special deals.

News from the front:
The Linux Newsletter

This online publication from WGS aims to keep you current with what is going on inside and outside the Linux community. Subscribing is easy, and best of all, it's free! Check the box on the order form, or send email to wgsnews@wgs.com with the word "subscribe" in the subject line or in the first line of the message. We are careful to keep our subscriber database up to date and avoid duplication. If you wish, you can unsubscribe at any time. Shipping weight is not applicable to this item.

wgsnews@wgs.com.......................................FREE!

Order Form for Offer #WB0011

Please print clearly.

Name ______________________________

Company Email ______________________________

Personal Email ______________________________

Company Name, if any ______________________________

Shipping Address* ______________________________

______________________________ Suite/Apt.# ______________

City ______________________ State ______________________

Postal Code ______________________ Country ______________________

*Please note: if you supply an address with a P.O. box, then we can ship only by U.S. Mail.

Work Phone ______________________ Home Phone ______________________

Company Fax ______________________ Home Fax ______________________

Fill out this section if using a credit card. Name on card ______________________

❑ Visa ❑ MC ❑ AmEx ❑ Discover Exp.______ Card number ______________________

Credit card billing address, if different from above: ______________________

____

❑ Check here to subscribe to our emailed monthly *Linux Newsletter*. No purchase required.

Part No.	Item	Weight	Qty.	Price	Total

Total shipping weight ______ Subtotal ______

If you are mailing or faxing your order, deduct 10% from the subtotal ______

Shipping ______

Total ______

Multiply total shipping weight by $2 per pound USA (min. $5), $3 per pound to Canada (min. $10), $10 per pound to other countries. Enter the result here.

The Linux Shopping Mall by WorkGroup Solutions, Inc. Department # WB0011.
U.S. Mail address: P.O. Box 460190, Aurora, CO 80046-0190 USA.
Phone: 1-800-234-7813 or 303-693-3321. Fax: 303-699-2793. http://www.wgs.com sales@wgs.com

LICENSE AGREEMENT AND LIMITED WARRANTY

READ THE FOLLOWING TERMS AND CONDITIONS CAREFULLY BEFORE OPENING THIS DISK PACKAGE. THIS LEGAL DOCUMENT IS AN AGREEMENT BETWEEN YOU AND PRENTICE-HALL, INC. (THE "COMPANY"). BY OPENING THIS SEALED DISK PACKAGE, YOU ARE AGREEING TO BE BOUND BY THESE TERMS AND CONDITIONS. IF YOU DO NOT AGREE WITH THESE TERMS AND CONDITIONS, DO NOT OPEN THE DISK PACKAGE. PROMPTLY RETURN THE UNOPENED DISK PACKAGE AND ALL ACCOMPANYING ITEMS TO THE PLACE YOU OBTAINED THEM FOR A FULL REFUND OF ANY SUMS YOU HAVE PAID.

1. **GRANT OF LICENSE:** In consideration of your payment of the license fee, which is part of the price you paid for this product, and your agreement to abide by the terms and conditions of this Agreement, the Company grants to you a nonexclusive right to use and display the copy of the enclosed software program (hereinafter the "SOFTWARE") on a single computer (i.e., with a single CPU) at a single location so long as you comply with the terms of this Agreement. The Company reserves all rights not expressly granted to you under this Agreement.

2. **OWNERSHIP OF SOFTWARE:** You own only the magnetic or physical media (the enclosed disks) on which the SOFTWARE is recorded or fixed, but the Company retains all the rights, title, and ownership to the SOFTWARE recorded on the original disk copy(ies) and all subsequent copies of the SOFTWARE, regardless of the form or media on which the original or other copies may exist. This license is not a sale of the original SOFTWARE or any copy to you.

3. **COPY RESTRICTIONS:** This SOFTWARE and the accompanying printed materials and user manual (the "Documentation") are the subject of copyright. You may not copy the Documentation or the SOFTWARE, except that you may make a single copy of the SOFTWARE for backup or archival purposes only. You may be held legally responsible for any copying or copyright infringement which is caused or encouraged by your failure to abide by the terms of this restriction.

4. **USE RESTRICTIONS:** You may not network the SOFTWARE or otherwise use it on more than one computer or computer terminal at the same time. You may physically transfer the SOFTWARE from one computer to another provided that the SOFTWARE is used on only one computer at a time. You may not distribute copies of the SOFTWARE or Documentation to others. You may not reverse engineer, disassemble, decompile, modify, adapt, translate, or create derivative works based on the SOFTWARE or the Documentation without the prior written consent of the Company.

5. **TRANSFER RESTRICTIONS:** The enclosed SOFTWARE is licensed only to you and may not be transferred to any one else without the prior written consent of the Company. Any unauthorized transfer of the SOFTWARE shall result in the immediate termination of this Agreement.

6. **TERMINATION:** This license is effective until terminated. This license will terminate automatically without notice from the Company and become null and void if you fail to comply with any provisions or limitations of this license. Upon termination, you shall destroy the Documentation and all copies of the SOFTWARE. All provisions of this Agreement as to warranties, limitation of liability, remedies or damages, and our ownership rights shall survive termination.

7. **MISCELLANEOUS:** This Agreement shall be construed in accordance with the laws of the United States of America and the State of New York and shall benefit the Company, its affiliates, and assignees.

8. **LIMITED WARRANTY AND DISCLAIMER OF WARRANTY:** The Company warrants that the SOFTWARE, when properly used in accordance with the Documentation, will operate in substantial conformity with the description of the SOFTWARE set forth in the Documentation. The Company does not warrant that the SOFT-

WARE will meet your requirements or that the operation of the SOFTWARE will be uninterrupted or error-free. The Company warrants that the media on which the SOFTWARE is delivered shall be free from defects in materials and workmanship under normal use for a period of thirty (30) days from the date of your purchase. Your only remedy and the Company's only obligation under these limited warranties is, at the Company's option, return of the warranted item for a refund of any amounts paid by you or replacement of the item. Any replacement of SOFTWARE or media under the warranties shall not extend the original warranty period. The limited warranty set forth above shall not apply to any SOFTWARE which the Company determines in good faith has been subject to misuse, neglect, improper installation, repair, alteration, or damage by you. EXCEPT FOR THE EXPRESSED WARRANTIES SET FORTH ABOVE, THE COMPANY DISCLAIMS ALL WARRANTIES, EXPRESS OR IMPLIED, INCLUDING WITHOUT LIMITATION, THE IMPLIED WARRANTIES OF MERCHANTABILITY AND FITNESS FOR A PARTICULAR PURPOSE. EXCEPT FOR THE EXPRESS WARRANTY SET FORTH ABOVE, THE COMPANY DOES NOT WARRANT, GUARANTEE, OR MAKE ANY REPRESENTATION REGARDING THE USE OR THE RESULTS OF THE USE OF THE SOFTWARE IN TERMS OF ITS CORRECTNESS, ACCURACY, RELIABILITY, CURRENTNESS, OR OTHERWISE.

IN NO EVENT, SHALL THE COMPANY OR ITS EMPLOYEES, AGENTS, SUPPLIERS, OR CONTRACTORS BE LIABLE FOR ANY INCIDENTAL, INDIRECT, SPECIAL, OR CONSEQUENTIAL DAMAGES ARISING OUT OF OR IN CONNECTION WITH THE LICENSE GRANTED UNDER THIS AGREEMENT, OR FOR LOSS OF USE, LOSS OF DATA, LOSS OF INCOME OR PROFIT, OR OTHER LOSSES, SUSTAINED AS A RESULT OF INJURY TO ANY PERSON, OR LOSS OF OR DAMAGE TO PROPERTY, OR CLAIMS OF THIRD PARTIES, EVEN IF THE COMPANY OR AN AUTHORIZED REPRESENTATIVE OF THE COMPANY HAS BEEN ADVISED OF THE POSSIBILITY OF SUCH DAMAGES. IN NO EVENT SHALL LIABILITY OF THE COMPANY FOR DAMAGES WITH RESPECT TO THE SOFTWARE EXCEED THE AMOUNTS ACTUALLY PAID BY YOU, IF ANY, FOR THE SOFTWARE.

SOME JURISDICTIONS DO NOT ALLOW THE LIMITATION OF IMPLIED WARRANTIES OR LIABILITY FOR INCIDENTAL, INDIRECT, SPECIAL, OR CONSEQUENTIAL DAMAGES, SO THE ABOVE LIMITATIONS MAY NOT ALWAYS APPLY. THE WARRANTIES IN THIS AGREEMENT GIVE YOU SPECIFIC LEGAL RIGHTS AND YOU MAY ALSO HAVE OTHER RIGHTS WHICH VARY IN ACCORDANCE WITH LOCAL LAW.

ACKNOWLEDGMENT

YOU ACKNOWLEDGE THAT YOU HAVE READ THIS AGREEMENT, UNDERSTAND IT, AND AGREE TO BE BOUND BY ITS TERMS AND CONDITIONS. YOU ALSO AGREE THAT THIS AGREEMENT IS THE COMPLETE AND EXCLUSIVE STATEMENT OF THE AGREEMENT BETWEEN YOU AND THE COMPANY AND SUPERSEDES ALL PROPOSALS OR PRIOR AGREEMENTS, ORAL, OR WRITTEN, AND ANY OTHER COMMUNICATIONS BETWEEN YOU AND THE COMPANY OR ANY REPRESENTATIVE OF THE COMPANY RELATING TO THE SUBJECT MATTER OF THIS AGREEMENT.

Should you have any questions concerning this Agreement or if you wish to contact the Company for any reason, please contact in writing at the address below.

Robin Short
Prentice Hall PTR
One Lake Street
Upper Saddle River, New Jersey 07458